DEPARTMENT OF EDUCATION AND SCIENCE

A language for life

Report of the Committee of Inquiry appointed by the Secretary of State for Education and Science under the Chairmanship of Sir Alan Bullock F.B.A.

LONDON
HER MAJESTY'S STATIONERY OFFICE

ISBN 0 11 270326 7*

Foreword

BY THE SECRETARY OF STATE FOR EDUCATION AND SCIENCE

This Report deserves to be widely read. All our education depends on the understanding and effective use of English as does success in so many aspects of adult life.

The Report concerns all who have responsibilities in education. Many recommendations are addressed to schools and teachers and call for a change of approach and redirection of effort rather than for additional resources. As the Committee acknowledges, recommendations with financial implications must be subject to current constraints; for the time being action on those which would involve additional resources must be postponed. Within this limitation I hope that local authorities and teachers at all levels will look carefully at the recommendations which concern them, as my Department will at those which concern the Government.

We are all greatly indebted to Sir Alan Bullock and his colleagues. They have given us an authoritative statement which will be of value as a basis for further discussion and development for many years to come.

DECEMBER 1974. REG PRENTICE.

Dear Secretary of State,

I have the honour to present the Report of the Committee set up by your predecessor, Mrs. Thatcher, in 1972 to inquire into the teaching in the schools of reading and the other uses of English. As the Committee's Chairman I should like to place on record the great help I have received from Dame Muriel Stewart, who has acted as Vice-Chairman throughout the inquiry. The Committee's debt to its Secretary, Mr. R. Arnold, H.M.I., is acknowledged in the Introductory chapter. I should like to express here my personal appreciation of the assistance he has given to the Chairman and of the close co-operation in which we have worked.

Yours sincerely,

ALAN BULLOCK,

(*Chairman*)

The Rt. Hon. Reg. E. Prentice, J.P., M.P.

MEMBERSHIP OF THE COMMITTEE

Sir Alan Bullock, F.B.A. (Chairman), Master of St. Catherine's College and Vice-Chancellor, University of Oxford.

Sister Basil Burbridge, Headmistress, St. Margaret Mary Junior and Infant School, Carlisle.

Professor J. N. Britton, Goldsmiths' Professor of Education in the University of London.

Mr. Alastair Burnet, Editor, The Economist.

Miss J. Derrick, Senior Lecturer, Language Teaching Centre, University of York.

Mr. J. J. Fairbairn, Head of Education Department, St. John's College, York.

Mr. H. K. Fowler, Chief Education Officer, Derbyshire.

Mr. Stuart Froome, Headmaster, St. Jude's C. of E. Junior School, Englefield Green, Surrey.

Mr. David Gadsby, Managing Director, A. & C. Black Ltd., Publishers.

Mr. C. R. Gillings, Headmaster, Midhurst Intermediate School, West Sussex (resigned 1 September, 1973 on appointment to H.M. Inspectorate).

Mr. W. K. Gardner, Lecturer, School of Education, University of Nottingham.

Mrs. D. M. R. Hutchcroft, O.B.E., Headmistress, Saltford Primary School, Bristol.

Miss A. M. Johns, Headmistress, Henry Fawcett Infant School, London, S.E.11.

Mr. D. Mackay, Adviser/Warden, Centre for Language in Primary Education, Inner London Education Authority (resigned 1 November, 1972 on appointment to a post in the West Indies).

Mr. Michael Marland, Headmaster, Woodberry Down Secondary School, London, N.4.

Professor J. E. Merritt, Professor of Educational Studies, Open University.

Mr. A. J. Puckey, Primary Adviser, Nottinghamshire L.E.A.

Mrs. V. Southgate Booth, Senior Lecturer in Curriculum Studies, School of Education, University of Manchester.

Dame Muriel Stewart, D.B.E., Chairman, Schools Council.

Professor J. Wrigley, Professor of Curriculum Research and Development, University of Reading; Director of Studies, Schools Council.

Mr. R. Arnold, H.M.I., Secretary.

Mrs. G. W. Dishart, Assistant Secretary.

Appointments shown are those held by members at the time the Committee was constituted.

The estimated cost of the production of the Report is £95,900, of which £14,700 represents the estimated cost of printing and publication, £68,700 the cost of administration, and £12,500 the travelling and other expenses of members.

Table of Contents

INTRODUCTION: The scope and nature of the Inquiry; and acknowledgements

PLAN OF THE REPORT

PART ONE

ATTITUDES AND STANDARDS

PART TWO

LANGUAGE IN THE EARLY YEARS

PART THREE

READING

TABLE OF CONTENTS

xi

TABLE OF CONTENTS

PART FOUR

LANGUAGE IN THE MIDDLE AND SECONDARY YEARS

CHAPTER 10   ORAL LANGUAGE

TALKING AND LISTENING: 10.1–10.31

xiii

TABLE OF CONTENTS

CHAPTER 11   WRITTEN LANGUAGE

INTRODUCTION: 11.1

PART SIX

READING AND LANGUAGE DIFFICULTIES

CHAPTER 17   SCREENING, DIAGNOSIS, AND RECORDING

SCREENING   17.1–17.14

DIAGNOSIS AND RECORDING: 17.15–17.25

TABLE OF CONTENTS

CHAPTER 22   TECHNOLOGICAL AIDS AND BROADCASTING

Part Eight

TEACHER EDUCATION AND TRAINING

PART NINE

THE SURVEY

PART TEN

SUMMARY OF CONCLUSIONS AND RECOMMENDATIONS

List of Tables and Diagrams

LIST OF TABLES AND DIAGRAMS

The diagrams listed below are all contained in Part Nine—The Survey.

INTRODUCTION

The Scope and Nature of the Inquiry; and Acknowledgments

The decision to set up the Committee of Inquiry was announced shortly after the publication of the N.F.E.R. Report, "The Trend of Reading Standards", and it was understandable that it should be widely regarded as an inquiry solely into reading. This was reflected in much press and public comment and in many of the letters we received. In fact it will be seen from our terms of reference that reading was not singled out for special attention but was placed in close association with other language skills within the context of teaching the use of English:

"To consider in relation to schools:

(*a*) all aspects of teaching the use of English, including reading, writing, and speech;

(*b*) how present practice might be improved and the role that initial and in-service training might play;

(*c*) to what extent arrangements for monitoring the general level of attainment in these skills can be introduced or improved;

and to make recommendations."

These terms of reference have allowed us to base our Report on the important principle that reading must be seen as part of a child's general language development and not as a discrete skill which can be considered in isolation from it. We have, in fact, interpreted our brief as language in education, and have ranged from the growth of language and reading ability in young children to the teaching of English in the secondary school. Indeed, we felt it necessary to begin with the years before a child comes to school and to examine the influence of the home on early language development.

It was obvious that we should have to consider some limits to our field of inquiry. We therefore decided to go as far as, but not beyond, the statutory age for leaving school. This means that apart from a reference to examinations in language we have excluded any specific consideration of sixth form work and higher and further education. At the same time we felt a particular concern about the needs of those pupils who leave school unable to read, and we have accordingly stretched our brief to include observations on adult illiteracy. We felt equal concern about the language problems of children from families of overseas origin and have included a chapter on their special needs. A good deal of our time was naturally spent in discussing the difficulties of children who are retarded in reading, but we have confined our attention to pupils being educated in ordinary schools. Our inquiry did not extend to children receiving special educational treatment in separate schools.

It became clear to us from our early discussions and from the evidence we received that we must give attention to the provision of resources and to the internal organisation of schools, since both have an important bearing on the development of language and the teaching of reading. Our first thought was to deal separately with primary and secondary education, allocating a part of the Report to each. We chose instead a form of presentation which would emphasise the continuity of English teaching, and this is explained in the plan of chapters which follows this introduction. Finally, we had to decide how far to go in discussing examinations. To have made a series of detailed recommendations about form and content would have extended our inquiry beyond what was practicable. At the same time it would have been unrealistic to leave examinations out of account, not least because they play a very large part in the experience of English of many pupils in the later years. We have therefore looked at some aspects of present examinations in English and at their influence on teaching and have given our views on the direction they ought to take.

Like many Committees before us, no doubt, we are anxious that the Report should be read and considered as a whole. Though individual chapters deal with given topics they are not intended to be self-contained, and those topics depend for their proper understanding on a knowledge of the background from which they emerge. This is particularly true of reading, not only for the reason we have already stated but because references to different aspects of the teaching of reading occur in various places throughout the Report. One of our main arguments is that there is no one method, medium, approach, device, or philosophy that holds the key to the process of learning to read. We believe that an essential condition for bringing about an improvement is a recognition that there is no simple nostrum and above all no substitute for a thorough understanding of all the factors at work. It is for this reason that we have made a policy of entering in places into considerable technical detail. We regard this kind of descriptive account as essential to an inquiry of this nature, since the Report is addressed to a wide audience. It is addressed in fact to all who are professionally engaged in education and to many more who have an interest in it—from parents to publishers. If there is one particular group, however, who have been in the forefront of our thinking it is the teachers in the schools. The quality of learning is fashioned in the day-to-day atmosphere of the classroom through the knowledge, intuitions and skill of individual teachers. Whatever else the Report may achieve we regard its first purpose as a support for them.

Throughout our work we have been made aware of the great public interest in the matters we have been investigating. From this point of view the setting up of an inquiry could hardly have been better timed. From two other points of view, however, the administrative and the financial, the publication of the Report comes at an awkward moment. The reform of local government has altered the shape and composition of many Authorities. Moreover, change is going forward in the structure of teacher training following the publication of the James Report and the subsequent White Paper "Education: A Framework for Expansion". With so much in a state of transition it has not always been easy to give our recommendations—for example in relation to professional centres and in-service training—the precision we should have wished. We hope, however, that the unsettling effects of change will be more than compensated for by the opportunities it creates to review existing practices. The financial circumstances of the country at the time when we were formulating our recommendations have impressed on us the need to be realistic. Some of the recommendations inevitably call for increased expenditure, and we recognise that it will take time before they can be implemented; but many could be put into operation by simple changes of practice which involve little if any increase in costs. By far the greatest number of our suggestions are intended for consideration by the schools themselves.

So much for the scope and limits of our inquiry. We pass next to the evidence on which we have been able to draw. The Committee agreed at its first meeting to obtain as complete a picture as possible of the actual practice in the schools. It was decided to draw up two questionnaires and these were completed in January 1973 by a random sample of 1,415 primary and 392 secondary schools. The survey was organised by the Secretary and Assistant Secretary to the Committee, and we are grateful for the help given them by statisticians of the Department of Education and Science, by Mr. Stephen Steadman of the Schools Council, and by members of H.M. Inspectorate. This is the first time a survey of English on this scale has been attempted in this country. It could not have been undertaken without the willing co-operation of the local authorities and the heads and staffs of the many schools involved, and we wish to express our great appreciation of the trouble they took to help us. As the survey contains much information likely to be of interest to anyone concerned with education, we have printed the questionnaires and the results in Chapter 25, together with a commentary upon the findings.

The Committee drew up a list of 66 individuals and 56 organisations from which it wished to receive written evidence, and a shorter list of those it wished to interview. At the same time, the Chairman issued a public invitation to anyone interested to submit written evidence, an invitation of which several hundred individuals and organisations took advantage. The evidence obtained from all these sources was the foundation on which the inquiry was built, enabling the Committee to draw upon an accumulation of experience, a wealth of research—both published and unpublished—and a very wide range of opinion. We are greatly indebted to all those who generously made these available to us, often at the cost of considerable trouble to themselves in preparing papers specially for the purpose. Another valuable source of evidence has been H.M. Inspectorate, and we have been grateful for the opportunity to draw upon their wide experience at various points in our work.

The Committee was also, of course, able to call upon a varied experience and expert knowledge from among its own members, several of whom produced drafts or papers of various kinds. 16 of the Committee are or have been teachers, 6 are involved with the training of teachers, either in universities or in colleges of education, and 5 have undertaken and published research relevant to the subject of the inquiry. We were also fortunate to have the expert advice of Professor J. Sinclair, who gave the Committee much valuable help in its discussions on the place of linguistics, and of Mr. A. Yates, Dr. R. Sumner and Mrs. C. Burstall, of the National Foundation for Educational Research.

Members of the Committee undertook a series of special visits to 100 schools, 21 colleges of education, and 6 reading or language centres. These visits, in various parts of the country, gave members the opportunity to see different methods of teaching and organisation and above all to talk to a large number of teachers in their classrooms. The Committee also studied, at first and second hand, the practice of certain other English-speaking countries. Evidence was received from Scotland, Canada, and the United States, and two members of the Committee, accompanied by the Secretary, paid a visit to North America, studying developments in schools, colleges, and universities. Over a period of two years the full Committee has met on 54 occasions, but the total of days devoted by individual members in visits and other kinds of consultation has run into many hundreds.

The Committee owes its gratitude to Mrs. G. W. Dishart, its Assistant Secretary, and the members of the supporting team—Mr. D. A. Robins, Mrs. K. F. Briggs, Mrs. P. Diegeler, and Mr. K. Price—who have been a personal help to members in so many ways throughout. To Mrs. Dishart we owe particular thanks for her special contribution, not least in clarifying for the Committee all the material produced by the survey and arranging it for presentation.

The Committee's greatest debt is to its Secretary, Mr. R. Arnold, H.M.I., who has been a constant source of energy, ideas, and invention at every stage of the inquiry. Throughout its course he has produced a stimulating flow of original material and drafts for the Committee, and his wide knowledge of all the aspects of our subject of inquiry has been an invaluable resource. The ability and efficiency with which he handled a formidable volume of organisation under great pressure have impressed us all. He has crowned two years' hard work by turning the views and judgements of the Committee into a coherent Report written by a single hand.

(signed)	Alan Bullock	Keith Gardner
	Sister Basil Burbridge	Diana M. Rought Hutchcroft
	James Britton	Audrey Johns
	J. W. A. Burnet	Michael Marland
	June Derrick	John E. Merritt
	James Fairbairn	Alan Puckey
	Henry Fowler	Vera Southgate Booth
	Stuart Froome	Muriel Stewart
	David Gadsby	Jack Wrigley

R. Arnold, H.M.I. (*Secretary*)

Plan of The Report

The design of the Report is intended to reflect the organic relationship between the various aspects of English, and to emphasise the need for continuity in their development throughout school life. It would have been a simple matter to deal separately with language, taking it right through the age range, and then to have done the same for reading. It would have been equally simple to divide the Report into separate sections for the primary and secondary years, each containing every aspect of the subject as it related to the needs of that particular age-group. However, both these methods would have conflicted with the principle that reading, writing, talking and listening should be treated as a unity, and that there should be unbroken continuity across the years. Against this has to be balanced the need to take certain topics out of context for concentrated attention, and it becomes obvious that some compromise is the best course. The chapters are therefore arranged in such a way as to avoid rigid divisions while at the same time allowing detailed examination of a given topic or the needs of a particular age-group.

Part One opens with a review of current attitudes to the teaching of English and then goes on to examine the question of standards of reading, considering evidence from the most recent N.F.E.R. survey and other sources. After introducing a number of issues which will be taken up in detail in subsequent chapters, the section ends with a case for a new system of monitoring national standards of reading and writing. As the introduction makes clear, we believe that the inquiry is essentially concerned with the development of language in education, and Part Two of the Report establishes this principle. It opens with a discussion of the way in which language and learning interact and goes on to propose various measures for improving language development in young children, particularly those from home backgrounds which put them at a disadvantage in certain ways. Only when it has been determined that reading is secondary to and dependent upon the growth of language competence in the early years is it introduced as a separate topic, and this is the subject of Part Three. We have already given our reasons for going to the length of setting out in detail what is involved in the process of learning to read. Chapters 6 and 7 are entitled respectively "The Reading Process" and "Reading in the Early Years", and they are intended to be complementary. Indeed, there is a deliberate overlap between them, and they should be read as one for a proper understanding of what is being advocated about the teaching of reading in the early stages. By the same token they should be related to other parts of the Report where topics given separate treatment have an important bearing on the development of reading. For example, the first two chapters of Part Five deal with organisation within schools and continuity between them, and implications for the teaching of reading enter into both. Even more relevant is the opening chapter of Part Six, where there is an examination of diagnostic procedures and the way they can be used to develop reading ability. Similarly, both chapters of Part Seven have much to say about reading, from the points of view respectively of the use of books and of technological aids.

The second half of Part Three deals with the later stages of reading and with literature. It leads into a study of language at the same age level, which is the burden of Part Four, and the chapter on literature is the point of juncture. Both parts have related chapters on reading and language across the curriculum. There are thus five consecutive chapters which associate language and reading in the middle and secondary years, covering the age-range 7 or 8 to 16 years.

Part Five examines organisational factors, with chapters devoted to primary and secondary schools linked by one on continuity. We have made a point of not dealing separately with middle schools, but the problems explored in relation to primary and secondary schools have equal relevance to them. The last chapter of this part of the Report extends the discussion of specialist support within the school to that of specialist support from outside, presenting a case for expanded L.E.A. advisory services.

After the development of language and reading has been considered across the age-range and placed within the organisational framework it is possible to consider in greater detail the question of special difficulties. Thus, what is said in Part Six depends upon an acquaintance with what has gone before. The section is introduced with a chapter on preventive measures in the form of screening and diagnosis, and this is followed by a consideration of provision for children with reading difficulties in primary and secondary schools. The subject is extended into the post-school years with a discussion of adult illiteracy and the steps that might be taken to reduce it. The section concludes with an examination of the special needs of children from families of overseas origin.

Part Seven of the Report is concerned with the role of books and technological aids in the school and relates them to suggestions made in earlier chapters. The section ranges from the use of the library to educational broadcasting and contains proposals for a review of allowances. Teacher training is the last major subject and its placing in Part Eight is determined by the need to show the range of concerns of which initial and in-service training need to take account.

The concluding two sections are a presentation of the results of the survey and a summary of the Report in the form of a list of conclusions and recommendations.

Part One

Attitudes and Standards

CHAPTER 1

Attitudes to the Teaching of English

1.1   In any anxiety over a contemporary situation there is likely to be a wistful look back to the past, with a conviction, often illusory, that times were better then than now. And the times people claim to have been better are generally within the span of their own lives. Nowadays few would consider the Code and Schedules of 1880 as a model from which we have fallen; so was there a point in time between then and now when we had arrived at the optimal? Was there a standard which we can regard, if not as ideal, at least as a criterion by which to judge other times and conditions? These are not trivial questions and certainly not contentious ones. If we are to decide what kind of English is right for our pupils they are the kind of questions that need to be asked.

1.2   Many allegations about lower standards today come from employers, who maintain that young people joining them from school cannot write grammatically, are poor spellers, and generally express themselves badly. The employers sometimes draw upon past experience for comparisons, but even where they do not there is a strong implication that at one time levels of performance were superior.   It is therefore interesting to find in the Newbolt Report[1] of 1921 observations of a very similar kind. There Messrs. Vickers Ltd. reported "great difficulty in obtaining junior clerks who can speak and write English clearly and correctly, especially those aged from 15 to 16 years". Messrs. Lever Bros. Ltd. said: "it is a great surprise and disappointment to us to find that our young employees are so hopelessly deficient in their command of English". Boots Pure Drug Co. remarked "teaching of English in the present day schools produces a very limited command of the English language. . . Our candidates do not appreciate the value of shades of meaning, and while able to do imaginative composition, show weakness in work which requires accurate description, or careful arrangement of detail". The last is very close to some of the observations made today, half a century later, and might almost have been taken from evidence submitted to us. We do not reproduce these to imply that things were never any better and that everything is therefore as it should be. To seek perspective is not to be complacent. But perspective *is* important, and a realistic assessment is the best point from which to move towards improvement. The issue is a complicated one. It is evident that the employers of 50 years ago were no less dissatisfied; but in any case we must ask with whom today's young employees are being compared. The situation is very much different from that before the war or for some time after it. Further and higher eduation has expanded enormously. More young people are staying on at school or going on to college, many of whom would at one time have gone into commerce and industry. Moreover, as the Central Statistical Office points out, there have been marked changes in the structure of employment in recent years. Agriculture and mining have employed a sharply declining proportion of the working population, manufacturing industry has remained at about the same level, and the service industries now absorb over half the total work force. The changing pattern of employment is making more widespread demands on reading and writing skills and therefore exposing deficiencies that may have escaped attention in the past. What is more, the expansion in junior management has been considerable, and one dimension of competence at this level is the ability to produce a written report.

1.3   Factors such as these should be taken into account when observations are made about the standards of school leavers. However, they do not alter the fact that these standards are not satisfying present day requirements. Furthermore, it has to be remembered that it is not only employers who express dissatisfaction. Further and higher education institutions often remark on the inability of their entrants to write correct and coherent English. The Committee was furnished with examples of essays by college of education students, with comments by the Professor of English who had submitted them. These essays contained numerous errors of spelling, punctuation, and construction, and were a disturbing indication that the students who wrote them were ill-equipped to cope with the language demands they would meet in schools. Observations to the same effect have been made to us by heads, who have complained of the poor standard of written expression of some of the young teachers who have joined their schools. These remarks by experienced educationists deserve to be taken seriously, the more so since they are not comparing the students with those of the past but measuring them against the demands of a professional function. It may be true that in commerce, industry, and higher education alike comparisons with past standards are misleading, but the clear implication is that standards need to be raised to fulfil the demands that are being made upon them.

1.4   In this chapter we shall be considering briefly the different approaches to English in schools today. Generalisations are commonly made to the effect that one or another set of attitudes has virtually swept the board. In fact, as our questionnaire results showed, and as our visits to schools confirmed, the variety of practice is wide. Some teachers see English as an instrument of personal growth, going so far as to declare that "English is about growing up". They believe that the activities which it involves give it a special opportunity to develop the pupil's sensibility and help him to adjust to the various pressures of life. Others feel that the emphasis should be placed on direct instruction in the skills of reading and writing and that a concern for the pupil's personal development should not obscure this priority.   There are those who would prefer English to be an instrument of social change. For them the ideal of 'bridging the social gap' by sharing a common culture is unacceptable, not simply as having failed to work but as implying the superiority of 'middle class culture'. Of course, even where a teacher subscribes to a particular approach he does not necessarily pursue it exclusively, neglecting all else. Nevertheless, these emphases do exist and in considering our own recommendations we must examine them, since we believe that in their extreme form they oversimplify what is in fact a very complex matter.

1.5   Nor is the debate on purpose and method exclusive to this country. The historical determinants in the United States of America are different from those in Britain, and this must be remembered when parallels are drawn. However, the same unease has expressed itself there. It gathered into a national head after 1957 when the Russians launched Sputnik, an event which caused the U.S.A. to look critically at many aspects of its education system. English was not identified with the national interest to the extent that the sciences and modern languages were. Nonetheless, its theorists and practitioners felt the same sense of urgency, and their self-examination emerged in "The National Interest and the Teaching of English" (N.C.T.E. 1961), a publication which expressed the deep concern of the time. In the previous year the College Entrance Examination Board had issued a short description of the proper divisions of the secondary school English curriculum: English consisted of language, literature and composition, a view summed up by the label 'The Tripod Curriculum'. Looked at in this light the study of English could be reduced to manageable proportions, and each unit invited a view of itself as a discipline capable of being structured. According to Muller[2], English in the U.S.A. was, until the structuring started, an amalgam of journalism, play-production, business letters, research techniques, use of the library, career counselling, use of the telephone, and advice on dating. He quotes Kitzhaber's remark that "An English teacher can teach almost anything without anyone, including the teacher, realising that it is no longer English that is being taught". Not surprisingly, the pressures we have noted issued in a definition of English which was as concerned with excluding the irrelevant as identifying the essential.

1.6 It is a characteristic of English that it does not hold together as a body of knowledge which can be identified, quantified, then transmitted. Literary studies lead constantly outside themselves, as Leavis put it; so, for that matter, does every other aspect of English. There are two possible responses for the teacher of English, at whatever level. One is to attempt to draw in the boundaries, to impose shape on what seems amorphous, rigour on what seems undisciplined. The other is to regard English as process, not content, and take the all-inclusiveness as an opportunity rather than as a handicap. The first response can lead to a concept of the subject as divisible into compartments, each of which answers to certain formal requirements.Thus there are many teachers, in both primary and secondary schools, who feel that English language should be extracted from context and studied as a separate entity. The weekly composition on a set title, comprehension, spelling, language exercises; this pattern is still common. The language work may take the form of a class activity or it may occur in a group or individual learning situation. If the latter, the nature of the experience can be governed by the assignment card. In either case the principle is that the child is engaging with the basic skills through the medium of controllable tasks. The second response can lead to a readiness to exploit the subject's vagueness of definition, to let it flow where the child's interests will take it. Its exponents feel that the complex of activities that go to make up English cannot be circumscribed, still less quantified; the variables are too numerous and the objects too subtle.

1.7 It would be absurdly oversimplifying to say that English teaching has, without light or shade, separated itself into factions with these ideas as the manifestos. For one thing few British teachers would subscribe to the notion of the 'Tripod Curriculum', mentioned above, still less to some of the practices that separate development gave rise to, e.g. the attention to rhetoric and analysis in the teaching of composition. (Indeed, it was by no means universally embraced in the U.S.A. One American educationist said that, like Caesar, they had divided the area into three parts and then found the division so convenient they had assumed God must have made them.) It is safe to assume that no-one would any longer see English in terms of the L.C.C. official Time-Table Form of 1920, which required the time allocation to be shown for each of the following 'subjects': (*a*) Composition, Written, (*b*) Composition, Oral, (*c*) Dictation, (*d*) Grammar, (*e*) Reading, (*f*)Recitation, (*g*) Word-building, (*h*) Handwriting, (*i*) Literature. Equally, not everyone would express a contemptuous disregard for standards and say that English was merely a free-wheeling vehicle for the child's emotional and social development. Thus, although there are certainly opposed emphases there is also an area of common occupation.

1.8   It is extremely difficult to say whether or not standards of written and spoken English have fallen. There is no convincing evidence available, and most opinions depend very largely upon subjective impressions. These are not to be dismissed out of hand, but we have already shown how difficult it is to make valid comparisons with the past. We have also remarked that any speculation about standards all too frequently relates them to a particular kind of teaching. We received many letters which suggested that 'creativity' is now reverenced and that 'formal' work has virtually been banished. This is a particular area of contention where personal impression clearly counts heavily, especially since 'creativity' and 'formality' are hazy concepts. Exact or even approximate comparability of standards may be elusive, but parents and teachers alike know there have been new approaches and that some schools have operated them with remarkable success, some have adopted them uncritically, and some have set their face against them. Moreover, these approaches have frequently been discussed in the press, and they have featured prominently in publications of one kind or another and in teachers' courses. What is far from certain is how widespread is this change of emphasis. It is commonly believed that English in most primary schools today consists largely of creative writing, free reading, topic or project work, and improvised drama, and that spelling and formal language work have no place. When certain teaching methods attract a good deal of attention it is understandable that people should assume them to have become the norm. But what *is* the situation in schools? How general has been the shift of emphasis away from the formal to the 'permissive'? We decided at the outset that we would find out by enquiring of the schools themselves by way of detailed questionnaires. This survey is described in detail elsewhere in the Report, and from the tables of results it will be seen that a good deal of time is allocated to formal practice in English. The answers we received certainly did not reveal a picture of the decay of such work in the midst of a climate of unchecked creativity. Sceptics may say that the schools told us what they thought we wanted to hear, or what they surmised would present them in a respectable light. We do not believe this for one moment, but even if it were true, one is still left with a picture of what primary schools feel is the *acceptable* way to be teaching. Our survey gives no evidence of a large body of teachers committed to the rejection of basic skills and not caring who knows it. It is facile to assume that all manner of weaknesses can be ascribed simply to the wholesale spread of a permissive philosophy. One has to look more deeply. This we hope to do in the course of the Report, when we shall develop some of the points made here.

1.9   We have in effect been discussing the first of the two responses described in paragraph 1.6, and we believe that the diagnosis and remedy it offers is an over-simplification. We take the same view of the second when it regards standards of performance as of slight consequence compared with the personal growth or social orientation of the pupil. Every good teacher is concerned with the social and psychological development of his pupil. But we refer here in particular to the notion of English in the secondary school as almost exclusively a source of material for personal response to social issues. Literature is experienced largely in the form of extracts and is filleted for its social yield. Talk is shepherded into the area of publicised questions, of acute issues of the day. The writing that emerges from both is to a large extent judged for its success by the measure of commitment it seems to reveal. Genuine personal response in such circumstances is not easy to express. These public issues have been dwelt upon at length by television and the press, and the cliché responses generated inevitably find their way into the children's writing and talk. We must make it clear that we are not contesting the place of social concern in the curriculum of the secondary school. But we are questioning the philosophy of those teachers for whom it has become the core and essence of the English programme. *Of course* it is part of the English teacher's task to develop social awareness and responsibility. By its very nature this subject involves the contemplation of immediate and vicarious experience into which such sensibility enters. Indeed, English is rooted in the processing of experience through language. The pupil uses language to represent the experience to himself, to come to terms with it, to possess it more completely. It is a major part of the teacher's skill to extend the range of that experience, at first hand and through literature, in such a way that new demands are made on language. It is our contention that for some pupils that range of experience has been narrowed. We know that some very sensitive writing and lively talk have emerged from encounters with contemporary social issues. We have read and heard it. But we have read and heard as much which has reflected the child's inability to produce a genuine felt response, where he has had to fall back on the ready-made cliché reaction.

1.10   Is it possible, then, to make some kind of provisional generalisation about standards? There may be little profit in attempting to compare today's standards with those of the past, but we underline our conviction that standards of writing, speaking, and reading can and should be raised. The first thing that is required is a redefinition of what is involved. These three abilities are usually described as 'the basic skills', but like the terms 'formal' and 'progressive' this is a phrase which merits more precise definition than it tends to receive. It is often read to mean that language abilities can somehow be extracted from context, taught in the abstract, and fed back in. The evidence is that one acquires language as a pattern, not as an inert collection of units added serially, a mechanical accumulation of abstracted parts of speech. So we are not suggesting that the answer to improved standards is to be found in some such simple formula as: more grammar exercises, more formal speech training, more comprehension extracts. We believe that language competence grows incrementally, through an interaction of writing, talk, reading, and experience, the body of resulting work forming an organic whole. But this does not mean that it can be taken for granted, that the teacher does not exercise a conscious influence on the nature and quality of this growth. The teacher's first concern should be to create the conditions necessary for fluency, but he then has a responsibility to help the child improve the technical control of his work. What is the quality of the child's verbalisation of his experience? With what fidelity and coherence does he communicate it to his readers? The child should be brought up to see this technical control not as an abstraction imposed from without but as the means of communicating with his audience in the most satisfying and appropriate manner. His development of this ability can be expressed in terms of increasing differentiation. He learns to carry his use of English into a much broader range of social situations, to differing kinds of audience. The purposes to which he puts language grow more complex, so that he moves from a narrative level of organising experience to one where he is capable of sustained generalisation. Considered in these terms the handling of language is a complex ability, and one that will not be developed simply by working through a series of text-book exercises. If we regard this approach as inadequate we have equal lack of sympathy with the notion that the forms of language can be left to look after themselves. On the contrary, we believe that the teacher should intervene, should constantly be looking for opportunities to improve the quality of utterance. In schools where the principles of modern primary school education have been misinterpreted this often does not happen. We have talked to young teachers who have so misunderstood them as to believe they should never directly teach the children.

1.11   If a teacher is to control the growth of competence he must be able to examine the verbal interaction of a class or group in terms of an explicit understanding of the operation of language. We believe that because of the nature of their training this is precisely what many teachers lack, and this has implications for initial and in-service training. In succeeding chapters we discuss language and its relation to learning, and in the course of the Report we emphasise that if standards of achievement are to be improved all teachers will have to be helped to acquire a deeper understanding of language in education. This includes teachers of other subjects than English, since it is one of our contentions that secondary schools should adopt a language policy across the curriculum. Many teachers lack an adequate understanding of the complexities of language development, and they often hold the English teacher responsible for language performance in contexts outside his control. A great deal of work remains to be done to help teachers learn more about the nature of children's language development, its application to their particular subject, and their own role in the process. There is also the important question of the deployment of staff in the teaching of English itself. The English in a secondary school is sometimes in the hands of as many as 15 teachers, only four or five of whom are specialists in the subject. Almost a third of the 12 year olds in our sample had their English with more than one teacher. In the survey the replies from heads suggested that no fewer than a third of all secondary teachers engaged in the teaching of English have no qualification in the subject (see table 72). It also revealed (table 70) that only 37 per cent of those teaching English spend all their time on it, while 38 per cent spend less than half. In some cases a shortage of qualified English teachers forces a head to assign a non-specialist to the subject. On the other hand there are schools where no strenuous efforts are made to acquire English specialists precisely because it is thought possible to make up English time from other members of staff. Similarly, if timetable construction is presenting a difficulty it is not unknown for the recalcitrant single period to be labelled English and given to whichever teacher is not already engaged. There are, of course, many examples of schools which go to great lengths to avoid any such disadvantages to English. Moreover, we are aware that some schools adopt as a deliberate policy the kind of integrated humanities work in which a teacher of another subject becomes responsible for the pupils' English. In the best of such schemes there is strong support from the English specialists, sound planning, and good resources. However, it remains true that large numbers of pupils are taught English in circumstances which would be considered unacceptable in many other subjects. The attitude still prevails that most teachers can turn their hand to it without appropriate initial qualifications or additional training. In our view such an attitude is based on an ignorance of the demands of English teaching and the knowledge required of its practitioners. In the course of the Report we shall attempt to illustrate these, since we believe that only if they are fully recognised can an advance in the teaching of English be achieved.

REFERENCES

1. *The Teaching of English in England* (The Newbolt Report): HMSO: 1921.
2. H. Muller: *The Uses of English:* Holt, Rinehart, and Winston Inc.: 1967.

CHAPTER 2

Standards of Reading

2.1   We have been discussing the general context of English and come now to the particular issue of standards of reading, about which a good deal of concern has been expressed. Many people who wrote to us took as their starting point the belief that standards of literacy had fallen. In the course of this chapter we shall examine the basis for this assumption by considering such objective evidence as we have been able to discover. An immediate difficulty is in arriving at a universally acceptable definition of the terms 'literacy', 'semi-literacy', and 'illiteracy', for the uncertainty surrounding them makes objective discussion far from simple. There is a good deal of emotion adhering to the terms, which too often robs them of the benefit of a true perspective. For example, in response to a survey on students' reading 52 university lecturers said all their students were "illiterate to some degree". One lecturer in medicine is reported to have said: "All my students are illiterate when they come to university—the best are literate when they leave". The 1950 Ministry of Education pamphlet "Reading Ability" put it succinctly: "In truth most definitions of illiteracy amount to this—'that he is illiterate who is not as literate as someone else thinks he ought to be'."

2.2   The same document defined 'literate' as "able to read and write for practical purposes of daily life". And in the following year U.N.E.S.C.O. proposed the criterion "A person is literate who can, with understanding, both read and write a short, simple statement on his everyday life". It is a feature of definitions of literacy that they progressively demand more of the person who is to be defined as literate. Thus, a decade later U.N.E.S.C.O. had modified its criterion to "A person is literate when he has acquired the essential knowledge and skills which enable him to engage in all those activities in which literacy is required for effective functioning in his group and community". The term 'functional literacy' was used by Gray in his 1956 international survey[1] to describe the minimal level of efficiency acceptable to the society in which the individual lived. He saw this in the case of the U.S.A. as the standard that would usually be achieved by pupils in grade IV (10 year-olds). But in recent years it has been argued that the threshold should be raised to at least grade IX (15 year olds), since much of the reading material to which the adult in society is exposed is written at levels of difficulty far beyond the understanding of one who can merely render print into spoken language. A telling illustration of this was provided by the 'Survival Literacy Study', conducted for the U.S. National Reading Council in 1970. The purpose of the study was to determine the percentage of Americans lacking the functional reading skills to 'survive' as participants in the social and economic life of the country. The reading material consisted of five application forms in common use in daily life, ranked in an ascending order of difficulty. The results showed that 3 per cent of all Americans were unable to read adequately the form of application for public assistance, 7 per cent a simple identification form, 8 per cent a request for a driving licence, 11 per cent an application for a personal bank loan, and 34 per cent an application for medical aid. In our own country it has been suggested[2] that there are at least a million adults with a reading age[3] of below 9·0 who cannot read simple recipes, 'social pamphlets', tax return guides, claims for industrial injuries, national insurance guides for married women, and most of the Highway Code. Indeed, in the study which analysed these reading tasks it was suggested that such material, and the writing in the simplest daily newspaper, required a reading age of 13 for "a reasonable level of comprehension". The ability to read a newspaper is obviously one of the most basic and important purposes of the achievement of literacy. In the U.S.A. one researcher[4] took a fairly representative sample of eight articles from news publications, applied a readability test to each, and administered the tests to pupils aged 9 to 18. He calculated that readers who could not answer at least 35 per cent of the items could gain little or no information from material at that level of difficulty. Only 33 per cent of the 12 year olds and 65 per cent of the 18 year olds reached this 35 per cent level, though the pupils were drawn from middle class homes in a residential suburb. In other words, one third of all his 18 year olds were unable to read and comprehend news publications they would be likely to encounter in everyday life. Many American government bureaux, publishers, and trade unions have retained consultants to help them simplify prose. But it has often been found that even when this has been done the lowest grade of difficulty at which complex subject matter can be written approximates to a reading age of about 15. In other words, the level required for participation in the affairs of modern society is far above that implied in earlier definitions. It is obvious that as society becomes more complex and makes higher demands in awareness and understanding of its members the criteria of literacy will rise.

2.3   It would clearly have been beyond our resources to study in depth the question of comparability with other countries, nor would it have been profitable. If definitions of literacy present difficulties it is obvious that attempts to compare standards between countries present bigger ones. In the present state of research there is little to be gained from speculation on whether any one nation has the advantage over any other. Downing[5] makes this clear when he refers to claims made in Japan, Germany, and Finland that the rate of illiteracy there is exceptionally low. He points out that the very low validity of comparative statistics on literacy rates casts grave doubts on the evidence. Moreover, literacy rates expressed as percentages do not indicate actual performance levels. Two countries may claim to have illiteracy levels as low as 1 per cent, yet the actual level of reading achievement in one of the two countries may far surpass that of the other. We are faced again with the question of relativity, for one country's concept of literacy may be very different from another's.   Even weaker is the subjective anecdotal evidence about the achievements of a country's children. In a recent survey[6] reading comprehension was tested across fifteen countries. It was found that "the differences among developed countries are of rather modest dimensions . . . the variations do not seem very important or readily inter-pretable". We can only conclude with Downing that 'league tables' of literacy levels based on current evidence can have little validity. Nevertheless, though it is difficult to compare standards objectively between the developed nations there is no doubt that some feel a sense of urgency about their own conditions. The U.S.A. is a notable example. In 1969 the then U.S. Commissioner of Education announced that one in four American pupils had "significant reading deficiencies". He believed there should be a major effort to ensure that by the end of the 1970s no-one would be leaving school "without the skill and the desire necessary to read to the full limits of his capability". In the following year the Right to Read Effort was established with the purpose of ensuring that by 1980 99 per cent of all Americans under 16 and 90 per cent of all over 16 would have functional literacy. Financed by the U.S. Office of Education, it reflects the anxiety felt in the U.S.A. about the 18 million people who have been estimated as unable to read effectively.

2.4   Various figures have been suggested for the probable total of such people in England and Wales. We referred earlier to the figure of a million as one estimate, but some people have put it at twice that number, or even higher. It is, of course, impossible to be certain. In "The Trend of Reading Standards" [7] 3·18 per cent of the 15 year olds in England were found to be semi-literate by the definition given in the 1950 Ministry of Education pamphlet. This defined a semi-literate as a person whose reading age was 7·0 years or more but less than 9·0 on the Watts-Vernon test. An illiterate was given as one with a reading age of less than 7·0. The percentage of 3·18 per cent represents nearly 15,000 young people on the basis of the known number of 15 year olds in school in 1970. The corresponding percentage of 'semi-literates' in 1948 was 4·3. Thus for the past 23 years or so between 3 and 4 per cent of the pupil population has been leaving school with this level of attainment. Given the total of 15 year olds in each year a simple multiplication sum would produce an indication of all the semi-literate adults who have left school since 1948. The result would, of course, leave many unanswered questions. All it would tell us is that when these people left school they had obtained a low score on a particular reading test. We cannot know what has happened to them since, though it is a reasonable assumption that their reading ability has remained poor. Extrapolation to discover the numbers of those who left with a similar attainment during or before the war would obviously be very unreliable. All estimates of the number of illiterates and semi-literates in the population must therefore be hedged about with reservations. Nevertheless, it is obvious that although they represent a small percentage of the total population their numbers are considerable. Strictly speaking, adult illiteracy does not fall within our terms of reference; but the more closely we have examined the evidence the more certain we have become that attention to it should be included in our recommendations. For it represents in human terms the consequences for those children whom a national survey shows as a statistic.

2.5   Before turning to the empirical evidence in detail we must mention another aspect of literacy which attracts a good deal of public attention. This is the influence of television, to which many references were made in the evidence we received. Some witnesses felt that the growth of visual methods of expression and communication has led to a decline in the use of language, and that this had contributed to an increase in reading difficulties. It was suggested to us that children today are more accustomed to watching television in their leisure time than to using the library for information, and that they are less likely than in the past to see their parents reading.

One large education authority, itself a pioneer in educational television services, said that the hours children spent in watching television reduced their felt need to read and write. There is certainly evidence to suggest that children of school age are spending an increasing amount of time before the television set. According to a recent issue of "Social Trends" [8] children between the ages of 5 and 14 watched an average of 21 hours of television a week in February 1969. By February of 1973 this had risen to 25 hours. Judging from the many letters we received, there is a widespread and strongly held view that this tendency is a growing threat to the development of literacy. Such opinions are essentially subjective, and there is, in fact, very little empirical evidence to show whether television has had any effects on standards of reading or on the amount that children read. In a major study [9] carried out in this country in the 1950s Himmelweit and her colleagues studied the effect of television upon children of two age-groups, 10–11 and 13–14. They had the advantage of a control group, matched by ability, social background, etc, which had virtually no access to television, a condition which can no longer be reproduced. The study showed that when children were first exposed to television they read fewer books, but by the time it had been in their homes for 3 years they read at least as many as before. Only the reading of comics seems to have been lastingly affected. One of the most significant conclusions was that comparatively little reading was taking place anyway. "It's not that they used to read a great deal and then television came and destroyed the ability; they always read extremely little." The 10 + children were found to be reading on average 2·7 books in a month, and the 13 + children 2·5.

2.6   These figures approximate to those revealed by a study of children's reading by Whitehead [10] and his colleagues. In 1971, some 16 years after Himmelweit's research, they found that the 10+ children in their sample read on average 3·0 books per month, the 12+ children 2·2, and the 14+ children 1·9. This very recent study gives the firmest available indication of a relationship between the amounts of time children spend reading and watching television: " . . . it is clear that the amount of television viewing accomplished by most children cannot but restrict the amount of time available for other leisure activities, including reading, and we have in fact found an inverse relationship between amount of television viewing and amount of reading". The authors point out, however, that behind this generalisation lie many individual variations. There exists a substantial number of light viewers (defined as those who watch television less than 3 hours per weekday evening) who read little or nothing; and of heavy viewers (more than 3 hours) who read a great deal. In interviewing the children Whitehead formed the impression that they could be ranged along a continuum. At one end would be those active or hyper-active children who participate in many activities, including reading, sport, hobbies, and television watching. At the other would be the rather inert and apathetic children with few discernible interests. Looked at in these terms the amount of reading a child does is one manifestation of his or her general temperament, personality, situation, and life-style. This having been said, it is still possible for there to have been a general 'displacement' of one form of occupation by another. It seems likely that each child has a fixed amount of time, appetite and energy available for leisure activities in general or 'media contact' in particular. If new activities or new media capture part of the available time and energy they will 'displace' by the same amount those which formerly played an equivalent part in the child's life. As children grow older they read less *and* watch television less, in proportion to the extent their social activities take them out of the home. Social Trends No. 4 (1973) shows that among the 15–19 year olds television viewing time had dropped to an average of 17 hours a week.

2.7   Though the experimental evidence is limited we believe that the general effect of television watching has been to reduce the amount of time spent in private reading. Enough has been said to show that such a conclusion must be qualified in certain particulars. For one thing it cannot be taken for granted that if there were no television, books would automatically be the magnet. The Himmelweit study showed that television had not produced a sudden aversion from books. The Whitehead survey suggested that many children give little time to either. What cannot be known is whether there would have been a steady increase in book-reading over the years if television had not intruded. It is a reasonable assumption, however, that at least a proportion of those 25 hours of weekly viewing would be spent in reading.

2.8   Another charge laid against television is that it develops a mass culture, sometimes dreary to the point of mindlessness. Many of our correspondents claimed that it not only reduced interest in the written language but debased the spoken language as well. Radio was held to be at least as guilty in this. Between them radio and television spread the catch phrase, the advertising jingle, and the frenetic trivia of the disc-jockey. This is a large question, involving a discussion of cultural change which would take us beyond our terms of reference, but it is clear that the content and form of much radio and television utterance makes the teacher's job a great deal more difficult. On the other hand, both media have effects on children's language growth which are by no means always negative, a point which is developed in Chapter 6. Moreover, there is no doubt that television and radio are sources of material of the highest quality, which can and should be put to good use in schools at all age levels. Recommendations to this effect are made in Chapter 22.

2.9   There is one issue that has to be faced squarely. Nothing this Committee can say in isolation will change the viewing pattern of those evening hours which children spend in front of a set. The control of programmes lies with the broadcasters and the bodies to which they are responsible; and the control of viewing lies with the family. We share the opinion of many of our witnesses about some of the material the children see, but the problem is a difficult one. The broadcasters will say that they have to offer adult entertainment and that the parent is responsible for what he allows his child to watch. The parent may see the issue in much less simple terms; he experiences influences and pressures which make domestic censorship hard to introduce or maintain. We have to take care not to go beyond our terms of reference in suggesting that much more serious thought should be given to the influence of television on children. This is a large issue, and we are confining ourselves to that part of it which relates to the use of language. Broadcasting still contains within it a vigorous tradition of public service, and it is not insensitive to constructive comment. The professional educator is particularly well placed to offer that comment. The child who is watching 25 hours of television a week is spending almost as much time in front of a set as he spends in a classroom. That fact alone makes it a part of his experience so influential as to generate serious obligations on the part of those who provide it.

2.10   In trying to reach conclusions about standards of literacy we had access to two sources of information. One was the testimony of expert witnesses; the other the empirical evidence of surveys. Though these witnesses were not unanimous they showed a common tendency to be cautious in stating an opinion on standards. The following are from the submissions of prominent researchers, who were among the few witnesses who commented directly on standards from a study of the statistical evidence:

> "There is no convincing evidence that there has been a reduction in standards. Nowadays, more people have wider needs for literacy in different contexts in everyday life, and where limited abilities occur they are brought before our attention".

> "The most that can probably be said about the movement of reading standards in the last third of a century is that there was a considerable downward movement during the war years followed by an upward movement in the 20 years after the war which may have levelled out in the last few years. Whether pre-war standards were caught up and overtaken is more difficult to say, but other evidence suggests that standards of older children are rather higher and those of younger children lower than those prevailing in the 1930s".

> "Though the N.F.E.R. Report showed that the improvement in reading standards appears to have ceased, the *improved* standard of 1960 has been maintained. Nevertheless, more and more children are leaving infant school unable to read, and fewer teachers in junior schools seem to be equipped to teach the basic reading skills".

Most witnesses did not commit themselves to a view, or where they did they acknowledged that it was essentially based on their own personal impressions. The unequivocal expressions of opinion were contained in the general correspondence we received, and here there was a majority view that standards had declined, or at any rate were at a standstill.

2.11   Later in the chapter we shall consider some of the reasons offered for this suggested lack of progress; but first we must examine the research evidence available to us. This is derived in the main from the series of national surveys carried out by the N.F.E.R. for the Ministry of Education and later for the Department of Education and Science. The first of these took place in 1948 and has provided the basis for comparison against which subsequent results have been measured. This and later surveys were summed up in the report "Progress in Reading 1948–1964"[11], prepared by G. F. Peaker H.M.I. for the Department of Education and Science. It was claimed that during the 16 years of the surveys there had been an advance of 17 months of reading age for 11 year olds, and 20–30 months for 15 year olds. Not all reviewers have agreed that this represents what the report described as a "remarkable improvement". Several pointed out that the 1948 test scores were naturally depressed as a result of the war and that they therefore presented a low baseline which would flatter subsequent results.

A fundamental reference point in the thinking of some witnesses was the pre-war situation. But it is very much open to question whether it is possible to relate present-day standards to those of before the war. In 1948, when the Watts-Vernon was calibrated against those tests employed pre-war, the sample used for the comparison was a judgmental one arrived at on a local basis. The pre-war tests themselves were not standardised by means of a national sample. Thus there is no firm statistical base for comparison, and in terms of tackling today's problems it is questionable whether there is anything to be gained from attempting it.

2.12   The most recent surveys in the series, and the first since the 1966 summary, were "The Trend of Reading Standards" (1972) and "The Reading Standards of Children in Wales" (1973).[12] It should be said at once that it is not easy to make accurate assessment of the results of such surveys without studying them in depth. Indeed, we found in taking evidence that informed people have interpreted the N.F.E.R. researches in different ways. We accept both publications as responsible and accurate research reports. The limitations of their research, which we shall describe below, are fully discussed in the publications by the authors themselves. It is to the English report to which this section will be largely devoted, since it has generated a good deal of concern about the reading standards of today as compared with those revealed by the 1964 survey.

2.13   The best point at which to begin is to consider the tests from which the results have been derived. The two tests, the Watts-Vernon and the National Survey Form Six (N.S.6.), are narrowly conceived. The first was devised in 1947 as a silent reading test of the incomplete sentence type. It has 35 items and lasts 10 minutes. The second was developed in 1954 along similar lines but with more items (60) and a longer duration (20 minutes). *We do not regard these tests as adequate measures of reading ability. What they measure is a narrow aspect of silent reading comprehension.* This is not the place to define reading ability, which is analysed in detail in a later chapter, but we must record here our view that the tests in question are able to assess only a limited aspect of it. Both tests are technically *reliable* in the sense that they measure the same features to the same degree on different occasions. But their doubtful *validity* is now apparent, in that they measure only in part what they purport to measure*.

2.14   The problem is therefore one of attempting to assess the product of a variety of contemporary aims and methods with instruments constructed many years ago. The Watts-Vernon test was 23 years old and the N.S.6. 16 years old at the time of the last survey. The report gave examples from them to illustrate how they had aged: the use of such words as "mannequin parade" and "wheelwright" in the N.S.6. and "haberdashers" in the Watts-Vernon. It pointed out that children of today were less likely to use the term "bathing" for "swimming", and may be unfamiliar with such expressions as "four rules of arithmetic" and "pacific settlement of disputes". This is a more

---

*". . . the format of the tests does set limits on what aspects of the ability to read with understanding they can and do measure. Since the largest unit of language in these tests is the sentence, they do not measure, at least not to any significant degree, what might be called the inferential aspects of reading, such aspects as the ability to follow an argument or extract a theme". (The Trend of Reading Standards: Start and Wells: p. 17).

telling limitation than might as first sight appear. If with the passage of time even two or three of the items become less familiar the effect upon the test results could be important. The comparable mean scores obtained over 23 years differ so slightly that this kind of increase in the difficulty of a few items can have a disproportionate influence upon the result. In other words, if in these items the pupils are at an artificial disadvantage compared with their predecessors then there is an underestimate of their ability. Where changes in mean scores are extremely small from one survey to the next, every item counts.

2.15   Another serious limitation of these tests is that they do not provide adequate discrimination for the more able 15 year old pupils. In other words, many of these pupils are capable of dealing with more difficult items than the tests contain. A fuller account of this 'ceiling effect', as it is called, is given as an annex. The 'ceiling effect' was noted as a defect of the Watts-Vernon test as long ago as 1956, and indeed the introduction of the N.S.6. was a response to it. There is now evidence to show that the 'ceiling effect' of the N.S.6. itself is causing problems, since at the senior level in particular many of the items are too easy. Indeed, according to the Welsh report it is perhaps now more serious than for the Watts-Vernon. The N.S.6. test was used alone in the 1972 survey[13] of reading standards in Northern Ireland. Because of the closeness of the achieved sample to the design sample it is possible to assess the special features of N.S.6. with somewhat more confidence than is possible from the English and Welsh surveys. And the most significant feature to emerge is the extent to which N.S.6. fails to allow able 15 year olds to score at a level which reflects their ability.

2.16   A histogram from the Northern Ireland report has been reproduced as Diagram 7 in the annex. This represents the scores for all the 11 and 15 year olds. The difference in the distribution is remarkable. It will be noted that the scores of the 11 year olds are well spread out but that those of the 15 year olds are 'piled up' towards the top end of the scale. This is a clear indication that the more able 15 year olds found the test too easy. The author of the report concludes that "scores for such pupils may be artificially depressed by the low ceiling of the test. It also follows that the test discriminates adequately only among the pupils whose reading scores are in the lower half of the range". Some idea of what this suggests about the performance of the more able readers can be gained from a scrutiny of the later items in the test. Quite apart from making demands upon vocabulary they require the reader to handle complex abstractions with some confidence. And yet questions of this calibre have proved too easy to stretch the older and brighter children. When these children are achieving near-maximum scores there is little scope for them to improve their performances and thus to affect the mean score. If in their case the kind of ability measured by the tests were improving, the tests themselves would probably be incapable of detecting it. This fact, and the ageing of the tests, would be sufficient to produce a levelling-off in the rate of increase in scores. The principle of extrapolation cannot be applied indiscriminately. It is not necessarily the case that a well-established trend in a certain direction must continue almost indefinitely. Thus, the roughly uniform increase of mean scores on the tests through the 1950s and into the early 1960s encouraged expectations of continued increase at the same rate.

This clearly could not happen. Improvements made by the poorer performers can raise the mean score for the age group, but the increase over the years can hardly be expected to go on at the same rate. For these reasons it is important to consider not only the mean scores but also the *distributions* of scores on tests which are suspected of having these limitations.

2.17   In both the English and Welsh surveys the sampling was inadequate in a number of respects. This was not the fault of the N.F.E.R. researchers—a postal strike played havoc with their plans—but the reports make clear the reservations of their authors. In the English survey only 60 per cent of the secondary schools were able to reply before the strike began, and 7 per cent of these declined to take part. The result was a sample of secondary schools numbering just over a half of those selected for inclusion. In such circumstances was the achieved sample still representative and random? Moreover, it was further affected by a high degree of pupil absenteeism, due largely to the fact that the testing took place in the last fortnight of the Lent term. There was some evidence to show that the proportion of Easter leavers absent for the tests was much greater than the corresponding proportion of pupils who were not leaving at Easter. This could have the effect of reducing the number of less able pupils taking part. The 1960 and 1961 senior surveys took place in the middle of the Autumn term, a time when the absentee rate of the less able was probably lower. The obvious inference is that the 1971 sample estimates for the 15 year olds could be artificially high, since if the absent pupils had in fact participated their scores might have lowered the mean. Start and Wells express it thus:

"... we must suspect that the less able are under-represented in our 1971 samples to a greater extent than in those of the last two surveys. In this case, the sample estimates for the present survey would be spuriously high in relation to those of the 1960 and 1961 surveys. Unfortunately it is not possible to estimate the extent to which the 1971 sample estimates may be spuriously high ... The extent may not be that great ... the Watts-Vernon test sample mean for all seniors would have been, at a very rough guess, 0·2 points of score less than the mean actually obtained. The corresponding figure for the N.S.6. would be 0·3 points of score lower".

There is one further factor which may have affected the estimate of standards. This is the possibility that the 11 year olds were handicapped by lack of familiarity with objective-style tests. Start and Wells observe that the children's 'test sophistication' may have been lower in 1970 than six or ten years earlier, when the 11+ examination was widespread and they were more accustomed to meeting tests of this kind.

2.18   In view of all these doubts and caveats it might be wondered whether any firm conclusions can be drawn from the most recent N.F.E.R. survey, and whether any safe comparisons can therefore be made with earlier surveys. There is, however, a degree of independent confirmation which has been little remarked. In the first place, the movement of scores obtained in England is comparable with those obtained in Wales, and this is evident at both senior and junior levels. In the second place, there is a degree of independence in the results obtained from the Watts-Vernon and N.S.6. testing of juniors. This is because separate but parallel samples of schools were drawn at the junior level in both the English and Welsh surveys. One sample was given the Watts-Vernon test, the other the N.S.6. When the trends are repeated in separate samples they give more grounds for confidence in them.

2.19   We have said enough about the limitations of the results derived from the national surveys, and we must add that it is not the fault of the authors that many people have ignored their reservations. Having expressed our own reservations about the tests and sampling we now turn to the tables of results. Reproduced below are the most important tables from the English report:

15 YEAR OLDS

Comparable mean scores with standard errors[14] for pupils aged 15·0 years Watts-Vernon Test (Maintained schools and direct grant grammar schools).

Table 1

Date of Survey	1948	1952	1956	1961*	1971
Mean score	20·79	21·52	21·71	(a) 23·6 (b) 24·1	23·46
Standard error	0·37	0·20	0·26	0·14	0·26

*Although only secondary modern and comprehensive children were tested in 1961, these figures are estimates of total school populations: (a) taking other schools at the 1956 level, (b) supposing other schools made the same advance as secondary modern schools between 1956 and 1961.

(Table 3.3 from "The Trend of Reading Standards", N.F.E.R.).

Comparable mean scores with standard errors for pupils aged 15·0 years. N.S.6. test (Maintained schools only).

Table 2

Date of survey	1955*	1960	1971
Mean score	42·18	44·57	44·65
Standard error	0·64	0·73	0·83

*England and Wales—scores would probably be slightly higher (0·20?) if England only were taken.

(Table 3.4 from "The Trend of Reading Standards", N.F.E.R.).

11 YEAR OLDS

Comparable mean scores with standard errors for pupils aged 11·0 years, since 1948.
Watts-Vernon test (Maintained schools only).

Table 3

Date of survey	1948	1952	1956	1964	1970
Mean score	11·59	12·42	13·30	15·00	14·19
Standard error	0·59	0·30	0·32	0·21	0·38

(Table 3.1 from "The Trend of Reading Standards", N.F.E.R.).

Comparable mean scores with standard errors for pupils aged 11 years 2 months, since 1955.

N.S.6. test (Maintained schools only).

Table 4

Date of survey	1955	1960	1970
Mean score	28·71	29·48	29·38
Standard error	0·55	0·52	0·92

(Table 3.2 from "The Trend of Reading Standards", N.F.E.R.).

Our considered view is that the results of the 15 year olds, presented in tables 3.1 and 3.2, are not disturbing in themselves, having regard to the limitations to be found in the tests. Scores on N.S.6. continue their slight increase, while those on Watts-Vernon increase until 1961 and then decrease slightly by 1971. The point to be emphasised is that the changes in the scores on both tests in the last decade are not large enough to be statistically significant; and the most reasonable conclusion is that the standards of 15 year olds have remained the same over the period 1960–71. The authors of the 1970/71 survey report made the point that "there seems to have been a steady increase in the weak tail of the 15 year olds over the past 23 years". This statement is easily misinterpreted, for it refers to the shape of the frequency distribution and not to the actual mean scores of the poorer readers. In the earlier surveys the range of scores which separated the best from the average reader was much the same as that separating the average reader from the weakest. But in later surveys the 'ceiling' of the maximum score has restricted the range of scores available to the above average and average readers. This has resulted in the spread of scores covered by the poorer readers, "the weak tail", becoming relatively more pronounced. We therefore cannot accept the suggestion made to us in evidence that "at the bottom of the scale a group approximating to a sixth of the school population has been showing a slight but steady decline in attainment for the last 23 years". Inspection of Table 3.6 and Figure 3.4 of "The Trend of Reading Standards" shows that the lowest standards have clearly risen during this period. Similarly, an examination of the difference in scores between the 10th and 90th percentiles at the age of 15 shows that this difference has *decreased* from 18·8 points of score in 1948 to 17·5 points in 1971. This apparent narrowing of the gap between the poor and the good reader emphasises the restrictions of the maximum score on the test used. The 'ceiling' has pegged back the top sixth, and the bottom sixth have been catching up as their scores improved*.

2.20   At junior level the following results are to be found:

(*a*) A steady increase of 3·41 points on Watts-Vernon from 1948 to 1964, then a decrease of 0·81 points between 1964 and 1970.

---

*This increase in the scores of the lowest achievers must not be confused with the issue of whether there is a rising proportion of poor readers among the children of un-skilled and semi-skilled workers. This important question is considered in detail later in the chapter.

(b) On N.S.6. an increase of 0·77 points between 1955 and 1960, then a decrease of 0·10 points between 1960 and 1970.

The picture here is thus one of steadily rising scores through the 1950s to a peak in the early 1960s, and a slight decline in scores (0·81 and 0·10) by 1970. We have also had access to the findings of other surveys of reading standards, but before discussing these we must add a word about how their results should be evaluated. If *national* standards are under discussion, then one needs either a national sample or a collection of a large number of local surveys which taken together represent accurately the national population. Such a collection does not exist, and it would in any case be extremely difficult to construct an adequate national sample from a series of local studies. One of the reasons why it is so easy to form a distorted view of the national picture is the fact that local surveys are often carried out in large urban areas not typical of the national situation.

2.21   Furthermore, as any survey obtains its results on the basis of sampling from a given population, it is very important to bear in mind any changes over time in the characteristics of the population from which the sample is drawn. If this population alters between surveys the trends they identify will be partly, and even mainly, sociologically determined. It will thus be extremely difficult to isolate valid interpretations of changes in standards of reading, or for that matter of other cognitive abilities. One good example of a changing population is to be found in recruitment to the Army, an organisation which monitors its intake so that year by year it is possible to record the mean score of each year's entrants. But little is known about the population of potential army recruits of which these intakes are samples. Indeed it is highly probable that the nature of the intake is decided by economic factors and other causes which fluctuate considerably in the short term. In times of economic boom the pool of potential army recruits is likely to be greatly reduced. Thus the mean scores recorded each year are derived from samples of a changing population, so that one cannot interpret trends with any certainty. A similar argument would apply to business concerns, or even individual schools, which draw their intake from an unspecified population subject to changes wrought by economics, the movement of social groups, or other influencing factors. It is clear, then, that local surveys have severe disadvantages for determining trends in national standards and that the basic difficulty is the well known one of estimating the standards of a definable population from a sample. National trends can only be properly evaluated by national surveys properly designed.

2.22   That having been said, the converse must be recognised. A national survey does not tell us anything about the circumstances of any given area. Local surveys have the considerable virtue that they allow the study of those psychological and sociological differences which might be ignored, avoided, or simply masked by national averages. They can complement the broad generalisations derived from a national survey and identify important local problems which might have equally important consequences for the nation as a whole. The survey carried out by the Inner London Education Authority is a case in point. Inner London is particularly atypical of the country at large. Totally urban, the population is skewed in social class towards the lower income groups, and the proportion of immigrants at the time of the survey was 17 per cent. The 1971 I.L.E.A. investigation was a follow-up of children who had been tested in 1968 when aged 8+. At the age of eleven 26,202 children were re-tested on two parallel versions of an N.F.E.R. sentence completion test. (The results of these cannot, of course, be directly compared with those derived from the Watts-Vernon and N.S.6.). It was found that the standardised scores of the children at 8+ and 11+ did not alter significantly; the change was from 94·6 to 94·9. It will be noted that the scores were markedly below the average (100) which was obtained by children of the same age when these tests were standardised on a national basis. Within the apparent stability from 8 to 11, however, the proportion of poor readers in the semi-skilled and unskilled groups increased from 17·9 per cent and 25·9 per cent respectively in 1968 to 22·0 per cent and 28·8 per cent in 1971.

2.23   In Aberdeen[15] in 1972 over 2,500 children were tested, representing 99 per cent of the two year groups concerned: 8 and 11. This was a repeat of an assessment carried out 10 years earlier in 1962, when the same coverage of 99 per cent was obtained and the same tests used: N.F.E.R. (Sentence) Reading Test A.D. and Test N.S.6. The results of this survey were of particular interest to us in two respects. Firstly, they are very much in line with those of the English survey, a fact to which the authors themselves draw attention: "The N.F.E.R. findings on recent trends in reading standards (i.e. in England) are confirmed by this study. While at the age of 8 years, the standard of performance in reading comprehension (in Scotland) is relatively unchanged, at age 11 there has been a slight decline in average standard. The difference between the 1962 and 1972 averages, however, is small—only two-thirds of one point of score in a test with 60 items. It would be reasonable to conclude therefore that standards are essentially unchanged over the past ten years". Secondly the results provide an interesting analysis by social class. It was found that among children with fathers in professsional or managerial jobs the average standard had improved, or at least been maintained. But among those with fathers in semi-skilled or unskilled jobs the average performance at 11 was seriously below the standard of the equivalent social group 10 years earlier.

2.24   As the national surveys in England and Wales did not record the social class of the pupils such information could not be obtained from them. However, there is further evidence to be obtained from other sources which confirms this relationship. For example, the National Child Development Study[16] revealed that 48 per cent of the children from social class V were poor readers at 7, compared with 8 per cent in social class I. Several studies have shown that the position worsens as the children grow older, there being a progressive decline in the performance of children of lower socio-economic groups between the ages of 7 and 11. The Educational Priority study[17] was applied to four educational priority areas, three in inner-city areas and the fourth in two small economically depressed mining towns. The children were given an N.F.E.R. sentence completion test, and a score of 80 was taken to distinguish non-readers or virtual non-readers. Excluding the immigrant children it was found that the proportions of children in this category in the four areas were 19 per cent, 35·8 per cent, 21·7 per cent and 17·7 per cent. The researchers concluded that the overall performance in E.P.A.s is not pulled down by a very low set of scores from a small group in an otherwise normal population. On the contrary, the results display a much more general pattern of low attainment, with very few children falling in the higher scoring groups.

2.25   We are aware that the effects of social class are not specific to reading. Several studies have shown that the correlation is with attainment in general. For example, in research carried out for the Plowden Committee[18], the most powerful variable was found to be the School Handicap Score (S.H.S.), a weighted sum of Father's Occupation, Father's Education, Mother's Education, Number of Books in the Home, and (minus) the number of siblings. Nevertheless, the relation with reading is a reality, and it seems to be universal. In a study in Swedish elementary schools Malmquist[19] found a distinct association between reading ability and social group; and evidence of a wider significance emerges from the comparative study of reading comprehension in 15 countries, in which the S.H.S. was again used. Differences in achievement among the developed countries were of modest dimensions, but they all had in common this important feature: that a child's family background gives a clear prediction of his achievement in reading at age 10 and age 14. There is evidence to suggest that the slight decline in scores at 11 years of age in the 1970/71 survey may well be linked to a rising proportion of poor readers among children of semi-skilled and unskilled workers. Such an influence does not, of course, conflict with our earlier observation that there has been no decline in the attainment of the bottom sixth of the school population. It is perfectly possible to find an increase in the *proportion* of children from a low socio-economic group and at the same time a narrowing of the gap between the best and the weakest readers. The two ideas are really unrelated, since one refers to proportions, the other to differences in the range of scores. What appears to be happening is that while reading standards at the lower end of the ability range have improved in most socio-economic groups, the poor readers among the children of the unskilled and semi-skilled have not improved their standards commensurately. The result is that the lower end of the ability range has an increased proportion of these children.

2.26   There remains the question of the national reading standards of 7 year olds. It is not, of course, the practice to carry out national surveys of the reading attainment of children of this age, and there is therefore no comparable evidence about their standards from which to draw conclusions. Nevertheless, there is much conjecture about the reading ability of 7 year olds today as compared to that in previous years. It is clear that for many people this is the age which causes the greatest concern. One recurring point in the correspondence we received was the belief that there is an increasing tendency for children to pass from the infant to the junior stage without a good grounding in reading. The research study[20] most often quoted is one carried out in the West Midlands in which it was found that between 1961 and 1967 the percentage who had not started to learn to read had risen sharply. In the earlier year it was true of 25 per cent of children in the sample of 2,000; by the end of the period the figure had risen to 40 per cent. There is a similar indication in the National Child Development Study[21], which said that in 1965: " . . . some 10 per cent of 7 year olds in the final term of their infant schooling had barely made a start with reading. A further 37 per cent had progressed beyond this stage but continued to need specific help". Both these studies were based on substantial samples and they can be taken as good indicators of a general situation. Their results are compatible with those of Morris[22] in Kent, where 45 per cent of 1st year juniors still required teaching help of the kind normally given in the infant school, and 19 per cent were virtually non-readers. Other local studies appear to substantiate these findings. Bookbinder[23] refers to three such studies—in Brighton, Salford, and Bristol—and suggests that children now start to read later but then make more rapid progress than in former times. From the evidence available there seems to be a 'prima facie' case for saying that children of 7 are not as advanced as formerly in those aspects of reading ability which are measured by tests. It can be put no more strongly than that, for the evidence has obvious limitations for purposes of generalisation. If there are doubts about the fact, there are even greater doubts about the putative cause. Much public comment is quite categorical in ascribing it to poor teacher training, or to a neglect of reading in favour of creative activities, which is cited as one of the effects of 'progressivism'. These propositions are examined in the appropriate chapters, but it is worth anticipating briefly in the case of the second, since this is the one most commonly advanced. In our survey we tested the hypothesis that infant schools neglect reading practice, and the relevant tables of results are reproduced in Chapter 13. A questionnaire of this kind obviously cannot assess quality, but it will be seen that in quantitative terms reading featured prominently in the infant schools in our sample, however they were organised. Our own visits to schools and our discussions with H.M. Inspectors confirm us in the belief that infant schools take seriously their responsibility for teaching children to read, though there are, of course, considerable variations in the extent to which they are successful.

2.27   There is a strong belief, reflected in much of the testimony we received, that if children surge ahead in their first or second year in the junior school they have not lost by starting late. This argument can be examined against a comparison of the West Midlands Study and National Child Development Study findings with those of "The Trend of Reading Standards". The samples are by no means a perfect fit, and any comparisons must be treated with appropriate caution. Allowing for this, however, it might be expected that the results of the first two would be reflected in the third. That is to say, a poor showing at 7 at the time of the earlier studies should predict a decline in standards at 11 at the time of the next national survey. To an extent, the prediction has proved true, in the sense that the progress shown in earlier national surveys has not been maintained. On the other hand, it could be argued that the performance of the 11 year olds is very much better than might have been expected from the prognostications, and that a good deal of productive learning has taken place in the junior years. Generalisations from this kind of comparison must not be taken too far. Between 1964 and 1970/71 the mean score of the 11 year olds decreased by 0·81 of an answer on the Watts-Vernon test, and between 1960 and 1970/71 by 0·1 of an answer on the N.S.6. test. It would clearly be impossible to evaluate this degree of decline in terms of the levels of achievement at 7 and the learning experiences of the children in the intervening years. The most that can be done is to consider the strength of alternative interpretations. As we have seen, one view would have it that there is no cause for alarm; that the decline at 11 is so slight as to be of little consequence, and that it does not justify increasing the pressure in the infant school. The other would say that anything less than a continued rise at 11 is evidence of falling standards, and that the junior schools are not properly equipped to make good the deficiencies of children who come to them as non-readers.

2.28   In Morris's study, cited above, it was found that 76 per cent of the junior school teachers in the sample had received no training in infant methods. 52 per cent lacked any infant school experience, and 18 per cent had no knowledge of how to teach children to read. The I.L.E.A. Literacy Survey showed that only 1 in 8 of the junior teachers had received specific training in reading techniques. Smaller-scale studies have pointed to similar conclusions and have suggested that as a general rule the junior school teacher is not equipped to cope in an expert fashion with children who have not made a start in reading. In evidence to the Committee many junior school heads have agreed that this is a difficulty with which they are faced. Their teachers have not received the training to enable them to assess when a child should have acquired a particular 'learning set' in reading, and how to contrive that he does. What is of particular concern to us is that the child who has not started to read might come to be regarded from an early stage as a 'remedial case'. Where the majority of children *have* made a good start to reading, and where the class teacher makes no claim to be able to teach the beginning stages, it is all too likely that the remainder will be 'withdrawn' for 'remedial' treatment very early in their junior school life. We would not be so unrealistic as to believe that every child should be a competent reader on leaving the infant school. But we would certainly be unhappy with a situation where the foundations of reading were not thoroughly laid there.

2.29   In summing up our conclusions about standards it is necessary to return first to the national survey. Despite all the reservations about the tests, absenteeism, and the size and nature of the achieved sample, the results of the N.F.E.R. survey still provide the best estimate of the country's reading standards. The remainder of the evidence has, on the whole, given us confidence in our interpretation of this estimate.

At the age of 11 no significant change in reading standards over the decade 1960–1970 emerges from the N.S.6. survey. But the movement in Watts-Vernon scores from 1964 to 1970 just achieves significance (at the 5 per cent level), so that such movement as did occur was in all probability downwards. The indications are that there may now be a growing proportion of poor readers among the children of unskilled and semi-skilled workers. Moreover, the national averages almost certainly mask falling reading standards in areas with severe social and educational problems.

At 15 years of age reading standards, as measured by the tests, have remained approximately the same over the period 1960–1971, again after an earlier period of steady increase from the 1948 baseline. We believe that the ceiling effect of the tests is causing such distortion in the score distributions that the computed mean scores must be viewed with considerable suspicion. The statistical results from the survey at both age points are not greatly disturbing, but neither do they leave room for complacency. We do not believe it is sufficient to rely on a 1948 baseline for measuring the movement in reading standards; nor are we satisfied that the present methods of monitoring them are adequate. We accordingly recommend that a new system of monitoring should be introduced.

2.30   In the chapters which follow we advocate those measures which we believe will lead to the development of the complex of skills that go to make up literacy. Reading must not be thought of as an uncomplicated skill like walking, acquired when young then left to look after itself. Reading, writing, talking and listening are associated abilities which the school should go on developing throughout a pupil's educational life. Teachers can do this only if they understand these abilities, and that means recognising them as an area of learning which demands expert knowledge. In the secondary school it means an end to the ill-informed view of English that because anyone can speak it anyone can teach it. And it means that all teachers should be made aware in their training of the complex role that language plays in their work, whatever they are teaching. Literacy is a corporate responsibility, in which the leadership should be provided by teachers with specialist knowledge but in which every other teacher shares. Standards will not be raised if the responsibility is seen as falling to a small part of the teaching population. To blame the infant teacher for every 'failed' reader is to misunderstand what reading is all about. To blame the English teacher for every mistake a pupil makes is to misunderstand how language and learning interact. Literacy demands a continuity and community of endeavour.

ANNEX.   THE 'CEILING EFFECT' OF READING TESTS.

Copyright

We are grateful to the following copyright holders for permission to reproduce diagrams: the Book Publishing Division, National Foundation for Educational Research for "The Trend of Reading Standards", and the Northern Ireland Council for Educational Research for "Reading Standards in Northern Ireland".

2.31   Suppose we want to measure attainment trends in reading over a long period of time. We do not know the shape of the distribution in the population, but for simplicity we assume it to be at least roughly normal (bell-shaped). What are the requirements of the measuring test?

The most fundamental is that it should be *valid*, in which case the test scores will be distributed over the full range of attainment. Should attainment improve, the range will either be extended upwards or shift bodily upwards, or both. Therefore there should be sufficient room upon the measurement scale for the whole distribution to move along it if improvement should occur in all parts of the range.

Diagram 1 illustrates this, exaggerating the movement.

Diagram 1

MOVEMENT OF DISTRIBUTIONS OF SCORES
SHOWING NO CEILING EFFECT

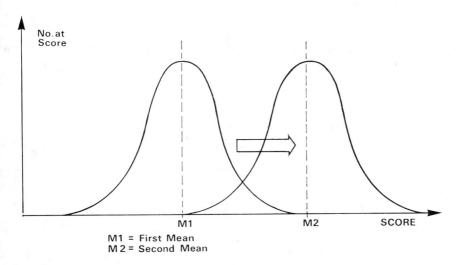

M1 = First Mean
M2 = Second Mean

This may be represented by means of percentile curves which are typically S-shaped when reflecting a normal distribution. See Diagram 2 below:

Diagram 2

MOVEMENT OF
CUMULATIVE DISTRIBUTION OF SCORES
SHOWING NO CEILING EFFECT

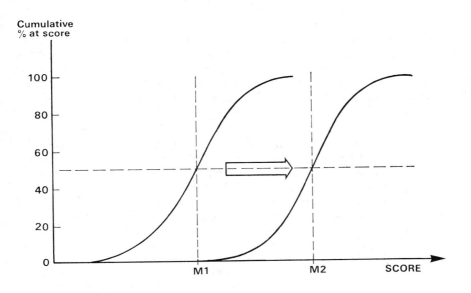

Now suppose we do not have a scale which has sufficient head-room for the whole distribution to move upward in score, since the more able pupils are capable of scoring more than the maximum number of items provided. What would be the effects?

2.32   The effects would be noticeable in the distribution of scores as a 'piling up' of scores at the ceiling of the test, shown here in exaggerated form:

Diagram 3

MOVEMENT OF DISTRIBUTION OF SCORES SHOWING A CEILING EFFECT

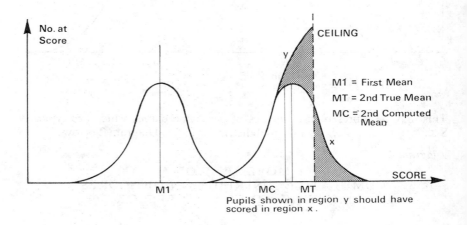

Pupils shown in region y should have scored in region x .

Those pupils who would have been capable of scoring in region x would be held to a score below the ceiling limit. In tests of the multiple choice form and/or with guessing corrections such pupils would not simply *all* score the maximum. (In a large sample some fluctuation could be expected if the test were retaken, as those who guessed right on one occasion might be wrong on another.)

In the N.S.6. a guessing correction is employed that terminates scoring if seven successive responses are incorrect. Only correct scores *before* the incorrect sequence of seven are counted, and those occurring after it are discounted as being probably guesses. Now it may happen that a pupil who answers correctly up to a number less than seven from the maximum could well continue to score beyond the maximum if additional items were available. Thus a small proportion who score as low as 54 on the N.S.6., which has a 60 maximum, are potential scorers in region x. The proportion is likely to be small because the N.S.6., like the W.V., is a highly reliable test; that is to say, the fluctuation of scores on re-testing would probably be low. In terms of the shape of the percentile score curve the effect would be as shown below:

Diagram 4

MOVEMENT OF
CUMULATIVE DISTRIBUTION OF SCORES
SHOWING A CEILING EFFECT

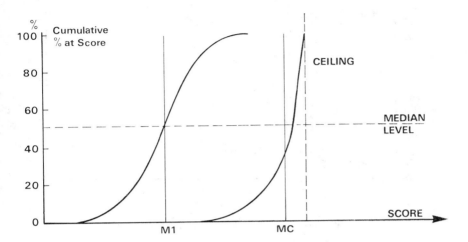

The top of the 'S' vanishes and there is 'bellying' of the lower portion of the curve. The mean would lie below the median and not on it as it would have done in an undistorted distribution.

What effects would the distortion produced by the ceiling have on the estimates of population parameters?

(*a*) As the distribution was no longer normal in form the sample standard deviation would not denote the same idea of measuring a symmetrical spread about the mean.

(*b*) As the sample standard deviation would be suspect, so too would the estimate of Standard Error which gives confidence in the probable position of the estimated mean for the population.

(*c*) The mean itself, though still computable, may be seen no longer to reflect the true attainment of the sample and hence no longer to provide an accurate estimate of the value within the population from which the sample is drawn.

2.33   Let us now examine how this exposition throws light on the results obtained with the W.V. and N.S.6. tests in the recent national surveys.

Figs 3.3 and 3.4 from page 38 of "The Trend of Reading Standards" show the situation on the Watts-Vernon test for 11 year old and 15 year old children respectively. Diagrams 5 and 6 reproduce these figures. Diagram 5 below (Fig 3.3) shows a parallel set of S-curves moving across the scale as standards rise. There is no ceiling effect with these 11 year olds, because even in 1964 the highest scoring pupil scored only 27, the maximum possible being 35.

Diagram 5

Scores in the reading tests of 1948–70 inclusive (11-year-old pupils in maintained schools)

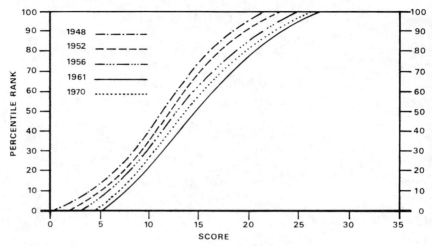

(Figure 3.3 from "The Trend of Reading Standards", N.F.E.R.).

Diagram 6 (Fig 3.4), on the other hand, shows that even in 1948 some 15 year old pupils were scoring the maximum. In succeeding years the 'top of the S' has almost disappeared and 'bellying' has increased as the distortion of the distribution of scores has become more marked. There is thus a definite ceiling on the W.V. at age 15, a fact which has been known since the early 1950s.

Diagram 6

Scores in the reading tests of 1948-71 inclusive (15-year-old pupils in maintained schools)

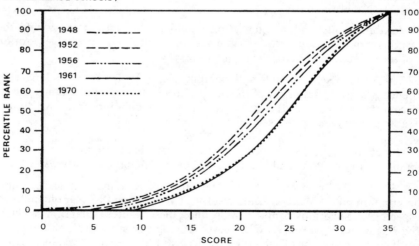

(Figure 3.4 from "The Trend of Reading Standards", N.F.E.R.).

Start and Wells give no comparable graph which presents a similar family of curves for the N.S.6., but they do give data for 1971 (see diagram 8).

The Northern Ireland survey of 1972 supplies a distribution of scores on N.S.6. at 15. Fig 3 from page 9 of that survey is reproduced here as diagram 7. There is a clear difference between the roughly normal distribution of reading attainment at age 11 and the distorted and curtailed distribution at age 15. The bell-shaped distribution of 11 year old scores is seen best if the page is turned sideways.

Diagram 7

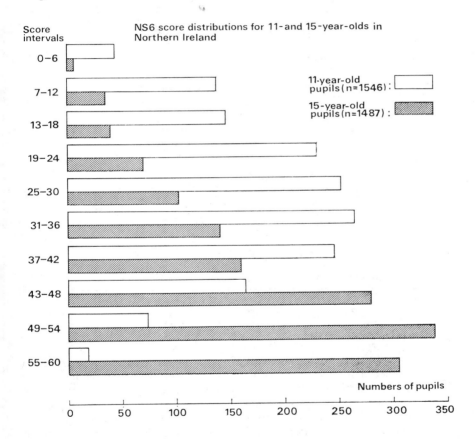

(Figure 3 from "Reading Standards in Northern Ireland", N.I.C.E.R.).

The following diagram depicts the percentile distribution for 15 year olds on both the N.S.6. and W.V. in the English survey of 1971. On the larger scales used in this diagram one can see that there is still some 'top to the S' left on the W.V. but none at all on the N.S.6. The ceiling effect of the N.S.6. is more severe at 15 than that of the W.V.

Diagram 8

PERCENTILE DISTRIBUTION OF SCORES
FOR 15 YEAR OLDS IN ALL MAINTAINED
SCHOOLS IN ENGLAND, 1971

Based on figures from Tables 4.3 and 4.4, Start and Wells, Page 59

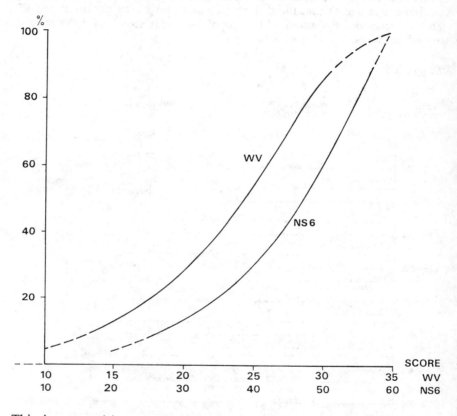

This is a surprising result. Many people expect the reverse to be true, because the introduction of N.S.6. in 1953 was in part an attempt to provide a test of higher ceiling than the W.V., whose ceiling had been recognised. It must be acknowledged that the attempt has failed. However, we cannot simply conclude on the basis of the ceiling effect alone that one test is better than the other, for while the Watts-Vernon test *appears* to be less affected by 'ceiling effects', the question of validity should be kept in mind, a point discussed in paragraph 2.14.

2.34   What are the implications of the test ceiling for the interpretation of results from the national surveys of reading standards?

Firstly, the meaning of the computed standard error of the mean is in doubt. When there is no longer a symmetrical normal distribution, computing the standard deviation of the sample scores in effect averages out the asymmetry. As it is the standard deviation which is used to estimate the standard error of the mean, the confidence limits set on the position of the mean must be interpreted with great care. More seriously the computed mean itself may be seen to underestimate the probable true mean reading attainment of 15 year olds. We must conclude that neither the W.V. nor N.S.6. can be used to give accurate estimates of reading ability at age 15. Sentence completion tests of this type do not appear capable of discriminating between the performances of the most able of these children. To this extent, reading ability has outstripped the available tests.

REFERENCES AND NOTES

1. W. S. Gray: *The Teaching of Reading and Writing:* U.N.E.S.C.O.: 1956.

2. D. Moyle *et al: Readability of Newspapers:* Edge Hill College of Education: 1973.

3. The term 'reading age' is used throughout this chapter, since it is the measure most commonly employed when standards of reading are being discussed. A reading age is obtained by transposing test scores on to a scale expressed in terms of years of development. We consider it in many ways a misleading concept which can obscure more than it reveals. Its use assumes that progress in reading can be equated with certain arbitrary units of time. In other words, learning to read is looked upon as consisting of equal steps which can be placed alongside another scale of equal steps, namely months and years. But there are no grounds whatever for supposing that reading progress is a linear process of this kind, and indeed there is evidence to the contrary. Nor is it reasonable to believe that the difference between reading ages of 6·6 years and 8·6 years is the same as the difference between those of 10·6 and 12·6. Even if these facts are disregarded, the concept of reading age is of limited practical value for teachers. If a statement like "a reading age of 7·0 years" is to have any real meaning, then the characteristics of "7 year old reading" must be known and defined. This would be difficult to achieve. The average 7 year old reader exists only as a statistical abstraction, and unless one can ascribe to reading ages attributes which have real meaning the term is highly misleading. It simply cannot be assumed that children having the same reading age read in the same way, require identical teaching, and will profit from similar books and materials.

4. J. R. Bormuth: *An operational definition of comprehension instruction:* in *Psycholinguistics and The Teaching of Reading:* International Reading Association: 1969.
J. R. Bormuth: *Development of Standards of Readability:* University of Chicago: 1971.

5. ed. J. Downing: *Comparative Reading:* Macmillan: New York: 1973.

6. R. L. Thorndike: *Reading Comprehension Education in Fifteen Countries: International Studies in Evaluation III:* International Association for the Evaluation of Educational Achievement: 1973.

7. K. B. Start and B. K. Wells: *The Trend of Reading Standards:* 1970–71 N.F.E.R.: 1972.

8. *Social Trends No. 4:* Government Statistical Service: H.M.S.O.: 1973. See also *Children as Viewers and Listeners:* B.B.C. 1974, which gives an interesting analysis of the viewing and listening preferences of children aged 5 to 14.

9. H. T. Himmelweit, A. N. Oppenheim & P. Vince: *Television and the Child:* O.U.P.: 1955.

10. F. Whitehead, A. C. Capey, W. Maddren: *Children's Reading Interests:* Schools Council: 1974.

11. *Progress in Reading 1948–1964:* Education Pamphlet No. 50: H.M.S.O.: 1966.

12. T. R. Horton: *The Reading Standards of Children in Wales:* N.F.E.R.: 1973.

13. J. A. Wilson: *Reading Standards in Northern Ireland:* N.I.C.E.R.: 1973.

14. Standard Error.   When a mean score is shown in the tables it has to be understood that this is an estimate of some unknown *true* mean score which would have been obtained if every child in the relevant population of 11 and 15 year olds had been tested. Obviously, it is impossible to test on this scale, so each survey has tested only a sample of children from each of the two age-groups. Thus, the mean value quoted for 11 year olds in 1970 on the W.V. test (Table 3) is an *estimate* of the *true* mean score for all the children of that age in that year.   Many different samples could be chosen without testing the same children, and if this were to happen one would get several *different* estimates of the *true* mean score of the whole age group. The chances that any one sample would give an estimated value precisely the same as the *true* mean score are, on commonsense expectations, small. We are in just that situation. We have one estimate of the *true* mean score for the whole population at that age. How close is it likely to be to the *true* value? The standard error quoted with each sample mean score gives us an answer to this question, but the answer has to acknowledge that the estimated mean score values one might obtain by repeated sampling would be sometimes higher and sometimes lower than the *true* value in the whole population. For instance, in 1964 (from Table 3) the sample of 11 year olds in maintained schools obtained a mean score of 15 on the Watts-Vernon test. The standard error was 0·21. This information tells us that the true mean score of the whole population of such pupils was close to 15. How close? If we said the true mean score for the age group was between 14·79 (15·00 − 0·21) and 15·21 we should be likely to be right 68 times out of 100 or roughly two-thirds of the time. It may not be thought adequate to be right two times out of three, but if we wish to be more certain of including the *true* population score we must widen the limits. We could thus be confident that in claiming the *true* mean score to lie between 14·58 and 15·42 (15 ± 2 × 0·21) we should be right 95 times out of 100. The combination of a mean score and a standard error derived from a sample must, therefore, be regarded as indicating *the range* of possible values of the *true* mean score. If, therefore, we are to be sure that from one year to any other year there has been a definite movement of the mean score, we must allow for the range of possibilities on each testing occasion. In drawing conclusions from the results it is not enough merely to note any difference in the mean scores. There must be no significant chance of an overlap due to either this sample or the one in the earlier test producing an estimate greatly removed from the true value in the age group at the time. And this means greatly that the difference must be sufficiently large for it to be clear that no such overlap has occurred.

15. J. Nisbet, J. Watt, J. Welsh: *Reading Standards in Aberdeen 1962–1972:* University of Aberdeen: 1972.

16. R. Davie, N. Butler, H. Goldstein: *From Birth to Seven:* Longman: 1972.

17. A. H. Halsey: *Educational Priority: Vol. 1:* H.M.S.O.: 1972.

18. *Children and Their Primary Schools:* H.M.S.O.: 1967.

19. E. Malmquist: *Factors relating to Reading Disabilities in the First Grade of Elementary Schools:* Stockholm: 1958.

20. K. Gardner: *The State of Reading:* in *Crisis in the Classroom*, ed. N. Smart: I.P.C.: 1968.

21. M. L. K. Pringle, N. R. Butler, R. Davie: *11,000 Seven Year Olds:* Longman: 1966.

22. J. Morris: *Reading in the Primary School:* N.F.E.R.: 1959: and *Standards and Progress in Reading:* N.F.E.R.: 1966.

23. G. E. Bookbinder: *Variations in Reading Test Norms:* Educational Research 12,2: 1970.

CHAPTER 3

Monitoring

3.1 Before we go on to consider how improvement can be secured in reading and the use of language we think it appropriate to complete this section on standards by setting out our conclusions on how these can be more effectively monitored. The national sample surveys carried out periodically by the National Foundation for Educational Research have provided useful indicators of progress in basic reading ability since 1948, but they have become increasingly difficult to interpret. In describing some of their shortcomings we have pointed out that the items represent only a limited sample of reading skills. The narrowness of the tests certainly ensured a high degree of precision in measurement, but it meant that their relevance was bound to be questioned. Tests which are limited to only one facet of a complex intermingling of skills clearly cannot supply information of a right quality. Such a conclusion poses an obvious question. Should some form of national survey be continued, and if so should it not be operated more systematically and according to more ambitious principles?

3.2 We are in no doubt of the importance of monitoring standards of achievement in literacy, and of doing so by using the most sophisticated methods possible. There will always be keen interest in the movement of standards, and it is perfectly natural that there should be. Where there is no information there will be speculation, and the absence of facts makes room for prejudice. We began the Report by pointing out how difficult it is to make reliable statements on standards of English today in comparison with those in the past. Opinion on this issue tends to polarise, and the lack of objective data is a serious handicap to rational discussion. Information of the right quality will be of value to teachers and researchers and will be a reference point for policy decisions at the level of central and local government.

3.3 We have also suggested that a wider and more demanding definition of literacy should be adopted. The existing criterion is determined by the reading standards of seven and nine year old children of many years ago on tests whose limitations are acknowledged. It should be replaced by a criterion capable of showing whether the reading and writing abilities of children are adequate to the demands made upon them in school and likely to face them in adult life. What we are proposing, then, is an entirely new approach. We are suggesting that monitoring should be extended beyond the limit of a single dimension to give more information than has ever been available before.

3.4 Obviously, no system of monitoring can encompass all the various objectives in English promoted by a wide variety of schools, let alone all the individual teachers within them. An ideal system would apply measurement continuously to the whole range of learning activity and weight the resulting indices according to importance. This is clearly far too ambitious. Nevertheless, our proposal is that the procedure should assess a wider range of attainments than has been attempted in the past. What is required, therefore, is an instrument that combines practicability with a more comprehensive and therefore more realistic sampling of the skills.

3.5 Monitoring should employ an array of techniques of a kind that will make assessment both reliable and valid. Ideally, it should not set up 'backwash' effects of any kind, and by design it should rule out the possibility of specific teaching to achieve good test results. Assessment is possible only by examining the explicit products of school activity, and the instruments of assessment should therefore include samples of performance considered to be important and representative of attainments. They should also be responsive to developments in the curriculum. This suggests that the instruments should incorporate the means for discarding out of date procedures and materials and for introducing and validating experimental methods. Monitoring should embrace teaching objectives for the entire ability range, since only by measuring the lowest and highest attainments is it possible to obtain sound general indices. We believe the device that would best answer these needs is the item pool, which is described at greater length later in the chapter. It entails the collection of a large stock of test items, wide enough in range to cover as many aspects of the various abilities as it is felt appropriate to assess. Selection from this pool would be made each time the monitoring instrument was applied. We recommend that monitoring should be administered on the basis of light sampling and frequent occurrence, and that the results should be published annually. This method, described later, would have many advantages, not the least of which would be that a continually accumulating body of information would replace the practice of sudden disclosures at four-yearly intervals. The responsibility for monitoring should lie with a national research organisation, such as the National Foundation for Educational Research, and the process should involve teachers and other educationists at all points, from the definition of objectives to the compilation of results. The nature of this involvement is outlined in paragraph 3.16, and it will be seen that an adequate period of preparation would be necessary. We recommend that 1977 should be the target date for the first application of the new monitoring procedure.

3.6 Before discussing the process in greater detail we must consider the question of the most appropriate age-points at which it should be applied. Clearly, the pupils must be able to work at a task without support or advice. Their capacity to use English *for themselves* is in itself an important aspect of enquiry. Moreover, it is one of our proposals that a selection of different assessment tasks should be distributed between the pupils in any one class. Eleven is still the age of transfer for most children, and the point where their education becomes more specialised. At this age pupils with reading and language difficulties face a situation where their deficiencies will be under still greater pressure. It is clearly a sensitive age point and one where objective information would be of particular value.

By the end of his school life a pupil should have reached certain levels of achievement in reading and producing language. The statutory leaving age might therefore seem a natural point to assess what proportion of young people have succeeded or failed in this objective. However, there are obvious arguments against choosing this as the point at which to apply the second stage of monitoring, not least the incidence of external examinations. We have therefore concluded that fifteen would be the most suitable age for the second application of the monitoring procedure. Eleven and fifteen, the ages at which previous surveys have been carried out, have obvious advantages and should continue to be the points at which tests are administered.

3.7   A criticism of many methods of assessment is that they are applied only to attainments that can be directly and objectively measured. Other attributes, arguably of greater importance, are excluded because the marking is felt to be too subjective or likely to be too cumbersome and costly. There is an undoubted logistical appeal in multiple choice items which can be machine scored, especially when the reliability of the test and the precision of the results are thereby increased. The limitations of this technique are obvious, but its alternatives would have to prove themselves valid, reliable, and logistically efficient on the scale required. The feasibility of such alternatives to multiple choice testing is considered below.

3.8   In agreeing that the present means of measuring standards is too narrow in concept we concluded that the *reading* test should assess a wider variety of reading skills. At the most obvious level the test should determine whether the child is able to extract meaning from the page. It should then assess whether he can discern implied as well as explicit meaning, evaluate the material in terms of its own internal logic and of other evidence, and re-organise it in terms of other frames of reference. Passages would be selected for readability and calibrated for difficulty, and span a range wide enough to encompass a number of functions. These would include the descriptive, the narrative, and the expository, all within the range typically encountered by children in their school experience. Chapter 8 contains recommendations about higher order skills and reading in the curriculum areas, and we see these activities as contributing to the item pool upon which the monitoring instrument will draw. The information resulting from all this would indicate far more effectively than earlier data the extent to which reading proficiency had been developed to serve personal and social needs. The survey instruments would include a balanced mixture, with multiple choice questions for the simpler items and open-ended questions for the more complex and evocative material. The first are attractive on the grounds of economy, objectivity, and ease of scoring. The second can be framed in such a way that the pupil's responses to a sentence or paragraph might be reliably scored by impression markings. These responses can provide a wealth of data to assist researchers and teachers alike in interpreting the empirical analyses. Answers to the open-ended questions will need the controlled subjectivity of multiple marking. This implies that skilled and experienced markers will be required and their performance assessed for consistency and accuracy, and that scoring rubrics will have to be developed through a series of trials. The establishment of item pools (see 3.15) will permit a far greater range of test materials to be collected and used in a survey than could be incorporated in a single test designed to be completed by pupils in about half an hour. As a temporary expedient the N.S.6. test should remain in operation to ensure a continuing baseline until a new datum can be established. This would be achieved by linking the test to items in the pool to relate the future results of all such items with the old data. We emphasise, however, that the existing tests should be dispensed with at the earliest opportunity.

3.9   So far there has been no attempt to monitor standards of achievement in *writing*, and we recommend that the practice should now be introduced. The reasons advanced for periodical measurement of reading apply with equal force to writing, and the two sets of results would be mutually illuminating. It has to be acknowledged that to test writing on this scale is not a simple matter. The first questions to be answered are: what features of writing should be tested? by what criteria is one to measure them? how are reliability and validity to be ensured? Writing is a highly complex activity, and no test would be adequate that measured a narrow segment of its spectrum. This constraint has to be reconciled with the need for as economical a marking system as possible, and the difficulties are at once plain. At first sight the most obvious prerequisite for assessing writing would seem to be an agreement upon what can be expected of a child at a given age. There are, however, so many variables at work that it soon becomes clear that this agreement is not possible. There have been several attempts to establish criteria for maturity in writing: mean length of composition, sentence length, the subordination index, the minimum terminable unit, etc. We can take the last-named as an example. The minimum terminable unit, or T-unit, is "roughly any sentence or part of a sentence that is an independent clause, possibly containing, however, one or more dependent clauses".[1] The average length of the T-unit, it has been argued, indicates 'syntactic maturity', and a child is seen to make slow but consistent progress as measured by this index. But a piece of writing might well have syntactic maturity and yet be wanting in organisation and content. Conversely, writing of high quality can employ a simple style that would not necessarily yield a high score as measured by the T-unit. Indeed, it is the mark of a mature writer to recognise the demands of his subject and construct his prose accordingly. Equally, it would be possible to work to a simple measure of correctness in grammar, usage, punctuation, and spelling; but important as these are, no one would suppose that they are the principal criteria by which the material should be judged. The conclusion is that writing can be adequately tested only by the scrutiny of a number of examples in which the child has had to cope with a variety of demands. An important measure of success in writing is to differentiate between the styles appropriate for particular purposes. To present tasks which call upon this ability would give more complete information than could be obtained from a single assignment. For example, at 11 the monitoring procedure might include writing that is autobiographical and narrative, explanatory and descriptive. At 15 it should be extended to involve higher levels of abstraction and greater complexity, and to include writing that answers the needs of various areas of the curriculum.

3.10   We therefore envisage the monitoring procedure in this area as consisting of a variety of tasks requiring different kinds of writing. Assessment of the scripts would involve 'impression marking' by small teams of markers, and in addition coding schemes would be applied for accuracy in spelling, punctuation, grammar and such other features as might be specified. There is convincing evidence to show that teams can achieve a good standard of consistency while dealing with large numbers of scripts.[2] It has been found, for example, that the averages of two sets of three persons marking by impression agree more closely than the impression marking of two individuals randomly chosen. It would, of course, be necessary to obtain a degree of consistency which would allow comparison with previous years, a feature essential to monitoring. This could be achieved by including in each batch of scripts a proportion from the first year's test. It is an essential principle of the item pooling system that assessment can reflect changes in the use of language and stylistic differences over the years.

3.11   There is no doubt that multiple marking of this kind is far more difficult to operate than mechanical marking, not to say more costly. However, the light sampling we advocate would mean that the number of scripts to be handled at any one time would be comparatively small. Moreover, we believe there is no substitute for specimens of children's actual writing as material for assessing standards. It has been argued that multiple marking of continuous writing adds very little to what can be gained from interlinear tests, in which the child is required to correct errors which have been deliberately introduced into a passage of prose. Nevertheless, we believe that the assessment should involve the generation of continuous language, not merely a response to it. Many teachers would feel as we do that a child's ability to write cannot be judged without studying what he has actually written. A test that relied solely on the child's ability to detect and correct errors in what someone else had written would be unlikely to command general confidence.

3.12   There is very much more to producing writing of quality than avoiding breaches of the accepted norms of standard English. Nevertheless, this aspect of the task is by common consent held to be important, and it should feature appropriately in any monitoring procedure. By applying the coding schemes the markers would be able to measure competence in it. Furthermore, the researcher responsible for the survey could take the scripts at any particular level and conduct an analysis of errors occurring in the writing. This would provide a descriptive comment on the standards obtained and a qualitative comment on the report itself. In addition to the application of coding schemes to the scripts, the monitoring process could include such objective measures as multiple choice and interlinear tests. These structure the situation in which a child is asked to demonstrate aspects of his mastery of written language, and we recommend that they be included in the pool of items from which tests are made up. The impression marking of scripts, the application of coded schemes, and the inclusion in the pool of objective items would together give a comprehensive assessment of standards of writing.

3.13   We discussed at length the feasibility of monitoring standards of *spoken English*, which is complicated by the increase in the number of variables and in the element of subjectivity. There has been a certain amount of research into the viability of testing speaking and listening, and there is the experience of examination boards to draw upon. These would be helpful sources of information if monitoring were to be extended into this field. In the course of our discussions we reviewed existing tests of the skills involved. We also considered such techniques as teacher-led group discussion, pupil-to-pupil conversation, response to taped speech and questions, and assessment of group production in contrast with individual contribution. It would not be difficult to devise 'test' situations which would call upon the use of different kinds of language. The logistics of the widespread involvement of teachers and use of apparatus would be challenging, but not as formidable as might at first appear. However, there are in our view certain fundamental obstacles. The nature of the activity is such that in testing it there is a danger of distorting it, and the problem of artificiality is a real one. Moreover, there is no doubt that many technical matters would have to be explored before tests of oral ability on this scale could be considered viable. The biggest problem would be that of comparing standards on a national basis and across the years. It would be necessary to store tapes in quantity to enable comparisons to be drawn, and the additional variables make this a less dependable device than the corresponding procedure in writing. We do not believe that in the present state of development it is practicable to introduce the monitoring of spoken English. This recommendation emerges from a consideration of the balance between gain and the difficulties of operation. The balance may shift if some of the latter can be removed, notably that of artificiality. Some useful research, both here and in the U.S.A., has already pointed the way, and we recommend that further research be conducted into the development of suitable monitoring instruments and economical procedures.

3.14   In the monitoring of reading and writing we recommend a new style of assessment which will allow for an extensive coverage of attainments without imposing a heavy testing load on individual pupils. The principle we suggest is the sharing of a selection of assessment tasks between a number of groups of pupils. At any one phase of assessment each group attempts a different set of exercises or items from that of every other group. The performance of the population is thus estimated by the performance of the separate groups taken together. The levels of attainment in a single test will be represented as the mean score obtained by each sample of pupils.

3.15   On every occasion when monitoring assessment takes place the test material presented to the pupils will be drawn from a large pool stocked with carefully developed items. The variety of sources from which this stock draws will ensure an extensive coverage of the area to be assessed, in contrast to the inevitably narrow forms of measurement afforded by a single test. From this central pool selections of different question types will be constituted into tests, i.e. concentrations of items following a predetermined pattern of characteristics. The sets of questions will be compiled in such a way as to be of roughly equal standard, each set containing items from the simple to the difficult. At the latter end of the scale the test can make considerable demands and thereby avoid a weakness of existing survey tests; namely their fixing of a 'ceiling' too low to measure the real capacity of the most able children. The approximate equivalence of the sets of questions will be assured statistically, by means of performance norms established over all the schools and pupils tested. The *exact* equivalence of each test is not essential, since they are being used to assess group performance, not to award marks to individuals.

3.16   In constructing the question pool the first task will be to specify the nature of the content and the objectives which it is hoped the pupils are achieving. This specification should be drawn up by the research officers in accordance with the advice of a consultative panel of teachers, L.E.A. advisers, and other educationists. The Department of Education and Science should be represented on the panel by H.M. Inspectorate. The result of this process will be a 'blueprint' to guide question writers, who will generally be teachers trained for the purpose. The questions thus prepared for the pool will be examined in the first instance by a review group of teachers to eliminate unsatisfactory items. The agreed questions will then be reviewed by expert test constructors to eliminate or amend questions which show technical faults. A period of development will be necessary for the items to be pre-tested. The characteristics of each item have to be known before it can be decided finally whether to accept or reject it, and the relative difficulties of collections of items in each part of the pool will have to be determined empirically. When this has been done separate tests, consisting of items calibrated into scales, can be compiled by drawing from the pool.

3.17   The pools could be augmented with single items which are not comparable with the main body in terms of the content or task. As such these would not be calibrated in relation to other scaled tests but could nevertheless be included in a monitoring 'sweep' to indicate trends, try out new ideas for measurement, or simply function as survey material. In this latter case the purpose would not be to assess standards but to gather information about a specific ability. The percentage performing adequately at the task would be reported, but the information would not form part of the monitoring data. The tasks could be varied at will according to the kind of ability it was felt revealing to explore at any given time.

3.18   A signal advantage of question-pooling is that it offers a degree of flexibility the single test can never provide. When the monitoring surveys are in train new exercises can be tried out alongside the calibrated items and thus 'chained in' at the appropriate point. Out of date material or examples found to be unsatisfactory can be discarded, while the repeated inclusion of an item will provide data which can be used to improve the accuracy of calibration. The major benefit of this flexibility is that it will be possible for the monitoring system to keep abreast of changes in the use of language and in teaching emphases in schools.

3.19   Until now, national assessment has involved administering one or two tests of reading of a 'large' sample and repeating the procedure with the same tests at roughly four-yearly intervals. We recommend that this form of assessment be replaced by one of light sampling, where the instruments are applied relatively frequently to a succession of 'small' samples. The principle is that monitoring should be applied once in every term, but to only 16 secondary or 32 primary schools on each occasion. 1,600 pupils would be required at one time, and eight of the tests from the pool would be divided among them, so that each test was completed by 200 children. By covering eight features of attainment in this manner it would be possible to gain a great deal of information without increasing the demand upon any one school or pupil. As a general rule a school would be selected only once in several decades, and a child would be unlikely to be involved more than once in his school life. Indeed, many children would complete their school days without ever encountering the monitoring process.

3.20   The figures we have cited are merely illustrative. The numbers would, of course, be subject to alteration according to the degree of precision required in estimating the Mean score, and that in turn would depend upon the reliabilities achieved in the tests. This emphasises the need for adequate resources to be provided for instrument development. If testing were carried out at termly intervals a rolling estimate of standards could be made over any given period of time. It would also be possible to acquire gradually an appreciation of how performance varies at different times of the school year, a matter on which little is known.

3.21 In the past, large surveys have been afflicted by unforeseen difficulties, e.g. gas and postal strikes. With light sampling such problems would become only temporary inconveniences. The few schools affected could be picked up as soon as administratively convenient, or in extreme circumstances omitted from the sequence of surveys altogether. The disruption would affect only a small proportion of the total sample entering the period over which Means were averaged to give rolling estimates. Spreading the amount of testing evenly over time and distributing the content and skills between pools of questions would reduce the demands on any one pupil's time to a very reasonable level; only one school period of about 45 minutes would be required. Moreover, the work required of participating schools would be no more onerous than under the old procedure. Careful organisation at the distribution stage would ensure that teachers were not asked to 'shuffle and deal' sets of tests. Instead they would be given a prepared package with the tests in order. Distributing different test forms to adjacent pupils would reduce the need for close supervision and the setting up of 'examination conditions' for whole year groups of children.

3.22 The operation of surveys in the past may have tended to underestimate the variation in reading difficulties in different parts of the country. It was suggested to us in evidence that there is a need for more detailed information about standards in certain localities, eg Educational Priority Areas. There seems to us a good case for monitoring to be selectively applied in this way where the information would be of additional value. The flexibility of the system we are recommending would allow such needs to be accommodated. We feel it necessary to emphasise, however, that the new system should be firmly established before any such extension is introduced and that the principle of light sampling should not be impugned.

3.23 Once the item pools have been established the survey can be operated by a small team supported by the consultative committee. The flow of work will be continuous, unlike that engendered by the large four-yearly survey which demanded an intensive effort over a short period from a temporary staff. This small team will be permanent in the sense that, although its members may change, it will maintain a continuity of function and experience. This will enable it to build up an expert knowledge of the growing body of data and its interpretation. One of its tasks will be to develop methods of presentation which will enable the results to be readily assimilated at all levels.

3.24 In conclusion we recommend that adequate research and development work should precede the introduction of such a system of monitoring. There are, of course, several aspects of it which would require investigation and detailed preparation. Fundamental to our concept of monitoring is an acceptance of the view that reading and writing are highly complex activities. If they are to be assessed with a subtlety which reflects this the instruments cannot depend entirely on simply scored objective measurements. There is an obvious difficulty when impression marking is introduced into the process. Nevertheless, the stability of this kind of scoring over a period of time can be ensured by taking appropriate steps: (i) careful selection and initial training of marker teams, (ii) preserving some continuity of markers over a number of years, (iii) recycling earlier scripts for comparison with current ones, (iv) periodic agreement trials with selected materials. We believe the benefits of impression marking to be considerable and that every effort should be made to overcome the difficulties.

3.25   It will also be necessary to conduct research into the nature of the materials most suitable for the assessment tasks we have suggested. This would be an essential prelude to the creation of item pools, the character of which would itself require a good deal of thought. In addition, consideration would have to be given to the cost and time required for the pre-testing programme referred to earlier. Objective tests and coded assessment would require proper validation. Consultation and experiment would be necessary for the specification of a suitable coding scheme, which would have to be simple, economical, and rigorous.

3.26   It seems to us beyond question that standards should be monitored, and that this should be done on a scale which will allow confidence in the accuracy and value of the findings. We do not underestimate the complexities involved in establishing such a system as we have outlined. Nevertheless, we believe that if a monitoring system is to command the confidence of both the teaching profession and the general public it must present a comprehensive picture of the various skills that constitute literacy.

REFERENCES

1.   W. Kellogg Hunt: *Grammatical Structures Written at Three Grade Levels:* National Council of Teachers of English Research Report No. 3: Urbana: Illinois: N.C.T.E.: 1965.

2.   J. N. Britton, N. C. Martin and H. Rosen: *Multiple Marking of English Compositions:* Schools Council Examination Bulletin No. 12: H.M.S.O.: 1966.

3.   See, for example, A. Wilkinson, L. Stratta, and P. Dudley: *The Quality of Listening:* Schools Council: 1974.

Part Two

Language in The Early Years

CHAPTER 4

Language and Learning

"Man interposes a network of words between the world and himself, and thereby becomes the master of the world".

Georges Gusdorf.

4.1 It is perfectly obvious that asking and telling play a persistent role in the day to day behaviour of human beings, and that without the exchange of information in words we should not be able to achieve a fraction of our customary activities. Add to this that we write and read letters, listen to radio and television, read newspapers and look things up in books, and it will be evident that verbalised information plays a crucial role in our affairs. This, however, if current theories are to be believed, is no more than the tip of the iceberg. It is the role that language plays in *generating* knowledge and *producing new forms* of behaviour that typifies human existence and distinguishes it from that of all other creatures.

4.2 These current theories stem from a powerful movement of ideas developed over the past fifty years, according to which man's individual, social and cultural achievements can be rightly understood only if we take into account the fact that he is essentially a *symbol-using animal*. By this account what makes us typically human is the fact that we symbolise, or represent to ourselves, the objects, people and events that make up our environment, and do so cumulatively, thus creating an inner representation of the world as we have encountered it. The accumulated representation is on the one hand a storehouse of past experience and on the other a body of expectations regarding what may yet happen to us. In this way we construct for ourselves a past and a future, a retrospect and a prospect; all our significant actions are performed within this extended field or framework, and no conscious act, however trivial, is uninfluenced by it. We interpret what we perceive at any given moment by relating it to our body of past experiences, and respond to it in the light of that interpretation. No doubt the processes of representation and storing are selective. Some things we are unable to interpret and their meaning is lost to us; some we may interpret but fail to store, and much that has been stored is certainly beyond the reach of deliberate recall. (Experiment[1] has shown, however, that this does not necessarily mean we cannot be influenced by such things in interpreting fresh experiences.)

4.3 Language is one of a number of ways in which we represent the world to ourselves, and if its workings are to be seen in perspective it is necessary first to look briefly at one of the other ways. The most obvious example of an 'inner representation' is probably the visual memory we carry away of some object we have looked at and can no longer see. It is this memory which enables us, in confronting a new scene on a later occasion, to recognise an acquaintance among a crowd of strangers. We could hardly expect however, that the person recognised will look *exactly* as he did on that first occasion. It must be that our memory enables us to generalise beyond the situations

47

on which it is based, or we should fail to recognise an old friend wearing a new expression. By generalising from our visual memories, in fact, we may make a good deal of sense of something we have never set eyes upon before. Thus, from much looking at many faces we come to recognise that a stranger is middle-aged rather than young, male rather than female, European rather than Oriental—not to mention the prior recognition that it is a human face that confronts us and not the face of a cat or an ape.

4.4   One of the keys to an understanding of language lies in realising that it is the prime means by which we construct *generalised* representations. At its simplest level of operation, a word that names an object is for a young child a filing-pin upon which he stores successive experiences of the objects themselves. As his experience grows, he uses the word to refer to an increasing range of objects, and applies it more and more consistently in the ways the adults do about him. He becomes increasingly aware of the characteristics of the category of objects named by the word. Thus he is employing language to assist him in generalising from visual (and indeed all other) modes of representing his experience. He does not, of course, do this without assistance. He may invent some words and apply them to categories of his own creation, but the vast majority of the words he uses will be taken over from the speech of the adults around him; and the objects these words refer to will be principally those to which the adults refer in using them. To sum up, then, we have to generalise from particular representations of past experiences in order to apply them to new ones, and language helps us to do this by providing a ready means of classifying these experiences. The important thing to remember is that as long as every event is experienced as unique and different from all other events we cannot set up expectations regarding the future. It is by recognising recurrences that we learn from our experience.

4.5   This brief account began at the simplest level of operation of language, with what *a word* can do. But of course, language is more than a mere inventory of words; it also includes highly complex rules for combining words into continuous speech or writing. An obvious example of such rules is the relation of the subject of a sentence to the predicate or the relation of a verb to its object. In addition to a vast array of grammatical rules, there are also lexical and semantic relationships built into language. The term 'flower', for example, is part of a hierarchy of terms: it subsumes the categories named by 'buttercup' and 'daisy' and is itself subsumed under other categories such as 'plant'. A speaker profits from the constraints upon his language behaviour, because they are the rules of the 'language game' that make communication possible. Having taken a word into his speech vocabulary, a child learns by degrees to use it for more purposes, for more complex purposes, and for purposes approximating more and more to adult uses. A similar process operates with respect to the rules governing language. For example, a child will first use the words 'buttercup', 'daisy', 'flower', and 'plant' without regard for their values in this hierarchy; later, however, when he is able to use the hierarchical distinctions, he will have acquired a very useful strategy of thinking, as any player of the 'Twenty Questions' game will recognise. Some psychologists go so far as to claim that the language rules gradually 'internalised' in this way "become the basic structures of thinking", indeed, that "a child's intellectual growth is contingent on his mastering the social means of thought, that is, language"[2]. For other psychologists, this would be too close an identification of thought with language. However, there is no need to enter this controversy, since it is enough to state what would be generally agreed: (a) that higher processes of thinking are normally achieved by the interaction of a child's language behaviour with his other mental and perceptual powers; and (b) that language behaviour represents the aspect of his thought processes most accessible to outside influences, including that of the teacher.

4.6 The plausibility of this claim has been greatly strengthened in recent years by the work of Chomsky and his associates in attempting to discover structural features to be found in all languages. If all languages embody some rules in common and those common rules are seen to be closely related to universal modes of human reasoning, then clearly the link between language and thinking is one that must be acknowleged. The simple fact would appear to be that people of all races have developed languages as their means of organising their experience of the world; and in doing so they have acquired, in common, characteristics specific to the human race. As a child gains mastery of his particular mother-tongue he learns by degrees to apply its organising power to his own experience, and as a result his mental processes take on new forms. So complete is the transformation that it is impossible for us to reverse the process and conceive of our situation in the way we saw it as inarticulate infants.

4.7 The familiar facts with which each of us goes armed to meet new experiences are in origin statements about the world, and we require language to make those statements. However, it would be perfectly possible to state here that the page the reader has before him is green in colour, and that is patently *not* a fact. Language used in that way is the language of hypothesis, the formulation of possibilities. It is crucial in the sense that *what is* can be said to exist in its own right, open to contemplation, whereas *what might be* takes a form in which it may be contemplated only when it is in some way represented or symbolised. It may be said that all behaviour is experimental: that, for example, as we walk from one part of a building to another, we test out the hypothesis that an aperture is indeed open and not protected by a plate glass door. And there may be occasions when the hypothesis is abruptly disproved. It would be very rash, however, to claim that in such a situation language had any direct role to play. It is when our behaviour moves into more problematic situations that the need arises for a hypothesis to be elaborated, to take on the form of a statement of the possibilities, and here we must use language. The effort to formulate a hypothesis, to put into words some possibility we have envisaged, results in a 'spelling out' to which we may then return, in the light of further experience and in search of further possibilities. By a kind of spiral, the formulation itself becomes a source from which we draw further questions, fresh hypotheses. The statement we have made becomes an object of our own contemplation and a spur to further thinking. It is probably true to say that the higher thought processes become possible to the child or adolescent who in this way learns to turn his linguistic activities back upon his own formulations.

4.8 If such claims are to seem feasible, two things must be remembered. One is that language provides us with a generalised representation of experience, and generalising has the effect of reducing the multiplicity of experience to a more manageable form. The other is that the complex rules governing the combination of elements when we speak or write impose order upon the experiences we succeed in putting into words. There are implications here for two familiar enough forms of classroom activity. In group discussion the spoken contribution of each member may be worked upon by speaker and listeners alike, and in the immediacy of face-to-face speech they make corporate enquiry a powerful mode of learning. Secondly, in the practice of writing the child left alone with his evolving utterance is engaged in generating knowledge for himself, particularly when the writing is frequent, brief, and strenuous rather than occasional and at length. At the same time he is developing mental operations which will afterwards be of service to him in writing, speaking, reading, listening or thinking.

4.9   It is a confusion of everyday thought that we tend to regard 'knowledge' as something that exists independently of someone who knows. 'What is known' must in fact be brought to life afresh within every 'knower' by his own efforts. To bring knowledge into being is a formulating process, and language is its ordinary means, whether in speaking or writing or the inner monologue of thought. Once it is understood that talking and writing are means to learning, those more obvious truths that we learn also from other people by listening and reading will take on a fuller meaning and fall into a proper perspective. Nothing has done more to confuse current educational debate than the simplistic notion that 'being told' is the polar opposite of 'finding out for oneself'. In order to accept what is offered when we are told something, we have to have somewhere to put it; and having somewhere to put it means that the framework of past knowledge and experience into which it must fit is adequate as a means of interpreting and apprehending it. Something approximating to 'finding out for ourselves' needs therefore to take place if we are to be successfully told. The development of this individual context for a new piece of information, the forging of the links that give it meaning, is a task that we customarily tackle by talking to other people.

4.10   In the Committee's view there are certain important inferences to be drawn from a study of the relationship between language and learning:

(i) all genuine learning involves discovery, and it is as ridiculous to suppose that teaching begins and ends with 'instruction' as it is to suppose that 'learning by discovery' means leaving children to their own resources;

(ii) language has a heuristic function; that is to say a child can learn by talking and writing as certainly as he can by listening and reading;

(iii) to exploit the process of discovery through language in all its uses is the surest means of enabling a child to master his mother tongue.

The ideas briefly set out in this chapter are intended, therefore, to provide a theoretical foundation for the chapters that follow.

REFERENCES

1. See, for example, A. R. Luria and O. S. Vinogradova: *The Dynamics of Semantic Systems:* British Journal of Psychology: Vol. 50: 1958.
2. L. S. Vygotsky: *Thought and Language:* Massachusetts Institute of Technology Press: 1962.

CHAPTER 5

Language in The Early Years

5.1   There has been a great deal of valuable work both here and on the other side of the Atlantic into the processes by which a child acquires language and the influences operating upon them. The chief of these is his home environment, and we shall recommend various ways in which parents may be helped to a better understanding of their own vitally important role. We shall also make suggestions about the kind of specific attention to language to be given within the nursery and infant school. Before this, however, it will be useful to review what is known about the way in which a child acquires language and the forces governing how it develops.

5.2   The point at which a child begins to connect two or three words is usually between the ages of 18 and 24 months. To reach this stage he has developed the capacity to imitate his parents, but he does not imitate unselectively. The words he reproduces are the content words, those which carry the essential information in what he has heard and what he is now saying for himself. These words are generally nouns, adjectives, and verbs, and they are the ones which tend to receive the stress in normal speech. It is natural that he should hear these more clearly and that they should be the ones that fix in his memory. He is less likely to hear the structural words, such as 'on', 'and', 'but', 'the', which are not essential at the level of meaning at which he is receiving. When the child produces his short sentences he puts them in an order which is syntactically correct, e.g. "Daddy come". He thus acquires early the basic rules of syntax, placing subject and predicate in their natural relationship, associating the noun with its modifier, and so on. At a surprisingly early age he responds to the intonation patterns of his parents' speech and adopts some of them. Thus a raising of the pitch on the second of the two words "Daddy come" enables him to utter them in question form. Indeed, it has often been noted that children will imitate intonation patterns in the non-speech sounds they make before they begin to speak.

5.3   The adult may well take up these contracted sentences and expand them in a manner which gradually opens up the child's area of verbal operation. Thus, the mother would be likely to expand the two words quoted above into "Yes, Daddy will be coming home soon". In one American experiment mothers were found to be expanding their children's simple utterances nearly a third of the time. The process is a two-way interaction. The child imitates the adult, and in turn the adult imitates the child, preserving the order of his words but adding inflections and attaching other words to them. The child reduces; the mother expands. This, however, is not the whole story. Anyone who has listened to a young child talking knows the inventiveness with which he tries out groups of words he is clearly not directly imitating. What he is doing is searching for the regularities of the language, and he naturally makes mistakes. The very fact that he does so shows how productive is this 'search'.

51

It is most obvious in the morphological mistakes he makes, i.e. in adding plural endings and forming tenses. When he says "I digged a hole", it is not because he has ever heard an adult say it; it is because he has learned that to add the sound /d/ or /t/ or /id/ to the verb converts it into the past. He has then overgeneralised, applying the rule in cases where it does not actually operate. His mastery of morphological rules comes later than his command of syntax, but together they amount to the discovery of latent structure, on which the child will work variations for the rest of his life. It has been suggested that by the age of four he will be in possession of the essential structures of the English language. Of course, this does not mean that he has complete command of the language. Recent research has shown that syntax is still being developed during the early years at school. A child's arrival at adult speech is the result of his working through a series of approximations to it.

5.4 This is a necessarily brief account of a highly complex process, but it is perhaps enough to show how important is the nature of the language exchange through which this process develops. The Plowden Report[1] said: "The educational disadvantage of being born the child of an unskilled worker is both financial and psychological". It could be added that it is also linguistic, but such a simple equation would be much less than the whole truth. There is an undeniable relationship between social class and language development, but we must qualify all that follows by pointing out that social class is a rather crude indicator. What is really at issue is the language environment in which the child grows up, and particularly the role played by language in his relationship with his mother. There is no shortage of terms to describe the kinds of environment in which language development prospers or is inhibited. We know the objections to the phrase 'cultural disadvantage' and to its suggestion of a deficit to be made up. Nevertheless it is a term which serves our purpose if it is understood that we do not assume a relentless correspondence between language development and social class. There are differences in language environment *between* socio-economic groups, but there are also differences *within* groups.

5.5 With these essential qualifications made we go on to consider what are the effects of different kinds of language environment. It has been suggested that the differences begin to be marked from about 24–30 months; and at this early stage they show up in what we have described above as the morphological rules. There are indications that the child in a favourable environment makes swifter progress in learning how to make plurals and use the right endings to make past tenses. Later he is found to show greater proficiency in complexity of sentence structure and indeed in the length of his sentences and the variety of vocabulary contained within them. Evidence from American experiments[2] suggests that the gap widens each year, so that the differences become more marked as children grow older.

5.6 Much the most influential work in this field of language and social environment has been carried out by Bernstein, and his terms 'restricted code' and 'elaborated code' have become widely known, though they are often misinterpreted. Bernstein[3] has emphasised that linguistic 'codes' are not related to social class as such but to the family organisation and the interaction between the individuals within it. In what we have called the culturally disadvantaged home a child's language will be limited by certain norms of relationship; there will be less opportunity for him to discuss the reasons for and the likely results of certain decisions. Intentions, possibilities, alternatives, consequences: he will lack occasions to explore these verbally. His more favoured counterpart, on the other hand, will have just this kind of experience. Within his family the part an individual plays in the interchange leading to decisions and judgments will depend less on his status than on his own personal qualities. He will be encouraged to talk things through; he will be given explanations and justification, to which he can offer alternatives. As a result, there is a premium on the need to develop more varied and more sophisticated uses of language.

5.7 An American study[4] set out to identify the patterns of mother-child instruction and relate these to the child's linguistic and cognitive development. This provided interesting illustrations of the contrasting techniques mothers used to teach their children simple tasks. The mother from the 'advantaged' home showed a greater tendency to anticipate an error and warn the child that he was about to reach a decision point. She would encourage him to reflect and to anticipate the consequences of his action in such a way as to avoid error; and she would do this in language that tended to be abstract and elaborated. Thus, he was helped to acquire the ability essential to any problem-solving situation: the capacity to reflect, to weigh decisions, and to choose among alternatives. All this took place in an experimental setting, and it cannot be taken for granted that replication in a British experiment would produce the same results. Nevertheless, it supports what is known from other sources, including the study of mother-child instruction in the natural environment of the home. Between the social groups there were marked differences in the range of purposes for which the mothers used language. The children from the advantaged homes experienced more sustained conversation, within which language was used for a greater variety of functions.

5.8 A study in this country by Tough[5] has suggested that all children between the ages of three and five seem to use language to protect their own rights and interests, open up and maintain relationships with others, report on present experiences, and direct their own and others' actions. But there is a range of uses which children from 'educating' homes seem to have developed more extensively than children without these home advantages. Among those Tough lists are the following:

to collaborate towards agreed ends

to project into the future, to anticipate and predict

to project and compare possible alternatives

to see causal and dependent relationships

to give explanations of how and why things happen

to deal with problems in the imagination and see possible solutions

to create experiences through the use of the imagination, often making a representation through the symbolic use of materials

to reflect upon their own and other people's feelings.

There is confirmation here of what is implied by the studies we have already described and many other British and American experiments; namely, that the child from the advantaged background is more likely to be led to use language of a higher order of complexity and greater abstraction. A child is at a disadvantage in lacking the means to explain, describe, inquire, hypothesize, analyse, compare, and deduce if language is seldom or never used for these purposes in his home. This is the kind of language that is of particular importance to the forming of higher order concepts; in short, to learning in the school situation.

5.9   But this difference should not be accepted with a kind of despairing determinism. The fact that some children from disadvantaged backgrounds make little use of an elaborated code does not of itself mean that they have no access to one. The context in which they use language and the nature of exchange does not *call for* the higher degree of complexity. If a child does not encounter situations in which he has to explore, recall, predict, plan, explain, and analyse, he cannot be expected to bring to school a ready made facility for such uses. But that is not the same thing as saying the ability is beyond him. What is needed is to create the contexts and conditions in which the ability can develop. What follows is a discussion of ways in which this can be done, both in and out of school, but first one further point needs to be made. The argument has been advanced, notably by Labov[6] in the U.S.A. but also by some people in this country, that to imply a superiority on the part of elaborated language is to think in terms of middle class values. Commenting on some of the American studies to which we have referred, Labov suggests that 'lower class' language need be no less effective, that it has its own equal validity, and that one should not look upon the child in terms of a deficiency to be remedied. This is a sincerely held view to which we may do less than justice in presenting it so baldly. It is a necessary corrective to the opinions of those teachers and educationists who believe the disadvantaged child brings nothing of his own to school. But it must not blind one to the reality of the situation as it exists. There is an indisputable gap between the language experiences that some families provide and the linguistic demands of school education. In our view it is not a condemnation of a language form to point out that there are some functions it will not adequately serve. But the fact that it will not serve them is at the heart of the matter. The important thing is that the child should not suffer limited opportunities because he does not have the range of language that society demands.

5.10   All children should be helped to acquire as wide a range as possible of the uses of language, and there are clearly two ways in which this can be achieved. The first consists in helping parents to understand the process of language development in their children and to take their part in it. The second resides in the skill and knowledge of the nursery and infant teacher, her measured attention to the child's precise language needs, and her inventiveness in creating situations which bring about their fulfilment. We will begin with the role of the parents.

5.11   Several of the witnesses urged on us that young people should be made aware of children's language development long before they become parents; that they should, in fact, encounter it while still at school. Some witnesses placed the emphasis on actual preparation for parenthood; others preferred to think in less personal terms. In both cases it was suggested that pupils from secondary schools should visit nursery and infant schools, where they would learn how to talk with young children in the context of constructive play, perhaps using toys they had themselves made. Alternatively or additionally the young children might come to them at the secondary school. We are very much in sympathy with the principle of introducing secondary school pupils to language growth in young children. With careful preparation many schools have developed excellent courses in parenthood, involving both boys and girls. Some have been evolved by the Home Economics department; others have become part of the curriculum for early leavers. A number have been shaped into C.S.E. courses, open to all fourth and fifth year pupils. Such courses often include general child development in the early years, taking account of health, dietetics, physical growth, and emotional needs. They usually have a vigorous practical element and involve the pupils in visits to playgroups and nursery classes. From our point of view the most interesting are those which are broadly-based and which direct the emphasis away from mothercraft to child growth as an aspect of human development. It has to be recognised that many adolescent pupils are simply not ready to cast themselves in the role of future parents, and for them a study of language in parenthood could well take the hypothetical even further. This is not to suggest that pupils still at school are not interested in young children. Indeed, there is plenty of evidence that they are. We are convinced that this interest can be extended to children's language without laying an overt emphasis on personal preparation for parenthood. Young people are deeply interested in human beings in all their variety: in their jobs, their environmental pressures, their life-styles, the things they do and the things they say. We feel that the language development of young children should be set in the wider context of the language human beings use. Within this context films, demonstrations, discussions, and practical experience would lead to an awareness of the adult's role in the young child's linguistic and cognitive development. This would include a study of the linguistic aspects of relationships, of the questions children ask, and of the value of discussion and explanation in controlling a child's behaviour as against simple prohibition.

5.12   To be successful any such study must be firmly based in practical experience. A theoretical study of language would not provide the kind of foundation which is necessary for the long-term objective. This means contact with young children within the schools, and this in its turn implies close co-operation between the teachers. In suggesting this we see clearly the problems of organisation which it sets. So far, only a relatively small number of secondary schools have developed contacts with nursery and infant schools. The widespread adoption of such a practice could produce obvious difficulties, and the teachers of young children could be forgiven for viewing the prospect with alarm. It must be made clear that we do not see this in terms of large numbers of secondary pupils invading the nursery and infant schools. The dominant consideration must be the interests of the young children themselves. But granted this, it should be possible for a pattern of visiting to be devised which would give a large number of pupils valuable experience. Provided it is carried out over a period of time, the receiving school need not feel any sense of intrusion. In any scheme of this kind a great deal will depend upon the interest and commitment of the individual pupil and the individual teacher, and some disappointments are inevitable. However, with proper planning the presence of these pupils will confer as much advantage as they themselves derive.

5.13   There is already sufficient experience to show that these are not impractical ideas. In one example, young children were taken along to a secondary school where they were given a mixture of objects likely to arouse their interest. In assembling these the older pupils had exercised considerable ingenuity and they used them to talk to the children on a one-to-one basis. Pupils have also been encouraged to write stories for five to seven year olds*, going to great lengths to match the language to the needs of the children, and in the process learning a good deal about them. We are suggesting, in fact, that although visits to young children in their learning situation are an important feature, the courses should go much further than that. When pupils plan their conversation sessions or prepare the material for their stories there will be a great deal of study and discussion, the more valuable because it is designed for a practical outcome. Whatever the nature of the personal contacts, they should be placed in a wider context, and this can relate first-hand experience to more general discussion. The following is a transcript** of a tape produced in a Manchester infant school by Staffordshire members of N.A.T.E. It was in fact produced for study by teachers some years ago, but it will illustrate the kind of material that can be used with older secondary school pupils. It is an example of 'participant'*** use of language, in which two young children talk their way into discovering the purpose of a land measuring tape they have been given. They have never seen one before, and the dialogue reveals how language is essential to their search; through it they work their way towards an understanding:

Boy It's got the date on it . . . it's blue, it's round, it's got a thing on what you hold.

Girl It's a kind of handle.

B   What you lock it up. What you lock it up.

G   A kind of handlebar.

B   Oh, that comes out. Oh, that comes out.

G   It's a tape measure, isn't it?

B   It's a tape measure. It looks like one.

G   Yes. It's a tape measure.

B   Hey, it only goes up to 9 and starts at one again. Hey, when you pull that out . . .

G   How do you put it back in?

B   Ah, I know. Oh, look, when you pull it out, the thing . . . the thing goes round and round. It's a handle. It's a handle.

G   Ah, that goes up. When you want it to go in you turn it back.

*There is a more detailed account of the possibilities of this kind of activity in Chapter 14, where we discuss ways of bringing about continuity between schools.

**We are grateful to Mr. Harold Stephenson for permission to use this extract.

***See paragraph 11.6 for a discussion of this concept.

B   Oh, yes, you turn it back. When you want it to go back *in*. Then if you want it to come back out . . .

G   Yes. You pull it out.

B   Hey, when you turn that round that goes round.

G   That goes round.

B   And when you turn it that way, that goes round. (laugh) When you press that, press that.

G   What number does it go up to? Starts at one.

B   Starts at one. It comes . . . what . . . it comes . . . first there's a red one and then there's a black one.

G   Well, now, that's one foot and then it starts on another foot.

B   Oh, yes.

G   And when it's a red one, it's two feet.

B   Two feet. How many feet does it go up to? Whoops! Seven feet now.

G   Lots of feet . . . 11, 12, 13, 14 . . .

B   16, 17, 18 . . .

G   I got to get it out. Is that one long or something . . . well it's all . . . (laughs).

B   31 there.

G   Yes, cor, more than a yard here.

B   Oh, yes, more than a yard.

G   I'll pull it all out and you hold it tight . . . Who will ever understand this, will they?

B   You've only got to wind it all back up again.

G   Well, Mark, it's a pieces in . . . 60.

B   Think it goes up to a hundred.

G   So do I. Oh, Mark, it's gone up to 66 feet.

B   66 feet it goes up to.

G   I can't turn it back again . . .

There is space to give only one such illustration, but obviously scope exists for many such enterprises. Tapes with transcripts, tape-slide sequences, video-recordings: these and similar extensions of personal experience can be put to good use in a study of children's language. It follows that such courses must be properly planned and equipped, and one cannot repeat too often that they imply a high degree of goodwill and co-operation between the schools. It also follows that the teachers who are organising them must have an up to date knowledge of language development, and appropriate in-service training will be necessary where it is intended to introduce such work.

5.14   After this the most productive point at which to introduce the subject of the language development of the young child is when young married couples are shortly to become parents. We believe it may well be in ante-natal clinics, which are attended by a high percentage of expectant mothers, that the case for children's language needs can be made with the greatest effect. Language is thus placed in the general context of child care, in which it can be shown to have an important place. It is accepted at once that this is not a simple matter. Ante-natal clinics already have a demanding task, with a range of preoccupations which must have priority. Nevertheless, we feel that the situation presents too valuable an opportunity to be missed, exemplified in the advice one health visitor gives to every expectant parent: "When you give your child a bath, bathe him in language". At the simplest level the clinics could be provided with pamphlets, posters, and other visual material. Videotapes and cassette playback machines with headsets offer interesting possibilities. Speech therapists and visiting nursery teachers could stimulate interest through discussion. In one inner city area a health visitor had started a Toddlers' Club for children from a few months old to nursery age. This was held weekly at the medical welfare clinic, and expectant mothers were invited to join in with the children's own mothers. There was close liaison between the health visitor and the head of the nearby infant school, who went along to take part with one or two of her nursery nurses. This was an interesting co-operative venture which, among other things, provided the expectant mothers with a valuable practical introduction to the subject of children's language needs. In ways such as these the ante-natal situation might become a point at which some very profitable foundations are laid. There is room for experiment into the means by which such possibilities might be realised. The problems are immediately obvious. Space, facilities, time, finance, the shortage of speech therapists: all these and more have to be taken account of when such arrangements are being considered. Nevertheless, the value of the outcome could be out of all proportion to the effort and expenditure involved. We see this early point of intervention as a key stage in the continuous help that should be offered to parents. In the following sections we go on to discuss the even more difficult question of how they might be helped within the home in the early years of the child's language growth. The creation of interest and awareness at the ante-natal stage would make this more natural and acceptable. Above all it would establish from the beginning that the child's language development takes its place alongside his physical and emotional growth as a matter of vital concern to parents. This is certainly an area of possibility which health and education authorities might co-operate to explore. Local situations will vary widely, and the greatest need will obviously be in the E.P.A.s, where pressures are already at their greatest. The resources of ante-natal clinics in these areas are often stretched, and the difficulties are not to be underestimated. Nevertheless, it is our central contention, and there is ample evidence from research to support it, that attention to language problems comes too late. The education process must be started earlier if the language deficiencies we have described are to be reduced. The difficulties of implementing such a policy at the ante-natal stage must not be allowed to obscure the need for one.

5.15   We come now to the possibilities for help within the home, and it must be acknowledged at once that home visiting is an activity which has to be conceived and carried out with the greatest delicacy and care. Almost all parents are keen that their children should have the best possible opportunity, but many set low expectations and assume that their child's performance will be governed by his innate ability. They regard the child's mental growth as controlled by maturation and capacity: something that simply happens up to a determined level by an automatic process. If he has it in him to do well he will, but this is something that his schooldays will discover. They do not recognise their own potential in furthering his educational development, and not uncommonly they are apprehensive that any attempt to 'teach' him or introduce him to books will conflict with the school's methods and thus confuse him. Moreover, there may be the natural suspicion on the part of the mother that a home visitor is bringing with her a critical attitude to the child's upbringing or the conditions of the home. In some cases anyone in an official position may be seen as representing authority. The father, whose co-operation is vital, may let his judgment of the situation be coloured by his experiences with 'officialdom' in other contexts. All this makes it an exercise requiring great tact and particular qualities on the part of the visitor. In recommending, as we shall, more initiatives in this field, we are also conscious of the implications for staffing and training. At this point we are discussing the pre-school situation, but we shall later examine home-school contacts. These can be given a strong foundation if the early relationship with a pre-school home visitor has proved rewarding. The qualities needed to achieve such a relationship speak for themselves. The visitor will have to be tolerant and understanding, imposing no judgment and hinting no censure. She will be setting up learning situations which are designed to advance the child's linguistic and cognitive development, and she will therefore need a good understanding of the processes at work.

5.16 There have been several home visiting programmes in the U.S.A., all of them concerned with children from culturally disadvantaged backgrounds. Some relied on purely voluntary participation; some went so far as to pay the mothers to take part. In certain cases the object was to equip the mother with the ability to work through a structured programme with her child. In others the mother was not actively involved at all, and the child received his 'tutoring' from the visitor. Many of these programmes appear to have been successful in what they set out to do, but they do not appeal to us as appropriate models for the kind of relationship we are suggesting. There have been a limited number of experiments in this country, mostly tentative and on a small scale. One particularly encouraging initiative came from a group of Norwich teachers who planned it as members of N.A.T.E. With the agreement of the City of Norwich education authority the teachers, in association with the English department of the college of education, volunteered to make monthly visits to families with a number of children one of whom was between 18 months and 2 years. The teachers worked with the parents and aimed to help them increase the range of linguistic opportunity for their children. The teachers themselves met monthly between visits to discuss their experiences, and they also provided transport to take the parents to the college to see films of interest to young mothers. The success of the first stage of the experiment led to an expansion of the number of teacher volunteers and an extension of the work to young married couples bringing up their first child.

5.17 The most fully documented experiment to date has been part of the West Riding E.P.A.[7] Project, and in this case the visitor worked with the children in the parents' presence. The organisers decided that they would not single out specific children as 'disadvantaged', but would take all the children in the district within a specific age-group. The children had in common the fact that they all lived within an E.P.A. and that their fathers were manual workers of varying degrees of skill. Nevertheless, there were considerable differences between the families, and it would have been possible to identify some children as in greater need than others. To have done so could have caused suspicion, not to say resentment, and the invitation to participate therefore went to all the families in one school catchment area. 20 children were involved, aged 19 months to 28 months, and they were visited every week for one to two hours over a period of a year. The visitor brought toys, books, tape recordings, etc., and in co-operation with the mother used these to develop a number of skills in the child. The initial attention of the Project was to examine and improve the child's educability, and though the sample was a small one there were clear indications that it succeeded in what it set out to do. Our particular interest here, however, is in its benefits in bringing about a growth of understanding in the parents. Their role in the child's linguistic and educational development was successfully demonstrated, and they acquired confidence and interest as they came to see what they could in fact achieve. One of the most valuable results of such enterprises is that they encourage a sense of partnership. It has been remarked above that many parents regard learning as the province of the school. Not only do they feel ill-equipped to anticipate it, but they do not see themselves as sharers in the process when their child starts school. This is sometimes born of indifference, but more often of apprehension. In a later section there will be a consideration of the ways in which parents can be brought into school. But it is worth emphasising again here that home visiting programmes should establish at an early stage the notion of partnership. The right kind of relationship with a home visitor can make the prospect of home-school contact a natural one in the mind of a parent.

5.18   It goes without saying that the parents should not be made to feel any sense of interference. The examples under discussion were experimental situations. They were of limited duration, had a declared objective, and were in the hands of highly skilled persons. In one sense the fact that they were experiments made their task more difficult. For many people the very notion of an experiment carries an unwelcome suggestion of being scrutinised. In the West Riding Project, for example, there was unease on the part of some parents at the idea of their child being tested by a psychologist. However, although an experiment presents problems it also has the advantage of providing a defined framework within which co-operation can be sought. The parent is helping the experimenter and can be made to feel she is taking part in an enterprise in which she and her child are not merely on the receiving end. If home visiting schemes were introduced on a large scale they would not have this advantage. It has to be acknowledged frankly that many of the families where this help would have most value would view it as one more addition to the social agencies with which they have so much contact. So much, then, depends upon the way in which the idea is broached and on the parents' earliest experiences of it in operation. Parents can become engrossed in their child's learning activities. When this happens any sense of receiving social aid will have been eclipsed. It is the feeling of being essential to the partnership that is the key. We feel that home visiting of this kind could be an important innovation, and one which might help to reduce the effect of cultural deprivation in the pre-school years. As local conditions vary so greatly there is little point in offering a blueprint of how such a scheme might operate. Authorities would have to assess the need in particular areas and then consider how they might find the resources for a programme and what should be its nature and duration. We recommend, however, that serious consideration should be given to such measures where cultural disadvantage is evident.

5.19   In recent years there has been a growth in the number of educational television programmes directed to young children.   They have often been criticised for being 'middle class' in tone and content. Television is discussed elsewhere in the Report, but we are concerned with the possibilities of the medium for increasing the kind of parental awareness we have been discussing.   One of the most valuable features of programmes for young children is that they offer to them and their parents a common experience to talk about. The most effective will be the programme that makes this a certain outcome, and it is not likely to happen if the mother's experience cannot so engage with what she is seeing as to draw her to elaborate upon it. This in itself is an argument for a tone and content with which she can find a good measure of identification.   Of particular interest is the possibility of using television to bring home to parents the language needs of their children and their own part in fulfilling them. There is no escaping the fact that educational programmes of this kind, directed at parents at an adult level of instruction, would be unlikely to be watched by the parents we are most concerned to help. It may be that the children's programmes themselves could be structured in such a way as to focus the parents' attention on these language needs in the process of fulfilling them. There is certainly room for research into the possibilities of television for the language interaction of parent and child. We would add that in our view the communication should be sustained and not simply occasional, and that it would be most effective if it complemented other measures of the kind we have been discussing.

5.20   This is an appropriate point at which to comment on the more general question of the influence on young children's language of television entertainment programmes. Although it seems to us regrettable that children of all ages should spend such long hours watching television (see paras. 2.5–2.9), we do not share the opinion that no good at all comes out of it. Certainly this view does not do justice to the undeniably good effects of television on some aspects of children's language. While it is certainly true that television popularises empty catchwords and current slang, it can also be shown to make the vocabulary of the moment eminently available to children. The vocabulary of politics, popular music, space travel, and industry is acquired by children not through the adult programmes of news and comment, but through cartoons, children's serials and tea-time entertainment programmes. It is a remarkable fact that infants have the vocabulary, if not the concepts, of the technological, polluted, divided world that television presents to them. Certain reading schemes in current use do not reflect the seventies; television does. It exposes children to a range of accents, idioms, and registers which they would not otherwise hear. Infants engaged in a space travel game show a knowledge not only of the words (e.g., rocket, countdown, capsule, splash-down), but of the way in which they are used. They reproduce as a matter of course the terse reporting style of the men in a moon landing. At other times they use the more leisurely and often hyperbolic register of the mid-Western cattleman. Observers are constantly struck by young children's response to puns and to rhyme which may feature very little in the speech of adults around them. It is a reasonable hypothesis that television, especially children's entertainment programmes, adult light entertainment, and to a mixed extent the commercial advertisements, has done much to sharpen children's response to this feature of language and to word-play in general. It is, of course, well known that children respond more than most adults to verbal play; what is not generally realised is that the language skills used in verbal play—repeating jingles, puns, riddles, matching rhymes etc.—may be very important in early reading. It is clear therefore that there are some important things to be considered about the impact of television on children's language. Parents and teachers need to be aware of this, and so do those responsible for planning and devising programmes. The programmes children watch between the end of afternoon school and tea-time seem to us to be particularly influential in this respect, and we recommend research into the whole of this very important field.

5.21   We shall return to the parents when we consider how schools can work in co-operation with them, but at this point we pass to the playgroup, nursery class, and infant school, and to the vitally important part played by the teacher in the child's language development. The teacher in these early stages is concerned to help the child move into an expanded set of relation-ships—with his peers, with adults other than his parents, and with the world reflected in a new range of experiences. Three or four year olds coming into school for the first time will often stand and stare, then flit from one activity to another, either silently or with excited chatter. There is just not enough time to take in everything, and the idea that all will still be there tomorrow is not easily accepted. As they become accustomed to the ordered provision children will begin to use materials more selectively and build on the remem-bered experience of the past. In this they are guided by experiment and by constant talk with their teacher, who helps them make sense of their ex-periences and prepares the way for new ones. Every encounter with clay, water, sand, 'junk', paint, book, and picture is used as an opportunity for talk. Excursions out of the classroom are made part of the process, and are constructed and reconstructed through anecdote and an exchange of question and answer. The teacher encourages the child to re-live his experience and embroiders it for him, helping him to draw out of it half-remembered detail. Meeting the same group of children day after day she is able to receive and deepen their interests, record their thoughts, and help them to share their discoveries with others. Thus in a very real sense the classroom and its extensions can constitute a language environment, with experience extending language, and language in turn interpreting experience.

5.22   Most nursery and infant teachers recognise that when young children are involved in some activity the talk that accompanies it becomes an important instrument for learning. Talk is a means by which they learn to work and live with one another. It enables them to gather information and build into their own experience the experience of others. Between themselves and with the teacher they 'process' or interpret the information, creating their own links between what is new and what is familiar. The continual reinterpretation of all that a child knows in the light of what he comes to learn is a characteristic of the talk that occurs in make-believe situations of his own creation. This takes many forms, from domestic scenes in the home corner to improvisations on story-book and television themes of heroes, adventurers, giants, and witches. It is fed by nursery rhymes and singing games, by the stories that teachers and children tell and the poems they read. Talk of this kind is a consolidating activity, a way of re-ordering experience to make it acceptable. Into this context of purposeful, sociable and consolidating talk, the infant teacher introduces the written language. What it brings is fresh material to be talked about, for the spoken word must mediate the written. In many infant schools concern for writing begins, one might say, with the making of 'books'. The teacher writes beneath a child's drawing or painting the caption he dictates to her. The child may be asked to trace over the writing, and later to copy it underneath. By degrees, beginning with the words he already knows, the child will take over the writing until the whole caption is his own work. The 'books' are collections of such pages. The child reads the sentence back to his teacher, and in this way this personal collection of captions and sentences becomes his first reading book. Sometimes they are the response of every member of the class to a particular stimulus, sometimes the work of a group sharing a common interest and anxious therefore to read other children's contributions as well as their own. Sometimes they are a collection of the work of a single child, his own book on his own topic. More often than not they are in the children's own handwriting and with their own illustrations, but we have seen excellent use of a Polaroid camera and a typewriter with a large 'Jumbo' type face which reproduces the kind of print used in most infant schools. Captions or labels of use and interest to the children are often to be found in the classroom. At first, the labels are accompanied by pictures that carry the same message, but as reading proficiency increases, there will no longer always be the same need for pictures. In some classrooms the walls become a kind of glossary of useful words in useful groupings, and the material changes as the interests of the class change and develop. Captions written by the children on maps or diagrams or models add to the verbal display. Where the whole effect is colourful and attractive, the right climate is produced for the development of pleasure in writing and reading and pride in the appearance of the handwriting*. The seeds are here for later developments. The nature of the books will change; what began as a full-page picture with caption will become by degrees a written page with illustrations, and then, where appropriate, a page of text unadorned.

5.23   There is, even in the earliest stages, no lack of things to write about. Young children will write about their homes and families, their pets and other animals, and the highlights of their day-to-day experience. They will write about a football match, a street accident, a snowfall or a thunderstorm, a visit to hospital, a television programme they have watched, or the things they bring into school, and they will write stories on fantasy themes involving witches or bandits, ghosts or gunmen. They describe objects or processes that have interested them, and in this way much of their writing arises from the practical activities in school. At the same time, they develop

*See Annex B to Chapter 11 for a discussion of handwriting.

a language adapted to the expression of feeling, a language of implicit rather than explicit statement; in short, a form of 'poetic' writing that is the counterpart of the consolidating talk we referred to above. Thus, writing serves them to give expression to their own versions of *what is*, and to create fascinating alternatives in terms of *what might be*. Across this range of purposes, however, their writing in these early stages is likely to remain expressive; it is likely, that is to say, to retain a close affinity with their speech. To begin to write is to put to a new use those linguistic resources that have so far been developed entirely by speaking and listening.

5.24   We have been describing the kind of language stimulus enjoyed by a child in a good school in his early years, and it is the foundation on which all else rests. But many witnesses have questioned whether this is enough for each and every child. The argument has been advanced that the kind of language for which we have urged the need will not necessarily be developed by the normal experiences offered in the nursery and infant school. It has been suggested that there is a need for a more precise definition of linguistic objectives and for the provision for some children of a more carefully planned language experience than is evident in most nursery and infant work at the present time. This is an important question and one which requires discussion. The best way to begin is by examining briefly one or two of the programmes that have been developed with this very object of directing attention to specific features of language. Several such experiments have been carried out in the U.S.A., and one of the most recent has been the tutorial language programme developed by M. Blank and F. Solomon[8]. This is based upon a regular one-to-one tutorial designed to develop 'abstract thinking' in the pre-school child by encouraging him to discuss situations not present before him. They involve him in explaining and predicting, two features of language which we have already noted as being less likely to be at the command of a disadvantaged child. They also require him to give and repeat instructions, to use language to compare and make choices, and to use relational words, such as 'between', 'under', 'before', 'after'. An interesting feature of the programme is the transcript of dialogues between teacher and child, with commentary by the authors on how language is actually being used. The one shows a teacher using the Blank and Solomon technique; the other reveals missed opportunities arising from a lack of conscious awareness of the language procedures on the part of the teacher. The authors claim that their method of tutoring with specific language goals produces marked behaviour changes and the use of more co-ordinated language patterns. They press a point which has in fact been made to us in a number of the submissions of evidence: that simply to expose a disadvantaged child to materials and put him into a one-to-one relationship with an interested adult will not necessarily bring about the language growth we are seeking.

5.25   The Bereiter and Engelmann programme[9] has received more publicity in this country and was criticised by many teachers on the ground that its methods seemed so alien to the generally accepted view of nursery education. The programme assumes very little language on the part of the children and it prescribes for them short periods of instruction each day. The main aims are to enable them to make affirmative and negative statements, to use prepositions, handle opposites, name basic colours, and make simple deductions. The authors emphasise that they are not bidding to replace the free and creative environment of the child's first school, merely to reinforce it. However, the range of language goals is undoubtedly narrow and the use of drill involving unison responses is an unattractive feature for most British teachers.

5.26   There is less intensity in the Peabody Language Development Kit, which was used in a radically modified form in the N.F.E.R. Pre-school Project. There are, in fact, four kits, and they aim to provide a language development programme from three to ten years of mental age. Each kit offers a complete programme which consists of 180 lessons of 20–30 minutes, and it is designed for use with groups of children rather than for a one-to-one situation. Within a general framework of language development it includes vocabulary building, sentence patterns, problem-solving and concept formation. The teacher is supplied with a manual, picture cards, posters, tapes or records, and puppets. At the lowest age level there are also toys and teaching aids for developing various skills, e.g. sorting and labelling. It is clear from the experiments carried out with these kits in Britain that the teachers involved were very divided in their reaction to them. This is not the place to detail the exchange of argument, but we are bound to record our own belief that at any rate in the British context programmes such as the Bereiter and Engelmann and Peabody do not provide a ready made answer. Moreover, their use may result in a narrowing of aims and a corresponding loss in the imagination and flexibility which are so vital to nursery education. There is an important place for guides of one kind or another to help the teacher to develop the child's language in the ways we have already indicated. There is also a place for programmes of a kind appropriate for English schools; they have a value in alerting the teacher to particular language needs, and they help her ensure *every* child's active involvement in small group work. But the guide should be a support for the teacher's initiative, not a substitute for it; and the programme should be an integral part of the rich environment she creates as a source of constant stimulus to language.

5.27   So far, the attempts described have been American, but in recent years there have been similar enterprises in Britain. These are different from one another in kind and often in philosophy, but they have one property in common; they are designed to extend children's language by deliberate procedures. In East London, Gahagan and Gahagan conducted[10] an experiment based on Bernstein's concept of 'restricted code'. It employed a language training programme that set tasks for which the former would not be adequate. The activities were designed to improve attention and auditory discrimination, to improve speech (extended narrative, explanation, detailed description, expression of uncertainty and the hypothetical, description of feeling and relationships), and to improve structure and vocabulary. The work involved the use of various games, and the teachers were asked to set aside 20 minutes a day for it. The same principle of a reserved daily allocation of time operated in part of the language development programme associated with the Swansea project[11]. This enterprise directed attention to the following language skills: listening, naming, describing, categorising, denoting position, sequencing, and reasoning. To give an example, the last three of these skills involve the use of 'relational' words such as

under, between	(relation of position)
before, after	(relation of time/events)
if, but	(relation of cause, effect and conditions).

These words are of the greatest importance to language development, and their use presents particular difficulty to young children. The programme therefore suggests activities which will lead the child to use them. Many of these are grounded in the normal experiences of the infant classroom, but some take the form of language games. The handbook provides a check list intended to help the teacher assemble a picture of the child's language through listening to his conversation in the normal classroom setting.

5.28   The notion of a check list or an inventory of language skills is one that attracts some controversy. On the one hand it is argued that a device of this kind offers the teacher a means of monitoring the child's progress; that it allows her to concentrate attention upon the deficiencies she detects. On the other it is contended that a check list puts the emphasis on surface structures rather than on the *context* of children's talk; that it induces the teacher to impose forms from without. This is the view of Tough[12], whose project has produced a teacher's guide to the appraisal of a child's use of language. This does not set out an inventory of language skills but shows teachers how they can keep their own record of observations. It directs attention to certain features of language, and in listing these the author emphasises that they are simply a framework to help the teacher identify uses of language she is already fostering in the normal course of her everyday work. The project does not suggest any games or special activities and goes no further in this direction than to provide two picture-story books and suggestions on how to use them to open up and guide the children's talk.

5.29   In making recommendations about the development of young children's language we have in mind an essential first principle. Granting what we have said about the need for more conscious procedures, how far can these be made to fit into the best nursery and infant practice of today? Our first point is that the more complex language uses can and should be developed within and as part of the normal classroom activity. However, the language programmes themselves point out that they are designed to complement this, not erode or replace it. They vary in the extent to which they 'stand outside' the normal daily routine in the sense of requiring a separate time allocation and a number of activities which have not emerged naturally from classroom experience. In our view the less the separation the more likely is the programme to match the normal way of working in schools, but with this caveat we are sure that teachers will find in some language programmes a very helpful support. Some teachers may prefer the assurance of guidelines, specified activities, and a daily time allocation. Others may regard the programmes as a source of useful suggestions which they will employ in their own fashion. Others again may find that 'language games' can make an interesting addition to the range of individual activities provided for children to choose from. Our own view is that the kind of language development under discussion will be more likely to take effect the more it uses as its medium the daily experiences of the classroom and the home. We emphasise again, however, that this cannot be left to chance, and we shall go on to argue for its place in teacher training and for the support of additional adults to enable the teacher to give attention to it.

5.30 We advocate, in short, planned intervention in the child's language development. At the level at present being discussed this will mean that the teacher recognises the need for the child to include in his experience the following uses of language, and that she will then keep an effective record of his progress in them:

Reporting on present and recalled experiences.

Collaborating towards agreed ends.

Projecting into the future; anticipating and predicting.

Projecting and comparing possible alternatives.

Perceiving causal and dependent relationships.

Giving explanations of how and why things happen.

Expressing and recognising tentativeness.

Dealing with problems in the imagination and seeing possible solutions.

Creating experiences through the use of imagination.

Justifying behaviour.

Reflecting on feelings, their own and other people's.

The experience of individual children will vary, and this means that the teacher's appraisal of each child's needs and achievement is the key to success. Children from advantaged backgrounds are likely to have plenty of opportunity at home to acquire such forms. It is the disadvantaged child who needs help with them, and through her appraisal the teacher can create the situation in which they are likely to be acquired.

5.31 We have discussed the kind of approach which we believe will produce the language development we regard as essential. This involves creating situations in which, to satisfy his own purposes, a child encounters the need to use more elaborate forms and is thus motivated to extend the complexity of language available to him. It also involves the teacher in charting the process by careful observation of the developing language skills. Before going on to say anything about the need for additional adults in the school we emphasise that success depends on the professional guidance of the teacher. The teacher is the organiser of the learning situation, working in close association with the helpers but planning the strategies which they are involved with her in realising.

5.32 We believe there should be more adults involved in the school to afford a one-one or one-two relationship with the children as often as possible. A proposal of this kind requires some elaboration, and we begin by distinguishing between two levels of language experience which such additional help would provide. In the first place it has to be recognised that increasing the opportunities for talk with a sympathetic adult will not necessarily develop more complex language forms in children who are unaccustomed to using them. As we have already suggested, situations have to be created from which such uses are bound to emerge. The person who plans these situations must have a knowledge of how language works, and the ability to appraise children's language and operate upon it accordingly. All this has implications for training and represents an increase in the professional responsibility of the teacher. It does this in two ways. The teacher of young children has always seen it as an important part of her task to add to their experience of language, and if these more sophisticated goals are to be achieved this new dimension is added to her work. Moreover, if other adults are to help it will be under her guidance and towards ends which she has shaped. To appraise each child's speech and keep a record of its features is asking a great deal of a teacher. In the first place she is operating in a situation where there is noise and movement and constant demands upon her time and attention. In the second place she has so much to do in the way of preparation that it is no easy matter for her to note and record speech on this scale. Nevertheless, appraisal and the keeping of some form of record is so important for the whole notion of developing the child's language that serious thought needs to be given to how it can be achieved. It is clearly not a skill lightly acquired nor a task that can be easily delegated.* It depends on more than a superficial understanding of language development, and should therefore rest with the teacher. But she needs support to accomplish it, especially in areas where there are many disadvantaged children. We suggest that the teacher should have the assistance of *trained* persons, the nature of whose participation she will herself decide according to the demands of the situation. In the nursery school the nursery nurse should have an important part to play in this process, since her training recognises the importance of language in children's early development. We suggest that this element in her training should be extended to take account of the factors we have been discussing. Language study at this level goes beyond that normally encountered by the student nursery nurse, and indeed by the nursery teacher herself.

5.33   We believe that in the infant and first school the teacher also needs the support of aides who have been properly trained. It is accepted at once that this is an issue which will require discussion and consultation. The Plowden Report[13] made a number of suggestions in its recommendation for the employment of aides, and it is not our intention here to re-examine these. What we want to stress is that aides working with young children should have as part of their training a course in language development in the early years. As a result of it the aide should be able to understand the teacher's policies and put them into practice, operating within situations the teacher has devised. The course would by its very nature call for a good deal of practical experience with young children, and theoretical aspects should be closely related to the work in the classroom. There is also scope for the use of film, tape/transcript, and video-recording, which would enable the student to study language in action and see it being successfully modified.

*One experienced infant headmistress gave us an example of how easy it is to over-estimate the young child's understanding of certain speech forms. When she was wrapping Christmas presents one six year old asked her if she wanted any more paper. She replied "Oh, I might do; I'll have to wait till I see if there's any more in my room". The boy repeated his question, and as she talked to him she realised that though her sentence was apparently just a simple sequence of monosyllables the expression of tentativeness meant nothing to him.

Ideally, such a course might be developed as a second stage course under the administration of the N.N.E.B., and be taken as an additional course after a period of experience in school.

5.34   Some Authorities have already taken steps to provide general training for aides working in their schools, and this training sometimes includes reference to the development of children's language. In many cases the schools themselves have been a source of valuable practical training, and the aides have learned a great deal about children's language needs through the guidance and example of the head and the teachers. These have been valuable starting points, but we are suggesting that there should now be a movement more deliberate and specific to enable aides to play their part in the ways we have indicated.

5.35   We have so far been discussing particular uses of language, those which are less likely to be at the command of the disadvantaged child. There is, however, great value in simply expanding the number of opportunities for talk with adults quite apart from the fulfilment of such specific aims. This is the second of the two levels of language experience, and one at which the nursery nurse or aide can operate widely and very profitably. What many children lack above all is the experience of having someone to listen to them. In the home their chatter may be disregarded, not out of any unkindness, but disregarded nevertheless. Their questions may receive casual answers and their remarks the briefest of acknowledgment. This may be particularly true in large families, and it is significant that several research studies have indicated a relationship between verbal ability and family size. Much of the mother's utterance is directed at regulating behaviour and establishing role, and a question or an observation from the child is quite likely to receive as a response an unexplained prohibition. Every child gets some measure of this, however little, but in some homes it is likely to be the dominant feature, especially where there are other children claiming attention. It is a likely outcome that the child will become accustomed not to expect answers, and in due course not to ask questions. This is not necessarily due to any lack of warmth or care on the part of the mother. Indeed her solicitude for appropriate behaviour is itself a token of her care. It may be, however, that sustained dialogue with her child, with herself in a teaching role, is not within her range of experience. Thus, unlike his more favoured counterpart, the child comes to school unused to the kind of conversation with an adult in which meanings are exchanged, past experiences reshaped, and questions posed and answered on both sides.

5.36   All these are features of language which the nursery and infant school should see as central to their verbal activity; and indeed the environment they create, the experiences they provide, have among their objects a stimulus to language growth. Paragraphs 5.21–5.23 described the way in which this is done. But when we come back to this matter of adult-child dialogue we are bound to ask whether the school is able to afford enough opportunities for it. To begin with it might be asked whether the teacher has sufficient opportunity simply to listen to the child talk. In her enthusiasm for what they are doing, her concern to give attention as widely as possible, she has much less time to listen than she would like. Some of the responses her questions attract go little further than the short utterance, perhaps a simple monosyllable.

The questions are often invitations to confirm or deny. A child's observation or anecdote will be warmly received, but its purport will sometimes be anticipated and a prompt will foreclose it. This is almost an inevitable consequence of having a large number of children to deal with. The teacher herself has insufficient time to recognise the possibilities of the exchange, to discern the direction in which she could edge the child to explore a particular idea. The nursery nurse and the aide should be able to make an important contribution here. Their training ought to have equipped them with the ability to 'read' a dialogue and to see where it might be encouraged to lead. It should have revealed how little profit there is for the child when the adult unconsciously manoeuvres him into making a closed-ended response. Perhaps above all else the teacher lacks time simply to listen, to let a child establish for himself a notion of the adult as someone who will reward a sustained verbal effort with her attention. It is here that there is great scope for voluntary participation, for the involvement of parents, students, and older secondary school pupils.

5.37   The participation of parents has been gradually increasing in recent years, particularly since the Plowden Report did much to encourage it. Many primary schools have worked hard to encourage parents to exercise a role in the life of the school, and a number have gone further than seeing this in terms of performing some kind of service. Parents act as escorts on journeys and in environmental studies outside school; they help in the school library, in the games period, in home studies areas. In all these situations they are involved in the learning process. We believe there is room for many more such initiatives, and our purpose in this chapter is to consider what parents can contribute in the nursery and infant school. It is no use pretending that the parent can slip easily into the learning situation. There are adjustments to be made and sensitivities on both sides to be respected. For example, it is all too easy for parents to misinterpret the situation and demand to know why their neighbour is 'teaching' their children. In E.P.A. areas in particular parents may well be diffident and feel ill at ease, though once these natural apprehensions are overcome the gains for them as well as for the children are striking. Conversely, unease on the part of the teacher is a natural possibility. It requires some adjustment to move from the accustomed circumstances of working alone or with a nursery nurse to sharing one's classroom with other adults. But evidence we have received suggests that once this unease has passed the teacher finds new opportunities are open to her. There is no question of her room suddenly becoming crowded. At any one time the numbers of parents involved will be small, and should certainly be no larger than the teacher herself thinks right for the situation. The grouping of related spaces—the alternative to the classroom concept of school planning—could contribute to the success of a pattern of shared working. Small withdrawal spaces would provide a degree of seclusion to the benefit of both children and adults, and at the same time enable the teacher to keep in touch with all that was taking place. Perhaps the first point to be made about parental involvement is that it may be courting disappointment to 'mount' it as a scheme. Where participation of other kinds is already well developed its extension into this field can probably be made very naturally. But in other circumstances it is better for the classroom involvement to develop from informal contacts.

5.38   Ideally, pre-school activity will have made these more easy to establish. If parents have been accustomed to home visiting or to pre-school playgroups they will find such contacts more natural. One school in a northern town took the initiative by going out to meet the mothers of two–three year olds in the community centre. The headmistress visited the centre once a week and after she had got to know them on personal terms she developed a kind of workshop situation. The following is her account of what happened when the relationship was well established:

"1st Session

This was a story-telling session. I gave what I considered the best way to tell a story to very young children and illustrated by telling "The Three Pigs"—"huffing and puffing and blowing the house down". Then parents volunteered to tell the group one of their own stories; there was no embarrassment, rather fun and a lot of laughter. The children (two and three year olds) were kept with the group for story telling, then were occupied in an adjacent room.

I considered this first meeting very important. It started or restarted bedtime stories at home. Parents had to borrow and read books from the Mobile Library to refresh their memories of stories heard long ago and to read up new ones.

2nd Session

1.   Children allowed to paint while parents watched and talked about colours and pictures.

2.   Parents took over for picture painting then (a) used large brushes to make Marian Richardson patterns—introductory writing, (b) used smaller brushes for letters, and (c) finally large graphite pencils for letters and words. Parents bought books to take home.

3rd–10th Session

At this period I had a very talented welfare assistant in the Reception Class. I asked if she could help these young mothers, knowing that she had much to give them. She could make almost anything, grow anything, and had a wealth of knowledge acquired through travel; most of all she loved children. These afternoons were a joy for all. Parents made dolls, clothes, and jewellery, painted pictures, and mended books. They prepared apparatus, mostly from scraps, bits and pieces from home, and odds and ends from city shops. This kind of work overflowed to the homes, involving fathers and older children. Fathers made geo-boards, clinometers and boxes for school mathematics."

Thus, although the children were not yet at school, the parents not only learned to appreciate the school's help and interest but made things for it for the benefit of other children. The sense of partnership which grew from this enterprise was ideal ground for the later participation we are discussing.

5.39   Another example comes from an East London infant school in an area of particular social difficulty. The head began by starting what she called the 'Wednesday Club', an opportunity for mothers to relax over a cup of tea and enjoy various activities ranging from cookery and hairdressing demonstrations to films and exhibitions of books. The mothers could bring their young children, who were looked after in a specially equipped playroom.

From this beginning she extended the activities to morning sessions, when she and members of her staff discussed with the parents various aspects of the education of young children. This led up to the making of a video tape of each class at work, with the mothers introducing each activity. The interest aroused encouraged the head to provide books, art materials, etc. for the parents to buy for use at home. The parents themselves raised the idea of opening a playgroup for their younger children, and the school is helping them to start this on a sound footing. This has given the head another opportunity to discuss with them the relationship between play and talk, and she is taking them to visit a number of good playgroups. The more we saw of this relationship the more we were impressed by the warmth and mutual trust it had generated. It had extended to visits by parents, children and teachers to the theatre and to the ballet, and there was no doubt at all of the benefit to the children's language development of all these shared experiences.

5.40   In another inner city area we found excellent co-operation between an infant and a nursery school to the same end. They founded a joint 'Mothers' Club', again with the initial emphasis on providing these young mothers with friendly social contact away from the four walls of their high rise flats. They developed a programme of talks, demonstrations, and practical activities, for some of which pupils of the nearby secondary school produced materials. The Club provided a collection of books for the parents themselves to read. They talked about these with one another and with the heads, who then led the discussion to children's books and the value of story-telling. The mothers worked out a rota for looking after their young children in the adjoining playroom and in this they were helped by a nursery nurse. From here it was a short step to drawing them into the nursery and infant schools themselves, and they were welcomed by the teachers into their classrooms and into the staffroom. We were again impressed by the quality of the relationship and cannot speak too highly of the determination of the teachers to make it work. It was not easy for them at first, and they do not disguise the fact. It meant a lot of hard work, patience, and adjustment, but they think the value out of all proportion to the initial cost, and they are in no doubt that it has made their own work more rewarding. The ways in which the services of parents are used must be for the school to decide, since circumstances will differ so widely as to make models unhelpful. The school will know what ratio of additional adults to children is most appropriate in its case, what patterns of encounter will be most rewarding, and what degree of 'tuition' the parents need. We recommend the practice as one that carries considerable benefit for all concerned, particularly for the children, and we should like to see its extension.

5.41   It should be recognised that individual and small group adult-child dialogue needs the right kind of accommodation, to which we have already made a passing reference. Nursery and infant schools are busy places, alive with noise and activity. Much of the additional language experience we are suggesting will, of course, take place in the context of normal classroom activity, with which we have suggested it should be closely associated. For example, the supporting adults will be engaged in talk with children at the sand or water tray, at the modelling table, or in the cookery corner. However, it would be an inadequate building that did not have spaces to which an adult could withdraw with an individual child or a small group to engage in uninterrupted talk, in language games, etc. This is not always a facility readily to be found, and we believe that school design should take account of the need for several such spaces to be distributed throughout the school.

5.42 It is likely that schools in educational priority areas would be helped in making and maintaining their contacts by having the services of an educational visitor or home liaison teacher, and indeed some such appointments have already been made. We believe that this kind of service is a valuable addition to a school's resources. It is never easy to separate educational and social concerns in the circumstances in which the teacher may be working, but we feel that the first should be emphasised. It should be his or her responsibility to help the parents into a co-operative relationship with the school and to encourage them to play a part in their own child's education. In this the visitor would be acting as one of the staff, not as an additional social worker, and should therefore have a teaching commitment. Heads with whom we discussed the possibilities of such appointments were all emphatic that they would not want a roving ambassador who simply used the school as a base. Indeed, their view was that each teacher should know the parents of all her children on these terms, doing the home visiting herself. They agreed that as a universal practice this would not be possible. Some teachers would find it difficult, and it would be unrealistic, not to say unfair, to ask it of probationers. A liaison teacher's role should be a flexible one, and it would involve her not only in visiting but in working with a class in school while their teacher was herself visiting. We believe that the liaison teacher should essentially be part of the school, and that the best results are to be obtained on this principle, not on the basis of a large 'case-load' across two or more schools.

5.43 Before passing on to the child's experience of reading we would conclude by emphasising once more the very great importance of a conscious policy for language development. We have argued that the language growth of very young children is a more complex matter than is often realised. We know that one of the principal concerns of teachers at this level is to help the children to use words freely in response to a variety of stimulating experiences. But we suggest it is now necessary to look more deeply into the process. More active steps should be taken to help parents in the early stages and then to show them how they can co-operate with the school to develop what has already been started. Teachers themselves need to know more about the way language works, and they should have support in planning and carrying out strategies to meet the children's language needs. There are obviously implications for a large-scale expansion in in-service courses and development work if these demands are to be met. Equally obviously there are implications for the staffing of nursery and infant schools. As so many of our recommendations for participation by additional adults depend on the involvement of an appropriately qualified teacher, the staffing ratio of infant and nursery schools should be improved to allow the additional responsibilities to be undertaken with full advantage.

REFERENCES

1. *Children and their Primary Schools:* H.M.S.O.: 1967.

2. M. Deutsch *et al.: The Disadvantaged Child:* Basic Books: 1967.

3. B. Bernstein: *Class, Codes, and Control:* Routledge and Kegan Paul: 1971.

4. R. Hess and V. Shipman: *Early Experiences and the Socialisation of the Cognitive Modes in Children:* Child Development, Vol. 36, No. 4: 1965.

5. Y. J. Tough: *Focus on Meaning: Talking to some Purpose with Young Children:* Allen and Unwin: 1973.

6. W. Labov: *The Logic of Non-Standard English:* in *Language and Poverty:* F. Williams (ed.): Markham, Chicago: 1970.

7. A. H. Halsey: *Educational Priority Vol. 1:* H.M.S.O.: 1972 and *West Riding Educational Priority Area Project: No. 5 The Home Visiting Project.*

8. M. Blank and F. Solomon: *A Tutorial Language Programme to develop abstract thinking in socially-disadvantaged pre-school children:* 1968–69 *et seq.*

9. C. Bereiter and S. Engelmann: *Teaching Disadvantaged Children in Pre-school:* Prentice Hall: 1966.

10. D. M. and G. A. Gahagan: *Talk Reform:* Routledge and Kegan Paul: 1970.

11. *Language Development and the Disadvantaged Child: Research and Development Project in Compensatory Education:* Schools Council (not yet published).

12. Y. J. Tough: *Listening to Children Talking:* to be published under the auspices of the Schools Council.

13. See 1. above.

Part Three

Reading

CHAPTER 6

The Reading Process

"I struggled through the alphabet as if it had been a bramble bush; getting considerably worried and scratched by every letter."

Charles Dickens: "Great Expectations."

"We are all of us learning to read all the time."—I. A. Richards.

6.1 Controversy about the teaching of reading has a long history, and throughout it there has been the assumption, or at least the hope, that a panacea can be found that will make everything right. This was reflected in much of the correspondence we received. There was an expectation that we would identify the one method in whose adoption lay the complete solution. Let us, therefore, express our conclusion at the outset in plain terms: there is no one method, medium, approach, device, or philosophy that holds the key to the process of learning to read. We believe that the knowledge does exist to improve the teaching of reading, but that it does not lie in the triumphant discovery, or re-discovery, of a particular formula. Simple endorsements of one or another nostrum are no service to the teaching of reading. A glance at the past reveals the truth of this. The main arguments about how reading should be taught have been repeated over and over again as the decades pass, but the problems remain.

6.2 A study of the way these arguments have been advanced, contested, revamped, discredited and rediscovered is a useful corrective to the idea that any one of them has a monopoly of truth[1]. In the last four centuries there has been a succession of them, making claims for word methods, sentence methods, experience methods, phonic methods, and so on. It is interesting to note that they were usually introduced with the description 'new' or 'natural' or 'logical'. Today's discovery was often yesterday's discard, unrecognised as such, or rehabilitated by some new presentation. This does not mean that there has been no advance, that nothing really new has emerged across the years. There have, of course, been many innovations of one kind or another, notably in materials. But the major arguments are substantially the same as they have always been, and to endorse one at the expense of the others is no more helpful today than it has proved in the past.

6.3 Among authorities on reading there is, in fact, considerable agreement, and in recent years they have done much to reduce the polarisation of opinion. There is no doubt, however, that this does still exist, and it characterised much of the evidence we received. One issue that has received more than its share of this kind of attention is that of approaches to the teaching of reading in the early stages. It is argued on the one hand that the essence of the process is 'breaking the code', converting print into sounds and then into words; it is argued on the other that this must take second place to securing and expanding the child's interest, keeping his curiosity alive, and giving reading a meaning. Immediately, a false conflict is created which leads to a number of unnecessary tensions. Some would put so much emphasis on the 'mechanics' of reading that certain children would be handicapped rather than helped. Others advocate so keenly the virtues of mature reading from the beginning that they are in danger of leaving it too much to trust that the skills will be acquired on the way. The children would thus be left ignorant of vital information about the nature of the written code. This emphasis fails to acknowledge that the majority of children also require precise, well-organised instruction if they are to become successful readers. In our view a large part of the controversy arises from the expression of unnecessarily extreme opinions, often more extreme than the real beliefs or practices of those who advance them. In addition, the contentious statements are often based on inadequate information. For example, we received many letters whose writers seemed convinced that the majority of infant teachers had abandoned the teaching of phonics; they argued that a return to the practice would raise standards dramatically. But the results of our survey showed that their supposition was far from correct. The teachers of six year olds in our sample were asked which approaches they were currently using. The results were as follows:

1. Look and Say (word recognition)   97%

2. Phonic 1 (letter sounds, digraphs, diphthongs)   97%

3. Phonic 2 (based on syllables)   70%

4. Sentence Method   51%

We believe that an improvement in the teaching of reading will not come from the acceptance of simplistic statements about phonics or any other single aspect of reading, but from a comprehensive study of all the factors at work and the influence that can be exerted upon them. In the course of this sequence of chapters, therefore, we shall outline what we believe to be necessary for the effective teaching of reading—from the earliest stages to the advanced skills required of the educated reader. We believe, however, that a fundamentally important question has to be answered before there can be any discussion of how the teaching of reading can be improved. What *is* Reading? Much of the misunderstanding surrounding the debate about reading results from the lack of a proper examination of what the process involves. Before considering the ways in which children can best learn the skill one must be clear about what is expected of them, in both the short and the long term. This knowledge should then inform decisions about the organisation of the teaching within the school, the kinds of initial and in-service training needed, and the resources required at each level. Thus a detailed understanding of the reading process is of critical importance in terms of its practical implications. It is for this reason that the account which follows includes a good deal of technical detail. We regard this as essential to our task, for we do not believe that a Report making recommendations about reading can examine the issues fairly without defining what is involved for a child when he is learning to read. We must also emphasise here that our discussion of reading is not confined to this section of the Report. Parts Six and Seven have a particular relevance to this one, but since references to reading occur throughout the Report we hope that all the chapters will be read in close association with one another.

6.4 It may be useful to begin by looking at some of the ways in which reading can be defined:

> "One can read in so far as he can respond to the language skills represented by graphic shapes as fully as he has learned to respond to the same language signals of his code represented by patterns of auditory shapes."

This statement by Fries[2] could be interpreted in a number of ways, but it reflects his view that the teaching of reading is largely a matter of developing the child's *ability to respond to letters and spelling patterns*. If these could be converted from print into spoken form then this could be regarded as reading. Goodman[3], on the other hand, emphasises the importance of teaching children to respond to meaning:

> "The purpose of reading is the reconstruction of meaning. Meaning is not in print, but it is meaning that the author begins with when he writes. Somehow the reader strives to *reconstruct* this meaning as he reads."

Reading is here taken to include all those processes necessary to arrive at some *reconstruction of the author's meaning*. Gray[4] elaborates on this theme in the following way:

> "A good reader understands not only the meaning of a passage, but its related meaning as well, which includes all the reader knows that enriches or illumines the literal meaning. Such knowledge may have been acquired through direct experience, through wide reading or through listening to others."

This means that reading is more than *a reconstruction of the author's meanings*. It is the perception of those meanings within *the total context of the relevant experiences of the reader*—a much more active and demanding process. Here the reader is required to engage in critical and creative thinking in order to relate what he reads to what he already knows; to evaluate the new knowledge in terms of the old and the old in terms of the new. By this definition reading includes all the intellectual and affective processes that take place in response to a printed text.

6.5 These three definitions may be represented as follows:

A response to graphic signals in terms of the words they represent

A response to graphic signals in terms of the words they represent	plus: A response to text in terms of the meanings the author intended to set down

A response to graphic signals in terms of the words they represent	A response to text in terms of the meanings the author intended to set down	plus: A response to the author's meanings in terms of all the relevant previous experience and present judgments of the reader

Finally, there is the view that looks beyond the reading process as such to the range of activities demanded of the adult reader, with all that they imply in social and economic terms. These implications are taken up in Chapter 8. There are, in effect, two basic approaches to the definition of reading. One is to start with the complexities of print. The other is to start with the potential reading demands of the modern world and to define as reading whatever is logically involved in meeting those demands. Taken together they give a more complete understanding than either one could afford alone.

6.6   The reader responds to print at a number of levels. At one level he recognises the shapes of separate letters, groups of letters, and whole words, and he associates appropriate sounds with those letters or collections of letters. The responses at this level are fundamental to reading, and the ability needed to make them may be regarded as 'Primary Skills'. The reader must have a reasonable mastery of this process of seeing a letter or group of letters as a discrete whole before he can respond at another level, i.e. to sequences. The ability to handle sequences—of letters, words, and larger units of meaning—is essential to fluent reading. The various skills involved have been described as 'Intermediate Skills' because they operate at a level above that of the primary skills but below the level of 'Comprehension' in the extended sense of Gray's definition. In examining each of these levels we need to consider three features. The first is the graphic element, the printed word or page; the second is the language element, the sounds, words and meanings to which the print relates; and the third is the pattern of relationships that may be established between the other two in the mind of the reader. An analysis of these will give an indication of the many points of possible difficulty at which a child may falter in learning to read. More positively, it can help the teacher to modify or extend the child's existing skills to lead him to a higher level of general reading competence.

6.7   At the level of the PRIMARY SKILLS the child has to learn to perceive separate units—individual letters or groups of letters, and individual whole words. To do this he must learn to respond to two fundamental attributes of letters: shape and orientation. It may seem rather obvious to the adult that a child has to learn to respond to letter *shape*. But letter outline may convey very little to a child unless it has been invested with some kind of special significance. He may get this by watching someone trace or draw letters, by doing so himself, or by exploring the shape of a three dimensional letter in wood or plastic. Without such experience his interest may be confined to the colour of the letter, its size in relation to the background, or some fanciful pattern that its appearance suggests to him, much as one sometimes sees fanciful images in clouds or ink-blots. To see letter shapes as adults see them is by no means a natural and automatic process. On the contrary, each child may have his own idiosyncratic ways of looking at letters, and to see them as the adult sees them means he has to develop a generalised 'learning set'. Since so many children respond to letter shape very readily it is easy to forget that many others may never have enjoyed opportunities which are necessary to accomplish this. Indeed there will be some who have actually acquired 'learning sets' which obstruct them when it comes to responding appropriately to letters. On the other hand, it is perhaps because parents have so often prepared the way fairly well that so many teachers think this aspect of reading requires little attention. This sometimes leads to their assuming mistakenly that there is something inherently wrong with the child if he happens to have difficulty in learning to recognise letters.

6.8   Learning that *orientation* is a critical aspect of letters may also present problems. For the first few years of his life a child learns to ignore orientation as a means of recognising objects. The doll or the toy train is still a doll or a train whether it is the right way up, upside down, facing left, facing right, or lying on its side. This is a critical part of what has been called "conservation of identity", the fact that things retain their identity over time and in spite of changes of position or temporary disappearance. At the same time, even the youngest children have little difficulty in orientating themselves correctly to objects when they want to. They can open doors the right way, turn book pages forwards or backwards, turn cups up the right way, and so on. However, when they come to letters they have a problem. They now have to learn that b is not d, p, or q; or that f is not t, and n is not u. If we include such similarities in shape as h : y and m : w, then it becomes clear that over half the letters of the alphabet are ambiguous in terms of the child's previous learning. It is not that children have particular difficulty with orientation as such. They can see as well as any adult that b is p upside down, just as well as they can see that the doll or train is upside down. Where they have trouble is in learning to recognise these reflected and rotated forms as entirely different letters. They would regard it as very odd if a doll had to be called Betty instead of Susan according to which way it faced, or the train was called a motor car when it reversed.

6.9   Of course, children are extraordinarily flexible in what they can learn to cope with when they are strongly motivated. Letters, however, are often much less fun than dolls and trains. The difficulty with letter orientation is that there is no strong incentive to acquire this particular 'learning set'. Moreover, as we have said, it seems to run completely counter to an existing 'set' that has already become very firmly established, i.e. "ignore orientation in identifying objects". The situation and materials must therefore be particularly well designed if the child is to 'un-learn' and then re-learn in the right way. Reversal tendencies are in fact quite persistent, even in normal readers. It is scarcely surprising that they represent an important proportion of the problems experienced by the children who have difficulty in the early stages of reading.

6.10   When children have learned to respond to a combination of shape and orientation they still have to learn each of the 26 letters of the alphabet. To these can be added the 17 shapes of those capital letters which are very different from the lower case forms, i.e.

A B D E F G H I J K L M N Q R T Y

This gives a total of 43 letter shapes. In addition to these there are also such typographical variations as:

Aaa Ggg Qqq Ttt Uuu Yyy

Encounter with such variations is inevitable, because of the wide range of printed materials to which children are exposed both before and after starting school. Children can, of course, learn all these individual variations. It is simply that they increase the total quantity to be learned and add to the burdens of the slow learning child an extra dimension of difficulty that he could well do without. This difficulty is probably even more marked when the child comes to write, since he may be confused in deciding which of the various forms to set down.

6.11   A more important problem relating to letter shape arises at the level of *word* perception, as distinct from letter perception. It is often argued that children should be taught to recognise whole words rather than respond to individual letters. Unfortunately, variations in letter shape multiply at the word level, as may be seen in the examples given below. Adults are so familiar with these variant word forms that it is hard for them to appreciate how different they are. The following set of unusual equivalent symbols will give an idea of what they may look like to a child:

AND ; And ; and ; and.   GO ; Go ; go ; go.

Moreover, the whole-word forms of certain *different* words, e.g. "hot" and "hat", are no more different than the variations of the *same* word e.g. "hat" and "hat".

hot △ □ ⑥

hat △ □ ⑥

hat △ ⎕ ⑥

In spite of this, fluent readers can readily cope with variations such as the following:

iT Is MOsT uNliKELy tHaT tHe

ReADer wiLL haVE preVIOusly

sEEn tHEse WholE WORD SHapES—

How DOes hE rECoGNise THem?

Similarly, children can often read each other's handwriting quite easily, even in the early stages of learning to read, though the writing may be almost as unusual as the above. It will be appreciated, therefore, that word recognition in English is not simply a matter of learning unique whole-word forms. Indeed, over-simplified ideas about word recognition just do not match the facts.

6.12 For a further comment on the nature of whole-word perception we must note that *detailed* vision is possible only for objects that fall within a maximum of 3° of visual angle. What this means for the young reader has been revealed by studies of eye movements. It was found,[5] for example, that among a group of seven year olds the average number of fixations was 2·4 per word. Though they could recognise some words at a single glance most words required an examination of individual letters or groups of letters. If the whole of a word does not fall within the area of clear vision this finding is scarcely surprising. Children do, of course, learn to identify words correctly in running text without scrutinising meticulously every single detail of them, and how this may be achieved is discussed later. Nevertheless, the accurate perception of individual letters and groups of letters is clearly an important factor in learning to read.

6.13 There is no doubt that if children are introduced to letters in inappropriate ways these can have a harmful effect on their subsequent learning. Unfortunately, this has sometimes been used as an argument that letter recognition should not be learned at all. We do not accept this argument. There is, in our view, any number of perfectly reasonable ways in which a teacher or parent may help a child to learn to recognise letters. These include such familiar practices as the following:

—drawing attention to the shapes of letters in an alphabet book;

—letter-matching activities (provided that there is some clear clue to help the child place letters the right way up, e.g. a coloured base line, or a jigsaw shape);

—tracing or colouring letter outlines;

—writing letters in a sequence which helps the child to establish letter differences (e.g. b=downstroke, then clockwise movement; d=anti-clockwise movement, then upstroke and downstroke);

—collecting variant forms of the same letters in a scrap-book (e.g. T, t, *t*);

—mnemonics (e.g. "S is for S-s-s-snake", or "O is for orange—you can tell by the shape".)

Any competent teacher of infants could add many more examples.

6.14   We do not suggest that children of *any* age should be subjected to a rigorous and systematic training programme of exercises based on this kind of activity. A limited number of such experiences will be quite sufficient to help most children learn to attend to the relevant characteristics of the letters. The important factors are precision in the design of the learning task and careful supervision. Letters will be learned more easily if the materials used are varied in such a way that only the *invariant* properties of the letters remain constant. Thus, the same letter shape may be presented in different colours, sizes, and materials, against different backgrounds, and in different forms (e.g. T, t, *t*). Many children learn their letters so quickly that a very limited experience of such activity is sufficient. For those who do not, these variations can help to sustain interest in a fairly limited learning task. Moreover, it will help the child to transfer his learning to the other contexts in which he will meet the letters he has learned, e.g. in word games or in books. Letters which are easily confused should be learned separately. Examples are b, which differs only in *orientation* from p, q, and d; and h, which has a similar *shape* to b. The longer an error is allowed to persist the harder it is to eradicate, and it is therefore much better if the initial confusion can be avoided. This may be achieved by the 'over-learning' of any one of the letters which are easily confused, and only then giving attention successively to each of the others.

6.15   Contrary to popular belief the majority of children are perfectly capable, well before they start school, of making the perceptual discriminations necessary for learning letter shapes. They learn to make extremely complex auditory discriminations in language, and show their ability with similarly complex visual discriminations in playing with many of their games and toys. There seems to us no obvious reason why they should be denied opportunities to become familiar with the letters of the alphabet before they start school. The question of reading readiness and the parents' contribution is discussed in greater detail in the next chapter.

6.16   We come next to the relationship between letters and sounds. Single letters, or groups of letters, represent sounds called "phonemes", which enable the reader to make distinctions between different words. There are approximately 44 phonemes in English. For children with normal hearing the ability to read depends, in the first place, on the ability to distinguish most of these phonemes in normal speech. Unfortunately, they are not quite such clear-cut units of sound as they may appear:

"A tape recorder can be used to confirm a number of remarkable findings of speech analysis. As an example, a tape recorder will demonstrate that "dim" and "doom" have no /d/ sound in common. If the two words are recorded, it is impossible to cut the tape in order to separate the /im/ or /oom/ from the /d/. Either one is left with a distinct /di/ or /doo/ sound or else the /d/ sound disappears altogether. One is left with two quite different kinds of whistle. There is no /d/ except as part of these quite different consonant-vowel combinations."[6]

6.17 What the variations within each phoneme have in common is some kind of preparatory position in the speaker's vocal apparatus, but this configuration changes as the sound is produced, depending on which sound is to follow. If, then, we teach a child how to pronounce a series of sounds and ask him to run them together to form a word he will indeed learn the trick of saying those separate sounds and of then saying the related word. But he has certainly not built up the word from the sounds he has pronounced first. As Daniels and Diack[7] pointed out many years ago, "kuh-a-tuh" does not produce "cat". The process is not yet fully understood by which children learn to imitate the sounds of speech and discriminate between them. To break up a word into what are thought to be its constituent elements does not, however, seem to us the best means of developing this process. We believe a better way is for teachers to rely upon methods that have a long history in the infant school but which have unaccountably fallen out of favour; namely, the use of rhymes, jingles and alliteration. These focus attention on the contrastive elements in words while avoiding the inevitable distortions of the more analytic approach. Another quite useful practice is to get the children to sort pictures into groups according to the initial sound of the object in the picture. If only one or two very easy sets are provided initially the children can then be encouraged to make up their own more extensive collections of pictures and play with them, following the rules for familiar games, such as Pairs and Rummy. Stories, and such verbal games as 'I-spy' and 'Knock-knock', encourage children to explore speech sounds and help them develop a better intuitive understanding of these sounds.

6.18 As there are only 26 letters but 44 phonemes certain letters have to be used more than once if each phoneme is to be separately represented. These additional sounds are often represented by two-letter combinations called digraphs, e.g. ch, th, ur, aw, ou, or by larger groups of letters such as *ough* for the last vowel sound in borough. Learning to respond to spelling patterns such as these should present no serious problem to the majority of children. Instead of learning the shapes of additional letters they simply have to learn to treat particular combinations of known letters as single units. Of much greater importance in this matter of establishing relationships between letters and sounds is the fact that there is no simple correspondence between the 26 letters and the 44 phonemes. If one were intent on constructing an alphabetic writing system from scratch the obvious course would be to aim at a one-to-one correspondence between phonemes and graphemes, the grapheme being any letter or combination of letters which represents a single phoneme. Some idea of the ways in which written English falls short of this alphabetic ideal may be seen in the following examples:

    i. <u>o</u>ne h<u>o</u>me c<u>o</u>mes w<u>o</u>men <u>of</u> <u>or</u> to d<u>o</u>

   ii. <u>ai</u>sle h<u>ei</u>ght <u>eye</u> <u>I</u> ph<u>i</u>al <u>i</u>ce h<u>igh</u> <u>i</u>sland b<u>uy</u> gu<u>i</u>de sty rh<u>y</u>me

In the first example a single letter is seen to take on eight different values in different contexts. In the second, a single phoneme is spelled in 12 different ways, and indeed other spellings could be added if less common words were included, e.g. ind<u>i</u>ct.

6.19   In one study the researchers[8] examined the 6,092 two-syllable words among the 9,000 words in the comprehension vocabularies of a group of six to nine year old children. They recorded 211 different spellings for the phonemes in these words, and these required 166 rules to govern their use. Over 10 per cent of the words still had to be left aside as 'exceptions'. Sixty of these rules applied to consonants, which are usually thought to be 'regular'. This means that even if a young child memorised these rules while learning to read he would still encounter hundreds of words not governed by them. Although there is certainly a great deal of value in learning to deal with the regularities that do occur, the problem for the beginner is that words do not come tagged to indicate the spelling family to which they belong.

6.20   The word printed below gives some impression of the kind of problem that confronts a child when he has to combine graphemes and phonemes in a phonic attack on an unfamiliar word. This word is in the vocabulary of most adults in this country, but it has been spelled here in an unusual way (though the spelling conventions that have been used are common enough in other contexts).

calmbost

Obviously, the word cannot be identified at a glance, and the following list gives some examples of sound values that are quite commonly represented by each of the letters:

   c: <u>c</u>entre; <u>c</u>andle; <u>c</u>ello

   a: m<u>a</u>n; c<u>a</u>ll; f<u>a</u>ther; c<u>a</u>ble; m<u>a</u>ny; w<u>a</u>nd; err<u>a</u>nd

   l: ca<u>l</u>m; co<u>l</u>t

   m: ha<u>m</u>

   b: cym<u>b</u>al; lam<u>b</u>ing

   o: fr<u>o</u>m; wh<u>o</u>m; t<u>o</u>morrow; c<u>o</u>me; h<u>o</u>me; w<u>o</u>men; f<u>o</u>rm

   s: lo<u>s</u>t; lo<u>s</u>e

   t: lis<u>t</u>en; sta<u>t</u>ion; los<u>t</u>

The adult reader will find this a difficult word* to decipher, for although the letters represent the sounds they commonly stand for in other words most

---

*the word is "chemist".

of them do offend against some of the more general spelling rules. This places him in a position similar to that of the child. The beginning reader does not know the rules, either consciously or at an intuitive level. He may therefore try both legitimate and illegitimate variations, as well as ignoring some of the various legitimate possibilities. And even when he knows the rules, the number of possible permutations is very great. If he had to work through them all with each unfamiliar word he would never learn to read. The idea that at this level reading consists of matching sounds and symbols in some simple way is therefore quite untenable. Teaching techniques based solely on this assumption can hamper subsequent reading development. That having been said, we must emphasise that this level of decoding *is* of particular inportance in the early stages of learning to read, and the complexity of English spelling patterns does appear to retard progress. So much seems clear from the British i.t.a. experiments.

6.21   English shares with French the disadvantage of being among the most complex in its spelling patterns. Italian, Dutch and German are rather better, but they in turn are less regular than Spanish. Finnish appears to come nearest to the perfect fit, at least in the European languages. Not surprisingly, it has been claimed for certain countries that the regularity of their phoneme-grapheme correspondence leads to a low incidence of reading disability. Finland and Japan are notable examples. Unfortunately, there are so many differences between each country in terms of pre-school experience, age of admission to school, teaching methods, modes of assessment, etc., that no firm conclusions can reasonably be drawn from comparative studies. Various solutions have been suggested to the problems presented by the irregular system of spelling in English, the most radical of which is its actual reform. We received evidence in favour of this measure, and it was suggested that we might include attention to it in our recommendations. The views of members of the Committee differ on the question of spelling reform, and this difference of opinion is probably a fair reflection of the range and intensity of the views held by teachers and the public at large. However, the majority of us remain unconvinced by the case for national reform of the system of spelling in English. We consider the issues involved too complex and the implications too far-reaching to enable us to stretch our brief to the extent of giving the subject the detailed study it needs. In the circumstances, therefore, we do not feel able to make a recommendation on it.

6.22   Other solutions devised to help the reader cope with the difficulties of irregular spelling are the use of diacritical marks or of colour coding, simplified spelling for the early stages of reading (e.g. the initial teaching alphabet), and vocabulary control of one kind or another.   All these are considered in the next chapter. One conclusion is inescapable at this stage: the teacher needs a sound understanding of the problems created for the learner by this evident irregularity in the phoneme-grapheme relationship of the English writing system.

6.23   Broadly speaking, there are two ways in which a child can learn the correspondences between phonemes and graphemes. One is by attending directly to the sounds and letters and the way they relate to one another. The other is by attending to whole words and their pronunciation, and over a period of time learning to make intuitive generalisations about phoneme-grapheme relationships. Even if there is no explicit teaching of phonics, many children will still work out phonic relationships for themselves. The above examples will have shown that although the child must steadily acquire a considerable amount of phonic knowledge he certainly does not use it in any simple way. We must therefore reject as highly suspect any phonic drill which causes children to pay more attention to single phoneme-grapheme relationships than to sequences. Competence in phonics is essential both for attacking unfamiliar words and for fluent reading. The question, then, is not whether or not to teach phonics; of this there can be no doubt. The question is how and when to do it.

6.24   We have already noted that letters pronounced in isolation tend to be very different from the phonemes they purport to represent. To teach a child that "kuh-a-tuh" says "cat" is to teach him something that is simply incorrect. It is very doubtful in fact whether in a strictly controlled experiment this way of attacking new words would prove to be much more effective than the old alphabetic method ("see-ay-tee" says "cat"). Both owe their initial success to what psychologists call "mediated learning", but at the expense of having the child acquire responses which must later be unlearned. A more common practice these days is for teachers to get children to synthesise rather larger units. The groupings are chosen in such a way as to reduce distortion and allow a genuine blending of sound, e.g., "bl-ack" says "black". It has been argued that the whole syllable is the more appropriate unit, since this produces the minimum of distortion. But even at the level of the syllable the child is still faced with difficulties. If he has been taught to treat "basket" as "bas-ket", he will find "wal-ked" of little use of him when trying to pronounce the superficially similar "walked". The rules for syllabification are no less complex than those for English spelling; by the time they are learned the child is past the stage of learning to read when they might have helped. More important, however, is the fact that they often conflict with the morphemic system; and morphemes,* not syllables, are the units of language. There is a case, therefore, for emphasising morphemes from a quite early stage. Thus, when a child encounters the word *hear* there is everything to be said for showing him that this is the base word in *hears* and *hearing*. In this way the emphasis is placed on the relationship between spellings and meanings and not just spellings and sounds. This point is taken up again in paragraph 6.38 after we have considered the importance of intermediate skills in developing word recognition.

6.25   A useful approach to teaching phoneme-grapheme relationships which is not in conflict with the various points we have made so far was pioneered by Daniels and Diack as the 'phonic-word' approach. It is the basis of what came to be called the 'linguistic' method, although modern linguistics has since made a much broader contribution to the teaching of reading. Like the phonic method, it calls for vocabulary control† of the 'cat-hat-mat' variety. However, instead of being explicitly taught the phonic elements, the child learns each whole word, sometimes through associated pictures. He is

---

*A morpheme is the smallest unit of meaning in language. Both 'hen' and 's' in 'hens' are morphemes. A syllable, on the other hand, relates essentially to pronunciation.

†Vocabulary control is the control of the rate at which new words are introduced and how often they are repeated.

then given exercises, games, or simple reading tasks which enable him to form and test his own hypotheses about the grapheme-phoneme correspondences. In our view this kind of approach is useful in helping a child to learn that letters and groups of letters do relate to sounds in a fairly systematic way. It will also help him in sorting out a particular set of relationships with which he is having difficulty. On the other hand, we would regard as mistaken any attempt to take a child through a programme of exercises which included anything more than a small number of the possible relationships. This would be a recipe for extreme boredom; it would provide little transfer, and it would place excessive emphasis on sounds at the expense of meaning.

6.26 Our analysis of the problem has led us to the view that it is better for children to learn phoneme-grapheme relations in the context of whole word recognition, at least in the early stages of reading. At this point, a programme for the explicit teaching of phonics may be as profitless as trying to instruct a pre-school child in the rules of grammar. However, children will be developing their own hypotheses about phoneme-grapheme correspondences, and this process should certainly be encouraged as opportunities arise. In the following section an examination of the intermediate skills throws further light on the best means of helping children to master phonics and to use context cues in responding to new or unfamiliar words. We therefore return to this question when we have considered some of the additional factors.

6.27 We described the INTERMEDIATE SKILLS as the ability to handle sequences of letters, words, and larger units of meaning. To acquire it the reader has to become familiar with the probability with which sequences occur. In other words, when he is reading a sequence he has to be able to anticipate what is most likely to follow it. By this means he reduces the number of possibilities to be considered when he encounters an unfamiliar word. Equally, he reduces the time taken to identify *familiar* words in fluent reading. He is also able to isolate the specific meaning of the word which changes its meaning according to context. It is important for the teacher to have some understanding of the process if he is to develop appropriate teaching methods. We shall therefore examine each of the levels at which the intermediate skills function.

6.28 A word consists of letters sequenced in a particular way. The left-to-right direction is, of course, an arbitrary convention, and there are languages in which it is right-to-left, or even vertical. Whatever the language, there are no strong reasons for thinking any one convention to be more 'natural' than any other. The important conclusion from this is that the direction in which letters or words are written and read does not come naturally; it is another 'learning set' that has to be acquired. As with the orientation of a single letter, this conflicts to some extent with 'learning sets' the child has already acquired. He may, for example, have learned to order the carriages in his train in a number of different ways, and to run it in any direction, but it still remains the same train. Little wonder, therefore, that many children are bemused by "on" and "no", "was" and "saw", "won" and "now", "stop" and "pots" etc; and these are only the more obvious examples. It is less generally appreciated that children often begin to attack a word correctly from left to right, reverse some of the medial letters, and end up, perhaps, with the correct final letters. Sometimes the reversal makes a real word, as when a child says "clot" for "colt" or "trail" for "trial", but he will often produce a nonsense word, assuming, perhaps, that this is a word he has not yet absorbed into his spoken vocabulary, e.g. "engery" for "energy". The fact that adults often make mistakes of this kind shows how persistent these faulty word attack habits can be, and how important it is to ensure that they do not get firmly established in the first place. The first essential is to recognise that children cannot take in unfamiliar whole words in a single fixation. This provides a starting point for considering possible ways in which these wrong habits can be avoided.

6.29   There are many letter sequences that occur rarely, if at all, in written English, e.g. dx, kng, wpvt. At the other extreme there are many that are very common, e.g. bl, str, atio. In principle, therefore, for any particular letter sequence one could calculate its frequency of occurrence in the reading experience of any child or adult. The more frequently a letter sequence occurs the more likely it is that the reader will come to expect the remaining letters to follow whenever he sees the first letter of that sequence. If, for example, he sees, the letter "p" in a particular fixation he may anticipate such letters as *a, e, h, i, l,* etc. at varying levels of probability. The expectancy that he will see such letters as *b, c, d, f, g,* etc. will be virtually zero. As he takes in more and more letters, however, the range of possibilities gradually reduces. Thus "pr . . ." produces a narrower range of expectancies than "p" alone, and "pri . . ." a still narrower one. Even if confronted by part of a nonsense word such as "redulanti . .", the majority of readers would be likely to anticipate only such possibilities as "ng", "on", "ous", "c", or "ne" to complete the 'word'. There is a good deal of evidence to suggest that speed in identifying letters is closely related to the degree of expectancy that the given letter will occur. If only one letter is possible, recognition will be virtually instantaneous. If the number is as many as five the perceptual task is slightly more complicated and takes more time. If any one of the 26 letters could be anticipated the problem becomes obviously very much greater and takes even longer. If, however, groups of letters, rather than single letters, can be anticipated the speed of response is much increased.

6.30   The swift identification of single letters, or groups of letters, is obviously of critical importance in fluent reading. However, teaching children to recognise isolated letters, or groups of letters, is only part of the problem. The other part is to help them develop the habit of anticipating likely letter sequences. Children must therefore learn to do two things at the same time, i.e. identify one letter, or group of letters, and anticipate the next. It follows that any excessive emphasis on one at the expense of the other may well hamper the development of this rather delicate complex of skills. The effects of inadequate teaching in either skill can be seen in the reading behaviour of certain children. There is the older child who still reads haltingly and falls back very quickly to an examination of letters. On the other hand there is the child who reads quickly and makes all manner of 'careless' mistakes.

6.31   All the points already made about letter sequence and probability apply equally to phoneme sequences. Thus, not only has a listener to recognise phonemes as they are uttered, but also to anticipate very efficiently those that are most likely to follow. Only by this means has he any chance of keeping up with a speaker's rapid flow of words. Even an incomplete nonsense word spoken aloud will cause anticipations of a limited number of possible endings, as did the written nonsense word "redulanti . . ." In tackling an unfamiliar word, therefore, the reader can call upon this knowledge of probable phonemic sequences to match the word on the page—as was no doubt evident to those who correctly deciphered the nonsense-spelling "calmbost" as "chemist" in paragraph 6.20. Most words do not present so many alternative possibilities. In many cases, an unfamiliar word may be decoded by a child as easily as an adult might decipher an unconventional spelling such as "trand", where the sounds "tr-nd" suggest the possibility of "trend", or "trained", in terms of known words. What we would emphasise here is the fundamental importance of prediction in attacking unfamiliar words. Words are recognised as a result of matching a small number of possibilities against the printed model rather than by mechanically working through all the possible sound values of the separate elements.

6.32   We have been discussing the implications for word attack of letter and phoneme sequences *within* a word. When it comes to reading groups of words the child has to acquire a 'learning set' to read successive *words* from left to right. This convention is simple enough to establish, but to achieve it there must be some teaching, or deliberate structuring of the learning experience. It should be learned early, or some initial confusion may provide yet another adverse reading experience. Though the child would acquire the skill in due course this early confusion could still contribute to a negative attitude to reading. It must be remembered, however, that even when it *is* established there is still a tendency for the eyes to move back and forth across a line of text. This is because additional factors are at work. A word might be incorrectly identified at first glance and this could become obvious from the words that follow. Moreover, it is not always possible for the reader to sort out the syntactic structure of a sentence at first reading. The structural cues provided by print are by no means as powerful as those of the intonation patterns of speech, and punctuation can sometimes confuse rather than make plain. Even when the structure is clear the meaning might not be, and this is another reason why it is often necessary to do a certain amount of back-tracking. There are, then, a number of different causes of regressive eye-movement. Once the habit has been established of reading from left-to-right, back-tracking is simply a sign that the reader is having problems with the text at some conceptual level. It is a case, then, of deciding whether or not he needs help at this level rather than of concentrating on the symptom.

6.33   As in the case of letters, words vary in the degree to which they can be expected to follow certain other words. Since the number of different words in use vastly exceeds the number of different letters, it follows that in the case of the former there is much less chance of being able to anticipate a particular sequence. Among the high frequency words, however, there is a slight tendency for some words to collocate, e.g. "on the", "in the". There are about a dozen high frequency words which together account for approximately a quarter of any piece of continuous written material. If the child learns these thoroughly and reads them frequently in running text a useful contribution can be made to his fluency. However, there should not be an undue emphasis on recognising them in isolation, since this could encourage the wrong kind of 'learning set'. Apart from these high frequency words there are others that tend to collocate in everyday speech, e.g. "bus stop", "telephone call", but they are not encountered so frequently as to make it worthwhile to give special attention to their visual forms.

6.34   Word recognition is also made easier by the ability to anticipate *syntactic* sequences. A number of studies show that a printed text is easier to read the more closely its structures are related to those used by the reader in normal speech. This means that for the young child certain kinds of reading material must present a problem. Such sequences as "look, look, see the elephant" do not come naturally off the tongue of the average five year old in everyday speech. Even the language of story books for young readers sometimes deviates appreciably from the speech patterns of those for whom they are intended. Since it also differs from the spoken language used in the various kinds of literature for older children and adults one wonders what is the justification for it. It certainly fails to provide a useful graphic representation of an acceptable linguistic style. Research has shown that pre-school children use a surprisingly wide range of sentence structures in their spoken language. Reading material which presents children with this unreal language therefore lacks predictability and prevents them from making use of the sequential probability in linguistic structure. The result is that they have to depend too much on a laboured phonic approach to unfamiliar words. This important issue is taken up in more detail in the next chapter.

6.35   The anticipation of sequences is also called into play at the level of *meaning*. It has been estimated[9] that the most common 500 words in English share between them some 14,050 meanings. The ambiguity of letters considered in isolation is almost trivial when compared to the ambiguity of isolated words. Only by using the surrounding sequences can the reader identify which of the many possible meanings an author intends in a given passage. The most effective teaching of reading, therefore, is that which gives the pupil the various skills he needs to make fullest possible use of *context cues* in searching for meaning. The habit of responding sensitively to context in order to detect significant nuances of meaning is not one that can be acquired quite simply in the early stages of reading. It develops over a life-time; and an important condition for its development is that in every reading task there should be an incentive to read with this kind of alertness. Anyone who has discussed with children the meaning of something they have been reading will appreciate how little use many of them make of the rich contextual cues that are available. This is scarcely surprising, as they are rarely taught how to do it. The teaching of reading virtually ceases once the child can read aloud with reasonable accuracy at a reasonable speed. Yet to discontinue instruction at this point is rather like halting the training of a pianist once he can play the scales and a few elementary tunes.

6.36   The point needs no labouring that the intermediate skills are important in word attack, in fluent reading, and in comprehension. What is less often realised is the very great potency of these skills when they operate in combination. Research has shown that the reading vocabulary of most children begins to widen considerably between the ages of seven and nine. This rapid acceleration almost certainly depends to a large extent on the effective development of intermediate skills, for it is these which enable the reader to cope with new words and new meanings in context. Dictionary skills are, of course, extremely important, but this enrichment of the reading vocabulary has as its primary source the ability we have been describing. Failure to develop this competence may partly explain the difficulties experienced by retarded readers in making progress beyond a reading age of eight or nine. Much 'remedial' work has emphasised word-building at the expense of reading for meaning, and this may be at least partly to blame.

6.37 If a child rapidly develops a reading vocabulary this does not in itself mean that he is developing as an effective reader. He may become skilled in recognising in print words he has previously heard, but he may still be unable to respond adequately to larger units of meaning in any given text. We are not able to recommend exclusively any one approach to helping children to respond to context cues. However, it may be useful to illustrate the possibilities with one instance. In recent years there has been a growing interest in the use of cloze procedure for developing the intermediate skills. Cloze procedure is the use of a piece of writing in which certain words have been deleted, and the pupil has to make the maximum possible use of the context cues available in predicting the missing words. There is no single 'right' answer in each case, as some of the words may be as suitable as the author's own words, or for that matter even more suitable. Merely filling in missing words as a routine exercise appears to have no measurable effect, but animated discussion on a piece of writing of real interest is a different matter entirely. When a cloze test is being prepared the deletions may be random, or they may be confined to certain parts of speech or words which are 'cued' in different ways. We would prefer to see approaches such as these as part of the teacher's repertoire rather than as part of a structured programme. They can be used with a whole class, a group, or an individual pupil as and when the need arises.

6.38 The great importance of anticipation has implications for the choice of words to be used in early reading material. If these are of the "Can Dan Fan Nan?" variety then the pattern of phonic expectancies built up at this critical period will be very much at odds with the spelling patterns of English. (The sentence quoted is an actual example from a book which follows the 'linguistic' method of teaching reading.) Several researchers have been highly critical of reading schemes in which the form of vocabulary control was to select similar words with regular spellings, a principle advocated by earlier linguists such as Bloomfield and Fries. One such critic[10] reviewed a number of studies which compared the early 'linguistic' reading schemes with basal* readers, and he concluded that the former "tend to produce inferior oral reading in both rate and accuracy". This judgment received some indirect support from a study[11] which showed that the learning of words with minimal contrasts, e.g. "rat", "fat", "hat", made it more difficult for the child to learn more complex words at a later stage. It was better to give the child more varied and complex words from the beginning, rather than restrict him to simple words with regular spellings. Other studies have shown

*The term 'basal readers' is used in the U.S.A. to refer to books which are graded in terms of difficulty and which form a reading scheme. The scheme will also include graded workbooks, teaching materials of various kinds, and one or more teachers' manuals.

that words which differ markedly from one another are more easily learned than those between which there is little contrast. One important advantage of not restricting vocabulary on a phonic or linguistic basis is that words can then be selected for their familiarity to the child, their interest, and their richness of meaning, all of which make them more easily remembered. If, in addition, his attention is drawn to morphemes, as we suggested in paragraph 6.24, the child who has met the words *hear, hears,* and *hearing* will have no difficulty with *heard* in a sentence such as "Peter had not heard his mother calling". His anticipations based on the context, combined with his response to the meaning of *hear,* will give him a very good chance of getting quickly to the meaning and hence to the pronunciation of the word *heard.* In conclusion, we must again lay emphasis on the need for the child to learn phoneme-grapheme relationships *within the context of actual reading.* To be able to do this he must develop an adequate sight vocabulary at an early stage, a subject discussed in the next chapter.

6.39   We turn now to the COMPREHENSION SKILLS, which will be introduced here briefly and discussed in more detail in Chapter 8. When a child reads fluently he is succeeding in extracting meaning from the printed page. In particular, he is deriving meanings as close as possible to those intended by the author. Comprehension skills, as we see them, relate to various kinds of interaction between those meanings and the reader's purpose for reading. In the course of these interactions he will reject some features of the author's thinking and assimilate others, modifying his previous ideas and attitudes in the process. There have been a number of attempts to categorise the various aspects of comprehension. Some have been based largely upon an intuitive assessment of the requirements of various kinds of reading task. Others have been based upon a statistical analysis of the results of reading tests. The following are some of the categories identified in these various attempts. They by no means exhaust the definitions, but they will give some indication of what is involved in the process of comprehension.

6.40   At the level of *literal comprehension* (para 8.15) the reader identifies material explicitly set down in the text that happens to relate to his purpose. To do this he has to be able to select significant detail and identify main ideas, which may be contained in descriptive or explanatory sequences, comparisons, and summarising statements. When he has achieved a grasp of the literal content the reader is then in a position to analyse, paraphrase, synthesise, and summarise it in whatever way suits his reading purpose. In varying degrees of difficulty this capacity for *reorganisation* is required of the child throughout his school work. The quality of comprehension at this literal level, however, is often very low. In project work, for example, many pupils have a strong tendency merely to string together sentences culled from various sources or, at best, to make only minor modifications in an attempt to paraphrase. This is clearly of very little value to them. If they are to reorganise and relate ideas, rather than confine their attention to specific phrases and sentences, they need to be taught particular skills. These include the ability to make well-structured notes, to integrate notes from various sources, and to use flow diagram techniques or other kinds of model.

6.41   When the reader goes beyond what is explicitly stated he is engaged in *inferential comprehension* (para 8.16). Here he interprets the significance of ideas or thoughts which might conceivably have been included or made explicit, but were not. This includes the interpretation of figurative language and the prediction of outcomes. Thus the reader is reading not only between the lines, but beyond the lines. Generally speaking this kind of reading receives scant attention in school except in the treatment of literature. The pupil has little incentive to respond sensitively to inferences in his reading in other curriculum areas. Another aspect of comprehension which receives little attention is *evaluation* (para 8.17), where the reader applies 'truth' tests to the material. He may, for example, need to evaluate the internal logic of a passage, and its authenticity, adequacy, and appropriateness. In spite of the very obvious shortcomings of much of the printed material placed before children, there is little systematic teaching designed to show them how to approach it in this critical fashion. The affective or aesthetic equivalent of evaluation is *appreciation*, which is usually regarded, in the secondary school at least, as being exclusively the province of the English specialist. It is discussed at length in the chapter devoted to the place of literature. Even in functional reading, however, there is everything to be said for developing the pupil's ability to respond to an author's use of language—to imagery, style, and structure. This should be seen as an integral feature in the development of other aspects of comprehension.

6.42 An important attribute of the competent reader is the ability to apply *flexible reading strategies*, according to his purpose and the nature of the material. Unfortunately, if most of their reading is of the single-speed kind, children will be habituated to becoming single-speed readers. The danger is then that the only technique they will ever use is inflexible, one-pace, line-by-line reading. Flexibility should be acquired at school and should be exercised throughout the curriculum. The only way in which it can be effectively developed is for the pupil to encounter a full range of reading tasks which make demands on the relevant skills.

6.43 Dealing efficiently with information must now be recognised as one of the major problems in modern society. It has been estimated that in the United States, for example, one third of the national product is currently used in producing information. Despite the growth of other media, the vast bulk of all information is recorded in printed form. So far in this chapter we have concentrated on the ability to read the various kinds of printed material in which this information is recorded. But dealing with information in the mass presents a broader set of problems of which the reading process itself is simply one element. It becomes increasingly necessary for a person not only to be able to cope with print efficiently, but to organise his own use of it. This means that he must be able to identify his own information needs, a much less simple matter than it sounds. He must then know the sources which will answer to them, judging the value of these from a wide range of material and selecting the limited amount which will serve him best. The first implication of this is that children should have extensive experience in defining their own purposes. They need to become skilled in working out exactly what questions they should seek to answer by reading. The second is that they should be given the opportunity to explore many different kinds of printed media, and learn how to obtain what they need. Pupils should be led to confidence in the use of bibliographical tools and in tapping sources of information in the community at large, and as the sources of information continue to change and multiply the teacher must be prepared to learn along-side his pupil.

6.44   Many individuals develop the various comprehension skills to a high level with very little guidance, but the majority need a great deal of positive help. Research (see paragraph 2.2) strongly suggests that as many as one third of the population may be incompetent in the kinds of reading comprehension to which we have referred. We also suspect that many people merely re-organise what they are reading in ways that confirm existing ideas and prejudices. If reading comprehension is to be significantly improved, then, an important principle has to be established. Every subject teacher in the secondary school must assume responsibility for developing all those kinds of skill that are needed by his pupils to read intelligently the material he presents to them. The ability to do this must therefore be seen as an essential element in the professional competence of the subject specialist, a principle elaborated in Chapter 8. It is a further reinforcement of our argument that reading should receive increasing attention from *all* teachers at each successive stage of education. We suggest later in the Report that each primary school should have a teacher responsible for advising his colleagues in language and reading, and this is one important area in which that teacher's contribution would be helpful. In the secondary school it would be an aspect of the policy of language across the curriculum, to which Chapter 12 is devoted.

REFERENCES

1.   H. Diack: *In Spite of the Alphabet:* Chatto and Windus: 1965.

2.   C. C. Fries: *Linguistics and Reading:* Holt, Rinehart and Winston: 1962.

3.   K. S. Goodman: *Behind the Eye: What Happens in Reading.*
     In: *Reading: Process and Program:* Urbana, Illinois: National Council of Teachers of English: 1970.

4.   W. S. Gray: *The Teaching of Reading and Writing: An International Survey:* Alfred: Paris-U.N.E.S.C.O. 1956.

5.   E. A. Taylor: *The Spans: Perception, Apprehension and Recognition:* American Journal of Ophthalmology: Vol. 44: 1957.

6.   F. Smith: *Understanding Reading:* Holt, Rinehart and Winston: 1971.

7.   J. C. Daniels and H. Diack: *Progress in Reading:* 1956.

8.   B. Berdiansky, B. Cronnel, and J. Koehler.
     Spelling—Sound Relations and Primary Form—Class Descriptions for Speech—Comprehension Vocabularies of 6–9 Year Olds. South West Regional Laboratory for Educational Research and Development, Technical Report, No. 15 (1969). Cited in: F. Smith: *Understanding Reading:* Holt, Rinehart and Winston: 1971.

9.   C. C. Fries: *Linguistics and Reading:* Holt, Rinehart and Winston: 1962.

10. G. P. Spache, and E. B. Spache: *Reading in the Elementary School:* Allyn and Bacon: Boston: 1973.

11. H. Levin, and J. Watson. *The Learning of Variable Grapheme to Phoneme Correspondence: Variations in the Initial Consonant Position.* Cornell University Cooperative Research Project No. 639: 1963.

CHAPTER 7

Reading In The Early Years

7.1 A recurring topic of discussion, and one which often arouses much feeling, is the age at which children should actually begin the process of learning to read. Understandably, the question is one of particular concern to parents, not least because they are uncertain of their own role in the matter. Should they give any kind of reading instruction before the child starts school? If not, how far should they be involved once the child has started school, and in what ways? Should it all be left to the teacher, with no home involvement beyond general encouragement? We have suggested in the previous chapter that the early stages of reading consist of various kinds of learning experience and that there is no one point to which the term 'reading readiness' can reasonably be applied. Decisions on the age at which preparatory reading activities should be introduced must be finely judged. If the process is unduly delayed the child is denied access to the many valuable opportunities that early reading opens up to him. If he makes too early a start the burden of learning may retard his reading development and make reading a chore rather than an enjoyable experience. There are many well attested cases of parents who have been highly successful in helping their children to learn to read. What is not known is the number whose efforts have been unsuccessful, or positively harmful. It would be instructive to know, for example, how many children with severe reading disability received misguided teaching from over-anxious parents in the pre-school years. Let us make it clear at once that we believe parents have an extremely important part to play. All we have said in Chapter 5 about the language climate of the home has a critical bearing on preparation for reading. There is, then, no doubt whatever of the value of parents' involvement in the early stages of reading. What needs careful thought is the *nature* of that involvement and the attitude they bring to it.

7.2 It has been said[1] that the best way to prepare the very young child for reading is to hold him on your lap and read aloud to him stories he likes, over and over again. The printed page, the physical comfort and security, the reassuring voice, the fascination of the story: all these combine in the child's mind to identify books as something which hold great pleasure. This is the most valuable piece of advice that a parent can be given, and we want to outline some of its implications before considering in greater detail the question of reading readiness. Before the child arrives at school he should have learned to look upon books as a source of absorbing pleasure. There are some households in which this is a virtual certainty from the beginning; there are very many more where there are few books of any kind and certainly none the child grows up with as his own. We believe that a priority need is to introduce children to books in their pre-school years and to help parents recognise the value of sharing the experience of them with their children. In this connection we have been impressed by the enterprise of such bodies as the Federation of Children's Book Groups in their aim to make books a part of the child's life from the outset. Many of the 90 or so groups in this organisation visit hospitals to read stories to young patients. Some take round book trolleys or tape-record stories and leave the cassettes for the children to play back. At least one group sells books for children at local factories where their parents work. Another encouraging development is the time allowed by some local radio stations for talks about children's books. We have already advocated the broadcasting of radio and television programmes directed to parents, and these should include guidance on how and what to read to children of different ages.

7.3   Potentially, the most important source of help is the Children's Librarian. One from whom we heard lends collections of books to the borough's hundred or so pre-school organisations, which include day nurseries, playgroups, and private nurseries. She and her colleagues visit as many of them as possible at fortnightly intervals to tell the children stories from picture books, and to get to know the supervisors and staff and the children's mothers. A travelling exhibition has been assembled, containing books for children up to the age of seven, and this visits health centres, teachers' centres, colleges of education, and community associations. Another proposal is to take a double decker bus to the areas of greatest need, determined by consultation with local community workers, health visitors, and social workers. The lower deck will be equipped with books for young children and their mothers, and the upper deck fitted out for story-telling and audio-visual programmes. This is similar in principle to the system in operation in a large county, where the same facilities are taken to the villages by touring vans. There are, however, some Authorities where no such pre-school activities have been considered, or where Children's Librarians are not empowered to lend books to playgroups and other voluntary organisations. We recommend that all Authorities should make possible and encourage enterprises of this kind.

7.4   Infant schools should be fully informed of pre-school activities of these and similar kinds so that they can take advantage of them. It is helpful, for example, if some of the books are familiar to the child in the midst of all the new material he meets. Where parents have been able to borrow books from the playgroup or nursery class it would obviously be a contraction of opportunity if the infant school did not continue the practice. Children should become accustomed as early as possible to easy access to books and a ready supply of them. There is evidence from our survey that schools are very much alive to this fact; 80 per cent of the six year olds in our sample were allowed to take books home at some time, though it is not possible to say on how regular a basis. There is inevitably a degree of risk when books are taken home by young children, but this has to be accepted. Parents should certainly not feel inhibited about borrowing them and should be reassured that the school takes a realistic attitude about the occasional book that has been torn or marked. Such a tolerance is unlikely to be abused, but in exercising it schools need to know they have the security of financial support and that replacements will be readily available. We should like to see more enterprises of the kind financed by one local Authority at the instigation of its English Adviser. Eight infant schools, most of them in areas of disadvantage, were each given a sum of money with which to set up libraries for parents. The intention was to encourage parents to choose books with the guidance of the teachers and to read aloud to their children both at home and at school. In their visits parents brought along their pre-school children and were also allowed to take books for them. The response from the home was extremely encouraging—as high as 60 per cent of the families at its best—and the Authority was encouraged to extend the scheme. The schools turned it to excellent advantage, the teachers exchanging ideas among themselves and bringing parents into the life of the school in a very practical way. As the adviser expressed it: "It has alerted many parents to the educational importance of reading and has perhaps brought a first book into some homes where reading has not hitherto formed part of the life pattern". Or in the words of one of the parents: "I bring my little ones into school when I come for books for our lad, and I can see them learning from the older children".

7.5 This is not the only example of its kind, and a few schools in various parts of the country have attempted similar schemes on their own initiative. Such enterprises are still comparatively rare, and we feel they deserve wider currency, but it is encouraging to see that more infant schools are devising ways of introducing parents to good quality books. Their methods include displays in entrance halls, Christmas present collections, and discussion sessions at parents' evenings. A number give parents the opportunity to buy books within the school, but it was evident from our survey that this is still a relatively uncommon facility, since it was available to only 16 per cent of the six year olds and 27 per cent of the nine year olds. (The practice was only marginally more common in secondary schools at 32 per cent.) In many areas there are no bookshops; in others the provision is extremely unsatisfactory, affording little choice. It therefore increasingly becomes the responsibility of the school to make it possible for children and parents together to see and select books which can be bought and taken home. Where there is a local bookshop with suitable books available it is possible for a parent or teacher to make a selection and sell the books at the school on a sale or return basis. This is particularly useful before Christmas and the long summer holidays. Some schools have obtained licences under the Publishers' Book Agency Scheme, which enables them to receive some of the discount given to the bookseller from which they buy them. An alternative is for the school to sell books through one of the various children's book clubs which operate through the post. All these suggestions for extension into the home are designed to erode the notion that 'real' books are of a lower order of importance for children who are only on the threshold of reading. Indeed it is at this critical stage of his development that the child is at his most responsive to influences which may form his future attitudes. This fact should be brought home to parents in every way possible. In our view, activity of this kind and on this scale is essential if parents are to be helped to play their part in preparing the child for the process of learning to read.

7.6 Every time a parent reads aloud to a child the child is learning that by some curious means the lines of print can be converted into stories which he can enjoy. When children are 'helping' with cooking and their mother reads aloud the directions from the cookery book they can see that this absorbing and enjoyable activity draws upon print. Letters, advertisements, labels, traffic signs are just a few examples of opportunities for parents to help children understand the purpose of reading and, on some occasions, to identify common words. The opportunities should be natural and not forced, and the outcomes of reading should be rewarding. In this way the parent can bring the child up with the right attitude towards the printed word, for it is by no means automatic that this will develop of itself. As Vygotsky[2] put it: "it is the abstract quality of written language that is the stumbling block". The child has "little motivation to learn writing when we begin to teach it. He feels no need for it and has only a vague idea of its usefulness". In a study of five year old children Reid[3] found that they had a "general lack of any specific expectancies of what reading was going to be like, of what the activity consisted, of the purpose and use of it". Thus it is important that before the child begins to read for himself he must come to look upon reading as an activity with a purpose. From the beginning it should be established as a thinking process, not simply as an exercise in identifying shapes and sounds.

7.7   A number of studies have suggested that a mental age of about six is necessary before reading instruction can be effective. These are mostly American studies, however, and in the American context, 'readiness' usually means that the child is ready to enter the first stage of a highly structured reading programme in classroom conditions different from our own. In any case, as long ago as 1937 a series of studies[4] showed that group size and flexibility make a very appreciable difference. Children with a mental age of four and a half to five can quite happily learn to read if they are given learning experiences which match their individual needs. There is ample evidence of children learning to read at home well before reaching even this kind of mental age. There is no virtue in denying a child access to early experience of reading, provided that it carries meaning and satisfaction for him. By one if not both of these criteria the use of drills is ruled out. It would be chilling to contemplate an image of earnest young parents holding up successions of flash cards and waiting with growing anxiety for their child to call the 'right' response. We are in no doubt that the help of parents —of the kind we advocate here and elsewhere in the Report—is of great value. But we are equally in no doubt that to communicate anxiety to the young child by driving him is a harmful practice. Let a child be put in situations which stimulate him, with materials that fascinate him, and there is no need to fret about the right mental age to start reading. It becomes almost an irrelevance.

7.8   Very high intelligence on the one hand and very low intelligence on the other certainly have a significant bearing on readiness. But apart from these extremes early reading success is not closely associated with intelligence test measures. A high score on an intelligence test may supply useful information to a teacher who has underestimated a child's potential capacity. A low score, however, is not in itself a dependable indicator that the child's capacity is limited. There is some evidence that when a teacher's expectations are based on intelligence test scores the pupil's achievements are affected accordingly. On the whole, therefore, it is reasonable to discount intelligence scores when considering reading readiness, except when the scores are high. A far better course is to judge the child's readiness for a particular step by the quality of his performance on the one that preceded it. There should always be a variety of challenging opportunities for a child to choose from, and if he is encouraged to experiment he may make those sudden forward leaps which occur when they are least expected.

7.9   The ability to read depends upon adequate *vision*, particularly at near point. If a child tends to grimace, to rub his eyes, to thrust his head forward in close work, or to avoid close work, he may well need to have his eyesight thoroughly tested. This should certainly be done before any conclusions are drawn about his readiness for a learning task that calls for careful visual discrimination. Even if a child's vision is satisfactory his visual perception will depend very much for its development on the experience he gets in exploring, identifying, and manipulating a wide variety of objects and shapes. Much has been written about the advisability of providing specific training in visual perception as part of a pre-reading programme. The evidence is inconclusive, but on balance such training seems only to be of value for children who have had a rather limited range of perceptual experience. Once a child has achieved a degree of proficiency there seems to be little gain in spending time on general perceptual learning. If such training is thought to be necessary it should consist of activities which will help the child to respond to form, orientation, and directionality and give him practice in systematic visual tracking. These activities need include nothing more dramatic than drawing, tracing, copying, matching, sequencing, tesselating, constructing, etc., which are the normal stock-in-trade of the nursery and infant school. In short, we feel that no child should be forced to follow a rigid programme of training in visual perception. The raw materials for its general development should be readily available in the home and in the classroom in the form of games and activities, and the way the child uses these provides the informed teacher with a useful diagnostic indicator.

7.10   The child's *hearing* is another important factor in readiness to begin reading, for impaired hearing can affect his ability to acquire phonic insight. If he has difficulty with high tones he is at a particular disadvantage. Hearing loss of this kind affects his capacity to hear such sounds as *p*, *b*, *s*, *t*, *k*, *v*, *sh*, *th*, and such blends as *cl*, *tr*, and *sp*. Thus, the child may not be able to distinguish between *p* and *b*, *s*, and *z*, *m* and *n*, or other sounds which are similar to one another in frequency, though most of the vowel sounds tend to be unaffected. Because the child can hear so many sounds with no difficulty this particular form of hearing loss is often overlooked in the critical early years. Children with suspected hearing loss should obviously be referred for appropriate medical treatment. However, poor auditory perception is a different kind of problem. There are children who have no significant hearing loss but seem unable to hear small differences between words or to appreciate rhymes. They may mispronounce words, substituting or transposing syllables, and they show related errors when they come to write. Some of these difficulties are to be found in many normal children and they tend to disappear of their own accord during the primary school years. In the early stages of reading these difficulties are a particular handicap where there is a marked emphasis on phonics. Poor auditory perception can therefore be taken as an indication that a child is not ready for reading experience, in which phonics are explicitly emphasised. However, this need not prevent him from making progress by concentrating on the visual discrimination of words, or from acquiring phonic insights inductively, as described earlier. In addition to this kind of activity there is everything to be said for games which give children pleasure in distinguishing between sounds, but we do not believe that a formal programme of training in auditory discrimination as such will significantly advance reading readiness.

7.11   It will be noted from what has been said here and in Chapter 6 that we have isolated no single point as the one at which learning to read begins. Instead, we regard the process as one of gradual evolution. A variety of pre-reading activities merges imperceptibly with activities that may only at some later stage be unhesitatingly described as reading. When children arrive at school they will be at different stages on a continuum. At one end some will already be reading; at the other there will be children who have had none of the preliminary experience we have described and will have little conception of what reading is. In her assessment the teacher will be guided by such points as the following:

the general confidence with which the child settles into school, his interest in trying new things, and his ability to concentrate on what he is doing at any moment in time;

his use of words and his ability to understand what is said to him;

his interest in attempting to read the various notices that appear in the classroom and about the school;

the amount of time he spends in the book corner, looking at books and trying to read;

the persistence with which he asks for help in reading: the early reader is often to be seen book in hand tracking down any adult who will listen to him read.

It cannot be emphasised too strongly that the teacher has to help the children towards readiness for beginning to read. There is no question of waiting for readiness to occur; for with many children it does not come 'naturally' and must be brought about by the teacher's positive measures to induce it.

7.12   In the early stages of reading the child should become familiar with individual letters, individual sounds, and at least some of the relationships between letters and sounds. This is rather like letting someone play with a ball and a bat, before he makes his first rudimentary attempts to play cricket. In reading, as in cricket, it is obviously helpful to introduce gradually the language of the game. Thus, there is no reason why children should not acquire the actual names of letters, and such terms as 'letter', and 'word'. These should be introduced quite unselfconsciously at appropriate moments, just as words like 'table' and 'chair' are learned without any fuss through normal use in the home. Of course, one of the early problems with reading is to find a suitable equivalent to play-ground cricket, i.e. to make reading itself an obviously worthwhile and interesting activity, even when the level of proficiency is still very low indeed. We have already indicated, however, that children may learn how enjoyable and useful reading can be, even before they can read for themselves, and the emphasis on purpose, meaning, and pleasure should be continued as the child begins to read independently.

7.13   The major difficulty in maintaining this interest when they do come to read for themselves is that of building up, at a reasonable rate, the number of words they can recognise on sight. The preparatory teaching of individual words from a reading scheme can be a rather barren exercise, divorced from the child's interest, and it does not develop a sufficient incentive for the child to build up an adequate sight vocabulary. The alternatives, however, seem equally unsatisfactory. If children are faced with texts containing more than a very small proportion of unfamiliar words they will spend far too much time struggling at frustration level and will derive neither meaning nor enjoyment. On the other hand, if a printed text contains only the small number of words they can instantly identify it is likely to be boring, if not downright banal. In either case, the children will not be able to make full use of their intermediate skills, so their already well developed linguistic abilities cannot be brought into action to make light work of what is otherwise a heavy burden. A sensible way out of this dilemma is to develop the child's interest in writing and reading his own work, and in reading the work of other children. This interaction can begin in the home, with the parent writing the child's name on labels on his clothing, on picture books or presents, on his drawings, or on any other items in which ownership or origin is of interest or importance. The child can then begin to write his own name, and odd words with which his parents help him. For instance, he can be helped to write the names of the dishes he likes best, perhaps against the days of the week when he has been promised them. He can add his name to letters to relatives, and his drawings can be decorated with one- or two-word captions in lower case letters his parents have shown him how to write. If he is given opportunities such as these, written words become a source of meaning and interest from the outset, and are thus so much more easily learned.

7.14   We described in paragraphs 5.22 and 5.23 how the good infant school develops the child's writing activities from small beginnings, and they should be read in close association with the argument presented here. Work of the kind discussed in those paragraphs is essential to the language experience approach to reading we are advocating. Each piece of writing by the children becomes part of the reading resources of the classroom. The advantage of this interaction between the child's writing and reading is that both are rooted in purpose and meaning. The vocabulary is familiar to the children, the sentence structures are those which they themselves use, and the discussions before and after every piece of writing and reading are excellent occasions for language development. It has been argued that handwriting is such a laborious process for young children that other means should be used to help them construct their own sentences. "Breakthrough to Literacy"[5] takes account of this by providing ready-made sets of carefully chosen words for teacher and children on printed cards. This has been of value in providing a stimulus to teachers to adopt the language experience approach and in offering them practical help. Whether or not the knowledgeable teacher needs this particular material once the approach is well established is open to question. And, of course, some teachers may prefer from the outset to use materials they have produced themselves for the same purpose. These decisions must be a matter for individual judgement and preference.

7.15   Of course, even where the climate of learning and the motivation are excellent, it does not follow that all children will build up a sight vocabulary at an adequate rate. Some have a remarkable facility for remembering a word and its spelling with little or no repetition, but it is obviously unreasonable to expect this of all children. It is a useful practice, therefore, to develop a word bank for storing words which have been used in talking and writing, so that these can be drawn upon and copied on later occasions. In our view there is a good case for beginning to draw the children's attention, even at this early stage, to the fact that there are different classes of words, and this may be achieved simply by the way the teacher organises the words in the different parts of the bank. Words might also be collected in their inflected forms, for the reasons given in paragraphs 6.24 and 6.38.

7.16   We have suggested that there is great value in using as reading material the children's own writing derived from their school experience and their life outside school. This is not to imply that commercially produced material becomes less important, and we believe that the teacher should be skilled in assessing its value and judging when and how to use it. The reading scheme is at the centre of this material in most young children's early experience of reading. We have argued for the parent to introduce the child to books before he starts school, but we do not include reading schemes among them. Once a child begins to read the first book of a graded series there is a great temptation for the parent to think in terms of rate of progress. When this happens, parent and child begin to lose the excitement and sheer pleasure that the first contact with books should provide. These qualities are replaced by a concern for measurable endeavour, and the desire to read may become secondary to a desire to perform to please the parent by progressing through the scheme. Much the same might be said of the use of reading schemes in the classroom, but the teacher is faced with an obvious problem of logistics. If she never had to cope with more than a few children she might well manage without a reading scheme, and indeed some teachers do so with great success, however large the class. Nevertheless, many more find it an invaluable resource. Unfortunately, all schemes have their shortcomings and the teacher often has too little time to compensate for them by giving additional attention to individual needs. This has two implications. The first of these need be mentioned only briefly here, since it is taken up in Chapter 13. The staffing of infant schools should be such as to allow a teacher to work with individuals and small groups as and when she believes it necessary. All too often at present she cannot do this without constant distraction. The second implication is that since reading schemes are a key resource in schools they need to be examined with a very critical eye, first in terms of their construction and then of the ways in which they can be put to the best use. Because of the importance of developing a sight vocabulary there was a strong tendency until recent years to design reading schemes in which the teaching of word recognition was the first consideration. There is no doubt of the great importance of this objective, but in pursuing it many reading schemes have failed to bring into play the intermediate skills and the comprehension skills. Thus, the debate about "whole words versus phonics" has been conducted at the wrong level. As we pointed out in the last chapter, this is far too simplistic a formulation of the problem.

7.17   It should go without saying that all early reading material should be attractive not only in presentation but in content. From a study of a wide range of currently available materials our general impression is that they are becoming increasingly colourful and well-illustrated. To improve the content is a more difficult matter, since the author has to work within the confines of a very limited vocabulary. A great deal of ingenuity has gone into the task, and content continues to improve, but there is still much to be done. All too often there is too little incentive to read the words rather than look at the pictures. The words and pictures should complement each other in such a way that the child needs to examine both with equal care. The printed word must be critical for any understanding of the action. Another important aspect of content is the effect upon children's attitudes, to which far too little attention has been given in the past. Any reading scheme should stand up to questions about how parental roles, sex roles, attitudes to authority, etc., are represented. Comparisons of primers in use in various countries show that there are marked and systematic differences in their content in this respect. Researchers[6] have also reported that the contents of primers display "a striking divergence from the realities of community, family, and child life, and from what is known about child development". We do not suggest that reading schemes should be passed through a kind of ideological or ethical scanner. But we do believe that children's experience should not be confined to a restricted range of reading matter presenting a narrow range of attitudes. It is particularly important to avoid this in these impressionable early years, for it is never too soon to start thinking about the ways in which attitudes may be influenced by reading.

7.18 The next feature to be examined in evaluating early reading materials is the extent to which the syntactic structures relate to the pattern of spoken language familiar to the child. This is an issue which was discussed in paragraph 6.34, and it is one to which we attach great importance. The significance of the relationship between the two kinds of language has been recognised fully only in the last decade, following a good deal of research. Unless there is a close match between the syntactic features of the text and the syntactic expectancies of the reader there will be a brake on the development of word identification. Certain reading schemes which have recently made their appearance have been expressly designed to take account of this. But it hardly needs to be added that there are schemes in widespread use whose language is stilted and unnatural, and far removed from anything the child ever hears in real life or uses himself. Children bring to school a spoken language far more complex than anything they encounter in these early readers. They use and can appreciate a wide range of sentence structures. Reading schemes which present highly contrived or artificial structures therefore lack predictability. They prevent children from developing the capacity to detect the sequential probability in linguistic structure.

7.19 This takes us to the question of the vocabulary used in the schemes. Traditionally, there have been two emphases in vocabulary control. One has been to select a very limited number of words which the child can learn as whole words. The other has been to select a larger number in which the spelling patterns are relatively simple. The first is usually associated with global approaches, such as the look-and-say sentence or look-and-say word method. The traditional look-and-say reading scheme assumes that there will be a major emphasis on teaching the recognition of whole words prior to any examination of letters and sounds. The principle is that the child will learn to recognise a word by associating it with a picture or by hearing it, and that each important word will be associated with various interesting activities before it is first encountered in the reading scheme. Word shape and length are regarded as useful cues for helping with word recognition in the early stages. There may be some structural *analysis*, i.e. examination of word parts, but the learning of letter sounds and attempts at *synthesis* come appreciably later. Since each word is to be presented as an undifferentiated whole the rate at which new words are introduced must be severely restricted. There must also be a high rate of repetition, so that the child 'over-learns' and is not confused by trying to cope with an ever-increasing number of half-learned words. Unfortunately, the authors of the older reading schemes, which are still widely in use, sacrificed other important considerations in restricting the vocabulary and repeating words frequently. Above all, they produced prose so unrealistic that it can no longer be regarded as an effective basis for reading instruction (see paragraph 6.34). In saying this we acknowledge that a great deal of research went into the selection of vocabulary for such schemes and into their general construction. If we now reject them we must at the same time record that the new schemes still owe them a great debt. The second of the two emphases we have mentioned is associated with an explicitly phonic approach. The traditional phonic scheme assumes that the child will learn letter sounds in the early stages. The principle is that if he is systematically taught how to synthesise sounds he will achieve independence in tackling unfamilar words. Thus the vocabulary control will be governed by the rate at which new phonic combinations are to be introduced. Needless to say, such a principle will have its own restricting effect on the range of words that can be used. As with the older look-and-say schemes, the prose in the early phonic readers cannot be regarded as acceptable for modern requirements (see paragraph 6.34).

7.20   In practice, it would be difficult for an observer to state with confidence whether any particular teacher was an advocate of phonics or look-and-say without examining the reading schemes she was using. And even that would not imply an exclusive commitment to one or the other method. When a child is trying to read an unfamilar word, a teacher will draw his attention to any clue she thinks may help at that particular moment—context, initial letter sound, initial blends, word length, outline, and so on. In addition, most teachers who adopt a look-and-say reading scheme will use supplementary material of the kind normally provided in a phonic scheme. Conversely, most teachers using a phonic scheme will encourage children to use a variety of supplementary readers in which the vocabulary is not strictly controlled according to phonic principles. Both groups will also have in common a variety of classroom activities related to reading. The great majority of teachers are in fact eclectic in their approach, and this came out very clearly in our survey. The major difference between teachers lies not in their allegiance to a method, but in the quality of their relationships with children, their degree of expert knowledge, and their sensitivity in matching what they do to each child's current learning needs. It must also be remembered that the child, too, is eclectic. He will have a certain amount of experience of looking at whole words that matter to him—on sweet cartons, food packs, television captions, and so on. And whether he is taught to or not he will develop a tendency to respond to letter sounds as part of his attack on new words. When a teacher is selecting reading schemes, then, she need not accept any limiting assumption the author may have had in mind when constructing it. What matters is the way in which the schemes can be used to the best advantage as part of the total 'mix' of reading and reading-related activities in the curriculum. This is a matter to which we now turn.

7.21   In what follows, we shall assume that before they start on a reading scheme children will have had a variety of pre-reading experiences of the kind described earlier in this chapter and in Chapter 6 and that they are able to read a few words they or other children have written. We shall also assume that language-experience activities will continue as an essential part of their daily school life. A child who is ready to make a start on a reading scheme will have acquired the general ability to respond to:

shape and orientation in discriminating between letters

letter sequence in terms of left-to-right directionality

letters and groups of letters as symbols that can represent sounds

letter sequences as orderly groups of symbols that can represent a temporal sequence of sounds

whole words as units of meaning, not primarily as symbols representing sounds

groups of words in terms of meaning, not as isolated words to be pronounced.

He should also know what the teacher means when she uses the terms 'letter', 'sound', and 'word'. Above all he should have learned to enjoy his encounters with words and sentences and with the meaning that lies behind them. We are not suggesting that children need have acquired more than *general tendencies* to respond in the ways listed above. There is no question of their having to achieve complete mastery in each before they go any further. The essential is that they should have made a good start with these and other general responses, which can be developed more systematically while they are following the reading scheme. The reading scheme can then be used to develop many of the great number of more specific responses on which skilled reading depends, i.e. to increasingly complex syntactic structures and to the wide variety of spelling patterns of English.

7.22   If a child has had a satisfactory preparation before tackling a reading scheme we believe that the choice of scheme matters less than the teacher's knowledge of what a given scheme can and cannot do, and her ability to supplement it in any way she may feel to be necessary. In the light of this principle we can examine the features of contemporary variations on the traditional themes, beginning with schemes based essentially on a look-and-say approach. The look-and-say scheme prompts three vital questions. How can a useful sight vocabulary be developed and enlarged? How are difficulties with phonic irregularity to be overcome? How can the child be helped to achieve independence in tackling unfamiliar words? When we come to phonic schemes there are questions of equal importance. How are children to be weaned from an early tendency to look for fairly simple relationships between letters and sounds? How can they be led to a greater dependence on context cues in handling unfamiliar words?

7.23   Broadly speaking, the vocabulary of a look-and-say reading scheme is selected on the principle that the words are easy to learn or are of high utility, that is to say frequently encountered. Words tend to be very easy to learn when they are of high interest value, e.g. *rocket, doll, engine, rabbit,* and such words have the additional advantage that they can be readily illustrated. They may also be easy to discriminate between because they vary in length and in the pattern in which the more conspicuous letters are arranged, i.e. those with ascenders and descenders such as *k, t, g*. Words of high utility, on the other hand, are inclined to have none of these properties. The words that occur most frequently in speech and writing are words such as *the, he, to, was, all, are, one, said*, etc. They tend to be of low interest value, are not so easily illustrated, and are less easily discriminated between in terms of length and configuration. Nevertheless, a dozen or so such words account for about a quarter of the words on a typical page of print, and a hundred or so account for about half the words on the page. It might therefore be thought that if these words are well and truly learned at an early stage a great deal has been achieved. This is to a large extent true, but it must be remembered that these utility words carry less information than the 'content' words, and the effect upon the reading performance is not so powerful as the numerical weight would imply. These high utility words are by their very nature the ones most likely to be used by children in their early attempts at writing. The high interest words they meet in their reading scheme can be added to the word bank so that they too can be brought into play in associated language-experience activities. This kind of reinforcement can reduce the need for excessive repetition of words in a look-and-say reading scheme, a possibility which is being taken into account in some recently published schemes. The treatment of phonics in a look-and-say scheme presents a problem. Children will tend to be confused by the complexity of the spelling patterns they encounter in the early stages of the scheme. From their knowledge of certain patterns they can generalise effectively to cope with words of similar pattern, but this does not help them when they meet irregularities. For example, a child is likely to be misled into pronouncing *bear* as *beer* by analogy with *hear*, and *beard* as *bird* by analogy with *heard*. This is where the ability to predict from context becomes so important. From the surrounding words (as, for instance, in the sentence "In the woods he met a big brown bear") the child must be able to derive enough information to help him recall the pronunciation and meaning of a word he has met in the word bank or used in his own writing. This implies that the teacher must be immediately at hand to help the child with the context where necessary and with the words that are altogether new to him. And this in turn implies that the teacher must have a well organised system that allows her to give a carefully judged amount of time to each child. Where this is not to be found the child working from a look-and-say scheme can experience difficulties. Most look-and-say schemes currently available do provide phonic activities, but usually as supplementary material. They do not help a child who has difficulty when attempting to cope with the complexities of any unfamiliar words he encounters in the actual text. We regard this as a disabling limitation of many otherwise very satisfactory look-and-say reading schemes. They do not afford direct assistance with phonics, and they provide little compensation for any lack of individual help the child may be receiving in the use of context cues.

7.24   We have already outlined the inadequacies of phonic reading schemes when they are made to carry the major burden of the instruction. However, when they are used within a general learning context of the kind we have advocated they become a quite different instrument. In the context of a language experience approach the use of texts in which the complexity of spelling patterns is reduced can help children to overcome some of their confusion about phonics. What we criticise is the unsubtle practice of encouraging children to build up words by 'sounding' letters as a routine practice. If the scheme is well designed, the phoneme-grapheme relationships should be self evident, and readily acquired by inductive learning with the absolute minimum of formal instruction. We have already stated our belief, however, that there should be an early switch from an emphasis on phonics to an emphasis on morphemic structure. Words in which the spellings do not coincide with patterns the child has met earlier in the scheme should be particularly well cued by context. There is a growing knowledge of ways in which words can be powerfully cued, but in our view this has not yet been applied with sufficient rigour in the preparation of phonic reading schemes. For the most part, they concentrate upon lower-order decoding processes. Where phonic schemes are not designed on narrowly conceived principles they are a valuable element in the reading curriculum.

7.25   We can sum up our view of the value of reading schemes in the reading curriculum by saying that we would welcome the further development of the kind of scheme to which it is as difficult to apply such simplistic labels as 'phonic', 'look-and-say', 'linguistic', etc. as it is to attach such labels to the methods of competent teachers. A good reading scheme is one which provides a sound basis for the development of all the reading skills in an integrated way. Performance on the scheme itself should provide the teacher with diagnostic information, and there should be a wide variety of supplementary materials for her to use with individual children who need extra practice or help of a particular kind. In saying this we must emphasise that we regard the reading scheme as an ancillary part of a school's reading programme, and nothing more. We are certainly not advocating that the school should necessarily use one, and we welcome the enterprise of those schools which have successfully planned the teaching of reading without the use of a graded series. Nor are we suggesting that if a school does decide to use a scheme it should confine itself to any particular one. Indeed, where a school has chosen to work in this way there should be books from several reading series available. Some schools draw from as many as twelve different schemes, not necessarily including all the books in any one of them. All this material, however, should form merely a part of the learning resources. The children's own writing should provide an ever-developing resource, and every infant class needs a wide range of books and other printed matter on the scale recommended in Chapter 21.

7.26   In paragraphs 6.21 and 6.22 we referred to cueing techniques and spelling modifications as a means of making the early stages of learning to read more manageable. We can now review these in the light of our comments on the value of reading schemes. There are two principal ways of providing additional cues to the value or function of letters: the use of colour, and the use of diacritical marks. In our survey one of the questions was designed to discover how widely these were employed in schools. Only 6 per cent of the classes were using colour and 2 per cent diacritical marks, which indicates that they are very much a minority practice in the country at large. At its simplest level, *colour* may be used in a fairly minimal way, for example to signal digraphs (ch, ea), silent letters (the "k" in "knife"), or a spelling pattern (a-e, i-e, o-e). At the other extreme there may be an attempt to use a very complex colour system so that every phoneme is unambiguously represented. The evidence for the value of colour systems is inconclusive. The more elaborate schemes may be said to exact too high a price in terms of the amount of attention they demand and the consequent distraction from meaning. Simpler schemes which signal more general functions (e.g. silent letters, the grouping of letters), rather than specific sound values may well have something to offer, though this has yet to be convincingly demonstrated. *Diacritical marking* is the application of marks of various kinds to signal letter function or value. As long ago as Elizabethan times a book of Aesop's fables was printed with such marks. Edgeworth and his daughter devised a diacritical system in 1798, and it was 're-invented' by Shearer in 1894. The most complete system and the one most commonly in use today is that devised by Fry. In an investigation[7] of its effectiveness he compared results from the use of an unmarked basal reading scheme, the same scheme adapted to his system, and an American i.t.a. scheme. His own system was not found to be superior. On the other hand, results which favoured the use of diacritical marking have been reported by Brimer[8] and Johnson[9]. It is fair to add that the first of these focussed only on decoding skills, and the teaching was limited to programmed learning techniques. In the second, the teacher variable was not controlled, and a word recognition test was the sole criterion of reading improvement. In the circumstances we do not feel there is sufficient evidence to enable us to recommend diacritics. We can sum up by saying that although there is no substantial evidence to support the use of cueing techniques of one kind or another they are certainly not discredited by research. Whether or not to adopt them is a decision for the school. We would add, however, that where schemes embodying cueing techniques are adopted, there is no need for the teacher to accept the limiting assumptions of authors about how they should be used.

7.27   The general reaction of many teachers to i.t.a. (the initial teaching alphabet) has been rather negative, and only 10 per cent of our sample schools containing infants were using the medium. Some of the more pressing advocacy of i.t.a. is likely to have been counter-productive. The experienced infant teacher can only be irritated by the suggestion that all that is needed to bring about general improvement in reading is the introduction of a simplified code. On the other hand, we have already noted the bewildering complexities of the English spelling system, and it is self-evident that a simplification of the relationship between sound and spellings must make it much easier for a child to make progress in the early stages. If there are fewer items to be learned this alone must reduce the time required, and if there are fewer ambiguities there will be less confusion. All this is amply confirmed by research. Following a careful review of the evidence the authors of the Schools Council Report[10] on i.t.a. came to this conclusion:

"There is no evidence whatsoever for the belief that the best way to learn to read in traditional orthography is to learn to read in traditional orthography. It would appear that the best way to learn to read in traditional orthography is to learn to read in the initial teaching alphabet."

Of course, as one of our witnesses pointed out, a spelling system that is most satisfactory in making word recognition easier at the stage of learning to read is not necessarily the best medium for rapid and effective reading in the literate adult. In Japan, for example, children first learn the 'kana' characters, each of which represents a syllable. They then learn 'kangi' characters, which are logographs and represent units of meaning. In a research study it was found that college students were able to read a script in kangi in just half the time it took to read a comparable script in kana. The 48 kana characters, on the other hand, are easily and quickly learned, and as all the words in the child's spoken vocabulary can be written in this syllable code the vocabulary of his early reading writing experiences is not restricted. The kangi characters are introduced gradually, so there is no sharp transition from one system to another. Certainly the co-existence of two writing systems during the introductory and transitional period does not seem to be a handicap. This observation coincides with the judgment of the Schools Council report that the difference between the alphabet used in school and that used outside does not represent a significant problem. It should, however, be remembered that where parents take the kind of active interest we have advocated in this chapter there is a possibility that some such confusion could occur.

7.28   As children become more fluent in reading they depend much less on a close scrutiny of every word, and their use of context comes to play an increasing part in identifying words. Individual spellings then become much less of a hindrance, a fact illustrated by the following sentence, which includes the word examined in paragraph 6.20.

"I gave the prescription to the calmbost" (i.e. chemist).

Similarly, though some of the characters in the following passage of i.t.a. are unfamiliar, one has little difficulty in reading it:

"wun ov the important tasks ov the infant scωl is tω begin teeching children tω reed, sins reeding is the kee tω much ov the lerning that will cum læter and tω the possibility ov independent study."

After one or two more paragraphs of the same kind the reader would be handling the text with scarcely any hesitation. By the same token, it is argued that the child who develops fluency in i.t.a. can transfer readily enough to t.o. The authors of the Schools Council report say that a head deciding to use i.t.a. as an initial medium can be confident that at the very least the children are unlikely to suffer, provided she has the support of the staff and can guarantee continuity of approach* when the children go on to junior school. Indeed, they go on to affirm that there is "a substantial body of evidence which indicates that most children will benefit in a variety of ways".

7.29   One obvious advantage of using a modified spelling system such as i.t.a. rather than a cueing technique (e.g. colour coding) is that it helps writing as well as reading. Children tend to learn quite quickly how to spell in i.t.a., and they then have ready access to almost every word in their spoken vocabulary. The value of this for language experience activities is obvious. When groups of t.o. and i.t.a. children were matched in the main

*See paragraph 14.2 for a discussion of this very important aspect of co-operation between schools.

British experiments[11], the writing produced by the latter was of consistently higher quality. (Downing and Latham[12] subsequently tested a sample of the children originally involved in this experiment and found that the i.t.a. pupils remained superior in t.o. reading and spelling even after five years at school, i.e. well beyond the transition stage). It is fair to add that many critics of i.t.a. do not accept that such gains are attributable to the medium itself. On the other hand, it also seems likely that many teachers who adopted i.t.a. have employed it in a rather narrowly conceived phonic approach. If this is so, the higher standards of reading and writing produced with i.t.a. may possibly have been even better had the medium been used differently. As a Committee we are not unanimous on the value of i.t.a., but we believe that as there is no evidence of adverse side effects at a later stage schools which choose to adopt it should be given every support. We also feel that teachers should examine the question of i.t.a. on its merits. We hope they will make their own objective assessment of the various arguments for and against, and not accept the tendentious statements that are still made by some of its advocates and opponents.

7.30   References occur in subsequent chapters to various organisational aspects of the teaching of reading, but we must introduce the main theme at this point. It is one thing to have an array of materials and techniques of the kind we have been discussing; it is quite another to be able to put these together coherently to provide an appropriate reading curriculum for each individual child as well as for the class as a whole. This calls for clear thinking about sequence and structure. The teacher has to decide whether a given objective is likely to be achieved most effectively by the child's independent effort, by work in small groups, or by direct class teaching. In planning her work she is faced with a number of decisions, each of which bears upon the organisation of the reading programme. For example, how much time should she spend on a particular reading activity in relation to other competing claims on her time? How should she evaluate the results of her own efforts as well as monitor the progress of each child? How can she make the best use of the assistance of additional adults, such as parents, aides, specialist or relief teachers, students and, indeed, older children? The ability to pose and answer such questions, and to organise accordingly, is the most important factor for success in the teaching of reading.

7.31   In our view every child should spend part of each day in reading or pre-reading activities, with the teacher keeping a meticulous check on progress. She will need to make qualitative observations by listening to every child read several times a week and by asking questions designed to develop the various kinds of comprehension. This will allow her to structure successive learning experiences for each child in such a way as to ensure a steady sequence of development through the various reading skills. Everyone would agree that additional attention should be given to children whose progress is unsatisfactory, but we would strongly emphasise the need to stimulate average and above average children to greater achievement. This means that the teacher should spend time with them individually, for it is not only the poor readers who warrant attention of this kind. A good deal of incentive can be provided by well organised small group work, where the interaction draws upon shared experiences in reading. (See Chapter 13 for a general discussion of group organisation). The children can be encouraged to discuss what they are reading, to ask questions and offer answers, and to compare their ideas of what the book said. They should become accustomed quite early to going back to the printed word and looking more carefully at something on which their talk has focussed. Co-operative reading of this kind can begin even in the earliest stages, when children can help one another in word recognition as well as interpretation. The teacher's own intervention in group work is of considerable importance, for as opportunities present themselves she can develop particular skills in a context in which the children are highly motivated and able to apply their learning with immediacy and purpose. There may be occasions where she wants to teach the whole class if this is the most effective and economical way of dealing with a specific reading skill, and the range of reading ability is not so wide as to make it impracticable. Indeed, the value of the collective class experience needs to be reaffirmed, and it is exemplified at its best when all the children are sharing the enjoyment of teacher's reading to them.

7.32   We therefore consider the best method of organising reading to be one where the teacher varies the experience between individual, group and class situations according to the purpose in hand. Fundamental to it all is a precise knowledge of the progress and needs of each individual child, and we consider this of such importance that it has been made the subject of a separate chapter (Chapter 17). We can anticipate it here by saying that a particularly important teaching skill is that of assessing the level of difficulty of books by applying measures of readability. The teacher who can do this is in a better position to match children to reading materials that answer their needs. In our visits to schools we came across many children who were not allowed to read 'real books' until they had completed the scheme. This is an artificial distinction and an unnatural restriction of reading experience. We also came across children who had made good progress through a scheme and were now struggling at frustration level in other kinds of reading, while others were bored by material that was making too few demands upon them. The effective teacher is one who has under her conscious control all the resources that can fulfil her purpose. By carefully assessing levels of difficulty she can draw from a variety of sources.

REFERENCES

1.   C. Lefevre: *Linguistics and The Teaching of Reading:* McGraw: 1964.

2.   L. S. Vygotsky: *Thought and Language:* Massachusetts Institute of Technology Press: 1962.

3.   J. T. Reid: *Learning to think about Reading:* Educational Research, 9: 1966.

4.   A. L. Gates: *The Necessary Mental Age for Beginning Reading:* Elementary School Journal, 37: 1937.

5.   D. Mackay, B. Thompson and P. Schaub: *Breakthrough to Literacy: Programme in Linguistics and English Teaching:* Schools Council/Longman: 1970.

6.   G. E. Blom, R. R. Waite, S. G. Zimet and S. Edge: *What the Story World is Like.* in: *What Children Read in School:* Grune and Stratton (editor S. G. Zimet) New York: 1972.

7. E. Fry: *A diacritical marking system to aid beginning reading instruction:* Elementary English, 41: pp. 526–9.

8. M. A. Brimer: *An experimental evaluation of coded scripts in initial reading:* New Research in Education: 1967.

9. H. Johnson, D. R. Jones, A. C. Cole and M. B. Walters: *The use of diacritical marks in teaching beginners to read:* The British Journal of Educational Psychology, Vol. 5, No. 42: 1972.

10. F. W. Warburton and V. Southgate: *i.t.a.: An Independent Evaluation:* Murray and Chambers: 1969.

11. J. A. Downing: *The i.t.a. Symposium:* N.F.E.R.: 1967.

12. J. A. Downing and W. Latham: *A follow-up of children in the first i.t.a. experiment:* British Journal of Educational Psychology, 39: 1969.

CHAPTER 8

Reading: The Later Stages

8.1 In the previous two chapters we have been anxious to establish the principle that young children should acquire from the beginning the skills that are employed in mature reading. These skills will obviously be used for more elaborate and demanding purposes as the child grows older, but the pattern is one that can be established early. We propose in this chapter to approach the matter from the other end of the age range and consider the fulfilment of some of these purposes. The development of reading skills is a progressive one, and there are no staging points to which one can attach any particular ages. We cannot therefore speak of kinds of reading ability as being specific to the middle years and as something essentially different from those used in the upper forms of the secondary school. The primary skills of the early years mature into the understanding of word structure and spelling patterns. The intermediate skills, so essential in word attack in the early stages, are at work in skimming, scanning, and the extraction of meaning in the more complex reading tasks of the later stages. The comprehension skills themselves do not change; it is in the increasing complexity of the purposes to which they are put as the pupils grow older that the difference lies. In the middle years there should be three major emphases. The first is to consolidate the work of the early years, and to give particular help to those children who for one reason or another have failed to make progress. The second is to maintain and extend the idea of reading as an activity which brings great pleasure and is a personal resource of limitless value. The third is to develop the pupils' reading from the general to the more specialised. We believe that the primary school teacher needs an understanding of the reading demands of the later years so that the line of development is clearly recognised.

8.2 What are these demands? This question is best answered in terms of three basic objectives, simple enough on paper but far from simple in the execution:

(i) the pupil needs to be able to cope with the reading required in each area of the curriculum;

(ii) he should acquire a level of competence which will enable him to meet his needs as an adult in society when he leaves school;

(iii) he should regard reading as a source of pleasure and personal development which will continue to be a rewarding activity throughout life.

8.3 The last of these will condition the other two. Functional reading, with which this chapter is largely concerned, should certainly not be seen as the onerous part of reading. The greater the pleasure of the task the more certainly will the skills become second nature. And the more capable the pupil becomes the more pleasure he will derive from reading. From this it will be seen that this particular objective is associated not simply with recreational reading but with all the other activities we shall go on to discuss.

Nevertheless, we believe that literature has a special role to play in fulfilling it and we have chosen to develop this aspect of reading in a chapter of its own.

8.4   The first of the three objectives is rarely recognised in schools as something that calls for explicit instruction. Specialist teachers generally believe that pupils need only to be fluent readers to cope with the reading demands of their subjects. We shall argue, however, that there are specific reading techniques which pupils can acquire to improve the efficiency of their learning, and that the subject teacher should help to develop these. We also believe that he should know something about levels of reading difficulty in the material he uses and about the capacity of individual pupils to cope with a particular book. This is more than simply a matter of intuitive feel; it involves the application of techniques of the kind described in paragraph 6.37. A general impression will not always tell the teacher whether a pupil is likely to find a certain book easy and undemanding, or readable if slightly challenging, or largely beyond his grasp.

8.5   The second of the two objectives is clearly a complex one. We have already referred to evidence (para. 2.2) which suggests that very many adults are unable to understand fully much of the reading material that directly relates to their lives and actions. To those we have given we might add a further illustration. This is again an American investigation[1], but it is reasonable to assume that the problems it reveals would also be found in some measure in this country. It took the form of a study of the reading proficiency of 7,500 adults. The material used to assess it was chosen according to such criteria as the extent to which it was in everyday use, its importance, and the time spent upon it. The most important reading matter . of the average day was held to include news, material associated with work, signs of various kinds, and print on consumer goods. The items used in the assessment reflected as closely as possible the level of difficulty involved for a proper understanding. 20 per cent of the adults in the sample were unable to achieve more than 47 per cent correct responses, and over half of them made more than 10 per cent incorrect responses. Evidence of this kind suggests that there is a good deal of inefficient reading among adults who are generally regarded as being "able to read". We are in no doubt that schools need to give serious consideration to the implication of conclusions such as these.

8.6   Broadly speaking there are two main approaches to extending the reading ability of older children. One is to timetable special periods for specific tuition and practice; the other is to extend skills in and through normal learning activities. On the face of it the case for separate lessons with specially designed reading programmes may seem quite strong. An obvious argument in its favour is that the teaching can be planned by a reading specialist whose understanding of the skills goes far beyond that possessed by the subject teacher or, for that matter, by most teachers of English. In our visit to America we studied this specialist approach in the High School grades. In some schools there was a 'Reading Consultant', in others a 'Reading Department' with its own head. Student schedules would sometimes include periods devoted to the activity as a subject in its own right, and we came across examples of teaching rooms specially fitted for the purpose. In one of these was an array of equipment ranging from speed-reading machines to devices for flashing letters on to a screen. Another consisted of a suite of rooms clustered about a central book area. The syllabuses of these departments listed such skills as inductive, inferential, and evaluative reading, and prescribed exercises for "locating the main idea" of a paragraph. (Indeed, we found this particular skill being practised through exercises early in the elementary school). The syllabuses assumed different reading requirements for different subjects, e.g. Science and Social studies, and counselled appropriate approaches.

8.7 Some aspects of this concentrated attention were impressive. In the first place it meant that there was in the school a highly trained member of staff who would offer specialised advice at every level. Secondly, it encouraged the idea that there could be no cut-off point beyond which it was taken for granted a pupil had all the reading skills he needed. We found well-motivated 16 year olds opting for Reading lessons for guidance in the techniques of tackling a substantial history text or improving their reading ability in science. However, in our view the disadvantages out-weighed the benefits. Although there was no 'horizontal split' in the teaching of reading, there was a very sharp 'vertical split' between Reading and English. Indeed, the teachers belonged to separate professional associations which scarcely communicated. The English teacher was able to feel he was teaching 'pure' literature and that he could presume the pupils' ability to read a text closely. He was thus tempted into abstract teaching *about* literature, rather than developing their reading abilities along with and by means of the exploration of meaning. Equally, the teachers of other subjects felt no concern to develop reading within their own subject, since reading was regarded as the preserve of the teacher responsible for it. Many of the specialist 'Reading' lessons contained a good deal of decontextualised vocabulary work, into which much of the supposed activity of "reading within subjects" resolved itself.

8.8 Associated with the notion of the specialised teaching of reading, both in the U.S.A. and here, is the commercially produced programme, sometimes called the 'reading workshop' or 'reading laboratory'. Again on the face of it such programmes appear to offer a ready made route to the development of reading skills. However, the fact that a pupil can become adept at completing the reading tasks in this rather narrow context does not mean that this ability will automatically transfer, and that he will be able to apply it at will in his other reading. Moreover, we have seen little evidence to support the view that there is any long term value in 'booster' courses using these programmes. Scores on reading tests are certainly raised in the short term, but gains do not appear to be sustained over a longer period. This does not necessarily mean that the kinds of experience provided by 'reading workshops' or 'laboratories' are of no value. Though the skills in which they offer practice will not *automatically* transfer, the teacher could take steps to ensure that they were applied to other reading tasks, notably within the subject areas. However, any real gain in reading development must come through the generation of a strong motivation, and this means reading to satisfy a purpose. This is more likely to arise from the wide-ranging opportunities of the curriculum than from the arbitrary stimulus of 'laboratory' materials. We therefore believe the real possibilities are to be found in the second of the two approaches we identified earlier, namely the extension of skills in and through normal learning activities.

8.9   Since reading is a major strategy for learning in virtually every aspect of education we believe it is the responsibility of every teacher to develop it. Unfortunately, it is difficult for most teachers, to whom reading and study skills may be second nature, to be fully aware of the complexity of these skills. If they are identified and described for them they may be inclined to dismiss them as being no more than common sense—as indeed they are. Nevertheless, this explicit awareness *is* necessary, for left to their own devices many of their pupils develop poor reading habits and others do not achieve the efficiency of which they are capable. In our view there should be certain commonly agreed approaches to reading as part of the school's policy for the development of language across the curriculum. We are not proposing any kind of prescription which would interfere with the teacher's ability to decide his own way of working. We are suggesting that by consultation all teachers should accept the responsibility for developing reading in their field, and that certain shared principles would help them to fulfil it.

8.10   The first is that reading for learning can be made more efficient. In *all* study situations, whether he is listening to a lecture, watching an instructional film, or reading a book, the learner calls upon his ability to reason, his existing knowledge, and his imagination. Thus, many of the abilities used in reading for learning are founded in the general approaches of the classroom. There are, however, certain conditions unique to reading. Because the print on a page is fixed and unchanging a reader can control his use of it by:

choosing the time, place and extent of his reading;

going back to earlier statements in the text, or looking ahead to future conclusions;

breaking the reading process to make notes, pause and think, or refer to other sources for comparison or illustration.

In other words, a reader has considerable control over the learning situation and he needs particular skills to take advantage of the possibilities this opens up to him. We can sum these up by saying that reading for learning will be most effective when the reader becomes an active interrogator of the text rather than a passive receiver of words. A second principle is that these skills should be developed in close association with the other aspects of language use, and in particular with the oral activity recommended in Chapter 10. Reading is an instrument for individual learning, but it is also a collective activity, and we believe that group discussion based on co-operative reading is a valuable means of learning.

8.11   The shaping of the policy is a matter for the individual school, but we believe that in guiding the studies of their pupils teachers in the middle and secondary years would find the following analysis useful:

 (i)   the formulation of the purposes of the reading;

 (ii)   organisation for reading;

(iii)   reading behaviour;

(iv)   assessment of reading activities.

8.12   (i) *The formulation of the purposes*

It will often be helpful for teachers to encourage their pupils to identify their purposes before they undertake a particular piece of reading. The major purpose behind any deliberate reading task can be expressed as a question, which gives rise to further questions and in turn to yet more specific ones. Pre-determined questions provide a framework within which the learning can be anchored. They make the reading more efficient by directing attention to those aspects of the text which are most relevant, and they help the pupil to retain what he reads. The pupil then brings into play scanning and skimming skills (see paragraph 8.18) instead of reading everything at the same pace. Properly applied, this approach can encourage habits of disciplined enquiry.

8.13   (ii) *Organisation for reading*

Pupils should learn how to organise their reading, firstly by being able to locate, evaluate and select the material they need, and secondly by applying organised study methods to the material itself. The practice of working from a single text book, or at most two, is nowadays much less prevalent than it used to be, and most subjects make use of a wider range of printed matter. Nevertheless, the pupils are often very dependent upon the teacher for what they shall read and lack the ability to make their own assessments and choose accordingly. Most of the individual bibliographical skills can be taught in a very short time and do not need a protracted series of practical exercises. After a basic introduction these skills can be developed through study activities in each subject area. The former practice is common enough, but rarely did we find the kind of staff co-operation which ensured the follow-up. All too often the pupils were taught how to locate and handle books but not given the immediate opportunity to put them to a useful purpose, as opposed to an artificially contrived one. We believe that in the course of the middle and secondary years pupils should acquire the following and become accustomed to applying them in the various areas of learning:

(i)   knowledge of available resources (e.g. books, magazines, files, pictures, tapes, cassettes, film) their location, and the way they are organised;

(ii)   ability to define an area of search by using reference books of various kinds and more specialised publications where necessary;

(iii)   ability to use subject index, classified catalogues, abstracts, and bibliographies, and to record sources systematically;

(iv)   ability to survey source material, making an assessment of author, publisher, and content.

In the last of these the pupil needs to be able to test the reliability of an author against other sources and to examine the way the book is organised. We met one biology master who made a point of giving his new fifth form pupils an introductory assignment and a list of six or eight books on which to draw. He deliberately chose books which conflicted in some point of information or opinion and when the pupils found out these contradictions for themselves he took them to a first-hand study to make their own judgement. This kind of activity brings home to pupils the importance of critically reviewing sources of information and of doing so economically and efficiently. Having chosen and surveyed the material, the pupils need to be able to plan their reading, deciding what can be read for a general impression and what must be given detailed attention. This can be applied equally where the study is individual and where the reading is to be shared by a group. They must then know how to deal with the information gained from the reading. A large number of pupils pass through school without ever learning to make notes efficiently. One has only to look at much 'project' work to see the truth of this. Unable to read selectively and to summarise the information, most pupils resort to copying verbatim from the books they are consulting. They should be taught various ways of making notes, including the use of topic cards and flow diagrams, listing their own sources, and of indicating their own comments or lines of further enquiry.

8.14   (iii) *Reading behaviour*

Comprehension work is standard practice in schools, and for most pupils it occupies a place in English lessons for the greater part of their school life. Much of this work is from text-book exercises designed for the purpose, and in recent years there has been an increase in the use of reading 'workshops' or 'laboratories', to which we have already referred in general terms. In our view, exercises in English text-books or in kits of one kind or another are inadequate for developing comprehension. They provide too restricting a context and do not take account of the fact that reading should satisfy some purpose on the part of the reader. This may be to derive pleasure, experience, or information; it may be serious, or it may be relatively trivial. But whichever it is the individual will read most rewardingly when he has a personal reason for reading, for he will then carry his own attitudes and values into the text and not simply respond passively to it. The declared "purpose" of so many of these exercises is to improve particular skills of comprehension. But even if there *is* any such result the improvement is so specific to the situation that it is unlikely to transfer to other reading tasks. This seemed to us conspicuously true of some exercises we saw in use in the U.S.A. These presented quite young children with such tasks as "locating the main ideas" in short passages. Even where the children succeeded in doing this in specific cases they had not grasped a concept which they could then generalise and apply to other situations. For this to happen the teacher must develop comprehension skills within the broader concept of purposeful reading. Another shortcoming of exercises in many English workbooks and kits is that they tend to give undue emphasis to literal comprehension, doubtless because it is much easier to frame multiple choice items at the literal level. The use of multiple choice items does not, however, represent a realistic approach to the development of comprehension even at this level. For it is one thing to match multiple choice items against the text but quite another to identify the relevant section of text without the aid of such pre-selected alternatives.

8.15   The development of *literal comprehension* is too important to be entrusted to exercises, even the best-designed of them. The principal object is to sharpen the reader's perception of the main theme and the idea sequences from which it is formed. He must be able to determine what is essential supporting detail and what is peripheral. Even when skimming at speed he must be able to pick out certain features and identify general structures and relationships. It may help pupils to acquire this ability if on occasion they make a close analysis of a passage to identify the significant words in sentences and the significant sentences in paragraphs, working out in group discussion the relationship between position and function. They would discover, for instance, that at the beginning of a paragraph a 'significant sentence' may do little more than introduce a theme; at the end it will often provide an informative summary or conclusion; in the middle it may be a major turning point in the argument. Its function is often indicated by a signpost phrase: "Nevertheless . . .", "In spite of this . . .", "On the other hand . . .", etc. By recognising the function of various sentences in the structure of the paragraph the pupils are helped to a grasp of the theme. From here they can go on to summarizing or paraphrasing the material or representing it in diagrammatic form. Our point is that the literal level cannot be taken for granted as an elementary aspect of comprehension and one that can be acquired by weekly exercises in answering set questions on a passage. It must be developed in a range of contexts where it is put to a practical purpose, and that means in the various subjects of the curriculum. The techniques themselves might be learnt in an English lesson, but the kind of co-operation we envisage would ensure that the subject teacher followed this up with practical application.

8.16   The same applies to the other levels of comprehension, of which the next is the *inferential*. This takes the pupil beyond the explicit statement to what the writer intended by implication or by assuming common ground with the reader. A large class, and the pressures of a particular syllabus, leave little time for the teacher to help individual pupils to explore the implications in much of what they read. Yet this he must certainly do if they are to get beyond the obvious meaning, or to question what might otherwise develop attitudes not readily accessible to reason. It is not only in the subject text-books that the pupil must learn to examine implications. He needs to gain experience in giving this kind of attention to a variety of printed media. These will include advertising brochures, newspaper editorials, employment particulars, and that whole range of material in which what is left unsaid is often no less important than the facts presented.

8.17   We gave earlier the example of the science teacher who led his pupils to question the reliability of certain books. This *evaluative* aspect of comprehension is common enough in English lessons, for example in the study of literature and in the critical examination of advertisements and newspapers, but it is much less evident in other subjects. There it is all too often taken for granted that the information in the text book is accurate and its opinion not seriously to be questioned—at least by the pupils. It is a striking feature of language in its printed form that words seem to take on an authority they much less commonly achieve in a spoken encounter, and it is one of the responsibilities of all teachers to ensure that this apparent authority receives critical attention. Comparative reading is a useful method, and one that can be employed with varying degrees of subtlety, for it is not simply a matter of deciding upon the respective merits of alternative versions. Pupils need also to recognise that they may bring prejudices of their own to their judgement of a set of opinions or of the emphasis given to certain facts.

8.18   An important aspect of reading behaviour is the ability to use different kinds of reading strategies according to the purpose and material. Consider, for example, the way one approaches the reading of different parts of a newspaper, a collection of advertising brochures, an income tax form, or a railway timetable. According to his purpose, interest, and time available, the efficient reader will glance through selectively or scrutinise in detail. Most of the reading done in school takes little account of this, and the pupil is generally expected to read all material fairly intensively. Yet there are many occasions when quite different kinds of approach are appropriate, in school just as in adult life. In both, the reader is exposed to more printed material than he can possibly find time to assimilate in detail. Much of it simply does not call for close examination. Very often the reader is concerned only to find a particular fact, or to locate a section of the text which he does want to examine carefully. This may demand of him the ability to *scan* the text to look for certain kinds of detail, or for some cue which will tell him whether what he is looking for is to be found in that section of it. On other occasions he may require to do no more than obtain a general impression of what a passage is about. This will call for the ability to *skim* through it, locating significant words and sentences, or sequences of particular kinds, all of which convey to him the general sense. It is thus possible to read at various levels of intensity to match a particular purpose. Unless pupils acquire these skills while still at school there is a likelihood that the only approach they will ever use is inflexible, one-pace, line by line reading. Judging by the number of 'crash' courses being taken up it is obvious that many adults find this limited reading technique a singular handicap in their work.

8.19   (iv) *Assessment of reading activities*

We have suggested that pupils should learn how to read for specific purposes, how to organise the material, and how to apply appropriate techniques. The fourth stage is their assessment of what they have achieved. This is a process by which the reader reviews his original questions and the material he has read, and examines the information he has gained from it. He can then assess whether the organisation of his reading might have been more efficient, and in what ways it could be improved on a future occasion. In short, he should be able to evaluate the product of his reading and the development of his own reading skills. We regard this capacity for self-evaluation as an important instrument for learning, and one which is by no means an automatic outcome of activities in which children learn by discovering. They need systematic help if they are to develop the habit of judging the effectiveness of their various reading activities in terms of their purpose. Another aspect of this process is the storage and indexing of the information gained from the reading. A great deal of what the pupil, or adult, derives from reading is lost because it is not preserved in a form in which it can be easily retrieved. We believe that older pupils can and should be taught how to index and cross-reference what they have recorded from their reading.

8.20   In recommending the development of a number of reading skills we have emphasised their value for learning throughout the curriculum. It will be obvious, however, that many of them apply equally to the kind of reading required of most adults. To this extent the work we have recommended will provide a good preparation for the reading demands of adult life. However, there remains the need to provide older pupils with a variety of reading which will give more specific experience of what they will encounter. In everyday life the consequences of mis-reading or a tendency to read carelessly can be quite serious. Pupils need experience in reading with an eye to consequences, for these will be waiting for them in insurance policies, guarantees, contracts, income tax forms, conditions of employment, works notices, trade union leaflets, and operating instructions, to name but a few. We do not suggest that these should be imported into the classroom *en masse* and studied one by one. Pupils do not pay income tax or take out insurance policies, and any training in reading and filling in forms would be quite unrelated to their present experience and concerns. Nevertheless, we believe that reading demands of this kind should certainly be discussed with the pupil before he leaves school. It is not a question of training in the handling of specific reading tasks but of learning to apply general principles to 'official' reading of one kind or another. There are many parallel forms of such reading that bear on the life and activities of the school, and these can be related to examples from the world of work and everyday life. Pupils could undertake a survey of the major areas of information for which most adults have a common need, e.g. home and family affairs, employment, leisure, community matters. They might then investigate the sources of information, and examine examples of it, particularly material which already concerns them or will do so as soon as they leave school. In some schools this kind of study is already to be found in courses for pupils in their final year, but we have not met any examples of specific attention to reading as an aspect of it. We regard this as an important part of preparation for adult life, and one that should not be confined to any one part of the ability range. We certainly do not believe that the reading needs of abler pupils are taken care of by their examination syllabuses. Explicit attention to skills of the kind recommended in this chapter is necessary if they are to become more efficient readers. Finally, we would again emphasise the part to be played by discussion and dialogue. They are an essential support to the pupil in the process of developing his skills as an independent reader.

REFERENCES

1. Richard T. Murphy: *Adults' Functional Reading Study, Project 1:* United States Office of Education: 1973.

CHAPTER 9

Literature

"I passed English all right because I had all that Beowulf and Lord Randal My Son stuff when I was at Whooton School. I mean I didn't have to do any work in English at all, hardly, except write compositions once in a while."
                    J. D. Salinger: "Catcher in the Rye".

"(he) . . . arrived at the conclusion, from which he never afterwards departed, that all the fancies of the poets, and lessons of the sages, were a mere collection of words and grammar, and had no other meaning in the world".
                    Charles Dickens: "Dombey and Son".

"It would have been impossible for me to have told anyone what I derived from these novels, for it was nothing less than a sense of life itself".
                    Richard Wright: "Black Boy".

9.1   This part of the Report would not be complete if it did not end with a discussion of literature, which to many teachers is the most rewarding form of the child's encounter with language. In the main, opinions converge upon the value of literature, if they take separate ways on the treatment it should receive in school. Much has been claimed for it: that it helps to shape the personality, refine the sensibility, sharpen the critical intelligence; that it is a powerful instrument for empathy, a medium through which the child can acquire his values. Writing in 1917, Nowell Smith[1] saw its purpose as "the formation of a personality fitted for civilized life". The Newsom Report[2], some 50 years later, said that "all pupils, including those of very limited attainments, need the civilizing experience of contact with great literature, and can respond to its universality". These are spirited credos, only two of many, and they represent a faith that English teaching needs. They have not, of course, gone unchallenged. In recent years it has been questioned whether literature does in fact make the reader a better and more sensitive human being. What was a matter of self-evident truth in the eighteenth and nine-teenth centuries is no longer exempt from question. Few would subscribe to the simple view that it offers models for living which the reader lifts from the pages. In fact, Sampson[3] made the point astringently 50 years ago, and few had a more passionate belief than he in the place of literature in school. ". . . let me beg teachers to take a sane view of literature.   Let us have no pose or affectation about it. Reading Blake to a class is not going to turn boys into saints". One American educationist has said bluntly that when it comes down to it there is no evidence that the reading of literature in schools produces in any way the social or emotional effects claimed for it. Another has argued that the teacher of English is not the custodian of ethics and character, and that in these matters he has no more and no less responsibility than his colleagues in other subjects. Many American teachers would accept his proposition that the prime responsibility of the English teacher in teaching literature is to teach literature. Thus it is not uncommon to find American high school pupils examining the generic characteristics of a work of literature and assembling patterns of image and symbol. This is not to say that teachers in the U.S.A. are single-mindedly concerned with the cognitive aspects of literature. It was, in fact, an American who attacked the writers of sequential curricula as "afraid to go where the feelings, perceptions, and questions of children would take them". Nevertheless, there is a difference in emphasis between the two countries in this as in other aspects of English teaching. This was apparent at the Dartmouth Seminar of 1966, when British and American teachers of English met to discuss the subject in depth.

9.2   In Britain the tradition of literature teaching is one which aims at personal and moral growth, and in the last two decades this emphasis has grown. It is a soundly based tradition, and properly interpreted is a powerful force in English teaching. Literature brings the child into an encounter with language in its most complex and varied forms. Through these complexities are presented the thoughts, experiences, and feelings of people who exist outside and beyond the reader's daily awareness. This process of bringing them within that circle of consciousness is where the greatest value of literature lies. It provides imaginative insight into what another person is feeling; it allows the contemplation of possible human experiences which the reader himself has not met. It has the capacity to develop that empathy of which Shelley was speaking when he said: "A man to be greatly good, must imagine intensively and comprehensively; he must put himself in the place of another and many others; the pains and pleasures of his species must become his own". Equally, it confronts the reader with problems similar to his own, and does it at the safety of one remove. He draws reassurance from realising that his personal difficulties and his feelings of deficiency are not unique to himself; that they are as likely to be the experience of others. Adolescents need this kind of reassurance, to be found in the sort of relieving awareness summed up in C. S. Lewis's remark: "Nothing, I suspect, is more astonishing in any man's life than the discovery that there do exist people very, very like himself". The media which influence their world often put a relentless emphasis on euphoria as the natural state of life. They encourage the inference that not to experience it is somehow to miss out and fall short of the norm. Most young people take a realistic view of this, but we can hardly be surprised that there are some who feel it as a pressure. This is only one uncertainty, and perhaps a minor one, but certainly reassurance is one of the available outcomes of this encounter with a wide range of possible human experience.

9.3   It may well be that we lack evidence of the "civilising" power of literature and that some of the claims made for it have seemed over-ambitious. But we can look to the results of various studies of children's reading as some indication of its value as a personal resource. These have suggested, for example, that children's favourite stories at different ages reflect the particular fantasies and emotional conflicts which are foremost in their experience at that time. The child gets most enjoyment from those stories which say something to his condition and help him to resolve these inner conflicts. Books compensate for the difficulties of growing up. They present the child with a vicarious satisfaction that takes him outside his own world and lets him identify for a time with someone else. They present him with controlled experience, which he can observe from the outside at the same time as being involved within it. Thus, the fulfilling of private wishes, the fabrication of an inner environment, is an important property of children's reading. It accounts for the conclusion that although the names of the most widely-read authors change from one decade to the next the characteristic features of their books remain much the same. The presentation is vivid and dramatic, the characters relatively unsubtle, and virtue triumphs in an ending which places everyone where he should be. As he works his way through the book the reader's sympathies will be engaged, his antipathies aroused. It is, of course, easy to say this, but less easy to escape its implications. Books may offer vicarious satisfaction and little else. Indeed many do, and the sympathies they engage and the antipathies they arouse may be far from what we would hope. The child will not necessarily, and not automatically, progress from books which simply vicariously fulfil his wishes to those where a complexity of relationships enlarges his understanding of the range of human possibilities. One would hope to develop the kind of response which is summed up in W. P. Ker's remark from "Imagination and Judgment": " . . . dramatic imagination enters into every question of justice. How can you understand other people's motives unless you act out a fragment or two of a play in which they are the characters?" The development of this response presents the teacher with one of his most delicate areas of operation, and one where his skill and knowledge play an extremely important part. One fact which becomes increasingly evident is the very great extent to which success lies in the contribution of the teacher. It is true in the initial acquisition of reading; it is true in the development of the reading habit; it is true in the growth of discernment. The first of these we have already discussed; the others we will now go on to consider.

9.4   There is no doubt at all in our minds that one of the most important tasks facing the teacher of older juniors and younger secondary pupils is to increase the amount and range of their voluntary reading. We believe that there is a strong association between this and reading attainment, and that private reading can make an important contribution to children's linguistic and experiential development. Before we go on to discuss what the school can and should do to promote it, it will be useful to spend a moment on what is known of children's reading habits. The most recent information on a large scale comes from Whitehead's survey[4] in his Schools Council research project. Almost half the 10 year olds in this survey claimed to have read three or more books during the previous month, the percentage dropping to some two fifths at 12+ and about a third at 14+. There is, however, a substantial minority of children who do not read books at all in their leisure time, and the number increases significantly with age. 13 per cent of Whitehead's 10+ sample had not read a book during the previous month, while at 12+ the corresponding figure was 29 per cent and at 14+ 36 per cent. At each age point this category contained a higher proportion of boys than of girls, and at 14+ the number among the former was as high as 40 per cent. When all else has been considered it seems that there is a fairly large group of children in secondary schools who have the reading skills but do not choose to read books outside school time. A great deal is obviously going to depend on the home environment. It hardly needs saying that where reading has no status and books no place the incentives to read will be slight. But it is clear to us that the school can make a very big difference to this situation. Various studies have revealed that teacher influence on a child's choice of book is considerable, particularly in the case of the less able pupil. Another important conclusion is that for the child who is not an habitual reader the simple fact of which book is where will often determine what he reads. These two factors —teacher influence and book provision—hold the key to an improvement in reading standards in the junior and secondary years.

9.5   We referred earlier to the damaging notion that once the child has mastered the decoding process he will make his own way. Few teachers would subscribe to it in such blunt terms, but it is nevertheless a notion that is implicit in much classroom procedure. In many junior schools there is a graded reader series to be completed before the child can go to a free choice of "real books". Some schools allow these to be read without such a graduation hurdle, but we often met the assumption that mastery of the graded series meant that the child could now read. The teachers were assiduous in their concern that the child should "learn to read", but when he could decode to their satisfaction they came to see him as self-supporting. In some schools the dependence on supplementary 'readers' was uncomfortably long, and the child had little experience of good children's literature. We found, in fact, that some capable readers almost never read a book in school. They dipped into reference and information books, many of which did not give occasion for sustained reading, but they did not read novels. We also noticed that this was related to the teacher's discontinuance of any kind of record of the child's reading. As long as the child was engaged on the reading scheme, or the graded readers supplementary to it, the teacher would usually keep a note of his progress through it. But we met few teachers who kept a record of what the child read after this. There were only comparatively rare instances of their knowing the pattern and balance of the children's reading, which in our opinion is one of the essential features of a policy of expanding its range.

9.6   A feature which ranks equally with this is the teacher's knowledge of what is available, especially in good modern children's literature. In the middle years of schooling in particular the range of emotional and intellectual development within any one class can be extremely wide, and a correspondingly wide range of fiction is needed. The indications are that narrative books are substantially outnumbered by non-fiction in most primary schools. With the increased emphasis on learning through discovery and personal interests schools have tended to acquire collections of information books to support this kind of work. These are to be found in encouraging profusion in book corners, entrance halls, corridors and bays, as well as in rooms designated as a central library. They are often supplemented by subject boxes or project loans from the school library service, and many primary schools still have their sets of class text-books. The result is a commanding majority of non-fiction material in the school at any one time. This profusion is encouraging only if it does not indicate a corresponding neglect of fiction. We have already discussed the value of good imaginative literature in its own right, but we would also suggest that it should be used more widely in association with information books. Suppose, for example, a teacher of older juniors or younger secondary pupils is setting up a study of the Vikings. There are plenty of information books on this topic, but it would be an incomplete experience if the child were to have access only to these. The teacher might therefore cluster about this core a modernised version of the Old English poem "The Battle of Maldon" and the Icelandic "Njal's Saga" or "The Saga of Grettir the Strong"; Madeleine Polland's novel "Beorn the Proud" and Walter Hodges' "The Namesake"; Patricia Beer's poem "Abbey Tomb", and Gael Turnbull's "Gunnar from his Burial Mound" from his group of poems "Five from the Sagas". All these complement one another and throw fresh light on the source books. Patricia Beer's poem, for instance, is about the fate of monks in a pillaged abbey; Madeleine Polland's novel includes an attack on a monastery from the Vikings' viewpoint. An encounter of this kind could be used to lead a child to wider reading of fiction through an awakened interest. To exploit a promising situation in this way the teacher needs to know what is relevant and available.

9.7   The third important feature of this process of developing self-initiated reading is ingenuity in 'promoting' books. At its simplest and most effective level this will be a case of the teacher's knowledge and enthusiasm bringing child, book, and situation together in a natural interaction. In the course of one visit two members of the Committee were in a primary school library during the lunch hour when a boy came in carrying a tin containing some maggots he had found. The teacher immediately showed a keen interest, talked to him about them, then led him to a shelf where there was a book on the subject. She generated such a curiosity about the book that the boy went off carrying it with his tin of maggots, promising to let her know more about them when he'd read it. This is a seemingly obvious procedure, but not as simple as it sounds, and not as common. There was no doubt of the boy's eagerness to read that book, but it was produced by the teacher's genuine interest in what he had to show her, and her knowing that there was just the book to turn the incident to a reading advantage. In short, it revealed an expert ability to bring the right book to the right child at the right time. Opportunities do not always arrive as such happy accidents, but they can be engineered. We came across similar instances in secondary schools, for example where the teacher had found for the pupil a short story which had something in common with one the pupil had written himself. In the teacher's words ,"the imaginative exploration of the pupil's work can provide a way into the more difficult adult work of fiction."

9.8   It is a particularly effective device for a teacher to stir demand by reading out arresting passages from new books. Television programmes likely to arouse a keen interest can be anticipated, and the teacher can have ready and waiting the appropriate books to catch the wave. There is almost no limit to the 'publicity' devices that might be conceived. For instance, in the display of dust jackets of new books arrows can lead off to large illustra-tions and short offprints of associated material. Pupils can be given a board on which to pin up extracts calculated to make the curious want to know more. The teacher might tape trailer passages on cassettes for children to listen to on headsets. Some pupils might produce advertisement posters or design alternative dust jackets from their knowledge of the book. And always the children should be encouraged to talk about what they have read, to the teacher and among themselves. By keeping a note of what children read he could bring three or four together who had had common experience of a particular book and let them explore one another's reactions to it. This is so much more productive and so much less forbidding than the obligatory written book review, where the pupil knows that his pleasure has inevitably to be followed by a chore.

9.9   All this kind of activity presupposes a wide range of books ready to hand and responsive to the teacher's controlling inventiveness. The acquisition of books and the promotional activities are essentially related, and anything less than a professionally informed policy will not achieve the object. The building up of book resources is often something of a piecemeal process rather than a planned response to defined objectives. School library services are an invaluable resource, but they are a support for the teacher, not a substitute for his control of the total learning situation. We discuss this question of book supply in Chapter 21 but mention it here to underscore the importance of keeping a flow of good imaginative literature at the children's fingertips. Various studies have shown that a large number of contemporary writers of good quality fiction are barely represented in many schools, despite the fact that quantitatively the school may be generally well stocked with books. The survey conducted by Whitehead revealed that at least 77 per cent of all the books read by his sample fell within the category of 'narrative', which included biographical writing as well as fiction. Though there was some evidence of a veering towards informational books among the older boys, the category of 'non-narrative' still accounted for only 14·5 per cent of all book-reading. It was clear that the narrative mode provided for children of all ages by far the strongest motivation towards the reading of books. The potential of this for a general increase in reading needs no elaboration, and the school should have the books both to create and meet the demand. It is a recognition of this fact that underlies the success of those schools which have achieved a remarkably high rate of voluntary reading.

9.10   We believe that this recognition cannot take place at too early an age, and that fantasy, fairy tale and folk-tale should take their place in the repertoire in the earliest stages of reading. J. R. R. Tolkien pointed out that fairy tales were not evolved for the nursery; they found their way there by historical accident. They contain the strength and simplicity of their origins, as well as their deep significance. The children will have had experience of them in a good pre-reading programme, when a teacher or parent will have read them aloud or will have told the stories. All too often when their own reading begins they lose this world in favour of a circumscribed domestic situation with narrow limits of action and feeling. We accept the argument that its commonest representation in early reading books offers few toe-holds for the working class child. But we do not believe that it should simply be replaced by one that is set in a working class environment. There is obviously an important place for such material, but we have heard the case for 'relevance' carried to the point of excluding fantasy or any stories with settings or characters unfamiliar to the pupils from their first-hand experience. We do not accept this view. Though we consider it important that much of a child's reading matter should offer contact at many points with the life he knows, we believe that true relevance lies in the way a piece of fiction engages with the reader's emotional concerns. A work like "Billy Liar", for example, has value for the older pupil not because of its environmental setting but because of its evocation of an aspect of adolescence and its exploration of family tensions.

9.11   We have emphasised that learning to read is a developmental process which continues over the years. To read intelligently is to read responsively; it is to ask questions of the text and use one's own framework of experience in interpreting it. In working his way through a book the reader imports, projects, anticipates, speculates on alternative outcomes; and nowhere is this process more active than in a work of imaginative literature. We strongly recommend that there should be a major effort to increase voluntary reading, which should be recognised as a powerful instrument for the improvement of standards. And in making this recommendation we recall a particularly telling remark from the evidence: pupils admitted to an adult literacy scheme had been asked to say why, in their opinion, they failed to learn to read at school. "Only one common factor emerges: they did not learn from the process of learning to read that it was something other people did for *pleasure*".

9.12   Most teachers of English would include among their most important aims a growth of discernment in their pupils. "Discernment" is a word that begs many questions, and it could be taken to mean that the task of every English teacher is to take every pupil up to a permanent relationship with the great classics. In the last decade this notion has increasingly drawn contention. On the one hand there are those teachers who see literature in terms of a heritage, with which they must endow their pupils. On the other hand there are those who argue that many pupils can never be expected to take literature into their lives in any such sense. There is an equal polarity of view on what should be done with literature in the classroom. To some teachers there is no question but that this should consist of a close and detailed examination of the text, each successive encounter an attempt to sharpen discrimination. For others the text is very little more than a point of departure, a springboard to be barely touched before taking off for the element of personal experience or social issue. Nor is this to be neatly equated with the ability of the pupils. In our visits we saw lessons where pupils of modest capacity were being pressed very closely to the text. And we saw able pupils engaged on experience-based programmes where the text was only perfunctorily visited. Nevertheless, the first approach is traditionally thought appropriate for pupils preparing for examinations and, by extension, for pupils whose road will in due course lead there.

9.13   The influence of examinations on literature teaching has come in for a good deal of assault, not least from those who could hardly be accused of anti-academic bias. Sampson, writing in 1921, said "If in any school something called literature is systematically taught, the efforts will usually be found to be directed towards literary history, or 'meanings', or the explanation of difficulties, or summaries of plays and stories, or descriptions of characters . . . . all of which are evasions of the real work before the teacher responsible for literature". And Aldous Huxley in "The Olive Tree" wrote that examinations in literature encourage pupils to repeat "mechanically and without reflection other people's judgements". C. Day Lewis saw the process as a threat to a true and sincere response. He described it as a lamentable practice to equip the students with highly sophisticated instruments of criticism, check that the poet responds positively to their tests, and then say "O.K. boys, now you may love him". Such censures gain force when applied to this approach to literature with pupils of lesser capacity. We have seen pupils preparing for "O" level and C.S.E. with a diet of activities corresponding very closely to those catalogued by George Sampson. The explanations and the summaries have expanded to take-over point; the literature has receded. We must seriously question what is being achieved when pupils are producing chapter summaries in sequence, taking endless notes to prepare model answers and writing stereotyped commentaries which carry no hint of a felt response. Yet this is the standard experience of very large numbers of fourth and fifth formers who spend a term or more on a modest novel which makes no claim to merit such long drawn out attention. We recognise the difficulty facing the teacher, who has the task of talking about a narrative the sequence of which the pupils have not grasped. There are substantial technical problems with which very many teachers have not yet managed to come to terms. These add up to knowing how to help pupils "through" a novel to the point of being able to respond to its experience without such unreal chores as chapter synopsis. We should like to see more professional discussion of appropriate teaching techniques for class approaches to a full-length novel.

9.14   There is no doubt that many secondary school pupils develop unsympathetic attitudes to literature as a result of their experience in preparing for an examination. We saw lessons in which a novel was treated as a hoard of factual information, with the pupils scoring marks for the facts they remembered. How many sheep did Gabriel Oak lose? What was the name of Bathsheba's maid? Where had Fanny Robins been working before she walked to Casterbridge? We saw pupils encountering poems as little more than comprehension passages, on which the teacher's information and interpretations were recorded as marginal notes. Yet in the same breath it must be said that the right relationship between teacher, text, and pupil can and does have a strikingly positive effect on attitudes to literature. In one fairly recent study[5] a substantial majority of a large sample of "O" level candidates of both sexes said they had no intention of reading more poetry after leaving school. But a study of the boys' responses showed that the small minority taking the opposite view came from just six of the twenty-nine classes in ten different schools. It is likely that the positive effect of the teachers of those six classes had been very strong. It is also clear that some of the recent developments in examining have encouraged extensive reading and imaginative teaching. In some of the C.S.E. classes we visited, pupils were responding sensitively to a wide variety of literature and deepening their understanding and enjoyment of it in the course of their study.

9.15   In a very real sense a pupil is himself being judged each time he responds in class to a piece of literature, particularly a poem. More is at stake than his knowledge of the text. Is the value-judgment he forms the one the teacher finds acceptable? Is he betraying himself, he may well ask, as one who lacks discrimination? In no other area of classroom operations is there quite the same degree of vulnerability, with poetry the most exposing element of all. Every skilled teacher has his own means of reducing this vulnerability, of balancing the need to explore the text with the need to preserve its appeal. Some of the most successful lessons we have seen have been those in which the teacher has contrived to stand alongside his pupils in this process of exploration. In other words, he has avoided using the text as a repository of answers to which he possesses the key. His curiosity about the work has remained alive and has not been extinguished by layers of acquired judgment. These are the most favourable conditions for any work of literature: when teacher and taught approach it in a common spirit of exploration. Inevitably and naturally the teacher will guide, but he will do this by devising situations which lead the pupils to their own insight. Nothing is served if the pupil simply learns to repeat "mechanically and without reflection other people's judgements", and if in the process he is lost to what literature has to offer him. As we see it, the main emphasis should be on extending the range of the pupil's reading. True discernment can come only from a breadth of experience. Learning how to appreciate with enthusiasm is more important than learning how to reject.

9.16   Over the past ten years or so there has been a growth in secondary schools of the organisation of thematic work. This has been felt to be particularly appropriate in mixed ability classes, since it enables pupils of varying capacity to work alongside one another productively. Sometimes the whole class may read certain poems or short stories together, while at others the material they are handling has been selected to suit their ability. Thematic work has thus provided the pupils with a common purpose, and by its very nature has encouraged an organic treatment of talk, reading, writing, and dramatisation. Literature has fared variously in such arrangements. It has certainly escaped what T. S. Eliot called the "dryness of schematic analysis", but sometimes the encounter has been so brief that the pupil has been denied anything but a fleeting consciousness of it. We have seen lessons where the pupil's acquaintance with literature, other than what he reads privately, has been confined to a passage used to introduce a discussion; not a discussion upon the passage, which has been barely visited, but upon an area of experience to which it is related. There were several occasions on which virtually no attention at all was given to the words on the page. "Have any of you had an experience like this?" is a tempting question after a first reading; but it becomes valuable only if the experience is then brought back to the text, and if there is a sharpening of response to the detail of the writing. An obvious danger in humanities lessons is for the literature to be selected solely on the ground that it matches the theme, however inappropriate it may be in other ways. Moreover, when a poem or story is enlisted to serve a theme it can become the property of that theme to the extent that its richness is over-simplified, its more rewarding complexities ignored. There is also a natural tendency to use collections of short extracts, so that the pupils' experience of complete books becomes minimal. We have a definite impression that fewer full-length novels are read. Anthologies are certainly a valuable resource, but they should open up opportunities, not constitute an end in themselves. The teacher's aim should always be to extend the range of writing to which the children can respond. Where anthologies are used we commend those that include complete pieces or substantial extracts, virtually artistic units on their own, rather than merely short snippets clipped out of their context.

9.17   The success of any innovation turns upon the manner and quality of its interpretation. At its best, thematic work has given to literature a self-proving eminence in the context of photograph, film, television, radio, and newspaper account which have been associated with it in developing the theme. We have seen excellent examples of work founded on such constellations of media. We have been particularly impressed by those situations, admittedly rarer, where the teacher has carefully chosen a core of poetry and drama and gathered about it prose texts which set up reverberations. By such means the words on the page can be brought into varying degrees of focus, and breadth achieved without loss of a controlled degree of depth. Many schools are successfully extending the range and variety of their pupils' reading with a large number of carefully selected titles from post-war fiction. These speak to the young adult, often on a helpfully simple level, and explore experiences of direct concern to him. In one small secondary modern school in an urban area we saw a fifth year class of moderate ability supporting their C.S.E. set book study with an extensive range of such titles, chosen by the teacher with an excellent eye for their appeal and relevance. There was no doubt of his success in developing his pupils' enjoyment of wide reading while at the same time preparing them for the examination.

9.18   These and similar forms of organisation demand not only professional skill but professional knowledge. Whatever the value of his contribution in other ways the teacher without specialist qualifications in English cannot be expected to have the same ready access to a wide range of sources. Where a team of teachers is co-operating on a theme, particularly with a humanities programme, the guidance of an English specialist is essential. It is by no means always the case that he is to be found there. If the child is to meet literature the extent, relevance and quality of that literature must not be a matter of chance but the informed judgment of one who has a wide and detailed knowledge of suitable texts. He may not actually be teaching the class, but his advice and support should be available to whichever of his colleagues is. In the best of such arrangements this goes without saying. Regular consultation, reviews and synopses of material, joint study of the books to be used: these and many other devices ensure that all the non-specialist teachers of English are fully resourced. But such planning is not universal, and it is still too readily assumed that anyone can turn his hand to English. This assumption all too often results in a narrower experience of literature, and the closing of opportunities that might have been opened up had the teacher only known of particular books that match them.

9.19   In recent years there has been a welcome growth in the practice of wide individualised reading within a class. This is a pattern which some teachers have long operated, and its advantages were pressed by Jenkinson[6] in his 1940 survey when he advocated small sets of books as opposed to the collective reading of the class novel. And yet the latter is still to be found in many schools as the standard, indeed the exclusive, procedure. We refer here not to the classes which are preparing for examinations, but lower and middle school groups. Its great disadvantage is that it usually entails a slow plod, in which the pupils' experience of the book is parcelled out over a term or part of a term at weekly intervals. There are likely to be pupils who read fewer books during the whole term in school than they read out of school in one month. Moreover, this pattern is often associated with the allocation to particular classes or year groups of certain novels. These lists are often interpreted quite strictly, so that a pupil has no official access to a book in a higher list. Such grading systems are more often than not quite arbitrary and are not based on anything other than an intuitive 'feel'. The intuition of an experienced teacher is a valuable instrument, but experience shows that assessments of suitability can vary widely. In one group of four comparable secondary schools there was only partial agreement as to where a particular book belonged. Of the following books, each to be found in the first or second years of at least two of the four schools, only three were prescribed for the same age point in every case: "Treasure Island", "Kidnapped", "Tanglewood Tales", "Jim Davis", "Tom Sawyer", "David Copperfield", "A Christmas Carol", "A Tale of Two Cities", and "Great Expectations". Indeed, certain of the books that appeared in one school's lower school list would be deferred by another until the third or fourth year. Where classes are of mixed ability the logic of such restrictions is further open to question.

9.20   At its most extreme the system of class reading at the rate of one or two books a term must put literature in a somewhat artificial light in the mind of the pupil. We have already remarked that children's voluntary reading is not as great in quantity as it should be, but there is no doubt as to its diversity and variety. The 6,000 children in Whitehead's sample who claimed to have read one or more books during the previous four weeks named more than 7,500 separate and distinct titles. In our view the teacher can have a marked effect on his pupils' reading by extending the individualised provision within the classroom and relating it to their reading outside school hours. We have argued that this implies a knowledge on his part of the wide range of good modern fiction available. Some of the book lists we saw in schools were remarkably well-informed on this score, but others contained little beyond the established 'classics', and reflected a stock which had not received an infusion of new (as opposed to replacement) material for some considerable time. It is equally important that the teacher should know something about the pupils' reading habits, and should discover what books they read in their previous school and the nature and extent of the work that has grown out of this reading. We hope he would then keep his own record of their reading in school and would discuss with them the books they read outside it. Perhaps it hardly needs adding that these will often disappoint him. Every survey so far carried out into children's reading reveals that much of it is ephemeral or well below what informed adults would consider to be good material. Nevertheless, the skilled teacher will not reject or denigrate it. The willingness to talk about it and take up the child's enthusiasm is essential to the process of encouraging him to widen his range.

9.21   In recommending an expansion of supported individualised reading in schools we see it as a complementary process to group attention to the text, which provides so valuable an opportunity to deepen the reading experience. Some of the best and most lasting effects of English teaching have come from the simultaneous encounter of teacher, pupil, and text. We have suggested above that this experience can be more universally enjoyed when it takes the form of a shared exploration. This is clearly not easy. The teacher has a deeper knowledge of literature in general and that work in particular than his pupils can possess. He brings to the situation a wider experience of life and a maturer view of it. To contain these in the process of sharing is a measure of his skill at its highest level. A child derives value from a work of literature in direct proportion to the genuineness of the response he is able to make to it. The teacher's skill lies in developing the subtlety and complexity of this response without catechism or a one-way traffic in apodictic judgments. This is particularly true in the case of poetry, which our visits showed to be receiving a wide range of treatment. At its best it was distinguished, and the children were being given an experience which was enviable and a pleasure to witness. At the other extreme some children rarely encountered poetry of any kind.

9.22   It has to be acknowledged that poetry starts at a disadvantage. In the public view it is something rather odd, certainly outside the current of normal life; it is either numinous, and therefore rarely to be invoked, or an object of comic derision. Definitions of poetry are almost limitless, but they always agree upon this central fact: that it is a man speaking to men, of his and their condition, in language which consists of the best words in the best order, language used with the greatest possible inclusiveness and power. Matthew Arnold said of it that it is "simply the most beautiful, impressive, and widely effective mode of saying things". To D. H. Lawrence " . . . the essential quality of poetry is that it makes a new effort of attention and 'discovers' a new world within the known world". Definitions can inspirit, but they can also deter. It is a reinforcement of the prejudice against poetry to present it as something precious, arcane, to be revered. This concept, a particularly tenacious one, sees poetry as "something more or less involuntarily secreted by the author", oozing from the unconscious in a manner quite unlike that of prose, which is consciously controlled. The teacher is often faced with the task of showing that poetry is not some inaccessible form of utterance, but that it speaks directly to children, as to anyone else, and has something to say which is relevant to their living here and now.

9.23   We have already referred to the analytical approach to poetry. This has been successively reinforced by every new examination which has been introduced, even where the authors of that examination have intended something quite different. T. S. Eliot once said of practical criticism: "It cannot be recommended to young people without grave danger of deadening their sensibility . . . and confounding the genuine development of taste with the sham acquisition of it". But it is to be found, in however skeletal or distorted a form, in some clearly inappropriate situations. We have seen C.S.E. classes working their way almost mechanistically through a set anthology, paraphrasing and answering endless comprehension questions on the way; and this is standard practice for many "O" level pupils. It is perhaps not surprising that in the survey mentioned earlier (paragraph 9.14) the pupils' attitude to poetry was a dispiriting one. Of 1,000 "O" level and "A" level students only 170 said they would read any more poetry after leaving school; 96 of the 800 "O" level students, 74 of the 200 "A" level students. Equally revealing was their attitude towards particular texts. The four "O" level poetry anthologies were conspicuously disliked, while at "A" level Milton's poetry, and particularly "Paradise Lost", was notably unpopular. It is at least possible that his standing was related to the degree of 'external' labour his poetry demands: factual knowledge, annotation, paraphrase, classical and biblical allusions.*

*Cf Sir Arthur Quiller-Couch: "On the Art of Reading" (1920): "You have (we will say) a class of thirty or forty in front of you . . . you will not (if you are wise) choose a passage from 'Paradise Lost': your knowledge telling you that 'Paradise Lost' was written, late in his life, by a great virtuoso, and older men (of whom I, sad to say, am one) assuring you that to taste the Milton of 'Paradise Lost' a man must have passed his thirtieth year".

9.24   Our argument here must not be construed as an attack on the notion of a close engagement with a poem; we have already expressed our faith in the value of a shared encounter with a work of literature. Eliot's remark about practical criticism can be balanced with his observation that where a poem is concerned understanding and enjoyment are essential to one another. By this reckoning what kind of understanding has the detailed study of poetry given to the large number of pupils who voted so feelingly against it? It is clear to us that this antipathy rests substantially in the *method* of teaching it; and the comprehension approach is by no means confined to the examination years. It is usually associated with the timetabled poetry lesson, which often assumes the shape of the Procrustean bed. Where this is the medium of encounter there is a temptation for the poem to be read, re-read, socratically worried, eviscerated for its figures of speech, even copied into exercise books. Clearly there are occasions when a poem needs a comfortable amount of time to be experienced, but poetry works best when it is wanted, not when the timetable decrees it. There will be times when a particular poem may make its maximum impact by being dropped suddenly, with neither preamble nor question, into a lull which calls out for it. There will be occasions when it seems the most natural thing in the world for a poem to be read at that particular moment. For instance, to read Anthony Hecht's poem "Tarantula" while discussing the Great Plague would be to give a new dimension to the subject. Edwin Muir's "The Interrogation" and Edwin Morgan's "The Suspect" graphically examine an experience of authority at its most unfeeling, each ending on a tempting question mark. The kind of talk that goes on in class always creates at some point the context for a poem that takes up the general feeling. The strength and relevance of the experience within it should engage the pupils' response and thus their willingness to grapple with the language. Some of the best lessons we saw were those where pupils and teacher were enjoying the exchange of opinions on points of vocabulary, attitude, atmosphere, and metaphor.

9.25   All this leads us back inevitably to the question of the teacher's knowledge of his material. Many schools simply do not have the resources to take this kind of opportunity. The anthologies, thematic source books, and collections of extracts are a great help, but they do not go far enough. Many of them are sensitively and intelligently compiled, and the editor has allowed his own good judgment to operate on his own very wide reading. Some, however, are simply anthologies of anthologies, yielding only a few new poems to supplement the very large overlap with collections that have gone before. A particular poem will appear time and again, though in fact it may not be either the most appealing or the most suitable of the very many the author has written. Inevitably, anthologies age, and where a school relies on class sets (sometimes, as we have seen, shared between two or three classes) the range of available material will become relatively narrower as time goes by. It is exceptionally difficult for the individual teacher to keep abreast of all the new poetry that is published. Indeed, except for those with a particular interest in it there is often a time-lag, so that the teacher is not aware of much of the work produced in the last two decades. A good anthology will do a great deal to introduce teacher and pupil alike to new and unfamiliar material, but it should not be a substitute for the extensive reading of poetry by the teacher himself. We know this is an ideal; but if the teacher wants to find material that he knows will be right for his pupils and the context he has created, this is the most rewarding way. There is some very good poetry published that never finds its way into an anthology, and much of it would appeal directly to the pupils. There is certainly everything to be said for teachers in a primary school and members of an English department maintaining a collective knowledge of what is being produced. We found that one of the strengths of the well qualified groups of specialists in some comprehensive schools was precisely this team approach to reading. Communally, the department had an impressive knowledge, upon which every individual member could draw. This awareness thus becomes a major contributor to the central resource collection a department creates for itself. Such a collection will contain print and non-print materials of all kinds, and one of its essentials should be a wide range of poetry gathered through teachers' first-hand reading of the work of individual poets. A resource point of this kind can be particularly helpful to a young teacher early in his first appointment. To enjoy so wide a choice, to be able to call freely on record, tape, or cassette, may make all the difference to his attitude to poetry in the classroom in that first year. Another valuable facility is the Arts Council/ D.E.S. 'Writers in Schools' scheme, which enables poets to visit schools to read and talk about their work. Where we have seen this in operation it has been very successful. Some schools have developed the interest it has generated by taking pupils to exhibitions of poetry and public readings.

9.26   We have placed some emphasis on contemporary poetry, but this is not to imply that we recommend it at the expense of older poetry. It is simply that much of the work of this half century, and perhaps particularly the last two decades of it, has a voice to which a larger number of young people can more readily respond. Moreover, it is fresh to many teachers themselves and some feel able to read it to their pupils with the pleasure of a new discovery. Poetry of this century and of earlier centuries can be read side by side, to the mutual illumination of both. And what we have said about going beyond anthologies applies with little less force to the latter.

9.27   Poetry has great educative power, but in many schools it suffers from lack of commitment, misunderstanding, and the wrong kind of orientation; above all it lacks adequate resources. There are few more rewarding experiences in all English teaching than when teacher and pupil meet in the enjoyment of a poem. We are not so unrealistic as to believe that all pupils can take away from school with them a lasting love of poetry. There will always be many people to whom it offers nothing. But we are certain that it does not reach as many as it might, and we believe this can be achieved.

9.28   We can sum up by saying that whatever else the pupil takes away from his experience of literature in school he should have learned to see it as a source of pleasure, as something that will continue to be a part of his life. The power to bring this about lies with the teacher, but it cannot be pretended that the task is easy. In outlining some of the difficulties we have inevitably had to be critical of certain approaches which we believe compound them. However, we must conclude with warm appreciation of the work we have seen in many of the schools we visited, which we believe is representative of the imaginative treatment literature is widely receiving. It is an aspect of English which has made some remarkable advances in recent years, and we feel that great credit belongs to the teachers who have done so much to bring these about.

REFERENCES

1. Nowell Smith: *Cambridge Essays on Education:* Editor A. C. Benson: Cambridge University Press: 1917.

2. *"Half our Future":* H.M.S.O.: 1963.

3. G. Sampson: *English for the English:* Cambridge University Press: 1921.

4. F. Whitehead, A. C. Capey and W. Maddren: *Children's Reading Interests:* Schools Council Working Paper No. 52: Evans/Methuen Educational: 1974.

5. G. Yarlott and W. S. Harpin: *1,000 Responses to English Literature:* Educational Research 13.1 and 13.2: 1972/73.

6. A. J. Jenkinson: *What do Boys and Girls Read?:* An investigation into reading habits with some suggestions about the teaching of literature in secondary and senior schools: Methuen: 1940.

Part Four

Language in the Middle
and Secondary Years

CHAPTER 10

Oral Language

TALKING AND LISTENING

> "*We children beg thee, oh teacher, to teach us to speak, because we are ignorant and speak incorrectly.*" "*What do you want to say?*" "*What do we care what we say, provided it is correct speech and useful and not foolish or bad*".
>
> *Grammar book of the early English scholar Aelfin.*

> "*Mrs. Durbeyfield habitually spoke the dialect; her daughter . . the dialect at home, more or less; ordinary English abroad and to persons of quality.*"
> *Thomas Hardy: "Tess of the D'Urbervilles"*

> "*I have forgotten the words I intended to say, and my thoughts, unembodied, return to the realm of the shadows*":
> *Osip Mandelstam.*

10.1 In his last term in the junior school a child may be with one teacher for the whole of the curriculum and for every session in the week. From his first week in the secondary school he may have different teachers for the ten or more subjects on the timetable, and may move to a different classroom every time the bell rings. In each situation he has to adapt to different styles of relationship, content, and methods of presentation. The implications of this change from one environment to another are considerable for the child and will affect his response as a talker and as a listener. The nature of the language encounter is shaped by the organisation of the pupil's learning experience. In many of his specialist subject lessons in the secondary school the experience is likely to give him much less scope for exploratory talk. There is a greater probability of direct teaching, with the teacher controlling the lesson by question and answer, and the pupils' responses shepherded within defined limits.

10.2 We need to begin by examining the nature of the language experience in the dialogue between teacher and class within this framework. By its very nature a lesson is a verbal encounter through which the teacher draws information from the class, elaborates and generalises it, and produces a synthesis. His skill is in selecting, prompting, improvising, and generally orchestrating the exchange. But in practice the course of any dialogue in which one person is managing 30 is only partly predictable. There will be false avenues and unexpected diversions. There will be minute by minute changes in the ratio of teacher-pupil contribution, depending upon how unfamiliar to the children the material becomes at any given point. In fact the class lesson is a very complex process. This complexity has always been intuitively recognised by teachers, but only comparatively recently has it been systematically studied. By an examination of tape transcripts Barnes[1] has illustrated the difficulties that face the pupil when a subject teacher is trying to 'implant concepts' by question and answer. It has also become clear what difficulties face the teacher if he is to encourage genuine exploration and learning on the part of his pupils, and not simply the game of guessing what he has in mind. What the teacher has in mind may well be the desirable destination of a thinking process; but a learner needs to trace the steps from the familiar to the new, from the fact or idea he possesses to that which he is to acquire. In other words, the learner has to make a journey in thought for himself. The kind of class lesson we are describing has therefore to be supported by others in which the pupils' own exploratory talk has much more scope. Where it builds upon such talk the class lesson can be an important way of encouraging the final steps by which a new piece of learning is securely reached. But it can achieve this only if the teacher-directed discussion takes up and uses the contributions of the pupils, for these indicate the stages at which pupils' thinking now stands, and they point the steps by which the destination can be reached. "Guessing what the teacher has in mind" becomes only too easily a substitute for this more arduous process.

10.3   One way for the teacher to avoid this is to watch that the questions he asks are open-ended rather than closed, and that the synthesis he brings about is seen to be the end point of the pupils' own thinking under his guidance. Genuine thinking may be more readily provoked when the teacher poses a *genuine problem* than when he asks a question to which he knows the answer. In a recent project Sinclair[2] has analysed the discourse of lessons to show how varieties of teacher utterance are related to varieties of pupil utterance, and vice versa. He shows, for example, that what may appear at first sight to be an alternation of two kinds of discourse, the question from the teacher and the answer from a pupil, is in fact very often an exchange containing three kinds of discourse: question (teacher), answer (pupil) and evaluation (teacher). 'Evaluation', in plainer terms, is the teacher's verdict on the pupil's answer. It may appear a rather elusive feature to anyone reading a transcript of a lesson, because it is often carried by the tone of voice rather than delivered in so many words, but it influences the discourse in such a way that the 'class discussion' is often no more than a series of disconnected endeavours to read the teacher's mind.

10.4   There is research evidence to suggest that on average the teacher talks for three quarters of the time in the usual teacher-class situation. It has been calculated from this that in a 45-minute period the amount of time left for a class of 30 to contribute is an average of some 20 seconds per pupil. Of course this does not happen in practice. Pupils have their own 'hidden agendas', and some will avoid any participation, given the chance this kind of situation affords. The rest may compete for attention, and the teacher determines not only who shall speak but what value their contribution is accorded. The exact nature of this control will depend upon the sensitivity and skill of the teacher, his view of the subject matter, and the pupils' understanding of what is expected of them. Teachers of young children, for instance, are more likely to be tolerant of anecdote than are those of older pupils. They recognise that an offering of wavering relevance may be essential to the child's way in to the dialogue. In the secondary school the subject teacher is usually concerned to achieve a step by step presentation of his material, and this often results in his asking the kinds of questions that elicit one-word answers. Some recent research in a number of American junior high schools showed that on average the teacher asked a new question every 12 seconds. It would be unwise to infer that the same rate would be found in this country. Nevertheless, it indicates that speed of questions, and therefore brevity of answers, is a likely feature where the dialogue is being used simply to transmit information. It is obvious that at this rate of exchange there can be little opportunity for genuine thinking. The teacher's effectiveness will be increased if he has an explicit awareness of the nature and characteristics of the discourse. If he denies himself the feedback from his pupils' reformulations of the stages in an argument, he cannot assess how successful he has been.

10.5   Before considering other forms of classroom dialogue it would be useful to pause on the question of the teacher's explicit understanding of his pupils' language. The point to be emphasised is that the child's language should be accepted, and most teachers appreciate the importance of this. To criticise a person's speech may be an attack on his self-esteem, and the extent to which the two are associated is evident from the status accorded to accent in society at large. There is a marked social element in the 'aesthetic' assessment of accents, in which researchers have found a hierarchy. At the top is Received Pronunciation, followed by certain foreign and regional accents, with industrial and 'town' accents in the lower reaches. In one survey Birmingham was placed firmly at the bottom, with Cockney only a little way above it. Research conducted in New York by Labov[3] found that the 'upwardly socially mobile' had a particularly sensitive perception of sounds in listening to spoken language. They were highly sensitive to the model to which they were aspiring and consequently to those sounds which they felt they should avoid. We believe that a child's accent should be accepted, and that to attempt to suppress it is irrational and neither humane nor necessary. The teacher's aim should be to indicate to his pupils the value of awareness and flexibility, so that they can make their own decisions and modify these as their views alter.

10.6   The question of conformity to acceptable standards of grammar and diction is rather more difficult and certainly one in which more teachers feel the need to change the speech habits of their pupils. However, a view that has long been held by linguists is that an utterance may be 'correct' in one linguistic situation but not in another. Any one person belongs to a number of speech communities, and correctness therefore becomes a matter of conforming to the linguistic behaviour appropriate to the situation in which he is talking. Many people find this notion of relativity hard to accept, but it seems to us far more reasonable to think in terms of appropriateness than of absolute correctness. This is to operate positively rather than negatively, in the sense that one is seeking to extend the child's range of language use, not restrict it. The aim is not to alienate the child from a form of language with which he has grown up and which serves him efficiently in the speech community of his neighbourhood. It is to enlarge his repertoire so that he can use language effectively in other speech situations and use standard forms when they are needed. This clearly cannot be achieved overnight, which is why we emphasise that the teacher should start where the child is and should accept the language he brings to school. In the course of the child's life in school there should be a gradual and growing extension of his powers of language to meet new demands and new situations, and this again takes us firmly to the need for an explicit knowledge by the teacher of how language operates.

10.7   There are other reasons why inappropriate evaluations are sometimes applied to the spoken word. Putting it very generally, not enough account is taken of the fundamental differences that exist between speech and writing. The writer must usually entrust his message to the words on the page. A spoken utterance, on the other hand, is not generally required to carry the full and final expression of a speaker's meaning, since he is in touch with his listeners and in the light of their responses can repeat, modify, or add to what he has said. Furthermore, a speaker uses more than words. He uses paralinguistic features, which supplement the words themselves and govern the *way* in which a thing is said. Intonation patterns and other paralinguistic features carry a great deal of the meaning. Tone of voice, pitch, intensity, timing, facial expression and physical gestures: all may contribute as part of his message. His pauses may range from mere hesitations to long silences, his gestures from the deliberate and formal to the unconscious expressiveness of bodily posture.

10.8   Written language has to take on a precision and complexity of linguistic structure that is not demanded of speech. If a reader wishes he can shut himself away with the text, giving it his whole attention. The words stand before him on the page, and he may vary his speed to match his comprehension, going back to re-read where he needs to, or pausing to make sure of a meaning before he reads on, cross-referencing for himself backwards and forwards in the text. A listener to speech, on the other hand, must catch his message on the wing. Thus it is that repetitions, re-phrasings, annotations, and extensions *en route*, all of them varieties of 'redundancy', are not only permissible in a way they would not be in writing, but may well indeed be essential. It is a tendency of the written language to transcend differences in time and place, and hence to offer some resistance to change. It is in the nature of the spoken language to change in response to changing demands, and for a variety of reasons. With such general differences as these in mind, one linguist[4] has gone as far as to claim that "serious written English may be regarded as a rather artificial dialect of our language".

10.9   In spoken language the paralinguistic features we have been describing strongly influence one person's judgment of another's effectiveness. This fact is tacitly recognised by most people, who know they can be charmed by nonsense and bored by sense. What they are largely unaware of is exactly how this is happening. Some teachers acquire a high degree of skill in assessing the spoken language of their pupils, but there is evidence[5] that very many find it difficult. We believe that an explicit understanding of the nature of spoken language would extend their ability to influence it. The teacher's own speech is a crucial factor in developing that of his pupils; even more important are the understanding and the informed attitudes he brings to the whole undertaking.

10.10   What then of ways in which verbal interaction can be organised to extend the pupils' ability to handle language? Throughout the primary and middle years the change of emphasis from teaching to learning has meant that talk now occupies a position of central importance. This is not, of course, to suggest that the classroom of the past operated simply on the principle that the teacher talked and the pupils listened, and that their output was through the medium of the pen. Nevertheless, new patterns of classroom organisation have changed the balance, so that primary school children spend more time discovering for themselves and talking about their discoveries. The teacher's role in this is vitally important and very demanding; for it is not enough to assume that, given a wide range of activities in a lively primary classroom, the child's language can be left to take care of itself. There is obviously great value in providing opportunities for children simply to talk freely and informally on whatever interests them, and nothing we say should be taken as detracting from this. But although such talk may serve many useful purposes it will not necessarily develop the children's ability to use language as an instrument for learning. The important question to ask is whether demands are being made upon their language by the nature of the problem and the process of arriving at a solution to it. Children need to represent to themselves and others what is being learnt, and a study of tape transcripts will show that in any group learning activity this is not an automatic outcome. It is even less likely to happen where children work individually through assignment cards or work sheets. As one among a variety of learning devices these have their place, but where they are used widely on an individual basis this limitation should be recognised.

10.11 The teacher's role should be one of planned intervention, and his purposes and the means of fulfilling them must be clear in his mind. Important among these purposes should be the intention to increase the complexity of the child's thinking, so that he does not rest on the mere expression of opinion but uses language in an exploratory way. The child should be encouraged to ask good questions as well as provide answers, to set up hypotheses and test them, and to develop the habit of trying out alternative explanations instead of being satisfied with one. This is unlikely to be managed easily in the full class situation, where the teacher has an obvious problem. If he allows the articulate to dominate he is doing nothing for the less articulate. If he tries to draw the latter into public participation they will often fail and their confidence will suffer further. Small group work, on the other hand, provides the security which encourages the less articulate to claim a greater share of the exchange. It is important that the teacher should spend time with each of the small groups to guide the language into fulfilling its purpose. "Guidance" is not used here in the sense of dominant intervention; indeed receptive silence is as much a part of it as the most persuasive utterance. The teacher has first to be a good listener, letting his genuine interest act as a stimulus. His questions will encourage the pupils to develop or clarify points in their thinking, or take them beyond it into the contemplation of other possibilities. We must not give the impression, however, that this is a simple matter and that there are no problems. The work of Sinclair and his colleagues has suggested that the reason children are not encouraged to ask questions is that so often they are placed in a non-initiating role. Moreover, as we have already pointed out, they are inevitably aware that there is something artificial about an exchange where the teacher's part is to evaluate their contribution and where he knows in advance what they are likely to say. These inhibiting factors cannot simply be wished away. The teacher must devise situations in which the pupils will naturally adopt the kind of behaviour he wants to encourage. In other words, he must structure the learning so that the child becomes positively aware of the need for a complicated utterance, and is impelled to make it. In this way the teacher's skilled and carefully controlled intervention is a valuable means of extending his pupils' thinking and making new demands upon their language. We have suggested that in primary schools the organisation of the work often makes it relatively easy for the teacher to arrange this kind of participation and that in the secondary school the picture is more complicated. Many English and humanities teachers plan such opportunities, but there are lessons in other subjects where no such flexibility is at work. We urge in a subsequent chapter that the role of language throughout the curriculum should be an important consideration in secondary schools. The child's need to organise knowledge through language should be recognised in all subjects.

10.12   When children bring language to bear on a problem within a small group their talk is often tentative, discursive, inexplicit, and uncertain of direction; the natural outcome of an encounter with unfamiliar ideas and material. The intimacy of the context allows all this to happen without any sense of strain. In an atmosphere of tolerance, of hesitant formulation, and of co-operative effort the children can 'stretch' their language to accommodate their own second thoughts and the opinions of others. They can 'float' their notions without fear of having them dismissed. Larger and more formal contexts make different demands, and the child should learn to be able to cope with these. The exploratory dialogue of the small group will obviously not serve when the pupil is presenting ideas to the whole class. For one thing the situation affords less security, since what could be chanced with the other members of a group of six will be less acceptable to a class of thirty. Tentativeness has to be replaced by an explicit sense of direction, and the pupil has to organise his thought for the benefit of a variety of listeners, whose attention he must try to hold. He has to think beyond his immediate words and be prepared to elaborate, since the larger group may seek further information where the small group would be content with what is immediately available. The two activities should be related, the one arising from the other in a purposeful way. Some small group work should have as its end a sharing of its conclusions with the whole class. This will impose upon it the need for shaping and organisation, and decisions as to how the material can be most effectively presented. Presentation can take many forms; it may be written, visual, or dramatic, or it may be through 'planned dialogue', with members of the group publicly exchanging views and afterwards summarising their conclusions. Some pupils may wish to make up a tape recording, supporting it with a film-strip they have made themselves. Easy-loading cameras and battery-operated portable tape recorders should be readily available for this purpose. If children want to incorporate into their main tape the interviews and sounds they have recorded outside the school they should have tape-copying facilities. In short the whole programme should have proper resources. The children must be able to feel that their efforts have had a real purpose and have been taken seriously. A good deal of the oral work we saw in schools suffered from a lack of contact with reality in the sense that it did not carry this conviction of real purpose. Its air of contrivance was apparent to the children themselves, and since their language was answering to no real need beyond that of an elaborate exercise it had an artificial restraint about it. This was particularly true of the weekly period devoted on lecturettes, 'formal' debates, and mock interviews.

10.13   There is a place for all these activities at some time or another, and the short talk has a particular claim. But all too often they have no relationship to the rest of the work and they lack context and support. Moreover, some of them are so organised that the majority of the class are passive listeners throughout the period. An example is a lesson we saw where a class of thirteen year olds was having mock interviews for a job. The teacher sat at his desk representing the employer, the pupil facing him with her back to the class. Only half the resulting dialogue could be heard, and the rest of the class had no opportunity for participation of any kind. The following diagram represents the pattern of voluntary participation observed in another lesson, where the teacher was attempting to involve as many pupils as possible in a class discussion:

Diagram 9

PATTERN OF PUPIL PARTICIPATION IN A CLASS DISCUSSION

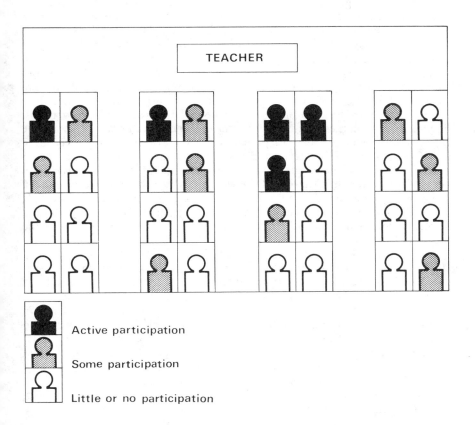

Active participation

Some participation

Little or no participation

It is at least possible that diagrams from a larger sample of English lessons devoted to 'discussion' would produce a similar pattern. In another school each child in a class of eleven year olds was giving a lecturette on a subject chosen by himself. The time for preparation was minimal and many of the children faltered to a halt without filling their allotted span. The feeling of contrivance was increased by the fact that each child had afterwards to submit to a public criticism and was allotted a grade by class vote.

10.14   The most successful example of this activity we encountered was where the children in a 'remedial' group were presenting what amounted to a series of demonstrations with commentary. They had about them all the raw materials of their interests and talked fluently as they handled them. One boy had constructed a model horse which he fitted with bridle, saddle, etc. in the process of his talk. All this was the outcome of the skill and enthusiasm of the teacher and was a natural element of the flow of work rather than a staged event. It is important to note that the children were being themselves, not obliged to play roles, or to see the situation as different from what it was in reality, or to imagine anything that was not the case. There is often great excitement and high motivation in simulation, role-playing, and constructing imaginary situations, but activities based on actualities ought not to be neglected. For some children, including the less confident and less gifted, such work can provide a firm base from which to undertake expeditions into imagined worlds. In one school we saw a class absorbed in a project which involved all the activities to be found in the formal 'speech lesson', but provided them with a context that gave them meaning. The children were asked to study the problem of the siting of a new airport and produce their solutions. The teacher had planned it meticulously, producing photographs, documents, and large-scale maps. Within their groups the pupils played the roles of interested parties and prepared for these roles by tape-recording conversations with a number of local people, e.g. museum curator, planning officer, and shopkeepers, and by writing personal profiles. All the group activity culminated in a sharing of the work, in which some pupils gave talks, some were interviewed, and others presented round table discussions. Throughout the project they had been given the opportunity to test hypotheses and solve problems and at the same time to project themselves into the feelings of others.

10.15   This capacity for projection, this readiness to speculate upon experience beyond one's own, is one of the great values of literature, and of talking about literature. Through talk about personal experience, and its objectification in books and stories, the child is able not merely to reshape his own but to accommodate that of others. An important task for the teacher is to encourage a view of discussion as a means of enlarging one's own personal world and modifying it to take account of other people's. So much formal discussion at adult level goes no further than the exchange of prejudices, or at the very least of inflexible points of view. Children should learn while at school that discussion is an opportunity to explore and illuminate a subject, not drive home relentlessly one's own personal opinions.

10.16   Some teachers have adopted the kind of approach recommended by the Schools Council Humanities Curriculum Project[6] in setting up discussions on controversial issues. This project was instituted in 1967 and in an evaluation of its effects it was found that statistically significant improvements were recorded on the Manchester Reading Test and the Mill Hill Vocabulary Test. The aim of the project has been to offer to secondary schools and to teachers "such stimulus, support and materials as may be appropriate to . . . enquiry-based courses which cross the traditional boundaries between English, history, geography, religious studies and social studies". Eight themes were illustrated by a great variety of materials—extracts from novels, history, drama, letters, reports, maps, advertisements, film, tape, slides, and other forms of 'evidence':

Education	People and Work
War and Society	Poverty
Family	Law and Order
Relations between the Sexes	Living in Cities

These were intended to lead to a wide range of practical and creative activities, the planning of which produced the opportunities for a great deal of purposeful talk. At the heart of the project was the small group discussion through which the pupils considered the evidence in the packs of materials. In the course of this the teacher was to submit to "the criterion of neutrality". He would take no sides in the controversy but would encourage "rationality rather than irrationality, sensitivity rather than insensitivity, imaginativeness rather than unimaginativeness, tolerance rather than intolerance". These are admirable objectives, and in our visits and our discussions we studied the extent to which they were being realised. We noted that some secondary schools have adopted an approach of this kind to the extent of cutting into the allocation of time for English to make way for it. This is a reasonable practice so long as (a) the pupils' experience is in no respect diminished from that which they would encounter in a normal range of English lessons; (b) the pupils are with teachers of English who understand their language needs and can ensure that the materials and activities are meeting them. We came across situations where these conditions were not being fulfilled and where the language work was lacking in direction. One reason for this was that the teacher sometimes lacked the skill to ensure that the quantity of documentary evidence did not outweigh the quality of expression. Even where this skill was present the evidence seemed sometimes to limit the value of the discussion rather than promote it.

10.17   We believe that those English teachers who have critically examined the relationship between materials and discourse have raised important questions. We also believe that the place of literature in such materials needs careful consideration. Some children are in danger of encountering literature only in the context of social controversy, and only then in the form of extract, short story, or poem. In the nature of things these tend to be chosen for their application to the theme rather than primarily for their quality or their relevance to the child's wider interests and needs. This is a shortcoming of much thematic work on social issues, some of which lacks the advantage of the detailed planning and collection of resources that went into the Schools Council Humanities Curriculum Project. We would be the last to deny the value of relating literature to live issues of human concern; indeed, elsewhere in the Report we urge that very relationship. But it is not the function of literature to provide a kind of social comprehension test; nor to serve as a glib and instant illustration, its true significances left unexplored.

10.18   The Humanities Curriculum Project has done a great deal to draw attention to the ways in which discussion can be inhibited by the 'hidden agenda' of the teacher, made manifest by implicit marks of approval or disapproval, and by questions which lead to passive acquiescence rather than deeper enquiry. Its best exponents deny that the procedural neutrality of the chairman implies abdication of responsibility. Yet fears have been expressed that in less competent hands the role might be interpreted in just this way, and be damagingly negative. The teacher-chairman's role is too complex to be circumscribed by simple notions of impartiality, and the Project, when properly understood, gives clear pointers to that complexity. We have expressed some reservations about the Project as it relates to the teaching of English, but we are in no doubt about its strengths. It is providing a helpful contribution to the growth of understanding about the nature of talk in the classroom, and of the teacher's vital part in developing in his pupils the attributes we have been advocating.

10.19   We move now to the question of listening. One or two witnesses gave it as their opinion that children are poorer listeners now than in the past. It was suggested that there has been a marked deterioration in children's ability to listen to instructions, to the teacher reading, and to radio broadcasts. We question whether there is evidence to support this contention. Opinions on such an issue are bound to be subjective, and only by the application of monitoring procedures could there be any certainty. Experiment has shown that students listening to lectures comprehend only about half the substance of them. The difficulty of listening is commonly underestimated, and it is another aspect of communication that deserves to be better understood. Human attention is limited, and the longer people are required to listen the less effectively they do it. Research findings on the amount of time pupils spend listening may now be out of date, but they have indicated that of the time devoted to listening, speaking, reading and writing, well over half is taken up by the first. Since much of this is purely passive its efficiency is limited. People listen best when they have to take some action upon the information they have received. Where they have the opportunity to reply or to participate through action their attention is stimulated.

10.20   To conclude that most listening is inefficient is to prompt the question: what can be done to improve it? A good deal of attention has been given to this question in the U.S.A., where experiments[7] have been conducted to isolate listening skills and evaluate techniques to improve them. The question is whether training can bring about a discernible improvement. To be persuaded of its value we would need evidence that it succeeds not only in the immediate situation but in the long-term, and that the improvement becomes general and transferable. The American experiments give no assurance of this, and even their short-term gains are open to question. An obvious difficulty of evaluation is that the testing situation itself is likely to influence the individual to try to perform better than he ordinarily does. For instance, it was found in the U.S.A. that the "actual listening behaviour" of a group of adults bore little relation to their test scores. Moreover, many of the listening tests and training programmes are based on the reading aloud of written language, which is certainly not representative of the listening skill the individual needs for the varied activities in which he is daily involved.

10.21   We cannot support the kind of 'listening exercise' which is applied to a whole class, irrespective of individual capacity and need. This device is to be found in some commercially produced kits, where the teacher reads out a passage and the children afterwards answer questions on a work-card. Wherever we saw this being practised it involved the whole of a mixed ability class, and in our view the exercise had little to recommend it. The able children could have been given more demanding listening experience, and the slow learners suffered from having their inadequacies made public. The essential question is whether listening skills can and should be dealt with in isolation. In our view listening ability cannot be regarded as something to be abstracted, remedied, and returned. It is part of a highly complex process in which it is related to the individual situation and to the knowledge and experience of the listener, the nature of his motivation, and the degree of his involvement. We have argued that the teacher should engineer situations designed to extend his pupils' ability to use language for a particular purpose. In the same way he should aim to extend their receptive capacity. To a large extent the two will obviously be interdependent, for when children are working together to an end, listening becomes essential to their success. But we again emphasise that a conscious policy on the part of the teacher is necessary. There may be no evidence to show that formal training procedures are lastingly effective, but there is an equal lack of evidence to suggest that the daily activity of the classroom is in itself sufficient. In our view the ability can best be developed as part of the normal work of the classroom and in association with other learning experiences. But deliberate strategies may be required, for it cannot be assumed that the improvement will take place automatically.

10.22   This has implications for equipment and resources, and we believe that the teacher should have ready access to anthologies of spoken language on tape. These anthologies should consist of language in use in a wide variety of real life situations, or as accurate a simulation of them as can be obtained. Groups of teachers have already shown what can be achieved in the preparation of tapes and transcripts. This kind of activity could be directed to the production of collections of spoken language, supplemented by recorded broadcast material not subject to copyright. In the early stages of development these might go into a centrally held bank maintained at the teachers' centre or by the local authority's audio-visual service. Where possible, however, they should be copied for each school which requests them. Some schools will prefer to build up their own collections. A secondary school and its contributory primary schools might co-operate to produce material that will ensure continuity across the point of transfer.

10.23   Work of the kind we have been describing must be supported by resources on a proper scale. Our survey (see Tables 36 and 37) revealed that many schools do not even have the use of a mains tape recorder for the teaching of English. Small primary schools suffer particularly in this respect. 93 per cent of schools of over 350 pupils used a mains tape recorder, but the figure was as low as 66 per cent in the case of schools of up to 70 pupils. The disparity was even greater in respect of battery-operated portable tape recorders, which we regard as a valuable aid in the development of oral language. The corresponding figures here were 58 per cent and 17 per cent respectively. A child has an equal right to such facilities whatever the size of school he attends. Indeed, it is surprising that there remain so many schools where English teaching lacks these essential pieces of equipment. The survey revealed that one in five of the sample primary schools had no mains tape recorder, while three in five had no battery-operated model. In our view the tape recorder is an indispensable instrument for oral work, and no teacher should be without ready access to one. In our survey of secondary schools we asked whether certain items of equipment were available for the teaching of English. The question was phrased in this way to take account of those schools where the equipment is held centrally and borrowed by departments when required. 98 per cent of schools had a mains tape recorder and 57 per cent a battery-operated portable. The first figure is highly encouraging, though it may mask many instances of difficulty for teachers. To be of greatest value a tape recorder should be ready for use at very short notice. It should certainly not be necessary to have to 'book' it for a particular lesson or send for it over some distance.

10.24 Continuity and development are difficult enough to ensure in children's writing, where the product can be re-examined and compared with earlier performance. They are still more difficult to identify in children's talking and listening, even with the help of a tape recorder to provide the aural equivalent of re-reading. We believe, however, that the notion of continuity and progress is an important one, and that it should be defined as clearly as possible within the teacher's mind. The following are suggested as guidelines to the kind of progression a teacher might hope to develop. They are not intended to be exhaustive, nor to apply to any given age-points, still less to provide finishing lines which every child must be expected to cross:

 (i) from simple anecdote, strung together mainly by co-ordinate syntax, to a shaped narrative, aided by voice qualities, timing, and emphasis;

 (ii) from limited to extended span; not only in the length of utterance, but in the ability to range backwards and forwards over the discussion, with an awareness of the relationship between its parts as it develops. When a pupil can say, at the appropriate point, "Ah, but you said just now that . . .", or "I want to pick up what X said . . .", he is demonstrating this very important quality;

(iii) from simple reiteration by the speaker of his own point of view to an openness to the complexity of the dialogue, so that he is able to modify his own viewpoint to accommodate the contributions of others, and encourage and interpret other opinions as part of a co-operative activity;

(iv) from the concrete to the abstract, the subjective to the objective, the present to the past and future.

In none of these is it a matter of shedding the former condition to adopt the latter, of developing one attribute at the expense of another. It is a matter of extending range, so that the pupil can move confidently within it according to the linguistic and social demands of the occasion, an ability which we believe should characterise the mature sixteen year old.

10.25 It has been the practice for a considerable time for some schools to enter pupils for examinations in spoken English. This facility has been offered by the English Speaking Board and by the Associated Board of the Royal Schools of Music for the past twenty years, and also by the Poetry Society. Our survey showed that 6 per cent of the secondary schools in the sample were represented in membership of the English Speaking Board. During the last ten years all the C.S.E. regional boards have introduced examinations in oral English, and it is also featured in trial English syllabuses for a single examination at 16+. In 1964 an experiment[8] was conducted by the Southern Regional Examinations Board in association with the University of Southampton to study the examining on a large scale of oral English. 450 candidates were divided into four groups, each of which took a different form of oral examination:

1. reading a passage and talking with the examiner.
2. making a short speech or lecture and answering questions.
3. talking to the examiner about a diagram previously studied.
4. participation in group discussion.

The four forms of examination were supported by tape recordings and by an assessment of the candidate's spoken English by his teachers. In its conclusions the study tentatively proposed that method two was the most "natural", rewarding, and successful; method three led to the cultivation of "civilised conversation", and method four measured ability unrevealed in the normal classroom situation. Habits in spoken English could be "sharpened, enriched and disciplined by intelligent and sensitive attention in the classroom and syllabus", and this attention could be focussed by C.S.E.

10.26   There was obvious interest in the possibilities of such examining, for C.S.E. boards have made oral English a compulsory element of their English examination. Some emphasise in their regulations that the examination is not intended as a test of elocution, and candidates are reassured that regional speech will not be penalised as long as it is clearly understandable. In the syllabuses the most commonly represented components are the prepared talk, conversation, and reading aloud. Certain of the boards include in the course work element such optional activities as improvised and scripted drama, debates, tape-recorded interviews, and aural comprehension. There are marked contrasts between some of the syllabuses. For example, the Associated Lancashire Schools Examining Board has a fixed requirement for a prepared talk and reading aloud, plus a straight option between group discussion and a duologue on a given topic. The neighbouring North Western Secondary Schools Examining Board, on the other hand, has no compulsory elements and rests on options from among nine widely ranging activities. It leaves the choice of speech situations to the school, with the provision that candidates should show ability to "(a) transmit ideas and feelings, (b) describe what has been experienced, (c) narrate, (d) present and discuss a point of view". The Middlesex Regional Board's examination consists simply of a group discussion among five or six candidates with an external examiner. The Yorkshire Regional Board requires only that "the test should cover such oral work as might take place during classwork and must include a conversation with the teacher on a topic provided by the candidate". The only G.C.E. "O" level examination in Spoken English at present available is that of the London Board, which gives as its aim "to test articulation and fluency". Its requirements are reading aloud and group and individual conversations with the examiner.

10.27   If C.S.E. Mode 3 syllabuses and the work of the English Speaking Board are added to the above the total represents a considerable volume of testing of spoken English. By no means all teachers are convinced that this is a good thing. We have talked to a number who believe that the concept itself is a questionable one and that all too often artificiality perverts such value as can be admitted. Such comments as the following sum up the misgivings that these teachers feel: "One of my most curious activities each year is helping to conduct a test in conversational English under the directions of my C.S.E. Examination Board. In this the candidate comes into my room to conduct a conversation with me and another 'examiner'; thereafter it is our task to solemnly award him a mark out of ten. Nothing less like a genuine conversational situation could be imagined . . . . Talk as a medium of social intercourse cannot be reduced to the level of an examination mark"[9]. There is, of course, a fundamental dilemma. The examination should assess the pupil's capacity in a natural and unforced way, and when an external examiner is present this is difficult to achieve. Moreover, the very prospect of his presence is likely to lead to rehearsal—even training—for the event, and this increases the artificiality. It is fair to point out that some of the examining boards have gone out of their way to eliminate this. They explain at length, either in the syllabus or in separate leaflets, the need to create an environment in which natural exchange of speech is possible. Some have allowed a good deal of freedom in the choice of activity, and have placed the emphasis on continuous assessment with external moderation. These are conditions also enjoyed by teachers who have devised their own Mode 3 syllabuses. These circumstances give rise in turn to the question: what then is the justification for examining spoken English? There might be an argument for the more formal, externally marked examination. Of course it is "unnatural", but the capacity to talk fluently and confidently in such a situation might itself be an achievement it was felt desirable to record. On the other hand, the further one goes to reduce the examination character of the activity, the more obvious becomes the question: why examine at all? Teachers to whom this question is posed say that the examination acts as an incentive to their pupils. However natural and incidental the continuous assessment, the pupil knows that it adds up to an examination result, and he therefore becomes conscious of the need to improve his speech habits.

10.28   As far as we are concerned there is one dominating criterion. Is an examination syllabus likely to further the objectives which we have outlined in this chapter? Is it likely to promote talk as an instrument for learning and for thinking? Will it help to extend a pupil's command over the varied resources of spoken language? Will it help him to look upon discussion as an activity in which it is as important to interpret and accommodate the view of others as to express his own? Will it develop in him the capacity to move from the concrete to the abstract, the immediate to the distant and the hypothetical? Expressed in this way these are unfair questions, for these attributes, and others we have suggested, are the equal concern of contexts outside the English lesson. They are, in fact, an important objective of the child's total education. The questions have nevertheless to be asked, for an examination which has a specialised concern with speech as such has admitted to itself a particular responsibility. In so far as the examining of spoken English can help to develop these qualities we support it. Where it does not we question its value. In our view it is sound practice for a school to set itself such objectives and then assess the extent to which it is fulfilling them. If it does this by public examination it is more likely to succeed with a Mode 3 syllabus it has devised for itself in such a way that the examination reflects the work and does not distort it. Failing this it will be served best by a Mode 1 syllabus which is sufficiently flexible to allow this essential condition to operate. We believe it is reasonable that certain accomplishments should be expected of a mature sixteen year old. Indeed, implicit in what we have advocated as a set of objectives is the ability, for example, to speak to a theme, to develop an argument, to present a case. What we question is the assumption that formal training will produce it, that 'speaking speech' as an end in itself is the best means of achieving such a purpose. We believe that all language activities should take place in a context where they have real, not contrived meaning. An examination syllabus states a requirement; it does not say how a pupil should be prepared to meet it. Nevertheless, we know from our visits that in many schools the preparation takes the form of set-piece exercises. A great deal of thoughtful work has gone into the preparation of C.S.E. syllabuses, and the boards are to be commended for the lead they have given. Some of them have produced particularly imaginative syllabuses which encourage schools to be equally imaginative in response to them. There remains, however, room for research into the manner in which syllabus and classroom practice interact. Comparative studies and other projects should seek to identify the kind of examination which will encourage the development of oral ability in the manner we have described in this section.

10.29   One valuable service performed by all the teachers involved in devising and administering oral examinations has been to generate interest in spoken language.   There has been intensive study and discussion involving many hundreds of teachers, and attention has been focussed on spoken English with more organised purpose than ever before. Throughout this part of the Report we emphasise the importance of the teacher in the development of children's spoken language. Only if he is well informed about the processes at work will he be able to appraise it and make decisions accordingly on how to extend an individual's repertoire. In Chapter 17 we recommend procedures involving close observation, and we believe that these should continue throughout the middle years. As children grow older the school makes progressively greater demands on their language. The teacher should have an explicit knowledge of the nature of these demands to enable him to help the child who is finding it difficult to meet them. We particularly appreciate the professional concern of those teachers who have had tape-recordings and transcripts produced of their own and their pupils' spoken language activities. These have provided admirable material for study, and we hope that more teachers will take advantage of this means of studying language in action. Such records provide a stimulating basis for discussion by groups of teachers in in-service and development work. We believe the teacher has an important role to play in research in this field, and the following are some examples of the topics of study that need to receive attention:

(i) the effects of school and classroom organisation on the pupils' language behaviour;

(ii) the formulation into a coherent body of advice of the intuitions of teachers who are skilful at conducting discussions. This is a subtle role, and one that should receive more detailed study to identify its characteristics. Teachers who fulfil it successfully generally have a well-developed body of intuitions. They are good chairmen, not in the sense that they can control an agenda expeditiously, but in the less explicit sense that they can bring the best out of the participants, raising the level of performance of each;

(iii) the comparative achievements of small groups of pupils talking together (*a*) to a brief given by the teacher (*b*) without guidance;
the most productive relationship between small-group and large-group work;

(iv) the relationship of children's oral language ability to their reading and writing;

(v) the effect of work in small groups of mixed ability on the language development of the less able.

10.30 We welcome the growth in interest in oral language in recent years, for we cannot emphasise too strongly our conviction of its importance in the education of the child. We have discussed at length the part it plays from the pre-school years onwards, its essential place in preparing a child for reading, its function as an instrument of learning and thinking, its role in social and emotional development. In today's society talk is taking on an ever growing significance. People are surrounded by words which are playing upon issues that will affect their lives in a variety of ways. The growth of television has brought these issues into the home in a manner and to an extent essentially different from anything that has been known in the past. As a consumer, a worker, a voter, a member of his community, each person has pressing reasons for being able to evaluate the words of others. He has equally pressing reasons for making his own voice heard. Too many people lack the ability to do either with confidence. Too many are unable to speak articulately in any context which might test their security. The result can be acquiescence, apathy, or a dependence upon entrenched and unexamined prejudices. In recent years many schools have gone a very long way to asserting this aspect of education as one of their most important responsibilities. But there is still a great deal to be done. A priority objective for *all* schools is a commitment to the speech needs of their pupils and a serious study of the role of oral language in learning.

DRAMA

10.31 Drama has an obvious and substantial contribution to make to the development of children's language, and its possibilities in this respect have yet to be fully explored. Before considering these we should make clear what we mean by the term 'drama' in the school context. Essentially, drama is a fundamental human activitity which may include such elements as play, ritual, simulations and role-playing, to give but a few examples. Where the spectators' role becomes dominant in all these activities they can be said to turn into theatre or conscious art form. Where spectators are absent, or where they become so involved that they cease to be spectators, what results is also a powerful form of drama. In the context of education this is sometimes called 'educational', 'creative' or 'free' drama. It is inescapably social, for it is about working in a group, often to solve a problem or make a decision. As a word on the school timetable, then, "drama" can imply either 'educational' drama or theatre, and these two main forms of activity themselves are extremely varied and fragmented.

10.32   Theatre implies performance to an audience and, generally speaking, performance based on a script or on the written word in some form. If we include activities in school clubs and societies it is still the most widespread form of 'dramatic' work in schools. Educational drama covers an extremely wide range of activities, verbal and non-verbal, whose common feature is that they depend very largely on improvisation of various sorts and do not, therefore, depend on the written word. Nor do they consider an audience to be of serious importance. Such activities may turn into the written word, i.e. become scripted, but generally speaking this does not happen unless a performance is envisaged. They may also arise out of the written word. There is still some tendency in schools for these two kinds of practice to be in sharp opposition to one another, even though in a varied and well-planned class drama lesson there will frequently be elements of the first of them. Quite often these two main activities do not exist under the same roof in the same school, or in the philosophy of the one drama teacher. Some teachers will have nothing to do with the scripted play; others take the view that improvisation is a waste of time. Fortunately, this polarisation of view, stemming from earlier training, is less prevalent now than in the past.

10.33   Neither extreme represents an adequate view of drama in schools. The ideal situation is one where the two forms of activity are complementary, so that the written word may become the spoken word and the spoken word the written. Improvisation can provide a physical context for the printed word to come to life. In Act I, Scene 2 of "Antony and Cleopatra" Shakespeare's words appear on the page thus:

Antony:	Fulvia is dead.
Enobarbus:	Sir?
Antony:	Fulvia is dead.
Enobarbus:	Fulvia!
Antony:	Dead.

On the page these words are unfulfilled, almost meaningless, until the whole relationship and all its implications have been fully experienced by trying them out in a convincing setting—physical, social and emotional. It is this 'situational context', as a linguist would term it, that calls for improvisation. There are countless occasions when written words—not just those in a play— are illuminated by being placed in a real context, which drama can help to realise. In its turn improvision can be enriched by the written word. This does not mean that the written word should be imposed upon the activity. It means that it can provide the origin and stimulus, the 'story', the 'situational contexts' for the work in improvisation.   In other words, improvisation can be initiated or given substance by literature, for here may be found the characters, relationships and situations for imaginative work in improvised drama. What is so often lacking in improvisation is stimulus and subject-matter of quality, and literature is an unequalled source of this. We have seen many improvised scenes in which the spontaneous language produced by the children was of limited range and interest, often rapidly degenerating into a trivial slanging match. Unless the stimulus of good writing (whether prose, verse, or drama) is offered from time to time the improvised dialogue will too often derive weakly from playground scraps and casual chats. The extending value of improvisation will then be lost.

Nevertheless, quite apart from its other qualities, it is improvisation, involving the complicated relationships between the written and the spoken word, which seems to us to have particular value for language development.

10.34   At this point it would be as well to emphasise that there are many other sides to drama at least as valuable as the language aspect we are discussing. We do not wish to imply that such activities as movement, dance, mime, and the work which drama prompts in related arts are less important than the more identifiable language activities. At the same time, we do emphasise that teachers should not retreat from language in their improvisation work for negative reasons; for example, because of the difficulties some pupils apparently experience with words.

10.35   There appears to be an important distinction between children's language in improvised drama and that of most of their written work. The one is open-ended, volatile, and incremental in structure and idiom; the other is relatively closed and formalistic. All writing, even when at its most creative, tends in school work to be a patterning of words within which thoughts and feelings have to be contained and ordered. In drama an element of invention lies round every corner, and dialogue has a way of surprising itself so that nothing is predictable. This inventiveness is often revealed by children improvising on a simple domestic theme, such as shopping or planning a holiday, with no more space than a few square yards of classroom floor cleared of the furniture. The group of six year olds who pile up their rostra, fruit boxes, and tables to make their castles or moon rockets are exercising imagination and intellect, physical co-ordination and social sense. And all the time they are using language as their means of bringing it to life. It is worth a thought that the higher up the school one goes the less likelihood is there of such open 'play' happening again, unless it is in the drama lesson. The following figures from our sample show that in the three years from six to nine the opportunities for this have decreased even there:

Table 5

IMPROVISED DRAMA IN CLASSES WITH 6 AND 9 YEAR OLD CHILDREN

	6 year olds	9 year olds
	%	%
In class time only	38	43
In optional time only ...	14	5
In both class and optional time	33	11
Not at all	15	42

10.36   An important aspect of the creativity of speech as distinct from writing is the inexhaustible fund of grammatical forms and idioms available to children from a very early age. If, as Chomsky[10] argues, "the normal use of language is innovative", it becomes a vital principle that the teacher should create opportunities most likely to produce innovation and generate 'natural' language in all its forms. An increasing number of teachers of drama, though they may not be prompted by Chomsky's linguistic theories, do in fact see their work as productive of such language. They would add that it helps to establish confidence in social intercourse, as well as familiarity with a variety of speech forms. They devise what might be described as a concentric series of situations. These vary from the known and the readily observed, such as family situations, to a wide range of less familiar situations, in which the pupils are led to resort to unfamiliar language patterns to suit the roles they are playing. Drama thus has the capacity for sensitizing the ear for appropriate registers and responses. It encourages linguistic adaptability, often accustoming the children to unfamiliar modes of language. What is said in drama will belong to a particular context of situation, which may take the form of a quarrel, a discussion among equals, persuasion, provocation or some similar language activity. By playing out roles and situations of this sort, some close to and some remote from his own experience, a child is using language for the development of his whole personality as well as for exploring personalities other than his own. And it must be added that the opportunity for fantasy roles, such as heroes, spirits, and monsters, usually through mythology, is at least as important as acting out the more familiar themes from everyday life.

10.37   The best of improvised drama can bring out unsuspected resources in children whose work in written English may not be promising. This is especially true if the stimulus material is well chosen for the language possibilities it contains. Owing to the difficulty of transcribing improvised speech in school drama, not many examples are readily available, but a good illustration occurs in the D.E.S. Drama Survey[11] of 1968. Here, some primary school children had been studying effects of the plague on a village in the 17th Century, and they improvised for 40 minutes on the story of a woman accused of being a witch.

10.38   The good teacher of drama, like the good teacher of any subject, needs to be able to say what he means by progression, not only from one kind of activity to another, but from one year to the next. Whether he regards himself as a teacher of English or more exclusively as a drama specialist, language cannot be denied an important place in his educational philosophy. His criteria of competence may differ from those of the English specialist, but the activities of the two cannot be divorced from one another without loss to both. Although drama offers scope for social language which is characteristically unplanned and open-ended, many teachers find it profitable to move from this into written English. The very young children in particular gain from such a transition; a common illustration would be the poems and stories produced by infant school children following dramatic improvisation on the themes of Hallowe'en or Guy Fawkes. Teachers claim that the quality of the writing gains in honesty and liveliness where drama has been a starting point, notably where it has been included in an integrated studies course of any kind. History, religious education and social studies, indeed all subjects, can benefit from a dramatic realisation of people and situations; and this will be as real to the pupil in terms of speech as in the feeling and imagination he is able to bring to it.

10.39   In spite of these arguments, however, it must be said that drama is still often unrecognised as a means of developing language in the secondary school. Though they would certainly regard drama as coming within their province, many English departments, even in large comprehensive schools, are without a member of staff confident enough or interested enough to make it a part of English. Of our sample of 939 teachers working with twelve year olds a mere 21 would regard themselves as trained drama specialists, either through a main course at a college of education or through a teaching qualification at a professional drama school. Of the 1,052 working with fourteen year olds, 26 had such a qualification. The survey also showed that opportunities for improvised work diminished sharply between the two agepoints, while the use of a printed text increased. The average weekly time on improvisation at fourteen was less than a third of that at twelve, and the time for work from a printed text had doubled.

10.40   Interesting developments are occurring in C.S.E. and "O" level, and the number of C.S.E. Mode 3 examinations has continued to grow. In the words of one county English and Drama adviser this has "already given drama teachers a much needed edge to their work". We welcome the growth in opportunities that this could promise, especially if it results in more experience of drama for older secondary school pupils. We do, however, have one important reservation. In devising the Mode 3 syllabuses a number of teachers are placing heavy emphasis on the 'history of theatre', with an undue weight on the learning of facts completely detached from any practical work. It would be unfortunate if a quest for 'academic respectability' for the subject led to an increase in syllabuses of this type. In our view the greatest value to be gained from the development of examination work would be in expansion of the kind of complementary activity described in paragraph 10.33.

10.41   Whatever view is taken of improvised drama by heads of English departments, there is too rarely any constructive or detailed discussion of its place in English teaching. Too little thought has been given to the various possible organisational models by which drama can be incorporated into a school timetable. We believe that every secondary school should examine such fundamental questions as the following, in relation to its own circumstances:

(i)   Should drama be a separate subject with its own department? If not, should it be taught by drama specialists within an English department, or by all English teachers? Is there greater value in a combination of both policies? (Our survey showed that 10 per cent of secondary schools in the sample had a separate drama department. 19 per cent of all the schools had a drama studio.)

(ii)   Should it be the policy of the drama or English department to encourage teachers in other subjects to use drama in their work?

(iii)   What language resources does drama call upon in individual pupils, according to their ability, background, etc? What are their speech patterns in the home, at play, and in the classroom, and how can drama be made to benefit these?

(iv)   What areas of language growth are neglected in other kinds of English teaching, and which of these may be regarded as particularly the province of drama?

(v)   Are there differences of criteria in language work from the points of view of drama specialist and English teacher?

(vi)   What is the role of the teacher in improvised drama, particularly in the development of language?

10.42 Some teachers will doubtless feel that our discussion of drama has neglected non-verbal forms of communication and over-emphasised the role of language. We acknowledge the value and high quality of much of this work, but it is our contention that in most schools drama has yet to realise its potential in helping the child to communicate with others, to express his own feelings and thoughts, and to gain confidence in a variety of contexts. Both in its close relation to literature and in its inherent shaping powers for speech, drama is a powerful instrument to this end. It warrants the serious study and professional discussion that are characteristics of those schools which are using it so effectively for this purpose.

REFERENCES

1. D. Barnes *et al*: *Language, the Learner, and the School:* Penguin Education: 1971.
2. J. Sinclair *et al.: The English Used by Teachers and Pupils:* unpublished research report: University of Birmingham.
3. W. Labov: *Phonological Correlates of Social Stratification:* American Anthropology, 66 No. 6(2): 1964.
4. H. Whitehall: *Structural Essentials of English:* (revised edition): Longmans: 1958.
5. *The Certificate of Secondary Education: Trial Examinations—Oral English:* Schools Council Examinations Bulletin No. 11: H.M.S.O.: 1966.
6. See L. Stenhouse: *The Humanities Project: An Introduction:* The Schools Council/Nuffield Humanities Project: Heinemann Educational Books Limited: 1970.
7. E. Pratt: *Experimental Evaluation of a Program for the Improvement of Listening:* Elementary School Journal, Vol. 56: March 1956.
8. *Op cit.* at 5 above.
9. A. Adams: *Free Talk and the Teaching of English:* Spoken English, Vol. 2 No. 2: English Speaking Board: 1969.
10. N. Chomsky: *Language and Mind:* Harcourt, Brace, and Ward: 1968.
11. *D.E.S. Education Survey 2: Drama:* (pp. 12-13) H.M.S.O.: 1968.

CHAPTER 11

Written Language

INTRODUCTION

11.1 We have considered talking and listening, two of the modes in which language is used, and have referred to the use of the spoken language in the special context of dramatic work. In earlier chapters we had much to say on a third, that of reading. We come now to writing, the fourth mode, but before approaching it we need to draw a clear distinction between those four modes on the one hand and another activity often closely associated with them in school, namely the *study* of language. We regard the distinction between *use* and *study* as crucial to any discussion of the place of language in the curriculum. The two are easily confused, since the use of language—for example in reading a difficult text or giving a written account of a complex idea—may be a strenuously 'studious' or thoughtful process. Let us give an illustration of the distinction as we see it. The reading of a paragraph to make out its meaning is an example of the *use* of language. If, however, the reader compares items from a paragraph with items from elsewhere, not to determine the meaning of the original but to make a generalisation about language, then that constitutes a *study*. In order to use language a person has, of course, to apply his knowledge of it. Some of that knowledge may have resulted from study, but much of it will have been picked up in the course of actually using language, and will remain implicit or unspecified. There is no satisfactory evidence to show how far an explicit knowledge of the rules governing language can reinforce an implicit knowledge, or substitute for it. This chapter is therefore based on the following premises:

(1) A child learns language primarily by using the four modes of talking, listening, writing and reading in close relationship with one another.

(2) Curiosity about language is widespread among children and enables them to engage successfully in occasional studies or linguistic 'experiments' arising out of their reading, writing, listening, and talking. The teacher encourages this curiosity and seizes the opportunity of pursuing some general question about language as it arises from usage, collecting and organising further examples for the purpose of answering the question. Studies of this kind may develop an experimental attitude towards language and provide a method of enquiry which helps pupils solve their own problems of language usage as they meet them.

(3) These *ad hoc* studies may in favourable circumstances, for example with older pupils, lead to *systematic* language studies. The value a pupil gains from these lies in the grasp of principles that may affect his understanding of himself and other people, rather than in any direct effect upon his language performance.

(4) Explicit rules and facts about language, that is to say the outcomes of other people's studies, have direct practical value to a pupil when (a) they solve particular problems in the tasks he is engaged on, or (b) he is able to reconstruct for himself the analysis that led to the rule.

WRITING

11.2 Writing has always been accorded a high prestige in our educational system, and this is due in large part to its traditional use as a means by which students put on record what they have learned. Written examinations have contributed to this emphasis, since they became the principal medium for judging achievement in most subjects of the curriculum. One result has been that until recent years spoken language has received relatively little attention. Another has been that most of the writing required of pupils is for purposes of record or assessment. A recent research study[1] on writing in the secondary school revealed that over 80 per cent of the written work in some subjects was judged to have been carried out for test purposes. In English itself the figure for the first year was 6 per cent but by the seventh year it had risen to 41 per cent. In junior schools in the past, the demands of the eleven plus examination often led to restrictions upon the kinds of writing the children were asked to produce. The removal of selection tests has undoubtedly expanded the range. What is open to question is whether this expansion has been as far-reaching as is sometimes believed.

11.3   It has, of course, long been the practice of most junior school teachers and secondary school English teachers to give their pupils opportunities for 'personal writing'. This is a loose term which distinguishes the writing from those 'impersonal' uses by which knowledge is acquired and recorded, and it ranges from the autobiographical to the fictional. The form that has attracted most attention is that which has become known as 'creative writing', a term which has acquired emotive associations and has sometimes polarised attitudes. Applied to the teaching of English it is a term of comparatively recent origin. In the Hadow Report of 1926 literature was described as "great creative art", but that was the only use of the word in the five pages devoted to English. It was in fact in the visual arts that teachers first discovered that children could express their individual responses to experience without first acquiring techniques by deliberate practice. It is perhaps surprising that a similar discovery in respect of writing should have come so much later in this country, since there was always plenty of evidence that children learn to speak without deliberate teaching and often achieve a high degree of fluency before coming to school. The discovery of spontaneity led in due course, principally in the secondary school, to a number of attempts to provoke or startle children into spontaneous utterance. 'Free writing' and 'creative writing' were names given to procedures that focussed upon the stimulus. This was usually some display or symbolic object to which the pupils would then be asked to respond in whatever way moved them.

11.4   This approach is still a popular one in many junior and secondary school classrooms, and indeed it has found its way into a number of course books. However, there is now more healthy scepticism about the value of this emphasis where it is at the expense of other kinds of writing. In their evidence a group of teachers gave their view of it in these words:

> "Many teachers see 'creative writing' as the high point of literacy. We need to re-think this: over-emphasis on it has distorted a whole view of language. It usually means, in actuality, colourful or fanciful language, not 'ordinary', using 'vivid imagery'. It is often false, artificially stimulated and pumped up by the teacher or written to an unconscious model which he has given to the children. It is very often divorced from real feeling."

This summarises how far removed is some 'creative writing' from what was intended by its early advocates. The truth is, of course, that 'creative writing' has come to mean many things. At its best it is an attempt to use language to recreate experience faithfully and with sincerity. It draws upon all the resources of language inventively yet in a form which is organic with the feelings or experience from which it grew. From this point there is a sliding scale of interpretations. Some teachers encourage children to strive for effect, to produce the purple patch, the stock response. Others have merely adopted the label and apply it to any kind of writing.

11.5   This lack of agreed definition reflects the absence of a clear rationale for the work to which it refers, and this applies equally to such terms as 'free', 'expression', and 'personal'. In our view the main stream of activity in the area of 'personal writing' should arise from a continually changing context, not from a prepared stimulus. This context will be created from the corporate enterprises of the classroom and the individual interests and experiences of the children, cumulatively shared with the teacher and the rest of the group. Moreover, the writing should be constantly developing in its capacity to fulfil the demands this context produces. Wherever spontaneity is exclusively valued this kind of development can be inhibited. Children reach a point where they need new techniques, having run through the satisfaction of their spontaneous performances. If the climate is one which is discouraging to such a concern there is inevitably stagnation. The solution lies in a recognition on the part of teachers that a writer's intention is prior to his need for techniques. The teacher who aims to extend the pupil's power as a writer must therefore work first upon his intentions, and *then* upon the techniques appropriate to them. When this is understood there is every reason why spontaneity should be an element in a great deal of what a child writes. Spontaneity then becomes capable of surviving the transition from artlessness to art; or in plainer terms, of supporting a writer in his search for new techniques appropriate to his novel intentions.

11.6   The difficulty of structuring development in writing, whether in English or in other subjects, has too often been regarded as insuperable, or as likely to lead to mechanical exercises and practices. There has not been enough thought given to the different varieties of English, and to the stages of language development at which children can begin to cope with them. Some categories are too rough and ready to be of much value—the division into subjective and objective writing, for example, or into narrative, descriptive, reflective, and argumentative. These still influence the setting of many "O" level examination papers, and not only the work of the pupils preparing for them but that of others much younger. We believe that a more useful frame of reference is to be found in the categories devised by the Schools Council Writing Research Unit[2]. These consist of three major functions superimposed upon a prior division into two modes of use: 'language in the role of participant' and 'language in the role of spectator'. In its participant role language is a means of getting something done in the world, such as giving instructions, setting up a hypothesis, exchanging information, or solving a problem. By contrast, language in the role of spectator is used to reconstruct past events or construct imagined ones. Putting the distinction in another way, an utterance in the role of participant is a means to an end beyond itself; an utterance in the role of spectator is an end *in* itself, something to be entered into and enjoyed by both writer and reader[3]. The three main categories superimposed upon these are Transactional, Expressive and Poetic. The Expressive is the central one. It is language 'close to the speaker', often the language used by intimates in a shared context. It relies upon a reader's interest in the writer as well as in what he has to say. Because of these qualities it has great educational importance, since it provides the tentative stage through which a pupil's new thinking must pass on its way to the comparative certainty of knowledge. This transitional process represents a continuum from the Expressive to the Transactional, which covers uses of language in the role of participant. As this role becomes more dominant it will demand greater explicitness in the writing, a more pressing concern for accuracy of reference. The other continuum, that between Expressive and Poetic, covers language in the role of spectator. As the demands of this role come to take precedence over the expressive needs of the writer, he finds organisation and formal patterning more and more essential to the fulfilment of his purpose. A gossipy letter and a work of literature are both examples of writing in the spectator role, but one is at the expressive end of the spectrum and the other at the poetic end. At the risk of repetition we must go a little more deeply here into this aspect of writing, and will defer until the next chapter a closer examination of the participant role.

11.7 We have already placed special emphasis on the importance of the pupil's intention as a writer and have suggested that this will arise out of the context of work in the class or the broader one of his out-of-school life, as shared with his teacher and classmates. It is upon these contexts that the teacher works with a view to arousing specific *individual* intentions, sometimes developing them tactfully in talk, and providing technical guidance as it is needed. If a teacher is to succeed in this he will need to learn all he can about the processes involved in writing and above all the satisfactions to be derived from it. In the case of Expressive and Poetic writing this is no easy matter, for the satisfactions lie well below the surface. We attempt here no more than brief indications:

1. When a child writes autobiographically he offers his experiences as a basis for forming a relationship of mutual interest and trust with the reader he has in mind. His satisfaction in the writing, if he succeeds, lies in the rewards of that relationship. Since for the teacher this mutuality is in fact a *professional* relationship and one that is necessary to the kind of teaching and learning we are concerned with here, he will aim at establishing it with every child he teaches.

2. When a child writes in the spectator role, whether autobiography or fiction, he exposes, by what he chooses to write about and the way he presents it, some part of his system of values, and his satisfaction lies in having his feelings and beliefs corroborated or modified. But this exchange is not indiscriminate; since trust between people is based above all on shared values, it is from those with whom the child has this kind of relationship that he derives most satisfaction in the exchange.

3. In offering his feelings and beliefs the child is in fact presenting himself in the light he would like to be seen in; acceptance of what he

offers confirms for him that picture, and this is probably the deepest kind of satisfaction to be had from the whole process. Again, this is not an indiscriminate undertaking; it matters who plays the part of respondent.

4. There is finally the sheer satisfaction of *making*, of bringing into existence a pleasing verbal object. Such satisfaction is likely to increase as the writing moves towards the poetic end of the spectrum.

11.8   We have given a necessarily brief summary of an analysis of writing that goes into much greater detail than it is possible to present here. It is an analysis which could help teachers of all subjects to relate their pupils' linguistic development to appropriate writing demands. We believe that progress in writing throughout the school years should be marked by an increasing differentiation in the kinds of writing a pupil can successfully tackle. The first task for the teacher is one of encouraging vitality and fluency in the expressive writing that is nearest to speech. Children will move out into other modes in their own various ways and at various times that no one can predict in any detail. Their reading interests will be an influential factor, particularly in the early stages. To develop, they must take in written forms of the language and articulate these with their own general language resources, built up by years of listening and speaking. And they must do this in such a way that the whole corpus is within call when they sit down to write.

11.9   There is one further feature of written communication which is no less important in the development of children's competence: the nature of the 'audience' to which the writing is addressed. The writer's sense of audience is one of the ways in which the quality of the communication can be assessed. It has long been realised, and research has confirmed the fact, that by far the largest amount of writing done in schools is explicitly or implicitly directed at the teacher. The remaining small proportion is divided between writing for self and writing for other pupils. Clearly the teacher has the responsibility of providing continuity in his capacity of principal receiver of what the children write. Nevertheless, we believe that writing for other audiences should be encouraged. If a child knows that what he is writing is going to interest and entertain others, he will be more careful with its presentation. Unfortunately, large numbers of children are still denied this assurance, and their work does not emerge from the covers of the exercise book. Children's writing should be attractively displayed, and they should have many opportunities to read aloud what they have written. This practice is most effective when it takes place in small groups as a naturally accepted activity. Where such opportunities are confined to very occasional readings to the whole class they can promote exhibitionism, resentment, or defeatism in some children. We welcome the development to encourage writing for audiences outside the classroom, where certain constraints and criteria offer additional challenges. (An example of this is writing for younger children, as described in para 14.14). By varying the demands the teacher will broaden the range of the pupils' writing experience. They should be faced with the need to analyse the specific task, to choose the language appropriate to it, and to establish criteria by which to judge what they have achieved.

11.10   We suggest in this chapter that there are wide-ranging possibilities for *ad hoc* study of language, and that such study may encourage experimental attitudes towards language in use. It follows from this that the child should not be made to feel that it does not pay to take risks. If a pupil is progressively to develop control in his handling of language he needs opportunity to experiment with new forms, and to do so with security. The teacher's first response to a piece of writing should be personal and positive. Only after responding to *what* has been said is it reasonable to turn attention to *how*. Correction and revision are then of unquestionable value. The best approach to these is for the teacher to go over the pupil's work with him, discussing persistent errors, suggesting solutions where the writing has run into difficulties, and talking over alternative ways of phrasing something. In much of the writing that takes place in school the pupil's first attempt is expected to be the finished article; there is not enough encouragement of the idea of a first draft to be followed by a second, more refined production. Merely to assign a grade to every piece of writing works against the notion of writing as communication. Obviously there will be occasions when the teacher wants to grade a piece of work for a specific reason. He may, for instance, have instructed the whole class in some technical point and feel the need to assess a sharply focussed writing task to follow. Assessment is not in question; it is when it becomes an automatic and unvaried process that it loses its value for both teacher and pupil. When every piece of work receives detailed scrutiny on every occasion teachers are marking against the clock, and this is a further pressure towards confining the corrections to surface points. There is less time for attention to such features as style, choice of word or image, or inappropriate colloquialism. And there is still less for engagement with the subject matter and for such discussion points as "can you find any point at which your main character behaves inconsistently, and explain why?" A useful approach the teacher might adapt to suit his own purposes is that of some C.S.E. Boards, where a candidate is able to offer for evaluation a selected proportion of the work of the past year. What the teacher needs is the time to give a proportion of each pupil's work the kind of close attention we have been advocating.

11.11   In recent years there has been a welcome increase in opportunities for teachers to discuss the assessment of children's written work. This has ranged from the experience of inter-school assessment and moderation in 16+ examinations to the informal study of primary school children's writing in teachers' centres. We should like to see such opportunities taken up more widely, for we have no doubt that the understanding that grows from them can have a considerable influence on the development of children's writing.

11.12   With regard to spelling, which is examined in greater detail in the annex, we believe the most important step the teacher can take is to improve the pupil's confidence in his own capacity. Repeated failure reinforces a poor self-image, and the correction of written work can make matters worse unless its purposes are carefully worked out. Earlier in the chapter it was pointed out that a child should have the opportunity to write for an audience, and that if he knows his writing is to be read with interest by others he will be more careful with its presentation. His experience of writing should not be one that leads him to look upon each assignment as a minor test, the almost certain outcome of which will be a number of spelling corrections to be written out three times. We have suggested that the most effective form of correction a teacher can practise is to discuss with each child the nature of his errors. How much time a teacher can spend with an individual pupil or a small group of two or three depends upon his classroom organisation. This should certainly be such as to allow personal attention for the children who need special support with their spelling. The teacher needs to be able to direct the pupil's attention to the essential features of the word, to accustom him to looking at it "with intent to remember". From this process the pupil's own word list will emerge, and he will be helped to learn those words for which he clearly experiences a need. For example, in one school we visited the children were required in some of their work to produce their first drafts in pencil on paper with a wide margin. The teacher then wrote the correct spelling in the margin as he discussed the piece of work with the child. The child erased his mistakes, substituting the correct spelling, and he was encouraged to do this from memory, having first learned the word. He then cut off the margin and clipped it into his folder of words essential to his own needs. We use the word 'learn' quite deliberately, for when the teacher has discussed the word with the child it is valuable for the directed visual perception to be reinforced in this way. It is a process of look, read, visualise, reconstitute, and reproduce. Clearly there must be no overloading. The teacher has to use his judgment as to which of the errors should receive specific attention, taking account of the child's measure of confidence, his expressed need for particular words, and so on. At the heart of the process is the concentration of attention on the internal structure of words, and this is something that rarely takes place when the conventional mark/correct procedure operates. We believe that in the course of their writing children should acquire a knowledge of the spelling rules and an ability to generalise about words, and that this should be rooted in the curiosity about language that the good teacher arouses. In some schools the mention of spelling rules has come to be regarded as almost heretical, but in our view this is to deprive the children of a valuable support. We were, in fact, encouraged to see schools whose commitment to a lively and imaginative approach to English included a recognition of the need for such a support. Typical was a large comprehensive school whose head of English had included spelling rules in the departmental guidance sheets he and his colleagues produced.

11.13   In the secondary school there is the additional complexity that the pupil is now writing for a number of different teachers and with an increased range of constraints. There are the words he needs for his own purposes but also the words the subject teacher requires him to have, and the uncertainty can be sharply increased within a matter of weeks. This calls for a high degree of patience and co-operation on the part of the staff. It is a common experience among English teachers to be constantly receiving criticism about the pupil's standards of writing in other subjects, and spelling is often the focal point of the censure. We believe that language production is a collective responsibility and that the subject teacher should be willing to co-operate by observing and recording in a way which will help his colleague. This in turn calls for an agreed policy based on an understanding of the factors at work in spelling weakness, a policy which will produce consistency of response to errors. Once a practice of consultation has been established the English teachers will be in a position to take continuing account of the words the pupil needs in other contexts. If the child is to be helped to an image of himself as a competent speller this co-operation and consistency of approach are essential.

11.14 In summary we must emphasise that in our view a systematic approach to spelling should be placed firmly in context. Any work on spelling should emerge from this context and its results should in turn become a contribution to it. System and purpose need to go together. When the child has been helped to perceive the essentials of the word he will find it easier to memorise and can go on attempting the word until he has assimilated it. But it will be his own word; one which answers to a real purpose or is likely to recur constantly in his writing. What is needed in attention to spelling is a sense of perspective. We believe it should be part of the fabric of normal classroom experience, neither dominating nor neglected. The climate should be such that the child has a motive for spelling correctly, and he should then be helped to it by an effective system.

LANGUAGE STUDY

11.15 For many people language study means the study of grammar, and this word featured prominently in the evidence, particularly the evidence of those witnesses who felt that standards of writing had fallen. What *are* the effects of grammar teaching on the ability to write? How much grammar should be taught, at what ages, and how? What, for that matter, is *meant* by grammar in the sense intended by those who suggest there should be more of it? In our discussions with teachers it became obvious that the term was often being used to include sentence construction, précis, paragraphing, vocabulary work, punctuation, and more besides. 'Grammar' has, of course, a highly specific and technical meaning, which we might roughly characterise as an analytical study of those formal arrangements of items in a language by which utterances have meaning. What is under discussion here, however, has a wider concern. It is the degree to which language *study* of several kinds, and practice arising from study, can be effective in improving a pupil's ability to *use* language in general. It is a central recommendation of this chapter that the teacher should take deliberate measures to improve his pupil's ability to handle language. The point at issue is what form these should take, and this is a question to which we have given much consideration.

11.16 The traditional view of language teaching was, and indeed in many schools still is, prescriptive. It identified a set of correct forms and prescribed that these should be taught. As they were mastered the pupil would become a more competent writer and aspire to a standard of 'correctness' that would serve him for all occasions. Such a prescriptive view of language was based on a comparison with classical Latin, and it also mistakenly assumed an unchanging quality in both grammatical rules and word meaning in English. In fact the view still prevails. Letters to the press are rarely more fierce than when complaining of the way in which a particular word is being misused or used in a new sense. 'Brutalise' and 'hopefully' are two recent examples, and there are many precedents. Dr. Johnson tried to eliminate 'fun', 'clever', 'budge', and 'mob'; and it is ironical that the very word Swift used for fixing the language in a permanent and authorised condition was "ascertain", which has completely altered its meaning since his day. One may regret some of the changes, which can deprive the language of valuable distinctions. One may decide to resist them and insist on keeping to existing forms, and this is natural and understandable. But if change is to occur it will in due time occur, since growth and change are essential characteristics of a language. Writing less than a hundred years ago Trollope used the past participle "gotten"; if it were uttered today it would be rejected as an intrusive Americanism. As one commentator has colourfully put it: "The living language is like a cowpath; it is the creation of the cows themselves, who, having created it, follow it or depart from it according to their whims and needs". Montaigne said as much in the 16th century, when he remarked that only a fool would fight custom with grammar. Many of the rules in use today were invented quite arbitrarily by grammarians in the 17th and 19th centuries, including the embargo on the split infinitive and on the ending of a sentence with a preposition. Before the 18th century they are both to be found in common use, along with other constructions proscribed today. John Donne regularly split infinitives, and Burns was no stranger to the practice. In a letter to "The Times" in 1907, Bernard Shaw wrote: "There is a busybody on your staff who devotes a lot of time to chasing split infinitives. Every good literary craftsman splits his infinitives when the sense demands it. I call for the immediate dismissal of this pedant. It is of no consequence whether he decides to go quickly, or quickly to go, or to quickly go. The important thing is that he should go at once." And, of course, there is Churchill's famous note in which he expressed his impatience with those who always struggled to avoid ending sentences with prepositions: "This is the sort of English up with which I will not put".

11.17   We give these examples not to suggest a free-for-all, but to put prescriptive attitudes in perspective. One of the disadvantages of the prescriptive approach to language teaching is its negative aspect. Ironically, many of these manufactured additions to the language took on a special status in school text-books, which often put the emphasis less on knowing what to say than on knowing what to avoid. Pupils not too certain of their ability with language would thus be looking for the gins and snares, to the equal detriment of their confidence and their writing. This kind of teaching has often inhibited a child's utterance without strengthening the fabric of his language. It has nurtured in many the expectation of failure and drilled others in what they already knew.

11.18   More fundamental, however, is the question of whether exercises in themselves and by themselves will improve the child's ability to write. Since the beginning of this century a good deal of research has been devoted to this subject, and though many believe its results to be inconclusive some of the individual experiments have carried much conviction. One[4] such study is particularly worth singling out for attention. One class in each of five schools was taught formal grammar over a period of two years, a corresponding class in each school having no grammar lessons during that time. The latter took instead what might be described as a 'composition course', consisting of practice in writing, revising, and editing, and an inductive approach to usage. At the end of the period both groups were given a writing test and a grammar test. In the writing test the 'non-grammar' classes gained significantly higher scores than the 'grammar' classes, and overall there was no effective correspondence between high scores in the grammar test and improvement in writing.

11.19   We do not conclude from this that a child should not be taught how to improve his use of language; quite the contrary. It has not been established by research that systematic attention to skill and technique has no beneficial effect on the handling of language. What has been shown is that the teaching of traditional analytic grammar does not appear to improve performance in writing. This is not to suggest that there is no place for any kind of exercises at any time and in any form. It may well be that a teacher will find this a valuable means of helping an individual child reinforce something he has learned. What *is* questionable is the practice of setting exercises for the whole class, irrespective of need, and assuming that this will improve every pupil's ability to handle English. What is also open to question is the *nature* of some of these exercises, where pupils are asked to fill in the blanks in sentences, convert masculine into feminine forms and singular into plural, insert collective nouns and give lists of opposites. Examples we saw included such tasks as: Change all words of masculine gender to words of feminine gender in "*Mr.* Parker's *father*-in-law was a bus *conductor*"; and: add the missing word in "As hungry as a . . . . . . ", "As flat as a . . . . . . ". It would be unjust to say that all the exercises in current use take this trivial form; but it is certainly true that an unwarrantably large number of them demand little more than one-word answers and afford no opportunity for the *generation* of language. Most give the child no useful insight into language and many actually mislead him.

11.20   In our visits to schools we found that the teaching of language through weekly exercises was still commonly to be found at all age levels, but particularly in the primary school. In some primary schools organised on 'informal' lines children would take an assignment card from the language corner for this purpose. In the main such work was not a reinforcement of something newly learned in the course of some other classroom activity, but a task performed outside any context which would give it meaning. Our questionnaire results show the extent of certain kinds of language work at the four age points: 6, 9, 12, 14. These are reproduced in tables 56, 57, 96 and 97, and it will be seen that they cast some doubt on the popular belief that primary schools spend very little time on 'formal' language teaching. For example, we asked whether during the week of the survey any planned attempt was made to extend the children's vocabulary by means of exercises. The answer "yes" was given by 67 per cent of the teachers of the nine year olds, and 50 per cent of those of the six year olds. For reasons explained in the statistical appendix to the survey it is not possible to draw direct comparisons between primary school and secondary school data. Nevertheless, it would seem that less time is spent in the secondary school on 'formal' language work. For instance, in the week of the survey only 21 per cent of the twelve year olds and 19 per cent of the fourteen year olds gave any time to vocabulary exercises. The figures for grammar exercises were 24 per cent and 10 per cent respectively and for punctuation exercises 16 per cent and 10 per cent respectively. In our discussions with secondary English teachers we found a good deal of uncertainty about the teaching of language. Some regarded language improvement as a by-product of the talk, writing, and literature which formed the core of their work; and they gave it no specific attention. Others set aside at least one period a week for it, usually working from a course book. A substantial number considered that the express teaching of prescriptive language forms had been discredited, but that nothing had been put in its place. They could no longer subscribe to the weekly period of exercises, but they felt uneasy because they were not giving language any regular attention. It seems to us that this uncertainty is fairly widespread, and that what many teachers now require is a readiness to develop fresh approaches to the teaching of language.

11.21   We believe that extensive reading and writing are of prime import- ance for language growth but that they should be supported by explicit instruction. We cannot accept that the development of language can be left to chance, on the principle that a 'relevant moment' will occur. There was an interesting comment on this practice in a report[5] by a visiting team of American educationists. In 1968 they spent 164 days observing the teaching of English in 42 British secondary schools, and on this issue they remarked:
"Most (i.e. teachers of English) suggested that whatever direct instruction in how to write might be needed by pupils could be presented by teachers during classroom writing lessons and could be based on actual experience in written communication. Yet hour after hour of classroom observation failed to reveal many efforts to provide such direct help."
In some of our own visits to secondary schools we formed a similar impression. It was not uncommon to find the despairing comment "Your punctuation must improve" on the writing of pupils who seemed to have received little or no specific instruction in it. Though in every instance the need should create the opportunity, the teacher ought to ensure that in a given period of time the pupils cover certain features of language, and for this purpose he might find a check-list useful. We believe these features should certainly include punctuation, some aspects of usage, the way words are built and the company they keep, and a knowledge of the modest collection of technical terms useful for discussion of language. We must emphasise, however, that everything depends upon the teacher's judgment and his ability to ensure that what is taught meets the needs of the pupil in his writing. Explicit instruction out of context is in our view of little value.

11.22   It is understandable that there should be many teachers who want to work through a series of items from a text book, for it gives the feeling of reassurance that progress is being made along a measurable line that will lead to total language competence. We have given our reasons for questioning this approach, but we have also made it clear that we are not opposed to the notion of levels of achievement, or of objectives described in terms of specific skills. It is certainly unrealistic to attempt to tie particular competencies to given age points; and it is not rewarding to treat language like a set of building bricks. But it *is* reasonable to set clear targets which the children recognise to be achievable. With this in view the teacher should determine appropriate language objectives, devise his own ways of fulfilling them, and assess the extent to which they have been achieved. Experienced teacher witnesses were critical of the kind of language teaching we have been questioning; but they were of one mind in their concern for recognisable progress in a child's command of language. As one head of department put it: "I would quarrel with the philosophy that problems sort *themselves* out by continued and increased exposure to books and good English".

11.23   The important thing is to define carefully what is meant by targets of achievement. It cannot mean that all the children in a class advance from one step to another at the same pace and at the same time. There is evidence of a general relationship between age and linguistic maturity in a pupil, as one would expect, but there is no simple correlation. Recent research[6], carried out at Nottingham University, suggested the following line of development: "The advance towards linguistic maturity is modest but steady over the first Junior school year, quickening somewhat in the second year, accelerating markedly in the third, and slowing to something like the first year pace in the fourth". Other evidence indicates a further acceleration in the first year of the secondary school, followed—on some variables, at least—by a plateau in the second year. The important thing to note is that the developmental pattern on a variety of language measures is not a simple one. Thus, although there is a general advance over the years, there are considerable variations, not only from one pupil to another but from one feature of language to another. It follows from this that to expect a whole class to maintain a steady and uniform advance along a line of linguistic achievement is unrealistic. The class lesson certainly has its part to play, but in response to particular situations, not as a timetabled substitute for a more comprehensive policy. The parts of speech are commonly made the subject of this kind of clockwork attention. It is perfectly reasonable that by the end of the middle years children should know about the parts of speech, but they should encounter them in the course of looking at language in a living context. For instance in the talk that precedes and surrounds the children's own writing the teacher might look with them at how another piece of writing has achieved its effects. In doing this he will not be offering models for imitation but getting pupils to look closely at language and what it can do.

11.24   If one were to apply this kind of purposeful attention to say, the following passage from "Martin Chuzzlewit" the pupil would learn with far greater effect what an adjective does than he would be underlining it in an exercise: "The mistress of the Blue Dragon was in outward appearance what a landlady should be: broad, buxom, comfortable, and good-looking . . . She had still a bright, black eye, and jet black hair, was comely, dimpled, plump and tight as a gooseberry". Or from the following anonymous passage, where the writer has carefully produced changes in the values of the adjectives by the way he has placed them in their context: "His plump hands waved persuasively and his smooth face took on a comfortable expression as he explained how he had made a handsome profit from the famine". "Plump", "smooth", "comfortable", and "handsome" normally have favourable connotations, but these positive values slip away from them in this context. The child who could recognise the connotative change in "plump" and "comfortable" in these two contexts would have learned something of much greater value than a label.

11.25   What we are suggesting, then, is that children should learn about language by experiencing it and experimenting with its use. There will be occasions when the whole class might receive specific instruction in some aspect of language. More frequently, however, the teacher will operate on the child's language competence at the point of need by individual or small group discussion. As a background to all this activity he should have in his own mind a clear picture of how far and in what directions this competence should be extended. This is best considered in terms of a succession of developments in the handling of language, all of which are likely to arise when a particular situation in writing creates the demand for them. The teacher should then provide for the range of writing experience to encompass these needs, and in doing this he should naturally take account of the pupil's capacity. The novel features in the task and the language it demands can be explored in discussion with the individual or the group, and supporting examples collected and worked upon. The child should thus be led to greater control over his writing, with a growing knowledge of how to vary its effects. This can happen only if the teacher has a clear understanding of the range of language experiences necessary to develop this control. Knowledge of this kind will help him design experiences which lead the pupils to experiment with language over a widening spectrum.

11.26   During recent years there has been a growing interest among teachers in the application of linguistics to English teaching. Fortunately, this has not taken the form of an attempt to introduce a "new grammar" into the classroom, as happened in the U.S.A. Many American educationists embraced the "new grammar" as somehow more likely to succeed than the old; and there was much discussion on the relative merits of structural* and transformational* grammar for high school students. The following is an extract from the English syllabus of a large high school we visited: "Of all the grammars available we have deliberately opted for Transformational -Generative Grammar (hereafter T.G.) as the one that gives us the most plausible 'platform' upon which to stand . . . T.G. is incomplete, but it is evolutionary, seeking to nurture traditional grammar scholarship, to provide a bridge from the past to the present, to make English come alive for the teacher and the student". But the majority of American teachers to whom we talked felt there was no useful place for this kind of work. Many had tried it and found it to be no more successful in improving their students' English than the grammar teaching it had replaced. In our view linguistics has a great contribution to make to the teaching of English, but not in this form. As one American[7] has expressed it: "The study of language is inseparable from the study of human situations . . . Is there anyone here who truly believes that it matters to anyone but a grammarian how you define a noun, or what the transformational rules are for forming the passive voice, or how many allomorphs there are of the plural morpheme?" We believe that the influence linguistics can exercise upon schools lies in this concept of the inseparability of language and the human situation.

11.27   It is this approach which provides the basis for the programme initiated by Professor Halliday in 1964 under the auspices of the Nuffield Foundation. The aim was to relate linguistics and English teaching, and after extensive trials a collection of materials was published as "Language in Use"[8] in 1971. There are 110 units, each centred upon a particular topic and

*See glossary.

providing an outline for a sequence of lessons. These topics are grouped under ten themes, which in turn are clustered under three main headings: Language—its nature and function; Language and individual man; Language and social man. Though the units were originally intended for the upper secondary years they are to be found in use throughout the 11–18 age range, and in colleges of education and of further education. The principle of the programme is to some extent like that of geographical and botanical field work, in that it involves studying 'specimens' of language. These might include the form of the language in which a policeman interviews a witness of an accident, or in which headlines are written, or in which the meteorologist gives his forecasts. The pupils will listen to tape-recordings, take evidence from a variety of people, study various texts, predict the occurrence of words in certain contexts, and so on. In these and similar analytical activities discussion plays a large part, involving work in groups of varying size. A number of the units include complementary activities in which pupils are asked to use their own language to create examples of the mode or register being studied. For instance, they might produce a letter to a newspaper complaining about the way in which other people use language, or a short sketch depicting two people in a professional relationship to one another, or a written record of a telephone conversation. We visited a lesson where a group of pupils of relatively low ability were completing a programme of work on regional speech; they were 'performing' some very creditable dialogues they had themselves written in a variety of dialects. In another school an English teacher had directed the pupils' attention to a series of separate items in a radio programme. Under his guidance, but without excessive direction, the class of 14–15 year olds were studying the language used by an eye-witness, an aggrieved victim of bureaucracy, and an enthusiast for an unusual hobby. They were then going on to compile their own pro-gramme, drawing upon their immediate experience and recent encounters.

11.28   It is, of course, up to the individual teacher to add to the assignments in each unit, or to omit from them what does not suit his purpose. The authors make clear that it is left to the teacher to decide "how any particular unit might meet the needs of a class . . . the actual shaping, pacing, and detailed content of the lesson is left in his hands". However, there is an inevitable danger that teachers might work mechanically through the units, and this possibility of misuse has attracted criticism. Where it happens—and there is little doubt that it does—both teacher and taught are working on the mistaken principle that language tasks can be fulfilled on a 'made to measure' basis. Language might come to be seen by some pupils as a series of stereotypes which can be produced to a specification. Unimaginatively used, the programme can be-come divorced from other aspects of English teaching. This has given rise to the further criticism that it does not commit itself to fundamental values; that it remains in essence a training in techniques. There is some justice in these reservations, but the programme makes no bid to provide the total language experience of the pupil in his work in English.

11.29   If used with the same dogged commitment as to a text-book, such materials as "Language in Use" will not fulfil their best purpose. Mediated by a teacher who can turn practical suggestion into imaginative reality, work of this kind has a valuable contribution to make. We have advocated throughout this section that children should progressively gain control over language by using it in response to a variety of demands. They can be helped to do this by studying how it works in various situations, not in any sense of choosing models or opting between stereotypes, but by insight into its richness and infinite possibilities. This will depend upon the teacher's imagination and inventiveness. Above all it will depend upon his knowledge of language and of his equal knowledge of his pupils' individual abilities, needs, and potential.

11.30   Many teachers, however, protest that the greatest constraint upon them in helping children to gain a progressive control over language is the public examination system, because there is so little variety in the demands it makes. This is a complaint of such long standing that it needs some examination itself, especially since there has been more change in the system in the last decade than in the half-century which preceded it.

11.31   Some ten years ago a forthright judgment was delivered on G.C.E. English Language examinations at Ordinary Level:

"We have considered most seriously whether we should advise the cessation of these examinations for educational reasons, as well as for reasons related to the changing demand for qualifications in English Language. We have come very near that conclusion."

This appeared in "The Examining of English Language"[9], the eighth and final report of the Secondary Schools Examination Council. The report was occasioned by "disquiet . . . about Ordinary Level Examinations and their effect on the teaching of English". Despite many changes since 1964 the unease remains, especially as the number of candidates has increased and the system has extended itself, with the introduction of C.S.E., to take in many pupils who handle words less easily. The arguments about the establishment of a Certificate of Extended Education examination have enlarged the area of disquiet. It is, indeed, impossible to dispel it completely. The schools are aware of the demands of higher education and employers for a 'pass' in English, and as long as the right of entry to succeeding stages of education or to particular kinds of employment is geared to the testing system, it is impossible for teachers to brush aside the particular demands of the English Language paper. For the same reason, the Examining Boards must continue to design papers, frame questions, and decide upon assessment procedures which will appear to offer comparable standards from board to board, from year to year. As long ago as 1921 the Newbolt Committee[10] said bluntly: "But for good or ill the examination system is with us. Nothing less than the total abolition of the examination system would serve the turn of those who object to examinations in English, and to make such a recommendation, even if we desired to make it, would be entirely futile."

11.32   The Newbolt Report suggested that examinations should be tests of the power of 'communication' in English rather than tests in grammar, analysis, and spelling. The only compulsory test it was prepared to recommend was one of the ability "to grasp the meaning of a piece of English of appropriate difficulty". The Committee also recommended that "oral examination should be resorted to more frequently" and urged that a reasonable standard of English should be required in all subjects of the curriculum. Two years earlier than the Newbolt Report the Secondary Schools Examination Council had recommended that there should be no separate test of formal grammar; awareness of grammar would be shown in candidates' writing. It also asked for more imaginative and fewer abstract essay subjects, but to no avail. The Council's recommendations, then and later, had no more effect than those produced by the Newbolt Committee. The Council had been set up in 1917 to carry out the Board of Education's new responsibility as a Co-ordinating Authority for Secondary School Examinations. Eight Examining Boards were approved, and the patterns of their papers were established by the early twenties; forty years later, in the early sixties, they had changed little. There was a précis, letter writing, paraphrase, analysis and other grammatical exercises, the correction of incorrect sentences, the punctuation of depunctuated passages and, of course, an essay, the titles of which in 1961 were sometimes indistinguishable from those of 1921.

11.33 Thus, when the report "The Examining of English Language" appeared in 1964 it was after a long period of relatively little change in basic attitudes to testing English. The report set out a number of criticisms, as follows:

the low standard of English among those who passed;
the large numbers entered, and the fact that teaching became a series of practice performances in examination techniques;
the negligible contribution of many of those techniques to the development of writing;
the unreliability of the examinations;
the unsuitability and irrelevance of many essay titles;
marking schemes for continuous writing might encourage teachers to give it less attention in their teaching;
the meagre literary merit of passages set for comprehension, and the trivial questions asked upon them;
the unreality of some of the summarising tasks, such as reduction to 'one third of the original';
questions on the 'correctness' of a particular usage out of context;
grammatical minutiae ("Some of the most eloquently critical of the replies we received from the schools were directed against these questions; we share the view that they are of doubtful utility in any examination of English language and that in their present form they do great harm").

It amounted to a formidable indictment, and in producing it the authors confessed that it was easier to find fault with the existing examinations than to suggest ways of improving them. However, they made the attempt and listed the following suggestions, which were elaborated in detail:

internal examinations with external moderation;
improvements to the existing examinations;
the separation of language and literature;
tests of spoken English.

The speed and eagerness with which the suggestions were seized upon, after such a long spell of torpor, reflected the concern of the teachers and examiners who were making their own re-assessment.

11.34 For the Examining Boards had grown restless on their own account, as can be illustrated by the following comment of the Joint Matriculation

Board made in 1960. "Comment . . . has concentrated mainly on the fact that to accept a pass in English Language at the Ordinary level has proved an unsatisfactory means of ensuring that at entry to a university all students are capable of using the English language with the degree of competence which is essential at that stage. Other universities than the five constituents of the Board are also making the same comment." After the publication of "The Examining of English Language" the Board organised what it modestly described as an experiment in school assessing in English Language. The project set out to devise (a) methods by which pupils could be taught without any direct preparation for any "O" level examination, (b) means of making school assessments which the Board could endorse as indicating that pupils had achieved not less than an "O" level pass standard in their writing and understanding of English. Since its inception the number of schools has increased from 10 to 34. The J.M.B. has also carried out its own enquiry into the reliability of examinations at Ordinary level. Both enquiries had financial support from the Department of Education and Science. We have used these experiments as an illustration because they have been comprehensively documented, but other Boards are conducting or are ready to consider internal examinations which are externally moderated. It is important to add that the Boards have always been willing to consider special syllabuses from schools (and applications from other schools to participate in these syllabuses once approved), but there have never been many applications.

11.35   While the G.C.E. Boards have responded in various positive ways to the criticisms made in the 1964 report, the new C.S.E. Boards have been free, indeed encouraged, to experiment much more widely. In the three years before that report was issued the Secondary School Examinations Council had published four which were concerned primarily with the Certificate of Secondary Education, and with the establishment of new examining bodies for it. The Council's first Examinations Bulletin, "The C.S.E.: some suggestions for teachers and examiners", asked the new Examining Boards to consider what English language examinations should be testing, and offered them a statement on English studies in school:

English, well-taught, should train a sixteen year old secondary school pupil to use the language confidently, appropriately and accurately, according to the circumstances in which it is used. He should be able to speak his own mind, to write what he has thought, and to have a care for the correctness of written and spoken English. He should be able to understand what he reads and hears, to master the ideas and re-state them in his own way. He should have some understanding of the different uses of language, of the language which relates, describes, evokes, persuades, and is the instrument of the creative imagination.

11.36   All fourteen C.S.E. Boards offer three modes of examination, of which the majority of schools take Mode 1, an external examination on syllabuses prepared by the Boards. The Mode 2 and Mode 3 syllabuses, to different degrees, met the 1964 report point that there should be internal examinations with external moderation. These syllabuses are so numerous and varied as to be impossible to summarise in so short a space. The Mode 1 syllabuses themselves vary a great deal, initially in whether they represent

English as a unitary study or whether there are separate 'language' and 'literature' syllabuses, candidates being able to offer both. There have been wrangles over the weighting to be given to unitary syllabuses, with no generally satisfactory solution in sight. The considerable developments the various syllabuses reveal may be summarised in this way:

(i) *Course Work*
All Boards offer opportunities for the presentation of course work, which allows the inclusion of a variety of writing, carried out on a variety of occasions. One Board, in making suggestions for the kinds of work which might be submitted for assessment, has for its eighth example: "Any other work which in the opinion of the candidates or the teacher might help to establish the candidates' ability in English". The very bulk of the work thus offered presents formidable problems of assessment and comparability, but the candidate is judged across a range of his writing. In Mode 3 syllabuses the scope is often wider still, extending to drama, film-making, tapes, and group work.

(ii) *Personal Writing*
Syllabuses which prescribe or permit course work allow a proportion of writing which is an entirely personal response to experience, direct or imaginative. Sometimes papers testing 'composition' also make room for such writing.

(iii) *Comprehension*
In paragraph 11.32 we remarked that the only compulsory test of English language the 1921 Newbolt Committee was prepared to recommend was "a test of power to grasp the meaning of a piece of English of appropriate difficulty". This concept survives in all C.S.E. syllabuses, though it is sometimes subsumed in a larger notion of 'response'. What is preserved is an anxiety that pupils should be able to read and understand, not just the 'sense' but also the feeling, tone, and attitude of the language they meet. And the language which stretches, which exercises them most is the language of literature. The choice of material has sometimes led to criticism from teachers that Boards not only provide the wrong texts but also ask the wrong questions. This is undoubtedly true in some instances, but the Boards are alert to the need to select with great care.

(iv) *Literature*
The Boards have experimented considerably, abandoning set texts, allowing texts to be used in the examination room, and providing a greatly extended list of books from which choice may be made. In particular, much more contemporary writing has been included. Mistakes have been made and some of the books chosen have been juvenile or trivial or not substantial enough for intensive reading. Nor could it be said that the Boards have succeeded universally in setting questions which, as Examinations Bulletin No. 1[11] put it, "are not so general as to be vague, or so obvious as to be anticipated by the text-book and the teacher's note".

11.37   Since 1965 and the first C.S.E. examination, Boards have been trying to meet the criticisms made in the 1964 report and to provide suitable ways of assessing the language competence and performance of children of a particular range of ability. The fundamental importance of some of the approaches that have been tried may be judged by their incorporation into feasibility studies for a common examination at 16+. There has not been time to evaluate them in detail, but it is worth mentioning two studies carried out by the National Association for the Teaching of English soon after the inception of C.S.E. These two, "C.S.E. English: an interim report"[12] and "Criteria of Success in English"[13] are a little outdated in minor detail, but the analysis made in them is still entirely pertinent. To these might be added the pamphlet "English Examined: a survey of "O" level papers"[14], published at the same time. The three together are a most valuable commentary on the problem of trying to come to terms with the paradox of language in examinations.

11.38   This is a necessarily brief account of the past and present situation of English language examinations, but it will serve to show how thoroughly and over how long a period the subject has been discussed. Our main reason for giving it is that our own views are founded upon those that others have expressed before us, both in recent years and in the distant past. In presenting our conclusion we must begin by affirming our belief that English should be assessed at 16+. The Newbolt Committee's wise remarks on the matter are no less true today than when they were made. The demand made by society and by parents for the evaluation of a pupil's performance is a perfectly reasonable one. What is more, many pupils themselves feel the need for such assessment, a factor that tends to be overlooked. We therefore welcome the extension of opportunities for assessment throughout the ability range and hope they will be made available to increasing numbers of pupils now that the school leaving age has been raised.

11.39   Our selective account of the evolution of examinations in English will have indicated the line of development we favour. English requires a wider and more flexible range of assessment than most other areas of the curriculum. We believe that rigid syllabuses are not the best means of achieving this and that there should be an increase in school-based assessment with external moderation. We hope that this assessment will increasingly reflect the kind of approach to language development which has been advocated in this chapter.

11.40   We have made it a policy in this Report to confine ourselves to discussing English for pupils up to the age of 16. Nevertheless, we must depart from this rule to make an observation on the question of a language examination at the conclusion of a sixth form course. The 1964 Report considered this possibility and recommended against in these words:

"We should not wish to see a separate language subject at advanced level, at least at the present time."

It did, however, recognise the value of making available a course which would include "a study of the structure of the language; the different types of English, the position of standard English, dialects and slang; and the relation of language to individual thought and behaviour and also its social implications". The suggestion was therefore that a linguistic section should be introduced into the existing "A" level examination. Since it was clearly out of the question to increase the burden of the syllabus this should take the form of an optional alternative to one of the existing papers. In the ten years since the report was published this development has not taken place. This seems to us an unfortunate loss of a valuable opportunity to take advantage of the relevance and interest of language studies for pupils of this age. We believe that the post "O" level English syllabus should contain a language element for all pupils who wish to opt for it, and we recommend that "A" level or whatever examination may replace it, should include a paper on this basis.

ANNEX A
SPELLING

11.41   Some years ago a philologist remarked that if one used all possible combinations the word 'scissors' might be spelt in 596,580 different ways. This was a hypothetical exercise, but a recent researcher[15] took a simpler example, the word 'saucer', and examined how 1,000 ten year old children tackled it. Fewer than half spelt it correctly, and those who wrote it incorrectly gave 209 alternative spellings. And yet according to the norms of the Schonell word recognition test 71 per cent of eight year old children can *read* the word 'saucer' correctly and without any supporting context. This is one of many indications of a fundamental difficulty: that many who have little trouble with reading may still spell uncertainly when they write.

11.42   Spelling is a complex skill, and one in which many adults and children fail. The reasons are various, and some carry greater weight than others. Poor spellers may have lower verbal intelligence. They may have difficulty in their visual perception of words and then in recalling them through imagery. They may be weak in generalising from the serial probability of letter occurrences. There are other determinants, but research has shown these to be the major ones. It has to be accepted at once that some people will have difficulty with spelling all their lives, but we believe that the teacher can bring about substantial improvement with the majority of children. No doubt the first question to be faced is: does it matter? It is sometimes suggested that spelling is a convention and that if it is of any consequence at all this is slight compared with so many other considerations in the teaching of English. There is no question about its being a convention, but in our view it is a convention that matters. It is of little relevance for today to argue that in "Faerie Queene" Spenser spelt 'hot' in at least six different ways: or that the Oxford English Dictionary lists 30 versions of 'little' by 16th and 17th century writers.

11.43   In the first place confidence in spelling frees the child to write to fulfil his purpose. In the second place spelling disability is an undoubted handicap in society, however many distinguished exceptions may be paraded to refute the view. But there is probably no need to press this point. Most of the contention surrounding spelling is concerned with timing and method rather than justification. Some teachers feel that so long as children leave school with spelling competence it should receive no special attention at the primary stage. Some believe that it can be acquired incidentally and that systematic teaching is the wrong approach. Few affect a total disregard for it.

11.44   The arguments about spelling go back a long way. Almost a century ago to this very year there was openly expressed anxiety about standards; and certainly around the turn of the century the debate was in progress as to whether spelling should be directly taught or could be breathed in naturally if the air was right. One of the first in the field was Rice, whose article "The Futility of the Spelling Grind" (1897) suggested that spelling received too much prominence in the timetable. He was followed by a succession of researchers who argued from objective data in favour either of a 'taught' or a 'caught' approach. Most of the research conducted in the last half century has been on spelling vocabulary, instruments for measuring spelling ability and for diagnosing errors, and the teaching methods by which children's spelling should be improved. The search to discover what words children should learn began quite early. Originally an arbitrary process, the compiling of lists became more systematic in adopting as a principle the frequency with which words occurred. Some were derived from children's own writing, some from that of adults. Lists have commonly come to be used as a teaching instrument, though many teachers have always relied upon their own observation of children's needs in deciding what words to present to them.

11.45   There is no need to trace the history of these lists, but certain of the more influential developments are worth pausing on. Many of the lists were derived from children's own writing, though a number were based on adult reading matter or correspondence. A major principle of selection is that of frequency of occurrence. For example, in the U.S.A. in 1926 Horn combined the results of earlier enquiries with his own word counts. His resulting "Basic Writing Vocabulary" contained the 10,000 words most likely to be written by adults. In 1944 Thorndike and Lorge, also in the U.S.A., produced "The Teacher's Word Book", a 30,000 word list again based on adult material. These two major enterprises provided the basis for one of the most popular lists in use in English schools today, though its author, Schonell, also incorporated extensive work of his own on the spelling and written material of English schoolchildren. He set out to distribute the words in his list on the broad principle that "the child should be taught the word when he wants to write it". But others suggested that lists could not be made to serve this principle, arguing that they are never able to supply the particular word a person should learn at a particular time. This is, of course, a central issue, and one which has an important bearing on the success of the teacher's efforts.

11.46   Two comparatively recent lists, produced by councils for educational research in Scotland and New Zealand, were planned to constitute teaching aids based on detailed field work. The aim of the Scottish Council for Research in Education was "to assemble a vocabulary based on familiar situations and bearing a close relationship to the child's own life". The result was a list derived from a count of the words in 70,000 pieces of writing by 7–12 year old Scottish children on matters of interest to them. The other list was compiled by the New Zealand Council for Educational Research. The 2,700 words were examined very carefully by inspectors and teachers in colleges and schools, and intensive checking followed. A feature of this list was that it enabled the child to ascertain the probability of his needing a particular word, and gave him specific guidance on how to learn. This interesting project therefore combined the principle of word count by frequency with a well ordered learning method that depended on the pupil's assessment of his own needs.

11.47   More conventional word lists have been criticised on the ground that they encourage ineffectual teaching. It is one thing to practise the spelling of words from a list but quite another to use them in writing. Not all pupils require practice on the same groups of words, and the permanence of the learning is a very uncertain outcome. Children may be able to cope with all the words in a given list after concentrated study, but they may still fail with the same words when they come to use them in writing. The fact is that success is most likely when their spelling is closely associated with the needs and purposes of their own writing. Young children have less difficulty with such words as 'orange', and 'penny' than with equally simple words like 'these' and 'outside' which have less meaning for them in terms of concrete experience. In saying this we are not advocating incidental learning, since we do not believe that all children will acquire spelling ability as an automatic and natural outcome of a healthy language environment. Certainly a child will have an excellent foundation if he is interested in language and curious about its workings, but he needs more than just the right climate.

11.48 Nisbet[16] estimated that the average child 'picks up' the spelling of only one new word out of every 25 he reads. Peters[17] concluded that spelling ability is 'caught', concurrently with other linguistic skills, by certain favoured children, but that less favoured children need to be taught, and taught rationally and systematically. Her results indicated that their attention should constantly be drawn to details of word structure, similarities of letter sequence, and the varying probabilities of such sequences. The importance of a favourable background diminishes in the junior and middle years, but it provides initial skills which help the child to develop good spelling habits. This accords with evidence submitted to the Committee from a number of sources, including workers in E.P.A.s, on the education of disadvantaged children. As one expressed it with particular reference to reading: "An incidental learning approach is hazardous for all children, but particularly so for those from disadvantaged homes". Research and opinion does not all run one way, and other experimenters have expressed more optimism about the success of incidental learning. However, our own view of the weight of experimental evidence is that the limitations of this approach can be no less marked than those of the rote memorisation of words bereft of context.

11.49 It is interesting to observe that in our own questionnaire only 10 per cent of the sample of nine year old children spent no time at all on spelling during the week of the survey. 67 per cent spent up to half an hour of class time on it, and 20 per cent more than half an hour. In another section the questionnaire inquired into the general methods in use in the class. The questions were directed to discover whether the children were:

(a) expected to learn spellings from their own or other children's errors and/or lists devised by the teacher,

(b) required to learn spellings from commercially produced lists,

(c) tested to see that they had learned these spellings.

95 per cent of classes employed the first method and 41 per cent the second; in other words many teachers at one time or another use both. 59 per cent of the classes were tested weekly, 33 per cent less frequently, and only 7 per

cent not at all. The secondary schools were asked how much weekly class time was spent on:

(a) spelling practice from lists,
(b) spelling practice by dictation of passages,
(c) spelling practice arising from written work,
(d) spelling tests.

The first two of these methods were little represented. During the survey week only 8 per cent of the twelve year olds and 3 per cent of the fourteen year olds had had spelling practice from lists. 13 per cent of the former had had spelling practice arising from their written work, and the same number had been given a spelling test. Among the fourth year pupils the corresponding figures were 9 per cent and 7 per cent. In the context of writing, teachers were asked about their practice in correcting errors. Only a handful of teachers said they did not correct any at all. The majority corrected some, while 24 per cent of the twelve year olds and 31 per cent of the fourteen year olds had *all* their errors corrected. 59 per cent of the younger and 41 per cent of the older pupils were required to write out the corrected spellings, and most were expected then to learn them. It is evident from these figures that many teachers are concerned about standards of spelling and that the errors the children actually make come in for a good deal of attention.

ANNEX B
HANDWRITING

11.50   The Ministry of Education pamphlet "Primary Education", published in 1959, said:

"It is a heartening thought that, in an age when so little of craftsmanship is expected of anyone, and when it is easy to say that few people care about quality and standards of work, very many are deeply concerned to give handwriting once more its proper dignity as the most universal of all crafts".

Would this statement hold true today? A view frequently expressed in the evidence was that handwriting is neglected in schools. In our survey we posed a question designed to establish how much time was spent on the activity by six year old and nine year old children. The results could be taken to suggest that there is some substance in the complaint, for as many as 12 per cent of the six year olds in our sample spent no time at all upon it, and among the nine year olds the figure was as high as 20 per cent. On the other hand, the results could be interpreted positively to suggest that most teachers still regard it as important, for the majority practice at both age-levels was to devote anything up to half an hour a week of class time to it.

11.51   The ability to write easily, quickly, and legibly affects the quality of a child's written output, for difficulty with handwriting can hamper his flow of thoughts and limit his fluency. If a child is left to develop his handwriting without instruction he is unlikely to develop a running hand which is simultaneously legible, fast-flowing, and individual and becomes effortless to produce. We therefore believe that the teacher should devote time to teaching it and to giving the children ample practice. The first requirement is that the school should decide which style of handwriting is to be adopted and should as far as possible do so in consultation with the schools to which the children will pass. We realise the difficulties of such consultation in some circumstances and have acknowledged them in Chapter 14. Nevertheless, there is no doubt that many children are confused by having to learn different models as they go from one school to the next. Liaison is not a simple matter when an infant school sends children to more than one junior school, but the remarks in paragraph 14.6 about continuity in the teaching of reading apply equally in this case.

11.52   We do not propose to enter into the question of which model is best, for this must be a decision for the schools themselves. There are, however, certain basic principles which need to be taken into account when the matter is being discussed. One question on which opposing views are often expressed is that of the kind of handwriting with which children should begin in the infant school. Some teachers believe that a print-script should be used and that this should be as near in appearance as possible to the type-face of the child's first books, so that he will have fewer characters to learn. There is certainly economy in using the same alphabet for both reading and writing, but the opponents of print-script contend that it ignores a fundamental requirement of handwriting—a continuous, linear, rhythmic movement. They observe that many children do not find it easy to change later to a cursive script, since there are no indications in the lower-case letters of print-script to suggest how they might eventually be joined. Conversely, they point out, a modified cursive or italic script makes possible a much smoother evolution to a running hand.

11.53   Whichever form is adopted there are certain conditions of general relevance, obvious enough in themselves to the experienced teacher but by no means fulfilled in every infant classroom. For example, the paper on which the children are to write should always be unlined and of a sufficient size to be unrestricting, and there should be plenty of suitable tools: soft pencils, crayons, and felt-tips, large enough in the barrel for small hands to manage them lightly and easily without strain. The correct hold should be encouraged from the outset, and the child helped to achieve the right sitting posture and relaxation of the muscles. He should also be shown how to form the letter shapes in the right way. For most children an upward stroke of the pencil seems to be the most natural movement, but if a child is allowed to form the habit of beginning letters from their bases the result will be a hampering movement which makes more difficult the development of a fast running hand. Brushwork and pattern-making and various well-tried kinaesthetic and tactile methods can reinforce the teaching of the initial downward movement and help a flowing technique to become established. If faulty techniques take root they are extremely difficult to correct, so the child has to be encouraged to persevere in what so often seems to him to be an awkward way to hold a pencil or a slow and unnatural way of forming letters. This points to the need for individual and small group teaching and for plenty of short, frequent practice, never of a length that leads to boredom or cramped fingers. In our view this instruction should not be intruded while children are actually at work in their own personal writing, for it is likely to interrupt their flow of thought. From the beginning there should be the proper kind of support and help for left-handed children, and when they come to use pens they should be given nibs specially suited to their needs.

11.54   As a child becomes more adept he should be encouraged to develop speed, for the laboured copying of individual letters will not lead to fluency. The need for regular practice continues throughout the early and middle years, particularly during the transition to a full cursive hand and when pens are introduced. Linking minuscules is a case in point, for ligaturing needs to be practised in a way that will ensure increase of speed and continuity of movement. It is best to classify the letters according to the method of joining, using the commoner letter pairs or letter groups, e.g. e d, ing, e a, o o. From these the child can progress to letter groups with a variety of ligatures, again in common use, such as tion, ous, ttle, ough. Practice with these not only helps to develop speed but has the advantage of reinforcing common spelling patterns. In the course of all this children should also be made aware of the rhythmical stresses of writing patterns and the affinity of letter forms which lead to a harmony of style.

11.55   We believe that the appearance of written work and the way it is set out deserves specific attention. Children should grow up accustomed to taking care in the way they present their work and to regarding its appearance as an important aspect of the whole production. This means that when their handwriting is being developed there needs to be attention not only to the shape of individual letters and words but to the spacing of words and lines, the relative heights of letters, the paragraph indentations, the form and style of headings, and the width and depth of surrounds. Practice in these matters should not take the form of drill, in which the child copies material of no other value. It should derive from activities where the task carries a purpose for the child, for instance in compiling a bound collection of his own writings or making fair copies of work which has involved personal investigation. The teacher will have many opportunities to organise situations which call for a high standard of presentation. Some of the more obvious are displays of work for other classes and for parents, and exchanges of work with other schools. Good handwriting is an important aspect of presentation and is an asset both in school and in later life, but we have tried to suggest that it is also an aid to the flow of thought during the process of writing. We believe that by the end of the middle years a pupil should have acquired his own personal style which is swift, economical of effort, relaxed, fluent, legible, and attractive.

REFERENCES

1.   *The Development of Writing Abilities 11–18:* Writing Research Unit: Schools Council: 1974.
2.   *Op. cit.*
3.   For the origin of this distinction see D. W. Harding: *The Role of the Onlooker:* Scrutiny, VI (3): 1937.
4.   R. J. Harris: *An Experimental Inquiry into the Functions and Value of Formal Grammar in the Teaching of English:* reported in Braddock, Lloyd Jones, and Schoer: *Research in Written Composition:* N.C.T.E.: 1963.
5.   *A Study of the Teaching of English in Selected British Secondary Schools:* U.S. Department of Health, Education, and Welfare: 1968.
6.   *Children's Language Development:* University of Nottingham: 1973.
7.   N. Postman: *English Journal:* November 1967.
8.   P. Doughty, J. Pearce, G. Thornton: *Language in Use:* Edward Arnold: 1971.
9.   *The Examining of English Language:* H.M.S.O.: 1964.

10. *The Teaching of English in England* (The Newbolt Report): H.M.S.O.: 1921.
11. *Schools Council Examinations Bulletin No. 1—The Certificate of Secondary Education:* H.M.S.O.: 1963.
12. *C.S.E. English: An Interim Report:* N.A.T.E. Bulletin Vol. 1, No. 3: 1964.
13. *Criteria of Success in English:* A critical survey of C.S.E. English syllabuses and specimen papers: N.A.T.E.: 1965.
14. *English Examined:* A Survey of "O" Level Papers: N.A.T.E.
15. M. L. Peters: *Success in Spelling:* Cambridge Institute of Education: 1970.
16. S. D. Nisbet: *Non-dictated Spelling Tests:* British Journal of Educational Psychology: IX, 1939.
17. M. L. Peters: *op. cit.*

CHAPTER 12

Language Across The Curriculum

12.1 In the two preceding chapters we have made several references to the role of language in other areas of the curriculum than English. It became clear to us in the early days of the inquiry that we could not do justice to the first term of reference if we did not direct our remarks to *all* teachers, whatever their subject. Indeed, we believe that the suggestions made in these chapters for improving the teaching of language could result in more effective teaching of subjects that lie right outside the terms of reference. For a proper appreciation of this concept the three chapters should be read as one. In this chapter we state a generalised case for the development of a school policy which might give effect to it.

12.2 It has been claimed that at no time in the life of an average person does he successfully achieve a more complex learning task than when he learns to speak, a task which is substantially completed before he is five years old. It has also been suggested that during the period from early infancy to five years old a child makes more rapid progress in learning about his environment than in any subsequent five-year span. The two processes cannot be independent. The effort a child needs to apply in learning language must derive from the satisfaction of evolving from helplessness to self-possession. Conversely, that very evolution must owe a great deal to the developing power of language as its instrument. What we advocate here is no more than that this interlocking of the means and the end should be maintained, if possible, throughout the years of schooling. To achieve this we must convince the teacher of history or of science, for example, that he has to understand the process by which his pupils take possession of the historical or scientific information that is offered them; and that such an understanding involves his paying particular attention to the part language plays in learning. The pupils' engagement with the subject may rely upon a linguistic process that his teaching procedures actually discourage.

12.3 The primary school teacher responsible for the whole or most of the school-work of his class already has it in his power to establish a language policy across the curriculum. Whether or not he is taking that opportunity will depend upon the extent to which the various uses of language permeate all the other learning activities, or to which, on the other hand, language learning is regarded as a separate activity. The distinction is a crucial one, and a great deal follows from it. For language to play its full role as a means of learning, the teacher must create in the classroom an environment which encourages a wide range of language uses. The effectiveness of this context for the purpose can be judged by the answers to a number of questions. For example, how often does a child share his personal interests and learning discoveries with others in the class? How far is the teacher able to enter such conversations without robbing the children of verbal initiative? Are the children accustomed to read to one another what they have written, and just as readily listen? Are they accustomed to solving co-operatively in talk the practical problems that arise when they work together? How much opportunity is there for the kind of talk by which children make sense in their own terms of the information offered by teacher or by book? What varieties of writing—story, personal record, comment, report, speculation, etc.—are produced in the course of a day? Over a longer span, what varieties occur in the output of a single child? These are straws in the wind. What they indicate is the degree to which learning and the acquisition of language are interlocked. We have argued elsewhere, and particularly in connection with reading, the need for a consensus among the staff of a primary school on matters of language learning. The individual teacher is in a position to devise a language policy across the various aspects of the curriculum, but there remains the need for a general policy to give expression to the aim and ensure consistency throughout the years of primary schooling.

12.4   By his training and experience, the primary school teacher is likely to conceive of his task in terms of integrated rather than subject-oriented work. In the secondary school, however, it is traditional practice to move more or less directly into a programme of specialist teaching and a subject timetable. Clearly it is here that the proposals to be made in this chapter principally apply. A primary school teacher may happen to be unaware of new conceptions of the role of language, but he would not generally regard them as matters outside his concern. However, they are certainly regarded in this way by secondary school teachers of most subjects. The move from an integrated to a specialist curriculum constitutes in itself a considerably increased demand upon the linguistic powers of the pupil, but the most obvious demand, that for a wider and more specialised vocabulary, is not the principal difficulty. In general, a curriculum subject, philosophically speaking, is a distinctive mode of analysis. While many teachers recognise that their aim is to initiate a student in a particular mode of analysis, they rarely recognise the linguistic implications of doing so. They do not recognise, in short, that the mental processes they seek to foster are the outcome of a development that originates in speech. A person's impulse to talk over a problem that his thinking has failed to solve is a natural one; what he is doing is to regress to an earlier, simpler form of problem-solving situation. Every teacher has known occasions when a child has solved his difficulties in the act of explaining what they are. Face to face speech is a very direct embodiment of the relationship between the speakers. If the relationship is one that gives the speaker confidence he will be understood, it acts as a powerful incentive to him to complete the train of thought he has begun. It has even been claimed that goodwill is enough in a listener, without understanding.

12.5   When we consider the working day in a secondary school the neglect of pupil talk as a valuable means of learning stands out sharply. To bring about a change will take time and persistence. Where pupil talk has been accorded little status in teaching methods, it is not surprising that when the opportunity does occur it tends to be filled by pointless chatter. But the cycle can be broken, as experience has amply shown. There is no need to repeat here the points we have made earlier in this section about the role of exploratory talk in the classroom. For such talk to flourish, the context must be as informal and relaxed as possible, and this is most likely to occur in small groups and in a well organised and controlled classroom. Once the practice has been established in such groups there is no reason why the exploratory talk should not succeed in due course with the whole class and the teacher together. The principle to be recognised, however, is that good 'class discussion' cannot be had simply on demand; it must be built up on work in small groups, and continue to be supported by it.

12.6   If the value of expressive talk is commonly overlooked in many subject areas, expressive writing often finds no place at all. In a recent research study[1] it was found that the teachers of a number of subjects did not encourage such writing, and this can be taken to mean that the children were often being asked to run before they could walk. They were being required to report conclusions in writing, their own or other people's, but not to produce the kind of writing that most effectively helps them to *arrive at* conclusions. The following passage[2] will illustrate the point. Asked to give an account of how to set up a wormery, a thirteen year old wrote:

> "I fetched a bucket of soil and a cup. A jar of sand and some chalk. I fetched a wormery glass which you can see through. I made layers of soil then sand and then powdered chalk. I continued like that. Then I put some water in it. I have marked with biro where the water ran. Then I placed four worms in the wormery. They did not stir when they were on top of the soil but later they will. I put the wormery into a dark cupboard which is closed."

At thirteen a writer might have been expected to produce a simple and practical statement in the style of a manual of instructions. In this light the comment made by his teacher, "Not very good", can be said to have been merited. What the pupil wrote, however, was an expressive statement reflecting his personal involvement. It is from such writing that the transactional must grow, and what the pupil wrote may have been appropriate to him at that particular stage.

We believe that expressive writing shares some of the virtues of expressive talk in helping a pupil to find his way into a subject. Moreover, it is an important stage on the way to a range of differentiated kinds of writing. To quote from the language policy document prepared by a secondary school we visited:

> "As well as providing opportunities for purposeful oral work within a given context, other subject areas might consider how they can enlist the personal involvement and interest of children in any writing required of them."

Or as Rosen[3] has put it: "The demand for transactional writing in school is ceaseless, but expressive language with all its vitality and richness is the only possible soil from which it can grow."

12.7   There is a sequence of ways, fairly obvious in themselves, in which children gather information. They can be listed in ascending order of difficulty as follows:

finding out from observation and first-hand experience;
finding out from someone who will explain and discuss;
finding out by listening to a spoken monologue, for example a radio talk;
finding out by reading.

These are not, of course, four independent processes; on the contrary, they must be seen as variants of a single activity, likely to be used in close conjunction. Moreover, it must be recognised that the child's speaking and writing are essential means by which he appropriates and uses the information he has gathered. This places reading firmly in a context of the use of language. 'Finding out by reading' puts the emphasis where we feel it belongs; the child reads because there is something he wants to find out, and this can be made to apply in any or every lesson on the timetable. This quest for information will call upon and promote the wide range of reading skills discussed in Chapter 8, but the child must be given the right kind of help. Subject teachers need to be aware of the processes involved, able to provide the variety of reading material that is appropriate, and willing to see it as their responsibility to help their pupils meet the reading demands of their subject. The variety of written forms a child encounters in reading will be an influence upon the development of his writing abilities. To restrict the first can result in limiting the second.

12.8   Furthermore, just as different tasks call upon different reading skills so also they demand a variety of modes of recording. Note making and other forms of record keeping associated with a pupil's reading can be valuable ways not simply of learning, but of 'learning to learn'. In the past attempts at teaching the art of learning have too often consisted in a few stereotyped methods of study, so generalised as to be of little value when applied in a real context. Subject teachers who know both the particular demands of their subjects and the individual needs of their pupils have an important contribution to make in this area.

12.9   This brief survey of language across the curriculum would not be complete if we failed to take account of the teacher's own language. There is no doubt that a well-prepared, extensive presentation by the teacher is sometimes the best way of handling a topic, particularly in the introductory stages of a course of study. It is likely to begin with the circulation of some material in the form of evidence, or data upon which conclusions can be based. The teacher marks out an area of concern and allows for a variety of approaches to it, and he does this through open-ended questions which elicit from his pupils the ideas and experiences upon which to work. The presentation is thus newly developed on each successive occasion. What the teacher is shaping by his probing is something to which both he and his pupils contribute. It may at the conclusion be an incomplete and modified version of what he intended, but it will be a truer representation of the understanding the group has reached than could have been derived from any direct exposition. In the course of working upon new concepts the teacher is bound to introduce new terms, but he can make good use of the pupils' own views and experiences to help them assimilate these. It is what the pupils do in following up the presentation that realises its value, and this is best achieved by the teacher's interaction with individuals and small groups. Getting children to talk to them is an art that most teachers acquire without giving the matter any thought. When it becomes evident to a teacher that his professional teaching relationship requires mutuality rather than distance, he is likely to find little difficulty in making the adjustment. The problem is that of reconciling this relationship with his role as a keeper of the peace, for he cannot avoid his responsibility for maintaining in the group an atmosphere in which learning may go on. There exist the two distinct roles of teaching and control, and the constant aim should be to develop the first to a point where it encompasses the second.

12.10   The notions we have been discussing here are gradually gaining currency, and we are encouraged by what has been achieved in the comparatively short time since their inception. The documentation has grown considerably in the last six years and now covers principles and practice, teaching and organisation. One of the earliest initiatives came from the London Association for the Teaching of English, which organised a series of conferences leading to the publication in 1969 of a discussion document[4], "A language policy across the curriculum". A number of schools responded to the suggestions this contained, and there followed valuable contacts with other subject associations, notably the Association of Teachers of Mathematics. The topic was taken up by the National Association for the Teaching of English, which invited teachers of all subjects to its 1971 annual conference[5] and devoted the programme to a series of working groups on various aspects of language across the curriculum. A teacher of mathematics afterwards reported:

"as children talk or write . . . in a mathematics lesson, or in the playground when they are sorting out the rules of a game of marbles, they are 'doing mathematics'. It is not just that language is *used* in mathematics: rather, it is that the language that is used *is* the mathematics. It was perhaps on this account that I did not feel myself too much of an eavesdropper when I went to Reading for the N.A.T.E. conference: the discussions were directly relevant to my own concerns."

And a teacher of biology:

"How might further developments take place? There was a strong feeling that local follow-up was essential, perhaps in Teachers' Centres. Objectives should be much more restricted, for example 'Reading' or 'Projects' or 'Discussion', and it will be necessary to consider the practical problems of small group work in the classroom. We all felt that other subject Associations should become involved".

The next major development was a series of Department of Education and Science short courses, beginning in 1972, which brought together on successive occasions heads of schools, advisers, heads of subject departments, and representatives of subject associations. The courses were planned as working parties, and a number of stimulating papers were produced on language across the curriculum. Another focal point for teacher activity has been the Writing Across the Curriculum project[6], at present being conducted for the Schools Council at the University of London Institute of Education. Several local authorities are now co-operating with the project team, and a large number of teachers are making a valuable contribution.

12.11   We have chosen these developments to illustrate the growth of interest in the notion of language across the curriculum, but it cannot be inferred from this that it has taken root in large numbers of schools. Despite such initiatives, and similar ones at local level, there are still comparatively few schools which have introduced it as a policy. This is understandable, for it cannot be pretended that a policy of this kind is easy to establish. The need is not obvious to every teacher, and the head of the school can best influence others if he is himself informed and convinced. This, however, is only the beginning, and the head cannot achieve alone the introduction and maintenance of the policy. We have considered various ways in which it might take effect, but to endorse any one would be to produce a prescription that would not suit the circumstances of every school. One possibility is for the responsibility to lie with a senior member of staff, experienced and appropriately qualified, whose status is at least equal to that of the heads of department with whom he will be working so closely. The advantage of such an appointment is that the teacher concerned would be able to concentrate his efforts upon the policy and carry the weight to enable him to persuade and exercise influence. The difficulty might be that it would not be easy to argue for another post to be added to the senior level of the school management structure. In some schools it would be possible for the function to be taken on by a member of the staff already occupying a senior post, for example, a director of studies or curriculum co-ordinator where he was qualified for the role.

12.12 Whatever form it took it would be important to establish a proper working relationship with the head of English department, whose own contribution to the policy must clearly be a considerable one. It could, of course, be argued that the head of department and his English specialist colleagues are in an ideal position to take on the responsibility themselves, and this is another possibility to be considered. The virtues are obvious, but we have argued elsewhere that English departments—and particularly the teachers in charge of them—are hard-pressed. To expect them to add this important task to their existing commitments would be asking a great deal. Moreover, it is conceivable that in some schools such an arrangement might make it harder for the concept to win acceptance among the staff. One approach might be to place the responsibility with a committee composed of heads of department, with the head teacher and the head of English giving a strong lead. This has the advantage of continuous consultation and collective responsibility, but it could be countered that it takes an individual hand to give real leadership. Clearly a great deal depends upon the circumstances of each school, not least its size and its present administrative structure. We strongly recommend that whatever the means chosen to implement it a policy for language across the curriculum should be adopted by every secondary school. We are convinced that the benefits would be out of all proportion to the effort it would demand, considerable though this would undoubtedly be.

REFERENCES

1. *The Development of Writing Abilities 11 to 18:* Writing Research Unit: Schools Council: 1974.
2. *Reproduced in "Language Across The Curriculum":* English in Education, Vol. 5, No. 2: 1971.
3. D. Barnes *et al.: Language, the Learner, and the School:* revised edition: Penguin Education: 1971.
4. Reproduced in D. Barnes *et al.: op. cit.*
5. Reported in *"Language Across the Curriculum": op. cit.*
6. See: *From Information to Understanding:* University of London Institute of Education: 1973.

Part Five

Organisation

CHAPTER 13

The Primary and Middle Years

13.1   The purpose of this chapter is to consider the organisation and staffing within schools as they affect English in general and language development and reading in particular, and to examine the implications of some of the suggestions we have made in earlier chapters and in certain of those which follow. We must, however, begin with a brief survey of pre-school provision, for it is important to recognise that children entering infant school start on a very uneven footing in this respect. In December 1972 proposals[1] were announced for the expansion of nursery education during the next decade. This should make possible a real advance in language development in young children, since it will allow more children to benefit from the kinds of experiences we described in Chapter 5. At present there is an immense range in the pre-school opportunities of young children, and an infinite variety in the extent and quality of the experience they eventually bring to the infant school. Some remain at home throughout the pre-school years with parents, relatives, au pair girls, or child minders, registered or un-registered. Some attend playgroups for up to six hours a week or spend as many as 45 hours a week in day nurseries and centres. Some receive full- or part-time education in nursery school or in nursery classes or units attached to primary schools, spending between 15 and 38 hours a week there.

13.2   It is difficult to make even the most general observation that would summarise the circumstances of children who are looked after by *unregistered child minders*[2]. In the nature of things it is hard to arrive with precision at either their numbers or the extent to which they are properly cared for. Nevertheless, there is every indication[3] that they run into many thousands and that the quality of care is often very poor, not simply because of unsatisfactory physical conditions but because of the absence of stimulus and attention to the child's developmental needs. In the case of *registered child minders*, local authority supervision is more likely to ensure satisfactory physical conditions, but the other aspects of the child's welfare must very often be just as inadequately served. Nearly 300,000 of the country's children attend *playgroups*. The playgroup movement sets out to create opportunities for socialisation and to provide a secure yet stimulating environment in which children can interact and in which parents can play a significant part. The staffing of the groups varies considerably, some being run entirely by parents, some by parents in association with trained colleagues, others by trained staff only. Equally variable is the quality of the provision, the materials available, and the kind of experience the children encounter. In the best groups the children hear stories, learn songs and rhymes, and are given plenty of opportunity for talk through the stimulus of their play. The *day nurseries*, both public and private, usually see their main purpose as providing nurture and care for children whose mothers are at work for long hours. However, there has been a growing awareness of the fact that different aspects of the child's development are interrelated. The result has been an increased concern for intellectual growth and the provision of book corners and interest areas in the better nurseries. This awareness is reflected in the training of the nursery nurses, who are encouraged to tell the children stories, help them enjoy picture/story books, and get them to talk about their experiences. Unfortunately, there is a shortage of trained nursery nurses and assistants, and the experience of children in public day nurseries is bound to vary a great deal. It is likely to vary even more in private day nurseries, since authorities apply differing standards with regard to training of staff, child/staff ratio, etc. in their requirements for registration. Lastly, there are the *nursery schools and classes*, which we have already discussed at length in terms of the important contribution they can make to language development and cognitive growth.

13.3   Within any one of these kinds of experience there is a great range in the nature and quality of language preparation. This fact is sometimes over-looked when comments are made about infant schools. In the best of cir-cumstances their task is a complex one; in areas of social difficulty the short-comings of language development impose additional and very con-siderable demands. The very diversity of all this pre-school experience underlines the need for contacts between infant school, nursery school, playgroup, and home, and there is great scope for initiative. For example, where children are already in a playgroup or nursery school the infant teacher can learn much by visiting them there, getting to know their back-ground and inviting the leader or nursery teacher to pay return visits. The pre-school child should be allowed to spend some time in the infant school with his mother in the term before he is due to be admitted. Admissions can be staggered over a period of some weeks, so that the teacher is given the chance to talk to small numbers of parents when they bring their children, and to give more individual attention to the children themselves. Some heads have found it useful to produce an illustrated booklet of suggestions to guide parents in preparing their child, and themselves, for his new experience. Parents should receive invitations to attend meetings of one kind or another in advance of their child's actually starting school. Where possible, facilities for borrowing and buying books should be extended to them, as another means of making them feel part of it at the earliest opportunity. Home-school liaison has already been dealt with at length in its relation to the child's language needs, but it is mentioned in this context to emphasise the value we place on a proper introduction to school life. Continuity and co-operation between home and school and between one stage of education and the next are vitally important to a child's development, linguistic and otherwise.

13.4   In recent years a considerable amount of time has been spent in discussing the internal organisation of schools and the way in which this affects the nature and quality of the teaching. The pattern from which large numbers of schools are held to have departed is that of the 'traditional' primary school, whose work is defined fairly precisely by a set timetable. This involves placing the 'basic skills' in the mornings, with the afternoons set aside for creative activities, history, geography, nature study, and some physical education. More often than not a scheme of work for reading and language sets out the appropriate form and content for each class. The advocates of this form of organisation say that these conditions lead to an assured attention to the 'basic skills', which results in a concern for correct-ness in written work and for measured progress in reading. They argue that there is a clearly defined purpose which can give teacher and pupil alike a feeling of security and achievement. As short-term objectives are sequentially attained there is a recognisable rate of progress, which parents can readily understand. Its critics contend that this kind of organisation limits the opportunities for learning. All too often the practice of reading and writing skills is totally unrelated to the pupils' other experiences and therefore lacks real meaning. Thus it is possible, as in mathematics, for a technique to be acquired without an understanding of what is involved in the process. They also suggest that such an approach implies a set of external standards which are an inadequate way of judging success. Before going on to discuss the implications of all this we are bound to say that extreme attitudes on either side are unhelpful. Moreover they represent a situation which does not exist in schools in any such extreme form. It seems to us unfortunate that public debate has tended in recent years to oversimplify a complex situation and has often been conducted through a series of slogan-like headings: progressive, formal, integration, basics, and several more. The conditions in which children learn most efficiently call for serious study, and in our view it is naive to believe that a particular form of organisation will in itself guarantee them.

13.5   Most primary schools still group children in classes according to the year in which they were born. Some are too small to do that, and their classes therefore have to contain children of different ages. Others produce this effect as a matter of policy, and their classes are then known as 'vertically grouped'. Normally, admission of children to infant schools on a termly basis can mean that some children are moved from one class to the next after only a term or two. There are four principal advantages claimed for vertical grouping: the children can remain with one teacher for a longer time; only a few new children need be taken into the class each term and they can therefore be settled easily; the younger children are encouraged to greater effort by the work of the older; slow learning children do not feel exposed. It is argued that the books and materials necessary to cover the wider age range offer an interest and challenge that is sometimes missing in classes for five year olds. Far from being hampered by the wide range of ability and age within the class the teacher can use it to good effect and give individual attention where it is necessary. There are several variant forms of vertical grouping. Some schools arrange for there to be the full infant age range in each class, while in others the 5s and younger 6s will be in one class, the 7s and older 6s in another. A number of schools re-group children for part of the week, either into or out of vertical groups. The critics of vertical grouping point out that continuity with one teacher is effective only where there is low staff mobility; the children may remain constant, but the teacher could well change frequently. Moreover, continuity can be a marked disadvantage to children if the teacher happens to be weak. A wide spread of ability within a class covering a three year age range demands considerable skill in planning and classroom organisation. It is argued that some teachers may make insufficient demands on the seven year olds or not provide appropriate help and materials for the younger children; or they may tend to overlook the needs of the middle group.

13.6   The infant schools that pioneered deliberate vertical grouping were those which had already introduced different forms of classroom organisation, sometimes summed up in the phrase 'the integrated day'. The variations on this theme are numerous, but the principal is that subject barriers are artificial for young children. Timetable constraints are therefore removed and there is greater flexibility for accommodating individual needs and interests. For a substantial part of the day individual children, or small groups, might be variously engaged at any one time in mathematics, painting, craft work, social play, reading, or writing a story or an account of some investigation. During this time the teacher moves among the children, helping, guiding, and teaching on an individual or group basis as the need arises. Balance is achieved by bringing the whole class together at certain times for physical education, making music, discussion, or some similar activity, such as listening to a story. This way of working takes account of differences in development, interest, and attention. Language skills become an integral part of the work, and the contexts for talk, reading, and writing are provided by a variety of experiences which the child finds highly motivating.

13.7   The chief criticism is that where children pursue their own interests almost exclusively they lack direction and due attention to the basic skills. Unless there is a meticulous system of record-keeping children can miss out important areas of experience and fail to make progress in certain directions. Some teachers might find it difficult to give sufficient help with reading on an individual or group basis when they are pulled in so many directions. It is the apparent excess of freedom of choice which has led some parents to worry that the basic skills are likely to suffer. The exponents of the integrated day accept that it needs skilful organising, but contend that where this is present the learning opportunities are increased. While a mixture of activities is in progress the teacher can engage one child or a group in the learning of the skill that must next be acquired. Where vertical grouping is in operation the teacher is better able by this means to cope with the wide range of attainment it must be expected to bring.

13.8   It was not possible in our survey to identify with precision the classes that were operating an integrated day in a full or partial sense. We were, however, able to do this for vertical grouping, and one of our objectives was to discover whether a commitment to it resulted in an emphasis on certain practices or in their comparative neglect. For instance it might be expected that teachers of deliberately vertically grouped classes would not set aside any particular part of the day for general attention to basic skills. The policy of setting aside time in this way was certainly common among the classes which were not vertically grouped; for it was adopted by 78 per cent of those containing six year olds. And yet as many as 52 per cent of the deliberately vertically grouped classes retained the same practice. In the case of the classes containing nine year olds there was an even greater incidence of the practice among the deliberately vertically grouped. Indeed, the proportion of classes doing their 'basic work' in the mornings was the same in both categories at 80 per cent. Similarly, it is sometimes suggested that vertical grouping and a disinclination to use phonic methods in the teaching of reading are associated. The following table reveals that although there is not a close correspondence in all methods the assumption about phonic work appears to be mistaken:

Table 6.

WAYS OF TEACHING READING—APPROACHES USED WITH 6 YEAR OLD CHILDREN
IN VERTICALLY GROUPED AND NON-VERTICALLY GROUPED CLASSES.

	Deliberately vertically grouped	*Not vertically grouped*	*Total*
Total number of classes	322(23%)	781(55%)	1,417
% of classes using:	%	%	%
Look and Say	97	96	97
Phonic 1	98	97	97
Phonic 2	68	72	70
Sentence Method	61	48	51
Pre-reading Exercises	61	21	35

Another example occurs in the numbers showing the frequency with which
teachers hear children read. The percentages, reproduced below, show that
there is no great difference between the categories:

Table 7.

THE FREQUENCY WITH WHICH TEACHERS HEAR CHILDREN READ—6 YEAR OLDS
AND 9 YEAR OLDS—IN VERTICALLY GROUPED AND NON-VERTICALLY GROUPED
CLASSES.

	Deliberately vertically grouped %	*Not vertically grouped* %
6 YEAR OLDS		
Ablest readers		
1. Daily	17	11
2. 3 or 4 times weekly	43	35
3. 1 or 2 times weekly	34	49
4. Less often	7	5
Average readers		
1. Daily	31	24
2. 3 or 4 times weekly	54	58
3. 1 or 2 times weekly	14	17
4. Less often	—	—
Poorest readers		
1. Daily	68	70
2. 3 or 4 times weekly	29	27
3. 1 or 2 times weekly	3	3
4. Less often	—	—

	Deliberately vertically grouped %	Not vertically grouped %
9 YEAR OLDS		
Ablest readers		
1. Daily	1	1
2. 3 or 4 times weekly	3	4
3. 1 or 2 times weekly	39	33
4. Less often	57	61
Average readers		
1. Daily	2	2
2. 3 or 4 times weekly	19	18
3. 1 or 2 times weekly	65	65
4. Less often	14	15
Poorest readers		
1. Daily	48	46
2. 3 or 4 times weekly	38	38
3. 1 or 2 times weekly	13	14
4. Less often	1	1

13.9 A further aspect of reading in which a comparison might be drawn is that of individual reading practice through graded schemes or other material. An analysis of this activity showed that the teachers of deliberately vertically grouped classes require it of their pupils with the same frequency as their counterparts in the other category.

Table 8.

THE FREQUENCY OF READING PRACTICE—6 YEAR OLD AND 9 YEAR OLD CHILDREN IN VERTICALLY GROUPED AND NON-VERTICALLY GROUPED CLASSES.

Reading practice, either from graded schemes or from other material	Deliberately vertically grouped %	Not vertically grouped %
6 year olds		
1. Daily	71	74
2. 3 or 4 times weekly	23	22
3. 1 or 2 times weekly	3	3
4. Less often	2	1
9 year olds		
1. Daily	59	58
2. 3 or 4 times weekly	28	28
3. 1 or 2 times weekly	11	11
4. Less often	1	2
5. Not applicable	1	1

It is not surprising that the differences revealed by these tables are modest, for the value of such techniques ought to depend on an assessment of the needs of individual children, not on the way the children are arranged into classes. If there is any occasion for surprise it is that so many of the deliberately vertically grouped classes should, like those in the other category, attempt to limit work on the basic skills to the morning period.

13.10 It is rightly pointed out that when vertical grouping is in operation the teacher must record with great care the progress and not merely the activities of each individual child. We argue at length in Chapter 17 that this is vitally important whatever the form of organisation. Nevertheless, it would have been disturbing if our survey had revealed less inclination for this practice on the part of teachers of vertically grouped classes. As the following table shows there was again little difference. In the case of the six year olds there were certain advantages in favour of the deliberately vertically grouped; with the nine year olds the position was reversed to a very slight degree:

Table 9.

RECORDS OF READING AND WRITING BY 6 YEAR OLD AND 9 YEAR OLD CHILDREN—IN VERTICALLY GROUPED AND NON-VERTICALLY GROUPED CLASSES.

	Deliberately vertically grouped %	*Not vertically grouped* %
Records are kept of:		
6 year olds		
1. Books read by each child	98	96
2. The occasions when a child has read to a teacher	94	95
3. Persistent individual weaknesses that require help from:		
i. specialist teachers of reading in the school	43	40
ii. specialist teachers of reading and/or educational psychologists outside the school	39	29
4. Assessment of written work	60	45
Examples of written work are kept from year to year as a progress record	52	31
Records are kept of:		
9 year olds		
1. Books read by each child	79	79
2. The occasions when a child has read to a teacher	69	71
3. Persistent individual weaknesses that require help from:		
i. specialist teachers of reading in the school	43	52
ii. specialist teachers of reading and/or educational psychologists outside the school	37	40
4. Assessment of written work	61	63
Examples of written work are kept from year to year as a progress record	43	39

We are not suggesting on the evidence of all the above tables that there is no difference of emphasis at any point between the different forms of organisation. A glance at the other tables in Chapter 25 will show where the variations occur. But we do suggest that it is mistaken to assume that any one form of teaching is tied exclusively to any given approach or provision.

13.11   How a school is organised should be based on a careful consideration of a number of essentials. Foremost among these are the educational needs of the children in question, the strengths and weaknesses of the teachers, and the quality of the other resources, material and human, both inside the school and out. The organisation can be considered successful if it brings together in the most effective way the best available combination of resources, and if it includes elements that allow it to change in the direction of becoming still more effective. It is not good enough simply to have adopted whatever is currently regarded as modish, nor simply to have clung to what was the best that could be managed in the past. As far as local circumstances allow, the organisation of schools and classes should reflect certain important facts, all seemingly obvious in themselves but by no means always taken into account. Children change as they grow older; children of the same age and of the same social background differ widely in their attainment and interests, and the differences between them do not remain constant; children learn best what is useful to them. These facts are sufficiently well argued elsewhere to need no further justification here.   Each has a bearing on the direction in which teachers should be attempting to modify their practices.

13.12   Our impression is that changes in organisation within schools in recent years have not generally been matched by changes in classroom practice. We have given the example of the schools where vertically grouped classes had their 'basic work' concentrated on the mornings. We visited some classes using the 'integrated day' form of organisation where the educational environment was less imaginative and demanding than that to be found in many 'traditional' classrooms. For example, when children moved to the 'language bay' they would take an assignment card and work to the instructions it gave. It might contain instructions to write a story; or a short passage with comprehension questions; or even some exercises, cut from a textbook and pasted on to the card. There was no interpenetration of language and the other learning experiences, and often little contact with the teacher. The system gave the appearance of allowing each child to work alone at his own pace. In fact, some of the work was as narrow in scope as the more 'formal' variety it had replaced, and it had the disadvantage of reducing the shared activity which gives opportunity for so much language. The important point is that when a new form of organisation is adopted the work within the classroom should be consonant with it in spirit and intent. This means that a good deal of careful thought should precede any organisational change. There is little to be gained from introducing a new system which merely carries on the practices of the one it has superseded and thus has its possible advantages neutralised. Moreover, new ways of working should not be adopted unless the staff has had a chance to prepare for them, and this has implications for in-service training. The most valuable innovations are likely to be those in which teachers are involved from the outset, and they should always result in an improvement upon previous practice.

13.13   As children mature they come to rely less on adults and more on themselves and one another. With their growing independence they welcome access to a number of teachers with more specialised knowledge than one class teacher can provide. The development is a gradual one, and is not uniform for all children. The change from one state of experience to the other has usually taken place on transfer from primary to secondary schools, often with an uncompromising abruptness. It is encouraging to see that a number of primary, middle, and secondary schools are nowadays evolving forms of organisation which modify this. We do not believe that there is an organisational solution for primary schools which is distinct from that for secondary schools and remains virtually unchanged throughout the primary years. We prefer to think in terms of a gradual development from the class/teacher situation through co-operative working to a degree of specialism for the older children. In practice this would work as follows. Between the ages of five and nine there would be a firmly based class-teacher relationship, but with a gradual extension of the involvement of other colleagues. There would be some need from a fairly early stage for the class teacher to refer to a colleague for more specialist help, but at this stage such help should be looked upon as supportive; that is to say, it would depend upon the occasion and the needs of individual children. It is likely, with five year olds, to involve only a small part of the school day for any individual child, and none at all for some children. The time required for this kind of supplementary help would gradually increase over the period between five and thirteen years, and it would probably be best arranged by having teachers work as teams. This would mean that teachers and children alike would have access to a member of staff with a particular interest in one aspect of the curriculum and a special contribution to make to it. Some of these contacts would be timetabled and some occur on an occasional basis in response to a particular need. Some would involve the whole class, some a number of children drawn from each class in the group. In certain subjects, such as French, music, and some aspects of physical education, there would be a case for full specialist teaching for the older children, but we do not envisage English as coming into this category. Since language permeates the curriculum we believe that it should not be abstracted from it in the primary school in the form of a specialist subject. Nevertheless, we emphasise strongly the importance of specialist help along the lines we have described above. The case for a member of staff with special responsibility in English in its widest sense is taken up in paragraph 13.23. It is important that the expert knowledge of such a teacher should be available where this kind of flexible grouping is being considered. Perhaps the most urgent need to enable these organisational patterns to develop is the provision of adequate time for staff consultation. Co-operative efforts, whether to initiate change or to adapt to it, cannot be effective unless there is time set aside for joint planning, for the interchange of discoveries, ideas, and experience, and for the expertise of some teachers to help with the problems of others.

13.14   Children of the same age differ in attainment and interests, but these differences do not remain constant over a period of time. The evidence of longitudinal studies is that children develop unevenly, a factor which adds to the demands created by individual differences. These differences call for corresponding variations of treatment, and these in turn suggest work in small groups and as individuals, with the teacher taking an active part. Group interaction is highly important in language activity and response to literature, and any decision to produce individual assignments and work-sheets should take account of this. Furthermore, opportunities of working together as a class should not be lost. In some classrooms this shared experience has almost entirely disappeared. We talked to teachers who never read a story or a poem to the class or talked to the children collectively. Indeed, some felt that they would be wrong to teach the class or any part of it directly, since this would compromise their commitment to a 'child-centred' programme. In our view this represents a serious narrowing of opportunities. Some of the conventions of language, for example, need to be taught directly; not necessarily to a full class, but *taught* none the less. The degree of 'structure' and the mode of learning will differ from one time and situation to another, and a teacher's repertoire of methods of organisation should be able to accommodate these various needs.

13.15   We might summarise our position by saying that our view of language learning has certain general implications for class and school organisation. Children learn to master their mother tongue at individual rates and by individual routes. All that goes on in a classroom may directly or indirectly contribute to the process, given an organisation flexible enough to allow this to happen. Independent work, by individuals and by groups, provides the best sustained context for effective instruction by the teacher and should therefore be the principal form of classroom activity. There will be some occasions when the teacher will find it appropriate to teach the whole class, or when the whole class will be watching or listening to something collectively. Where an organisation of this flexible kind is working successfully, frequent and regular timetable breaks are likely to amount to an interruption to learning.

13.16   Many witnesses urged that classes should be smaller, and in the questionnaire we took steps to find out the distribution of class size in our sample. They were as follows:

Table 10.

DISTRIBUTION OF CLASS SIZE FOR 6 AND 9 YEAR OLD PUPILS
(*Percentages*)

	Range of class sizes							All Classes
	1–15	16–20	21–25	26–30	31–35	36–40	41–45	
6 year old classes	2	4	10	25	40	19	—	100
9 year old classes	1	5	10	19	36	26	3	100
All 6 and 9 year old classes	1	4	10	22	38	22	2	100

This table tells its own story, and in our view there are still far too many classes which are larger than they should be. We would be going beyond our brief in recommending any particular level of pupil-teacher ratio. This is an issue which concerns the school situation in general, and not simply that part of it into which we have been inquiring. Nevertheless, the question of class size is important to our considerations, and it was certainly regarded as such in the schools we visited. Many teachers told us that with large classes they were unable to give individual attention with sufficient frequency and in sufficient depth. This is of particular importance in the early stages of reading, and unless the teacher can spend time with the individual child the kind of suggestions outlined in Chapter 7 cannot be effected. We recommend as a first step that schools should be staffed in September according to the largest number of children expected during the coming school year. At present many are staffed according to the expected average for the year. Since many schools with infants continue to take children at subsequent points in the year the result is generally a disturbance of the pattern of work. There is often an unsettling rearrangement of children and teachers, which almost invariably hampers progress. Even where the school contrives to avoid this rearrangement the arrival of new children progressively reduces the teacher's freedom to give individual attention. If the school were staffed at the maximum point at the beginning of the school year these disadvantages could be reduced.

13.17   Research evidence conflicts on the question of whether there is a correspondence between class size and standards. There was an interesting observation upon this matter in a large-scale comparative study[4] of reading in a number of countries: "it does not seem at all odd that no systematic relationship between class size and reading attainments had been found. The variety of experience in the classrooms of different countries is so complex that it would be surprising to find any simple connection of such a kind". The investigators said this held true despite quite large differences in class size from country to country, e.g. Sweden 25; Denmark 28; Norway 30; Germany 38; France, sometimes over 50. It was suggested, therefore, that other factors "overwhelm the differential effect of class size within this range of 25 to 50 pupils per teacher". The N.F.E.R. publication "A Pattern of Disadvantage"[5] comments usefully on the difference between teachers' views and research findings: "The findings (that is on class size and standards of attainment) relate to the measurable outcomes of education rather than to the more diffused concepts of quality in education"; "The fact that the majority of teachers will reject the evidence relating to class size is perhaps a reflection on the wear and tear they experience in handling large classes day after day". This is a helpful observation, for it seems to us a matter of commonsense that a teacher with a large number of children in his or her daily charge will find the situation more difficult to organise effectively than if the number were smaller. We emphasise the words "daily charge" and the "day after day" used in the N.F.E.R. publication. For there can be no strong grounds for arguing that teaching groups should invariably be confined to a given size. We have no hesitation in saying there should be an improvement in the pupil-teacher ratio, but it is not a simple matter of recommending a straight reduction in average class size. It is a question of relating improved resources to the demands *of any given situation* in as productive a manner as possible. A straightforward reduction in the number of children per class would be welcomed by teachers; of this there is no doubt. But schools should also be able to organise their classes in such a way that group size is matched to the needs of the work at any particular time. For example, it should be possible for whole classes or groups of classes to be divided, evenly or unevenly, from time to time to allow different kinds of activity. In some circumstances this would mean one or more teachers free of a main responsibility for a class, and therefore one or more other teachers temporarily having a larger group of children than usual. This would be one consequence of a flexibility where a group of teachers divide or re-divide the children between them. We believe that most teachers would accept this concept and that what they find most limiting is the constant and unrelieved pressure of working with a large class. In our view most primary schools are reaching a stage in their development where the chance to create very small groups as occasion demands would be more profitable to them than a simple reduction of average class size. The international study[6] cited experience in Denmark, where in recent years some classes have been divided into smaller units for lessons in the native language. The result, according to the Danish contributor to the report, has been that "division of classes for a few lessons has proved more satisfactory in its results than previous efforts directed at reducing the size of the whole class, for example from 32 to 28". We believe there can be considerable advantages where teachers work with a group of classes and divide and re-divide them to form clusters of varying abilities, interests, and numbers. There are, however, certain conditions essential to its success. The teachers should be committed to the idea, and the arrangement should not be introduced until they are able and willing to adapt their separate ways of working to the new demands. This implies careful planning and consultation, a clear understanding of the whole programme, and adequate facilities.

13.18   Before continuing the discussion of staffing we might consider briefly the last of these provisos, that of facilities. Later chapters are devoted to resources of various kinds, but we refer here to physical accommodation, for which flexibility of the sort we have been describing poses obvious questions. It would be wrong to assume that nothing can be done unless the spaces are purpose-designed. Some schools have been very successful in introducing patterns of variable grouping in premises offering no special facilities. Teachers have exercised great ingenuity in improvising to make old buildings and old furniture serve modern purposes. It is obvious, though, that where the building does not impose constraints the opportunities are so much the greater, and this has implications for primary school design. The best design recognises that educational methods and patterns of organisation are in a continuous process of evolution. This means that a building should offer its users a range of choices which will enable them to develop their work along a variety of lines. As a recent D.E.S. Design Note[7] expresses it: "The wide range of activities taking place in schools needs to be matched by equally varied facilities. Some activities are compatible, but others conflict and require separation. Each has its own requirements for a suitable teaching environment. Thus it is necessary to provide the right balance of spaces with different environmental conditions". A concept of this kind will allow for various small groupings, but also for a large number of children to be taught as a class. It will allow for freedom of movement where necessary, but also for reading and writing in the privacy and quiet of the enclosed space. Design should also take account of the involvement of parents and other adults in the daily life of the school, and the Design Note quoted above gives an interesting illustration. In our own recommendations we suggest that young children's language development will be furthered by increased opportunities for 1-to-1 conversation with adults. We believe that in the design of new nursery and infant schools the brief should include a requirement for several spaces to which an adult could withdraw with an individual child or a small group. When L.E.A.s are considering the most effective use of minor works money for modifications to school buildings, the value of this facility should be taken into account.

13.19   This takes us back to the question of staffing and to our recommendations for the extension of language work with young children. There is no need to repeat them here, but we would draw attention to the staffing implications of the extra demands they would create. For example, where a school is working with parents and accepting secondary school pupils (paragraphs 5.37; 5.11) the pressures on teacher time and attention are increased, and the authority's staffing policy should take account of this. We have suggested (paragraph 5.42) that it would be valuable for some schools to have facilities for visiting parents in their homes. Heads to whom we talked about this possibility preferred that members of their staff should have this opportunity rather than that an educational visitor be appointed for the purpose. The ideal might be an additional teacher whose home liaison role involved her not only in visiting but in working with a class while their teacher was herself visiting. These and associated suggestions in Chapter 5 are particularly relevant to the special needs of schools in inner city areas and other areas of marked social disadvantage. We are in no doubt that such schools require additional help. An examination of the difficulties they face makes it obvious that they need a more favourable staffing situation than schools which do not encounter them. These difficulties have been discussed in detail elsewhere in the Report, notably in Chapters 2 and 18, but we refer again to them here to emphasise the strain to which some schools are subject.

13.20   The National Child Development Study[8] pointed to certain environmental features which could be related to poor performance in reading, e.g. overcrowding and absence of amenities in the home. Family size was another factor, and the difference in reading attainment between first and fourth or later born children was equivalent to 16 months of reading age at the age of seven. The additional effect of two or more younger siblings could mean a loss of a further 7 months' reading age. The relationship between home environment and reading achievement was confirmed in all the developed countries in a recent international study[9]. It was found that home and family background provided an appreciably accurate prediction of the reading achievement of individual pupils and of the average achievement of children in a school. Several studies confirm that many backward readers display restlessness, antisocial behaviour, and a rebellious attitude. There is, then, ample evidence of a link between reading failure and socio-economic disadvantage and a relationship with emotional disturbance. The I.L.E.A. research department found that among children in Inner London schools there is a markedly higher incidence of emotional disturbance than the national average. The I.L.E.A. 1968 Literacy Survey revealed that at the age of eight one in six children was a poor reader compared with one in twelve nationally. The school questionnaire associated with that survey showed that on average 22 per cent of the school roll received special help with reading, mainly in small withdrawal groups. In our national sample

11 per cent of the twelve year old secondary pupils were in 'remedial' or withdrawal groups for this purpose.

13.21 We visited a number of inner city schools in London and elsewhere in the country whose difficulties derived from the severe social problems of the area. In one such school 47 per cent of the children were having free school dinners, 30 per cent were from one parent families, and the staff judged that 53 per cent came from 'problem families'. 50 per cent of the fourth year juniors were non-readers. Some schools draw almost all their pupils from areas where there is an extremely high incidence of overcrowding, crime, rent arrears, debt, lack of standard housing amenities, people living in one or two rooms, children in care, and referrals to social services departments. We are in no doubt that such schools need additional teachers, but we do not underestimate the difficulty of recruiting them. Some of the schools have an abnormally high rate of staff turnover[10], and we spoke to heads whose staffs had undergone two complete changes of personnel in three years. This mobility is often matched by that of the children themselves, and we visited one school where as many as 32 per cent of the eleven year olds had not started there at seven. Almost as high a proportion would have left the area before completing a secondary school course. In circumstances such as these the picture is one of shifting encounters, against a background which creates a need for sustained relationships and a sense of security. It is clear that steps so far taken, as in E.P.A. areas, have proved to be inadequate, and that this is a serious problem which calls for vigorous action involving more than simply educational agencies. We welcome the action of the Secretary of State in setting up a unit within the Department to study the problems of the disadvantaged, and his approval of an increased allowance to teachers working in stress areas.

13.22 There remains the important question of staff support within the school in language work and the teaching of reading. There is clear evidence that when above-scale payments are being allocated in primary schools English is all too often not even considered. Our own survey showed that of the schools with the power to award above-scale posts only 29 per cent have assigned one to responsibility for advising other teachers in the teaching of English. We feel this situation is unsatisfactory, and that it reflects a mistaken belief that any teacher can cope with all the varied aspects of English without additional training or specialist advice. We believe that every school should have a teacher with this responsibility, and that where authorities and schools have the power to make additional payment for it they should do so.

13.23 We have used the term English in order to emphasise the inclusiveness of the role. Several witnesses suggested that each school should have a teacher responsible for supporting his colleagues in the teaching of reading. This is a recommendation which we readily endorse, but we would broaden it to include the development of language in general. The task would be a demanding one, and a consideration of what it would involve makes it all the more surprising that such an important role is filled in so few schools. In the first place the teacher would act as consultant to his colleagues on matters of reading and language. It would fall to him to assess the results of screening and to discuss with his colleagues the diagnostic procedures and special help required by individual children. It is important to emphasise, however, that his concern extends beyond the language and reading needs of the slow learner, and should equally involve those of the able child. He would obviously need to be well informed of current developments and new materials, and this would include a knowledge of children's literature, since one of his responsibilities would be the guidance discussed in Chapter 21. As a teacher with a special contribution to make in a particular area of the curriculum he would play an important part in any re-grouping arrangements of the kind described earlier. It would be unprofitable for us to attempt to define too closely the extent of such a teacher's function. To do so would be to risk circumscribing it or extending it beyond the practicable, for a great deal will depend upon the size of the school. For example, in a small school it would be reasonable for the post to include responsibility for library books. In a large school this would clearly need to lie with another member of staff, though both teachers would work in close co-operation. For this recommendation to have the best effect there would have to be adequate preparation. Though there are many teachers in primary schools with a keen interest in language development and reading, there is a limit to the number with a special knowledge of them. This would mean effective in-service training provision for the teachers selected for these posts. It would also mean sustained support from the local authority advisory team, whose role we consider in a later chapter. At present neither of these forms of support is sufficiently well developed in most authorities to perform the task, or, for that matter, the more general one of helping schools to a better understanding of English teaching. We emphasise that all teachers in the primary school must carry equal responsibility for language and that for this reason they should receive support of these two kinds in the teaching of English in all its aspects.

13.24   The importance of good leadership by the head cannot be overstated. This was identified by Morris[11] in her Kent survey as a characteristic of those schools which achieved good reading standards and progress. The heads produced carefully defined goals and the organisation necessary to attain them. They were enthusiastic teachers, involving themselves in the work of the classroom and providing an example to their staff. A similar conclusion emerged from the Co-operative Reading Studies of the U.S. Office of Education, where an important factor in success was found to be "the amount of interest and attention given to the organisation of the reading programme by the school administration". Our own visits left us in no doubt that where the head sets a high value on language development an essential precondition for success has been established. This reveals itself in a variety of ways, of which concern to raise every child's level of achievement is the most apparent. There is a positive expectation for every child, and the staff are encouraged to keep careful records of each child's progress. There is a receptivity to new ideas and approaches, which are not adopted uncritically but evaluated carefully. The head discusses them with his staff and puts them into practice only where the conditions are right and an improvement in standards is likely to result. This is an aspect of the notion of the school as its own in-service training unit. Sometimes courses will be held within the school, and whenever a member of staff attends an outside course its benefits are shared with colleagues. The head's own part in this process is of vital importance, and his leadership can often find its best expression when he works alongside his colleagues in the classroom. The appointment of a teacher with a responsibility for language and reading would not diminish the importance of this leadership. Indeed, support of this kind would help the head to realise the policy more effectively. It cannot be emphasised too strongly that the teacher is the biggest single factor for success in learning to read and use language. The school with high standards of reading is the one where the teachers are knowledgeable about it and are united in ascribing to it a very high priority. A coherent strategy, understood and agreed by the staff, is the best instrument for improving standards of reading and language, and the head's part in the process is central to its success. In small schools, where the head is called upon to take responsibility for a class for a substantial part of the time, there should be some provision to enable him to fulfil this role, including generous secretarial assistance.

REFERENCES

1. *Education: A Framework for Expansion:* H.M.S.O.: 1972 and Circular No. 2/73: Department of Education and Science: 1973.
2. S. Yudkin: *0–5: A report on the Care of Pre-School Children:* National Society of Children's Nurseries: 1967.
3. *The Illegal Child Minders:* Priority Area Children: 1972.
4. J. Downing (ed.): *Comparative Reading:* Macmillan, New York: 1973.
5. D. Donnison (ed.): *A Pattern of Disadvantage:* N.F.E.R.: 1972.
6. J. Downing (ed.): *op. cit.*
7. *Design Note 11: Chaucer Infant and Nursery School, Ilkeston, Derbyshire:* Architects and Building Branch, Department of Education and Science: H.M.S.O.: 1973.
8. R. Davie, N. Butler, and H. Goldstein: *From Birth to Seven:* Longmans: 1972.
9. R. L. Thorndike: *Reading Comprehension Education in Fifteen Countries: International Studies in Evaluation III:* International Association for the Evaluation of Educational Achievement: 1973.
10. See Report on Education No. 79, *Teacher Turnover:* Department of Education and Science: 1974.
11. J. M. Morris: *Standards and Progress in Reading:* N.F.E.R.: 1966.

CHAPTER 14

Continuity Between Schools

INFANT AND FIRST SCHOOL—JUNIOR AND MIDDLE SCHOOL

14.1   Over 40 years ago the Hadow Report[1] urged that there should be no sharp division between infant, junior, and post-primary stages, and that the transition from any given stage to the succeeding one should be as smooth and gradual as possible. The Plowden Report[2] developed the same theme, remarking that though contacts between schools were still inadequately cultivated there was evidence of a real improvement. This improvement has continued, so that at any rate it is uncommon to find a school that does not recognise the importance of the principle. This is particularly true where it concerns transition from infant to junior school, with which we are concerned in this section. It was the experience of our visits that the relationship often does not go far beyond an obvious goodwill and a readiness to co-operate in general terms. However, a number of schools have developed a range of useful joint activities. In the first place they have recognised that at the point of transfer a young child has a particular need of security and reassurance. They have therefore arranged an exchange of teachers so that the first year junior teacher becomes an accustomed figure to the young children who will soon be going up to her; or the children themselves have spent days in small groups in the classroom which will be their home the following term. Correspondingly, a teacher from the infants has spent part of each day in the junior school, keeping contact with those recently transferred and in particular the ones who still need help with reading. Schools occupying the same building have set up common working and quiet areas in corridors or other available spaces. There have been joint assemblies, plays, and outings. All these are admirable developments which enable separate schools to achieve the kind of sharing that is available to the 5–11 school. Moreover, they are the translation into action of a philosophy of continuity based on regular inter-staff discussion. We are concerned in these paragraphs with the extent and quality of co-operation as it relates to the development of language and reading skills. This is likely to be most successful where it is an aspect of the kind of linked identity we have described. It must be emphasised, however, that continuity in respect of language and reading development needs to receive detailed attention in its own right.

14.2   The first essential is a thorough knowledge of the other school's approaches and methods. If the infant school has followed the practice of observing and recording the children's language development (see Chapters 5 and 17) the junior school must be aware of what has been achieved. Equally, it would be regrettable if a school were to involve parents in the work of the classroom only for the practice to be brought to a sudden end at the point of transfer. Such sharp severances do occur. We encountered situations where the infant school was committed to i.t.a. and the junior school hostile to it. The latter would have no i.t.a. books in the school, so that when the children arrived they were uncompromisingly presented with traditional orthography whether or not they had managed the transition. This kind of thing is a symptom of a general lack of sympathy between the schools concerned. And a lack of sympathy results from and results in an inadequate understanding of the other school's objectives and methods. The teaching of reading offers a good example of this. We talked to some junior school teachers who expected every child to be sent up to them 'able to read', or at any rate regarded any who couldn't as the infant school's failures. A number of the letters we received reflected the same opinion. This is to take a very limited view of reading, not to mention the nature of individual differences in children. Moreover, it overlooks the fact that up to a third of the children may have spent only six terms in the infant school and some will have been in the country for only a few months or even weeks. Reading is the subject of too much recrimination. The idea that reading is a once for all process, learned when young and afterwards possessed as a fixed skill, has the effect that the blame is always passed downwards. In the nature of things the infant school is held ultimately responsible. If reading were seen for what it is—a developmental process of which decoding is only one stage—there would be a better chance of mutual understanding. It is unrealistic to insist that certain objectives are the sole responsibility of the infant school, and that the junior school should be able to plan a programme on an assured base line. The recognition of this is a feature of those schools which have developed a high degree of co-operation. Where they exchange teachers, have a regular programme of meetings, and discuss examples of children's work, they will come to understand and perhaps share one another's approach. They will arrive at a set of realistic objectives which are regarded not as fixed goals for each age-group, but rather as a series of 'landmarks' attainable over the years.

14.3   When a group of children move into a junior school or department at the beginning of the school year the range of their capability, performance, experience and circumstances is considerable. In some areas the summer-born will have had the disadvantage of completing only six or seven terms in their first school, while others will have had a full nine terms*. Some children will have passed the entire five or six weeks' holiday without access to a word of print, and their reading ability might well have regressed. Others will have read to their parents every day and had stories read to them, and they will have gained in fluency. Missing the support of the constructive talk of the infant school, some will have had very little sustained two-way conversation in the home. Others will have been encouraged to talk about their experiences and will have had long conversations with their parents. The receiving teacher should be informed of all this. She is likely to know that a child has had less than the full nine terms in his first school. She is less likely to know his experience of language in general and reading in particular within the home. Older brothers and sisters are a guide, and schools grow to know some families extremely well as one child follows another. However, for all its apparent predictive reliability this is a crude indicator. Every child is an individual, and the receiving teacher needs detailed information about the children who come to her. Ideally she will have met and perhaps worked with the child and his teacher frequently over the past year, in his classroom and her own. She will know what her colleague has been doing to develop the child's linguistic repertoire. She will have met the

*In Barker Lunn's study ("Educational Research" Vol. 14 No. 2) 26 per cent of the children were found to have completed nine terms in the infant school: 24 per cent had completed eight terms, 24 per cent seven terms, and 26 per cent six terms.

parents in the infant school. We accept that what we have described is an ideal and may be rarely attainable in full, particularly where large junior and middle schools draw children from a number of sources. Nevertheless, we believe it can and should be done by all schools to some degree, and the more highly developed the relationship the better. To be effective it requires the commitment of the teachers, above all of the heads, and collaborative planning of the right kind.

14.4   There is no substitute for first-hand knowledge of the children and of the kind of learning situation in which they have been involved. But this should be supported by a full set of records which gives the receiving teacher information in several dimensions. Diagnosis and recording are discussed in Chapter 17, and it is sufficient here to say that the records which accompany a child from the first or infant school are all too often inadequate. Rarely are there indications of a child's specific strengths and weaknesses, recorded in such a way as to help the teacher at the next level to give special attention to them. We have recommended that the teacher in the nursery and infant school should appraise the children's language in order to develop their ability to use more complex forms. It is essential that the information gathered in the course of this appraisal should be passed on to the junior school, which has the responsibility of continuing the process of language development. The same need for precise information applies to progress in reading. It is not sufficient to supply a reading age or indicate the page the child has reached in the book of a particular reading scheme. The nature of a child's reading difficulties should be identified, recorded, and handed on. The results of our survey revealed that a substantial number of junior schools tested the children's reading during their first term in the school. It can be inferred from this that the receiving schools did not feel they had sufficient information about the child and needed to establish his standard of attainment. However, our survey also showed (Table 39) that the majority of schools administer a simple word recognition test, which when used to obtain a reading age will not reveal the child's points of weakness. Moreover, it is clearly better to avoid submitting the child to tests so soon after entry. Records of the kind we are recommending would direct the attention of the child's new teacher to features of his reading which were continuing to give difficulty. They would also be a valuable part of the screening procedure which we go on to recommend, the two essential features of which are close observation in the infant school and in some cases the administration of a test towards the end of the child's first term in the junior school or department (see Chapter 17). The fact that the screening process might extend across the point of transfer is another argument for close collaboration.

14.5   Our survey showed that 39 per cent of the teachers of the six year olds kept examples of children's written work from year to year as a progress record. What the responses could not tell us was whether this accumulation of written work was passed on with the child to his next school. Such a 'profile' would obviously be of great value to the junior school, and we recommend that all schools should consider adopting this practice. Only three or four examples a year need be included; too copious a collection would defeat the purpose. One important benefit would be to help teachers towards realistic expectations. Wiseman[3] and others have pointed out that a teacher's expectation of a pupil's performance can have a powerful influence on the quality of that performance. If teachers frequently discuss actual examples of children's work and such folders are compiled then the assessment will be more soundly based.

14.6   Just as some of a child's writing should accompany him, so should his reading material. One outcome of the kind of co-operation we have advocated would be a continuity of approach between the two schools. We have already referred to the kind of acute disjuncture sometimes to be found where a junior school is hostile to the i.t.a. through which the child has begun to learn to read. A less severe and more common practice is to introduce a reading scheme completely different from the one with which the child has been familiar. The security of familiarity is essential to a child who is still having some difficulty with reading, and he will respond better to the spur of new material when he is working from a well-established base. On the other hand, the child who is reading well will welcome the stimulus of a variety of new books, and any continuity of approach should take account of individual need for fresh enterprises. Ideally, the two schools should plan together a joint programme for the development of reading. Elsewhere in the Report we have recommended book-selling activities in school. We hope that where a child has become accustomed to this facility he will not lose it at the next stage. When an infant and junior school occupy the same building they might share book-club or book-shop facilities. Where this is not the case the schools should discuss ways in which they can co-operate to expand the children's reading opportunities.

JUNIOR AND MIDDLE SCHOOL—SECONDARY SCHOOL

14.7   There has been a gradual increase in the development of liaison between primary, middle, and secondary schools, and some excellent schemes have been evolved. Some secondary schools have appointed a member of staff, usually a teacher of first year pupils, to maintain contact with the contributory schools. In a few instances the secondary school sends the children's first year progress reports to their former school to let their teachers see how they have settled in. Schools on both sides of the point of transfer have organised joint events, and the younger pupils have learned to feel at home in the upper school well before they have come to join it. Members of staff have exchanged visits and in some cases teaching assignments. Activity of this kind is by no means the general rule, but there have been some highly encouraging enterprises.

14.8   There are, of course, many schools where the only intimation of a child's earlier education is what is contained in the authority's record card which precedes or accompanies him. These naturally vary a good deal, but they may contain little more than columns for Reading, Speech, Written English, Number, and Intelligence, with assessment on a five-point lettering scale. At their most elaborate they may contain a wide range of diagnostic information and extensive teacher comment. How much does a C against Speech tell about a child's oral ability? Does such a shadowy assessment incline the receiving school to distrust and therefore disregard it? On the other hand does detailed information set up teacher expectations that may 'type' the child before he appears? Questions of this kind tempt some teachers into an unfortunate doubt about the value of transmitted records, and in the absence of inter-school contacts the two phases may work in relative isolation from one another.

14.9   The English teacher may feel that within a comparatively short time he will be able to assess his new pupils on the strength of the work they produce for him. He may therefore ask whether there is much value in his knowing what has happened before they reach him. We have made clear our conviction that there is, and that a knowledge of their language experience in all its forms is essential to him. Where there is a well-organised policy of general liaison at school level this will be easier to acquire, but in our view continuity is so important that links should certainly be established between secondary school English departments and the contributory primary schools.

14.10   Transmitted records are but one aspect of this policy of continuity, and the information they contain should be such as to give genuine guidance to the secondary school English department and to teachers of other subjects. Vagueness of definition is unhelpful and is paradoxically more likely to set up confining expectations than is an extensive array of information. The right degree of detail enables teachers at both levels to meet on commonly understood ground. Subjective assessment is valuable, but it is the more revealing for being supported by objective data and actual evidence of performance. As in the case of infant to junior school transfer we have in mind a profile which would include diagnostic information and examples of written work. The essential thing about diagnostic data is that they should help the receiving teacher to plan his work in respect of the particular pupil. Again a bare reading age is not enough; the teacher in the secondary school should have access to the experience of the child that other teachers have accumulated over the years. Several have worked with him, have had opportunities to identify his difficulties, and know what has succeeded and what has failed. All this valuable information should not be allowed to go to waste.

14.11   In the matter of language continuity there seems to us no substitute for a study of children's actual production. This is why we suggest that the developmental profile should contain examples of pupils' written work to the extent of three to four pieces per year. This cumulative record of language development, supported by teacher comment, would be of considerable practical value to successive teachers. It should be accompanied by an indication of the books the pupil has read and by the results of informal reading inventories (see Chapter 17). We have suggested that an increase in voluntary reading is an important factor in the improvement of reading attainment in the late junior and early secondary years. Obviously, a teacher cannot know everything a child reads, but as comprehensive a picture as possible of his reading habits would be a valuable instrument. At the most obvious level it tells the teacher a great deal about that particular pupil and provides a foundation from which to develop his future reading. It seems to us a haphazard procedure when a secondary school teacher can receive a child without any information on his experience of reading beyond what he can glean from the child himself. We regard it as fundamental that this kind of information should be recorded and should form part of the profile which one teacher passes on to another.

14.12   Behind the word 'continuity' there lies the implication of a positive attitude to co-operation between the phases. It is our experience that primary and secondary schools often know little of one another's methods and aims. Where they do, there is usually sympathy; where they do not there is the possibility of misunderstanding, prejudice, and an inclination to denigrate. The stereotype is that primary school methods are always to be identified with process, creativity, and self-determination; secondary school methods with content, rigour, and direct instruction. This, it need hardly be said, is far from the truth. We are arguing here not simply for the transmitted knowledge of a particular pupil's capacities and needs but for a mutual understanding of what has been and will be involved in his experience of language. A child can leave the primary school with a well-defined awareness of his teacher's range of response to his writing. Within weeks he is in a school where several teachers are making different kinds of demand on his written language. He does not know their expectations, and indeed he may well be quite unprepared for the linguistic demands made upon him.

14.13   Expectations need to be realistic and they need to be informed by a first-hand study of how children write and talk in response to the needs of a given situation. In Chapter 12 we recommended the development of a language policy across the curriculum in secondary schools. At this point we are suggesting that a valuable first step might be a joint study by primary and secondary teachers of children's written and spoken language. This could be associated with an exchange of teaching assignments. We are aware that this is not as simple as it sounds. One secondary school we encountered received pupils from 40 contributory primary schools. This is untypical, but in much less extreme situations there could still be considerable difficulty in arranging this kind of co-operation. Nevertheless, there seems to us a good case for accepting it as a principle. It is impracticable to expect secondary school teachers to sustain separate discussions with each of a large number of primary schools, still less teach in all of them. But joint conferences are a viable proposition, and the opportunity can be created for various groupings for this purpose.

14.14   It is not only at the level of staff contact that possibilities exist for co-operation between primary and secondary schools. There is scope for the kind of activity in which older children work with and for younger ones. This might, for example, take the form of the writing of stories for six or seven year olds by fourth year junior pupils. They would need to talk with the younger children about their interests and their favourite kinds of story as part of the preparation for writing. After drafting the stories they would ask fifth and sixth year secondary pupils to act as editors, and from the resulting discussion the stories would emerge. Their writers would then read them to some of the younger children and listen to others using the stories as part of their own reading material. By applying an informal reading inventory the writers would be able to refashion their stories to adjust readability levels, and this would entail further visits to their editors, with whom all the implications would be discussed. Finally the stories, attractively printed, would take their place among the young children's reading matter. In a project of this kind, which is capable of many variations, children are co-operating at various levels for a real purpose. The junior and secondary pupils are involved in discussions about shaping language to do a particular job, and they have to study the needs and interests of young children to do it.

14.15 In their role as providers the older pupils gain at least as much as the ones they are helping, and this is a characteristic of 'cross-age tutoring'. This is an activity which has been employed extensively in the U.S.A. and is being tried by some schools in this country, often with the help of Community Service Volunteers. Older pupils give individual tuition to younger ones in their own or another school, deriving help and support from their teachers in sustaining it. This has been found to develop a relationship from which the younger child gains a new kind of support and the older pupil a feeling of responsibility and achievement. The schools which have adopted it do not minimise the difficulties and the obvious need for patience and diplomacy in organising such a scheme. But they are almost always enthusiastic about its benefits, both direct and indirect. Given the right degree of commitment this kind of work can be a profitable form of co-operation between schools.

14.16 It has to be frankly acknowledged that despite advances there are still many schools which have almost no contact with the one that precedes or follows them. In our view effective liaison is a priority need, and if it can include practical activities of the kind we have been describing there will be a considerable gain in the understanding of one another's objectives. We have urged that reading be regarded as a continuously developing skill and that language be extended to meet increasingly complex demands as the child grows older. Neither aim can be achieved without close co-operation and mutual confidence.

REFERENCES

1. *Reports of the Consultative Committee:* H.M.S.O.: 1926, 1931, 1933.
2. *Children and their Primary Schools:* H.M.S.O.: 1967.
3. S. Wiseman: *The Educational obstacle race: Factors that hinder pupil progress:* Educational Research, 15, 87–93: 1973.

CHAPTER 15

The Secondary School

15.1 We suggested earlier that since language pervades the curriculum there is no place for specialisation in English in the primary school. We also suggested that liaison between primary and secondary school should be so close as to allow the child to go on perceiving English as a continuous experience without sharp breaks. Our visits to schools led us to conclude that this is all too rarely achieved. On transfer the majority of children move into a situation where work in English is abruptly separated from all their other activities. In recent years there has been much talk of 'breaking subject barriers' and 'new integrated approaches', particularly with reference to first and second year pupils and those in their last year of statutory schooling. The intention in the case of the former is to reduce the sense of fragmentation in the minds of pupils who have always been accustomed to one teacher for most of the working day. Sometimes the practice is for the form tutor to take them for several subjects, of which English is one. Sometimes the teachers of a number of subjects (e.g., history, geography, religious education, social studies, English) work together as a team and jointly plan the course. This kind of organisation is variously interpreted, and it ranges from a situation where the subjects are linked in a loose interrelationship to one in which they lose definition altogether. Occasionally it is the practice to timetable one or two additional periods of English separately. With the fourth year pupils the purpose of 'integration' is usually to provide courses that school leavers might find relevant and attractive, and this generally means the involvement of several teachers in one or other variation of the pattern just mentioned.

15.2 When such arrangements have been discussed English has almost invariably been one of the subjects assumed to be an obvious participant. Perhaps unexpectedly, therefore, we found that 93 per cent of the twelve year olds in our sample were taught English as a separately timetabled subject. Only 7 per cent experienced it in the context of one or another form of integrated studies. The figures for the fourteen year olds were similar at 94 per cent and 6 per cent respectively. Our sample pupils did not include eleven year olds, and the survey could not therefore identify situations where children were timetabled for integrated studies in their first year before passing to specialist English in their second. However, since only 2 per cent of the schools organised English as part of a 'multi-subject' department it seems likely that most of the eleven year olds went straight into 'specialist' English. It is necessary to qualify the term 'specialist' before we go any further, since it cannot be taken to mean that they necessarily receive their English at the hands of a teacher with qualifications in the subject. Indeed, our survey showed that one third of the teachers teaching some English in secondary schools had no such qualifications, a point to which we return later.

15.3 We must begin our brief evaluation of integration and specialisation by pointing out that we are concerned here only with its effects upon the teaching of English. Our remit does not take us as far as an examination of its value in general terms, though we would suggest that for integration to be successful it must take place in the mind of the child and not remain a notion in the mind of the teacher. An arrangement we encountered in our visits to schools was one in which each form tutor takes the pupils for several subjects, including English. Unfortunately, although they may be responsible for four or five subjects many of the teachers do not attempt to 'integrate' them, but teach them as separate entities. Whether or not they are successful depends to a very large extent on the support and guidance they receive from heads of department. A teacher whose training and background is in another subject often lacks any knowledge of children's literature and any acquaintance with current ideas about language development. It is a serious disservice to him and to the pupils to allocate him a course book, a poetry anthology, and some sets of class readers and assume he can take it from there. Only by being drawn into the life and thinking of the English department can he be properly sustained. This exposes a fundamental problem of the arrangement by which the form tutor teaches several subjects, for what applies to English applies equally to the others. A teacher cannot be expected to make himself an integral part of several separate departments without a great deal of help.

15.4   Where integrated studies are taught by a team of teachers from a number of subject areas there are varying degrees of sophistication in the way of working. Perhaps the commonest is where they decide upon a theme which will occupy a given number of weeks and through which the various subject interests will find expression. It is often launched by a 'key lesson', or audio-visual presentation, at which the whole year group is present. In the weeks that follow the pupils work in groups or individually with assignment cards or work sheets, which the teachers have co-operated to prepare. In principle this and similar forms of co-operative arrangement hold much more promise than the one we described above. They must, however, be able to stand up to the same kind of question if the school is to be certain that the teaching of English is not to suffer. The plain truth is that before any school makes a decision on whether English should be integrated in some way or taught separately there are several questions it must ask itself. If English is to be associated with three or four other subjects what is likely to be the effect upon the pupil's experience of oral and written language? Will this experience be restricted or expanded by the demands of the other constituents? Will the teachers be able to create situations in which literature illuminates the other elements in the course and in turn gains a dimension from them? How well equipped are the teachers to handle what becomes an exacting situation? It has been argued against such a form of organisation that it weakens the control of the learning process, that it leaves to chance what could otherwise be guaranteed. It has also been suggested that the experience it embodies lacks depth and any true organic quality. The pupils' writing becomes narrow in range, with the factual predominating and the imaginative finding little place. Literature tends to be either neglected or bent to conform with the dictates of the other components. As one of our witnesses put it, "There is a danger that the poem or story can be subtly distorted because it is used as an illustration of a pre-announced theme, whereas in reality, if its true nature were attended to, it would have to be recognised as more complex, and indeed multi-thematic rather than mono-thematic. There is a danger also that the poem or story may be used as a starting off point for discussion or writing rather than valued as an experience in itself, a situation which may lead to overemphasis on material which is moved through quickly *en route* to another goal, rather than on material which is dwelt on, savoured, and fully enjoyed". There is much substance in such objections, and in the even more serious one that the teachers involved may lack any knowledge of English teaching. For example, we visited schools where the first and second years experienced English only in the context of humanities but where the involvement of a teacher of English was quite fortuitous. In one or two such instances the head of English department was outside the arrangement to the point of not knowing what the children were encountering in the way of English during those two years; his responsibility began when the pupils entered the third year. We cannot emphasise too strongly the need for strong specialist representation where English is part of an integrated programme, whatever form this may take.

15.5   But if English can lack identity in such schemes it is not immune from a lack of purpose when taught in its own right. This occurs when it is not backed by a well thought out policy, by a unifying intention which has emerged from a sense of direction worked out in staff discussions. This lack of clearly understood purpose reveals itself in the separate development of the various 'compartments', the writing being unrelated to the talk, the talk to the literature. It is often manifest in the written work, where there is a 'bittiness', a lack of a supporting framework, a sense of the piece existing in a vacuum. We believe, then, that to divide the English programme into a number of compartments, unrelated and separated by timetable boundaries, is a very limiting procedure. At the same time we must acknowledge that the abandonment of this practice, though an immense gain for well-organised and imaginative teachers, has sometimes left others without a sense of direction. In such cases there is a confusion about how a teacher is to devise a sequence of activity that will fulfil his aims and give the pupils a sense of purpose. This is a matter in which the head of department's leadership is of vital importance, and it is one of the main reasons for the prominence we give later in the chapter to the development of an 'instrument of policy'.

15.6   We regard the opposition of specialised English and integrated studies as a false issue, for it is evading the fundamentals to regard them as mutually exclusive. These fundamentals can be reduced quite simply to objective planning. Specialist areas of interest exist whether they remain separate or are 'folded into' others, and the school has to decide what are its objectives for each. What is needed as a basic principle is not that English should necessarily claim for itself 'separate development' but that it should truly *inform* the other areas of interest. If it becomes part of an integrated scheme it must retain a valid presence, sustained by specialist knowledge and adequate resources. This means that the kind of work described in Chapters 9, 10 and 11 must be represented to the same extent and in the same depth as if English were taught separately. If it is timetabled as a separate subject it must reach out to other areas of interest, drawing upon them for its material through close co-operation with the teachers concerned. Our own view is that there should be other forms of working than two straight alternatives. For example, certain aspects of the work might emerge from the integrated pattern, crystallise outside its context, form the subject of separate study, and then be re-immersed. The theme described in paragraph 9.6 is an illustration of this. Without proper planning such a topic would depend upon information books for its associated reading. But if the literature is expertly assembled it can come into its own outside the programme, gaining from the context in which it was first introduced and contributing to it by return.

15.7   We are not prepared to recommend a simple organisational solution which would imply that a given structure will solve the various problems. It is spirit, clear aims, understanding, and planning that achieve the results, and none of these is the automatic by-product of a system of organisation. We believe that talk is more fluent, writing more committed, and reading more avid when English in seen as a complex and organic interaction between them and the whole range of the child's experience. The decision that faces the school is how best to bring this interaction about in the light of its own particular circumstances.

15.8   We gave close consideration to suggestions made to us that *reading* might be taught by a separate 'specialised' approach. It was argued by some witnesses that since there is a hierarchy of reading skills it is illogical to confine the specialist teaching to those pupils who are still experiencing difficulty with the most fundamental of them. We have considered the merits of this argument in Chapter 8 and do not feel able to support the notion of separate and specialised teaching of reading. However, we believe that if it is not to exist in this form there must be firm measures to ensure that its positive features are available in equivalent strength. This means that every teacher must be able and prepared to teach children to read within his own subject. We have recommended that this should form a part of teacher training, and in the meantime it calls for support within the schools. At present most schools have no policy for developing reading across the curriculum, and English departments do not see it as one of their functions. We believe that the English department should consider the development of reading skills at all levels and in all its aspects as one of its most important responsibilities. As part of the school's policy for language across the curriculum it should offer guidance in the extension of this ability in all the pupil's learning activities. For this purpose it is desirable there should be at least one member of staff with advanced qualifications in reading. The effect of modern approaches in many subjects is to put a higher premium than ever on the ability to read. There is increasing use of assignment cards and work-sheets. All too often these and the tasks they prescribe make no allowance for individual differences in reading ability, and the advice given to subject departments should include a concern for readability levels in the material being used.

15.9   In the section on *drama* we suggested that secondary schools should ponder in relation to their own circumstances whether it should be taught as part of English or within a separate department. We hinted a third possibility: that both practices might exist in combination. 84 per cent of the secondary schools in our sample taught drama "as part of the work of the English department". We have already made clear our views on the value of drama for language development, and where drama is integrated with English the link can be exploited at will by the teacher who is responsible for both. On the other hand complete integration has real practical difficulties, not the least of which is that many excellent teachers of English are unqualified by training, experience, or temperament to handle improvised drama. Further, there are good arguments for the separate existence of drama to provide a run of time when its themes and developments can be pursued in their own terms. This is particularly true for the older adolescent years, and in our visits we saw some splendid dramatic work with fourth and fifth year pupils in separate drama options. Ideally, then, we would recommend that in the secondary school drama should be an essential part of work in English while at the same time having scope as an activity in its own right. If constraints of time, staffing, or accommodation rule this out we would urge that there should be compensatory measures. For instance, where drama exists only within the English department one of its members should be appropriately qualified and carry the responsibility of supporting and advising his colleagues. If drama has come to be concentrated within a separate department it is of the utmost importance that the teachers involved in it should work in very close co-operation with the English department. In either case, the teachers responsible should look for opportunities to relate drama to pupils' work in other areas of the curriculum.

15.10   We have been discussing various aspects of the position of English as a specialist area and must now pursue the fundamentals of objectives and planning. First, the question of pupil grouping. It is not part of our brief to assess the respective general merits of various forms of grouping, such as streaming, setting, broad banding, and mixed ability. That issue has, in any case, been exhaustively discussed elsewhere, and our concern here is confined to the implications for English of certain of the variations. Diagram 10 shows the distribution of pupil groupings for the teaching of English in our sample secondary schools. It will be seen that the practice of mixed ability teaching, comparatively uncommon in secondary schools at one time, has become fairly widespread, especially for the twelve year olds. 18 per cent were in groups which drew from the whole of the school's ability range, while another 14 per cent were in groups which excluded only the 'remedial' pupils. Speaking purely for English, most of us have reservations about arrangements by which pupils are streamed or setted according to ability. However careful the process, classifying individuals in this way makes different pupils in the same group seem more similar than they are, and similar pupils in different groups seem more different than they are. Moreover, we believe that even if it were possible to grade children accurately according to language ability it would be to deprive the less able of the stimulus they so badly need. Less commonly acknowledged, but equally important, is the fact that it would steadily deprive the more able of opportunities to communicate with the linguistically less accomplished. Of course, the actual effect in the classroom of mixed ability grouping varies widely according to the spectrum of ability within the school's intake. Such a group in an inner city area is very different from one in a suburban area. A good deal also depends on the size of the group (for example, there is a great difference between a mixed ability class of 20 pupils and one of 30) and on such factors as accommodation and the pastoral organisation of the school.

Diagram 10

METHODS OF GROUPING FOR THE TEACHING OF ENGLISH IN THE SAMPLE
SECONDARY SCHOOLS—

12 AND 14 YEAR OLDS

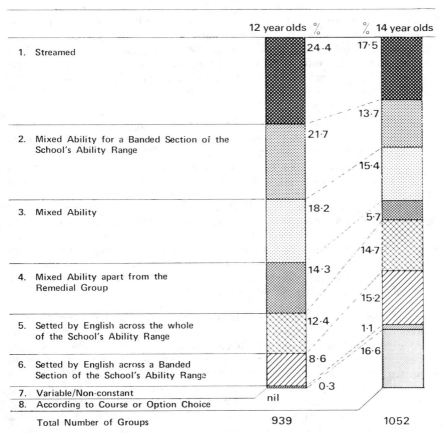

	12 year olds %	% 14 year olds
1. Streamed	24·4	17·5
		13·7
2. Mixed Ability for a Banded Section of the School's Ability Range	21·7	
		15·4
3. Mixed Ability	18·2	5·7
		14·7
4. Mixed Ability apart from the Remedial Group	14·3	
		15·2
5. Setted by English across the whole of the School's Ability Range	12·4	1·1
		16·6
6. Setted by English across a Banded Section of the School's Ability Range	8·6	
7. Variable/Non-constant	0·3	
8. According to Course or Option Choice	nil	
Total Number of Groups	939	1052

15.11   Before a school decides to adopt this kind of grouping for the teaching of English there are a number of questions it has to ask itself, of which the following are merely examples. How can the children with serious reading difficulties be given the kind of individual help they require within a class totally mixed in ability? Is it proposed to withdraw them for at least part of the time, or alternatively to have additional teachers in the classroom to give support? Is there a risk that the small group interaction so valuable in English will be lost in favour of almost continuous individual activity? How can the shared study of pieces of writing, and particularly full length works, be managed with so wide a range of ability? The first and second of these questions are of particular importance, and mixed ability grouping should certainly not be introduced until the school has worked out detailed plans in response to it. Indeed, we are bound to express our own reservations about the kind of grouping which goes so far as to include children who are experiencing difficulties of this kind. The third question is

K

fundamental to an understanding of the complex organisation required if this kind of grouping is to be successful. In some of the mixed ability classes we visited the children were being taught as if they were a homogeneous group, much of their experience being direct class teaching aimed at the middle of the range. In others the work was so finely individualised that the class rarely came together for a collective experience. Between these extremes were examples of imaginative planning to give the pupils a variety of learning experiences. The plain truth is that mixed ability teaching requires sound classroom control of the pupils, and considerable skill in teaching and the organisation of learning resources. The above questions raise issues about which misgivings were expressed in the evidence we received. These can be seen in the words of a witness who in principle was warmly in favour of mixed ability teaching:

"The full nature of the problem may perhaps be brought home by a reminder that in a first-year secondary school class containing the full range of ability, the English teacher may encounter an extraordinarily wide spread in reading age (e.g., from seven to fourteen), and an accompanying wide divergence in maturity of reading interest and taste. . . . What may tend to happen is a concentration, sometimes unnoticed, on these areas of English teaching (talk, dramatisation, writing) in which divergence of reading level is minimised, and in which, therefore, the mixed ability class can be held together as a cohesive unit, within which groups are at any rate doing related things, even if not necessarily doing the same things at the same time". "What often seems to go unrecognised . . . is the really massive and massively varied provision of books which is absolutely essential if the class library is genuinely to meet the needs of a secondary class of fully mixed ability".

15.12   Observations of this kind are useful reminders that the complexities inherent in mixed ability teaching are considerable. They do not alter the views of those of us who are convinced that where it is practicable this is the form of grouping which offers most hope for English teaching, but they do reinforce our common belief that it requires a great deal of thought and planning. There should be carefully judged opportunities for learning as a class, and a flexible pattern of group and individual work. For this, thematic work is a valuable unifying device, but it should be so conceived as to avoid the limitations we described in paragraph 9.16. We were fortunate to see some excellent examples of mixed ability teaching in our visits to schools, and they all had one feature in common. They had the unanimous support of the teachers involved, who had all been consulted before the system was introduced and then drawn into the planning. We must repeat the observation we made in the corresponding chapter on the primary school: innovations of any kind are of real value only if teachers are able to assimilate them properly and use them to improve upon their previous practice.

15.13   As we have said, the more complex the teaching arrangements the more is demanded of the teachers in terms of skill, organising ability, and knowledge of resources. This takes us to the question of the supply of qualified English teachers, a matter to which we made brief reference earlier in the chapter. English teaching has been fortunate in the quality of the people taking it up since the war. It has attracted men and women of ability and energy with a wide range of interests and a commitment to young people and social improvements. Nevertheless, the staffing situation is not a happy one, and in our enquiries we found that schools were experiencing many difficulties. For one thing there is too great a mobility of teachers, a problem which English shares with other subjects. 11 per cent of our sample were in their first year of teaching, and 24 per cent in their first year in their present school. This has disquieting implications for continuity of teaching and the development of English department policy. In our opinion, English is a field which has a particular need of continuity, since so much depends upon the teacher's observation and nurture of his pupil's language growth. Measured against this need the turnover figures give cause for concern. Furthermore, just under one tenth of the teachers of English in our sample were part-time. There is no doubt of the value of their contribution, but we think it unsatisfactory that so substantial a proportion of the teachers responsible for English should not be in school for the full week. Not only is this kind of arrangement another source of discontinuity but it adds to the problems of a head of English who is trying to develop within the department a policy of continuing dialogue and collective planning.

15.14   We approach with some diffidence the analysis of formal qualifications among teachers of English, as we are aware of the excellent work done by many who do not possess them. Moreover, we are equally aware that the supposedly appropriate qualifications are not always suitable for the task. These reservations made, we find the distribution of qualifications in Table 11 considerably disturbing.

Table 11

QUALIFICATIONS FOR TEACHERS TEACHING ENGLISH IN SECONDARY SCHOOLS, AS SUPPLIED BY HEADS OF THE SCHOOLS

	Number	%
(a) An honours degree in English with a post-graduate certificate in Education	479	*14·1*
(b) A degree in which English is one of the subjects, with a post-graduate certificate in Education	310	*9·1*
(c) Followed a main or advanced course in English (leading to a teaching certificate or B.Ed.) at College of Education or Education Department of a Polytechnic, for teaching in		
(i) secondary schools	745	*21·9*
(ii) junior/secondary schools	331	*9·7*
(iii) junior schools	70	*2·1*
(d) An honours degree in English	105	*3·1*
(e) A degree in which English is one of the subjects	107	*3·1*
(f) A main or advanced qualification in drama	137	*4·0*
(g) None of the above	1,113	*32·8*
Total Teachers	3,397	*100*

The final figure is the most striking; a third of those involved in English teaching have no discernible qualification for the role*. Of course, many of these may well be teaching English to only one or two classes, spending most of their time in some other subject. But this in itself is a significant feature and another disquieting aspect of the situation. Of the teachers engaged in English, only 37 per cent spent all their time on it. 25 per cent were teaching it more than half their time, and 38 per cent less than half:

Diagram 11

PROPORTIONS OF TIME SPENT BY TEACHERS IN ENGLISH TEACHING, BY TYPE OF SCHOOL

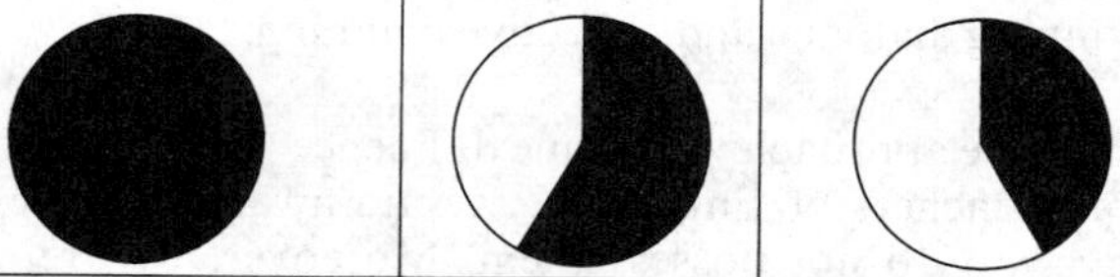

	ALL THE TIME	MORE THAN HALF THE TIME	LESS THAN HALF THE TIME
Modern	27%	29%	44%
Grammar	60%	19%	20%
Comprehensive	39%	24%	37%
All other	48%	26%	26%
Average for all schools	37%	25%	38%

(An expansion of this distribution, giving a more detailed breakdown of the data by size and type of school, is to be found in Table 70, Chapter 25.)

There can be no other secondary school subject which is staffed by such a large proportion of people without appropriate qualifications. Nor can there

*It should be noted that this was the figure supplied by heads to indicate the qualifications of ALL the teachers in their schools who were teaching English. In the class section of the questionnaire we directed the question specifically to the teachers taking English with the sample twelve and fourteen year old pupils. Details of their replies are given in Tables 77 and 78.

be any subject which 'borrows' so many teachers from other areas of the curriculum and assumes they can fill the role with little or no preparation. Where the English teaching is shared among many the problems of co-ordination can become acute, and several heads of department told us that they found it difficult to develop a coherent policy and keep it refreshed by discussion.

15.15   Considerations of this kind depend in large measure on the degree of priority accorded to English by the head of the school, and its status is reflected in the construction of the timetable. For example, the disposition of total time affects the length of the English sessions, their placing across the week, and whether or not the English of a group of classes is 'blocked', i.e. taught simultaneously. There is a wide variation from school to school in the extent to which the English department is consulted on those three questions, and in the extent to which its wishes can be met. Nevertheless, the impression we carried away from our visits and our discussions with teachers was that English very often has a lower priority than other subjects. It is expected to make fewer and simpler timetable demands, and those demands it does make are less often met. Any firm request from any subject for a particular use of time is a constraint upon the timetable. One example is a generous allocation of double periods; another is the 'blocking' to which we referred above. The latter is a difficult requirement to meet too often in a timetable, as it demands that a number of teachers must all be available at the same time. In most schools the number of such 'vertical locks' the timetable can carry is acutely limited, and English faces the problem that many other subjects have traditionally become accepted as having greater claim on this and similar timetable constraints. French and mathematics, for instance, usually demand setting and thus frequently exhaust the school's blocking capacity, while science and craft make heavy claims on double periods. Some subjects need to be taught in specially equipped rooms, and they inevitably take an early place in the timetabler's thoughts.

15.16   All these factors, singly or in combination, often put English at a disadvantage when the timetable is being constructed. One or two illustrations will be sufficient to show how this can work in practice. We visited one large school which worked an eight period day. Whereas every other subject had double periods, mathematics requested single periods and setting. To permit this, English was always timetabled in singles and paired with mathematics to make 'false doubles'. Thus, English always preceded or followed a lesson change, and though it felt the need for double periods as acutely as the other subject did for singles it never had a longer spell of time than 35 minutes. (Almost 40 per cent of the twelve year olds in our survey sample had none of their lessons in periods of more than an hour.) A similar conflict of interests was seen in another school, where staff availability was a problem when the fourth year 'G.C.E. band' was being setted. The outcome of the situation was that the four English sets were constituted according to the pupils' ability in mathematics. We found it a common practice for English to be used to fill in the single periods left over at odd times of the week. In a number of schools which allocated English five periods it was said to be "not possible" for one class to have all five with the same teacher. Indeed, we found one school in which a few classes had three teachers each for their English. It must be added at once that we met heads who went to very great trouble to accord to English the same timetabling advantages as any other subject. Nevertheless, our general impression was that in too many schools English was used by the timetabler as the lubricant that allowed other subjects to slip into their favoured place. We strongly urge that English should be given a high priority when heads are devising their staffing and timetabling policy.

15.17   For the reasons we have given, and others we shall go on to adduce, the role of the head of the school in the teaching of English has never been so important. One measure of it is the support he gives to his head of English department, and this includes securing him time for the thought and planning the task demands. In recent years the role of the head of department has grown in complexity. Not only has the subject increased in scope and widely diversified, but greater flexibility has been required of it to meet individual needs and interests. This demands of the head of department a much wider knowledge of available books and materials and of developments in teaching methods. In effect his responsibility extends from the management of resources to a concern for the in-service training needs of the department. His relationship with his colleagues is the key to the success of English teaching in the school. As one witness put it, "I see the role of head of department as concerned first of all with teachers. Unless he can lead his department so that it is a unity I don't think one can progress very far".

15.18   Our visits left us in no doubt how demanding a job this is, especially in large schools. The problems we have been describing were common to very many of the heads of English we met. They were experiencing considerable pressures, and they had insufficient time and help available to them. Despite this, the majority were managing remarkably well and were succeeding in developing a strong team approach. These included teachers who had had to cope with the sudden expansion of their department as a small school became a large one on reorganisation. Inevitably, however, this situation produced problems to which some were not so readily able to adjust. Accustomed to working with two or three colleagues and with children from a restricted ability range, they found themselves with problems on a daunting scale. The pupils were now drawn from almost the entire ability range, and the staff of the department became a heterogeneous collection of teachers with widely differing views on how English should be taught. Equally under pressure were some heads of departments who had been virtually catapulted into promotion after only a short period of teaching. Their intelligence, energy, and ambitions for their subject often outstripped their experience, resources, and strength. This situation has resulted in some areas from the extreme difficulty of finding heads of English department. Candidates with reasonable experience and qualifications are in very short supply for a number of reasons. Apart from the more general one of a shortage of qualified teachers of English, these have included a variety of attractions into other fields. For one thing there is a well-documented tendency for arts teachers in general, and English teachers in particular, to be drawn to middle and senior pastoral posts. As one writer[1] expresses it: "Scientists feel that they have more to lose by moving into the pastoral area, whereas arts teachers, in moving in that direction, feel that they are extending interests and skills that have been important to them in their teaching function". Other reasons that have been put to us are the growing opportunities for the teaching of English as a second language, the attraction of posts in further education, and the increased appeal among English graduates of teaching in primary schools.

15.19   Advisers, heads, and L.E.A. officers in various parts of the country, but above all in inner-city areas, told us of their difficulty in appointing heads of English departments. Some said it was not uncommon to have to advertise three or four times for one good candidate. Another factor which is operating is the effect of the 1971 Burnham salary structure, which has been to narrow the differentials. The highest post (Scale 5) that can be awarded to a head of department can be acquired in, for instance, a grammar school of 600 or a comprehensive school of 1,000. Beyond that the financial reward remains the same, however large the school, except in the few cases where a small 'senior teacher' allowance is allocated. This is, of course, a problem common to all subjects, but it seems to have been felt particularly acutely by English, which shares with mathematics the largest teacher-period loading in the school. In large schools of up to 2,000 the number of teachers involved in the teaching of English is often very considerable. It has to be acknowledged that experienced heads of department in medium-sized schools are often deterred from taking on the additional responsibility in larger schools by the absence of any further salary gain. We are not in a position to recommend that English be singled out for special treatment in the form of an increased differential. On the other hand, to make a recommendation that would include all subject departments would take us beyond our terms of reference. Nevertheless, we feel it necessary to draw attention in urgent terms to the general problem of appointing heads of English department in some areas and to the particular one facing large schools. Quite apart from the matter of financial reward there are various steps that could be taken to ease the difficulty for heads of English department who are subject to considerable pressure. The staffing ratio of the department should be improved to allow more time for consultation and planning. There should be a generous allocation of above-scale posts to allow the head of department to delegate effectively, and he should be given secretarial and ancillary help. We are aware of the many and various staffing demands that heads have to reconcile, but we urge that they give sympathetic consideration to the first two of these suggestions. The fulfilment of the third, to which we now turn, lies with the local authority.

15.20   In our discussions with heads of English department, clerical help emerged as one of the needs they felt most keenly; and yet only 8 per cent of the schools in our sample had any such help for the exclusive use of their

English department. In our view the improvement likely to result from this relatively modest addition to the resources would be out of all proportion to the cost. We offer the analogy of the assistants available to science departments, and frequently to art and craft departments. It has long been accepted, for instance, that in the science laboratory ancillary help is required with the organisation of 'the teaching materials'. The same is no less necessary for English, the 'materials' of which are duplicated sheets, press-clippings, files, photographs, and so on. A simple distinction can be made between two kinds of ancillary help. Firstly, there is the preparation of teaching material—typing, duplicating, mounting illustrations, and other aspects of reprographic work. Into this category also comes the preparation of audio-visual material—recordings, slides, overhead projector transparencies, etc. Secondly, there is the handling of existing or purchased material: ordering, receiving, accessing, issuing, stock-checking, and progress-chasing. This is an exacting enough job for printed books, but it becomes much greater when there is a continuing demand for ephemeral or occasional material. An English department requires help of both kinds, the first of which might well be offered centrally through a school resource centre. The advantage of this arrangement would be that it meets the need of a reprographic unit to have a constant 'through-put'. The management of audio-visual resources is discussed in a subsequent chapter, but we would emphasise here that whatever form the provision takes the needs of English must be met with no less readiness than if the department managed its own. We strongly recommend that every English department should have internal ancillary help of the second kind. The extent of the provision would depend on the degree of central help available for the preparation of materials, for if this were not available the department's own ancillary assistance would need to be increased. Assuming the existence of such central support we believe that a minimum of 20 hours' 'internal' assistance a week should be authorised for every five forms of entry in an 11-18 school, and pro rata.

15.21   Another important influence on the achievements of an English department is accommodation. One of the side-effects of the notion that 'Every teacher is a teacher of English' has been its extension to 'Any room is suitable for English'. Many heads to whom we spoke recognised the fallacy of this assumption and took great pains to avoid it when drawing up the room timetable. In some schools, however, it was obvious that English was deemed to have no requirements that could not be answered by any classroom that happened to be free. One timetable we studied placed a first-year teacher in six different rooms for his English teaching. An even more extreme case was that of a large comprehensive school where one of the teachers taught 37 periods out of 40 in 13 different rooms. Not only was he constantly moving about the school, but he did not even have the same room for one class throughout the week. These are instances of inadequate concern for the needs of English teaching and of subsequent unsatisfactory timetabling. We have deliberately chosen them as extreme examples, and we do not, of course, assert that such practice is widespread. The survey provided us with an opportunity to discover the pattern across our sample of schools, and the result was as follows:

Table 12

ALLOCATION OF ROOMS FOR ENGLISH
IN SECONDARY SCHOOLS

| | Teachers taking English: | | |
	Mostly in the same room	In class bases (i.e. where pupils are static and teachers mobile)	No regular base
Type of school:	%	%	%
Modern	75·1	17·8	7·1
Grammar	32·9	56·4	10·7
Comprehensive	61·4	27·4	11·2
All other	53·3	30·4	16·3
Average for all schools in the survey	63·1	27·3	9·6

It is quite clear from this table that a substantial proportion of English teachers—over one third—are itinerant within the school, carrying their books about with them from one lesson to another. Even where they have the use of a regular room for their English lessons, this is by no means necessarily one designated as an English room. Thus, many teachers are unable to establish an environment in which they can exhibit work, put up illustrations and posters, mount displays and models, etc. We regard this as unsatisfactory, and believe that all English teachers should have the stability that is so essential to the kind of work we envisage. We acknowledge that some schools make it a policy to keep pupils of the most recent intake in one room to give them the security of a home base. This is clearly a case in which there would have to be compromise to the principle we are suggesting, and there will be others like it. Nevertheless, we believe it important to establish the principle that the English department should have accommodation of its own which the teachers working within it share, and which can afford every member with a full programme of English a teaching base of his own.

15.22   Our visits convinced us that where a teacher was assured of this stability he had a much better chance of creating the right atmosphere and fulfilling his plans. One of our teacher witnesses urged that "English should be taught exclusively in rooms resourced, looked after and seen to be the responsiblity of the English department". We support this principle, while acknowledging that some schools will find advantages in a degree of shared accommodation not only within a department but between subjects. As a basic tenet we strongly recommend that when rooms are being allocated the needs of English should receive the same consideration as those of any other subject. We apply the same recommendation to the planning of new accommodation, to the implications of which we now turn.

15.23   By comparison with some other subjects the space, furniture, and equipment required for activities in English might appear at first sight to present few problems. But a closer examination makes it clear that the demands on space are not at all simple and that though the special requirements are less obvious they are no less real. We talked to many English teachers and studied expressions of opinion from several other sources, and though they differed in emphasis and detail they all centred upon the need for better space provision. This is where our own priority lies. In our visits to schools rarely did we see pupils with the space to spread their papers, or the degree of 'psychological insulation' for individual reading and writing that adults would expect for themselves. Group work requires the space to allow tables and chairs to be re-arranged into clusters. Discussion operates best when the pupils are sitting round a group of tables or in a horseshoe of chairs. These examples alone—and they are chosen as the most obvious— indicate how important to English teaching is generous space. The first essential is for the flexibility which allows the teachers a number of options. It should be possible for a teacher to spend a major part of his time in his own base. It should also be possible for a group of teachers to share a cluster of spaces which are adapted to the needs of varying activities and varying numbers of pupils. In most existing buildings this would be hard to achieve without structural alteration, but we found several schools which were attempting to group their English rooms to create a suite. It is a commendable measure which makes possible co-operative activity, the easy sharing of equipment and facilities, and ready access to what might be called the department's headquarters.

15.24   If the grouping of English rooms is considered in relation to other subject groupings the possibilities of shared facilities are increased. It is in such circumstances that we see the place for a projection theatre capable of seating a hundred or so children. This should be fitted with sound-proof projector booth, wired-in good quality speakers, and a large permanent screen. Another facility of value to the English department, on the same shared basis, is a sound recording studio. High quality recording is difficult in even the best equipped classroom, for this is an activity that requires 'laboratory' conditions if it is to do justice to some aspects of the oral language work it is designed to serve. Drama in a secondary school can operate in a variety of forms and at a variety of levels. The fundamental need is for the kind of space a teacher can use for informal work and improvisation, and since this often develops naturally from other activities it must be a space immediately to hand. In addition there should be a larger and more elaborately equipped area which is shared with other subjects. Elsewhere in the Report we have advocated the use of film and videotape in such circum- stances as to make them a part of the normal texture of lessons. If this is to happen it must be possible to bring the equipment into the room easily and without fuss, and if necessary at short notice. This becomes a much simpler matter if the English rooms are *en suite*, with the equipment shared between them, and ideally, certain of the rooms should have the equipment built in. This recommendation is not in conflict with our expectation that shared accommodation might include the use of a projection theatre. There is a good case for a school to be equipped with a facility of this kind and for English teachers to have access to it, particularly when they want to show a full- length film. But there is also a case for independent facilities if videotape and film, notably in the form of short extracts, are to be used as part of the normal lesson situation in the way we have suggested in Chapter 22.

15.25   We believe one of the most pressing needs of English teachers is a departmental centre to house the ancillary help we have recommended and the teaching material the department assembles or produces. Many English departments have serious problems of storage and retrieval for even their most modest requirements, let alone the more elaborate resources we should like to see developed. We have already pointed out that in addition to books much use is made by many teachers of press clippings, photographs, printed extracts, and all manner of ephemeral material. Moreover, the books themselves are moved about more freely than in the past, when it was common for a teacher to be issued with a course book and one or two other full sets, which he might keep for a term or even a year. What is required is a departmental centre which houses stock and catalogues of material and has the facilities for the ancillary helper to maintain them. Correspondingly, every English teaching room should have ample storage space. In our visits we found that many teachers were handicapped by the lack of it, and makeshift arrangements were quite common. In one school a teacher had to store his books in a small cloakroom under the stairs; in another they were kept in cupboards some distance from the classrooms. And surprisingly, in several of the schools we visited the classrooms did not even have open bookshelves. We regard this whole question of storage and retrieval as an important factor in the teaching of English, for the facilities with which we saw many teachers having to manage were dispiriting and restricting. Much the same can be said of furniture and fittings, which were often of a kind that frustrated attempts to work in new ways.

15.26   We do not underestimate the financial problems of equipping English departments in the ways we have suggested. A realistic view makes it obvious that sweeping changes and improvements cannot be effected over-night. Nevertheless, we do believe that where building improvements are being planned or new projects designed opportunities such as those we have described should not be missed. We are anxious not to prescribe accommoda-tion requirements in such detail as to limit discussion, and for this reason we have resisted the temptation to reproduce plans in this chapter. We have confined ourselves to what we consider certain fundamental requirements, which we hope local authorities will accept as essential provision. We strongly recommend that when new buildings or extensions are being designed there should be full consultation between architects, the authority's English advisory staff, and teachers. Some of the best design currently to be found has resulted from this kind of professional co-operation.

15.27   We have been discussing ways in which English teachers can be helped by organisational and other means to develop their work, and we return now to the operation of the department itself. Before considering the articulation of the department's policy we must say something about the question of classroom control. In our visits we were acutely aware that some teachers were experiencing considerable problems, and there is evidence to suggest that such problems are far from uncommon. The general causes obviously lie beyond our brief, but we have formed the opinion that in the wrong circumstances some English teaching methods can actually contribute to these difficulties, since they put an additional strain on teachers who are weak in their control. If we are to be realistic we must draw attention to these disciplinary problems, for obviously the subtle aims we have outlined in the Report cannot be achieved unless there is peace in the classroom. We believe that English departments should consider the control implications of their approaches and should not commit themselves to ways of working which will be impracticable in the circumstances and likely to aggravate the difficulties.

15.28 In this chapter we have laid emphasis on the need for consultation between the teachers of English and for effective leadership by the head of department. How is the agreed policy to be articulated? Our visits left us with the impression that the 'syllabus' or 'scheme of work' has lost favour with many teachers of English. The passing of a certain kind of syllabus will certainly not be lamented. We refer to the document that spelt out in close detail every step each teacher was to take, to the extent that if he followed it he would have virtually no freedom of thought or action. It prescribed which points of grammar he was to teach, and in what order, and which books he might read with the children. Such schemes of work were often unworkable if the English teaching was to contain any life and variety. Not surprisingly they were allowed to gather dust, and in many schools were never replaced. Some able young teachers, reacting against syllabuses that were clearly inadequate, have opposed the notion of any kind of written document. We are bound to say from our experience that their sense of freedom has often proved illusory, as it has led to much fragmented teaching. This has been the case even in some departments with a tradition of discussion between its members. Indeed, informal exchange, though immensely valuable, can carry the risk of masking lack of coherence. In one school it was only in the course of our conversation that one teacher revealed to another that he had been using a certain kind of exercise for some time. In another school a teacher said of work with a third year class: "I'm mostly living from hand to mouth, hoping that something one week will trigger off something for the next". He admitted that his choice of work was neither planned nor a studied response to the interests of the class, but was determined largely by impulse. This kind of directionless drift is clearly related to questions of leadership, consultation, and joint planning within the department, but the absence of a working document is an aspect of these.

15.29 If the experience of English in the years of secondary education is to be coherent it must be more than a series of chance encounters. If there is no agreed statement of purpose, every teacher is on his own. Several of our witnesses pressed the importance of some form of documentation, but they differed in their interpretation of the idea. One believed that among other things it should record "specific departmental policies such as hearing the children read aloud, the availability of homework for inspection, and the amount of writing that should be produced over a period of time". For another it was "essentially a 'position paper', outlining the philosophy and aims, so that the collective wisdom of the team is recorded for mutual benefit and that of newcomers". A third preferred to see it as "basically related to classroom practice, and not to theory; to short-term aims, rather than long-term aim". A number drew attention to its value for the school in which there were many new young teachers or a large and disparate group of teachers who "took some English".

15.30　We believe with our witnesses that every English department should produce a document making clear its purposes and the means it proposes to fulfil them. We have already argued that the head of department should create a climate in which there is continuing professional discussion among his colleagues. He should encourage them to share with him the responsibility for keeping up with new developments and knowledge, for a dialogue which fashions the English teaching in a school needs to be an informed dialogue. We believe that the thinking that emerges from it should take shape in a manifesto, reflecting the spirit and purpose of the department and responsive to the continuing exchange of views within it. We suggest that the term 'instrument of policy' would represent this more accurately than 'syllabus' or 'scheme of work'. We envisage it as a cumulative and slowly changing document, from which loose-leaf sections are withdrawn for revision as the department's ideas evolve. Its first purpose is to support the English teacher in the classroom, but those who devise it should also bear in mind its importance for the head and other colleagues in the school, for new teachers, students on teaching practice and their tutors, and for outside advisers. The document should contain a clear account of the aims and purposes of the department and of the balance of activities designed to fulfil them, and it might include an anthology of teaching ideas, an outline of any specific points which the department has agreed should be taught, the administrative procedure for stock, pupil records, etc., and lists of books and other material available. Such a document would help teachers give shape, coherence and sequence to the work they devise for the pupils.

15.31　Much of what has been suggested in this chapter depends for its success on the head's vision and commitment. We are in no doubt of the great importance to the school as a whole of his attitude to English. If heads are in a position to help create a strong English department they are also uniquely placed to encourage the development of a language policy across the curriculum, the case for which is argued in Part Four. Such a policy means in effect that every teacher in the school should accept it as part of his responsibility to develop the pupils' reading, writing, and speaking ability in and through the subject or activity for which he is responsible. It also means that he should have an awareness of his own use of language and understand how the nature of the verbal exchange between himself and his pupils can affect the quality of the learning.

If the success of language and reading in the primary school depends upon the orientation of the whole school, the success of the secondary school can be said to depend very considerably on the level of achievement in reading and language. Unless the pupil can read, write, and talk competently he cannot benefit from the range of learning which the secondary school provides. The responsibility for language growth in adolescents extends beyond the English department and becomes an important part of 'school management'. Our recommendations must therefore be addressed to heads as much as to English teachers, for we believe the time has come to raise language to a high priority in the complex life of the secondary school.

REFERENCES

1.　E. Richardson: *"The Teacher, The School, and the Task of Management"*: Heinemann Educational Books: 1973.

CHAPTER 16
L.E.A. Advisory Services

16.1 Local authority advisory* services and their role in support of the school are an appropriate conclusion to this part of the Report. The first thing that needs to be said is that in national terms this support is inadequate in extent. In November 1971 the Arbitration Tribunal deciding the Soulbury Salary Scales for Inspectors and Advisers asked local authorities for information about the numbers of posts in all subjects. 130 of the 147 L.E.A.s in England gave the following details of the numbers in their employ at that time.

Table 13

L.E.A. ADVISORY SERVICES IN ENGLAND: DISTRIBUTION OF ADVISORY POSTS BY SUBJECT

	Advisers	*Assistant Advisers*
Physical Education	176	78
Music	97	16
Home Economics	60	14
Handicraft	37	—
Science	34	—
Art	33	—
Drama	33	—
Mathematics	30	—
Modern Languages	25	—
English	18	—

The Education Committees Year Book[1] of 1973/74 shows 22 authorities as having English advisers, though four of these are listed as English with Modern Languages, English and Drama, English and allied subjects, and General and English. In addition, six authorities have advisers for Humanities which presumably includes responsibility for English. To these can be added some general inspectors and advisers who maintain an interest in English, but the figures for these are not known since this information is naturally not included. There has thus been a slight growth since 1971, but the fact clearly remains that there are far too few advisers with an interest in English and a recognised responsibility for supporting the schools in this area of their work. In view of the central importance of English in the whole educational process we find this situation a matter for great concern. We strongly recommend that local authorities should give urgent consideration to appointing advisers with this specific responsibility where they do not already exist.

16.2 We argued in the last chapter that English has been given too low a priority in staffing and resources in many schools. To the reason already suggested another should be added. English has not had the benefit of the impetus that a strong advisory team can give to a subject. This impetus

*Various authorities use different forms of designation. Some distinguish between 'inspectors' and 'advisers'; some use the term 'adviser' for all such posts, and the word 'organiser' is sometimes to be found. For the purposes of this chapter we have chosen to use the term 'adviser' throughout.

expresses itself in terms of additional resources, increased local development work, and expanded in-service training, to mention but a few. We are not suggesting that in authorities without an English adviser other subjects are deliberately advanced at its expense. It is rather that the subject's needs are not articulated; in consequence they are often underestimated because it is assumed that they are not so great as those for which a strong case is made in other subjects. Moreover, it is the practice of some authorities to allocate money to an adviser to enable him to encourage development work in his subject or provide additional equipment. English has all too often missed this advantage. If advances are to be made in the teaching of English in all its aspects the need for this specialist support must be recognised. It seems to us deplorable that an area of the curriculum so complex in its demands should be so poorly represented in L.E.A. advisory services. The figures quoted above speak for themselves.

16.3   It is important at this point to define the kind of advisory support we think necessary. In using the term 'English' here we envisage an area of responsibility which extends from language and reading in the early years to English studies at the highest level of the secondary school. This at once raises questions. Is it feasible, or for that matter desirable, for one person to have responsibility for advising across such a wide spectrum? What is the position of the general primary adviser who already has a keen and active interest in reading? Let it be said at once that the general advisers in many authorities have done exceptionally good work in promoting reading and language work in primary schools. Without their continued involvement the co-operative or 'team' concept we are proposing could not operate. This in itself provides the answer to the first question. It is clearly both unrealistic and limiting to think in terms of one person taking sole responsibility for all English advisory work throughout an authority's schools. The 'team' should involve a number of people able to make contributions from a variety of points of strength. It should have a specialist English adviser, and should draw for its membership from the general primary and secondary advisers, advisory teachers on secondment from schools, and specialists in reading, learning difficulties, drama and 'immigrant' language teaching.

16.4   In appointing their general primary advisers some authorities try to ensure a coverage of those aspects of the curriculum not accounted for by the specialists in music, physical education, etc. Thus, in addition to their general assignments some advisers will promote the interests of mathematics across all the primary schools, while others will take a particular interest in environmental studies or in English in at least some of its aspects. There is, of course, wide variation in the depth of knowledge general advisers bring to this side of their work. Some of those with a particular concern for English have developed a special interest in children's talking and writing, while others have a detailed knowledge of books for children. Many primary advisers, whatever their other curricular emphases, have had experience in the teaching of reading and maintain their interest in it. Moreover, since language pervades the curriculum they are concerned with children's ability to handle it in various contexts. It is clear, therefore, that the involvement of the general primary adviser in the work of the English advisory team is vitally important.

16.5   It might be argued that since there is clearly so much experience and interest already available in the person of the general adviser the need for a specialist is reduced. Indeed, it is doubtless this view that has influenced so many authorities to rely upon their non-specialists. We regard this argument as untenable for a number of reasons. Apart from the fact that it takes no account of the needs of the secondary school it demands more of the general primary advisers than they can reasonably be expected to give. Their duties are numerous and wide-ranging and often involve administrative work. In the schools themselves they are concerned with educational progress in its widest sense, and the amount of time they can give to children's literature or the growth of language, for example, is limited. This is true of those general advisers with a special interest in English; it is even more true of their colleagues. Furthermore, though their combined knowledge is valuable it will not necessarily include an expert understanding of children's language development. When one considers the secondary school the case is even stronger. General advisers for secondary education come from a wide variety of subject fields. An unpublished survey carried out by N.A.T.E. suggests that in only a relatively small number of cases do their general duties include a particular interest in English. Moreover, the general adviser for secondary schools is quite likely to have even less time to devote to any particular subject. It seems to us unsatisfactory for a local authority to depend upon such a person on the strength of his personal interest in the subject rather than appoint a full-time adviser.

16.6 If English in all its aspects cannot be left to the general adviser it is equally true that it cannot be left solely to the specialist. English advisers already in post have for the most part displayed great adaptability. Their own background is generally that of the secondary school, but they have become increasingly interested in language development in general. Nevertheless, few would feel confident that they could cover alone all aspects of their field from early reading to "A" level literature. However committed to professional renewal they could not maintain a knowledge of every element at the same high level. It is for this reason that we advocate the notion of co-operative action, where the specialist English adviser is supported by the experience and knowledge of his general colleagues and by a number of advisory teachers. We envisage the advisory teachers as being drawn from among those whose appointment we recommended in paragraph 13.23 and from English teachers in secondary schools. They would be seconded for a period of 2–3 years, and one of their most valuable functions would be to work alongside teachers in their classrooms. They would help in providing in-service training and stimulating local development work. There are, of course, advisory teachers already employed in some authorities, though not necessarily in the field with which we are concerned here. In some cases they work in co-operation with advisers, but in others they are a substitute for them. We regard this second course as unsatisfactory. A specialist adviser is essential to the kind of co-operative activity we are recommending.

16.7 It was suggested to us in evidence that authorities with large numbers of children from families of overseas origin should have appropriate specialist advisers. We have described in Chapter 20 the language problems of these children, who represent in some areas a considerable proportion of the school population. It seems to us essential that schools in these areas should have the support of an adviser with special knowledge of the needs of Caribbean dialect speaking pupils and of teaching English as a second language. It would be unreasonable to expect the English adviser to command this kind of knowledge, and a specialist appointment would be necessary. At the same time it would be unfortunate if the 'immigrant specialist' were to work in relative isolation. It is as important at the advisory level as in the school that the work of the specialist should be related closely to the curriculum at all points. We therefore recommend that where an authority appoints an adviser with such responsibilities he should work with the advisory team responsible for all aspects of English. As an expert in language in general as well as in specialised terms he would have a valuable part to play in its work.

16.8   There is scarcely need to list the possible activities of the 'team', since the compass of these is contained in the pages of this Report. At the most fundamental level its rôle would be to support teachers throughout the age-range, keeping them informed of new developments, disseminating good practice, and providing in-service training. In co-operation with the warden(s) of teachers' centre(s) it would encourage teachers in such activities as the development of new materials and the study of children's spoken and written language. Where the authority provides an independent language centre the English adviser might have overall responsibility for it and for links with the teachers' centre(s). Equally, where a language centre is in a college of education the team should have a close working relationship with the staff of the college. One of the advisory team's most valuable services would be to support teachers in their induction year in co-operation with professional tutors.

16.9   The following is a sample of the activities in which the team would be involved. It has been selected from the Report in such a way as to indicate the wide range of concerns that would be brought—for the first time in most authorities—into the same field of vision:

(i)   Language development in the early years, and support for the kind of initiatives recommended in Chapter 5.

(ii) Involvement in the screening procedure advocated in Chapter 17. This system would be the product of co-operation between the English advisory team, the Schools Psychological Service, and the schools themselves. The advisers and the educational psychologists would be jointly concerned with guidance to the schools on professional observation to be made during the infant years, administration of the test in the junior school, and follow-up support for the teachers at both stages. We have emphasised that a screening system is of value only if it results in appropriate help for every child who needs it. This would be the most important element of the joint responsibility.

(iii) Support for schools in improving the teaching of reading and the evaluation of new materials. This would extend beyond early reading and include the development of higher order skills in primary and secondary schools and reading within the 'content areas'.

(iv) Advice on books of various kinds and in particular recently published children's literature. Co-operation with the various agencies, e.g. the School Library Service, in exhibitions and the kinds of activity recommended in Chapter 21.

   (v) Encouraging the adoption of a 'language across the curriculum' policy in secondary schools. This would entail consultation with general secondary advisers and advisers in other subjects, whose co-operation would be to the mutual advantage of all involved.

  (vi) Responding to requests for advice from secondary school English departments on the devising of syllabuses in C.S.E. and other examinations in which they may be approved.

 (vii) Providing professional advice when new buildings and extensions are being planned. The team should be consulted on accommodation needs of the kind discussed at various points in the Report.

This list is merely a sample of the responsibility that would fall to an English advisory team. In effect the Report itself represents the extent of its range of work.

16.10   The notion of co-operative activity needs to be properly interpreted if it is to be recognised as a workable proposition. It is obvious from an examination of its area of work that the various members will have widely different contributions to make. We see the team as a group of people brought together for a particular purpose but working in a variety of ways to achieve it. Some have major responsibilities which lie outside it, but their involvement is essential to its success. We believe that English in all its aspects, different as they may seem, should be recognised as a unity, and that the various contributions should come together in this way to give it expression as such.

REFERENCES

1.   *Education Committees Year Book 1973–74:* Councils and Educational Press Ltd.

Part Six

Reading and Language Difficulties

CHAPTER 17

Screening, Diagnosis, and Recording

17.1 Schools have long played a part in preventive and curative medicine for children by means of the School Health Service. We believe it is now time to introduce a far more systematic procedure for the prevention and cure of educational difficulties. Early detection of educational failure is of the greatest importance in the development of each child, since once he has begun to falter and is allowed to continue struggling unaided, he is less and less likely to make sound progress. We have therefore considered carefully the proposal made to us by many witnesses that every L.E.A. might institute a screening programme.

17.2 It is first necessary to define the issue clearly to avoid confusion in the use of terms. In the written evidence the term "at risk" was applied equally to young children who were likely to fail and to older children who were already encountering failure. 'Screening' is a concept drawn from the field of medicine, where large-scale X-ray tests for chest conditions are a familiar form of it. Screening of pre-school children at intervals between birth and entry to school has been the practice in many local authorities for a number of years. It has consisted of physical examination and developmental tests, intended to identify as soon as possible any organic disorder or any delay in acquiring important sensory-motor skills. Translated into educational terms, screening implies the application of one or more procedures to a defined population of pupils, usually a whole age group, which would identify pupils likely to experience learning problems. This information would alert teachers to preventive action and indicate the need for further investigation in specific cases. Defined in this way screening is a process which would be applied at the beginning of the child's school life, before his growing involvement with the process of learning to read gives him an experience of failure. In other words, it identifies the child "at risk" in the sense that though failure is to some extent predictable in his case he has not yet encountered it. Equally, screening can be applied at a later age, say after two years of schooling, where it would be designed to give information about the reading disabilities children had *already* begun to reveal. Both concepts were represented in the views of witnesses with whom we discussed the subject. There was a division of opinion among them as to the most appropriate age at which to introduce screening, and this is an issue to which we have given close consideration.

17.3 However, before arriving at any conclusions about the detailed operation of screening procedures we invited 145 L.E.A.s in England to tell us how they identified their children likely to experience reading and language difficulties. The results of this inquiry*, which was carried out before the reorganisation of local government, are given at the end of the chapter. The 93 replies ranged from accounts of relatively informal and subjective

---

*(1) An account of the results of the inquiry appears as Annex A.

(2) Included as Annex B are descriptions of the screening practice of three local authorities whose contrasting systems we present as examples.

procedures to data from fully standardised tests administered with statistical support. In some cases the tests were supplemented by carefully designed checklists on which the teacher recorded her observations over a period of time. Equally varied was the extent to which these surveys did in fact function as effective identification measures. Some identified the schools with particular problems, but not the individual child who was failing. They were therefore unable to yield the information which would lead to individual attention, and could not, by our definition, be called screening. Others were so organised that they enabled additional help to be concentrated on the children shown to need it. It is our central contention in this chapter that the provision of special help should be an automatic sequel to a screening and diagnostic programme, and that it should be given immediately to every child shown to be in need of it. Indeed, we believe it essential that a plan for subsequent action should be worked out in detail *before* any policy of screening is adopted.

17.4   Some teachers and researchers have raised two main objections to screening. Firstly they believe that its results are in danger of shaping or reinforcing the teacher's expectations of the pupil. Secondly they feel it is wrong to set out predictions at a time when deficiencies are capable of spontaneous remission. Their argument is that many children at risk at age five would, with normal primary teaching, be making satisfactory progress at seven. These are points of view to be respected. It would be quite wrong to involve children in self-fulfilling prophecies, and we agree that there is a good deal of work to be done on the question of teacher expectation. Nevertheless, we believe that the risks associated with the predictive aspects of screening are not so great as those created by missing a child in need of special help. There is ample evidence that children in poor socio-economic circumstances are more likely to experience difficulty in learning to read than those more fortunately placed. For a variety of reasons, some immigrant children are at risk. So are children with a family history of delay in learning to read or in speaking. Indeed, any child who has shown significant delay in talking can be regarded as at risk in terms of reading and language development. Other relevant factors of a medical or neuro-developmental kind are disturbances in auditory and visual perception, certain speech defects, fluctuations in mood, and poorly co-ordinated movement. In short, there are many known indicators of a likelihood of difficulty in learning to read, and we believe that evidence of this kind is too valuable to neglect.

17.5   This takes us to the question of the age at which screening procedures should be administered, and to the nature of those procedures. A useful starting point for our discussions of this was the recommendation of the Secretary of State's Advisory Committee[1]:

"Teachers will notice any indications of reading disability during the first years at school, but at some stage a systematic screening of all children will be necessary. The end of the infant school will be a good time for this: at the age of 7–8 children should be sufficiently advanced in their reading for meaningful results to be obtained from the screening process; and it would be a suitably early age to begin remedial treatment for disabilities which are revealed. Screening should be the responsibility of teachers, who should, however, collaborate with educational psychologists in devising means to identify those children with severe reading difficulties".

17.6   From our survey of L.E.A.s it became clear that by far the most popular times for carrying out some kind of assessment, whether or not it could be called screening, were the first term and the second year of the junior school. Witnesses with whom we discussed the question were divided in their opinions, some preferring screening to start in the infant school, others favouring a delay until the age of seven or eight. The arguments in favour of beginning in the infant school are (a) structured observation can be used which directs teachers' attention to the learning characteristics of the individual child; (b) severe problems can be identified in time for treatment to begin before failure becomes cumulative. The recording process it involves will lead to greater continuity of appropriate teaching from the succession of infant teachers who come into contact with the child. Those who favour the later age contend that children are in danger of being 'labelled' too early. They feel, moreover, that the channelling of teachers' observation could result in the infant school narrowing its aims. It might direct its teaching towards improving the children's performance on the criteria involved in the screening. This point was not accepted by teachers who had experience of operating screening procedures which involved 'channelled' observation. They reported that the checklists offered a useful framework for their normal assessment of children, and that this was in no way distorted by them. Nor, they felt, were their aims and teaching methods adversely influenced. The chief argument advanced against the later age for screening is that the child who has failed to learn to read by the age of eight has a rapidly diminishing chance of ever succeeding. The earlier the identification, the sooner the special help can be given and the more likely a successful outcome.

17.7   There are certain other factors to be considered when decisions are being reached on the most appropriate age for screening. Any testing of all children at the end of the infant school would normally be carried out by teachers whose responsibility for teaching them would shortly cease. If, on the other hand, it were to take place early in the junior school the teachers administering it would be those who would go on to devise the necessary help. It would be quite wrong to face children with a test situation at the beginning of their life in a new school, when they have to adjust to new teachers, new companions, and new surroundings after a long summer holiday. A date towards the middle of the first term would be a good compromise. A month or so usually gives the children time to settle down, and the second term would be to delay too long the appropriate measures to be taken when the analysis of the results was complete. Our own view, therefore, is that if tests are used they should be introduced not earlier than the middle of the first term of the junior school and not later than the beginning of the second term.

17.8   We believe the most important part of the procedure is careful observation and recording. Of course, every good infant teacher sees this as a vital part of her normal work. She is continually observing her pupils and noting their difficulties, and she is often responsible for the first step in referring children to the educational psychologist, the school health service doctor, the speech therapist, or the social worker. The question is whether such practice should be systematised, so that a checklist ensuring consistency of observation is completed by every teacher and becomes part of the screening profile. An instance is to be seen in the first of the illustrations in Annex B, where teachers, administrators, advisers, and educational psychologists co-operated to produce such a checklist. It has proved useful in giving teachers a common and agreed framework for their assessment of children's development. It has also been a support to young and inexperienced teachers, of whom there are many in this area of high staff turnover.

17.9   In our view there is a strong case for systematic observation as a first stage of the screening process from the time the child enters school. In recommending the principle we would add that if checklists are to be introduced they should be developed in full consultation with the teachers who are to use them. This will involve a good deal of preparatory activity on the part of teachers, advisers, and educational psychologists. The agreed structure should emerge from a programme of meetings and study groups and should be supported by in-service training at both general and school level. We do not underestimate the scale of effort this will require on the part of the authority, but we feel it is fully justified in its benefits. We have been impressed by the results where the educational psychologists have seen themselves as closely associated with the teachers in their work.

17.10   As a foundation for its careful observation the infant school should start with the advantage of information from the pre-school stage. Some parents are prompt to supply information on such matters as delayed speech and defective hearing, but others are either unaware that there is an abnormality or for one reason or another do not let the school know.   For this reason it is important that the teacher should be informed in confidence of the results of the child's medical examination, whether this is carried out just before or just after admission. The school doctor and the health visitor are valuable sources of information to the school, and the latter is particularly well placed to note evidence of speech delay[2]. We welcome the recognition now being given to educational implications in school-entrant medical examinations and to the need for improved communications between school doctors and teachers. Equally important is the information that can come from the educational welfare officer, the social worker, and the speech therapist[3].

17.11   The results of the systematic observation in the infant school should be recorded in such a way that the development of the child "at risk" can be closely followed. The Sheldon Committee Report[4] encouraged arrangements for the medical screening of young children, and recommended that local health authorities should maintain a register of children found to be developmentally at risk. In this way the children could be kept under special observation until the presence of any disorder or delay were proved or disproved. By analogy it is pertinent to consider whether there would be an advantage in recommending that L.E.A.s should keep a register of children at risk in *educational* terms. The experience of local health authorities who have used 'at risk registers' has not proved entirely satisfactory. As the authors of "From Birth to Seven"[5] point out: "The Registers have tended to become too large for practical use and substantial numbers of handicaps have been missed in low risk children who were not on the register". This seems to us a serious limitation, and there is every reason to believe that the same criticism would apply to registers used as a sole means of identifying children who might need special help with reading and language. The essential is that no child who is for any reason missed should continue to be missed. More reliable and productive would be a detailed profile of every child's strengths and weaknesses, and this should be used to plan an appropriate learning programme. All this implies the closest co-operation between the schools, the School Psychological Service, and the L.E.A. Advisory Service, with information where appropriate from the School Health Service.

17.12   Central to the whole procedure is the notion that the information can be applied to the child's needs however frequently he changes school. It is sometimes suggested that in areas where there is little or no social disadvantage there is no need to screen. This is a questionable argument, but in any case it presupposes a situation of general stability, with teacher and family mobility low. Nowadays, such stability is less and less common, and schools in many relatively affluent areas experience constant changes of both teachers and families. It is a recurring emphasis of this chapter that the detailed recording of a child's performance is essential, with the results of screening an important foundation for it. In poorer areas, where there is likely to be a higher proportion of children "at risk", the argument applies with still greater force. In localities where housing problems, uncongenial surroundings and poor school buildings contribute to a high teacher turnover, the new and inexperienced teacher must be alerted to the needs of individual children. Here too there is a high rate of family mobility, if for a different set of reasons. This is well illustrated by the fact that 50 per cent of children move out of Inner London before reaching their 14th birthdays. The case hardly needs pressing that in such circumstances some substantial record of every child should go with him to his next school, a point which is elaborated later in the chapter.

17.13   We confess to some doubts about the setting of a standardised test for all the children in the age group, and these doubts stem from what we regard as two principal difficulties. The first is the nature of the test itself. Those most widely used at present are of the simple word recognition variety. They have the advantage of being easy to administer and of being familiar in the schools. They would serve a screening function to the limited degree that failure to recognise graded words beyond a given point suggests the child has some measure of disability, even though it may prove to be transient. However, such a measure may be quite at odds with the range of skills the infant school has been aiming to develop. In our view, if such tests are used for screening in the first year of the junior school they should take account of the critical processes at work in reading for meaning and not be restricted to word recognition. They should combine simplicity of operation with a recognition of the holistic nature of language learning. Moreover, they should ideally have been developed and evaluated within the last ten years. Such a set of criteria at once limits the choice at present available. Our second reservation relates to the question of how the test results are used. We see no advantage in mass testing and centrally stored data unless the outcome is special and individualised help directed precisely at the children who need it. It can be argued that for that to happen there is no need for a test to be given, without any kind of discrimination, to every child in an authority. The more logical course would be for the teacher's systematised observation to provide first-level identification, followed where necessary by more detailed scrutiny. Against this can be placed the argument that universal testing at a given age ensures that no child is overlooked. The plain truth is that everything depends upon the diagnostic skill of the teacher. She is the one in close daily contact with the child and is best placed to relate his reading development to his intellectual endowment, his linguistic competence, and his home circumstances. Compared with an assessment of this kind, the results of other measures to detect failure in reading are bound to be crude. If we were satisfied that every teacher was equipped with this professional skill we should consider the mass test of very doubtful value. If we were convinced that the observation and recording throughout an Authority's schools was comprehensive and consistent we should consider the mass test altogether superfluous. In our view the best system of screening is one of systematic observation and recording, with selective testing of those pupils about whom detailed and specific information is required. However, we are emphatic that a system of observation, recording and selective testing must have well-developed support services and in-service training of high quality. Until these conditions operate the testing of the whole age group, despite its limitations, has to be seen as the most practical course. Indeed, we accept that for some local authorities it is an essential part of their procedure, particularly in the present circumstances of high teacher mobility and a large proportion of children likely to reveal learning difficulties.

17.14   One further point needs to be made. At present it is common practice to test for the purpose of ascertaining comparative reading levels by schools. A norm-based approach will reveal among other things the great disparities which exist between areas and between schools within those areas. It could therefore be used to help an authority concentrate additional resources where they were most needed. Where tests are used there is everything to be said for employing the results to determine where extra teachers, equipment or money should be allocated to the best effect. Some authorities have already used this device effectively. We emphasise, however, that the first aim of screening must always be to identify the needs of individual children. Undeniably, information to guide policy decisions is important, but nothing should take precedence over this primary objective. It is perhaps wise to reaffirm at this point our belief in the importance of the daily concern of the teacher for the learning experiences of the children in his or her care. What we have described in this section is intended to support good teaching, and if our proposals were implemented in such a way as to interfere with it we should consider this a backward step.

DIAGNOSIS, AND RECORDING

17.15   We see the screening procedure as only the first stage in what should be a continuous process of diagnosis. Whatever the level of a child's reading ability, at whatever age, a scrutiny of the way in which he is functioning will enable the teacher to design reading experiences which will take his skill further. It is clear from the letters we received and from our conversations in schools that teachers take very seriously their responsibility for detecting children's reading difficulties. Many witnesses suggested that teachers should be equipped with new tests, simple of administration, to help them in this task. On the other hand, we talked to teachers who had grown accustomed to the idea that testing was the province of the educational psychologist.

Some were suspicious of testing, believing that it occupied valuable time which would be better spent in teaching. We shall take up later the question of the relationship between teacher and educational psychologist, but would like to dispose of the other argument at this early point. Testing should never be carried out without a real purpose. If it is done simply to complete a column beside a child's name then the critic is right; the time *would* have been better spent in teaching. A basic principle can be stated: testing should always lead to more efficient teaching, which it is designed to serve. It should be seen as an essential dimension of the process of teaching reading, not a parasitic growth upon it. In these paragraphs we consider the ways in which teachers can strengthen their teaching by the use of diagnostic instruments, and these are not confined to tests.

17.16   What steps do teachers take at present to test their children's reading, and what do they do with the information? No fair generalisation can be made, but there are several pointers. Our survey confirmed existing research findings that the most widely used test in schools is the Schonell Graded Word Reading Test. Table 39 indicates the numbers of schools using certain tests, and it will be seen that this particular one was used by 73 per cent of 936 primary schools. The Burt and Holborn tests, also of the word recognition type, were next in popularity, though even when added together they did not equal Schonell in prevalence. It is interesting to note that the largest schools were more inclined to use certain of the less common tests than were the smallest. The Neale Analysis, for example, was in use in 23 per cent of the schools with over 350 on roll, as against 9 per cent in those with fewer than 71. There have been suggestions that teachers are not sufficiently informed about the range of tests available. This table would seem to give some support to this view, since tests other than Schonell, Burt, and Holborn ranked low in frequency, and the first of these was in use in no fewer than 84 per cent of the largest schools in the sample. On the other hand, it is equally fair to infer that they are the most widely used because teachers find them the most helpful. There is no questioning the usefulness of a word recognition test for certain purposes, but so heavy a reliance on this form does suggest a narrow view of testing. In our opinion it is essential that before any test is applied it should be assessed for its appropriateness for given purposes. For example, the skills required to identify words in isolation are different from those required in making constructive use of context. A child's score on a word recognition test is a helpful piece of information about his level of achievement in one particular skill. But it will not provide any information about the words with which he is having difficulty in his current reading. Nor will it give an accurate picture of his ability to discriminate between particular sounds, or to link sounds with letters, or to understand phonic rules. It can be inferred from the child's performance in the test that he has this or that degree of ability to discriminate visually between word shapes, and very likely between letter shapes. But in itself that is insufficient information. A low score is a helpful indicator that a weakness exists and that the child needs help, but in order to decide what specific help is needed the teacher needs more precise information.

17.17   In another section of the questionnaire (page 458) teachers were asked whether they tested the child before he moved from one book to the next. 88 per cent of the infant teachers and 77 per cent of the junior teachers said they did. It is likely that the manner of testing here was closely related to the intention, and that it took the form of hearing the child read. Ability to cope with one book would thus be the criterion for being allowed to progress to a more difficult one. There is independent evidence to show that this is in fact the most prevalent method employed by teachers, particularly those in infant schools. Where a graded reading scheme is in use the system has the virtue of simplicity and logic. But for purposes of diagnosis it is, of course, of little value simply to record the titles or numbers of books a child has read. All this tells the teacher in effect is that the child is or is not able to cope with a certain book at a particular level in a particular scheme. Different reading schemes may have at any given level different words in a different quantity arranged in a different complexity of sentence structure. In short, the teacher is not able to generalise from this relatively crude measure about the child's reading ability, still less identify his weakness. However, there is one great virtue in this method of assessing a child's progress; it means that the teacher regularly hears him read aloud. This is one of the most valuable techniques at the teacher's disposal, but the indications are that its diagnostic possibilities are largely unrealised. In research carried out in infant schools Goodacre[6] found that when listening to children read only one in five teachers recorded particular errors and only one in ten a knowledge of letter 'sounds'.

17.18   There is no doubt of the importance attached in schools to the practice of hearing children read. In our survey we asked how often during a week children of different ability read to the teacher. The results were as follows:

Table 14.

NUMBER OF OCCASIONS ON WHICH 6 AND 9 YEAR OLDS READ TO THE TEACHER
IN A WEEK, BY READING ABILITY OF THE PUPILS

(*Percentages*)

	Daily	3 or 4 times	1 or 2 times	Less Often
6 year olds:				
The ablest reader	17	36	41	6
An average reader	31	54	15	—
The poorest reader	72	26	2	—
9 year olds:				
The ablest reader	1	4	35	59
An average reader	3	19	64	14
The poorest reader	48	38	13	1

These figures reveal many points of interest, the most obvious of which is that teachers extensively use the process of hearing children read as a means of giving practice to those who seem most in need of it and of monitoring their progress. Since so much time is devoted to this important activity the best possible use should be made of it, and this means that it should be an essential part of the diagnostic process. Our observations showed that this is rarely the case. Most teachers, in striving for fluency, set a premium on a quick, confident, and unhesitating delivery of the words.   This might well discourage a child from dealing adequately with points of difficulty, and the tendency will be reinforced if the teacher is given to excessive prompting. The technique of hearing children read is at its most effective when errors are seen as miscues which provide a "continuous window into the reading process". We have discussed in Part Three the notion of reading as a process of producing the most reliable prediction with the minimum cues available. We are suggesting here that the teacher should be aware when the child is reading of why he is making particular errors. She can then base her teaching on her understanding of the kinds of context cues to which the child is not making an adequate response. The teacher's observation and interpretation are extremely important instruments of diagnosis, but they depend upon a thorough knowledge of what reading is and the sub-skills it involves. We made this same point when discussing language development in the early years. Expert observation by the teacher cannot be valued too highly. It is a major teaching skill, and one upon which all effective diagnosis is founded.

17.19   If a teacher is to plan individual instruction to meet specific needs her first task is to assess the attainment level of every child and provide each with reading material of the right level of readability. This sounds obvious, but it is not common to find the process carried out with the necessary precision. A simple and effective means of approaching the task of matching child and material is the use of informal reading inventories, which are in effect structured observations of reading performance. These consist of passages selected by the teacher from the child's everyday reading material. As the child reads aloud the teacher notes his errors systematically and may ask him questions to assess his understanding of the passage when he has read it again silently. By this means the teacher is able to assess the child's reading ability in relation to a task whose difficulty level he has already established. He is then able to refer him to the right kind of material for further reading. These inventories have a distinct advantage over standardised tests in this situation. They appraise the child's level of ability in a particular task without reference to the performance of others. Norms are unimportant when a teacher is setting out to design a reading programme tailor-made for an individual. The informal reading inventory described below enables the teacher to determine at which of three important levels the child is operating with any given piece of material. This method was developed in the U.S.A., and we do not suggest that the error-rates as given here will necessarily apply in the English classroom. They are reproduced to illustrate the principle, which we think a valuable one. At the *independent* level, the child is able to read aloud in a natural and easy manner, without help from the teacher and with 99 per cent accuracy in word recognition. If the child makes more than one error in a hundred running words or has less than a 90 per cent* comprehension of the passage he is not reading at this level. The teacher can then determine whether he is at the *instructional* level with this particular material. This involves 95 per cent word recognition, the child making no more than 5 errors in a hundred running words, and he should be able to give a satisfactory answer to 75 per cent of the questions asked by the teacher. At this standard of performance the child can be expected to reach independent level on that material in response to appropriate teaching. Below

---

*It will be obvious that the percentages are arbitrary figures which lack the objectivity of those applied to the word recognition rate. They are an indication to the teacher of the extent of correct answers the child gives to questions she considers it reasonable to ask.

it he can be said to be operating at the *frustration* level, and the material is too difficult for him. This is indicated by a word recognition rate of 90 per cent or less (10 or more errors in 100 running words) and a comprehension ability of 50 per cent or below. There will also be revealing behavioural characteristics, such as lack of vocal expression and inaccurate observation of punctuation.

17.20   The informal reading inventory has the advantage that it can be produced from any reading material the teacher chooses, and we would expect that she would be advised in this by the teacher with special responsibility for language and reading. It allows her to prescribe for each child reading material appropriate to his needs. She may decide, for example, to reinforce his confidence by providing reading material for him at his independent level, or she may decide he is ready for something more challenging at the instructional level. She will certainly steer him away from reading at his frustration level, except when he is highly motivated to look at a particular passage for some reason of his own. By using the informal reading inventory the teacher is able to gauge exactly the kind of material which will yield further diagnostic information. A child faced with material at the frustration level will be likely to add or omit words, mispronounce, substitute or silently wait to be told. We have suggested that efficient reading consists not in scrutinising each letter and each word, but in using all the available context cues in the most economical and productive manner. When a child makes a 'miscue' the teacher should record it as such and ask herself why he made that particular one. Research has suggested that 4 out of 5 errors are in the nature of substitutions, the others being mainly omissions or insertions. Both proficient and weak readers conform to this pattern at their respective frustration levels, but the former more often suggest a word that is graphically similar. One study showed that about a quarter of their substitutions deviated from the word in the text by only one letter. Thus the more able reader may read 'man' for 'men', but the weaker may read 'man' for 'monkey'. By recording and analysing the miscues the teacher can detect specific weaknesses in a child's word attack, e.g. in the use of context, or in medial sounds. If the teacher is skilled in interpreting the errors an informal reading inventory is in effect a changing battery of test materials which provides her with a comprehensive record. It has the peculiar strength of making the testing process a learning situation for both teacher and child. Moreover it can be used not only to detect and remedy the poor reader's deficiencies, but to help the capable reader to read better. We have been able here to describe the device only briefly and at its simplest level; but it can, of course, be used in varied and sophisticated forms to develop higher reading strategies in children who are fluent readers. Diagnosis and teaching thus become a single process.

17.21   Diagnosis by structured observation requires thoughtful recording if it is to be turned to advantage, and we regard recording as an essential element in the actual teaching process. The record must show which particular reading skills need most attention if progress is to be ensured; and therefore the precise steps that must be taken to supply it. Our survey showed that records which might be put to this use were to be found in only a minority of schools. Only 37 per cent of the teachers of six year olds and 46 per cent of those of nine year olds said they kept records of persistent individual weaknesses that might require additional help within the school. The figures relating to outside help were even lower at 32 per cent and 38 per cent respectively (page 459). However able the teacher, we do not believe that appropriate measures can be developed to meet varying individual needs unless the characteristics of these are sequentially noted. Recording can take many forms, from the keeping of fairly simple notes to elaborate inventories with spaces to check off sub-skills. We are referring here not to the checklist an authority may devise as a standard element of its screening system, but to that which a school may use for its own teaching purposes. Opinions are divided on the respective merits of simple and detailed checklists. Of the one it is said that it has the virtue of being attractively easy to use but the defect of being a relatively blunt instrument; of the other that it is a very precise tool but too time-consuming. This must be a matter for individual choice which will depend in large measure on the extent of the teacher's experience in assessing reading ability. Inventories of skills, e.g. the blending of sounds, will be of considerable help to teachers who want a ready-made system of visual checking. Others may prefer to indicate errors on a duplicate copy or an acetate sheet in accordance with an agreed code, e.g. the circling of omissions and the underlining of mispronunciations, showing whether the child uses initial-sound or shape-of-word clues. The important thing is that the recording should be in a form which is helpful to other teachers and can be interpreted expertly and used constructively to advance the child's reading competence. This applies at all levels of ability, and structured observation should be equally at the service of the good reader whose skills can be taken further. A good system of recording will reflect the teacher's planning for each child's reading development. In a classroom organised on 'informal' lines, with a good deal of individual work in progress, effective recording of the kind we have been discussing is of the greatest importance. As pupils grow older there should be increasing opportunities for self-appraisal. Some pupils can be encouraged to develop a responsibility for their own progress, recording their strengths and difficulties, and using the record as an aid towards the growth of higher level skills.

17.22 So far we have been discussing diagnosis in terms of structured observation, which is the first stage in the process. For some children it will be the *only* stage, since in the hands of the experienced teacher it provides in itself a series of insights sufficient to ensure their progress along a line of potential development. There will be many children, however, whose weaknesses as revealed by this method will call for deeper investigation through the application of tests. There are in existence several diagnostic tests which teachers can use to follow up the initial identification they made through their controlled observation. Some witnesses suggested that there was an acute need for more of these. We recommend that new diagnostic tests[7] should be devised and that these should combine the maximum of practical information with ease of administration. In saying this we would emphasise that the availability of new tests is not a solution in itself. We have already referred to survey results which showed what little use is made of tests other than a very small number of well known ones. None of these tests is designed for diagnosis in the terms we are discussing here. The indications are that many schools are not aware of the variety of diagnostic instruments at present available, or at least are unfamiliar with their use. This has important advisory and in-service training implications, for the ability to diagnose should be part of the professional competence of every primary school teacher. He should have access to a range of tests which he can draw upon where necessary to supplement his own observational procedures.

17.23 The third stage in the diagnostic process is referral to the school doctor and the educational psychologist, and this will involve an even smaller number of children. The relationship between teacher, educational psychologist, and doctor should be such as to encourage a team approach. In the case of most children the teacher will be able to diagnose at a level which will reveal to him the best means of helping the child. But there will be cases where he will find it appropriate to involve other members of the team. Where a child fails to respond to help this should be done without delay, so that further investigations can be carried out and the parent brought into consultation. The first step is to enquire of the school doctor whether there are any medical factors that may be relevant to the child's difficulty in learning to read. This will give the doctor the opportunity to re-examine the child, and the medical information should then be made available to the teacher and to the educational psychologist who will investigate the child's learning difficulties. It may also be helpful in appropriate situations to refer to the educational welfare officer and social worker. It was suggested to us in evidence that at present too many children are referred to the school psychological service with reading problems. It was also pointed out that if psychologists were more readily available for consultation *in schools* there would be fewer referrals necessary. Our case is that with proper training the teacher should be able to make finer judgments in this matter of bringing in his colleagues, whose participation in the school setting is important. He should be able to perceive that a difficulty revealed by diagnostic test requires further investigation of a kind that lies with them. All too commonly the contacts between teacher and educational psychologist are few, and in the past there has been a tradition of quite distinct functions. It is more profitable to think in terms of different emphases rather than different roles, and in some authorities this concept is taking encouraging shape. This is particularly true where a large-scale venture such as the introduction of a screening programme gives rise to joint planning.

17.24 We believe that educational psychologists have an important part to play in in-service training, notably in helping teachers to a more detailed knowledge of diagnostic techniques. The provision of courses and information for teaching was the subject of a survey[8] carried out in 1973. Authorities were asked whether their Schools Psychological Service or Remedial Education Service had provided during the last year any courses in which the uses and limitations of reading tests formed a significant part. Of the 159 responding only 27 per cent had arranged more than two such courses, and 39 per cent had not provided any at all. At the other end of the range 2 per cent had organised over 30. 33 per cent produced pamphlets or other materials giving information about reading tests, and these ranged from single sheets to 30-page booklets. Only one pamphlet contained a description of informal reading inventories, though it is not known to what extent the use of these was featured in the courses. The survey revealed that 36 per cent of authorities had not provided either courses or pamphlets during the year in question. It would be unjust and incorrect to infer from these results that some Schools Psychological Services and Remedial Education Services do not supply teachers with any information at all about tests. Much useful help in this respect is given in the everyday work of the services, especially when the test results of particular children are being discussed. Moreover, there are other bodies, such as University Departments and Schools of Education, which arrange courses and supply information. Nevertheless, we believe that there is scope for a considerable expansion of in-service training activity in which educational psychologists and teachers are jointly involved. This is not simply a question of the one arranging courses of lectures for the other. It should entail a great deal of practical work and follow-up within schools. Much of this might well be based on actual case studies and evaluation of special teaching programmes designed by teachers and psychologists working together. There is undoubtedly a considerable demand from teachers for in-service training in the field of diagnosis, and it is hoped that the new authorities will find it possible to effect an expansion to meet it.

17.25   Finally, we would again emphasise that the aim of diagnosis is to improve the teaching in relation to the needs of the individual child. An effective system of diagnosis and recording should be an important source of intelligence to head and staff, helping in decisions about individual teaching programmes and the materials and books needed to support them.

ANNEX A:

RESULTS OF AN INQUIRY INTO ASSESSMENT PROCEDURES APPLIED BY LOCAL AUTHORITIES

17.26   Authorities were asked to supply information about any surveys into reading they had carried out during the last three years. They were also asked to give details of any arrangements for identifying at an early age children likely to have reading and language difficulties. 93 of the 146 authorities responded, 56 of them County Boroughs and 37 County Councils. The information they submitted was extremely varied. It ranged from highly detailed statistical analyses to brief general comments. There was an equally wide variation in the methods employed. On the one hand there was the periodical survey, sophisticated in design and employing several different techniques; on the other there was no testing at all, but a policy of general consultation between schools and other agencies, especially the Schools Psychological Service. The variety was also evident in the extent to which specialist help was available to the child experiencing reading difficulties. There was often a relationship between the extent and quality of this help and the criteria applied to discover which children were in need of it.

17.27   Of the 93 authorities which responded, 50 provided empirical data based on objective assessments, i.e. tests given to groups of pupils. A minority had carried out surveys on a regular basis for a number of years, but most had conducted a single survey or one or two pilot studies in individual schools. Some authorities placed the emphasis on directing help to the individual child in need, while others combined this with identifying schools to which extra resources should be allocated. A few were concerned to monitor local standards across the years. The figures reproduced below show that the number of surveys has increased during the period to which our inquiry referred. As the authorities were approached during 1973 the figure for that year is not complete:

1970 : 18   *1971 :* 25   *1972 :* 37   *1973 :* 26

In some cases testing was carried out at two or occasionally three stages during a child's schooling, but the most usual practice was for it to occur once early in the primary school. Several authorities had changed the age for testing within the last three years.

Table 15

ASSESSMENT OF READING ABILITY BY L.E.A.S—AGE AT WHICH PUPILS WERE TESTED AND NUMBER OF INSTANCES

Age at which pupils were tested:	Number of instances
7+ last year in infant school	8
7+ first term of junior school	28
8+ second year in junior school	16
9+ third year in junior school	3
10+ first term of fourth year in junior school	2
11+ last term of fourth year in junior school	10
12+ last year of middle school	1
14+ third year of secondary school	1
15+ fourth year of secondary school	1

17.28   There was wide variety in the tests used; no fewer than 21 different kinds. Several authorities used the same ones on successive occasions; a few employed different tests according to age group in any one year. The following table shows the incidence of use of the various tests:

Table 16

ASSESSMENT OF READING ABILITY BY L.E.A.S—VARIETIES OF TESTS AND INCIDENCE OF USE

Tests	Incidence of tests
(a) Individual:	
Schonell Graded Word Reading Test	11
Burt (Vernon) Revised Word Reading Test	6
Holborn Sentence Reading Test	6
Standard Reading Tests (Daniels and Diack)	3
Vernon Word Reading Test	1
(b) Group:	
Young Group Reading Test	11
Southgate Group Reading Test	7
Wide Span Reading Test	2
Carver	2
Spooncer	2
English Picture Vocabulary Test	2
Renfrew Picture Action Test	1
Gates McGintie (New N.F.E.R. British Standardisation)	1
Litsart (Purpose designed test, produced by an L.E.A.)	1
N.F.E.R. Reading Test A	1
,, ,, ,, B.D.	3
,, ,, ,, S.R.A.	1
,, ,, ,, A.D.	1
,, ,, ,, D.E.	1
,, ,, ,, N.S.45	1

The individual tests were usually administered by classroom teachers as part of the general assessment of children's progress. In such cases the survey consisted of a request to the schools for the data to be passed to the authority by a specified date. The assessment itself was therefore not necessarily carried out on any particular date or even at roughly the same time in different schools.

17.29 A particularly interesting feature of the inquiry was the variation it revealed in the criteria used for determining reading disability. These are shown below in three basic categories, within each of which different criteria were applied:

(a) Reading disability determined by a discrepancy between reading age and chronological age. The following shows the variety of yardsticks used by different authorities:

   (i) Reading age of 12.5 at chronological age of 15
   (ii)   ,,   ,,   9.5 at time of 11+ survey
 (iii)   ,,   ,,   9.0 at chronological age of 11.06 (4 L.E.A.s)
 (iv)   ,,   ,,   8.6   ,,   ,,   11.04
  (v)   ,,   ,,   8.4 at time of 9+ survey
 (vi)   ,,   ,,   8.0 at chronological age of 8.9
 (vii)   ,,   ,,   6.0 at time of 8+ survey (7 L.E.A.s)
(viii)   ,,   ,,   6.6 at chronological age of 7.7
 (ix)   ,,   ,,   6.0   ,,   ,,   7.06
  (x)   ,,   ,,   6.9   ,,   ,,   7.4
 (xi)   ,,   ,,   6.0   ,,   ,,   7.3 (3 L.E.A.s)
 (xii)   ,,   ,,   6.8   ,,   ,,   7.2

Note: Three authorities simply stated a one year discrepancy at whatever age the test might be applied, while two others left the discrepancy unspecified.

(b) Reading disability determined by standardised score, incorporating age allowance:

   (i) Less than 90 on the English Picture Vocabulary Test
   (ii)   ,,   ,, 85   ,,   Young Group Reading Test (2 L.E.A.s)
 (iii)   ,,   ,, 85   ,,   N.F.E.R. S.R.A.
 (iv)   ,,   ,, 85   ,,   Wide Span Reading Test
  (v)   ,,   ,, 80   ,,   N.F.E.R. B.D.
 (vi)   ,,   ,, 80   ,,   N.F.E.R. S.R.A.
 (vii)   ,,   ,, 80   ,,   Young Group Reading Test (4 L.E.A.s)
(viii)   ,,   ,, 80   ,,   Gates McGintie
 (ix)   ,,   ,, 71   ,,   Young Group Reading Test

(c) Other criteria quoted by authorities were:

   (i) inability to read 10 words at 7+ and 20 words at 8+ on the Schonell Graded Word Reading Test
   (ii) "below chronological age"
 (iii) "non-readers"

17.30 As might be expected, the variety of criteria resulted in different proportions of children regarded as displaying reading disability. These are shown in the following table, where the figures to the right of the percentage column indicate the number of times each percentage was reported.

Table 17

ASSESSMENT OF READING ABILITY BY L.E.A.S—PERCENTAGES OF CHILDREN ASSESSED AS HAVING READING DIFFICULTIES

Percentage of children assessed as having reading difficulties	Age at Testing						
	7	8	9	10	11	14	15
under 5 per cent	4	—	—	1	2	1	—
6—10 per cent.	12	—	2	1	3	1	—
11—15 per cent.	8	2	—	—	6	—	—
16—20 per cent.	5	3	—	—	2	—	—
21—25 per cent.	8	3	—	—	—	—	1
26—30 per cent.	2	2	—	—	—	—	—
31 per cent and over	4	—	—	—	1	—	—
Number of L.E.A.s testing	43	10	2	2	14	2	1

These figures reflect the wide variation in choice of criteria as well as the *actual* proportions of children with reading difficulties. For seven year olds the range is from 'non-readers' (approximately 2 per cent of children, reported twice) to 'below chronological age' (approximately 42 per cent of children, reported once). When the extremes are disregarded it would seem that at this age between 10 per cent and 25 per cent of children are identified as needing special help; by the age of eleven the proportion has reduced to between 7 per cent and 15 per cent.

17.31   Nine of the authorities added that it was also their practice to ascertain the extent of higher standards of reading performance. Six of them used the criterion of reading age, and the proportions of children whose reading age was two years in advance of their chronological age ranged from 5 per cent to 57 per cent. The remainder used the standardised score, taking one standard deviation above the mean as the criterion, i.e. scores of 116 or over. The proportions here ranged from 9 per cent to 20 per cent.

17.32   There was little reference to the effect upon reading age norms of the rise in standards between 1948 and 1968. For example, 'the norm' for children of 7.5 in 1950, defined in terms of the number of words read aloud from a word recognition test, would differ from the 'norm' for children of the same age in 1970. Nor was there reference to the gradual ageing of certain tests, or the steady decline of the reading age concept in favour of the standardised score on a test designed for the age group in question. In some authorities regular testing had been the practice over the last few years, involving the same standardised test, the same mean age of pupils, and the same criteria for interpreting scores. There is no doubt that this consistency rewarded them with superior information for judging the movement of standards and allocating additional resources. Where conditions of administration varied the information carried far less conviction, principally because a history of local norms had not been founded.

17.33   We have said little about the descriptive accounts which were not based on a testing programme. They consisted largely of general statements about the administrative provision for 'remedial' teaching. There was frank acknowledgement that the subjective judgment at work could result in variable standards. On the other hand several authorities felt that the liaison they had developed was adequate to the task and that a survey involving testing would add little useful information. It is clear that there is widespread concern among authorities to help children with learning difficulties and to strengthen those schools where they are in the greatest number. It is equally clear that the methods used to identify these children vary widely in the degree of precision they attain.

ANNEX B:

DESCRIPTIONS OF THREE DIFFERENT FORMS OF SCREENING PROCEDURE

17.34 On analysing the replies to our inquiry about screening procedures we invited three authorities to describe in greater detail the methods they had developed. The following are the accounts provided by these authorities:

Example 1: AN OUTER SUBURBAN AREA

As a result of concern about the teaching of reading a working group was established to enquire into the feasibility and timing of a form of standardised testing to reveal children "at risk" in language development. The group consisted of the authority's inspectors, educational psychologists, and representative primary school heads.

There followed a decision to assess each child early in his life in the infant school in order to avert the depressing experience of cumulative failure which some children face. The working party's first task was to decide on the kind of instrument to be used. Their criteria were: (*a*) that it should be short and easy to score, (*b*) that it should give an accurate general picture of each child's abilities and skills, particularly those involved in the reading process, and (*c*) that it should be sensitive enough to distinguish between slow-learning children and those whose progress gave no cause for concern. The discussion resulted in the design of a checklist to provide a series of structured observations by the teacher. The objects of this checklist were to assess each child's readiness to begin reading, to identify possible areas of learning difficulty, and to provide appropriate help promptly for teacher and child. The working party allowed for the uneven nature of the maturational process. The checklist is made up of a list of 19 simple questions on the child's development in the four main areas most important to the learning process, namely: (*a*) speech and communication, (*b*) perceptual-motor, (*c*) emotional-social and (*d*) the child's response to learning situations. The teacher gives a "yes" or "no" answer to each question, and space is provided for further comment. At various points during the infant years the teacher will again mark up the checklist, thus producing a continuous record of the child's early progress. This material is regarded as an early stage in the process of identifying children "at risk". Subsequent stages in the screening procedure are as follows:

(i) Assessment at the end of infant schooling; one further entry is made on the checklist before the child transfers to the junior school. In addition each child attempts the first two pages of the Neale Analysis of Reading Ability.

(ii) At the end of the second year in the juniors the children take the Young Group Reading Test.

(iii) Final testing in the primary school: in the last term of the fourth year all children who have appeared "at risk" in earlier tests are re-tested on the complete Neale Analysis to determine a reading age, which is entered on each child's record card.

Copies of the checklist and all reading ages are sent to a central point and are analysed by the L.E.A. computer. First results indicate that there is correlation between the checklist and the child's reading age.

The success of such a scheme depends upon the skill and commitment of those who operate it. In each infant and junior school the authority has appointed one teacher with a special allowance for taking responsibility for screening in the school. These teachers are in contact with centralised resources and training plans, and they are involved in in-service training on screening and diagnostic testing. They provide a focal point for other members of staff, particularly probationary teachers, and they give advice to ensure that the statistical data provided by the screening procedures is used to the best effect by their colleagues. Some have taken on additional and related responsibilities. For example, they advise on book purchase or organise the time-tables of part-time teachers. Several have become increasingly interested in language development throughout the school.

The inspectors and educational psychologists have provided in-service training courses to take advantage of these developing interests. For teachers new to screening, the authority provides a series of practical pamphlets, and they have the sustained support of the Primary and English inspectors. A Language Centre has been established as an additional resource. Teachers are welcomed there to visit the standing exhibition of language development materials and equipment, talk over problems with the specialists, prepare their own materials, and hold discussion groups.

17.35   *Example 2:* A SOUTHERN COUNTY AREA

The authority introduced screening for the following reasons:

  (i) to identify the children needing special help in learning to read;
 (ii) to allocate extra teachers where they were most needed;
(iii) to indicate the extent of in-service teacher training need in this aspect of the curriculum;
(iv) to ensure appropriate help for children experiencing learning difficulties —help either through remedial teaching in normal school or through special school attendance.

Every year the staff of the psychological service carries out a two-part survey of reading problems in primary schools throughout the county. At the beginning of each spring term primary school heads are asked to list those children in the 7/8+ age group whose reading ages fall two years or more below their chronological ages, and to identify those children due to move up to middle or secondary schools who might benefit more from transfer to special schools. The 7/8+ age group children experiencing reading difficulties are listed on criteria provided by individual word recognition tests rather than by group tests administered to the whole age range. It is acknowledged within the authority that this procedure has the disadvantage that some children may be missed, as class teachers are being asked to use subjective judgments in selecting anticipated slow learners for reading testing. On the other hand, one of the factors influencing the decision in favour of the individual test was that it provides the teacher with a face-to-face experience of each child's problems.

The second part of the survey is that heads are asked to arrange for administration of the Non-Readers' Intelligence Test (constructed and standardised by Dennis Young, and published by University of London Press) to those children listed as slow learners. This group test is designed to measure verbal intelligence independently of reading skills, so that children experiencing specific reading difficulties will not be handicapped by these when completing it. The aim of this screening test is to distinguish between those slow readers who can probably be helped best by periodic remedial teaching in normal schools and those whose general intellectual handicaps may be such that they will be helped most appropriately through full-time special schooling. Children obtaining low scores on the group intelligence test are assessed developmentally by educational psychologists, who discuss the children's special needs with parents and teachers. After staffing increases in the psychological service it has been found in recent years that the majority of children scoring low on the group intelligence test have already been the subjects of consultation between head teachers and psychologists; consequently this second screen is now regarded as serving no more than a 'mopping up' purpose, and may be discontinued in the future.

Survey returns provide the basis for consultation between remedial advisory teachers, educational psychologists, advisers and education officers, and are taken into account in education officers' allocations of teaching time for the following school year. In some cases, time is allocated specifically for remedial work; in others remedial teaching time is incorporated into a general allocation. Whether or not they receive specific remedial teaching allocations, most heads manage to timetable work in small groups for children in need of special help. These groups are often conducted by qualified married women who have returned to teaching part-time. At the beginning of 1974, with the county school population at approximately 81,000, specific remedial teaching allocation for primary schools was about the equivalent of 30 full-time teachers.

Although word recognition tests are judged to be useful in identifying slow learners they are of little value in providing teachers with practical guidance on teaching methods appropriate for particular children. An important feature of arrangements for helping children with reading difficulties has been the provision of regular in-service training sessions. Through these courses, conducted mainly by the county's two remedial advisory teachers, teachers have been helped to make use of tests designed to diagnose children's reading difficulties and to link their findings with appropriate teaching methods. To complement these courses, educational psychologists and remedial advisory teachers have together produced a series of booklets detailing examples of diagnostic and teaching techniques.

17.36 *Example* 3: AN INNER CITY AREA

The authority has an extensive remedial service, provided partly in special centres and classes, partly by allocating extra teachers to individual schools, and partly through peripatetic teachers. Over the past two years the school psychological service has provided a series of in-service training workshop courses in the assessment and 'remediation' of specific reading difficulties.

The extensive study of case histories in these courses underlined the great importance of the initial identification of children in need of special help. An equally important factor was the increasing responsibility taken by the remedial teachers for initial assessment and advisory work in schools. If the special services are to be used with maximum efficiency and if help is to be given at the appropriate time it is essential that such children be identified early by means of a systematic screening procedure.

One of the educational psychologists introduced a screening instrument to identify children with learning problems. Its purposes may be defined as follows:

1. To provide a profile of the individual child's abilities as a guide to his educational needs.
2. To provide a continuous monitoring of pupil standards—possibly at three different age levels, e.g. final year of infant school; mid-junior; and first year secondary level.
3. To provide a basis of comparison when evaluating various educational methods.
4. To identify those children who may be "at risk" in the learning situation and those requiring further diagnostic investigation or an adaptation of educational programmes.
5. To provide some standardised information about general levels of competence. Such information might help teachers, particularly subject specialists, to start with realistic expectations about pupils' levels of performance and so avoid presenting of oral and written material beyond their level of comprehension.

The authority's psychological service has been giving attention to developing the screening procedure for children in the final year of the infant school. It was decided that the screening instrument should give a measure of the child's reading attainment and word-attack skills, together with some information on aspects of perceptual, cognitive and language skills and of personality attributes relevant to the learning process. Such an instrument needs to be reliable and yet economical in terms both of cost and teacher time. Members of the psychological service and specialist teachers therefore began to build up a series of tests and assessment procedures, some already published, some purpose-designed, which a teacher could use within the classroom situation. A small-scale pilot study was carried out on some 250 six to eight year old children. The outcome of this study was a body of information on each child's functioning in such areas as motor co-ordination, eye-motor control, visual and auditory discrimination and memory, active and passive vocabulary, comprehension and attainment in spelling, and reading and phonic skills, together with some indication of relevant environmental and motivational factors. The data were analysed, and a purpose-designed screening instrument compiled which could be used with children in their final year in infants' school. This was applied initially in one division early in 1974. The instrument consists of a pupil's work-book containing a variety of exercises which can be completed by the children as a group activity in the classroom. The work-book is contained in a pupil's folder on which the teacher completes a short pupil-behaviour questionnaire and records such relevant data as the child's vision, hearing, speech, laterality, attendance, and number of schools attended. The teacher's handbook contains instructions for administering and scoring the work-book exercises.

It is intended to run in-service training courses and to produce a videotape programme on the administration of the screening procedure. These will be followed up by further teachers' courses and by published handbooks on planning educational programmes relevant to the needs of the pupils. The psychologists and the remedial teachers working with them will carry out further investigations of children identified as "at risk" by the initial screening. These children may require remedial help within the school or at local remedial centres. Profiles will be provided of pupils' areas of strength and weakness at an early age, and teaching programmes within the school will be adapted accordingly. It is hoped that these measures will prevent the development of some types of early learning difficulty. This will allow specialist services to concentrate on pupils with severe problems which fall outside the scope of ordinary classroom programmes.

REFERENCES

1. *Children with Specific Reading Difficulties.* H.M.S.O. 1973.
2. See *The Role of the Health Visitor in Relation to Speech Development:* The College of Speech Therapists.
3. See *Speech Therapy Services:* H.M.S.O.: 1972.
4. *Child Welfare Centres: a report of the sub-committee of the Standing Medical Advisory Committee of the Central Health Services Council:* H.M.S.O.: 1967.
5. R. Davie, N. Butler, and H. Goldstein: *"From Birth to Seven":* A report of the National Child Development Study: Longmans: 1972.
6. E. Goodacre: *Hearing Children Read:* Centre for the Teaching of Reading: Reading University School of Education: 1972.
7. An up to date review of diagnostic tests currently available in this country and the U.S.A. is to be found in *Reading Tests and Assessment Techniques:* P. D. Pumfrey: U.L.P.: 1974.
8. P. D. Pumfrey: *The contribution of L.E.A. Schools' Psychological Services and Remedial Education Services to the provision of courses on, and pamphlets concerning, the uses and limitations of reading tests: a survey of current practice in England and Wales:* University of Manchester: 1973.

CHAPTER 18

Children with Reading Difficulties

18.1   In this chapter we have drawn together some of the issues relating to children in ordinary schools who are experiencing failure with reading. It will be obvious, however, that their difficulties and the provision they need are by no means confined to this part of the Report. In all we have so far said about language and reading there is the insistence, in some places explicit and everywhere implicit, that careful attention should be given to those children who show signs of experiencing particular difficulty. Indeed, the entire sections on language and reading in the early years should be read in association with this chapter. Equally, we have the needs of these children very much in mind in the parts of the Report where we discuss organisation, resources, and teacher training.

18.2   Children with reading difficulties are usually described as 'retarded' or 'backward', and the term 'slow learner' is sometimes used as a substitute for the second. A backward reader is generally regarded as one who is below the average for his age[1]. Thus, if a ten year old child has a reading age[2] of 9.0 he is backward by twelve months. The notion can also be expressed in terms of a reading quotient. The 1950 Ministry of Education pamphlet gave the critical quotient as 80; below this a child could be considered a backward reader. He may be working to the limit of his capacity and yet register this low score. The retarded reader, on the other hand, is defined as one whose attainments are low in relation to his intelligence. His achievements are not being judged against those of his contemporaries but in relation to his own mental capacity. By these terms some children are backward, some are retarded, and some are both. Thus, the last-named will be achieving below the norm for their age and also below the average for children of similarly low ability.

18.3   This is a necessarily brief account of what is in fact a complicated issue, but it serves to provide a background for what we consider an important qualification of the notion of 'failure'. There is first of all the failure which is legitimate in the sense that the child can see that success is possible but is eluding him. Provided he can be helped to identify and then overcome the causes of his failure the experience is a valid one, for in these terms failure becomes acceptable and manageable. The second sense in which the word can be used is where the child is faced with objectives which are at the time completely beyond his powers. He is unable to understand the causes of his failure, which is inevitable and inescapable. The child's awareness of failure of this kind can have serious consequences in terms of personal feelings, attitudes, expectations and achievement. A very real possibility is that the backward child can also become a retarded one in circumstances where unrealistic achievements are being expected of him. The notion of failure, however defined, should be approached with circumspection. Defeatism on the part of parents or teacher will soon spread to the children themselves. It is more constructive to think and plan in terms of greater progress for *all* children. The pupil formerly considered as 'failing' will then be seen as one who is making slow progress and who can be helped to improved achievement if certain positive measures are taken.

266

18.4   It is clear that there are many children leaving infant school who are still finding great difficulty in learning to read and are likely to continue to need special help in the junior school, particularly those summer-born children who may have had only two years of early schooling. While we acknowledge that children vary in the ages at which they are ready for the more formal aspects of learning to read, we do not accept that this stage of readiness should be seen merely as an aspect of maturation, to be patiently awaited. Carefully planned activities will give the child the preparation he needs for the more formal beginnings of reading and writing. We are convinced that a more systematic approach to such preparation would reduce the number of children with reading problems in the junior school. Delay in making even a modest beginning in reading beyond the age of seven puts the child at educational risk, not merely because a great deal of later learning depends on the ability to read, but because the poor reader is less likely to receive skilled attention the older he becomes. A survey[3] carried out by the Inner London Education Authority into the literacy of 31,308 children revealed that 63 per cent of the junior schools had no full-time teacher who "had received specific/detailed training (i.e. more than a few general lectures) to teach reading at training college or specialist course". Indeed, fewer than one in eight of the full-time teachers in junior schools had been trained to teach reading. It is significant that in the National Child Development Study a follow-up of eleven year olds surveyed four years earlier revealed that the majority of those who were retarded at seven had fallen behind even further. It is equally clear that the number of children continuing to need help in their secondary school is also considerable. In replying to our questionnaire 13 per cent of secondary schools judged that at least a quarter of their pupils aged twelve required "special provision" on account of reading and language difficulties. In 10 per cent of the schools the same number of pupils were held to be in similar need at age fourteen. Children in the Isle of Wight[4] who had reading difficulties at the end of their junior school subsequently continued to experience difficulty; the group as a whole made only 10 months' progress in reading during the 28 month period of the follow-up. A further examination of the group at the age of fourteen showed that the majority of children found to have severe reading difficulties in their primary schools continued to lag far behind in reading as they approached the end of their statutory school life.

18.5   The causes of reading failure are no less complex today than they were when Sir Cyril Burt examined London children some 50 years ago. In many cases the cause may be found in the circumstances of a child's upbringing, which restrict his experiences and provide little or no encouragement for him to learn. Children who come from homes where conversation is limited and books unknown are likely to be slower in their linguistic growth and to find greater difficulty in learning to read than those who come from more favoured backgrounds. Some children have limited natural ability, or a sensory defect, particularly hearing, which adversely affects their capacity to develop language. Children of limited mental ability reach their developmental milestones, including those of speech and language, more slowly than normal children. In the Isle of Wight survey it was found that 23.4 per cent of the "intellectually retarded" children spoke their first words at 25 months of age or later, compared with 2.3 per cent of the normal population. Some children may be anxious or depressed, so that they cannot apply their minds to learning; they may have lost confidence in themselves and in their capacity to learn because they have already failed in school. Lastly, there is a rather smaller group of children who experience a difficulty in learning to read that cannot be accounted for by limited ability or by emotional or extraneous factors. The term 'dyslexic' is commonly applied to these children. We believe that this term serves little useful purpose other than to draw attention to the fact that the problem of these children can be chronic and severe. It is not susceptible to precise operational definition; nor does it indicate any clearly defined course of treatment. Most of the children, however, do find difficulties in auditory and visual discrimination and in associating visual symbols with the sounds they represent, and it has been suggested that these difficulties are caused by delayed maturation of the co-ordinating processes of the nervous system. A more helpful term to describe the situation of these children is 'specific reading retardation'. This has been defined as "a syndrome characterised by severe reading difficulties which are not accountable for in terms of low intelligence and which are not explicable merely in terms of the lower end of a normal distribution of reading skills"[5]. Given a skilled analysis of the nature of their difficulties, followed by intensive help and support, most of these pupils eventually learn to read, though their spelling may remain idiosyncratic throughout their lives. Arrangements for making this help available to them are discussed in para 18.18.

18.6   The level of a child's intellectual capacity inevitably affects his ability to acquire linguistic skills. But it must be remembered that intelligence itself is a developmental concept, and disadvantaged children brought up in circumstances which fail to nourish intellect can make considerable gains if placed in a favourable learning environment. It has been claimed[6] that increments are possible not merely during the early years but at *any* time during the years of a child's development. For a teacher to know that a certain slow reader is of high intelligence may usefully lead him to expect and encourage a higher attainment in the child. In contrast, the knowledge that a child is of below average intelligence may lead to an acceptance of below average reading standards. Yet many such children do become better than average readers, and one of the factors at work may well be positive expectations on the part of the teacher. The relationship between reading success and intelligence can be more easily identified with averages than with individual children. One would be justified in expecting that a group of children whose average intelligence quotient was higher than that of another group would have higher average reading scores. But in the first group there would almost certainly be some poor readers, while in the second there would be children with reading attainments above the level their intelligence might have suggested. The divergences in each case would represent the other factors in operation, for example, motivation, parental interest, perseverance, and the presence or absence of appropriate teaching. As a group of psychologists expressed it in a paper submitted in evidence: "If children are apparently unable to learn, we should assume that we have not as yet found the right way to teach them". Slow progress in reading is undoubtedly characteristic of children with limited natural endowments, and to expect their reading progress to be at the same rate as that of their more able peers would be unrealistic. However, with good teaching they should be able to make steady, continuous progress throughout their school lives.

18.7   The close association between retardation in reading and emotional disorders has been frequently noted, and has been referred to in much of the evidence we have received. It has been pointed out[7] that 'over-reacting' types of behaviour disturbance become increasingly severe up to the age of nine—i.e. during a critical period for the acquisition of reading and writing skills. Boys retarded in reading are more than twice as likely as other children to show anxiety or lack of concentration, and are three times as likely to experience irrational fears and anxieties; poor readers as a whole are almost four times as likely to show signs of maladjustment in school as children whose performance in reading is normal. In the Isle of Wight study a third of the children retarded in reading exhibited anti-social behaviour; similarly, of the group of children identified as anti-social over a third were at least 28 months retarded in their reading. Though the exact nature of the association between reading failure and emotional disorder is unclear, the association is so marked that "one might suppose that the relation is in most cases reciprocal. From the teachers' point of view, this suggests that emotional or behavioural disturbance is at any age a danger signal that learning failure may follow; similarly, failure to learn, for whatever reason, is a cue for action before it has emotional consequences of a lasting and compounding sort"[8].

18.8   It is now over half a century since Burt observed that backwardness and poverty were closely interrelated. A few years ago, when Wiseman carried out his survey for the Plowden Committee[9], the association was found to be with *psychological* poverty—lack of books, low parental interest, and a linguistic expectation at variance with the language used in the school. Recent investigations carried out by a number of L.E.A.s in underprivileged industrial areas in the North West revealed a disturbingly high incidence of reading retardation at the age of eight. In some of the schools serving these areas almost a quarter of the age group had "low reading ability"; in a few schools in re-housing areas, where parental interest was minimal and vandalism rife, the number of children with "very limited" reading ability rose to 40 per cent, and the number of non-readers to as many as one in five. We have discussed in Chapter 2 some of the recent studies that have confirmed the relationship between low attainment and home circumstances. One of these was the first report of the National Child Development Study, which showed that at seven years of age "the chances of an unskilled manual worker's child being a poor reader are six times greater than those of a professional worker's child . . .; the chances of a Social Class V child being a non-reader are 15 times greater than those of a Social Class I child". Put in more general terms, "the difference between children from Social Classes I and II and those from Social Class V is equivalent to nearly 17 months of reading age". Even more startling is the evidence that has recently become available from the follow-up study of the same group of children four years later, which shows that their retardation at age eleven, so far from being alleviated, has actually increased: "the differences between Social Classes I and II and V was about 27 months compared to about 17 months at the age of seven". This evidence is in accord with the findings of earlier surveys such as those of Douglas[10] and others, whose later work indicates that retardation of this kind often persists until the end of a child's school days. There can therefore be no doubt that active intervention is needed at an early age to compensate as far as possible for the cumulative effects of social handicap.

18.9   Among the factors which contribute to retardation in reading the local authorities and the schools themselves have not escaped criticism. Present facilities for helping children with difficulties in reading and in the use of language have been described as "sorely inadequate" by some of our witnesses. We believe there to be some truth in this assertion, supported as it is by the findings of a number of surveys and investigations. There are undoubted differences in standards of reading and language in schools serving very similar residential areas, as the Newsom Report showed[11], and startling improvements in reading levels have been claimed as a result of a determined effort to improve standards. Some local authorities have augmented the resources of those schools with the largest numbers of poor readers, and by so doing have helped them to bring about significant improvements. On the other hand, it has to be acknowledged that there are many schools where these children are exposed to the unsettling effect of rapid teacher turnover or are taught by inexperienced teachers.

18.10   The arrangements for providing 'remedial education' vary greatly; from remedial classes or withdrawal groups within an individual school to peripatetic advisory services, area classes, or specialised help in remedial centres. How effective are these measures? This would seem at first sight to be a relatively easy question to answer, but the results of efforts to do so over a number of years have proved controversial, not least on account of the many different types of provision and approach, and the varied criteria for selecting the children to be given help. It might be expected that some broad consensus of opinion would emerge to indicate whether or not 'remedial' treatment is likely to be successful; but the evidence from research is neither unanimous nor particularly encouraging. One of the earliest studies[12] proved promising: children who had hitherto made little or no progress in reading began to do so when given remedial teaching. The average gain during the six monthly period was 1.9 years for the 64 children for whom there were complete results. Collins[13], in a now well known monograph, reviewed the progress of groups of children who had received such education at the Remedial Education Centre at Birmingham University Institute of Education. He, too, found that the immediate effects of remedial treatment appeared to have been beneficial; the children who completed the course made an average gain of two years reading age in one year one month, and the behaviour difficulties of rather more than half of them improved. But a subsequent experiment gave rise to doubts. Two groups of children were given remedial education, one in the Remedial Centre and one elsewhere, and the results were compared with those of a control group who received only normal teaching in their ordinary class. In the short term, gains of the remedial groups were shown to be limited: "only in the mechanical aspects of word recognition were treated children markedly different from controls". Even more significant was the finding that "the long term effects of treatment were negligible". Later studies[14] have tended to confirm these results: children who received remedial education showed considerable short-term gains, particularly in the more mechanical aspects of reading such as word recognition, but this progress was not sustained.

18.11   In seeking to discover the reasons for these seemingly depressing results, those responsible for the studies have drawn attention to the difficulties of making a just evaluation of measures which vary so greatly in approach and resources. Remedial education can consist of an hour or two a week in a centre or clinic or a daily period in school. It can be closely related to the rest of the child's work in school or it can be entirely dissociated from it, even to the extent of using a different orthography. It can range from unskilled treatment, based on inadequate understanding of individual differences, to expert help from a teacher with specialised training and long experience. We believe the discouraging findings reported by most research workers should not lead to a conviction that all such measures are bound to be ineffective. The success of these measures in some schools is there to be seen, as we noted earlier. When attention is focussed upon children who *do* learn to read it is apparent that many successful readers overcome difficulties which have been considered important as causes of failure. Put another way, although a number of children in difficulty do have below average test intelligence, some degree of hearing impairment, or indeterminate laterality, the same may be said of large numbers of successful readers. There are, however, certain factors which are essential if success is to be broad and lasting.

18.12   (1) The particular nature of each child's difficulties must be seen in relation to his whole linguistic development. There is no mystique about remedial education, nor are its methods intrinsically different from those employed by successful teachers anywhere. The essence of remedial work is that the teacher is able to give additional time and resources to adapting these methods to the individual child's needs and difficulties.

(2) Fundamental is the teacher's ability to create warm and sympathetic individual relationships with the pupils, so that they are encouraged to learn through the stimulus of success. Again, it is not a question of devising special 'remedial methods', but of applying good teaching in such a way that failure is replaced by a sense of achievement, with all that this means for a child's confidence and self respect. This is particularly important with young and immature children, who are the most easily discouraged by failure; for them it is more than ever important not only that they achieve a high rate of success, but that this is reinforced by the constant encouragement and approval of the teacher. From this it should be evident that remedial work is not work for the inexperienced or indifferent teacher, but for the one who combines a high level of teaching skill with an understanding of the children's emotional and developmental needs.

(3) Remedial help in learning to read should wherever possible be closely related to the rest of a child's learning. Children who are in need of special help sometimes have their weaknesses exposed by the very efforts designed to remedy them, particularly if these result in fewer opportunities to achieve success in other activities, such as art, crafts, drama, and music. This can be particularly true of older children for whom a monotonous and prolonged emphasis on remedial work in the basic skills occupies a major part of the time. Where this is at the expense of other parts of the curriculum which may offer them greater chances of success the policy can be self-defeating.

(4) There should be every effort to involve parents and help them to understand the nature of their children's difficulties. Evidence from the Educational Priority experiment[15] and from schools themselves shows that lack of interest on the part of the parents can be too readily assumed. The more the interest of parents can be aroused, the more they are likely to play a constructive part in helping their children at home. This is a matter we have dealt with at length in Chapter 5 and referred to elsewhere in the Report.

18.13   After stating these general principles we can look more closely at the organisation of additional remedial help in the school. In the primary school patterns of organisation within the classroom can go far to reduce the likelihood of failure. Opportunities for co-operative and individual work allow the varying requirements of children to be fulfilled. But there inevitably comes a time when one teacher, however skilled, cannot alone provide for the wide range of individual needs, including those of children whose difficulties call for additional help if they are not to fall still further behind. In some primary schools, where the ratio of staff to children is particularly favourable, the responsibility for giving help to these children may lie with every teacher. This arrangement certainly avoids the danger of dissociating reading from the rest of the child's learning, but it may deny him the special help he needs unless all the teachers are equally capable of providing it. The most common arrangement is for children in need of additional help to be taken separately by another teacher, sometimes by the head. Our survey revealed that 69 per cent of the teachers taking 'remedial' or withdrawal groups in the primary schools were part-timers. Part-time teachers used for this purpose include peripatetic remedial teachers, highly skilled in the teaching of reading and with additional training to equip them for the task. However, the indications are that there are many part-time teachers who have no recent experience of teaching reading and no in-service training to prepare them. There were 22,762 pupils in the 3,816 groups in our sample, which means an average of six pupils per group, and of the 'remedial' six and nine year olds 75 per cent were in groups of up to ten. In our visits to schools we talked to several class teachers who found this kind of arrangement unsatisfactory. Some would rather the part-time teacher were used to release them to give extra help to the children in need of it. Others believed that the part-timer should work alongside the regular teacher, who knows the child's background and can ensure that special help with reading is not divorced from the rest of his work. These are approaches with which more schools might experiment, bearing in mind the essential condition that the teachers concerned should find it a congenial way of working. This is not to say that one system should simply be substituted for another. In some circumstances there may well be much in favour of the part-time or peripatetic teacher withdrawing individuals or small groups on occasions. What we are suggesting is a flexibility which permits a variety of practice. At present the part-time teacher and the class teacher often work independently, and few schools have a member of staff with special responsibility for co-ordinating the work and advising.

18.14   This question of the relationship between remedial help and the general curriculum is of the greatest importance. Children who are taught in special groups are sometimes returned to general class work without the level of reading competence they need to enable them to make independent progress. Through lack of support they fail to continue the rate of progress they had made in the remedial group. Closer liaison between remedial teachers and class teacher is essential if the progress is to be maintained. There is, however, much more to it than that. We have argued elsewhere in the Report that in the primary school every teacher should consciously plan a reading programme which is designed to cater for the various levels of ability within the class. In our view this should be a school's explicit policy whether or not it decides to give additional special help by a withdrawal system. When a child comes to spend all his time with his class he should have the right kind of reading programme to take him on from that point.

18.15   In secondary schools the problem is more complex. Where there is a specialist organisation, or where grouping by ability is not favoured, it is unrealistic to expect every teacher to find the time or to possess the necessary knowledge and experience to help pupils who are retarded in language and reading. In about two-thirds of the schools which replied to our questionnaire children were withdrawn from their regular class group either regularly or occasionally for additional help in reading; in the remaining cases help was given in special classes or 'remedial departments'. The first of these practices has the disadvantage that the remedial reading tuition is separated from the remainder of the pupil's learning. On the other hand it has the virtue of allowing the pupil to take his place with his peers for the greater part of the week. This kind of arrangement seems to us to be particularly suitable for those whose reading is at a lower level than that of their general ability to learn and who are likely to profit from this specific and intensive tuition. With these pupils the separation can work effectively, but we recommend that the tuition should be related to the rest of the pupil's learning where possible. We came across one way of doing this in what the school called a 'support option', where an extraction system was being used in close co-operation with the main teaching. Fourth and fifth year pupils with reading difficulties followed the normal option timetable but took one subject fewer than their peers. In the time thus released they attended small group sessions for 'support'. The teacher responsible for this had the task of helping the pupils prepare for their work in various subjects, looking over chapters of text-books and helping them with their writing. One pupil who was to take part in a play reading later in the day was being helped with his part by the support teacher. We should like to see more initiatives of this kind, which we believe have considerable promise. It has also been suggested[16] that if retarded readers are able to receive counselling they regain confidence and show an increased capacity to learn. This may consist of nothing more than regular informal conversation with sympathetic adults, not necessarily teachers. We feel that more use could be made of this kind of voluntary help, provided that control remains in the hands of the teachers. The second practice, namely the allocation of pupils to special classes or 'remedial' departments, allows the teaching of reading to be integrated with the special curriculum that has been devised for the group of slow learners, making it possible to give both specific and incidental attention to reading and language development. We do not favour this practice when it results in the pupils being separated for most of the week, but it does seem a practicable arrangement for some pupils for part of it, say between one and two-thirds of the time. These classes are frequently called 'remedial' but are better thought of as slow learners' groups. There should be close co-operation between the teachers in charge of them and their colleagues with whom the pupils spend the remainder of the time. Consultation and exchange of information can ensure that the work and methods in all areas of the curriculum are suited to the pupils' particular needs. A third form of provision, though far less common, is for remedial specialists to join the pupils in their normal specialist lessons, such as history and geography. They act as tutors and counsellors in close association with the subject teacher to enable each pupil to keep up with and take a full part in the class work. This is another initiative which we believe should receive every encouragement and which more schools might consider.

18.16   Given the widely differing circumstances of secondary schools, we do not believe it possible to prescribe a particular pattern of organisation as the best, but we are convinced that whatever pattern is adopted it will prove successful only if it is based upon the principles we have already set out. Thus, additional teaching assistance should always be related to a child's interests and as far as possible to the rest of his learning. It should not isolate him unnecessarily from his class or group, nor prevent him from taking part in those aspects of the curriculum which he finds particularly satisfying and enjoyable. Additional teaching resources and other supportive services (such as the school psychological service) should be made available in sufficient strength to enable the great majority of such children to receive help within, or at least in close association with, their normal learning situation.

18.17   In many secondary schools, work with 'slow learners' seems unhappily to rank low in the list of priorities. These children commonly attract less than their fair share of resources, and their educational needs appear to be inadequately recognised. Their real need is a curriculum designed as much to develop their strengths and extend their interests as to remedy their weaknesses. It is not always easy to distinguish the needs of individual children, but failure to differentiate between their educational requirements is the source of much bewilderment, frustration and mis-directed effort. It is no part of our brief to consider in any detail the total curricular needs of slow learners, which are at present the subject of detailed investigation elsewhere. Nevertheless, we are convinced that their learning *must* be based on what seems to them interesting and real, and must provide them with opportunities to achieve "something in their school lives which they can look on with pride and which they . . . know others can look on with respect"[17]. Otherwise, there will be little on which to base realistic and effective language work and reading. It is important that general responsibility for these children should lie with a senior member of staff who is able to co-ordinate all the school's resources on their behalf. Where the school has a remedial department its head should have the status to enable him to carry out this role. Where a different form of organisation exists the teacher responsible should have comparable authority. Whoever exercises this responsibility should work in close consultation with the heads of other departments.

18.18   It will be apparent from what we have said above that we find ourselves in agreement with the view expressed by the Secretary of State's Advisory Committee[18] that the great majority of children with reading difficulties should be given the help they need in their own schools. However, as we have remarked, there are some children who experience a difficulty in learning to read that cannot be accounted for by limited ability or by emotional or extraneous factors, i.e. the children often referred to as 'dyslexic'. These pupils are likely to need more intensive treatment than the ordinary school can provide, and this may best be given in a remedial centre or reading clinic, a facility which should be available in every authority. They should be able to offer, or at least should have access to, a comprehensive diagnostic service, calling as necessary upon the skills of doctor and psychologist to complement the skills of an experienced staff of teachers. Ideally, they should not only provide skilled diagnosis, assessment and treatment for the comparatively small number of children with severe difficulties who attend them, but should also offer an advisory service for teachers in the schools. Their staff would be closely involved in the operation and follow-up of the screening procedure and in the provision of courses of the kind mentioned in the last chapter. They could also play a valuable role in evaluating books and other materials for backward readers, in disseminating information, and in making their experience available to teachers generally. In all these activities they would work closely with the adviser with special responsibility for children experiencing learning difficulties, and through him would be supported by the English advisory group advocated in Chapter 16. We regard the support of a specialist adviser as essential, and recommend that every authority should make such an appointment where one does not exist.

18.19   In conclusion we feel it important to single out again for emphasis the fact that the majority of the pupils who leave school with an inadequate command of reading come from areas of social and economic depression. The problem is more than one of teaching reading, and a combined effort by the social services, teachers and administrators is required over the whole period of a child's school life. One thing emerges clearly; the longer reading failure is allowed to persist the more difficult it is to overcome. Preventive measures are likely to be far more productive than remedial ones. It is essential to prevent early failure from becoming a source of emotional disorder for the pupil. Whatever the causes of failure may be, the chances of future improvement are impaired when a pupil becomes nervous, dispirited, over-anxious or alienated. It would be unrealistic to expect that conditions for learning will ever be ideal and there will always be children who for various reasons fall behind. But a very great deal can be done to prevent reading disability by raising the quality of teaching generally and by giving skilled individual help before a sense of failure has led the child to lose confidence. As Sir Cyril Burt once observed: "Never let the child lose heart—for once he has lost heart he has lost everything".

REFERENCES

1.   This concept appears simple but can be misleading if taken at face value. It has rightly been pointed out that 18 months' backwardness at the age of eight is more serious than 18 months' backwardness at fourteen. There has also been criticism of the practice of assessing achievement by comparing children with others of the same age. For example, "Comparing a child's

attainment with that of his contemporaries implies that potentially every pupil can reach a level of educational achievement commensurate with his chronological age. But this is not the case. Since about ten per cent of children are intellectually dull, they cannot by definition achieve the same standard as the majority of their contemporaries". (M. L. Kellmer Pringle: *"The backward child: dull or retarded"*—Times Educational Supplement: 12 October 1956.)

2. See References to Chapter 2 for discussion of the notion of reading age.
3. *Literacy Survey:* Inner London Education Authority: 1968.
4. M. Rutter, J. Tizard, K. Whitmore: *Education, Health, and Behaviour:* Longman: 1970.
5. M. Rutter and W. Yule: *Specific Reading Retardation,* in *The Review of Special Education:* ed. L. Mann and D. Sabatino: Buttonwood Farms Inc.: 1973.
6. A. D. B. Clarke and A. M. Clarke: *Consistency and Variability in the Growth of Human Characteristics,* in *Advances in Educational Psychology,* ed. W. D. Wall and V. P. Varma: U.L.P.: 1972.
7. D. H. Scott, N. C. Marston, S. J. Bouchard: *Behaviour Disturbance in Children:* University of Guelph: 1970.
8. W. D. Wall: *The Problem Child in School:* in *London Educational Review,* Vol. 2, No. 2.
9. *Children and their Primary Schools: Vol. 2 Research and Surveys:* H.M.S.O.: 1967.
10. J. W. B. Douglas: *The Home and the School:* MacGibbon and Kee: 1964.
11. *Half Our Future:* Report of the Central Advisory Council: H.M.S.O.: 1963.
12. L. B. Birch: *The Remedial Treatment of Reading Disability:* Educational Review: 1948.
13. J. E. Collins: *The Effects of Remedial Education:* Oliver and Boyd: 1961.
14. A. Cashdan and P. D. Pumfrey: *Some Effects of the Remedial Teaching of Reading:* Educational Research; 11, 2: 1969.
    A. Cashdan, P. D. Pumfrey, and E. A. Lunzer: *Children Receiving Remedial Teaching in Reading:* Educational Research; 13, 2: 1971.
15. E. Midwinter: *Setting up the Triangle:* Times Educational Supplement: 27 June 1973.
16. D. Lawrence: *Counselling of Retarded Readers by Non-Professionals:* Educational Research, 15: 1972.
17. *Enquiry No. 1:* Schools Council: H.M.S.O.: 1968.
18. *Children with Specific Reading Difficulties:* H.M.S.O.: 1972.

CHAPTER 19

Adult Illiteracy

*"The result was that she could not read. . .She lived in fear that the truth might
emerge, and conducted all transactions with wariness and distance . . .
She carried her head above her tragedy, and her secret was her own."*
Ivy Compton-Burnett: "Manservant and Maidservant".

19.1   It is a disturbing fact that if a young person leaves school unable to
read effectively he is quite likely to receive no further help for the .rest
of his life. For most adolescents the statutory leaving age marks the point
at which in practice their literacy ceases to be a public responsibility and
becomes purely their own. In the nature of things they are not well equipped
to take on this responsibility, and even if they were they could not always
count on finding adequate support. In the first year or so of their working
life many young people may not find their lack of reading and writing ability
a serious handicap. They are often in jobs which make no demands upon it,
and in their private life they contrive to manage without it. But that does not
mean it is matter of no concern to them. They often feel a sense of inadequacy,
which reveals itself in pretended indifference or in attitudes of hostility.
They adjust to their deficiency by a narrowing of their world to exclude
print, but before long they find that this kind of rejection will not keep the
problem at a distance. The need to be able to read and write intrudes increasingly upon their lives. Even if their job remains undemanding they may
feel more and more exposed in their personal lives. Modern society assumes
an ability to handle print, and the adult who does not possess it can feel
vulnerable and alienated. Some young people never overcome their feelings
of hostility, but many who would be glad to receive help have no idea where
to go, or lack the confidence to take the first step.

19.2   There are three main tasks to be faced. The first is to remove the
apathy, guilt, or hostility and convince the adolescent and adult that he need
not resign himself to failure. The second is to make known to him where the
right support can be found. These both imply the need for a counselling
situation, since the contacts have to be more personal than can usually be
afforded in normal enrolment for adult education. The third task is to
provide this support on a much more comprehensive scale than is at present
available.

19.3   It has to be acknowledged that when an adolescent leaves school with
a long experience of failure the urge to put it permanently behind him can be
very powerful. He is likely to have withdrawn in spirit while he is still there,
but the act of leaving has a special significance. It marks the end of a way of
life which, whatever its other compensations, has become associated with low
self-esteem. This is a time, then, when he is least likely to want to return to a
teaching situation, especially if the feeling of freedom is still relatively
uncomplicated by serious embarrassments. For some this is the beginning of
a long alienation from the idea of verbal learning, with a steadily diminishing
prospect of ever returning to it. They will be conscious of the stigma, but will
adjust to their deficiency through a life-style that entails as little exposure to
it as possible. Others will be made aware of it more quickly, more painfully,

and more often. Some of them will want to make good their loss, and succeed where they once repeatedly failed.

19.4   In a survey conducted by the National Association for Remedial Education[1] an attempt was made to find the specific causes impelling people to seek help. Most of the men gave reasons associated with their jobs. They found that their deficiency robbed them of promotion prospects or exposed them to constant embarrassment where any kind of documentation was involved. One voluntary scheme told us that men applying for tuition gave such reasons as "I've turned down promotion to foreman because I can't cope with the reports", "When I go for a job and they give me a form I just walk out", "The wife has to do my time-sheet". The N.A.R.E. survey showed women to be chiefly concerned with "self-improvement", and they made frequent reference to the prospects of finding and keeping a boy friend. Married members of both sexes are sometimes distressed at the difficulties to be faced when their children come to start school. The kind of remark they make is eloquent of their disturbance of mind: "The kids keep asking questions, and I can't read to them", "My child must never know".

19.5   Evidence such as this, and the experience of the voluntary schemes, suggests that there are strong motives driving non-reading adults to remedy their disability. What is not known is the proportion who do anything about it. Recent research[2] conducted at Reading University showed that since 1950 adult literacy programmes in England have provided at least 30,700 adults with instruction for a period of 6 months or one school term. The figure for 1972 alone was at least 5,170. This is almost a sixth of the total, and it indicates that there has been a considerable increase in the number enrolling for instruction. The growth of opportunities has been particularly rapid since 1967, and indeed 38 programmes began during 1973 alone. These are encouraging developments, but there are no exact figures to reveal what proportion of the total need is being met. It is impossible to say with complete accuracy how many adult illiterates and semi-literates there are, but we have examined some of the indications in paragraphs 2.2 and 2.4. One thing is certain: the 5,170 or so receiving instruction in 1972 were only a fraction of those who stand in need of help at one level or another. The Russell Report[3] acknowledged the importance of improved provision in its comment that adult education included a concern for basic literacy. "First there is the improvement of general education from the point where initial schooling ceased. For some this may go back to basic education of an elementary kind, including functional literacy and numeracy". Another expression of the growing concern is the interest aroused by the initiative of the British Association of Settlements[4], which has rightly pressed for adult illiteracy to be made an immediate objective for action.

19.6   As a source of help the school often finds itself in an anomalous position. At the point of leaving, these young people are not always likely to heed advice on how to keep up the process of learning, which to them means failing. Nevertheless there is evidence that some schools do successfully guide their pupils to post-school opportunities, and more could be done in this respect. The evidence of our own visits to schools suggests that large numbers of pupils with very low reading ability leave without any kind of guidance. While realising the difficulties we think this an unfortunate omission. If a young person reaches the end of his statutory school life unable to read the education system has failed him in one vital respect, and that should not be the end of the matter. Every step should be taken to provide continuity, and with its knowledge of the pupil's learning difficulties the school has the first responsibility.

19.7 The indications are that most of those receiving instruction are persuaded to it by relatives and friends, who are often guided by Adult Education publicity material. Press, radio, and television play a substantial part by drawing attention periodically to the problems and the available solutions, and it would be valuable if references could be worked into popular programmes with large audiences. Local radio and the Public Library Service could be useful sources of immediate guidance, and specific publicity could be regularly featured in local newspapers. The local authority should inform employers and the various social agencies of opportunities. The latter are particularly well placed to give advice, since their role and contacts put them in a good position to recognise adults with reading and writing difficulties. They include the Social Service Departments, Youth Service Departments, probation officers, and officers of the L.E.A. Careers Service and of the Employment Service. All have an important part to play in helping the adult illiterate. To fulfil this properly they need to be able to guide him to an efficient referral point, where counselling is available and where he can be introduced to the kind of tuition best designed to suit his needs. All this suggests carefully organised co-ordination on a scale not at present available.

19.8 We have remarked on the expansion of facilities for adult literacy instruction. The questions to be asked are: are there enough of them, and are they effective? The answer to the first can only be that provision nationally still falls far short of what it should be. There must be many young people, particularly in small towns and rural areas, who are without ready access to facilities. The majority of local education authorities offer, or are prepared to offer on demand, some form of instruction to adult illiterates. Most of the provision is in classes in evening institutions and adult education centres or in colleges of further education. Occasionally they are based on schools, and a few authorities offer individual help on a one-to-one basis. There is a relatively small number of voluntary schemes, of which the Cambridge House Literacy Scheme in Camberwell was the influential pioneer. They have established the value of a one-to-one approach with adults and are exercising increasing influence over general thinking about ways of dealing with adult illiteracy. In February 1973 prisons and borstals accounted for 116 programmes between them, and the Army School of Preliminary Education provides a very thorough course for entrants in need. Of the programmes described in the Reading University research report 40 per cent averaged two hours' instruction per week, and 36 per cent between three and six hours'. As might be expected, certain of the prisons and borstals were able to exceed this amount. One possibility which has not yet been sufficiently explored is that of using the work situation as a place where literacy improvement could be achieved. Part-time day education is a device which could be particularly effective with young employees. Certainly there is scope for greater involvement on the part of employers, unions and the industrial training agencies.

19.9   We are not able to comment on the quality and effectiveness of the courses, which lie outside our terms of reference. However, we are in no doubt that very great credit is due to the organisers of many of these programmes, official and voluntary, and to the teachers involved in them. Of course, facilities and circumstances vary enormously from one situation to another. Many pupils are taught in groups of up to fifteen, though a considerable number of programmes keep the size to a maximum of five. A minority manage to achieve individual tuition, and this is usually the aim of private schemes. In the U.S.A. adult literacy programmes operating on the group principle have been found to achieve disappointing results. The Committee on Reading of the National Academy of Education reported that pupils make very slow progress and frequently drop out before the goals have been reached. The failure of the courses has been attributed to a shortage of well-trained instructors, ineffective teaching techniques, inappropriate teaching materials, and difficulty in "protecting the privacy and dignity of the learner". One cannot infer from this that similar problems in this country would necessarily produce the same incidence of failure. But these difficulties also exist in the English situation, and it would be surprising if they did not substantially reduce the likelihood of success, particularly where they occur in combination. Some experienced witnesses were severely critical of the pattern of much group instruction. They identified the shortcomings as absence of proper training for instructors, lack of cohesion in the teaching groups, and a high rate of student turnover. The instructors, they said, were often drawn from local primary schools and had no experience of working with adults. Adolescents and adults, differing widely in age, appearance and intelligence, and each with his own individual problem, were all in the same room with the same tutor. Class registers at the end of any session showed that a large number of students attended irregularly and dropped out before the end of the course. This picture is not necessarily representative, but one or more of these shortcomings must be true of many adult literacy courses.

19.10   The 'basic' class is faced with 3 built-in difficulties. The problems of the non-reader are deeply personal, and for a variety of obvious reasons the group experience is often quite unsuitable for him, at least in the early stages. His teacher, however competent, is accustomed to a different learning context, and cannot without further training be expected to be expert in the special needs of the adult or post-school adolescent. Finally, the class is likely to be held in a school building, the ambience and associations of which are scarcely right for a fresh start. Despite these limiting conditions a great deal of devoted work is done, but it is reasonable to ask whether it is fair to teacher or taught that they should continue to be restricted by them.

19.11   We believe that individuals taking the first step towards renewing their contact with education should be able to expect privacy. Enough has been said of the vulnerability felt by many of them to make it obvious that the first impression may determine the success or failure of their whole venture. Individual tuition will result not only in a better adjustment to the learning process but in a positive attitude to the task. The right kind of personal relationship will give the student the support he needs to persevere. Research[5] has indicated that with schoolchildren a sympathetic individual relationship can in itself result in improved performance, even where no actual tuition is involved. It cannot be emphasised too strongly and too often that what the failing reader most needs, whatever his age, is the encouragement which will change his image of himself. With adults this has a much better chance of occurring in a one-to-one situation than in a group, where there may be other students who come with higher standards or make faster progress. It is, of course, simpler to recommend individual tuition than to create the number of tutors needed to make it available. The various voluntary schemes are making an excellent contribution, but they are still few in number and are to be found only in certain centres of population. Some authorities have already given a good lead by making grants to them, and some provide individual tuition themselves. We believe that more should do both and that they should help organisations into existence where local people show an interest in forming one. These schemes are an example of the community service at its best, and whenever a new one is founded it attracts a large number of offers from people who are willing to act as tutors. While it is encouraging that such schemes are supported by voluntary financial contributions, we do not believe that this source alone is sufficient to provide a sound foundation. Too often the organisations are forced to expend excessive amounts of time and energy in fund raising. Moreover, it is vitally important that once tuition has been started there should be no possibility of its being discontinued for lack of financial support. We therefore believe that local authorities should provide generous grants to these schemes and should help them maintain and extend their activities.

19.12 Local authority provision and voluntary private schemes hold the key between them. In their co-operation lies the opportunity for help on a new scale, with an extension of individual support and better counselling services. The major contribution will continue to rest with the local authority, and the new authorities will have the opportunity to take stock and assess what can be done to improve provision. We have already talked of the need to co-ordinate information services. The authority must reach out to more people, telling them what kind of help is available. An expansion in publicity would inevitably result in the need for more staff. The work of one of the private schemes received a good deal of attention in the Press, on radio, on television and in a large-circulation women's magazine. There was an immediate and large increase in the number of self-referrals, and this response has been maintained ever since. One brief item on adult illiteracy in a B.B.C. regional programme resulted in 300 enquiries in a single local authority. A local authority stepping up its 'open' publicity and at the same time making the various social agencies more aware would need to prepare for the resulting pressure on its facilities. Any further enterprise by the broadcasting organisations to provide televised courses, such as the series recently introduced by the B.B.C., would be almost certain to create a follow-up demand with similar effect. There would already be need for a considerable expansion of resources if a policy were adopted for a degree of individual tuition. We accept that an authority could not provide a private tutor for every student. Nevertheless, flexibility of staffing would allow private tuition where it was most needed or as an introduction for all students. There should be links between trained volunteers and trained teachers, and a mixture of one-to-one tuition and group work. In short, there should be a range of individual and group provision at different levels to meet different needs. Ideally, the personal relationship once formed should be maintained, and whatever grouping arrangements might later supervene the student should have the continuing support of this contact with his tutor-counsellor. Some authorities might have difficulty in providing accommodation other than in schools, but as far as possible it should be in surroundings which do not carry the disadvantage of earlier associations[6]. The voluntary schemes work on the home-learning principle, and go to some lengths to match tutor and student. This seems to us an excellent principle, since it presupposes a careful study of each entrant's individual needs. A reading age is simply not enough, for the student's condition involves far more than a given level of mechanical ability, and the approach and methods should be matched to his previous experience and present needs.

19.13 Some of the volunteer tutors in the private schemes are trained teachers, but the majority are from other and various walks of life, in the main unconnected with education. Most receive some training for the work, but the organisers say there is often a problem in finding experienced people to teach the tutors and to give them follow-up advisory support. There is no doubt that the ability to make the right relationship is the most important quality a tutor can possess. Nevertheless, he will operate more effectively and his own confidence will be the greater if he receives a good grounding in the skills of teaching reading. Not all trained teachers will have had the advantage of this, and even where they have they will need some help in adjusting their approaches to the situation of the adult or post-school adolescent. The local authority should make provision in its in-service training programme for all who are acting as tutors in adult literacy work.

19.14 Members of immigrant groups, usually men and boys, add considerably to the numbers of those requiring help with literacy. Many of them are non-native speakers of English who have acquired a fluency in speech—often at work—but have never learnt to read or write the language. Some of these may be illiterate even in their mother tongue and need help at the most fundamental level. Others come to literacy classes when they should properly be attending language classes, for they have very little knowledge indeed of spoken English. Then there is the adult of Caribbean origin, who may speak a form of English heavily influenced by the grammar and lexis of his own dialect. With the probable exception of the first group to be mentioned it is hard to see how the varying needs of these different kinds of illiterates can be met within a class of native speakers. They require tutors who have an understanding of the language difficulties of members of the different immigrant groups. These tutors should maintain close contact with those responsible for other types of language instruction at adult education level. Several voluntary schemes exist which deal exclusively with home tutoring for immigrant families; these are supported in some cases by the L.E.A. and in others by such organisations as the local Community Relations Council. We urge that this support should be strengthened.

19.15 One of the most pressing needs of people involved in adult literacy work, under whatever auspices, is more suitable teaching materials. Many would like to make greater use of audio-visual aids, and all would welcome a wider range of reading material appropriate to the interests and needs of adult students. These do not exist in anything like the quantity that is necessary, but an expansion in provision is likely to lead to a correspondingly greater interest on the part of publishers. There is also a need for conferences for tutors at regional level. The Advisory Councils for Further Education could play a significant part in the development of such work. The effectiveness of the various forms of provision and of methods and materials should be evaluated, and the results widely disseminated. There is at present a lack of adequate centrally collected information on adult illiteracy. Our own information was gathered from a variety of sources, both individual and institutional, and we believe that provision should be made nationally to develop and evaluate materials and resources, give advice, and organise seminars and conferences. We recommend that the Secretary of State should consider ways in which these functions might be carried out most effectively.

19.16 Adult illiterates are not necessarily the best placed to say what caused them to fail at school. Understandably, they sometimes rationalise or seek reasons which put them in the best light. On the other hand they may denigrate themselves to avoid criticism. Nevertheless, the reasons they do present are instructive and they tend to follow a common pattern. Principal among them are illness during childhood, problems of hearing and sight not diagnosed early enough, frequent absence from school including truancy, repeated change of school, family disharmony or break-up, and poor teaching. Many of them reveal a long history of poor motivation, and from their stories it is clear that neither their parents nor their teachers were able to get over to them the value and rewards of learning to read: "I didn't do anything at school. I just sat". "We did the same useless things, year after year". A surprising number do not know whether their brothers and sisters are literate, and many maintain that their parents are not aware they have left school unable to read properly. In their homes the subject is simply never discussed. Those who have recently left school are often critical of the 'remedial' teaching they received, saying that it was skimped and that the teacher was not trained for the work. Whatever the bias of the respondents these causes are all real enough. In the long term the solution to the problem of adult illiteracy lies in preventive measures, and these paragraphs should therefore be read in company with what we have said about children with reading and language difficulties. But we again emphasise that the young person who leaves school with these difficulties unresolved should not be left to his own devices. The day of his leaving school should not be a dividing line beyond which further help is a matter of chance.

REFERENCES AND NOTES

1. *Adult Illiteracy:* National Association for Remedial Education: 1972.
2. *Survey of Provision for Adult Illiteracy in England:* R. M. Haviland: Centre for the Teaching of Reading: Reading University School of Education: 1973.
3. *Adult Education: A Plan for Development:* H.M.S.O.: 1973.
4. See, for example, *A Right to Read: Action for a Literate Britain:* British Association of Settlements: 1974.
5. D. Lawrence: *The Effects of Counselling on Retarded Readers:* Educational Research: Vol. 13, No. 2: 1971.
6. In the U.S.A. the Right to Read Effort has recommended that public libraries should accommodate adult literacy work, and that where these are not available community centres, community schools, churches and office buildings should be used.

CHAPTER 20

Children from Families of Overseas Origin

20.1 Since the mid-1950s schools in most large cities in England have received children whose parents are of overseas origin. The majority of these are children from the West Indies, India, Bangladesh and Pakistan, whose parents have come to seek work in Britain. Others are children of Italian, Spanish and Cypriot workers. In addition there is a scatter of Chinese children whose parents are engaged in the catering industry. There are considerable numbers of Asians from East Africa, including the refugees expelled from Uganda in the last two years. Some of the families have now been settled in Britain a decade or more, and their youngest members have been born in this country. The great majority of the children, born here or brought from overseas, have a big adjustment to make when entering school. For most of them this adjustment includes a linguistic factor, either that of learning English as a new language, or of learning Standard English as a new dialect. The children's linguistic adjustment relates in many ways to their educational progress, and it is to this issue that we turn in this chapter.

20.2 It is, of course, helpful to have some idea of the number of children of families of overseas origin at school in Britain, though there is considerable difficulty in arriving at useful statistics. In 1973, by the D.E.S. definition[1] then existing, there were 284,754 'immigrant children' in maintained primary and secondary schools in England and Wales, comprising 3·3 per cent of the total school population. More significantly, since immigrant populations are concentrated largely upon Greater London and industrial cities in the Midlands and North, individual local education authorities can have as high a proportion of immigrant children on roll as 27 per cent. Raw statistics such as these help to show why such a large measure of attention has to be paid in some areas, much more than in others, to the educational needs of the children labelled 'immigrant'. Obviously what is needed is as sharp a measure as possible of these special educational needs. An immigrant child does not present problems to a school simply because he is an immigrant child. Centrally collected figures cannot, for instance, indicate exactly the numbers of children with linguistic needs nor give any measure of these needs. The only people who can do this satisfactorily are the people on the spot, the teachers in the schools and the local education authorities. A few authorities have already had considerable practice in making such assessments. Bradford is notable in having carried out for several years an annual survey of immigrant children in its schools, distinguishing between their different ethnic origins, identifying their levels of proficiency in English, and making flexible educational arrangements accordingly. We recommend that all authorities with immigrant children should make similar surveys regularly, in order to achieve a greater refinement in their educational arrangements. Now that the N.F.E.R.'s English language tests[2] are available, it should be possible to give an accurate assessment of proficiency in understanding, speaking, reading and writing English on the part of children for whom it is not their native language. It is clear from the available reports that comparatively little provision is made in some areas, that the education of children of overseas parentage is given a low priority, and that many of the

284

existing arrangements do little more than meet the initial language and adjustment needs of new arrivals. It is, of course, at that point that the need for intervention is most sharply felt in the schools, but the adjustment of immigrant children to their new environment and to learning elementary English is only the beginning of what for most is a long process. It is a process that consists primarily of learning to live in or between two cultures, and of learning to handle two languages or dialects.

20.3   The term 'immigrant' is sometimes used in a very general sense, often to mean anyone of overseas parentage, or with a black skin. It is not uncommon to meet teachers and members of the public to whom all Asian immigrants are the same, irrespective of their country of origin, and for whom there is no difference between India and the West Indies. It goes without saying that teachers and others should have an informed and sympathetic understanding of the children's different origins, the cultures of their homes, and the very real link between some of their countries and Britain. No-one should accept a stereotype of 'the immigrant child', but should acknowledge the very great differences there are between children who fall into this general category. There are differences not only of language and culture, but in the manner in which families succeed or fail in settling here, and in providing a secure home for the children. Many immigrant children come from stable supportive families in which the relative affluence of the parents is evident; others face grave problems of insecurity and hardship, and in many respects resemble some of the indigenous families in the same inner city area.

20.4   In urging a greater measure of attention to the education of immigrant children, we want to emphasise the long-term nature of the issues involved. The inflow of newcomers and their families has slowed down considerably in the 1970s, but the needs of the children who are already here are continuing ones. They cannot be dealt with briefly and then forgotten. Although there has been little sustained research describing the comparative performance of children of minority groups at school in Britain, there is enough to show a disturbingly low pattern of attainment. The Community Relations Commission underlined this in its evidence to the Committee, and in its report to the Home Secretary,[3] as did I.L.E.A. in the details provided of the 1968 Literacy Survey in its schools. This survey included a census of the reading attainment of eight year old children in I.L.E.A. primary schools, and it is worth remarking that in 1972 23·3 per cent of the immigrant children in school in England and Wales were concentrated in I.L.E.A. The evidence as we received it made no distinction between children of West Indian and Asian origin, and it is clear that there are special reasons for the failings of both groups. The figures are disturbing in showing the markedly lower reading standards of immigrants. A high proportion come into the category of poor readers: 28·5 per cent as compared with 14·8 per cent of non-immigrants. Conversely there is a low proportion in the category of good readers: 3·5 per cent as compared with 11·4 per cent non-immigrants. An unpublished analysis of all I.L.E.A. pupils transferring to secondary schools (quoted in the Community Relations Commission report referred to above) indicates that of immigrant children who have received their full education in this country, those of Asian origin are in fact performing at a level comparable with the indigenous population. Pupils of West Indian origin, on the other hand, are performing well below average. The E.P.A. study in Birmingham was another source of disturbing results, and a good deal of publicity has been given to the high proportion of West Indian children in E.S.N. schools in London. This is partly attributable to their poor performance in primary schools, particularly in the skills of reading and writing. Further evidence, relating to the nation at large, comes from the N.F.E.R. studies, which show the generally low placement of West Indian pupils in streamed schools (lower than that of Indian and Pakistani pupils), and a low transfer rate to selective schools: 4 per cent for West Indians, 9 per cent for Indians, 9 per cent for Pakistanis, 25 per cent for non-immigrants. In common with the Asians the majority of West Indian pupils staying on for fifth and sixth form courses tend to take either low-level examinations or no examinations at all; only a small proportion of West Indian pupils take "A" levels, a disturbing fact again in view of the long-term needs of the community.

20.5   Immigrant children's attainment in tests and at school in general is related not only to language but to several other issues, particularly those of cultural identity and cultural knowledge. No child should be expected to cast off the language and culture of the home as he crosses the school threshold, nor to live and act as though school and home represent two totally separate and different cultures which have to be kept firmly apart. The curriculum should reflect many elements of that part of his life which a child lives outside school. Some schools and authorities are already dealing wisely and boldly with these matters, and there are interesting examples in the recent Schools Council Working Paper, "Multiracial education: need and innovation".[4] But many more schools in multiracial areas turn a blind eye to the fact that the community they serve has radically altered over the last ten years and is now one in which new cultures are represented. We see implications here for the education of all children, not just those of families of overseas origin. One aspect of the question which we believe merits urgent attention is the nature of the reading material that is used in schools. In their verbal representation of society, and in their visual content, books do a great deal to shape children's attitudes. We would urge that teachers and librarians should have this in mind when selecting books for schools. If the school serves a multiracial society, does it have books about the homelands of its immigrant families, about their religions and cultures and their experiences in this country? The Library Association catalogue[5] of books for the multi-racial classroom makes some useful suggestions of titles. Even more important, has the school removed from its shelves books which have a strong ethnocentric bias and contain outdated or insulting views of people of other cultures? These questions are relevant across the entire age range. The reading material used in infant schools should be truthful and unsentimental in its visual and verbal content. Equally, the social studies texts in the secondary school should place in fair perspective the events and movements in history which have affected the peoples from whom the immigrant families spring. A survey[6] of children's books revealed much inaccurate, thoughtless and downright offensive writing about people from other countries. We strongly recommend the report of this survey, published by The Institute of Race Relations, to all who have responsibility for book selection in multiracial schools. Similar surveys could be carried out by groups of teachers, who would be providing a useful practical service while developing their own sensitivity to the issues involved. These and related questions should also enter the initial training of teachers, for whether or not they go to teach in schools with immigrant children it is right that they should have this kind of awareness. This is an appropriate point to record our conclusion that there are not enough books available which represent children of overseas back-grounds in the ways we have been describing. We address this observation to publishers, whose contribution in this whole area is potentially very considerable.

20.6   In discussing the language needs of immigrant children it is important to distinguish between two broad groups. The first consists of families from the Caribbean, whose mother tongue is English—even if in several respects it differs from the kind of English spoken in England. The second group is made up of those whose mother tongue is a totally different language and who speak little or no English on arrival. We will consider these in turn. The 1972 D.E.S. statistics revealed that there were 101,898 children of West Indian origin (including Guyana) in the schools. Other evidence suggests that about half of these were from Jamaica, the remainder from the smaller islands in the group. For most of them the language of childhood and of the home is an English-based Creole, a variety or dialect of English. Jamaican Creole has been extensively studied and described over the last 20 years. It is recognised by linguists as being a well-developed language, with a sound system, grammar, and vocabulary of its own, and capable—like other varieties of English—of being used expressively and richly. However, the West Indian situation is very complex, since in most schools in the islands a standard form of English, very close to Standard English in England, is the medium for formal education and is the language the children are ex-pected to read and write. There are already, then, linguistic difficulties for pupils and teachers alike in the schools of Jamaica and other Caribbean islands; and there are difficulties, if of a rather different order, for the West Indian children at school in Britain. For most of them the language of infancy and of the home will almost certainly be a form of dialect, though some members of the family will be able to switch to a more standard dialect for certain purposes. The child attending school will be likely to have teachers who know no Creole at all and who will expect him to understand and res-pond to a dialect that may at first be very strange to him. The teacher's ignorance of Creole, and perhaps his traditional attitudes to non-standard forms of English, will tend to make him dismiss Creole features in the West Indian child's speech as incorrect or 'sloppy' English. The issue of dialect thus raises many problems. It is clearly important that teachers should be fully aware of these and that they should recognise dialects for what they are. In assisting children to master Standard English, which in effect is the dialect of school, they should do so without making children feel marked out by the form of language they bring with them and to which they revert outside class. A positive attitude to West Indian dialect—as to West Indian culture—would help teachers and children alike in multiracial city schools. This area of study should therefore receive attention in both initial and in-service teacher training. Useful support for this work can be derived from the findings of the Schools Council project on the teaching of English to West Indian children[7], and we would draw attention to the strong interest . in Creole language studies in several university departments of linguistics in this country. The information and expert guidance is available for those willing to draw upon it.

20.7   The Schools Council project carried out tests which showed that dialect impeded the children's learning of English in the areas of oral comprehension, spoken intelligibility, reading, writing and spelling. It also developed some material to help teachers counter the effect of dialect interference in children's written work. The main effort, however, was directed to materials for promoting communication skills in the multiracial class, and neither this project nor any other as far as we know has studied the specific problems experienced by West Indian children in learning to read. It is reasonable to assume that if these problems were better understood by teachers there would be a general improvement in the literacy skills of West Indian children, with possibly far-reaching implications for their all-round performance at school and their social adjustment. There is urgent need for work of this kind to be carried out and for its results to be disseminated on a wide scale, and we believe that support should be given to appropriate research and development projects.

20.8   Little evidence was received about positive measures carried out in schools or centres to help West Indian children develop their language skills. However, we were impressed by what we heard of one outer London borough which has organised a 'supplementary service' for West Indian pupils. The children are selected according to need and taught in small groups for an hour a day, considerable emphasis being placed upon language. They are helped to distinguish Standard English from other forms, and to practise those English structures where there is most interference from dialect. This part of the teaching is fairly formal. The children are also encouraged to talk about themselves, and they have books and pictures in which black children figure as well as white. An important part of the work is helping children to have a positive attitude to themselves and to school, and West Indian teachers are among those who teach the groups. The scheme operates flexibly, with the teachers meeting once a week to discuss their work and plan materials. Similar schemes could be operated in other authorities where there are concentrations of West Indian pupils. Schools should also be encouraged to try different approaches, and to share their findings with one another. Work relating both to dialect and to improving the ability to communicate should be encouraged on a much larger scale. In our visits to primary schools we saw some good use of the Schools Council project materials referred to above. One component of these, 'The Dialect Unit', can give teachers insights into some Creole speakers' problems in writing Standard English, and it can also provide a springboard for further work initiated by teachers and children themselves. In some cases it is said that West Indian parents resent their children being singled out for special attention, and also resent the implication that "they do not speak proper English". But many West Indian parents are concerned about their children's progress and, from their own experience of learning to switch dialects in the West Indies, can understand the present difficulties of their children in this country. Consultation with them can often result in new approaches being developed to help their children, and schools should look for opportunities to draw on the support that parents and community can give. By getting to know some of the minority bookshops that now exist in London and elsewhere, and by using some of the excellent resource centres of local Community Relations Councils, teachers can obtain books and papers published in the Caribbean. They will find that these can provide stimulating new material for use in school, and at the same time give a useful insight into Caribbean life. We reaffirm that in order to teach West Indian children effectively teachers need to have an understanding of their dialect and culture.

20.9   There is general agreement that at first sight the language problems of non-English speaking children are easier to deal with than those of the dialect or Creole speakers. They have to learn English as a second or even a third language, but what they know, namely their original language, and what they need to learn, are clearly distinguished in the teacher's mind. There is by now a considerable body of methodology available and some very useful materials, at least for the initial stage of learning English as a second language. The different types of organisation set up in L.E.A.s are fully documented in the Schools Council Working Paper[8] and the Townsend study[9]. In some of the large authorities with immigrant populations there are flourishing teachers' centres and a strong system of support and in-service training for teachers of English as a second language. Considerable practical knowledge has been contributed to the field by teachers and college lecturers returning from teaching posts overseas. However, these teachers tend to move on again, and there is in any case a high staff turnover in the inner city schools where most of the work is done. These factors contribute to a shortage of teachers able to teach English as a second language and of people to train them, a problem noted by the Parliamentary Select Committee[10]. There are, of course, no easy remedies to teacher shortages of this kind, though more should certainly be done to make it easier for teachers returning from overseas postings to be recruited into language teaching for immigrant children.

20.10   The organisation of this teaching within a school and within an authority should measure up to the demand. The situation can be summed up as one in which the teaching often starts too late and ends too soon. In some areas even the provision of places for the limited number of new entrants in a special class or language centre is inadequate. Children may consequently have to wait several months to begin to be taught English; in a few places not even this provision exists. This cannot be justified on the ground that the children will pick up English anyway and that special language teaching is unnecessary. We believe that it *is* necessary, and that it must be provided. It is outside the scope of this Report to examine the advantages and disadvantages of the different types of provision made for teaching English as a second language. Common sense would suggest that the best arrangement is usually one where the immigrant children are not cut off from the social and educational life of a normal school. The money spent on transporting children to other schools or centres, or peripatetic teachers from school to school, might sometimes be much better allocated to the appointment of full-time language experts to the schools where the children are on roll. Where there is a very small number of such children in several schools, then bringing them together for sessions of specialist teaching may be more practicable. Some of the special centres set up for this purpose

M

provide highly professional language teaching. We are, however, aware that this teaching is often carried out in complete isolation from the child's school, and that his other teachers, including the head, may be unaware of what he is learning and of the methods used to teach him. Specialist language teachers need to work in close liaison with other teachers. In whatever circumstances they operate, they should be given time to consult with these teachers in the schools and to be in touch with the child's education as a whole.

20.11 Another worrying aspect of this *initial* provision is the fact that it absorbs almost all the trained teachers who know anything about the teaching of English as a second language. Very few are to be found giving sustained language help to immigrant language learners *beyond* the initial stage. In statements of policy L.E.A.s often claim that the aim of initial language teaching is to bring the immigrant child to the level of English at which he can profit from the normal school curriculum in company with his English-speaking peer-group. This generally means a year or less, or at most 18 months. In most cases, however, it is unrealistic to think that the immigrant can reach that level of proficiency in English in 18 months or less. His whole experience of English, the language and the culture, has more or less to be mediated through school. The Indian child virtually goes home to India every night. His participation in mixed social activities outside school is limited, and this is particularly true in the case of girls. Weekends and holidays are times when the child may hear next to no English spoken at all. Although after a year he may seem able to follow the normal school curriculum, especially where oral work is concerned, the limitations to his English may be disguised; they become immediately apparent when he reads and writes. He reads slowly, and often without a full understanding of vocabulary and syntax, let alone the nuances of expression. His writing betrays his lack of grasp of the subject and a very unsteady control of syntax and style. His mistakes, or deviations from Standard English, often bear a superficial resemblance to those of the slow-learning native speaker, whom he resembles in his limited range of expression. But many of the mistakes are essentially those of the second-language learner, such as a failure to use articles in a way that comes automatically to the native speaker, or inaccurate verb forms and confused morphology. Coupled with this, his handwriting is often that of someone who has never been taught systematically how to form and link the letters of the Roman alphabet in an acceptable cursive style. We regard it as a grave disservice to such children to deprive them of sustained language teaching after they have been learning English for only a comparatively short time. In our view they need far more intensive help with language in English lessons. This should be the task of a specialist language teacher, whose aim should be to help them achieve fluency in all the language skills. In oral work the emphasis might be on expression, on vocabulary extension, on finding the right style for the right occasion, and on achieving an acceptable pronunciation. In reading and writing teachers need to follow a developmental programme, using a graded language scheme or following a planned course. Non-native speakers are known to experience difficulty in reading extensively and at a reasonable speed. This indicates the need for a planned reading curriculum, in which texts are used with appropriately graded language and content. But there was little evidence in the schools and centres we visited of really advanced English language work of this nature, and of a good supply of well chosen books which were contributing to children's language development.

20.12   It is also clear that the children need linguistic help right across the curriculum, and that here the language specialist's task in the secondary school merges with that of the subject specialists. Broadly speaking, all subject teachers need to be much more aware of the linguistic demands their specialisations make on pupils. It is no easy task to help teachers to this awareness, and co-operation and experiment are called for within and between schools. We were impressed by the efforts of schools we visited in Bolton[11] and Bradford, where the specially appointed language specialists had devised a flexible co-operative system within the school. They functioned both as teachers and consultants, sitting in on subject classes, analysing the linguistic demands made on immigrant learners in different areas of the curriculum, and offering running help to the children as the class proceeded. This is a much more effective way of working than dealing with pupils in comparative seclusion, which is bad both linguistically and socially. It is feasible for language experts to work in this fashion not simply with second-language learners but also with Creole-speaking children. Arrangements of the kind we have described demand trust and co-operation between language specialist and subject staff, and the role of the head and of heads of departments is obviously vital in creating the right atmosphere. There should be more initiatives to establish a new role for the language teacher in a multi-racial school, one of consultant and adviser across the curriculum rather than of teacher confined to a single room. As a matter of urgency teachers able to work in this way should be appointed extra to complement wherever secondary schools have on roll a significant number of children who are no longer classed as initial language learners but need linguistic help. We recognise that this recommendation would be costly to implement in some authorities, and we acknowledge the difficulty of recruiting teachers with the appropriate skill and experience. Nevertheless, we see no other realistic solution for the linguistic and social problems posed by the presence of large numbers of second-stage language learners in schools.

20.13   We have suggested that those authorities with areas of immigrant settlement should maintain a continuous assessment of the language needs of immigrant pupils in their schools. For the most part these are not accurately assessed unless there is a member of the advisory staff with a major responsibility for immigrant education in the authority. We would strongly urge the appointment of advisers with special responsibility for the language development of immigrant children, able to provide suitable and sustained in-service training and to support groups of teachers in their response to local problems. Needless to say, it is as important for these advisers to liaise with the authority's other advisers as it is for the language specialists in a school to co-operate with other teachers. They should certainly work in close association with their colleagues responsible for advisory work in English, a concept discussed in Chapter 16. The specialist adviser needs to have a clear view not only of what is required, but of the way in which existing strengths can best be used. For instance, some trained teachers of English as a second language could profitably be deflected from initial language work in a reception centre to dealing with the more complex needs of second stage language learners. Unless there is a person responsible within the authority such informed use of resources tends not to occur.

20.14   A special word needs to be added about children of overseas parentage in infant and nursery classes. In the first place we see the provision of nursery classes in inner city areas as having great importance for the early language development of immigrant children. This is true both for those from non-English speaking homes and for those from West Indian homes. It is known that many West Indian parents leave children with child minders in circumstances which encourage passive response from the children and which must often have harmful effects on their development, both linguistic and general. It is often reported that they find it difficult to adjust to the informal environment of the nursery or infant reception class, that they are bewildered rather than delighted by the variety of activities offered them, and that they find it hard to concentrate even for a short period on any single activity. There are special difficulties, too, for very young children from non-English speaking families, children born in Britain but brought up in homes where neither the language in use nor the culture is English. Teachers of these young children have shown reluctance to do any 'formal' language work with them, usually on the ground that in the good infant or nursery class they would learn to speak English anyway, without any intervention on the teacher's part. But these children, after a full two years in infant classes, often reach junior school seriously lacking in fluency in English. To meet the special needs of these children, teachers in nursery and infant classes should be willing to modify their traditional organisation. The child bewildered by a choice of activities might be given a more limited number of alternatives. For children with language difficulties it is essential that for a short period every day a teacher should sit with individuals or small groups and talk with them. The experiments conducted in the pre-school and infant centres and classes of Bradford and other towns have already shown that special language tuition can be provided early and saves time and trouble later. There is nothing to suggest that it need in any way be too formal, nor need it take much time from the other important learning opportunities that nursery and infant classes would normally want to provide. Valuable guidance for language work with non-English speaking infants is contained in a forthcoming Schools Council publication in the *Scope*[12] series. Another recent development is the extension of the work of the Schools Council project "Communication Skills in Early Childhood" to nursery classes in which there are children of families of overseas origin. Both these sources of information should help nursery and infant teachers to focus on priority areas of language and deliberately extend the young child's use of English.

20.15   Until now there has been a shortage of nursery provision in many of the areas where there are large numbers of overseas families. The promised expansion of nursery education will do something to remedy this, but there are two important points to be made. First, it is clear that the conventional training of nursery and infant teachers has normally lacked a component that will help them understand the specific language difficulties and cultural values of children from families of overseas origin. There is a need for both these aspects to be taken into account in teacher-training programmes and in-service education. Secondly, new approaches may be necessary if these children are to be reached in their early years. The links of such families with the existing schools are often tenuous. Mothers may be at work all day, or live in purdah, or speak no English; fathers may be permanently on night shift. Notices sent from school are sometimes not read, or are misinterpreted. The parents sometimes want to delegate to the school full responsibility for social training. In some instances they know nothing of the possibilities of nursery education and feel unable to take advantage of it where it exists. In the case of many of these families the conventional channels of communication between school and home do not function, and quite different strategies are needed.

20.16   There are good arguments for a more sustained and systematic service linking home and school, especially in the areas of intensive immigrant settlement. In some areas there is evidence of good results ensuing from various systems of home visiting, sometimes involving a teaching member of a school staff, himself a member of an immigrant community, sometimes the provision of social welfare assistants attached to infant schools. In the West Riding, after the success of the home visiting scheme in the E.P.A. project, there has been a development whereby a home visitor teaches a little English to housebound Pakistani mothers and to their young children through the medium of simple educational toys. In a summer holiday project students worked on a one-to-one basis with immigrant school children, and one of the most profitable achievements was to build up a pre-reception class for rising-5s, immigrant children unable to speak English but due to enter school the following autumn. There were three weeks of small-group and individual play involving a great deal of language interaction with willing student teachers and an experienced infant teacher in charge. The result was that the children developed the confidence to speak English and become familiar with the apparatus and activities of an infant class. An additional benefit was the informal contact between teacher and parent, a valuable foundation for the coming school year. Obviously, none of these approaches provides a complete answer and all of them need adequate financing. Professional advice should be available for the personnel involved, whether they be trained teachers or nursery helpers, social workers, home visitors, or student volunteers. Members of the advisory service should provide them with training in language development and in understanding the social and cultural values of families of overseas origin; and the role of members of the minority communities themselves is obviously vital in this work of mediating between the different communities. Children of overseas origin should see people of their own communities in the role of teacher and helper. L.E.A.s should be alert to the needs of providing training, or re-training, to immigrants who will be able to perform this important function.

20.17   The importance of bilingualism, both in education and for society in general, has been increasingly recognised in Europe and in the U.S.A. We believe that its implications for Britain should receive equally serious study. When bilingualism in Britain is discussed it is seldom if ever with reference to the inner city immigrant populations, yet over half the immigrant pupils in our schools have a mother-tongue which is not English, and in some schools this means over 75 per cent of the total number on roll. The language of the home and of a great deal of the central experience of their life is one of the Indian languages, or Greek, Turkish, Italian or Spanish. These children are genuine bilinguals, but this fact is often ignored or unrecognised by the schools. Their bilingualism is of great importance to the children and their families, and also to society as a whole. In a linguistically conscious nation in the modern world we should see it as an asset, as something to be nurtured, and one of the agencies which should nurture it is the school. Certainly the school should adopt a positive attitude to its pupils' bilingualism and wherever possible should help maintain and deepen their knowledge of their mother-tongues. The school that really welcomes its immigrant parents must also be prepared to welcome their languages, to display notices and other materials written in them, and even to adopt some of the rhymes and songs learnt by the young children at home. At least one authority is experimenting with an even greater investment in bilingualism by encouraging pre-reading experiences and early play in the language of the home in pre-school and infant classes. Confidence and ability in this language will help the children to the same qualities in their second language, English. Schools in neighbourhoods where many languages are spoken, as in North London, would find suggestions of this kind impracticable, but there is every reason for adopting them in areas where there is a fairly homogeneous language situation. In any event, bilingual pupils should be encouraged to maintain their mother-tongue throughout their schooling. There is a great deal to be said for their entering for "O" and "A" level examinations in their first language. The Townsend study[13] shows that though schools often encourage this, few if any actually give tuition in any Indian language. The immigrant communities themselves are reported as teaching their own languages, and the range encompasses Greek, Punjabi, Urdu, Gujurati, Hindi, Italian, Polish, Arabic and a cluster of others. Little is known about the effectiveness of such provision, and we recommend that further study should be made of this and other aspects of bilingualism in schools. It has an important contribution to make to what we suggest is the central recommendation of this chapter: a sensitivity and openness to language in all its forms.

REFERENCES

1. The Department of Education and Science used the following definition in its Form 7(i) when collecting annual statistics of immigrant children until 1973: (i) children born outside the British Isles who have come to this country with, or to join, parents or guardians whose countries of origin were abroad; and (ii) children born in the United Kingdom to parents whose countries of origin were abroad and who came to the United Kingdom on or after 1 January ten years before the collection of the information.
2. *Tests of proficiency in English:* N.F.E.R.: Ginn: 1973.
3. *Educational Needs of Children from Minority Groups:* Community Relations Commission: 1974.
4. *Multiracial education: need and innovation:* Schools Council Working Paper 50: Evans/Methuen Educational: 1973.
5. J. Elkin *et al.: Books for the Multiracial Classroom:* A Select List of Children's Books, showing the backgrounds of India, Pakistan, and the West Indies: The Library Association Youth Libraries Group: 1971.
6. J. Hill *et al.: Books for Children: The Homelands of Immigrants in Britain:* Institute of Race Relations: 1971.

7.   *Teaching English to West Indian Children:* Schools Council Working Paper 29: Evans/Methuen Educational: 1970.
8.   *English for the Children of Immigrants:* Schools Council Working Paper 13: H.M.S.O.: 1967.
9.   H. E. R. Townsend: *Immigrant Pupils in England:* N.F.E.R.: 1971.
10. Select Committee on Race Relations and Immigration: Session 1972/73: *Education: Vol. 1: Report:* H.M.S.O.
11. A film depicting the co-operative system at Deane High School, Bolton, is available on loan from The Central Film Library, Government Film Building, Bromyard Avenue, Acton, London, W.3. The title is *English as a second language: first and second phase teaching.*
12. *English for Immigrant Children in the Infant School:* Scope Handbook 3: Longman: not yet published.
13. H. E. R. Townsend: *op. cit.*

Part Seven

Resources

CHAPTER 21

Books

"All that mankind has done, thought, gained or been; it is lying as in magic preservation in the pages of books".

Carlyle.

21.1   In the written evidence we received there were occasional pessimistic references to the future of the printed word in education. Some witnesses feared that its importance was declining; a few would hasten that decline. One asked that we should "counter a persistent bias towards 'books' as the almost exclusive medium of learning". Another suggested that ". . . the day has come when educationists should seriously question the extent to which the printed and spoken word should predominate in education to the exclusion of the image". We respect these views, which we recognise as representing certain movements of thought in recent years. But we cannot accept the belief that the printed word should learn to adjust to a modified status. In analysing the reading process we argued that the medium of print occupies, and will continue to occupy, a position of the highest importance in the educational process. We do not accept that there is too much attention to print in schools. Quite the contrary. We believe that schools can make better use of the books and other material they at present possess, and that many schools are in urgent need of more. In this chapter we shall examine the acquisition and deployment of books within the school and conclude with implications for expenditure.

21.2   In some quite wealthy school districts in the U.S.A. the book environment in schools for younger children is surprisingly poor, and in certain other countries a variety of books for infants is seen as "a waste of money, because the children cannot yet read them". In contrast, the wealth of books in many English infant schools is a delight to experience. In some they are deployed so skilfully as to give the feel that the whole school is a book environment. They are displayed with natural objects and artefacts, surrounded by colour, and placed at points where the child is constantly encountering them. Book areas or corners are made inviting by carpeting and a few chairs. In fact, they come to be seen by the child as a natural and necessary part of his daily life. We cannot pretend that all infant and junior schools present books in this manner and on this scale. Some feel their physical conditions to be against them; some assign books a relatively low priority when ordering stock, and do not go far beyond reading schemes and instructional materials; some, particularly small schools, lack sufficient money to buy the books they want. It is, of course, an easier matter to display books enticingly in modern surroundings, but some of the most attractive displays of books we saw were in old schools in inner city areas. Schools should be given the kind of furniture and accessories that will allow them to produce the right conditions for creating a reading environment, such as sloping bookshelves of good depth where books can be displayed with the picture visible on the front cover. And, of course, there is also a great deal of scope for improvisation, in which many parents would be glad to help.

21.3   If a school is to regard books as a means of developing children's language and experience it needs a conscious design in acquiring them. For one thing, it should know the proportions of books at various reading levels and the extent to which these match the range of ability of the children. Whenever any school buys or borrows a book it has a reason for doing so, but that in itself will not ensure that the stock does not grow by a process of random accretion. What is required is a book policy which reflects a set of objectives understood and accepted by the staff. All this points to the case for one member of staff to have responsibility for carrying out this policy. In very many primary schools books are ordered by the head, who consults his staff, scans the various sources of information for himself, and decides what proportion of the capitation allowance shall be spent on them. Clearly, the disposition of the school's total financial resources is the head's responsibility; but except in the smallest schools he cannot always be expected to have the time necessary to organise the supply and flow of books.

21.4   Ideally, every teacher should have a first-hand knowledge of children's books, and in some schools, for instance, the staff undertake to read a book each every month. There is no denying that many schools face considerable difficulty in selecting books. They lack the facilities to view them in quantity at first hand and often rely on publishers' catalogues. We believe that authorities should devise ways of helping in this matter. Some authorities have set up their own 'book rooms' or enable teachers to visit exhibitions at colleges and teachers' centres by closing the school for the day and giving a travel allowance. As the larger authorities come into being there should be increased scope for such enterprises. A number of new authorities may be planning the building of new library centres for the expanded area, and there would be an admirable opportunity for including within each an educational book-room. To supplement local provision, permanent exhibitions, which are regularly revised, might be established in regional centres. We envisage these as offering a wider scope than can normally be provided at teachers' centres, where exhibitions of books will need to be limited either in range of material or in duration. They should be sources of professional guidance open to parents as well as teachers, with an organised programme of such activities as discussions, films, and talks by authors. They should contain a range of children's books and journals on the scale of the collection maintained by the Department of Education and Science, or the Children's Reference Library at the National Book League. Every school should have periodic opportunities to see a very wide range of books at first hand and should consider extending these opportunities to the children themselves. Pupils should be drawn into the discussions which are an important part of it.

21.5   Our survey revealed that 12 per cent of the primary schools and 57 per cent of the secondary schools were members of the School Library Association. This is one of a number of valuable sources of information about books, and well-informed reviews of new material are a facility of which much greater use could be made. There should be a free exchange of opinion and information, and reading and study groups at teachers' centres are a way of achieving this. All this activity will be no less necessary if a teacher is appointed to take general responsibility for books. He should have a wider and more specialised knowledge and therefore be in a position to advise, but responsibility for books remains a collective one. He would help his colleagues to realise their objectives, but they in turn would help him to develop the overall book policy of the school. Our survey revealed that 61 per cent of the primary and middle schools large enough to qualify for above-scale posts had a teacher receiving payment for the responsibility of "organising the library". We did not inquire in the questionnaires into the precise duties this entailed, but the evidence of our visits suggests that in few schools does the teacher exercise the kind of role we are recommending. The teachers were keenly involved in the care of books, but often their responsibilities were of a fairly simple administrative kind. It was the exception to find them guiding colleagues on the sources of information about children's fiction. It was equally uncommon to find them organising a policy for acquiring books according to present and predicted need, and charting their dispersal within the school. For this kind of work a teacher needs support. Resources of any kind should reflect a school's curriculum, not determine it, and though the teacher with responsibility for books has a key role he is only a part of this process.

21.6   A book policy implies that the school should have a record of all that it possesses. The ideal situation is where any book in the school can be obtained by any child at any time, but in practice this is not always easy to fulfil. Where a given topic is to be studied the teacher can plan ahead and assemble a collection of appropriate books; but the need for a particular book is often created quite spontaneously. It may be prompted by a chance remark, or a question arising from a discussion, or a material being used in art or craft. A child may want to find out what substance is indigo, what are the characteristics of a mute swan, what is the diet of a blackbird, or the direction of the trade winds. These will arise from some immediate situation and need an immediate solution; to refer to a distant central collection is wasteful in time and may even suggest that books are occasional to the process of learning and discovering rather than central to it. Every primary school classroom should therefore have a book corner, partly enclosed and occupying the quietest area of the room. Here will be found an encyclopaedia, a good dictionary, a good atlas, a collection of books ranging across the children's interests and touching all the major areas of the curriculum, a shelf of poetry, and a range of fiction. (It should be remembered that books can lose their attraction for children if they remain unchanged from week to week and term to term. It is particularly important that there should be constant refreshment of stock in vertically grouped classrooms where children can often be in the same environment for a considerable time.) This localised source should be supplemented by a central collection, which might include non-print material of various kinds. The ebb and flow of books into and out of this collection will be a continuous process. The important thing is that there should be a clear and recognised system of organisation which allows everyone to know what are the school's resources and how they are dispersed.

21.7   Books from a School Library Service[1] should become an organic part of this system and not be treated as something apart. There are, of course, occasions when a particular class obtains a project loan or 'book box' for a specific purpose and on a short-term basis, but in speaking of School Library Service stock we refer to the facilities by which schools are supplied with a substantial number of books on a semi-permanent basis. As the various services differ so much it is difficult to generalise, but some schools tend to keep books obtained in this way in a separate category. This sometimes leads to the practice of buying only one kind of book and relying for the other upon the external source. We visited some schools where the fiction came from one source and the non-fiction from the other, and they were housed separately. We also encountered anomalous situations in which the school would allow only its own books to be taken home, or vice versa. This seems to us an unnecessary distinction, and the school's entire stock of books should be regarded for all purposes as a unified resource. Some School Library Services find that when a mobile collection visits a school one teacher will select what another has just returned. Such instances suggest an inadequate control of resources, and reinforce the need for planning and co-ordination within the school.

21.8   Our survey revealed that of the schools from which the sample six year olds were drawn 80 per cent obtained books from the School Library Service. For the nine year olds the figure was 87 per cent, and for the secondary schools 64 per cent. Used properly the School Library Service is an excellent aid, and is one of the most valuable developments of recent years. The example we give to illustrate our case is a composite one, incorporating features of three actual services. There are, of course, other variants, and this is not offered as a simple blueprint. There is a central collection for children at the principal public library, and each of the nine branches has a children's specialist. A mobile library visits each school once a term, carrying on its rounds 2,500 books. A school is allowed to take 100 books on each visit and is not required to return them. As one librarian puts it: "The only time we require the books back is when they are worn out, in need of repair, or are of no use to the school". If teachers prefer they can visit the Library Stack and select books from the shelves instead of waiting for the van's visit. Either way the advice of the children's librarian is available. The range is extremely comprehensive, but a school may order lists of specific titles and if these are not in stock they will be obtained and made over to the school. In addition to this steady flow there are project collections, which can be ordered to meet any predicted or short-term curriculum need. These books, too, automatically pass into the stock of the school library and do not have to be returned. Thus, the school has a very generous source of books and other material and the benefit of expert advice. The important thing is that such an aid should not be used passively. Its advantages are diminished if schools lean on it as a prop and their own self-reliance is reduced. Schools should continue to acquire books through their own financial resources. The School Library Service may do the purchasing and processing on their behalf, but it is important that they should exercise the choice. A school should maintain its own expert knowledge of children's reading material, and the relationship with the children's specialists at the library should be a partnership. Both are in fact engaged in the same enterprise, with much in common between their respective emphases.

21.9   There is a great deal to be said for joint courses and study groups for teachers and children's librarians, and for joint panels to review new publications and prepare lists. This would emphasise the inter-professional consultation element, which is essential if the School Library Service is not to be simply a source of largesse of which the school makes demands and from which it automatically receives. We found evidence of a growing sense of partnership and an increasing range of joint activities. Teachers review and evaluate books for children's librarians, and they visit publishers' and book-sellers' exhibitions together. The School Library Service provides book displays for parents' evenings and for teachers' centres, and it organises book clubs both in term and holiday time. In one case a number of primary heads formed themselves into a reading group to extend their knowledge of modern children's fiction and try out a range of it with their pupils. The service arranged book exhibitions, gave introductory talks, and supplied the books. The idea spread from small beginnings and was afterwards extended to parents. Already some services carry material other than books, and schools welcome this kind of extension. For example, there is much to be said for their preparing maps for environmental studies, or facsimile docu-ments for local history, in which the help of the county archivist could be sought. A number of these would be standard, but it should be possible for a school to ask for special ones to be prepared when planning ahead for a particular piece of work. Where possible they should be associated with the resources of the museum service and local archives, so that book, illustration, document, broadsheet, and real object come together. Libraries also have a part to play in maintaining collections of records, tapes, cassettes, film strips, and film loops, which will supplement those the schools should acquire or make for themselves.

21.10   We believe there is great potential in the kind of partnership we have been discussing, but this presupposes the expansion of School Library Services. The reorganisation of local government will afford new opportuni-ties for this. Library authorities will generally be co-extensive with education authorities, and libraries themselves will be grouped into larger units, making possible the provision of more specialised staff and services. There should be an appraisal of the kind of support schools can be given, and this points the need for close consultation between the education authority's advisers, the schools themselves, and the library staff. It is necessary to add that there are still authorities which have not appointed a children's librarian, and we strongly recommend that there should be one in every authority.

21.11   Much of what we have been saying relates equally to primary and secondary schools, and our recommendations about co-operation with the School Library Service apply at all levels. Pupils between 8 and 13 have a common need in terms of book provision and range, and whether they are in primary, middle, or secondary school this need should receive comparable fulfilment. Some children's experience of books is subject to acute change on transfer from one phase to another. This is sometimes liberatingly for the better, sometimes restrictingly for the worse. Where a primary school has narrowed its book acquisition to little more than advanced primers, sup-plementary readers, and reference books, the child's encounter with a secondary school library can be an exciting experience for him. He may, on the other hand, leave a primary school where books of all kinds can be picked up at will and read without hindrance. And he may exchange this for a school where the library is open only at certain times to certain classes and even kept locked for part of the day. Both sets of conditions obtain, and both are unsatisfactory. There should be no time in a child's school life at which books become more difficult of access. The reading habit should be established early, and should receive unqualified encouragement from that point onwards.

21.12   In secondary schools the nature of the organisation is such that responsibility for the library is part of the staffing structure. This is not to say that the appointment necessarily carries an above-scale post, and some teachers are designated librarian with neither an allowance nor any extra time for doing the job. At the other end of the spectrum are schools with full-time chartered librarians or teacher-librarians and a quota of ancillary staff, sometimes with the responsibility of administering a resource centre of which books are only one element. We shall be going on to discuss resource centres, but we must emphasise at this point that many secondary schools fall far short of satisfactory basic library provision, let alone more sophisticated facilities. Some have a room which has the title of library but is continually in use as a teaching space or even serves as a class-base. Our survey showed that while 47 per cent of the secondary schools used their library only as a library, a disturbing 19 per cent were timetabling it for other purposes for more than half the week. It is this kind of accommodation which can degenerate into a place that opens two or three times a week for book borrowing in the lunch hour or after school. Even when the library is not used for teaching, lack of facilities for constant supervision can result in the locked door. A simple dilemma faces many schools: to conserve book stock by locking it away for most of the week, or to risk losing it by allowing unsupervised open access. We believe that every secondary school should have the accommodation and staffing facilities to ensure that this kind of question does not arise. The library is at the heart of the school's resources for learning, and it is simply unacceptable that this kind of weakness should exist. We do not propose to recommend a formula for the numbers of librarians, assistant librarians and ancillary staff in schools of various sizes. A great deal depends upon the use made of the library in any particular school, and we would be reluctant to recommend figures which come to be regarded as maxima. Various proposals[2] have been made which provide a useful basis for discussion, and we recommend that the staffing of libraries, including ancillary help, should be on as generous a scale as possible.

21.13   The task of the librarian within a school has a dual nature, and there has therefore been some debate as to who should perform it. It is suggested on the one hand that the chartered librarian has the indispensable skills of management and bibliography and a knowledge of children's literature. It is argued on the other that since the library ought to be an integral part of the educational function of the school the librarian should have training and experience in teaching. One difficulty has been that except for the Teacher-Librarians' Certificate* there have been few opportunities for teachers to acquire help in how to organise and manage a library. Several authorities have adopted a policy of appointing chartered librarians to their larger secondary schools, and it has been estimated that there are now 400 or so in schools in England and Wales. In general there has been no doubt of the substantial benefit of this full-time professional skill. The only disadvantage has been where it has led to teachers taking less interest in the library. If the

*Awarded jointly by the Library Association and the School Library Association.

librarian is fully involved in the development of resources for learning this should not happen. In our view he should have a seat at all head of department meetings, and departments should involve him in their own internal planning.

21.14   We believe that more extensive use should be made of the training facilities available for library work in schools. Many opportunities already exist, and there have been a number of interesting developments. There are several undergraduate courses which aim to produce librarians well qualified to play their part in the educational life of the school, for example at Liverpool Polytechnic and Newcastle-upon-Tyne Polytechnic, where the courses lead to C.N.A.A. degrees. Loughborough University is establishing a 4-year sandwich course in librarianship and education, culminating in an honours degree and qualified teacher status. Graduates with a B.A. in Librarianship may enter the teaching profession by taking a postgraduate Certificate in Education. For qualified librarians Garnett College of Education (Technical) offers a one-year course leading to qualified teacher status, and the Froebel Institute is introducing a course which has the same purpose. Similarly, there are opportunities for serving teachers to become qualified in librarianship, and 15 of the 16 schools of librarianship in the United Kingdom offer a one-year full-time post-graduate diploma course open to teachers. Leeds Polytechnic also provides facilities for part-time study of a kind which takes qualified teachers to a C.N.A.A. bachelor's degree in Library Studies. These examples are perhaps sufficient to indicate that appropriate qualifications may be achieved by a variety of routes. Ideally, all school librarians should be doubly qualified in teaching and librarianship and we hope this will be the pattern of future development.

21.15   Resource centres[3] have potentially a considerable contribution to make to the teaching of English, and we welcome them as an important development. They are still a comparative rarity, but they are increasing in number and interest in them will continue to grow. Resource centres acknowledge that books should be supplemented by other media to give the maximum support for learning situations. These will include a wide variety of audio-visual aids, so that the pupil is able not only to look up books and other print materials but also study slides and film loops and listen to tapes and cassettes. The centres will be served by reprographic facilities* which can make available at short notice quantities of newspaper cuttings, children's writing, photographs, facsimiles of documents, pamphlets, prints, and so on. Cassette copiers will do the same for sound materials. All these enrich the possibilities open to the teacher, but the resource centre is effective in proportion to the ease with which pupils can themselves use it. This implies adequate and expandable storage capacity and a retrieval system which is easily understood. We would suggest that when retrieval systems are being set up their organisers should incorporate information on the readability level of each printed text. A simple form of coding would enable the pupil to select material at an appropriate level and would save confusion and frustration.

*It is proper to add that the school needs to be aware of any copyright limitations when the copying of material is proposed. Copyright laws are at present under study by the Committee chaired by Mr. Justice Whitford.

21.16   Resource centres are not simple to establish, and their implications for staffing, accommodation, curriculum planning, and timetabling are considerable. These and related factors should be studied carefully before a school takes the first steps to establish one. To make available a new range of resources will not automatically improve the quality of the learning. A school should feel the *need* for more elaborate and far-reaching resources, and its development of them should be in response to the requirements of its own curriculum planning. In operation a resource centre is only as good as the demands made upon it, and as the thinking that has gone into creating them. Nevertheless, it would be a lost opportunity not to take account of the need for a resource centre when new buildings are being planned. Equally, when existing buildings are being expanded the need for a resource centre should be anticipated. Assuming the school library is to be the nucleus it should be possible to relate to it additional spaces suitable for the future development of a centre but used in the meantime for general teaching purposes.

21.17   Any discussion of standards of book provision, to which we now turn, must draw attention to an extremely wide range of existing conditions. Generalisations are out of the question, and the only one we will allow ourselves is that schools do not have enough fiction of the right range and quality. One factor complicating book provision in general within secondary schools is the effect of examinations and curriculum development. Any area of the curriculum in which there is development tends to attract relatively heavy expenditure, and within English the turnover of examination texts creates a recurring demand. Many English departments find it necessary to spend such disproportionate sums on new set books that fiction for the lower forms is seriously neglected. Good imaginative literature in single copies or small sets is sacrificed not only to the demands of the literature examination syllabus but also to the priority accorded to expensive course books. The stock rooms of many English departments have successive generations of such books, each set replacing one favoured by an earlier head of department. Some of the books have received relatively little use, and their accumulation prompts questions about the department's corporate planning and purchasing policy. English departments are undoubtedly faced with many demands upon the money allocated to them. As one witness put it: "What often seems to go unrecognised is the really massive and massively varied provision of books which is absolutely essential if the class library is genuinely to meet the needs of a secondary class of lively mixed ability". Some are more successful than others in making the most effective use of their allocation, and their success results from thoughtful planning based on a clear view of their aims. We acknowledge that the demands of literature examinations can be onerous, but we repeat our belief that a good supply of fiction for younger pupils will pay dividends. We have already made a similar point in respect of primary schools, where information books tend to predominate and where sets of course books and 'laboratory type' materials sometimes absorb a large part of the allowance.

21.18   A few years ago the average number of library books in secondary schools was 5 or 6 per head; in grammar schools it was rather higher at 7 or 8, though the provision was often heavily weighted in favour of the older pupils. We asked our sample of secondary schools how many library books they had in stock. On average the number was about 8 per pupil, but that average conceals a disturbingly low figure in many of the schools, as the following diagram shows:

Diagram 12

AVERAGE NUMBER OF LIBRARY BOOKS PER PUPIL IN SECONDARY SCHOOLS

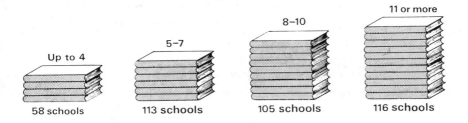

Until comparatively recently over half the schools in the country had to finance their libraries on allowances of between 15p and 40p per pupil, and the range of grants was between this 15p lower limit and the recommended figures of the Association of Education Committees. In the financial year 1972/73 the Association recommended expenditure on secondary school libraries at the rate of £1.50 per head per annum for pupils of 11–16, and £2.25 for pupils of 16 and over, with an additional grant of not less than £25 per annum for small schools. The Association went on to make the reservation that its suggested allowances applied in full only to schools which bought all their own library books. Where part of the requirement was met by direct loans of books the allowance would be appropriately reduced.

21.19   The variation in the amounts allowed for both secondary and primary schools by authorities has aroused much criticism, particularly from teachers. Each year the Chartered Institute of Public Finance and Accountancy (formerly the I.M.T.A.) and the Society of County Treasurers publish "Education Statistics". The 1971/72 issue included, *inter alia*, tables which showed the amount each individual L.E.A. spent per child on 'class books' and library books. The range for English primary schools was from 82p to £3.22, and for secondary schools from £1.83 to £5.36. These figures should be set against the sums recommended as 'reasonable' by the Association of Education Committees. In 1971 the Association recommended the following allowances to apply in the year 1972/73:

Table 18

CAPITATION AND BOOK ALLOWANCES TO PRIMARY
SCHOOLS: 1972/73. RECOMMENDED FIGURES OF A.E.C.

Primary	*Capitation*	*Sum for class books*
	£	£
Up to 9 years		
Good allowance	4·25	2·20
Reasonable allowance	3·50	1·75
9–11 years		
Good allowance	5·00	2·50
Reasonable allowance	4·20	2·20

These primary school figures do not include any provision for library books, for which it is recommended that additional provision should be made.

Table 19

CAPITATION AND BOOK ALLOWANCES TO SECONDARY
SCHOOLS: 1972/73. RECOMMENDED FIGURES OF A.E.C.

Secondary	*Capitation*	*Sum for class books*
	£	£
Up to 16 years		
Good allowance	7·50	3·50
Reasonable allowance	6·75	3·00
Over 16 years		
Good allowance	11·25	5·00
Reasonable allowance	10·00	4·50

(The above secondary school figures do not include the recommended provision for library books, which is mentioned in the previous paragraph.)

In a recent booklet[4], the Educational Publishers' Council recorded that more than half the L.E.A.s in England and Wales in 1971/72 failed to spend the recommended 'reasonable' allowance at both primary and secondary levels. Comparative expenditure figures need to be read with caution, since authorities vary widely in their accounting methods. There is also variation in the extent to which capitation allowances are supplemented by other centralised services, or by special arrangements for particular subject areas or particular types of school. What might seem an unpardonably low *per capita* sum allocated to the school may disguise the fact that the authority provides an excellent school library service. These are necessary qualifications to the figures, but after they have been made it remains true that some authorities make inadequate provision for books, notably those that provide neither a supportive service nor go beyond minimal expenditure on school library resources.

21.20   In several of the submissions of evidence we were urged to recommend that all authorities should make provision for books up to a certain standard and that there should be an increase in the general capitation allowances.

In considering the question of the level of capitation allowances it is necessary to understand what they are intended to cover and their position within the complete spectrum of public expenditure. For the purposes of calculating public expenditure and the operation of Rate Support Grant, the cost of text and library books falls within a larger block of expenditure known as 'non-teaching costs'. This includes on the one hand educational equipment, stationery and other consumables, and on the other the services of ancillary staff and the maintenance of school premises and grounds. Recurrent expenditure on text books and library books in 1972/73 amounted to £9·701m on primary and £12·971m on secondary schools, which represents a mere 5·36 per cent of the total of primary and secondary non-teaching costs. The fact that expenditure on books is part of a larger block has the important practical consequence that it is in competition for the funds available within the whole allotment of non-teaching costs. Pressures for increasing ancillary staff in schools continue to grow, while maintenance and repair bills are in the long term unavoidable. We believe that books are in a particularly vulnerable position in relation to the other items covered by non-teaching expenditure.

21.21 Authority practice in the disposition of capitation allowances to schools varies enormously. At one extreme, expenditure is rigidly controlled under specific 'heads', with no virement of any kind. At the other, at least one authority now delegates global responsibility to the headteachers of individual schools. In consultation with their governors they are free to determine how they will divide their total sum between teaching staff, ancillaries, text books, library books, audio-visual aids, stationery and materials, and so on. Several authorities are looking for a middle way, of a kind, for example, which allows full virement but lays down minimum and maximum standards. Allowances of money to schools are based in the main upon the number and age of the pupils. The exact arrangements again vary from one authority to another in respect of the amount per child, the pupil ages at which the rates change, and the extent to which other money is provided. Some authorities follow the A.E.C. recommendations and increase their allowances according to the age of the pupils; namely at nine, eleven and sixteen. Some maintain the same *per capita* allowance throughout the primary stage, while others increase it at the beginning of junior school or of middle school. All L.E.A.s increase their allowance at the beginning of secondary school, but while some have only two scales, for under and over sixteen, others create an intermediate allowance to cater for the book needs of their fifteen and sixteen year old pupils, who include examination candidates.

21.22 The disparity between individual schools in terms of both resources and money available is likely to be considerably greater than is suggested by the published figures of the average expenditure of individual L.E.A.s. Indeed, variations from these published figures can be such that some schools in 'low spending L.E.A.s' have a higher actual income than some in 'high spending L.E.A.s'. The resources available to schools are sometimes distributed in a very uneven manner, and those with meagre funds are not necessarily compensated in other ways. Some schools have access to bulk buying which tends to increase the effectiveness of their purchasing power, while others receive special allocations of money from time to time. Energetic and influential L.E.A. advisory staff can have a considerable effect upon a school's resources in their own subject fields. As we have remarked elsewhere, English is very poorly provided with specialist advisers, and therefore stands to benefit little in this way. Some comprehensive schools operate in split premises, and though they are compensated with additional teaching staff there is often no recognition of their need for extra resources. Schools in old buildings sometimes suffer from the fact that their intended replacement makes it uneconomical to put new resources within old fabric; unfortunately this can give them the worst of both worlds for an unconscionable time. For one reason or another, then, disparity between the best-provided and worst-provided schools is undoubtedly great. Indeed, it is probable that one could find two maintained primary schools identical in size, staffing, and accommodation but with the difference that one has an income three times greater than the other. We find this disparity disturbing and are by no means assured that the best use is being made of scarce resources.

21.23   There is a fundamental problem in the allocating of resources to schools: how to reconcile the objective of fairness with that of building on strengths. The first leads to a general improvement of provision on a broad front, but inevitably some schools under-use the facilities while others will not have enough to match their initiative. The second means allocating resources where enthusiasm and expertise suggest that they will be well used; but, of course, either or both can vanish with staff shortages. Another disadvantage of the first is that it tends to take the form of 'pro rata inputs', despite the fact that many of a school's needs are not in a linear relationship with the number of pupils. Library books are a case in point. If x books are required for a library of a school of a given size, one twice as big does not require 2x books. One aspect of the 'pro rata' system which we find particularly disturbing is the effect upon smaller schools. In January 1973 out of a total of 21,175 schools of primary age range in England, there were 4,319 with 100 or fewer pupils. A further 4,818 had between 101 and 200 pupils. 5,989 or 66 per cent of the schools with up to 200 pupils covered the whole primary age range from under five to eleven years old. Some L.E.A.s take steps to reduce the disadvantage to these schools of the simple *per capita* allowance. At least one Authority calculates its allowance for *all* primary schools in two parts, a basic lump sum, plus a *per capita* amount. Some Authorities with schools of under 100 pupils round up the number on roll to the nearest 50 and calculate their *per capita* allowance on that basis. The size of lump sums varies widely, and so, for that matter, does the L.E.A.'s definition of a 'small school'. One L.E.A. with a number of small schools recognises their special problems by making provision for them according to the following table (1973 figures):

Table 20

FORMULA FOR ADDITIONAL ALLOWANCE TO SMALL SCHOOLS:
EXAMPLE OF POLICY OF ONE L.E.A.

	Number of pupils	*Lump sum in addition to* per capita *allowance*
		£
Primary	Under 20	40
	21–40	30
	41–100	20
Secondary	Under 300	200
	301–500	100

21.24   We are convinced that the simple *per capita* basis for calculating allowances to schools is too crude. A better formula might be reached if two basic figures were used: a *per capita* figure sufficient for mainly consumable materials, and a second figure for those items which it is not sensible to reckon on this basis, such as library books. We mentioned above the effect upon library resources of placing them in a linear relationship with the number of pupils. For example, a school of 400 children with 2,000 books is in a very much better position than a school of 100 with 500 books. Both have the same number of books per head, but the range of choice in the smaller school is far more limited, despite the fact that the needs of an individual child are the same, whatever the size of the school he attends. The majority of small schools cover the age range from five to eleven. It is perfectly clear that a school with 70 children from five to eleven needs a wider range of books than if it had 70 children all eight years old. This difficulty could be met by allowing for the first 70 in a school at the highest rate, with successive reductions for each of the next four groups of 70. Alternatively, every school might be given the same lump sum, with an additional amount determined on the *per capita* basis.

21.25   The disadvantage to the small school is a particularly pressing illustration of the larger problems we have already mentioned: that of allocating resources to schools in a manner which is both equitable and effective. In this chapter we have set out to show some of the existing anomalies and problems. In our view the whole question of allowances to schools, and how they are distributed, needs detailed examination. We recommend that for this purpose a standing working party should be formed, made up of representatives of the D.E.S. and of L.E.A.s. The first task of this working party should be to recommend minimum figures for book provision, and these should be kept under annual review to take account of inflation and other factors.

21.26   Schools are finding it increasingly difficult to maintain a good supply of books in the face of rising costs. Moreover, changing methods of organisation and of teaching affect quite drastically the number of books available to the school from its allowance. For example, many primary schools have moved away from a reliance upon basic course books, in English as in other subjects. These are printed in large quantities and so relatively cheap. When the school changes to practices which demand a wider variety of books as a support for individual and group work it is likely to get fewer for its money. These books are often produced in colour and inevitably cannot always command the large print runs of text books. They are therefore more expensive, and this makes it difficult for schools to provide a good range within existing capitation allowances. Fiction in hard back is particularly expensive to buy, since it is printed in relatively small numbers. The secondary school is having to cater for an increased ability range and to make provision for course options, an expansion in examination courses, and curriculum innovation in various subjects. Metrication has presented all schools, primary and secondary alike, with the need for a whole new generation of mathematics books.

21.27   Expenditure on books accounts for only a very small proportion of the total net L.E.A. expenditure, a mere 0.85 per cent in 1971/72. It is extremely discouraging that so many authorities continue to spend so little on the basic tools of education as compared with the remainder of their total budget. Indeed, we are particularly concerned about the likely effects upon them of the current economic climate. The economy measures of May 1973 called for a reduction of £81m (at November 1972 prices) in the Rate Support Grant relevant expenditure of English and Welsh local authorities for 1974/75. Education's share of this cut was £24.6m. The further reductions in public expenditure required by the Chancellor of the Exchequer on 17 December 1973 included a 10 per cent reduction in procurement expenditure during 1974/75. This cut amounted to £51m (at November 1973 prices) for Education in England and Wales. We note that the joint circular from D.O.E., D.E.S. and other Departments concerned (D.E.S. Circular 2/74, 31 January 1974) included the following paragraph relating to the education service:

"The scope for securing savings among these different items (i.e. the items making up 'procurement' expenditure) will vary somewhat and it will rest with each local authority to secure the required reduction of 10 per cent in their prospective expenditure in this field. The Secretary of State is aware that, as in the case of other services provided by the local authorities which will be subject to similar reductions in procurement expenditure, some reductions in standards of material provision will occur in schools and colleges during 1974/75. However, *she hopes that authorities will generally recognise the desirability of maintaining adequate levels of expenditure on books used in schools and colleges, even though this may entail a rather higher proportionate reduction in some other procurement items*".

These reductions in expenditure are serious enough by themselves, but we strongly doubt whether in very many local authorities in recent years there has been adequate provision for the eroding effects of inflation on the purchasing power of capitation, etc. allowances. Indeed an article in "Education" of 25 January 1974 puts the position:

". . . The provision for books and stationery or for *per capita* allowances to schools has not in recent years kept pace with the increase in prices. The purchasing power, therefore, of such allowances has been dropping. In the present year . . . the increase necessary on *per capita* allowances might be as much as 20 per cent, if purchasing power were to be maintained".

We acknowledge the difficulties authorities face and the many constraints upon them. Nevertheless, in our view it is unfortunate that books and associated materials are in the forefront when cuts are made at times of economic stringency. After each percentage cut the new lower figure becomes the baseline for the next calculation. Until such time as the suggested working party is able to produce new recommended figures for book provision in primary and secondary schools we believe that the A.E.C.'s most recent recommended levels should be regarded as a minimum and that all authorities should meet them.

REFERENCES

1. The School Library Service is a support service for schools and is commonly based on the public library. For a description of a desirable range of library support services to schools see: *The Public Library Service: Re-organisation and After* (Library Information Series No. 2): D.E.S.: H.M.S.O.: 1973.

2. See, for example, *School Library Resource Centres:* The Library Association: 1972.
3. See *School Library Resource Centres, op. cit.,* and *School Resource Centres:* Schools Council Working Paper 43: 1972.
4. *Books in School: Needs and Provision:* Educational Publishers' Council: 1973.

CHAPTER 22

Technological Aids and Broadcasting

22.1   There are two points that deserve to be emphasised at the beginning of a discussion of technological aids. The first is that there is no question of the machine taking over the job of the teacher. The second is that we cannot look to any machine to provide of itself some kind of breakthrough in the teaching of reading. Both fallacies are frequently met, and both are based on a misunderstanding of the role of the teacher. However brilliant a technological innovation, success depends on the skill with which the teacher integrates it into his work. It depends on the way in which the new element in a child's learning is supported by and derives meaning from all the other elements. We might begin, then, with a fundamental principle. The equipment is not in itself significant; what is important is the quality of the materials and the use to which they are put. In themselves these are no more prone to poor use than any other teaching materials; but neither do they have any special qualities which will make them succeed independently of the teacher who is using them. This kind of realism is necessary, for technological aids have suffered equally from distrust and from over-enthusiasm.

22.2   These reservations made, we have no doubt that aids of this kind have a considerable contribution to make to language development and the teaching of reading. They give the teacher extended opportunities at various levels of activity, from individual tuition to full class involvement. Most children quickly acquire confidence in their use. Indeed there is a considerable degree of sophistication in the attitude of quite young children to pieces of equipment of various kinds, many of which they are accustomed to handling at home. A child who has learned to control a machine and can operate it at will often acquires a new motivation, especially when he has failed with pencil and paper. A statement as simple as that brings us back to the organisational demands upon the teacher. In his continuous assessment of each child's progress and needs he should see technical aids as another resource available to him to prescribe for a particular situation. And that means knowing the child, knowing the strengths and limitations of various pieces of equipment, and knowing whether any one of them is appropriate for that child on that occasion. This is no small order, and it is not surprising that many teachers feel unable to cope with it. Some are ready to welcome equipment into their classrooms but do not fit it into their programme of work in any planned way. Others find that the attention they must give to one child or a small group operating an audio-visual aid is more than they feel able to justify.

22.3   Teachers require a good deal of help if they are to recognise what audio-visual aids can and cannot do to further their work. They need help not only to understand and feel confident with particular pieces of equipment, but above all to evaluate the material which they present. This means that they must be able to depend upon prompt maintenance and technical advice, and indeed many authorities provide a service which responds promptly to requests for either. Moreover, some of the practices we describe below would make considerable demands upon teachers' time if they were expected to prepare all the tapes, slides, charts and whatever else they might need. We believe that the teacher's rôle is to organise the learning situation, and that he should be able to rely upon help with the preparation of the materials. How this is provided will depend upon local circumstances, but the experiments carried out by various authorities have indicated some interesting possibilities. For example, some schools can look to a centre which has the task of preparing packs of materials using a variety of audio-visual media, and of providing certain advisory and information services. In at least one authority most of the secondary schools and some primary schools have a Media Resources Officer whose role is to assist in the organisation and preparations of materials and keep the staff informed on current developments in the field. They work with teachers in devising and producing tapes, slides, films, charts, etc., and in this situation they have an important in-service training function. They are also responsible for first-line maintenance of equipment, though not as technicians. A third measure is the grouping of a secondary school and two adjacent primary schools for the sharing of equipment and the joint production and use of resources, each group being provided with ancillary help. Some authorities have concentrated equipment and materials in Teachers' Centres, where teachers can experiment, seek advice, and prepare tapes, etc. on the spot to take back to their schools. A few authorities produce their own television programmes for relay to the schools by a cable system, and this draws teachers into the planning and presentation of content.

22.4   Television is discussed later in this chapter, where we recommend that in common with the other audio-visual media it should be put to more widespread and constructive use in schools. Many young teachers enter their first appointments with little preparation in the use of educational broadcasting. We believe that the information services of the B.B.C. and I.B.A. should be exploited more vigorously in teacher training. There is a wide range of demonstration material which the Schools Broadcasting Council makes available to colleges. In particular, it has some 80 study boxes, 17 of them devoted to series related to the teaching of English, and these contain film, radio tapes, slides, documentation, and teacher comment and classroom discussion. Not enough use is made of these and other opportunities. Before going on to consider the characteristics and use of a number of individual items of equipment, we must again emphasise the importance of the teacher's control over the media. They must serve his curriculum planning, not dictate to it. This is why it is so important for the subject to be explored in initial and in-service training. We do not suggest that the young teacher should emerge from college with the technical mastery of a wide range of equipment. But we do believe that he should have learned how the media can be made to serve his purposes, and should have had experience of their use in the teaching he himself received.

22.5   After radio, by far the most popular item of equipment is the mains tape recorder. We have discussed its use in the chapter on Oral Language, where we described it as a virtually indispensable instrument. Great advances have been made in the last few years in the development of magnetic recording, and there is now a very varied selection of equipment to choose from. Our survey showed that 80 per cent of the primary schools and 98 per cent of the secondary schools had mains tape recorders, and 14 per cent of the latter had a recording room. Reel-to-reel mains recorders were certainly more common than battery-operated models, which were found in only 57 per cent of secondary and 42 per cent of primary schools. Many schools will have purchased their spool recorders before cassette recorders were fully developed, and the next generation of equipment will probably reflect a recognition of the particular advantages for language work of the battery-operated cassette models. On technical grounds alone these have many virtues: simple controls, protection against accidental erasure, automatic sound levels when recording, private listening with earphones, and a sound quality which is satisfactory for most situations. Above all they are portable, which means that a pupil can carry one round for recording conversations with adults or other pupils. This ready manoeuvrability tends to make children use them more naturally than they sometimes feel able to do when grouped round a static machine. The Primary Extension Programme, promoted by the Council for Educational Technology, produced some interesting initiatives in the use of the simple cassette recorder. Nursery rhymes and stories for four and five year olds were recorded on C30 cassettes, some for simple listening, some inviting the children's oral response or participation with flannelgraph and cut-out figures. Each child was given his own ear-piece, and the machines were put in the book-corner for free use. The children returned to them again and again, and the stimulus to talk was highly productive. This kind of situation is particularly suitable for young children but can be reproduced throughout the age-range with appropriate material, particularly with slow learning children. One useful technique is for the teacher to cover up the text of a book, leaving only the pictures exposed. Two or three children are asked to make up and record their own story based on the pictures. When this is transcribed it becomes their own reading book, and they later hear and read the story written by the author of the original.

22.6   Additional equipment can be related to the recorder, so that the visual and aural reinforce one another. For example, easy-loading cameras can be used to produce stills and filmstrips, which are then linked to tape-recorded material. Many teachers, both in their own classrooms and at Teachers' Centres, have developed this kind of work in a variety of ways. All those to whom we talked said they found the cassette recorder an indispensable item. Among the uses they listed for it were: developing childrens' ability to listen and to follow instructions in completing a task, helping them to record results of personal investigations, giving practice to slow readers by linking cassette to text, recording sounds for a stimulus to talk and writing, interviewing adults and other children, composing commentaries to accompany slide sequences or film, recording stories and poems to build up a library of tapes, and producing sound effects for improvised drama. The most common use we found was the recording of a story or other reading material which the child followed from the book as he listened. Sometimes this simply reinforced the defects of the text, and this again underlines the importance of the teacher's role in evaluating the material. Merely to add a taped reproduction to poor reading matter is to gain nothing. This can be even more true of phonic practice provided in this way, if sound and symbol are not very carefully related. For example, we came across one commercially produced programme where the letters 'b', 'd' and 'p', often a source of difficulty to children, were dealt with in a manner likely to add to confusion rather than remove it. More often than not, however, the examples we saw of the use of cassette/print were very encouraging. Sometimes well-designed commercial products were being used, where book, cassette, slide and film strip made up a unit, each component bearing on the same topic. Also popular were the B.B.C. Radiovision units, where a filmstrip purchased in advance provides the visual element for the radio programme, which can be recorded by the teacher. A minority of teachers had developed their own materials, sometimes using pictures which the children had taken themselves with simple cameras. Children from one inner-city school had visited a cattle market and recorded their impressions visually and orally by way of cine and still cameras and taped interviews, to be linked later to their own written accounts. There is scope for much more imaginative work of this kind, not to mention teacher preparation of materials at the simpler tape/print level. Where an authority has a high speed tape-copier available in its audio-visual services, this can be shared between a number of schools, thus permitting an exchange of recorded stories and reference material. For some of the work we have been describing the cassette playback machine will be adequate. This has the disadvantage that it cannot record, but it is very much cheaper than the cassette recorder itself. Two or three fitted with junction boxes and headsets can provide several children with the opportunity to listen to pre-recorded material. We have singled out the portable machine as a particularly valuable instrument, but do not intend by this to minimise the importance of the mains tape recorder. There are many occasions when the latter is the obvious piece of equipment for a particular purpose, and every teacher should have ready access to one. We see the cassette recorder as supplementary to it, and we should like to see one of these in every classroom where the teacher regards it as essential to his work.

22.7 A number of infant teachers now make much use of various specialised machines which use recorded sound to supplement written and pictorial information. With at least one of these machines the pupil can record his own voice, replay, and match his attempt with a master recording. Some machines are moderately expensive (of the same order of cost as a good reel-to-reel recorder) but are still within the budget limits of most schools, including small primary schools. We asked about three such machines in our survey in an attempt to discover to what extent this kind of aid is employed. The most widely used of them was to be found in 10 per cent or so of the schools containing six year olds and 17 per cent of the junior and middle schools. 14 per cent of the secondary schools had one or other of such pieces of equipment. The machines differ in detail and in method of operation, but they work on the same principle of letting the child hear what he is reading. We met teachers who found them a very great help, and their commitment to them was proving a valuable element in their teaching of reading. Cost was obviously an important factor with the heads to whom we talked, and not only initial cost but recurrent expenditure on consumable material where this is required to operate the machine. Another wise criterion was whether the teacher could make materials herself to suit her own approach and fulfil the needs of individual pupils as she assessed them. We feel that machines which allow this kind of teacher independence have an important advantage over those which operate only with specially produced materials. These materials may well be of excellent design but they often present schools with the problem of continuous replacement of consumable items. More important, they limit the use of the equipment in the sense that it cannot be linked directly and at will to work the child has been doing in the course of other activities. Machines can be a useful reinforcement in the process of teaching a child to read, but they make their best contribution when they can be integrated with the rest of the work the teacher has devised for the teaching of reading. Another technique which deserves mention in this context is the use of the typewriter, especially for older children with reading and writing difficulties. Several teachers have found it a useful stimulus, and one system which uses an audio-visual method of training typewriting skills claims considerable additional benefits for motivation and progress in reading.

22.8   We have mentioned visual material as one component in the successful linking of sight and sound. The 16mm film projector and the 35mm strip projector are old-established aids, and though more common in secondary than in primary schools they have been increasingly evident at all age levels during the last ten years or so. In our survey sample (see table 37) 65 per cent of the junior and middle schools had a slide/filmstrip/loop projector and 39 per cent a film projector. The corresponding figures for the secondary schools, almost a quarter of which had a projection room, were 86 per cent and 92 per cent respectively. This last is a high figure, but it seems probable that in many schools the 16mm film projector is under-used. It tends to be wheeled out for the showing of a film to a whole class, and the occasion has the flavour of a special event. It is understandable that to make the most of the hiring costs a school should want to let as many children as possible see the film, and this often leads to the large audience. We have, for example, seen situations where as many as three classes have been assembled to watch a film whose atmosphere could not survive such conditions. In terms of the value to be derived by each child it was a false economy. Schools should aim where possible to arrange more small group viewings of the kind which give rise to so much valuable interaction and follow-up. Some authorities organise their own 16mm film library, and when this happens film often plays a more prominent part in the teaching of English. The British Film Institute is an excellent source of complete films and short extracts, and will undertake the booking arrangements for films from other sources.

22.9   We have seen the work of some teachers who make excellent use of film as a focal point for talking and writing, as an aid in thematic work, where it is associated with related literature, and as a medium for study in its own right. In devising a course for fourth and fifth year pupils one English department had tried over a hundred films in the space of a few years, most of them hired from the British Film Institute. These were rarely full-length feature films. As one teacher put it: "There are many excellent short films which are shown in Film Festivals and then are seen no more. Like short stories, they fit well into double lessons". One such short film is "A Time Out of War", where two Union soldiers and a Confederate strike a temporary personal truce at the height of the American Civil War. The following are extracts from pieces of writing by two boys who had seen and talked about the film:

"The trees around the river were generously covered with leaves, birds sang on their still branches, it was a beautiful day. The river was low and heavy, slowed down by the thick mass of reeds. This was a day in which nature excelled itself, a day for anything except war. This was the reason the men didn't want to fight and even if they did it was stalemate. Neither side could move and it was too hot to fight. After the truce had been agreed by both sides they went down to the river, for an hour of freedom from the pressures of the war".

"Alden, the other Republican, using a hard grey rock as a soft white pillow, lay next to the crisp rippling stream which swiftly whirled by on to curves and bends, and sped through the bright green energy-filled reeds which were forced into a leaning position. This was what war was destroying. The natural beauty of life, warm and pleasant. Then the one fishing disturbed the quiet for what he thought was a fish biting on the line. His friend hurried across to discover it was a dead fellow soldier. They buried him under a dark lifeless tree and then gave him a soldier's salute. When the truce had begun and they were relaxing, cannon fire was heard bellowing out of the distance. This was appropriate as it kept reminding the soldiers who thought of peace as they rested in peace, that the war was still in motion. The water, reeds and sunlight showed the natural way of life which the soldiers tried to turn to. The dead tree was in respect to the men who were dead, which also was true in nature".

In our view film has an important contribution to make to the teaching of English at all age-levels. It needs imaginative preparation, with its exact role and the associated activity carefully thought out for every situation in which it is used.

22.10 The 35mm film strip projector and the slide projector have been developed considerably in the last decade. Lamps run cooler, and projectors have been made safe for children to handle themselves. Teachers and children have found them increasingly helpful as a classroom aid, and a wide range of commercially produced material is available. Some publishers produce packs which contain slides, printed matter, and disc or cassette. In our visits to schools we were impressed by the inventiveness of many teachers in helping the children to produce their own units. We have referred earlier to some of this work, where children used cameras and cassette recorders to devise their own slide/tape sequences. Some have made photoplays to illustrate a story or give a visual interpretation of a piece of music, and these have always given rise to a great deal of oral and writing activity. Work of this kind, where there is a well-defined task, high motivation, and a rewarding end-product, is ideal for the kind of language development we discussed in the chapter on Oral Language. Since much of it is dependent upon activity in small groups the equipment should include small screens and viewers for slides and filmstrips. The overhead projector is another machine which can be employed for language work, with the children cutting out silhouettes and adding colour, captions, and sound. All manner of material, e.g. woven fabrics, cotton wool, grasses, can be used to create visual effects, and children's ingenuity in this matter is almost limitless. The technique used for making captions can also be employed to produce material for teaching reading. Letters and words can be written on transparent acetates and then cut out. The idea of using letters and words on separate strips that can be moved round at will is a simple one, but it seems comparatively rare for the overhead projector to be put to this service. One obvious advantage of this technique is that whatever the size of group the children can see clearly what is happening; and this cannot always be said for the moving of cut-out card on a table.

22.11   A brief mention has already been made of reprographic facilities, the demand for which has increased considerably in recent years. Printed material remains the most important and prolific of resources, and a large amount of it is hand-made by teachers themselves, from simple work-sheets to cards and booklets intended for synchronised use with recorded sound. A means of copying and duplicating is essential, and most schools have some system, however simple. In our survey we asked secondary schools whether repro-graphic facilities were available for the teaching of English, and 76 per cent replied that they were. This figure is, of course, open to a wide interpretation. According to the school's own view of its equipment it can cover a range from one simple spirit duplicator to a high-speed automatic machine backed by an electronic stencil cutter. The same range will be found in primary schools, though few are likely to possess the more elaborate and expensive equipment. This is not to say that their needs for material are any less de-manding than those of the secondary school; far from it. It is simply that few but the largest schools can afford such equipment, and this means that the majority of schools—primary and secondary alike—do not possess the most sophisticated facilities. Many authorities do their utmost to ensure that this lack does not handicap the schools, and they have organised central reprographic facilities, either in the Teachers' Centre or in a separate unit. For example, in one Teachers' Centre we visited it was common for a teacher to ask for anything up to 200 copies of diagrams, pictures, or cut-outs, and have them despatched almost by return. It would be unrealistic of us to make a simple recommendation that *every* school should have an electronic scanner and a high-speed photocopier and a punch-binding machine and an electric laminator. Some schools could put them to full-time service every day of the week and still not exhaust the possibilities, while others would make little use of them. We would naturally like to see every school with the range of facilities to meet its expanding curriculum demands, and we certainly believe that these should never be thwarted for want of access to such facilities. This access might be made available through the Teachers' Centre or other unit, or through a system of sharing between schools, say a secondary school and two or three primary schools. Such an arrangement would impose an important condition: it would need proper staffing and a range of equipment able to produce material in great quantity to the right specifications and at relatively short notice. In our visits to schools we have seen some highly promising curriculum developments hampered by want of good reprographic facilities, and we believe that all schools should be able to count on fast high quality reproduction of the materials they need.

22.12   There remains the question of the extent to which each school should be equipped with audio-visual aids. We have selected certain ones as having a particular contribution to make to the teaching of reading and of English in general, but the selection does not, of course, imply that any not mentioned are discounted. The record player, for example, is well known as a valuable aid in the teaching of English, and many schools have built up extensive collections of recorded poetry and plays. As we have already remarked in the case of reprographic facilities, it would be unrealistic for us to recommend that every school should have a full range of audio-visual equipment. There are obvious reasons why this would be unhelpful, but for us the principal one lies in our central contention that the demand for aids should be created by the teacher's curriculum planning; they should not be imposed upon it. We have visited more than one school where a video recorder has never been unpacked from its box, or where the film projector has been brought out of the storeroom twice a year at the most. Simply to make a piece of machinery standard issue would not guarantee its use. Nor should it, for the use of the equipment should be in response to the needs generated by the work. The teacher must first be persuaded that by adopting it he will create a number of opportunities for learning that did not exist before. This is a matter for in-service training and for guidance from L.E.A. advisers, and we have already remarked on its relevance to the preparation of the intending teacher. It might be argued that to equip a school with a particular facility would lead it to experiment with its use. We have suggested that this by no means follows, and though there will doubtless be many instances of a successful outcome we nevertheless believe that this approach is the wrong way round. There is, of course, an important converse to this argument that automatic issue cannot be recommended. This is that a request from the school should meet with a positive response. In considering the provision of facilities within schools there are clearly too many variables to make it possible to produce a simple formula, but our recommendation is plain. We believe that where the school has a curricular need for a particular audio-visual aid every effort should be made to provide it. Some items of equipment might be shared with other schools, as in the grouping system described earlier. In many situations this will not be possible, and in any case there are certain pieces of equipment, such as cassette recorders, playback machines, and cameras, of which a school should have exclusive use on the basis of one per class. And here we must again mention the situation of the small school. 29 per cent of the schools in our primary sample had no more than 150 on the roll. Table 36 shows the extent to which primary schools of various sizes possessed certain items of equipment, and it will be seen that the small schools were poorly off in this respect. The fact that one school has less than a third the number of pupils of another does not mean that it thereby needs a narrower range of equipment.

22.13 Educational broadcasting, both radio and television, is a very important resource for reading and language development, and one which deserves detailed attention. It is interesting to note that in our survey sample more of the secondary schools were equipped with television than with radio, the figures being 91 per cent and 83 per cent respectively. The same was true of the junior and middle schools, where television and radio were represented in the ratio 96 per cent : 92 per cent. In the infant and first schools the position was reversed at 64 per cent : 85 per cent. Many schools are able to tape radio programmes, but in some cases not without considerable difficulty. Radio broadcasts are commonly relayed to classrooms from a central receiver, and if the mains tape recorder is not available a programme is lost. There is a good deal to be said for the combined V.H.F. radio-cassette recorder, which is immediately to hand, is simple to operate, and needs no careful timing. In addition to the considerable output of national radio there is now a source of valuable material in local radio, where the broadcasters co-operate closely with teachers. Groups of teachers take part voluntarily in a series, and the practice has grown among L.E.A.s of seconding teachers to work with the education producers at the stations in developing programmes for local schools. These programmes can provide the teacher with much useful and stimulating material for language development, geared more closely to local needs than the national networks can sometimes achieve.

22.14   One of the most powerful sources of vivid experience is the general output programmes of television, particularly documentaries and drama. Many teachers are already basing a good deal of classroom work on such programmes. In some primary schools they use after-school programmes as a stimulus for talking and writing, and assemble collections of books to exploit the interest the programmes arouse. In secondary schools the practice is more widespread, and we met teachers who brought the experience of the television screen into the classroom, preparing for evening programmes and following them up the next day. Some classes were reading the texts of television plays with enjoyment and others were writing scenes for themselves. In a few schools we came across serious study of the medium of television itself. We were impressed by such work as we did see but are concerned that a decade after the publication of the Newsom Report there is still little evidence of the kind of study it recommended: "We should wish to add a strong claim for the study of film and television in their own right"[1]. We believe that in relation to English there is a case for the view that a school should use it not as an aid but as a disseminator of experience. In this spirit we recommend an extension of this work. Although there is unquestioned value in developing a critical approach to television, as to listening and reading, we would place the emphasis on extending and deepening the pupils' appreciation. This could be achieved by three complementary approaches:

(a) the group study of television programmes, extracts, and scripts alongside other media dealing with the same theme;

(b) the study of a full-length television work in its own right, with associated discussion and writing;

(c) the study of television as a medium, with some exploration of production methods, comparison with other media, and analysis of the output of programmes.

In addition to home viewing such activities would involve the play-back in school hours of video-recorded evening programmes, and some reading of the literature of television.

22.15   The B.B.C. and I.B.A. have continued to expand their education output in recent years, with valuable attention to reading and English in general. The educational output of both is influenced by advisory committees on which teachers and other educationists sit. Their discussion is supplemented by advice and information gained at first hand in the schools by the organisations' own education officers, most of whom are themselves drawn from the teaching profession. Both networks have been at pains to give shape to their professional interest in language and reading, their only hesitations being over time and money in relation to the other demands of the school curriculum. At regular meetings the two bodies exchange plans and timetables, and they jointly carry out statistical surveys of the audiences in schools. These statistics show that in 1972/73 98 per cent of all primary schools in the United Kingdom used school radio broadcasts, and the same percentage used television. The figures for secondary schools were 65 per cent and 62 per cent respectively. A mere 2 per cent of the primary schools with television sets did not use them to receive educational programmes, but the corresponding figure for the secondary schools was 33 per cent. In the case of radio, the figures show an almost identical disparity between primary and secondary schools. B.B.C. programmes with an important language ingredient, such as "Watch" (television, older infants), "Merry-go-round" (television, 7-9), and "Let's Join In" (radio, infants) have been used in 70 per cent, 70 per cent and 47 per cent respectively of the schools for which they were designed and which are equipped to receive them. The television series "Look and Read", first devised in 1967 for 7-9 year olds needing extra help in reading, was taken in 35 per cent of the equipped schools. Audience figures in general fall off among secondary schools, notably when the programmes are experimental, but the "Listening and Writing" series was taken by 21 per cent of schools. The schools service of the I.B.A. has also played an important part in this aspect of the curriculum, and among its English programmes are "It's Fun to Read", "Picture Box" and "Writer's Workshop". Both organisations produce supporting material, much of which is an essential part of the provision. It takes the form of attractive publications, worksheets, film-strips, etc., and detailed notes which frequently contain a wealth of ideas on which teachers can draw to relate the broadcast material to their own pattern of working. Thus radio and television programmes provide children and teachers with a common experience which can be adapted to the needs and capabilities of individual pupils. There is a tremendous potential in educational broadcasting, and we believe that teachers should continue to be provided with this valuable source of stimulus for talking, reading and writing. It goes without saying that the use of broadcasting material involves the teacher in careful preparation if it is to be effectively integrated with the rest of the children's activity. When this is done successfully the quality of the resulting work is such as to suggest to us that those teachers who do not attempt it are missing promising opportunities.

22.16 A particularly creditable feature of the whole broadcasting effort is the amount of audience study and consultation that has gone into most of the programmes. Some, such as "Look and Read", are influenced by the results of more rigorous research, but generally speaking inquiry of this kind is extremely expensive and beyond the means of the broadcasters themselves. Some programmes, especially if they are breaking new ground either in form or content, are 'piloted'. Sample programmes are produced and recorded, then taken in a small number of trial schools, and the resulting response is used to modify the proposals as necessary before a published series is begun. Research may well be an area which should receive more attention and which could attract funds from external sources, a point to which we return below. In only rare cases, notably in such programmes as "Young Scientist of the Year" and in educational broadcasts by B.B.C. Local Radio stations, have teachers and children themselves been involved in programmes. We feel this practice could be extended.

22.17   The use of television in schools at the present time is limited by several factors. In a number of schools there is only a single television set and this is frequently ill-tuned, ill-serviced, and ill-sited. Even where the school is better served than this there is still the problem of using a single transmission most effectively, especially when time-tabling is a further constraint. The use of a video-recorder is a valuable aid, since it enables the teacher to record television programmes on magnetic tape and re-show them at times and in circumstances best suited to the needs of the pupils and the school organisation. Current developments with video-cassette recorders promise to make this technique even easier. There has been a fairly rapid increase in the last few years in the number of schools equipped with recording facilities, and currently some 29 per cent of all schools have video-tape recorders. However, many of these are large secondary schools and there are very few primary schools among them. Indeed, it is estimated that 49 per cent of secondary schools with more than 800 pupils have video-tape recorders. In our own survey, only 18 per cent of the sample secondary schools were able to use recordings in the teaching of English. We welcome the efforts of L.E.A.s to provide these items of equipment in all their schools, but in our recommendations we would go further. What is required is a complete system for recording television and sound programmes, involving not only the video-recorder itself but a stock of magnetic tape large enough to permit a small library of tapes to be held for up to a year without the need for constant erasing. There should be good aerials designed and sited to give adequate signal strength, and an efficient system of maintenance and repair. In some schools, twin recorders will be necessary to permit recording and playback to go on at the same time. We are particularly concerned that the small schools should not be denied facilities of this kind, and we believe that the needs of nursery and infant schools should be given urgent consideration. Although financial restraints are likely to make it difficult for schools to acquire colour television receivers on a large scale in the immediate future, it appears to us that over the next few years there will be a gradual move in schools to colour reception. The video-cassette recorder already records in colour at no extra cost, and the educational broadcasting output will be entirely in colour by 1976 at the latest.

22.18   The wealth of broadcast material can be fully exploited by schools only if they are able to record programmes and use them in ways and at times that suit their purposes. We acknowledge that writers, artists, and performers have rights which are protected by law, and we appreciate the efforts made by broadcasters and by copyright holders themselves to allow schools to copy certain types of transmission. Nevertheless, much more could be done, both by a revision of the law of copyright and by an extension of agreements to make available to teachers a far greater proportion of the material. For example, a system of licensing might be negotiated, broadly based upon the amount of use intended, and applicable to all broadcast material. A working group of the Council for Educational Technology has been considering in detail the problems of copyright within education. We welcome this enterprise and the Council's submission of evidence to the Committee chaired by Mr. Justice Whitford which is at present looking into the whole issue of the laws of copyright.

22.19   Educational broadcasters are seldom short of ideas; what they lack is money to carry out research. Although there have been some informative pioneer studies to discover what pupils have learned from specific broadcasts, it remains true that there is still too little research and evaluation, both of which are of the greatest importance to programme planners and producers. Both the I.B.A. Education Advisory Council and the Schools Broadcasting Council are aware of this need and they have initiated their own evaluative studies from time to time, the most recent being a co-operative exercise involving nearly 60 L.E.A.s and 120 schools. Ideally, what is required is the involvement of qualified educational research teams, so that evaluation can be linked closely to production. This evaluation should aim at determining such effects as (a) interest, (b) increase in knowledge or skill, (c) the discrepancies in benefits to individual children and how these can be remedied, (d) the contribution of each component in the programme package, (e) how and in what ways the effectiveness of a programme differs between individual teachers. Such work would give production teams a firmer base on which to test their programme ideas. Any substantial effort along these lines would require special funding, but we believe that this is a time when wide experimentation in programmes, drawing upon rigorous research and evaluation, would pay dividends for literacy.

22.20   It has to be recognised that finance is now a major problem in educational broadcasting, so that it seems very unlikely that either authority can afford to carry out unaided any significant extension on its own. The B.B.C., over the years, has been able to allot annually some £6m of licence revenues to meeting the broadcasting needs of the education world generally, excluding the Open University. It has itself raised the question of "whether some alternative sources of funds can be found, at least for that part of the service which is directed towards schools and colleges". That would be a major break with the tenets of the past. If it is indeed a pointer to the future it would seem that only public funds, possibly with some selective help from charitable foundations (e.g. to finance the research elements), could meet the extra cost needed for an expanded broadcasting effort directed to reading and language development. The B.B.C.'s school broadcasting budget in 1972/73 was £2½m, nearly two-thirds of it spent on television. The I.B.A. companies' incomes are subject to fluctuation, but it may be assumed that their combined spending on all school programmes is between £1m and £2m a year. These are not small sums, but the financial constraint plainly limits the opportunity for any major new initiative.

22.21   It would be impractical for us to recommend a massive increase in programmes on the teaching of English at all levels. Quite apart from the cost, we have already pointed out that much remains to be done to encourage and enable schools to make more widespread and constructive use of what is already provided. But there are certain areas where we feel that there is an urgent need for expansion. These are in the pre-school years, in the early stages of schooling, and for older children with learning difficulties. We referred to the first of these in Chapter 5, where we suggested the use of television to help parents understand the language needs of their children. This is most likely if the children's programmes themselves could be structured in such a way as to focus the parents' attention on these language needs in the process of fulfilling them. We believe that programmes should be developed to help the language interaction of parent and child, and that they should be based on thorough research, for the objectives we are pressing will not be achieved simply by providing entertaining sequences. Again we acknowledge the pioneering work of the broadcasters, particularly with such recent series as "Rainbow", "Mr. Trimble", "Playtime" and "You and Me". These are attempting to involve adults and children in a common experience and provide opportunities for talk. If programmes are to reach those parents and children where the need is greatest it will be necessary in some areas for schools and social agencies to promote active participation. The habit of passive viewing needs to be broken and parents made aware of their rôle in using television constructively, not merely as a means of keeping children out of mischief. We believe, moreover, that the programmes we are advocating, and others directed specifically to parents, should be shown on video-tape at ante-natal clinics. There is no escaping the fact that this would not be easy to fulfil, but we are convinced that the dividends would be out of all proportion to the cost and effort.

22.22 Ideally, programmes directed to pre-school children, at home and in the nursery class, should have virtually a year-long daily output. This is what "Sesame Street" aimed to provide in the U.S.A., where it was transmitted for an hour a day, five days a week. It used animations, puppets, film-clips, and adult actors, and it exploited the techniques of commercials to produce the maximum impact. In Britain it was initially shown for only an hour a week—on Saturday mornings—for some 13 weeks, and only in two I.B.A. areas. The controversy it aroused is well known and there is no need to detail it here. The I.B.A.'s research[2] showed that many parents found it stimulating and valuable for their children, but its critics maintained that its manner was alien to British educational ideas and way of life. One observation was that it might have been better received had it been 'translated' into English, as it was successfully translated into German and Spanish. A more recent American series, "The Electric Company", a trial selection from which will be broadcast by the B.B.C. in summer 1975, appears to have proved more acceptable in Britain. This series is designed for school viewing by seven to ten year olds as an aid to the development of basic reading skills. It is highly entertaining and uses songs, humour, short sketches, and numerous other devices, including electronic computer-generated graphics and animation. We must again emphasise that in our view the value of such programmes lies in offering a common experience which the teacher can adapt, and not in providing a series of direct lessons. For pre-school children a programme similar to "Sesame Street" can provide useful background experience in an entertaining way. Once they are in school, however, both time and learning experiences are organised more deliberately in terms of individual needs. Clearly, if children cannot be expected to work at the same pace through a reading scheme it is not to be expected that their learning needs can be closely matched to the pre-determined sequence and pace of a series of television broadcasts. Programmes used for their general interest continue to be useful, but to employ them for skill-building with the whole class can have serious drawbacks. Techniques of the kind used in "Sesame Street" and in "The Electric Company" for teaching specific skills would be of more value if available to the teacher in the form of video-tapes or short film loops for use with individuals or small groups.

22.23   18 months' research and testing took place before "The Electric Company" 's first experimental run of 130 daily half hour programmes over 26 weeks. Some idea of the total cost, which was met jointly by the U.S. Office of Education and certain industrial charitable foundations, can be deduced from the fact that each individual programme cost not less than £5,000 to make. This kind of outlay, and the £3.3m. spent on "Sesame Street", suggests that a British equivalent of either would be likely to swallow up a disproportionate part of the total available resources. With due realism we cannot recommend expenditure on this scale. Nevertheless, we do believe that extra funds concentrated upon programmes for pre-school children would have considerable educational and social value. We also feel that there should be a greater investment in programmes produced for children with reading difficulties, particularly in the age-range at which "The Electric Company" is directed, provided they are able to be used in the way we have suggested above. With the appropriate modifications, both types of programme could draw profitably on some of the techniques used in "The Electric Company" and "Sesame Street". Programmes aimed to help adults with reading difficulties have recently been introduced. This is a commendable enterprise, and it presents another argument for allocating to minority audiences a proportion of the limited resources available.

22.24   The suggestion has been made that national interest in literacy might be encouraged by exploring the issues and problems in a popular entertainment series, rather as one of the aims of "The Archers" was to ventilate matters of interest to the farming community. Whether this is practicable is a question for broadcasters, but it does raise a related possibility of introducing the right kind of reference into established popular programmes. If the theme were to come up naturally in a highly popular series like "Crossroads" or "Coronation Street", some parents might be given an insight into their children's language needs or reading difficulties. At another level young adults might be encouraged to take the first steps towards help because their difficulty was represented sympathetically. If some aspect of the subject were to be introduced into a major programme or play or into any episode in a popular dramatic series there would need to be deliberate planning. For the maximum effect to be achieved advance information and guidance would be necessary for the various interested agencies. These suggestions would require a closer liaison between broadcasters responsible for general output and those responsible for educational programmes. These links do exist but are perhaps too tenuous, and in our view a closer interaction between these two sides of broadcasting could result in considerable benefit to literacy in its widest sense. We believe that these ideas deserve consideration and that their practicability and implications should be examined.

REFERENCES

1. *"Half Our Future"*: HMSO: 1963
2. *Reactions to "Sesame Street" in Britain*: Independent Broadcasting Authority: 1971

Part Eight

Teacher Education and Training

CHAPTER 23

Initial Training

23.1   Our Report emerges at a critical and uncertain time in the development of teacher training. Following the James Report[1], the White Paper "Education: A Framework for Expansion"[2] has established the pattern for the future. This is gradually being put into effect, but aspects of it still await interpretation. The disposition of the various institutions and hence the types of course is not yet known, and such concepts as the professional tutor and the professional centre are still being discussed. This chapter, and to some extent the next, must be conditioned by this uncertainty. Our discussions and visits have taken place during what is essentially a transitional period for teacher training. The training of teachers for the future is clear in outline, but not in detail. We must therefore reach our conclusions within these limits, tempering some of our recommendations, and taking the risk that others might prove difficult to implement.

23.2   A recurring theme in the evidence we received was that colleges of education give too little attention to language in general and reading in particular. One after another of the written submissions quoted the experience of young teachers who claimed to have completed their training with only the most cursory attention to the teaching of reading. Generalisations are bound to be unfair to many individual colleges, and we acknowledge this in detailing some of the criticisms. These are summaries of general tendencies, and it would be a mistake to assume that they apply to all colleges. It would equally be a mistake to underestimate the efforts that have been and are being made to improve provision, and we shall go on to discuss some of the positive developments.

23.3   A good deal of our evidence was received from the colleges themselves, and we supplemented this by our visits and our discussions with lecturers, students, and teachers, particularly probationers. A frequent observation was that in some colleges there is still surprisingly slight attention given to the teaching of reading, with students receiving little more than a few lectures of an hour's duration. More common than this extreme is the practice of a good introduction in the first year of the course but no subsequent development. Many students have therefore lost both knowledge and confidence by the end of their third year when they are about to start their teaching life. Furthermore, there is often an uncertain relationship between theory and practice. Not only are they not interwoven but one is sometimes emphasised at the expense of the other. Thus there may be a good deal of general discussion about practice but no sound theoretical base. Conversely, students may receive a series of lectures on the theoretical aspects of reading but never have the opportunity to work with children at the relevant point in the course. Students all too rarely get the chance to study an individual child's reading and help him to improve it. Indeed, within the block teaching practice they may have little opportunity to teach reading at all, particularly in certain forms of classroom organisation. The extent to which they receive help from the teacher varies greatly, and their supervisor is sometimes not well placed to relate the practical experience to the work in college. Too much reliance is placed on unaided observation by the students, and there is no systematic feedback. Though there have been significant advances in individual colleges there is generally scant use made of technological aids, particularly video-tapes, which enable students to evaluate and build upon practical experience. In most colleges the teaching of reading is the responsibility of general practitioners who are highly experienced in infant, junior or remedial work. Only comparatively rarely are they strengthened by the presence of a colleague well qualified in reading by training or experience, and this is reflected in an uncertainty about the needs of students who intend to teach in junior and secondary schools. There is little attention to aspects of reading beyond the initial stages and to remedial measures for pupils who are still having mechanical difficulties.

23.4   These are the shortcomings brought most insistently to our attention, and they are common enough to be presented as qualified generalisations. Two principal conclusions emerge from the evidence and from our discussions and visits. First, there is a remarkably wide variation in the importance attached to reading and language development in different institutions. Secondly, colleges find it difficult to provide enough time to deal adequately with these aspects in the face of the conflicting claims of other elements of professional training. To put these conclusions in context it will be helpful to consider briefly the background of the present situation. During the past twenty years colleges have given steadily increasing status to 'academic' subjects of study in teacher training. This was in keeping with the hope expressed in the Ministry of Education pamphlet of 1957[3] that the students' personal education should be strengthened. The result of this trend has been that these subjects, which can now be studied to degree level, have made major demands on time. In this context English as a main subject has developed largely as a study of literature, with language occupying a minor role, though in recent years some colleges have introduced major courses in linguistics. Education—which includes elements from psychology, sociology, philosophy, and the history of education—has itself developed as an 'academic' subject; and it has not necessarily been directly related to the immediate needs of the beginning teacher. In short, there has been a tendency for an emphasis on the 'academic' training of the student to emerge at the expense of the professional element. During the period in which all this has taken place the length of the course of teacher training has been increased from two years to three, and for some students it extends to four. Language and the teaching of reading did not automatically gain when the course was lengthened, nor when there were moves to restore the balance between personal and professional education. Priority often went to psychology, sociology, and child development.

23.5   In the mid-1960s, because of increasing disquiet among teachers, there was an attempt to give greater prominence to reading and language, but the structure did not make it easy to bring about the necessary changes. In the curriculum of the colleges there are sections which call for the detailed study of child development, language growth, social constraints, classroom organisation, remedial work, reading, and the practice of teaching. It is obvious that the lecturers themselves have a clear picture of the relationship between these various features, widely separated in the curriculum, and see them as adding up to a coherent preparation for the intending teacher. It is equally certain that few students, preoccupied as they are with immediate objectives, manage to achieve the same. Indeed, many consider their theory course to be irrelevant to their own specific tasks in the classroom. Some observers feel that this is because the students lack experience with children before they undertake the theory studies. This is clearly a factor of great importance and one to which we shall return, but it is not an explanation in itself. It is the *fragmentation* which prevents theory from being linked with practice within a coherent intellectual framework. Some colleges have attempted to overcome this by giving a member of staff the responsibility of co-ordination. Such a task presents formidable difficulties and we do not believe it is the solution. In our view the answer lies in constructing a new type of course.

23.6 Before considering the form it should take we must look at some of the efforts made by colleges to improve the position of language and reading within the existing framework. In our visits we found that college staffs were giving a good deal of thought to the introduction of new courses and in some cases these were in operation. In one college, for example, all students had an introduction to 'language in education' in their first year, and this was linked to a study of reading at first, middle, and secondary school levels. Students could then go on to choose from a range of options which included language and communication, language in a multi-racial society, and the needs of backward children, all of which could be taken to B.Ed. (Hons.) level. In another college a foundation course, staffed by a team drawn from the Education and English departments, aimed to develop an awareness of function and variety in language, using the students' own language as a medium. This was followed by a professional course which applied the work to the classroom and gave the students practical experience with small groups of children. In their second year the students took a course entitled "Language and Reading" at first/middle school levels or one on language across the curriculum at secondary level. There was then the possibility of a study of Language and Communication to B.Ed. (Hons.).

This course is worth reproducing in detail as an example of the productive thinking that has been taking place in some colleges:

"*Aims* (i) to help the individual student meet the urgent demands for practical mastery of language in new situations (in college as well as school), and for new roles (as teacher and learner);

(ii) given some success in (i), to encourage reflection on language in use by teacher and learner for a given task; to consider beforehand the range of choices available, and to judge afterwards the effectiveness of the use of language;

(iii) given some success in the first two, to relate particular observations of language in use to theory, and to learn to apply theoretical concepts to classroom and personal problems that involve language.

General Thus, during the basic courses there is a shifting focus for the tutors
methods: who advise individual students and small groups on the language element in their own work. How far (iii) is emphasised will depend on the tutor's judgement and the student's readiness.

YEAR I (all students)

LANGUAGE AIMS	ACTIVITIES	FEATURES IN FOCUS
		implicitly and, given progress, explicitly.
1. Effective use of the voice in speaking to a larger group and in story telling.	Preparation for and practice in making contact with children through story; group discussion and practical criticism.	Stress, intonation and attitudes. Interaction, particularly questioning.
2. Widening the varieties of speech and writing a student can confidently use; developing initial awareness of the range of choice and how this relates to purpose; supplementing the language functions already developing in a student's 'main' course.	Environmental and thematic work with teams of tutors, using language to understand, come to terms with, extend and communicate a wide variety of personal experiences. Diaries, a display presentation, and a personal assign-ment (often a folder of writing) are discussed with tutors.	Expressive, poetic and transactional varieties, and the writer's intentions; the heuristic function in diaries and group discussion; interaction of visual and verbal in displays.
3. Understanding some classroom uses of talk, writing and reading in primary school.	Preparation of material to encourage children's talk etc.; discussion with tutors of specific schemes of work.	Exploratory talk (and drama) and the move-ment towards considered and shaped formulation; effects on language of involvement in task.
4. Observation and elementary analysis of a specific aspect of language in use in a primary classroom.	Selection of aspect; observations in first teaching practice, focussed on detailed items (avoiding over-generalisation) and written up for essay; discussed with tutor.	Aspects selected include: questioning and its functions; oral/written questions; the language of instruction in small/ large groups, for new skills or new ideas; language and social role; level of abstraction; notions of correctness.

YEAR II (course for primary and middle years)

1. Understanding of a child's uses of language at different stages of development and in specific contexts; moving towards a view of the teacher as organiser of linguistic (and other) resources and of situations for learning.	Examination of child language on tape, transcript and video; preparation followed by work with groups of children, aiming to use and extend language in a variety of contexts; on-going discussions with tutors.	Didactic and exploratory uses; speech and social role/ relationship; differentiation of language varieties and functions; provision for a range of functions and levels of abstraction.

LANGUAGE AIMS	ACTIVITIES	FEATURES IN FOCUS
2. Understanding of appropriate techniques and resources for the teaching of literacy.	Examination of teaching materials and tests; classroom procedures. Practical teaching with a group of children; preparation of materials. For junior study specific remedial methods; for infants the enrichment of oral language as a step to literacy.	Graphic symbol and sound correspondences; notions of correctness; standard English and dialect.
3. Understanding of language as one medium among others for learning and the expression of thought and feeling.	Examination of resources and preparation of schemes of work with a variety of focus, but in each case considering the language element, including linguistic resources and anticipated use of language by the children; planning of classroom organisation to enable this approach. All discussed with a team of tutors.	Enacting and the development of verbalisation; symbol and representation.

23.7   Some colleges have made it a policy to spread their treatment of language and reading over three years, with substantial work on them in the third year. In a number of institutes of education university lecturers have given strong support in language work to lecturers in the colleges. During the past two years some colleges have been looking quite seriously at new course structures involving the unit or module approach, a form of organisation to which we return later in the chapter.

23.8   There has also been much discussion in colleges of the problem of giving students adequate practical experience with children, and we came across numerous experiments. One practice was to bring children into the colleges, so that students could work with small groups, with their lecturers and the children's teacher at hand for consultation and follow-up. Another was for students to work with children in the schools for, say, half a day a week for two terms, taking responsibility for individual children or for small groups. Experience of such kinds is not always easy to organise, and lecturers told us that schools were sometimes unable or unwilling to co-operate. They were sometimes able to compromise by such devices as collecting information about an actual class of children and basing simulation exercises upon it. One or two colleges used video-recordings through which students could discuss with their lecturers and other students their work in schools. Some colleges relied upon sharpening the focus on reading and language work in the course of normal teaching practice. The students would be given special assignments such as keeping detailed records of a number of children and planning work to match individual needs. Another useful form of school-college contact has been the extensive collections of children's books, assembled by colleges and open for use by local teachers as well as by students. Many lecturers work in close association with teachers at Teachers' Centres and are involved in in-service education and local development work.

23.9   Few aspects of teacher training are more important than the development of profitable co-operation between colleges and schools, for upon it rests the successful integration of theory and practice. We believe that the student should have early access to practical experience, so that theory will take hold. Precisely how early will depend upon the nature of the route the student takes into teaching and the point at which he commits himself. The terms of the White Paper certainly ensure that an intending teacher can select the units of his work in such a way as to gain early practical experience, and a theoretical and conceptual framework that will prepare him for the third and fourth year. We were impressed by attempts in a few colleges and U.D.E.s to put the relationship on a sound footing through the appointment of a teacher-tutor. To quote from the evidence of one college:

> "The person appointed has full responsibility for the entire normal curriculum of a class of twenty 11-12 year old children in a local Middle School. He is supernumerary to the school's establishment . . . and the College aspects of his work require him to pay particular attention to the role of language in learning of the children in his class. His tutorial function is to help students to develop this same expertise: much of his work is done at the school and his brief is to include other members of the school staff whenever possible, thus providing an opportunity for effective individual in-service training of a co-operative kind. We think this type of post, which enables us to have a few students working in a carefully controlled situation, is unlike other Teacher/ Tutor appointments . . . teachers involved are not withdrawn from the school—nor is the *tutor* withdrawn from the teaching of children".

There is room for more enterprises of this kind, which seem to us to hold considerable promise for the development of a productive relationship between theory and practice.

23.10   We have remarked that some colleges have been considering a unit-based structure, and there is clearly a good deal of thinking in process at the present time as colleges plan to diversify their courses. It seems likely that there will be a growth in the provision of modular courses to give students more choice and provide a wider range of outcomes. Main subjects of study will be built up as units to contribute to a Diploma in Higher Education or a first Degree, and there will be some flexibility in the aggregation. The professional training element will also be influenced by this modular structure and, depending on the time at which he commits himself to teaching, a student will be able to make choices relevant to his purpose. We believe it is essential that all teachers in training, irrespective of the age range they intend to teach, should complete satisfactorily a substantial course in language and the teaching of reading. We are in no doubt of the formidable teaching task this represents and the time demands it will make. Our justification for it rests in the arguments presented in this Report. We have urged throughout that the most important single factor is the teacher, and therefore, by extension, his initial and continuing professional education. To give point to this we reproduce here some of our specific recommendations which depend for their fulfilment on a course of such substance and quality:

All children should be helped to acquire as wide a range as possible of the uses of language. In nursery and infant schools there should be planned attention to children's language development. It should be the school's conscious policy to develop in all children the ability to use increasingly complex forms.

5.4–5.10; 5.30

As part of their professional knowledge teachers should have an explicit understanding of the processes at work in classroom discourse, and the ability to appraise the pupil's spoken language and the means of extending it.

10.2–10.7

The teacher should take deliberate measures to improve his pupils' ability to handle language. They should be led to a greater control over their writing, with a growing knowledge of how to vary its effects.

11.5, 11.8–11.9; 11.15, 11.22–11.23, 11.25

A stimulating classroom environment will not necessarily of itself develop the children's ability to use language as an instrument of learning. The teacher has a vital part to play and his role should be one of planned intervention.

10.10–10.11

In the secondary school subject teachers need to be aware of:

(i) the linguistic processes by which the pupils acquire information and understanding, and the implications for the teacher's own use of language.

12.1–12.2; 12.4–12.10

(ii) the reading demands of their own subjects and ways in which the pupils can be helped to meet them.

8.9–8.19; 12.10–12.11

An improvement in the teaching of reading can come only from a comprehensive study of all the factors at work and the influence that can be exerted upon them. The teacher should be able to organise a detailed reading programme based upon this knowledge and upon his skilled diagnosis of each child's needs.

6.1–6.3; 7.30–7.32; 17.16–17.22; 18.14

23.11 This sample is sufficient in itself to illustrate our argument that language should occupy a central position in teacher training. The one feature shared by all educational institutions is that they make heavy demands on the language of those who learn and those who teach. We believe, therefore, that among the modules that go to make up the professional training element there should be a compulsory one on language in education. In addition to this there should be optional units which introduce new areas of study or allow the student to take certain aspects of the course to a more advanced level. For example, we would expect extensions of an appropriate kind for teachers preparing to teach in an infant school or to become English specialists in a secondary school. We consider that the basic course should occupy at least 100 hours, and preferably 150. It will be obvious at once that such a commitment of time would scarcely be feasible in a one-year course of professional training, and we give separate consideration below to the problem of the P.G.C.E. and Dip. H.E. student.

23.12   To indicate what we believe the basic module should contain we have chosen to present two examples as an annex to this chapter. They are not offered as blueprints and they do not pretend to have explored all the possibilities. For that reason they differ intentionally in emphasis and approach. It is not for us to be prescriptive but to offer starting points for discussion among teacher trainers. We have set out what we think should be the scope but the precise nature of the course and the way in which it is organised must rest with the colleges themselves. We would only add that the value of such a course to the teacher will depend upon the success with which theory and practice are successfully integrated. It is therefore assumed in both examples that the theoretical aspects are being closely related to the student's classroom experience.

23.13   A form of teacher training which has shown a considerable expansion in recent years is the one-year course for graduates, leading to a post-graduate certificate of education. The numbers entering teaching by this route have grown steadily, and this trend is expected to continue. In 1963, 3,883 students started their postgraduate year of training; ten years later, in 1973, they totalled 10,759; current thinking is that by 1980 their numbers may have risen a considerable way beyond this. In other words, in view of the planned reduction in recruitment to three- and four-year courses of training in the colleges, the total annual intake of students to training may by 1980 be about equally divided between the two sources.

23.14   It is therefore clearly necessary to give consideration to the kind of language study which would be appropriate for graduates taking the one-year P.G.C.E. form of training, and important to bear in mind that this takes different forms and is provided in different kinds of institutions. Rather more than half the graduate students now opt to take their professional course in a college of education rather than in a university department of education. Traditionally, the P.G.C.E. has trained specialist teachers for grammar schools, and it is still true that intending specialists for the various kinds of secondary school form a majority. However, increasing numbers are following P.G.C.E. courses which equip them for other kinds of teaching—in primary or middle schools, for non-specialist teaching in secondary schools, and for teaching in the overlapping area of upper secondary and further education. No one form of language provision can be suitable for all of them, though obviously there will be important common elements.

23.15   At present the post-graduate certificate of education courses vary considerably from institution to institution, but all are comparatively brief, lasting three terms, and up to a third of the time is normally given to school-based teaching practice. The period left for academic work is therefore strictly limited. Existing courses make varied provision for teaching students something about language in relation to education. Some offer a series of lectures on 'Language' or 'Language in Schools', and electives such as 'English as a Second Language'. Others offer—if only implicitly, through the theoretical core in educational philosophy, psychology and sociology—insights into the operation of language. These might include, for example, the rôle language plays in determining the social awareness of children, or the developmental stages through which they progress towards conceptual understanding. And, of course, all P.G.C.E. courses include work on approaches to teaching. Where this deals with the principles as well as the methods of teaching there is a major opportunity for considering both the communicative and the heuristic aspects of language.

23.16 In our discussions we gave much thought to the position of the P.G.C.E., since we were reluctant to compromise on the principle that every teacher entering the profession should have had a course of equal substance in language and reading. However, it is obvious that since the time available in the one-year P.G.C.E. course is so limited, a language component conceived simply as an addition could cause severe strain. It follows that a course of the scope we have exemplified in the annex must be modified in the case of the P.G.C.E. student, but we have produced what we consider should be regarded as minimum specifications. With varying emphases, according to the age-level for which the student is preparing, we would expect language work in a P.G.C.E. course to include the following:

i Some knowledge of the nature of language: the implications of language as a system of rules governing relationships; modifications brought about by social and geographical features as well as by subject matter; varieties and dialects.

ii the functions of language: a study of the wide range of purposes of language; language as a fundamental instrument in the personal growth of the individual; the classification of language from various viewpoints.

iii The relationship of language to thought: the way in which language is said to structure reality, both in the young child's view of his universe and in the adult's culturally determined view of phenomena.

iv The relationship of language to learning, which is the central problem for the teacher: the rôle of exploratory language and the influence upon it of classroom organisation; how language offers and develops concepts; the technical vocabularies of subjects and their characteristic ways of expressing things; how the language of the teacher promotes or interferes with learning; language across the curriculum.

v The acquisition of language: the general stages of early language growth; the nature of the child-adult dialogue in the acquisition of language; the influence of family structure.

vi The development of language: the variation of language performance from situation to situation, and between speaking and writing; the effect of teaching children abstract grammatical categories.

vii Reading: reading in the context of other linguistic skills; the general factors affecting the acquisition of reading; approaches to the teaching of initial reading; the reading demands of subjects; study skills.

23.17   How are these requirements to be met? We have argued earlier that the best means of ensuring that language is coherently presented is to make it the subject of a separate course. We should prefer this to be the model for the P.G.C.E., and indeed in some places it is already provided in this way in the form of an option. Another possibility of which there has been some experience is inter-disciplinary studies, based on 'problems in education' or 'centres of interest'. Students come together in large and small group sessions for up to a week. They are given tasks prepared by members of staff from different disciplines and make their contribution from their various subject positions. A radical solution would be to regard language as one central synthesising force which would serve to relate certain elements taught in philosophy, psychology, and sociology courses, and otherwise to dispense with these as separate disciplines. The most likely choice will probably be the co-ordination of work done on language in the different components of the P.G.C.E. course. Where this is adopted we believe it should involve team-teaching, with a linguist a member of the team and every member of staff committed to emphasising the underlying unity of language studies. The lecturers in educational philosophy, psychology, and sociology should aim to ensure that their contributions to the students' understanding of language are mutually supportive and reinforcing. They should have as a common objective the indispensable basis of linguistic awareness urged under the heading 'minimum specifications'. It is worth introducing here a cautionary note from the evidence submitted by a group of linguists working in teacher training:

"Sociological or psychological approaches to the study of language are valuable, but only if language' *as well as* social structure is studied, if language *as well as* developmental psychology is studied."

The language work must be given specific focus on teaching practice, and this means knowledge and involvement on the part of the tutors and supervisors. They have the responsibility of demonstrating its application not only in the classroom in general but also within individual subjects. Whether a student is preparing to teach science, mathematics, or an arts subject he must have a good grasp of the way the children acquire knowledge in his subject. For example, pupils may learn its specialised and abstract vocabulary and even apply it with apparent correctness but still have only an uncertain understanding of what they are doing. The student must be trained to assess how far the linguistic structure of his subject as he teaches it is grounded in the experience of the pupils. Indeed, he must acquire an understanding of all that is implied in the term 'language across the curriculum' as we have elaborated it in Part Four. The preparation he receives should be placed as closely as possible in contexts that simulate the kind of teaching he is being trained for.

23.18   We have weighted this discussion of the P.G.C.E. towards the U.D.E., its traditional provider. This emphasis is intentional, since we are anxious to establish the importance of language in the training of the large numbers of teachers who will continue to enter teaching by this route. We have already pointed out that a substantial proportion of graduates take their professional training at colleges of education, and that increasing numbers are preparing to teach in primary schools. We regard the seven specifications we listed as a *minimum* requirement for all post-graduate education students, and we hope that the language component will be more substantial for all who are training to teach in primary schools or as English specialists in secondary schools.

23.19   At this stage it is not possible to predict with precision how many students will enter teaching with only one year of professional training after taking a Diploma in Higher Education (Dip. H.E.) which has had no education content. It is not part of our brief to comment generally on future plans for teacher training, but speaking purely for our own area of concern we are disturbed at the possible implications of that particular method of entry. We have presented in the form of two examples what we believe should be the language/reading component of a teacher training course. It would be very difficult for this to be covered in a one-year post-Diploma course of this kind. We are aware of the significance of the induction year as the fourth year of training and have taken account of that in drawing up our models. It will not do, therefore, to argue that for our particular purpose the induction year will make good what could not be included in the third year. A course of the kind we envisage could not be provided within a one-year professional training course, where the pressure upon time will be acute. Either the language/reading course would have to be drastically reduced or something else would have to go. We have admitted the case of a modified language/reading element in the post-graduate certificate of education, while acknowledging that it is less than our ideal. However, to make the same recommendation for post-Diploma students—many of whom are likely to teach in primary schools—would leave us with a sense of having compromised too far.

23.20   There is an obvious dilemma here, and one for which in the present state of knowledge there is no obvious solution. A great deal depends on the extent to which this route into teaching is taken up, and the kind of provision colleges make for it. For example, we have heard of some colleges which are proposing that Dip. H.E. students should opt into teaching at the end of their first year rather than on the completion of their diploma. This extension of the professionalising period would, of course, change the situation. On the other hand, there may be some institutions which will provide a straight one-year teacher training course for students who have obtained the Dip. H.E. there or in another college. An influencing factor here will be whether a general study of language was one of the subjects which made up the Diploma. We believe that language should become a well-established option in Dip. H.E. courses and that institutions selecting for a professionalising year should look upon it as an important qualification for acceptance. In the event, it may be that relatively few students will choose to enter teaching with no more than one year of professional education following a Dip. H.E. without a language component. It is, however, our considered view that if this should prove a popular route the time available will be inadequate for the kind of professional preparation we think necessary. In doing so we reflect the unease of several of our witnesses and many people with whom we discussed teacher training in our visits to schools and colleges.

23.21   Our recommendations in this chapter have clear implications for staffing and resources. The most evident of these is that teacher training will require more people qualified in language in education, including reading. In the last four or five years there has been some expansion in the provision by universities and polytechnics of courses in linguistics, socio- and psycho-linguistics, and reading studies, and more appropriately trained specialists are becoming available as a result. However, the position in colleges of education is still very uneven, and present provision would not be sufficient to meet the demands our recommendations would create. We believe that lecturers appropriately qualified by experience and specialist training have an essential contribution to make to the courses we have recommended and that the staffing of teacher training institutions should take full account of that fact. We believe also that experienced lecturers already in colleges of education should be given ample opportunities to take advanced courses in language and reading, a point to which there is further reference in paragraph 24.14.

23.22   From our discussions and our visits to colleges we became aware of marked differences in the quality and quantity of resources made available for work in language and reading. We welcome the initiative of those colleges which have established reading centres, some of which have been developed to the point where they are providing students and local teachers alike with an excellent resource. Such distinguished exceptions aside, how-ever, we are left with the impression that facilities for work in language and reading are inadequate. In many cases they do not begin to compare with those of main subject areas, particularly in terms of ancillary help and specially equipped rooms. Rarely do they have their own accommodation, properly fitted out for practical work, and all too often the work is time-tabled wherever a room is available. We believe it extremely important that language courses of the kind we are advocating should start on a sound footing, and we recommend that they should have their own properly equipped accommodation and ancillary help.

23.23   Before passing on to the induction stage of the teacher's training we must consider a question which was of some concern to many of our witnesses: the language ability of the students themselves and their compe-tence in study skills. In Chapter 1 we referred to evidence which complained of the standards of written English of some college of education students. Heads of schools have written to make similar observations about some young teachers who have taken up their first appointments with them. The position should not be exaggerated, and generalisations are certainly out of the question. Nevertheless, we find it disturbing that there should be any cause for disquiet of this kind. In our view the teacher's competence in all aspects of language should be beyond question. We hope that as entry requirements become more stringent this competence will be more exactly taken into account. In the meantime what can be done by colleges for those of their students whose English needs to be improved? The measure that appeals to us least is what its advocates called a 'remedial' course, where the students would have formal practice in writing essays, revising punctuation and spelling, etc. This has overtones of the 'freshman composition' courses in some American colleges. We believe that the students' own language should receive serious attention in college but that a separate 'remedial' course is not the best means. It is unlikely that such a course would bring about any lasting improvement which would survive transfer from the narrow context in which it took place. In our view a better way is to use the students' own spoken and written language as a starting point in the course on language. In learning about the nature and operation of language, students should become more explicitly aware of their own practices. This is a sound principle in any circumstances, but it is of particular relevance for those students whose own use of language is uncertain.

23.24   We can sum up our basic recommendation by saying that during their pre-service training all teachers should acquire a more complete understanding of language in education than has ever been required of them in the past. However, we must emphasise that we regard this as only the first stage in a continuing process, the next phase of which—the induction year—opens our discussion of in-service education.

23.25   TWO EXAMPLES OF A BASIC LANGUAGE COURSE (see 23.12)

Example 1

(1)   THE NATURE AND FUNCTION OF LANGUAGE
(based on (a) the students' own language and (b) the language of school children).
Language as rule-governed behaviour: reference to phonology, grammar, lexis.
Accents, dialect, standards.
Spoken and written media.
The functions of language—some theoretical models.

(2)   LANGUAGE ACQUISITION
Pre-speech behaviour in the family.
'Speech for oneself' and the regulative role of language.
Speech and the development of higher mental processes (Piaget, Vygotsky).
Creativity and language (Chomsky).
The development of syntax; transitional grammars.

(3)   SPEAKING AND WRITING AS SOCIAL PROCESSES
The context of situation.
Language and role relations.
Language and social control.
Language and the presentation of self.
Conversation and the validation of social reality.

(4)   THE PROCESSING OF CODED INFORMATION
Stages in data-processing (a) perceptual, (b) encoded in speech, (c) encoded in writing.
'Ear language' and 'Eye language'.
'Linguistic awareness' and reading.
Storage and retrieval of information.

(5) LEARNING TO READ

The initial stages: sight vocabulary, phonics, reading for meaning, context cues, the role of expectations.
Reading and the internalisation of written language forms.
Reading and the purposes of the curriculum.
Developmental reading: suiting the skill to the purpose.
Diagnosis, testing, observational techniques.
The rôle of fiction in developing reading.
Children's literature and patterns of individual reading.

(6) LANGUAGE IN SCHOOL

The language behaviour of the teacher (the language of instruction, of questioning, of control; the teacher as listener).
The language of text books.
The heuristic function of language—talking and writing as ways of learning.
The development of expressive, transactional, and poetic writing.
Literature as language.
Language across the curriculum—a language policy for a school.
Organisation: class organisation for talk, for writing, for reading.
                 organisation of resources.
                 diagnosis and recording.

Evaluation: educational aims and the uses of language in school.

23.26 *Example 2*

(1) INTRODUCTION

(a) An historical introduction to language change and stability.

(b) A sketch of linguistic theory, with psychological and sociological links.

(2) COMMUNICATION IN THE CONTEXT OF COGNITIVE AND AFFECTIVE DEVELOPMENT

(a) Goals of communication in speech and writing: Information needs; negotiation processes; control processes; thinking; forms of self-expression.

(b) Sociological and psychological factors affecting communication

(i) accents and dialects; styles of print and writing; conventions of presentation; linguistic constraints in a multi-cultural society; attitudes and preconceptions; knowledge structures; motivations.

(ii) social context and style; comparative study of a range of texts; the kinds of writing required of children at school; the kinds of writing relevant to a teacher's professional role.

(3) THE COMMUNICATIVE EVENT

(i) Strategies and tactics used in accomplishing communication goals.

(ii) Receptive organisation—information access and selection procedures.

(4) SKILLS AND STRUCTURES

(a) Primary skills—Language substance.

(i) the sound system of English, with an emphasis on intonation, auditory perception and discrimination.

(ii) the graphic system of English, including punctuation, visual perception of letter shapes and groupings.

(iii) correspondences and anomalies in the sound and graphic systems. Auditory and visual association.

(b) Intermediate skills—Language form.

(i) Syntactic structures in speech and writing.

(ii) semantic structure: words and collocations
semantic relationships.

(iii) inter-sentential structures in speech and writing; the paragraph and beyond.

(iv) redundancy as a feature of natural language: context cues in reading and listening, writing and speaking, arising from redundancy; stochastic processes.

(c) Comprehension skills—Language function.

(i) kinds of comprehension—literal, interpretative, reorganisation, inferential, evaluative, appreciative, applicative.

(ii) factors affecting comprehension.

(a) reader/listener preconceptions; reader/listener goals.

(b) behaviour of speaker/writer: language variation (e.g. restricted codes); sensitivity to situations (e.g. registers, language for special purposes); awareness of audience— aiming at target groups of listeners/readers.

(iii) Aids to comprehension: questions; note-taking techniques, models and diagrams.

(5) SELF-DEVELOPMENT, SKILLS AND STRATEGIES

(a) Developmental analysis and evaluation.

(b) Learning to use verbal skills in communication; self-evaluation, recording techniques and personal resource management.

(c) Interdependence of resources and skills: the limiting effect of deficiencies in either: techniques for overcoming transitory and developmental deficiencies.

(6) ORGANISATION OF LANGUAGE AND READING IN THE CURRICULUM

   (a) Varieties of media for learning.

      A.   Reading: reading schemes and workshops
                     subject-area textbooks and materials
                     other types of printed media

      B.   Speech: the language of the teacher
                     verbal styles and strategies
                     recorded and broadcast speech
                     other varieties of spoken language
                     language interaction in group learning situations.

   (b) Evaluation of media for learning.

      A.   intelligibility, legibility, readability of media.

      B.   analysis of content: logical and ideological.

   (c) Language across the curriculum.

      (i)   activities for developing the full range of language/reading behaviour in each curriculum area.

      (ii) organisation of learning situations within the normal curriculum.

(7) TEACHING THE INDIVIDUAL CHILD

      (i)   Assessment of individual language and reading performance; record keeping.

            Creative analysis of the child's idiolect, using the skills acquired earlier in the course.

      (ii) Devising of individual learning activities based on the assessment of analysis.

            Assessment and selection of appropriate materials to match individual needs.

      (iii) Special individual problems in language and reading; an awareness of the various influencing factors.

(8) DEVELOPMENT OF THE LANGUAGE CURRICULUM

   (a) Evaluation of teaching materials and procedures in use.

   (b) Resource development.

      (i)   storage and retrieval systems for the teacher.

      (ii) management of audio-visual resources.

REFERENCES

1. *Teacher Education and Training:* H.M.S.O.: 1972.
2. *Education: A Framework for Expansion:* H.M.S.O.: 1972.
3. Ministry of Education pamphlet No. 34 *"The Training of Teachers":* H.M.S.O.: 1957.

CHAPTER 24

In-Service Education

24.1   We start from the premise that everyone now accepts pre-service and in-service training to be parts of a single continuous process. This view is reflected in the White Paper "Education: A Framework for Expansion"[1] and in the James Report[2], which preceded it. Pre-service education is not a phase in which the intending teacher must stockpile resources for a lifetime. Nor is in-service education simply a phase for remedying deficiencies or decay in the original supply. This movement in the direction of a unified process has been strengthened by the notion of the induction year in place of the period of probation. The change in terminology is significant. It marks a shift from simply allowing the realities of classroom responsibility to test the personal and professional adequacy of the teacher and, by implication, the quality of his initial training. The situation is replaced by one in which the newly qualified teacher is supported in his adjustment to the responsibility. Part of the process is the opportunity to continue his training, including those elements of it which may be more appropriate here than in the pre-service stage. These two aspects of the induction year find expression in the notion of the teacher tutor or professional tutor and of the professional centre. There has been a good deal of discussion of the idea of the teacher tutor, but rather less of the professional centre to add to the description given in the James Report. It is clearly envisaged both there and in the White Paper that the centres should occupy an important place in the continued education of teachers during their induction year. Later in the chapter we shall consider how they might play their part in helping the teacher to his understanding of language and reading. In the meantime we must consider in greater detail the characteristics of the induction year and the needs of the young teacher leaving college or U.D.E.

24.2   First, he or she will need to be inducted into the procedures of the particular school, and this means learning the answers to some fundamental questions. What, for example, is the school's attitude to language development and its strategy in the teaching of reading? What resources are available and to which colleagues should one turn for advice? What is the policy for record-keeping? These are only a few of the many facts, some articulated, some left implicit, that the new teacher will have to learn about the school's way of working. Even more important will be his need to discover as much as possible about the backgrounds and interests of the children. It is during this period of orientation that the support of head, teacher tutor, and colleagues will be of the greatest importance. As the teacher comes to know his class and the educational and social context better he will become more aware of the points at which his own knowledge needs filling out. This is the stage where the expert assistance and resources of the professional centre should be available in an essentially practical application. The young teacher may need help in exploring the materials available for the teaching of reading and perhaps preparing his own; he may need advice on specific language difficulties or on matters of classroom organisation. This work is best organised on a small group basis, so that he can explore with his peers these and other problems of mutual interest. Another important element in his continued professional studies must be the opportunity to re-examine in the light of his classroom experience some of the material on language and reading which he encountered during his initial training.

24.3   We have used as an illustration the newcomer to the primary school, but of course his secondary colleagues will be faced with the same general problems and many of the particular ones. Young teachers from both phases should come together frequently in the induction year to discuss such aspects of continuity as those we outlined in Chapter 14, and in particular the children's language development. We apply this recommendation to all secondary school teachers, whatever their subject, for an essential aim of the induction year should be to sensitize the young teacher not only to the children's language but to his own use of language in the classroom. We have discussed this at length earlier in the Report, but must include a brief additional reference to it in this context as one of a number of features we regard as essential in in-service training. Simple realism makes it obvious that one cannot expect every serving teacher to enrol for courses on language in learning; and this is one reason why we go on to propose what might be done by and within the school itself. But the induction year gives a unique opportunity for teachers of different subjects engaged with different age groups to acquire the kind of knowledge and awareness embodied in Part Four of this Report.

24.4   The growing preference for the term 'in-service education' signals some important convictions about the position of the teacher as a full partner in the enterprise rather than as the object of a training programme. It is a concept which we believe of great importance for the improvement of language work and reading in schools. The principle was expressed in the written evidence of witnesses who are themselves actively engaged in promoting it:—

> "Professional education implies not simply learning for oneself but learning to apply in school: this is the weakest part of our present system, since it demands a steady interaction between working in the classroom and detaching oneself to consider more objectively what has been going on, and what alternative choices might be made. This suggests that the present system of continuing education, with its main emphasis on either evening courses or release for a term or a year, needs extending and a new emphasis to be given to a flexible interaction between practice and theory".

> ". . . any theoretical knowledge offered to teachers must be integrated with the intuitive knowledge on which their teaching is based. Knowledge of linguistic theory alone has little impact on teachers' classroom behaviour".

There is growing evidence of disenchantment with what has been described as the 'solution-centred approach', where the emphasis is on promoting a supposed solution to educational problems. In our discussions with teachers we heard many complaints about the kind of course where a series of lectures was delivered to a large audience, with the short 'question time' excluding most of those present from any kind of participation. It is interesting to note that in a survey carried out by Nottingham University School of Education[3] only 25 per cent of the teachers preferred the idea of "a prescribed, taught course of study". The remainder opted for one or other of a number of alternatives which involved more active participation. From these 36 per cent chose "to work within a group of teachers on a problem of professional interest".

24.5 This is all part of the question of how innovation comes about in schools. Not all in-service education is directly concerned with promoting innovation for curriculum change, but much of it has this intention. When the efforts have met with only modest success, as not infrequently happens, there has been a tendency to ascribe this to the school's natural resistance to the ideas the returning teacher brings with him. From this it has often been assumed that the remedy lies in an increase in the dose. However, it has rightly been argued[4] that to rely exclusively upon formal courses is to mis-judge the school as a social organism and underrate the part the teacher himself plays in initiating change. We believe that the individual school is a highly important focal point in in-service education, and that there should be an expansion in school-based approaches. For example, with the help of one or more members of the English advisory team as a catalyst, an entire primary school staff might study how the teaching of reading could be improved. This could result in several experimental measures and an agreed common policy arising from discussion among the teachers themselves. In addition, it might lead to identifying areas in which further outside help was needed. A staff that has played a part in deciding its own in-service education needs will be likely to receive and evaluate collectively the ideas that are brought back, not reject them unexamined. The head has a crucial role in this process, in which he should be supported by the teacher with responsi-bility for language, and we regard opportunities for in-service training for heads as of the first importance. There should be more experiments of the kind initiated by one reading centre, which ran a one-month course for eight primary school heads, followed by a course of twenty half days for a member of staff from each of the eight schools. We recognise that there are particular difficulties in all this for very small schools, and we urge the generous use of supply teachers to allow heads and teachers to attend in-service activities outside the school and to exchange visits with other schools.

24.6 The appropriate unit for in-service education in the secondary school will more frequently be the English department, and clearly the head of English has a particular responsibility for helping in the continuing pro-fessional education of his colleagues within the department. This implies a long-term view of the shaping and direction of the English teaching in the school, and the opportunity for every member of the department to share in it. Thus, the head of department should keep his colleagues up to date with information on new developments, maintain a continuing dialogue on policy, and encourage shared decisions on where the English teaching can be strengthened by help from outside the school. We have already suggested in Chapter 15 that this becomes extremely difficult where the English teaching involves several teachers who spend only part of their time in it, but it be-comes correspondingly more important. Heads of department should receive every help and encouragement in developing this aspect of their role, and some schools will need more support than others from the L.E.A. English advisory team. The English department will also have an important part to play in sustaining a language policy across the curriculum. We have discussed this at length earlier in the Report but believe that it deserves mention in this context as an example of school-based in-service education at its most productive.

24.7   It is clear from the evidence we received that large numbers of teachers believe there are not enough courses in reading. When the D.E.S. published "Survey of In-Service Training for Teachers"[5] in 1967 the results showed that in the year 1966/67:

Table 21

NUMBERS OF TEACHERS ATTENDING IN-SERVICE TRAINING COURSES
DURING THE YEAR 1966/67

5,591	teachers attended		81	Reading	courses
11,616	,,	,,	244	English	,,
18,178	,,	,,	603	Science	,,
34,140	,,	,,	901	Mathematics	,,
30,945	,,	,,	1,163	P.E.	,,

Various surveys have revealed that reading occupies the highest priority when teachers in primary schools are asked to say for what aspect of their work there should be more in-service provision. Since the 1967 figures, quoted above, there is likely to have been a considerable expansion in the number of courses on reading, but it seems certain that the demand still greatly exceeds supply. We believe that L.E.A.s and other providing agencies should increase the availability of courses on reading and on the various other aspects of English to which we have drawn particular attention in the Report. Two that we regard as of primary importance are the role of language in the classroom and the use of diagnosis in the teaching of reading.

24.8   In-service education in reading should include courses which deal with the teaching of advanced skills. The majority at present available do not go beyond the teaching of reading in the early stages. It is therefore not surprising that teachers of English in secondary schools have not shown a marked interest in attending reading courses. In the D.E.S. "Survey of In-Service Training for Teachers", Table 25 gave details of courses for which teachers felt there was a future need. 35 per cent of English teachers believed there should be more courses on the teaching of English, but only 5 per cent felt the same about courses on the teaching of reading. (The corresponding figures for lecturers in the English departments of colleges of education were 87 per cent and 2 per cent). Such figures can certainly be taken to indicate that a need is not always recognised, but they can also be taken to reflect on the course provision itself. A reading course with the kind of structure they felt appropriate to the pupils they were teaching might evoke a quite different response from secondary school teachers of English.

24.9 We recommend that there should be a variety of kinds of provision, with the emphasis on a flexible interaction between practice and theory.

These might include:

(i) One to four week workshops held in the summer and planned to lead to a term's follow-up work in school.

(ii) Provision for courses involving half-day release, with afternoon and evening sessions, for teachers engaged in such follow-up work.

(iii) School-based investigations and case studies over a term, discussed and guided weekly in afternoon and evening courses.

(iv) Courses and workshops for a weekend or a full week, both to initiate such school-based investigations and to draw together conclusions.

24.10 Complementary to the substantial increase in the range and volume of local in-service training in recent years, there has been a developing pattern of planning on a regional basis. The merits of such a strategy are obvious, for it enables the best use to be made of scarce resources, particularly people expert in the field of language and reading. It becomes possible to provide courses which it would be impossible or uneconomic for local authorities to organise themselves. Moreover, it provides the stimulus that comes from working with teachers from different areas and circumstances, and with different problems. The most important single advance here has been that of the regional courses arranged jointly by the Area Training Organisation and the Department of Education and Science. These A.T.O./D.E.S. courses, of which there have been a number in reading and various aspects of English, have broken new ground in drawing together all major partners in in-service education in the region—teachers, local authorities, colleges and universities, and H.M. Inspectorate. They have provided a type of course which lies between the shorter sessional courses of a local character and the full-time ones which require secondment. The pattern of movement between participation in the course and work in the classroom has enabled principles to be studied and applied, and then reconsidered in the light of practical experience. We hope that under whatever title or auspices A.T.O./D.E.S. courses continue in the future there will be an expansion of the number concerned with the field we are discussing. There is a particular need for more courses on a regional basis for teachers of English in secondary schools.

24.11 An important source of in-service education for experienced teachers is the full-time courses on reading, language, or general English provided by some colleges and university institutes. These courses, of one-term or one-year duration, are at present few in number and they have encountered some problems of recruitment in recent years owing to the difficulties teachers face in securing secondment. Our survey showed that few teachers had attended either kind of course during the past year, and particularly those of one term's length. Yet the indications are that teachers recognise the value of such courses and would welcome the opportunity to attend them. In the Nottingham survey referred to earlier a majority of teachers said they would prefer one-term release to a number of other alternatives. We strongly recommend that local authorities should do everything possible to second more teachers to attend these courses and that the courses should be increased in number. In-service education at this level has a vital part to play in expanding within an authority the number of teachers who have added to their classroom experience a period of sustained study. At least some of the advisory teachers referred to in Chapter 16 could be expected to come from among this group.

24.12   Full-time diploma or higher degree courses, drawing upon a national rather than local or regional constituency, make up only a relatively small part of the total in-service training activity.   We believe the number of such courses in language and reading should be increased. The quality of in-service education at local and regional level depends upon the people who will be available to provide informed leadership. Expansion of the kind we have suggested requires more such people than are at present available. Practical experience needs to be combined with an understanding of fundamental principles which has been developed by advanced study. Every effort should therefore be made to involve teachers who have already taken substantial courses in the various in-service courses and workshops that may be organised.

24.13   Opportunities for part-time study have been increased in number and range through the degree and post-experience courses offered by the Open University. It is significant that among the post-experience courses the one on Reading Development has had the largest enrolment. This is the more impressive when it is remembered that many of the teachers enrolling receive no financial help from their local authority. In itself it is yet another indication of the importance teachers attach to learning more about the teaching of reading. It also says much for the attraction of an interplay between professional experience and academic study which makes considerable intellectual demands. We consider this course a significant forward step and believe that its methods and materials provide a valuable model.

24.14   We would summarise these various opportunities as converging upon one over-riding need: a substantial increase in the number of teachers who can provide the tutorial and advisory help upon which developments in initial training, induction, and in-service education depend. There are not enough teachers equipped to act as language consultants within schools, as advisers and advisory teachers for a local authority, or as specialist lecturers for students in training. At other points in the Report we have emphasised the importance we ascribe to these functions if there is to be a growth in the quality of the teaching of reading and English. For this to happen there must be a systematic and progressive programme of in-service education which opens up possibilities of career development. A suggested pattern would be as follows:—

(a) (i) local part-time courses for teachers who are, or might become, language and reading consultants within the primary or middle school. These courses should extend over at least two terms, preferably on the pattern of A.T.O./D.E.S. courses, and might include a residential element. They would have a common core with options. In addition, the teacher should undertake in his own school a supervised investigation into some aspects of language or reading, e.g. the demands of writing in various areas of the curriculum, or the diagnosis of individual reading difficulties.

(ii) courses of corresponding length, type, and quality for English teachers in secondary schools.

(*b*) one-term full-time courses which would extend the range and depth of the topics covered in the part-time local courses. They should follow a similar pattern with a common core and options. These one-term courses would be at a level which would provide appropriate preparation for work as an advisory teacher for the local authority. Entrants to such a course would profit from having attended a local course of the kind described above or studied to a level equal to that of the Reading Development course of the Open University.

(*c*) advanced courses at diploma and higher degree level to provide an appropriate training for local authority advisers and those engaged in the initial training of teachers. Entry to these would be determined by existing qualifications, but we hope that in the long term many of the entrants would have completed courses at the two lower levels.

24.15 From their continuous contact with schools the authority's English advisory team will be an important influence in assessing local in-service education needs and in devising ways of meeting them. Among these will be development work at Teachers' Centres, where the provision for work in language and reading should be strengthened. As the first point of reference outside the school they are in a position to bring home to teachers, whatever their purpose in attending, the central importance of language throughout the curriculum. There is great variation in the facilities of Teachers' Centres and in the range of activities that take place in them. In some, language activities are already well developed; in others there is little more than elementary attention to them. In addition to the general Teachers' Centres there are a number of specialist centres in reading and a few in language, and certain of these have come to attract teachers from all over the country, notably the Centre at Reading. We visited some of these centres and were impressed by the service they were offering to teachers, not only as focal points for in-service education but in their collection and evaluation of materials. They indicate clearly how great a need there is for sources of expert knowledge and advice at this level. Several colleges of education have also established reading centres, which are simultaneously meeting the requirements of students in training and of serving teachers. Of particular value are their large and comprehensive collections of materials and equipment which teachers may examine, sample, and discuss. Frequently, there is co-operation between these centres and local Teachers' Centres, and this is a welcome development. Equally welcome are the signs of growing co-operation between the different kinds of centre and the professional associations in reading and English. In varying degrees these associations make a valuable contribution to in-service education, both directly and through publications and general influence.

24.16 We recommend that language/reading centres should be developed on such a scale that teachers in every authority can have access to one. In making this recommendation we prefer to think in terms of function rather than of institution. As we have remarked, a few such centres already exist, and they should be strengthened. Some Teachers' Centres have the potential to build up the language/reading element to the status of a specialist unit.

The same is true of a number of colleges. In some authorities none of these circumstances obtains, and it may therefore be necessary to build up a specialist centre, either as an independent unit or upon an existing institution. In short, it would be unrealistic of us to recommend a uniform pattern. The variety of circumstances is so great that to do so would be a recipe for duplication and redundancy. Our fundamental concern is that every teacher should have access to a stage in provision at which expert knowledge and an extensive collection of materials is available. Where this is housed will depend upon the local circumstances, but we would expect a flexibility of administration which will allow joint participation by full-time professional staff, the L.E.A. English advisory team, and lecturers from the college of education.

24.17   The relationship of such centres to the professional centres needs to be carefully considered if they are to be mutually supporting. In the future pattern of regional planning for in-service education the professional centres promise to become a significant feature. They will be concerned not only to support newly qualified teachers in their induction year, but to augment the in-service provision for experienced teachers. Their role and function still await full articulation, though these will probably evolve from working experience rather than spring fully armed from an *a priori* definition. However, it is reasonable to anticipate that these centres, based upon existing institutions and providing good accommodation and resources, will be able to help the serving teacher in at least three ways:

(*a*) Short full-time courses, or courses on the A.T.O./D.E.S. pattern and opportunities for private study in a variety of fields. These opportunities would be open to teachers in the new larger authorities in which the centres were situated. Where the centre has developed a particular competence they would be available to teachers from other parts of the region.

(*b*) Research and practical enquiry work of particular relevance to the educational needs of the authority or the region.

(*c*) The production of experimental teaching materials; support for teachers who are engaged in curriculum development in their own schools and need help in the design and preparation of appropriate material.

Professional centres may be expected to draw upon existing agencies, reinforcing rather than attempting to replace them. Indeed, one of their functions will be to help create links between these agencies, both national and local, and the teachers in the area. We would expect that where a language/reading centre is established—in any of the forms we have suggested—it will operate as the arm of the professional centre for that aspect of the curriculum. And, of course, it may fall to the professional centre itself to develop the language/reading centre if in a given situation it is more appropriate than any of the variations we have suggested. The pattern of provision must be governed by local circumstances, and the range of possibilities must be wide enough to allow these to be used to the best advantage.

24.18 The suggestion was put to us in evidence that there should be one or more national focal points for developments in the teaching of the various aspects of English. There were a number of variations of this recommendation:

> "For various reasons the study of reading and English lacks a national organisation that commands authority. I would recommend the establishing of a National Centre for the Teaching of English at all levels."

> "Encouragement should be given to the establishment of one or more English Study Units which would represent all aspects of English teaching and would carry out curriculum development and other projects and continuously review the state of the subject."

> "It may well be that consideration will need to be given to the establishment of a national body specifically concerned with the teaching of English to provide a central focus and to co-ordinate the activities of the regional bodies in this field."

> "There is no central body in this country with responsibility for initiating, guiding, co-ordinating and disseminating the results of investigations and experiments in the teaching of reading and related fields (e.g. language and early education). This position needs rectifying, and L.E.A./University interaction will need to be established and maintained in order that theory and practice can progress together."

The emphases are different but these and similar suggestions converge upon an idea for which we believe there is a sound case: there should be a national reference point for language in education, which includes the teaching of English in all its forms and at all levels. Before considering the possible activities of such an institution we feel it important to emphasise this comprehensiveness of interest. We do not accept that there should be a national centre concerned only with the teaching of reading. Nor would we advocate a national centre for the teaching of English which was identified with a literature-based view of the subject and concerned largely with the secondary or older primary pupil. Our notion of such a centre is that it should embrace all aspects of English teaching—from pre-school language and early reading to advanced reading and English studies in the sixth form. We see its activities as including:—

(i) Providing a consultancy service for all who are involved, in whatever capacity, in the teaching of English in its various aspects.

(ii) Building up an extensive library and providing an abstracting service.

(iii) Assembling information on research in this country and abroad, and analysing research needs; supplying information at all levels of demand, and disseminating the results of research and development work.

(iv) Organising seminars, courses, and conferences.

Our own view, and it is no more than a tentative suggestion, is that for logistical reasons the centre should be sited on a university campus, though with its own governing body and staff. This would enable it to draw upon the resources of the university while remaining independent. However, we believe that the question of siting and funding should be the subject of consultation and further discussion. We therefore recommend the principle of a national centre and suggest that interested parties should be called together by the Secretary of State to consider the details of location, organisation, and function.

REFERENCES

1. *Education: A Framework for Expansion:* H.M.S.O.: 1972.

2. *Teacher Education and Training:* H.M.S.O.: 1972.

3. H. Bradley: *In-Service Education after the White Paper:* University of Nottingham School of Education: 1974.

4. R. G. Havelock: *The Utilisation of Educational Research and Development:* British Journal of Educational Technology, Vol. 2, No. 2: 1971.

5. *Survey of In-Service Training for Teachers:* Department of Education and Science: H.M.S.O.: 1967.

Part Nine

The Survey

CHAPTER 25

The Survey

I INTRODUCTION

25.1 In the face of so much subjective comment on present-day practices in the teaching of English we decided to seek as wide a range of objective information as possible. The obvious way was to send a questionnaire to a substantial number of the maintained primary and secondary schools throughout England. Over 2,000 schools were invited to take part, and it is a measure of the interest aroused by the inquiry that so high a proportion (87.5 per cent) responded. The result is that this has been the most comprehensive survey ever undertaken in this country of the teaching of various aspects of English in primary and secondary schools. We are extremely grateful to the thousands of teachers who were involved in completing the questionnaires, and to the many who offered additional comment and opinion. Section IV of this chapter reproduces the questionnaires and the total or percentage responses, and certain of these have also been used throughout the Report where appropriate.

25.2 The survey sought information about the organisation of the schools and their staffing and resources as these affected the teaching of English. It also enquired into the extent and nature of the teaching itself, with the intention of constructing a picture of the range of activities that a child might experience during a typical week at school. It would clearly not have been feasible to examine the situation at every stage from nursery to "O" level, so we selected four age groups to study. These were the children aged 6, 9, 12 and 14 on 31 August 1972. Between them they could be relied upon to give a fair representation of primary and secondary school practice. At one extreme they included children in the earliest stages of learning to read, at the other those who had started a course leading to an external examination. Our enquiries were directed at the range of English activities of children in each of the four age groups.

Details of the Sampling

25.3 Our sampling design allowed us, in one operation, to gather information about the schools themselves and about pupils of the relevant age groups. A list was prepared of all maintained primary and secondary schools in England. This grouped them according to type and size of school as recorded in January 1972. Systematic sampling with a random start was then used to select one in 10 secondary and one in 20 primary schools. Children of the specified ages were randomly selected from within these schools, according to the criteria given in paragraph 25.6 below, so that in each chosen school one child came from every class containing at least five children of the specified age. The activities of each child were thus a 'sample' of the activities of the class. Details of the stratification by school type and size are given below. The schools were grouped by type to enable us to pick sample children of the specified ages. Grouping of the schools by size made it possible to check whether certain aspects of organisation and provision were affected by school size.

359

Type of School

PRIMARY:

    i. Infant schools; First schools for age ranges 5-7, 5-8 and 5-9;

    ii. Junior with Infant schools; First and Middle schools; First schools for the age range 5-10;

    iii. Junior schools; First schools for the age range 7-10; Middle schools deemed primary for the age range 8-12.

SECONDARY:

    iv. Junior tier comprehensives with an age range 11-13, 11-14, and 11-16 with optional transfer at 13 or 14;

    v. Senior tier comprehensives with an age range 13-18 and 14-18; comprehensive upper schools starting at age 13;

    vi. Modern; grammar; comprehensive upper schools starting at age 12; 'all-through' comprehensives for the age ranges 11-16 and 11-18; 'other' secondary schools (mostly those formerly known as bilateral and multi-lateral).

Size of School (number of full time pupils)

PRIMARY

    up to 150
    151 to 250
    251 and over.

SECONDARY

    up to 500
    501 to 1,000
    1,001 and over.

First schools constitute a very small proportion of all schools. For the purposes of our inquiry we have grouped them with Infant schools where their age range did not exceed 5 to 9, and with Junior and Infant schools where it extended from 5 to 10. Omitted from the sample altogether were the 9-13 or 10-13 middle schools which existed at the time of the survey.

25.4   The category ii primary schools contain both 6 and 9 year old pupils and, since it would have been unreasonable to present these schools with sets of questions for both age groups, twice as many of those in this category were included in the survey. One half of them were asked to report on the activities of 6 year olds while the other half reported upon 9 year olds. This arrangement has been taken into account in compiling the tables which give data on the Primary schools sample.

25.5   Below are set out the size and response characteristics of the sample of schools compared with the total population of schools from which it was drawn:—

Table 22.

SIZE AND RESPONSE CHARACTERISTICS OF THE SURVEY SAMPLE OF SCHOOLS
COMPARED WITH THE TOTAL POPULATION OF SCHOOLS FROM WHICH IT WAS
DRAWN.

	Number of schools			
	In population		*Approached*	*Replied*
Type of school	*January 1973**	*January 1972**		
Primary				
(i)	5,683	5,425	269	246
(ii)	10,936	11,147	1,106†	964†
(iii)	4,556	4,578	226	205
Secondary				
(iv)	224	229	} 42	38
(v)	234	187		354
(vi)	4,089	4,298	380	354

*Figures are given for the total number of schools in 1972 and 1973, because although
the survey was conducted in 1973 the sample had to be drawn from the 1972 list of
schools.

†Half of these schools contributed to the 6 year olds sample and half to the 9 year
olds sample.

Note: See paragraph 25.41 in Section V of this chapter for an alternative description
of the sample characteristics.

Usable responses were obtained from 88 per cent of the primary schools, and
85 per cent of the secondary schools. The questionnaires were distributed by
courtesy of L.E.A.s, and we selected the week beginning 22 January 1973 as
the one for which schools should be asked to complete them. This particular
week was chosen as being free of features which would make it untypical of a
full normal working week. It was in the second term of a school year and
sufficiently far from a holiday closure to make uninterrupted working likely.
Lastly, it was the week in which the schools would be collecting annual
D.E.S. statistical data which were relevant to our own inquiry and afforded
a useful overlap.

The Sampling of Children within Schools

25.6   The first part of the questionnaire was directed at obtaining information about the organisation and resources of the SCHOOL as such. The
second consisted of a section for each CLASS in which there were at least
five pupils of the specified age, defined as at 31 August 1972. The class section
of the Primary Questionnaire was completed by the teacher in charge of the
Registration class, and that of the Secondary Questionnaire by the teacher
responsible for the teaching of English to the class or group. Where more
than one teacher was involved in teaching the class English we asked that
the task be undertaken by the one with the greatest share of the teaching.
Where this was divided equally the task fell to the teacher whose name was
first alphabetically. We chose as our sample pupil the boy OR girl whose
name was first ALPHABETICALLY (not necessarily the first on the

register) and who was present for the whole of the week beginning 22 January 1973. The teacher was asked to fill in the form in relation to the activities of this pupil during that particular week.

25.7   It was understandable that a few teachers should have had some misgivings about our sampling of activities by reference to individual children. The activities of the child who was to be the subject of this section of the questionnaire may have been far from typical of the activities of his class as a whole. However, by adopting this selection procedure we would ensure that the full range of children's activities was obtained, and it was our purpose to describe the whole age group rather than any one individual class.

DETAILS OF THE QUESTIONNAIRES ON INDIVIDUAL PUPILS

Primary

25.8   In Part One of the Report we discussed opinion on the relationship between standards of achievement and certain kinds of school organisation and teaching method. We pointed out there how subjective such opinion was bound to be, and in framing the questionnaire we considered the feasibility of testing various hypotheses frequently advanced. It is notoriously difficult to produce objective criteria by which to define differing teaching 'regimes', but we considered that the attempt should be made. One of the most common opinions expressed in the correspondence we received was that 'vertical grouping' resulted in the neglect of certain practices. It so happens that this is one of the easiest forms of classroom organisation to define in a fashion suitable for use in a questionnaire. We therefore chose to identify it in the sample and to examine the extent to which the children in such classes experienced teaching different from those in 'conventional' classes. Our identification of vertically grouped classes rested upon answers to question 1H in the class sections of the Primary Questionnaire.

A "deliberately vertically grouped class" was defined as a class for which the answer to question 1H was "yes" AND,
for 6 year old classes, the class was in either:

(i) an Infant or First school with more than 70 pupils;

or (ii) a Junior with Infant or First and Middle school with more than 200 pupils;

for 9 year olds, the class was in either:

(i) a Junior with Infant or First and Middle school with more than 200 pupils;

or (ii) a Junior or Middle school with more than 150 pupils.

A class "not deliberately vertically grouped" was defined as a class for which the answer to question 1H was "yes" and was in a school smaller than those shown above for "deliberately vertically grouped" classes.

A class "not vertically grouped" was defined as any class where the answer to question 1H was "no" AND the class was in a school as large as those shown for "deliberately vertically grouped" classes above.

The distinction between "deliberate" and "not deliberate" groupings was thus made on the assumption that in small schools vertical grouping is not altogether a matter of choice. In part II of this chapter the results are given of certain comparisons between the different classes.

25.9   One obvious problem in obtaining information about specific activities is that in primary schools English is not a clearly defined subject on a time-table. The extension of language experience, the development of writing, the time spent in reading: all are fundamental parts of the total primary school experience, whether the children are making a model, learning about weight and volume, or investigating some aspect of local history. When we asked teachers to try to estimate the amount of time spent on particular activities in English we were aware that our questions had an air of artificiality about them. In the questionnaire we provided a series of thirty-minute time slots, and the fact that many of the replies ranged so widely over these probably results from the teachers' differing interpretation of our questions. Some teachers will have held strictly to the categories we listed, and may well organise their work very much along such lines. Others will have had diffi-culty in deciding how much time any one activity occupied in a week's work in which no divisions were made. Where activities are very specific the answers are likely to be more reliable. For example, work on spelling or comprehension exercises can be clearly defined and quantified. Oral language work, on the other hand, permeates the curriculum and the answers will almost inevitably underestimate the time spent upon it. For these reasons, essentially educational rather than statistical, we have not attempted to give total times spent on English in primary schools in the same way as has been possible for secondary schools.

Secondary

25.10   A point we felt it necessary to determine at the outset in respect of the secondary school was the extent to which English is still taught as a separate subject. In recent years there has been much discussion of integrated studies of one kind or another, and it has generally been taken for granted that where they are adopted English should be part of the package. We therefore asked whether the 12 and 14 year old pupils in the sample were in classes where English was experienced in this way. We distinguished two possible forms this might take: (i) where English was taught as a separately recognisable element in an integrated scheme, (ii) where it was completely assimilated into an integrated scheme of which it was an indistinguishable element. It will be seen from paragraph 15.2 that only a very small number of schools had adopted either. The form of integration defined in (ii) above accounted for only 2 per cent of classes with 12 year olds and 3 per cent of classes with 14 year olds. Since this kind of organisation is not consistent with identifiable English activities, these sample pupils were left out of the activities data. Consequently, the totals for some tables will be found to be short of the total of schools and pupils in the achieved sample. This is noted in the footnotes to the appropriate tables.

25.11   The 14 year olds were divided into three distinct categories: "examina-tion pupils", "non-examination pupils", and "remedial pupils". There are, of course, some schools which adopt a policy of entering ALL pupils for an external examination, whatever their level of ability. In our data, therefore, there may be instances where a pupil whom a different school would have placed in a 'remedial' group has been entered by the respondent school as belonging to an examination group.

25.12   In the questionnaire the English teaching activities at both age-levels were presented under four main heads: Writing, Language Study, Reading and Oral English. These were subdivided into 45 specific activities in school, and 28 homework activities (i.e. excluding Oral English). Our aim was to obtain a very detailed picture of English teaching, but this inevitably led to substantial difficulties of interpretation. For each of the activities we presented the question in a form which divided the time spent during the week into half-hour intervals. This exhaustive use of sub-divisions meant that many more activities were listed than any one teacher could cover in the course of a week's teaching. It was therefore necessary to provide a zero time slot to allow respondents to record a 'nil return' for some activities. In the analysis of the data this presented some problems, which are explained in the technical notes at the end of the chapter. Nevertheless, we have been able to calculate average teaching times for each specific activity as well as for the four main groupings. These average teaching times are presented in terms of time spent (a) by all the sample classes, and (b) by only those classes which included the activity in their English lessons during the week in question. We would emphasise that all these calculated times should be interpreted with caution in respect of individual sub-activities. The safest interpretation will always be in terms of the total time devoted to the teaching of English or to the main division totals for Writing, Language Study, Reading and Oral English. Because of the lack of rigorous definition of the individual sub-activities, comparisons between them are obviously less reliable than comparisons between any of the four main activities which make up the total time devoted to the teaching of English.

25.13   In fact we were able to make an independent check upon the total English teaching time which we had calculated from the records of individual activities in the half-hour times intervals. In a separate question, teachers were asked to state the total time allowed for English during one week. To discover the average times spent on individual activities we had used the mid-point of each time interval. If these procedures were adequate, the resulting totals should agree with those gained from asking directly for the total time given to English. The table below shows the agreement to have been remarkably close for "all pupils" in the two age-groups.

Table 23

TOTAL TIME DEVOTED TO TEACHING ENGLISH IN SECONDARY SCHOOLS

	Direct Response	*Sum of Activities*	*Difference*
All 12 year olds	3 hrs. 22 mins.	3 hrs. 26 mins.	4 mins.
All 14 year olds	3 hrs. 16 mins.	3 hrs. 14 mins.	2 mins.

Note: The full range of information about the English activities of the secondary pupils is shown in Tables 96 and 97 of the Secondary Commentary.

25.14   It remains only to say that we do not claim to have made an exhaustive study of all the data in the Primary and Secondary Commentaries which follow. Given the time at our disposal we have confined ourselves to a limited range and depth of comment. However, both sections include a variety of cross-tabulations for more extensive study by interested readers, and we have made reference to these and to other data in various chapters of the Report.

II PRIMARY COMMENTARY

25.15 INTRODUCTION

(i) The Questionnaire Forms

The Primary Questionnaire was in two sections, a General and a Class section.

The General section was completed by the heads and enquired into aspects of staffing, resources, aids to reading, testing policy and provision for poor readers across the whole age-range of the school. The Class section related specifically to the classes containing six or nine year olds. It was filled in by the class teacher and provided details of class organisation, the teaching of reading, the use of books, record-keeping and the children's work.

(ii) Reading

The Primary Questionnaire did not set out to collect again the kind of information on reading standards which was brought together by the N.F.E.R. survey, the results of which were published in "The Trend of Reading Standards". Nevertheless, in view of the interest in this subject it was felt appropriate to place a special emphasis on the teaching of reading. A number of questions were therefore asked about class policy on reading practice, the use of reading schemes and other books, and the amount of time the children spent on reading. The teachers were also asked how they would assess the reading standard of the sample child in comparison with nationally recognised norms. Much of the subsequent information collected was cross-analysed against the teachers' answers to this question, and thus three distinct pictures emerged of the experiences of children who were rated as "above average", "average", and "below average" in reading ability.

25.16 THE SCHOOLS

(i) The Sample Schools

Table 24

SIZE AND TYPE OF SCHOOLS IN THE SAMPLE

	Number of schools with the following number of pupils on roll						All schools
	Up to 70	71–150	151–200	201–250	251–350	351 and over	
Infant and First	10	46	56	62	66	12	252
Infant with Junior, and First and Middle	118	97	57	56	82	70	480
Junior, and Middle (8–12)	1	4	15	22	84	78	204
All schools	129	147	128	140	232	160	936

All tables relating to the school, as distinct from the class, are drawn from the responses of these 936 schools.

(ii) The Classes

Tables relating to classes containing 6 year old and 9 year old children are drawn from a larger sample of 1,415 schools. A more detailed explanation of the sampling can be found in the introduction to this chapter. Information was collected about 6 year olds in 1,417 classes and 9 year olds in 1,253 classes. In the 'school' sample there were 214,494 full-time pupils covering the whole primary age range. These pupils were organised into 6,936 classes, giving an average class size of 31 children. What that average figure meant in practice for the sample classes containing 6 year old and 9 year old children can be seen in the histograms below. (Diagram 13.)

(iii) Pupil Teacher Ratio

There were 7,917 full-time and 977 part-time qualified teachers in the sample of schools. If we take part-time teachers as fractions of full-time teachers, the whole staff complement amounted to the equivalent of 8,394 full-time teachers. This gives a pupil-teacher ratio for the schools of 25.6:1, which is comparable with the ratio of 25.5:1 for all primary schools in England in January 1973. The figures included the head as a member of the teaching staff, but not the peripatetic teachers who visit schools for various types of specialist teaching. Inclusion of the peripatetic teachers would, of course, have made a marginal improvement in the staffing ratio.

(iv) The Organisation of Classes

Chapter 13 examines different kinds of organisation which may be encountered in primary schools. In drawing up the questionnaire we attempted to assess the effect upon the teaching of English of adopting one of these methods, namely vertical grouping. For the purposes of our survey a class was adjudged to be "deliberately vertically grouped" if by deliberate choice it contained an age-range of at least 18 months and the school fulfilled a specific minimum size criterion. Where a class had an age-range of at least 18 months but the school itself did not reach the minimum size stipulated, we have termed it "not deliberately vertically grouped". Obviously, if a school is too small to have one teacher per age group an age span of at least 18 months in a class is dictated as much by circumstance as by policy. (A fuller explanation of our definition of vertical grouping for the purposes of the survey appears in the introduction to this chapter.) The questionnaire results revealed the incidence of vertical grouping shown in Table 25.

Diagram 13

HISTOGRAMS SHOWING SIZES OF CLASSES OF 9 AND 6 YEAR OLDS

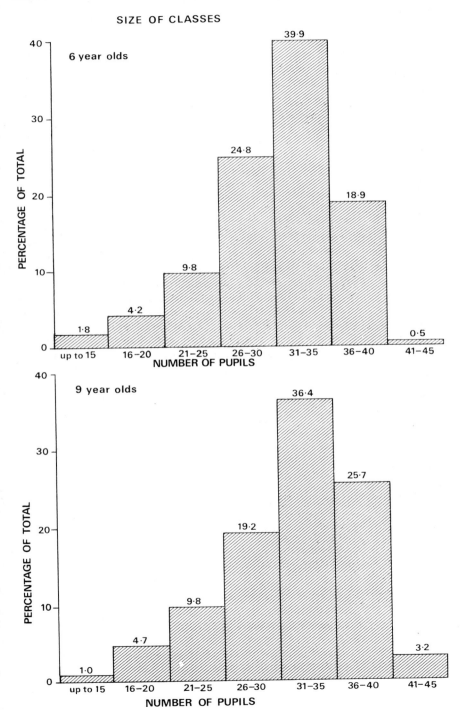

SIZE OF CLASSES

Table 25

ORGANISATION OF CLASSES: VERTICAL GROUPING

	Deliberately vertically grouped	*Not deliberately vertically grouped*	*Not vertically grouped*	*All classes*
6 year olds				
Number of classes	322	314	781	1,417
Percentage	*22·7*	*22·7*	*55·1*	*100·0*
Number of children	4,788	3,383	21,715	29,886
Percentage	*16·0*	*11·3*	*72·7*	*100·0*
9 year olds				
Number of classes	348	157	748	1,253
Percentage	*27·8*	*12·5*	*59·7*	*100·0*
Number of children	5,612	1,583	21,271	28,466
Percentage	*19·7*	*5·6*	*74·7*	*100·0*

Note: It is not, of course, possible to derive average class sizes from these figures, since whether or not a class is vertically grouped the number of 6 or 9 year olds it contains will not represent the whole possible membership of that class.

By stratifying the questionnaire data according to whether or not the class was vertically grouped, we have been able to provide some comparisons of particular reading methods in relation to the overall organisation of work within the different classes. For example, it emerged that 61 per cent of the vertically grouped classes containing 6 year olds used a 'sentence method' approach to reading compared to only 48 per cent of those "not vertically grouped". Among the classes containing 9 year olds, however, this difference of practice no longer existed. The 'sentence method' was used there by about 30 per cent of classes from each kind of grouping.

There were other instances where the practices of the three groups diverged noticeably, and these are taken up later in this chapter, particularly in the reading section.

25.17 TEACHERS

(i) Staffing

Table 26

NUMBER OF TEACHERS AND ABOVE-SCALE POSTS

Full-time	
Head teachers	936
Holders of above-scale posts (including deputy heads)	2,772
Others	4,209
Total	7,917
Part-time	
Total	977
All teachers in sample schools	8,894

(a) Above-Scale Posts

39.7 per cent of the full-time teachers other than heads received salary payments above Scale 1, but of these only 6.9 per cent were for advising other teachers in the teaching of English. The current Burnham Salary Document (operative from 1.4.73) lays down that only primary schools with a points score of 201 or more (i.e. more than 133 children on roll) are entitled to assistant teacher posts above Scale 1, and from this we calculated that just over 660 (70.5 per cent) of the primary schools in our sample were entitled to one or more such posts. However, of the 660 or so schools which could have appointed a teacher to advise colleagues in the teaching of English only 192 (29 per cent) had chosen to do so. We have argued earlier in the Report that this reflects the mistaken but all too prevalent view that any teacher can cope with all the varied aspects of English without additional training or specialist advice.

(b) Other Teachers

A check was made upon the totals of full and part-time teachers in order to discover how many schools had a teacher complement exceeding the number of registration classes. In all, 746 (79.7 per cent) of schools had teachers "in excess" of total registration classes; the number of such teachers in terms of full-time equivalents amounted to 1,416. When the incidence of these teachers was related to the size of the schools, it was found that 26 per cent of schools with fewer than 70 pupils and 61 per cent of those with 71-150 had "excess teachers", compared with over 93 per cent of all schools with more than 150 pupils. 29 per cent of schools had two such teachers while 17 per cent had three or more. As might be expected, "excess teachers" were most commonly found in the larger schools.

In addition L.E.A.s employ a number of peripatetic teachers for specific subjects and the survey found 186 of them who taught reading in the sample schools for a total of 470 half-day sessions during the survey week.

(c) Length of Service in School

The class teachers of the 6 and 9 year olds were asked to say how long they had served in their present schools. On average a fifth had served there for less than one year, a third between one and three years and the remainder more than three years. These figures were analysed by class organisation in order to determine whether this factor affected teacher mobility. Only two differences of pattern were found. Firstly, 41 per cent of the teachers of "deliberately vertically grouped" classes containing 6 year olds had been in post for three years, compared with 52 per cent of the teachers of "not vertically grouped" classes. Secondly, in the classes containing 9 year olds, 59 per cent of the teachers of the "not deliberately vertically grouped" classes (i.e. from some of the smaller schools) had been in post for more than three years, compared with 49 per cent in "deliberately vertically grouped" classes and 43 per cent in "not vertically grouped" classes.

(ii) Teachers' Centres

We were interested to know whether one or more of the teachers in each of the sample primary schools had made use of a Teachers' Centre in connection with any aspect of the teaching of English during the five month period from

September 1972 to January 1973. 58 per cent of the schools had at least one teacher who had done so. This information was cross-tabulated against the number of teachers in each school, in the expectation that those from the smallest schools might find it most difficult to attend the centres, either through lack of substitutions or because the school was in a remote area far away from one. The results were as follows:

Table 27

SCHOOLS WHICH MADE USE OF A TEACHERS' CENTRE IN CONNECTION WITH THE TEACHING OF ENGLISH

| | | *Schools with the following numbers of teachers:* | | | | *All schools* |
		Up to 5	*6–9*	*10–12*	*13 or more*	
All schools		239	294	216	187	936
Schools which used Teachers' Centres:	Number	106	163	141	134	544
	%	*44·4*	*55·4*	*65·3*	*71·7*	*58·1*
Schools which did not use Teachers' Centres:	Number	133	131	75	53	392
	%	*55·6*	*44·6*	*34·7*	*28·3*	*41·9*

As might be expected, the table shows that the larger the number of teachers in a school, the higher was the probability that at least one teacher would have attended a Teachers' Centre for some activity connected with the teaching of English during the specified period. On the other hand, well over a quarter of those with 10 or more teachers had had no one attending a Teachers' Centre for any purposes connected with English. By comparison, and despite their smaller staffs, in 44 per cent of schools with fewer than six teachers one or more of the staff had attended a centre during the period.

(iii) In-service Training

We asked the class teachers of the 6 and 9 year olds whether they had attended a course concerned mainly with one or more aspects of teaching English. For the shorter courses respondents were asked to limit their replies to those they had attended within the three years prior to January 1973, but no such time limit was imposed on courses involving at least six months' full-time study. The results appear in Table 28 below.

Table 28

ATTENDANCE BY TEACHERS OF 6 AND 9 YEAR OLDS AT COURSES ON ASPECTS
OF THE TEACHING OF ENGLISH

	Classes of 6 year olds		Classes of 9 year olds	
	Number	%	*Number*	%
Length of course attended:				
At least 6 sessions	404	*28·5*	316	*25·2*
30 days to 6 months full-time or 6–12 months part-time	22	*1·6*	27	*2·1*
6 months full-time or more than 1 year part-time	23	*1·6*	39	*3·1*
Total number of courses attended	449	*31·7*	382	*30·4*
All class teachers	1,417	*100·0*	1,253	*100·0*

The table shows that almost one in every three class teachers in our sample
had taken advantage of the very short courses, which at their best can keep
teachers in touch with developments and stimulate ideas. However, if one
takes into account the fact that we stipulated a three-year time span, the
results can be taken to mean that on average no more than about one in ten
class teachers attended even the shortest of courses in connection with
English in one year. The take-up of longer courses in our sample was very
low, even after making allowance for the likely numbers of new entrants to
teaching, who would not yet be eligible to enrol for them.

(iv) Associations concerned with reading and the teaching of English in
schools

Several teachers complained in their evidence about the lack of sources of
up-to-date information relevant to their work. One such source of which
relatively little use seems to be made is the specialist organisations concerned with various aspects of English teaching. Our questionnaire asked for
details of school affiliations to certain of these associations. The response
rate was as follows:

Table 29

ASSOCIATIONS CONCERNED WITH READING AND THE TEACHING OF ENGLISH, ETC

Percentage of schools which were affiliated to the following organisations (or which had one or more members of staff who were members):	
United Kingdom Reading Association	*5·6*
National Association for the Teaching of English	*4·7*
School Library Association	*12·5*
Association for the Education of Pupils from Overseas	*1·9*
All schools (100 per cent)	936

25.18 READING

For reasons we have given, the Primary Questionnaire placed considerable emphasis upon reading and enquired into the different methods, media and materials employed by teachers, and the amount of time the children spent on reading.

(i) Methods

The class teachers were asked whether they had used any of a specified list of methods with any of the children during the survey week. The results were as follows:

Table 30

METHODS OF TEACHING READING TO 6 YEAR OLDS

	Percentage of teachers using each method
Method:	
Alphabetic Analysis	*59·5*
Look and Say	*96·6*
Phonic 1	*97·2*
Phonic 2	*69·7*
Sentence Method	*51·3*
Pre-reading Exercises	*35·4*
All classes (100 per cent)	1,417

The principles underlying these methods are discussed in Chapters 6 and 7, and it is sufficient to say here that Alphabetic Analysis, Phonic 1 and Phonic 2 aim to give the child early independence in word attack through teaching him to synthesise letter sounds, while Look and Say and Sentence Method lay emphasis on teaching the child to recognise whole words or larger units of meaning. Pre-reading exercises lend themselves less easily to concise definition, but are explained in the glossary.

Table 30 shows that most teachers in the sample adopted an eclectic approach to the teaching of reading. It is particularly noteworthy that both Phonic 1 and Look and Say were used by 97 per cent of all teachers of 6 year olds, which suggests they regarded these two approaches not as alternatives but as complements.

A further analysis of these figures enabled us to compare the practices of the "deliberately vertically grouped" and the "not vertically grouped" classes. Table 31 shows the results of this comparison for the classes containing 6 year olds.

Table 31

METHODS OF TEACHING READING TO 6 YEAR OLDS IN VERTICALLY GROUPED AND
NON-VERTICALLY GROUPED CLASSES

	Deliberately vertically grouped	*Not vertically grouped*
Percentage of classes using:		
Alphabetic Analysis	*68·9*	*55·6*
Look and Say	*96·9*	*96·3*
Phonic 1	*97·5*	*97·1*
Phonic 2	*68·3*	*71·6*
Sentence Method	*60·6*	*47·5*
Pre-reading Exercises	*61·2*	*21·1*
Number of classes (100 per cent)	322	781

Only Alphabetic Analysis, Sentence Method and Pre-reading Exercises in
Table 31 are significantly different at or beyond the 5 per cent level* in the
two types of class. More of the "deliberately vertically grouped" containing 6 year olds used the first two than did those which were "not vertically
grouped". Pre-reading exercises were used by very many more of the
"deliberately vertically grouped" classes containing 6 year olds than by
"not vertically grouped" 6 year olds. This was undoubtedly due to the fact
that only the "vertically grouped" would contain reception-stage children.
There was no significant difference in the use of any of the six methods by
the classes containing 9 year olds.

*Reference should be made to paragraph 25.37 for a technical note on significance
testing.

(ii) The Use of Reading Schemes and Other Books

Teachers were asked to what extent they used reading schemes in the teaching
of reading. 19 per cent of the 6 year old classes in the sample and 6 per cent
of the 9 year old classes used only one commercial reading scheme for reading
practice. Over half the 6 year olds (53 per cent) drew upon several schemes
supplemented with other books which the teachers themselves had graded
in order of difficulty, while the remaining 28 per cent used commercial
schemes together with other books, not all of which were graded. 37 per
cent of the 9 year olds used reading schemes and other books graded by the
teacher, while the majority (54 per cent) used both graded and non-graded
books. Just 2.9 per cent of 9 year olds and a mere six classes of 6 year olds
(0.4 per cent.) used for reading practice books and materials which did not
fall into any of these categories.

Most of the commercially produced reading schemes provide supplementary
books which may be read between the major steps of the graded series. The
survey showed that these were widely used, by 78 per cent of the 6 year olds
and 61 per cent of the 9 year olds. Before the child was allowed to move

from one graded reader to the next most teachers usually tested him by hearing him read. This was the practice of 88 per cent of the teachers of 6 year olds and 77 per cent of the teachers of 9 year olds. One-third of all teachers of both 6 and 9 year olds required poor readers to re-read their books if their performances were unsatisfactory, while 3 per cent sometimes made them repeat a book more than once. There was no difference between the practices of vertically grouped and other classes.

(iii) Media and Schemes, etc.

A section of the questionnaire was designed to provide quantitative data about the use of the various media and schemes for the teaching of reading, information which has never before been collected on such a large scale in England.

A list was compiled which incorporated the best-known of the systems in current use. Table 32, which is based on the school sample, indicates how commonly each was employed, and the information has been cross-tabulated by *size* of school. Table 33 shows their incidence by *type* of school. By far the most frequently used were the Key Words (79 per cent) and "other controlled vocabulary" types of reading scheme (89 per cent).

In recent years much attention has been focussed upon various means of dealing with the difficulties of phoneme/grapheme correspondence, a subject discussed in Chapters 6 and 7. The questionnaire listed a number of different media to discover to what extent these had been adopted.

Table 32

MEDIA AND SCHEMES ETC. USED IN THE TEACHING OF READING, BY SIZE OF SCHOOL

	Size of school						All schools
	Up to 70	71–150	151–200	201–250	251–350	351 and over	
Percentage of schools using							
Initial Teaching Alphabet	3·8	4·1	10·9	12·9	11·6	9·4	9·1
Colour coded schemes	4·7	5·4	5·5	5·7	6·5	6·9	5·9
Diacritical Marking	1·6	—	2·3	0·7	3·5	2·5	1·9
Key Words reading scheme	80·6	78·9	71·9	67·1	80·2	90·0	78·6
Other controlled vocabulary	87·6	89·1	87·5	91·4	89·7	88·1	89·0
Breakthrough to Literacy	24·8	22·5	33·6	31·4	32·8	40·6	31·3
Reading laboratories	10·1	17·0	21·1	24·3	29·3	43·8	25·3
Stott's Programmed Reading Kit	15·5	23·8	27·3	21·4	36·2	45·6	29·6
All schools (100 per cent)	129	147	128	140	232	160	936

Table 33

MEDIA AND SCHEMES ETC. USED IN THE TEACHING OF READING, BY TYPE OF SCHOOL

	Infant and First	*Junior with Infant; First and Middle*	*Junior and Middle*
Percentage of schools using			
Initial Teaching Alphabet	*11·9*	*9·2*	*5·4*
Colour coded schemes	*3·6*	*6·3*	*7·8*
Diacritical Marking	*1·2*	*1·5*	*3·9*
Key Words reading scheme	*64·7*	*81·7*	*88·7*
Other controlled vocabulary	*89·7*	*88·8*	*88·7*
Breakthrough to Literacy	*33·7*	*29·6*	*32·4*
Reading laboratories	*8·7*	*25·4*	*45·6*
Stott's Programmed Reading Kit	*19·8*	*27·9*	*45·6*
All schools (100 per cent)	252	480	204

The Initial Teaching Alphabet (i.t.a.) was used by 10.1 per cent of schools containing infants. Naturally enough it was most strongly represented in infant classes, but it was also in use in some junior classes, probably those where some children had yet to make the transition to traditional ortho-graphy. The other media we listed, colour coding and diacritical marking, were less commonly used, the first in 6 per cent of schools and the second in only 2 per cent.

(iv) Time Spent on Reading

The class teachers were asked to state the amount of time spent by the sample child on reading activities during the survey week. The detailed tables of results appear as Tables 54 and 55. In brief they show that 99 per cent of the 6 year olds spent time on 'reading practice', while over 90 per cent also spent some time on reading stories for themselves. Among the 9 year olds the figures were 75 per cent and 95 per cent respectively. The detailed figures show that the amount of time devoted to reading was often substantial.

Three-quarters of the 6 year olds were expected to read daily from the books used for reading practice, and almost all the rest at least three or four times a week. Among the 9 year olds 59 per cent were expected to read from these books daily, 28 per cent three or four times a week and the remainder less often. We were interested to discover whether the fact that a class was vertically grouped altered the picture at all. It was found that in the main the practice of the "deliberately vertically grouped" was identical in both age-groups with that of other classes.

When answering the question "How often does the child read to a teacher during a week?" the class teacher was asked to identify, and comment in terms of, "the ablest", "an average" and "the poorest reader in the class". The percentages reproduced in Table 34 below show, as might be expected, that the greatest emphasis was on hearing the poorest achievers read. However, over half the teachers of 6 year olds heard *all* their children read at least three or four times a week. There was no great difference between the "deliberately vertically grouped" and "not vertically grouped" classes, but a higher percentage of children of both age-groups in the "not deliberately vertically grouped" classes, (i.e. those in the smaller schools), read to their teachers more often. One suggestion is that the size of classes in these schools is small enough to make this possible, and the comparative staffing ratios (17.5:1 in schools of up to 70 pupils, compared with 25.5:1 in all schools) would support this hypothesis.

Table 34

NUMBER OF OCCASIONS ON WHICH 6 AND 9 YEAR OLDS READ TO THE TEACHER IN A WEEK IN VERTICALLY GROUPED AND NON-VERTICALLY GROUPED CLASSES

	Deliberately vertically grouped classes		*Not deliberately vertically grouped classes*		*Not vertically grouped classes*		*All classes*	
	Number	*%*	*Number*	*%*	*Number*	*%*	*Number*	*%*
6 year olds								
Ablest reader								
Daily	54	*16·8*	106	*33·8*	86	*11·0*	246	*17·4*
3 or 4 times	138	*42·9*	97	*30·9*	275	*35·2*	510	*36·0*
1 or 2 times	108	*33·5*	94	*29·9*	380	*48·7*	582	*41·0*
Less often	22	*6·8*	17	*5·4*	40	*5·1*	79	*5·6*
Average reader								
Daily	100	*31·1*	149	*47·5*	189	*24·2*	438	*30·9*
3 or 4 times	175	*54·3*	131	*41·7*	455	*58·3*	761	*53·7*
1 or 2 times	46	*14·3*	34	*10·8*	136	*17·4*	216	*15·2*
Less often	1	*0·3*	—	—	1	*0·1*	2	*0·1*
Poorest reader								
Daily	219	*68·0*	242	*77·1*	548	*70·2*	1,009	*71·2*
3 or 4 times	93	*28·9*	69	*22·0*	213	*27·3*	375	*26·5*
1 or 2 times	9	*2·8*	3	*1·0*	20	*2·6*	32	*2·3*
Less often	1	*0·3*	—	—	—	—	1	*0·1*
All 6 year olds	322	*100·0*	314	*100·0*	781	*100·0*	1,417	*100·0*
9 year olds								
Ablest reader								
Daily	2	*0·6*	4	*2·5*	9	*1·2*	15	*1·2*
3 or 4 times	11	*3·2*	9	*5·7*	33	*4·4*	53	*4·2*
1 or 2 times	135	*38·8*	60	*38·2*	248	*33·2*	443	*35·4*
Less often	200	*57·5*	84	*53·5*	458	*61·2*	742	*59·2*
Average reader								
Daily	7	*2·0*	13	*8·3*	14	*1·9*	34	*2·7*
3 or 4 times	67	*19·3*	43	*27·4*	134	*17·9*	244	*19·5*
1 or 2 times	225	*64·7*	86	*54·8*	486	*65·0*	797	*63·6*
Less often	49	*14·1*	15	*9·5*	114	*15·2*	178	*14·2*
Poorest reader								
Daily	166	*47·7*	86	*54·8*	347	*46·4*	75	*47·8*
3 or 4 times	131	*37·6*	55	*35·0*	286	*38·2*	465	*37·7*
1 or 2 times	46	*13·2*	14	*8·9*	104	*13·9*	36	*13·1*
Less often	5	*1·4*	2	*1·3*	11	*1·5*	677	*1·4*
All 9 year olds	348	*100·0*	157	*100·0*	748	*100·0*	1,253	*100·0*

25.19 RESOURCES: BOOKS AND AUDIO-VISUAL AIDS

(i) Libraries and the Use of Books

The survey showed that of the 660 or so schools entitled to posts above Scale 1, 402 or 61 per cent had awarded one to the teachers in charge of the library. The evidence of our visits was that most of these teachers were involved in such administrative duties as the ordering, organising and cataloguing of books, but that their activities seldom extended beyond into such areas as shaping book-buying policy or advising other teachers on children's books. Where a school's book resources are to be used to best effect, the school needs a person to assume these additional responsibilities, an argument developed in Chapter 21. In that chapter we drew attention to the importance of having books immediately available in the classroom as well as in a central collection. In our sample 98 per cent of the 6 year olds and 95 per cent of the 9 year olds had classroom libraries, while 82 per cent of the 6 year olds and 90 per cent of the 9 year olds had access to books elsewhere in the school, in a central library collection, a corridor or another classroom. About a quarter of the teachers arranged set times when children could borrow books from elsewhere in the school, while 81 per cent of the 6 year olds and 89 per cent of the 9 year olds could do so at any time, provided they had the class teacher's permission. 80 per cent of our sample 6 year olds and 93 per cent of the 9 year olds were allowed to take books home. This suggests a welcome improvement since the Plowden Committee's finding, reported in 1967, that only 65 per cent of the primary schools in its survey allowed children to take books home.

16 per cent of the schools attended by 6 year olds and 27 per cent of those attended by 9 year olds provided some facilities to enable children or their parents to buy books, though the limited evidence of our visits was that those schools which did sell books did so only very infrequently.

The survey gave evidence of the substantial support given to primary schools by school library services. Schools were asked: "Are books on loan from the L.E.A./County/County Borough library?", and the results were as follows. For purposes of comparison the response of secondary schools to the same question has been included in the table:

Table 35

LOAN OF BOOKS BY THE L.E.A./COUNTY/COUNTY BOROUGH LIBRARY TO PRIMARY AND SECONDARY SCHOOLS

Primary schools	
6 year old classes	
Number of classes	1,417
Percentage having books on loan from	
L.E.A./County/County Borough Library	*79·4*
9 year old classes	
Number of classes	1,253
Percentage having books on loan from	
L.E.A./County/County Borough Library	*87·4*
Secondary schools	
Number of schools	392
Percentage having books on loan from	
L.E.A./County/County Borough Library	*64·0*

(ii) Audio-Visual Aids

The questionnaire sought to discover which items of equipment the schools used in the teaching of English, and a fairly comprehensive list was drawn up for the purpose. Tables 36 and 37 show the extent to which the equipment was available and how schools of different size and type compared. It will be seen that the highest percentages are to be found in the schools with over 350 on roll. Certain of the more common items, such as radio and television, are represented fairly evenly across the range of school size; but others, such as the battery tape recorder, offer a telling contrast. The situation of small schools in respect of equipment and other facilities is given special attention in paragraph 25.23. Table 37 reveals a marked difference between infant/first and junior/middle schools in the availability of a television set.

Table 36

INCIDENCE OF AUDIO-VISUAL AIDS BY SIZE OF SCHOOL

	Size of school						All schools
	Up to 70	71– 150	151– 200	201– 250	251– 350	351 and over	
Percentage of schools using							
Record player	62·8	68·0	80·5	79·3	81·9	80·6	76·3
Mains tape recorder	65·9	76·9	80·5	72·9	84·1	93·1	79·8
Battery tape recorder	17·1	25·9	36·7	45·0	57·8	58·1	42·4
Filmstrip/Slide/ Loop projector	44·2	50·3	63·3	50·0	62·9	67·5	57·3
Film projector	11·6	12·2	24·2	20·7	26·7	38·8	23·2
Radio	86·1	84·4	88·3	89·3	87·5	91·9	87·9
Television	80·6	75·5	80·5	78·6	86·2	93·8	83·1
Language Master	4·7	8·2	11·7	6·4	14·2	19·4	11·3
Talking Page	0·8	1·4	0·8	—	3·0	2·5	1·6
Synchrofax	0·8	0·7	—	2·1	2·2	6·9	2·2
Other teaching machines	5·4	6·8	7·8	5·7	9·5	13·8	8·4
Number of schools	129	147	128	140	232	160	936

Table 37

INCIDENCE OF AUDIO-VISUAL AIDS BY TYPE OF SCHOOL

	Infant and First	*Junior with Infant; First and Middle*	*Junior and Middle*
Percentage of schools using			
Record player	*73·8*	*74·0*	*84·8*
Mains tape recorder	*66·7*	*81·9*	*91·2*
Battery tape recorder	*41·3*	*36·9*	*56·9*
Filmstrip/Slide/Loop projector	*50·0*	*57·7*	*65·2*
Film projector	*12·3*	*22·3*	*38·7*
Radio	*84·5*	*88·1*	*91·7*
Television	*63·9*	*87·9*	*95·6*
Language Master	*10·7*	*9·4*	*16·7*
Talking Page	*2·0*	*1·3*	*2·0*
Synchrofax	*2·0*	*1·7*	*3·9*
Other teaching machines	*7·5*	*9·0*	*8·3*
Number of schools (100 per cent.)	252	480	204

25.20 TESTING AND RECORDING

Chapter 17 argues the importance of an effective system of diagnosis and recording based on the teacher's structured observation and on the use of suitable tests. In the survey we aimed to ascertain how the children's progress was assessed and their problems identified, and the steps that were taken to record the findings. The following tables relate to the use of tests.

Table 38

TESTING OF CHILDREN WITH PUBLISHED READING TESTS, BY TYPE OF SCHOOL

	Percentage of schools which test all children			
	Infant and First	*Junior with Infant; First and Middle*	*Junior and Middle*	*All schools*
	%	%	%	%
Time tested:				
First term	*2·0*	*11·9*	*78·4*	*23·7*
Last year	*61·1*	*65·0*	*75·5*	*66·2*
Some other time	*27·4*	*92·7*	*93·1*	*75·2*
All schools (100 per cent)	252	480	204	936

Of the 936 schools, a quarter tested children in their first term in school. Two-thirds tested them during their last year in school and three out of four at some other time. On average, therefore, it seems that most children stand a good chance of being formally tested at least twice during their primary years. It will be seen that a high proportion of the junior and middle school children were tested during their last year, though it is not possible to state the extent to which results were passed on to the next school.

All schools were asked to indicate which tests they used, and a table of the results from our 936 'sample' schools follows. Table 39 refers. The most marked feature of this table is the heavy reliance placed upon the Schonell Graded Word Reading Test, which was used by 72 per cent of the schools in our sample. It was first published in 1945, and has not subsequently been revised or restandardised. Goodacre commented upon its prevalence in findings from an N.F.E.R. survey in 1959, and it is clear from our own survey that this test continues to be the one with which most schools are familiar. The table shows that 93 per cent of all schools used tests of one kind or another. On average those with fewer pupils tended to use two or three different tests, the larger ones three or four. 17 per cent of schools placed some reliance upon tests other than those we had specified; these probably included some of their own devising. We tried to find out whether size of school had any pronounced effect upon testing policy, but were unable to discover any discernible trends. The evidence of our visits suggests that the application of reading tests is the main method, indeed in some schools the only method, used to determine which children should receive special help. Of the 936 schools in the sample 644 (69 per cent) were allocating special help to children whose test score fell below a certain level.

Chapter 17 gives details of the features we consider necessary in the recording of children's work and progress, and certain of these were included in the questions. The results reveal that almost all the teachers of 6 year olds kept records of the books read by each child, and of the occasions they heard the child read. The figures for these practices were 95 per cent and 94 per cent respectively, and the comparable figures for the teachers of 9 year olds were 78 per cent and 70 per cent. Assessments of written work were kept by 47 per cent of the teachers of 6 year olds and 60 per cent of the teachers of 9 year olds.

Table 39

USE OF DIFFERENT READING TESTS, BY SIZE OF SCHOOL

	Size of school						All schools
	Up to 70	71–150	151–200	201–250	251–350	351 and over	
Percentage of schools using each test:							
None	7·8	10·9	10·9	6·4	8·2	0·6	7·4
Burt Rearranged Word Reading Test	24·0	29·9	28·9	35·0	39·7	42·5	34·3
Schonell Graded Word Reading Test	75·2	59·9	70·3	71·4	73·3	83·8	72·5
Schonell Silent Reading Test A	27·9	23·1	18·8	22·9	22·8	33·1	24·8
Schonell Silent Reading Test B	27·1	22·5	18·0	21·4	21·6	33·1	23·9
Vernon Graded Word Reading Test	3·1	4·8	1·6	4·3	3·0	5·0	3·6
Holborn Reading Scale	25·6	18·4	21·9	25·7	29·7	38·8	27·2
NFER Reading Test AD	14·0	17·7	11·7	10·7	16·4	18·1	15·0
Neale Analysis of Reading Ability	9·3	14·3	19·5	12·9	18·1	23·1	16·6
Standard Test of Reading Skill	8·5	13·6	18·0	12·1	21·6	28·1	17·7
Word Recognition Test	1·6	—	1·6	0·7	2·2	2·5	1·5
Young Group Reading Test	9·3	6·8	4·7	5·0	4·3	7·5	6·1
Southgate Group Reading Test 1 —Word Selection	9·3	3·4	7·8	5·7	6·0	8·8	6·7
Southgate Group Reading Test 2 —Sentence Completion	7·0	3·4	5·5	2·9	3·5	5·6	4·5
Other	10·9	20·4	13·3	17·9	21·6	16·3	17·3
Number of schools	129	147	128	140	232	160	936

One of our questions was designed to determine how many teachers kept records of persistent individual errors that might indicate the need for help from (a) specialist teachers of reading within the school, and (b) specialist teachers and/or educational psychologists from outside. 37 per cent of the teachers of 6 year olds and 46 per cent of those of 9 year olds kept such records for the first of these purposes and 32 per cent and 38 per cent respectively for the second. Specialist help with reading is obviously less relevant in the case of 6 year old children, but it is perhaps surprising that the figures for the 9 year olds are so low. Chapter 17 makes out a case for the importance of keeping systematic records and one measure recommended is that of building up a collection of a child's written work over a period of time. In the survey we found that only some 40 per cent of the teachers of both age-groups kept children's work for this purpose.

25.21   PUPILS WITH READING AND LANGUAGE DIFFICULTIES

(i) General

The term 'remedial' is applied in primary schools to a not very precisely defined band of children along the continuum of ability. When the questionnaire was devised we chose not to attach any objective criteria to the term, and we have therefore to recognise that as used in the questionnaire and in this commentary it applies to children with a fairly diverse range of abilities and problems. The questionnaire results relate to those children whose schools had identified them as being in need of special help, and who were in fact receiving such help. It emerged that 22,762 (10.6 per cent) of the children of the whole primary age range fell into this category.

Schools were asked whether any of these children were being taught reading for any part of the time in classes, groups or individually outside the registration classes. The question specifically excluded 'group work' within the class unless an additional teacher was being brought in for the purpose.

Table 40

CLASSES, GROUPS OR INDIVIDUAL TUITION IN READING OUTSIDE
REGISTRATION CLASSES, BY TYPE OF SCHOOL

	Infant and First	*Junior with Infant; First and Middle*	*Junior and Middle*	*All schools*
Percentage of schools providing tuition in reading outside registration classes:				
Throughout the full age range	*29·4*	*24·2*	*58·3*	*33·0*
For part of the age range	*40·5*	*47·3*	*34·8*	*42·7*
Not at all	*30·1*	*28·5*	*6·9*	*24·3*
All schools (100 per cent)	252	480	204	936

709 (76 per cent) of the 936 schools had at least one group* for poor readers. There were 3,816 of these groups, an average of four in every school which possessed them. Taking into account all the different forms of provision for poor readers, we calculated that the size of their groups was most commonly in the range of 2-10 pupils, the average being 6. Indeed, this was true of 67.8 per cent of the schools, while at least another 8.9 per cent always gave individual attention to their poor readers.

Note: These figures do not include groups specially formed for children whose first language was not English.

*The word 'group' must be taken here to include individual children, or groups of two or more who are withdrawn from their ordinary classes for remedial reading.

111 (11.9 per cent) of the 936 sample schools organised one or more special registration classes for poor readers, as follows:

Table 41

SPECIAL REGISTRATION CLASSES FOR POOR READERS

	Number of classes*				All schools
	0	1	2–3	4–5	
Schools					
Number	825	80	24	7	936
Percentage	*88·1*	*8·5*	*2·6*	*0·7*	*100·0*

*Including any registration classes in centres outside the schools.

(ii) Provision of Special Help

The heads were asked whether special help was given to children who achieved low scores on reading tests.

Table 42

SPECIAL HELP GIVEN TO CHILDREN WITH LOW SCORES ON READING TESTS, BY TYPE OF SCHOOL

	Infant and First	Junior with Infant: First and Middle	Junior and Middle	All schools
Percentage of schools which:				
Tested and gave special help	*31·8*	*77·5*	*94·1*	*68·8*
Tested and gave no special help	*46·4*	*19·8*	*5·4*	*23·8*
Did not test	*21·8*	*2·7*	*0·5*	*7·4*
All schools (100 per cent)	252	480	204	936

(iii) The Reading Ability of the Child

In addition to information about children receiving remedial teaching, the questionnaire provided other data which we cross-analysed against the reading ability of the child.

The primary school teachers were asked to rate the sample children in terms of their reading ability. Consequently all references to "ability" in this section should be taken to refer specifically to the teacher's rating of the child's reading ability. The teachers were asked to assume that on average 25 per cent of children were good readers for their age, 50 per cent average readers, and 25 per cent poor readers. We would have expected to obtain results which corresponded roughly to these proportions. In fact the results were as follows:

Table 43

TEACHER RATING OF READING ABILITY—6 AND 9 YEAR OLDS

	6 year olds	9 year olds
	%	%
Good reader	30·8	41·1
Average reader	47·0	37·4
Poor reader	22·2	21·5
Number of children	1,417	1,253

One possible interpretation of this table is that teachers are over-rating the ability of the children, in particular the 9 year olds. This could in turn mean that the teachers may be teaching a disquietingly high proportion of their pupils at an inappropriately advanced level. Another factor we cannot rule out is the possibility of an unknown but relevant bias in the selection of the sample child.

One hypothesis which the questionnaire data confirmed was that the "below average" child was likely to meet more teachers in a week than his more able peers. This might be because of a tendency in some schools to ask any teacher to take a single lesson now and again with the "below average" children, or it might reflect the common practice of using the help of part-time and peripatetic teachers with the remedial children.

(iv) The Teachers

Table 44

NUMBER OF TEACHERS BY WHOM 6 AND 9 YEAR OLDS ARE TAUGHT IN A WEEK, ACCORDING TO READING ABILITY

	6 year olds			9 year olds		
	Above average	*Average*	*Below average*	*Above average*	*Average*	*Below average*
Average number of teachers teaching the child in a week	2·1	2·1	2·4	3·2	3·2	3·4
Percentage of children being taught by the following number of teachers:						
1 teacher	35·2	34·8	27·1	8·5	10·4	8·5
2 teachers	34·6	32·6	30·6	24·5	24·3	18·2
3 teachers	18·8	21·5	24·8	28·3	28·8	27·5
4 teachers	8·7	7·5	10·5	19·4	20·2	25·3
5 or more teachers	2·7	3·6	7·0	19·2	16·2	20·4
Number of children	437	666	314	515	469	269

At all ability levels the 9 year old children were likely to encounter more teachers than the 6 year olds in the course of one week. However, in both age groups the children of below average reading ability were taught by more teachers than the average and above average children. 18 per cent of the below average 6 year olds were taught by 4 or more teachers, compared with 11 per cent of the average and above average children. Among the 9 year olds 46 per cent were taught by 4 or more teachers, compared with 36 per cent of the average and 38 per cent of the above average. We cannot be certain how the time was allocated among the teachers, but if it meant that the children went to different teachers for separate lessons we find the figure of 18 per cent particularly disturbing. If the children are experiencing reading difficulties at this age, they are in particular need of security, continuity, and stability.

Just over 29 per cent of the sample schools entitled to posts above Scale 1 had appointed a teacher to such a post because of his special responsibility for teaching poor readers. Over 10 per cent of the teachers with special responsibilities relating to English undertook two of the duties we listed, namely organising the library, advising their colleagues in the teaching of English, and the teaching of poor readers. In all, 813 teachers were involved in teaching registration classes or withdrawal groups for poor readers. Of the total, 557 (69 per cent) were teachers working only part-time in the school. Indeed we discovered that 57 per cent of all the part-time teachers in all the 936 primary schools were engaged in some teaching of remedial groups. In addition to their full and part-time staff, about one in five of the sample schools had one or more qualified teachers who visited the school at least once a week to assist and advise in the teaching of reading. These 188 peripatetic teachers provided a total of 470 half-day sessions for the schools in the survey week. It is clear from these results that the schools in the sample made very considerable use of peripatetic and part-time teachers for the teaching of reading. Teachers employed in this way are normally employed in teaching small withdrawal groups, leaving the class teacher free to work with the rest of his class. The fact that so many teachers may be involved in working with these children can cause considerable problems unless the class teacher is able to maintain constant contact with his part-time colleagues over the progress of the children in the withdrawal groups. Much of the benefit of the extra teaching may be lost if the class teacher is unable to build upon it within the normal classroom experience.

Excluding the peripatetics, we enquired how many of the teachers engaged in teaching the withdrawal groups or classes had attended relevant training courses. The results were as follows:

Table 45
ATTENDANCE AT RELEVANT COURSES BY TEACHERS OF WITHDRAWAL
GROUPS OR CLASSES

Percentage of teachers attending courses of the following duration:	
6 months*	*11·7*
6 weeks to 6 months*	*12·2*
Less than 6 weeks*	*46·9*
Percentage of teachers attending no courses	*29·2*
All teachers (100 per cent)	813

*Part-time courses are included within the appropriate full-time equivalent.

P

(v) Books

The questionnaire data also proved useful in testing the hypothesis that the able readers were more likely to have more books in their possession in school than the less able. The table below shows that in terms of average numbers of books the hypothesis was borne out:

Table 46

NUMBER OF BOOKS IN THE POSSESSION OF 6 AND 9 YEAR OLDS ACCORDING TO READING ABILITY

	6 year olds			9 year olds		
	Above average	*Average*	*Below average*	*Above average*	*Average*	*Below average*
Average number of books in the child's possession	3·0	2·7	2·2	3·6	3·5	3·3
Percentage of children with the following number of books:						
None	*1·3*	*4·2*	*6·7*	*1·0*	*1·0*	*1·8*
1	*12·1*	*16·5*	*29·0*	*5·4*	*7·9*	*10·8*
2	*31·1*	*35·7*	*34·1*	*20·0*	*22·6*	*25·6*
3–5	*49·8*	*39·9*	*29·0*	*57·7*	*53·5*	*50·9*
More than 5	*5·7*	*3·6*	*1·2*	*15·9*	*14·9*	*10·8*
Number of children	437	666	314	515	469	269

Two other factors are noticeable:

(a) There was a marked difference between the number of above average and below average 6 year olds without any books in their possession.

(b) There is a wide variety of practice between schools. There was a far greater difference between the practices of different schools in providing books the children could retain than there was in the provision they made for children of different reading abilities.

(vi) Nature of the Children's Written Work

We thought it likely that the teacher's rating of the child's reading ability might affect the balance of the written work he was asked to perform. The results given in Table 47 enable us to examine that hypothesis in the light of different kinds of written work children normally produce in school.

Table 47

VARIETY OF WRITING BY 6 AND 9 YEAR OLDS, ACCORDING TO READING
ABILITY

	Child's reading ability		
	Above average	*Average*	*Below average*
6 year olds			
Percentage of children writing on the following subjects:			
Original stories	*79·4*	*64·3*	*44·6*
Stories rewritten in own words	*81·5*	*74·9*	*67·8*
Writing derived from model making—			
art and craft	*44·8*	*39·2*	*40·8*
Personal investigations—science	*40·9*	*38·0*	*26·7*
Other aspects of daily life	*86·5*	*82·6*	*77·4*
Number of children	437	666	314
9 year olds			
Percentage of children writing on the following subjects:			
Original stories	*84·5*	*82·5*	*75·1*
Stories rewritten in own words	*85·6*	*84·0*	*85·1*
Writing derived from model making—			
art and craft	*31·1*	*30·7*	*29·4*
Personal investigations—science	*55·9*	*45·4*	*38·3*
Other aspects of daily life	*58·4*	*52·9*	*56·1*
Number of children	515	469	269

As might be expected, fewer of the below average 6 year olds were producing
writing. Moreover, the balance of their writing activities was found to be
different. There was little to choose between the three groups in their experience of writing based on model making or art and craft activities, and much
the same applies to writing on "other aspects of daily life". The rewriting of
stories in their own words was a little less common for the below average
6 year old, but the striking differences occurred in the writing of original
stories and in writing based upon personal investigations in science. These
aspects figured much less frequently in the work of the less able 6 year olds.
By the age of 9 the differences in the writing experience of children of varying
abilities were less pronounced, and the below average children were now
much more likely to be writing original stories and accounts of work in
science.

25.22 THE PUPILS AND THEIR WORK

The individual pupil sections of the questionnaire directed the class teachers'
attention to twelve distinct aspects of English taught in the primary school.
Each class teacher was asked to state the amount of time spent by the sample
child on each of the activities, both in class and optional time. "Class time"

is that time when the whole class is engaged in the same activity. The tables show that there are some aspects which the majority of teachers teach almost exclusively in class time. "Optional time", as its name suggests, denotes those times in the day when individual children are given some freedom in what they do, within certain prescribed limits.

The comments at the foot of each table attempt to draw out the main points of interest in the figures. They do not pretend to be an exhaustive analysis of the tables.

Table 48

TIME SPENT ON POETRY AND VERSE BY 6 AND 9 YEAR OLDS

	Classes spending these amounts of class time (minutes)						All classes	
	0	*1–30*	*31–60*	*61–90*	*91–120*	*121–150*	*151 or more*	*No.*	*%*
6 year olds Optional time (minutes)									
0	42	708	230	28	4			1,012	*71·4*
1–30	11	240	106	12	1			370	*26·1*
31–60		16	10	4				30	*2·1*
61–90		1		1				2	*0·1*
91–120									
121–150			3					3	*0·2*
151 or more									
All classes	53	965	349	45	5			1,417	
As a percentage of all classes	*3·7*	*68·1*	*24·6*	*3·2*	*0·4*				*100·0*
9 year olds Optional time (minutes)									
0	182	547	113	5	1			848	*67·7*
1–30	40	227	85	6				358	*28·6*
31–60	6	19	17					42	*3·4*
61–90			2	1				3	*0·2*
91–120	1							1	*0·1*
121–150									
151 or more			1					1	*0·1*
All classes	229	793	218	12	1			1,253	
As a percentage of all classes	*18·3*	*63·3*	*17·4*	*1·0*	*0·1*				*100·0*

Almost exactly 50 per cent of the 6 year old pupils spend up to half an hour a week of class time on poetry, and no optional time. This has declined to 44 per cent by the age of 9, and the percentage who spend no time at all on poetry has risen to 14 per cent from just under 3 per cent. The proportion of children experiencing it in class time in excess of 30 minutes dropped from 28 per cent at 6 years old to 18 per cent at 9, and there was no compensating increase in optional time. Fewer than a third of the children of either age group spent optional time on poetry, and then it was normally less than half an hour.

Table 49

TIME SPENT LISTENING TO STORIES READ OR TOLD BY THE TEACHER OR FROM A
SCHOOL BROADCAST (RADIO OR TV) BY 6 AND 9 YEAR OLDS

	Classes spending these amounts of class time (minutes)							All classes	
	0	1–30	31–60	61–90	91–120	121–150	151 or more	No.	%
6 year olds Optional time (minutes)									
0	1	30	120	281	356	258	134	1,180	83·3
1–30		8	18	32	34	31	5	128	9·0
31–60	1	1	2	15	17	16	4	56	4·0
61–90		1	1	9	4	5	7	27	1·9
91–120				3	3	3		9	0·6
121–150				3	2	5		10	0·7
151 or more				1			6	7	0·5
All classes	2	40	141	344	416	318	156	1,417	
As a percentage of all classes	0·1	2·8	10·0	24·3	29·4	22·4	11·0		100·0
9 year olds Optional time (minutes)									
0	38	302	427	204	75	30	16	1,092	87·2
1–30	3	29	42	14	4	3	2	97	7·7
31–60	2	6	21	9	2			40	3·2
61–90	1	1	8	2	1			13	1·0
91–120			2	3	3			8	0·6
121–150			2			1		3	0·2
151 or more									
All classes	44	338	502	232	85	34	18	1,253	
As a percentage of all classes	3·5	27·0	40·1	18·5	6·8	2·7	1·4		100·0

If one takes class and optional time together, nearly 90 per cent of the 6 year olds had over an hour a week listening to stories, while 35 per cent had over two hours, which is equivalent to just over 20 minutes a day. 17 per cent of the children heard stories as an option, and it seems likely that some of this might represent time spent listening to tape-recorded stories on headsets, either individually or in small groups. Only 30 per cent of the 9 year olds had over an hour a week of listening to stories, a figure which includes about 10 per cent with more than 1½ hours. Of the remainder 40 per cent had up to an hour a week, 27 per cent up to half an hour and the rest none at all. The drop in participation in this activity at age 9 was not compensated for by an increase in optional time. Indeed listening to stories was normally seen for both age-groups as a class activity and few devoted optional time to it. By age 9, most children would be capable of reading stories independently, but the schools still apparently recognised the value for children of hearing a good story well told.

Table 50

TIME SPENT ON ORAL ENGLISH (CONVERSATION, LANGUAGE GAMES, PLANNING WORK, DISCUSSION, REPORTING) BY 6 AND 9 YEAR OLDS

	Classes spending these amounts of class time (minutes)							All classes	
	0	*1–30*	*31–60*	*61–90*	*91–120*	*121–150*	*151 or more*	*No.*	*%*
6 year olds Optional time (minutes)									
0	11	105	152	140	80	46	46	580	*40·9*
1–30	6	83	140	102	56	27	26	440	*31·1*
31–60	6	11	53	52	27	25	13	187	*13·2*
61–90	3	4	11	30	14	13	16	91	*6·4*
91–120		3	3	6	12	3	1	28	*2·0*
121–150	1	1	2	6	3	4	5	22	*1·6*
151 or more		6	10	5	8	6	34	69	*4·9*
All classes	27	213	371	341	200	124	141	1,417	
As a percentage of all classes	*1·9*	*15·0*	*26·2*	*24·1*	*14·1*	*8·8*	*10·0*		*100·0*
9 year olds Optional time (minutes)									
0	42	249	238	104	46	15	12	706	*56·3*
1–30	28	105	123	70	17	7	9	359	*28·7*
31–60	8	20	39	37	17		3	124	*9·9*
61–90	2	4	11	9	4	5		35	*2·8*
91–120	2		2	4	5	2	2	17	*1·4*
121–150		1			4			5	*0·4*
151 or more	1			1			5	7	*0·6*
All classes	83	379	413	225	93	29	31	1,253	
As a percentage of all classes	*6·6*	*30·3*	*33·0*	*18·0*	*7·4*	*2·3*	*2·5*		*100·0*

Since oral work pervades almost the whole of the work in the primary school, it must be acknowledged that a question asking how much time was spent on it in a week has an element of artificiality. It may be that the various interpretations used by different teachers have accounted for the wide spread of times spent shown in the table above. Oral English was experienced by almost all the children in class time, while 59 per cent of 6 year olds and 44 per cent of 9 year olds also spent some optional time on it, usually up to half an hour, though occasionally more. As we have defined it, oral work includes "planning work, discussion and reporting", exploratory aspects of talk which can successfully operate with small groups in optional time. Nevertheless 41 per cent of 6 year olds and 56 per cent of 9 year olds spent no optional time at all on oral work. Overall only 66 per cent of the 9 year olds spent more than half an hour a week of both class *and* optional time on it. The corresponding figure for 6 year olds was 86 per cent. The distribution of higher time allocations shows that the amount of explicit attention to oral English declines substantially from 6 years old to 9 years old.

Table 51

TIME SPENT ON IMPROVISED DRAMA (SOCIAL/DRAMATIC PLAY, ETC)
BY 6 AND 9 YEAR OLDS

	Classes spending these amounts of class time (minutes)						All classes	
	0	1–30	31–60	61–90	91–120	121–150	151 or more	No.	%
6 year olds Optional time (minutes)									
0	212	392	101	24	10	3	2	744	52·5
1–30	117	204	63	12	3	2		401	28·3
31–60	49	55	49	9	3	1		166	11·7
61–90	18	18	17	7	3	4		67	4·7
91–120	8	3	5	1	2			19	1·3
121–150	1	5	1		1	1		9	0·6
151 or more	3	2	2				4	11	0·8
All classes	408	679	238	53	22	11	6	1,417	
As a percentage of all classes	28·8	47·9	16·8	3·7	1·6	0·8	0·4		100·0
9 year olds Optional time (minutes)									
0	520	375	134	25	1		3	1,058	84·4
1–30	41	66	37	6			1	151	12·1
31–60	16	7	13	3				39	3·1
61–90		1		2				3	0·2
91–120	1							1	0·1
121–150	1							1	0·1
151 or more									
All classes	579	449	184	36	1		4	1,253	
As a percentage of all classes	46·2	35·8	14·7	2·9	0·1		0·3		100·0

Very many more of the 6 year olds had improvised drama than the 9 year olds, both in class and optional time. As many as 42 per cent of the 9 year old classes had *no* improvised drama at all. The figure for the 6 year olds is much lower at 15 per cent. In optional time almost half of the 6 year olds had some improvised drama, compared with only 15 per cent of the 9 year olds. This movement, like the similar one in poetry, is a revealing illustration of a diminution in 'imaginative work' as the child grows older.

Table 52

TIME SPENT ON WRITING (STORIES, PERSONAL ACCOUNTS, CREATIVE, ETC)
BY 6 AND 9 YEAR OLDS

	Classes spending these amounts of class time (minutes)							All classes	
	0	1–30	31–60	61–90	91–120	121–150	151 or more	No.	%
6 year olds Optional time (minutes)									
0	23	72	127	145	137	88	55	647	45·7
1–30	20	34	84	96	57	44	29	364	25·7
31–60	22	8	35	41	46	29	19	200	14·1
61–90	17	2	10	19	11	9	9	77	5·4
91–120	26	5	4	6	14	9	6	70	4·9
121–151	16		3			6	2	27	1·9
151 or more	22		1	1		2	6	32	2·3
All classes	146	121	264	308	265	187	126	1,417	
As a percentage of all classes	10·3	8·5	18·6	21·7	18·7	13·2	8·9		100·0
9 year olds Optional time (minutes)									
0	23	66	261	179	66	21	17	633	50·5
1–30	11	32	156	78	41	17	10	345	27·5
31–60	12	18	60	41	33	15	6	185	14·8
61–90	14	6	13	9	5	2	3	52	4·2
91–120	8	4	2	3	2	3	2	24	1·9
121–150	4	1	2		1			8	0·6
151 or more	1	2		2	1			6	0·5
All classes	73	129	494	312	149	58	38	1,253	
As a percentage of all classes	5·8	10·8	39·4	24·9	11·9	4·6	3·0		100·0

Among the 6 year olds there is a marked contrast between extremes of experience of this work. Between 1 per cent and 2 per cent of the children of each age group did no writing of this kind at all in the week, while 21 per cent of the 6 year olds and 11 per cent of 9 year olds were shown as devoting to it over 1½ hours of class time and some optional time, usually up to half an hour or an hour. It is clear that in a substantial number of schools writing is taken as a class activity. 46 per cent of the 6 year olds did their writing entirely this way, with no optional time allocation, while 8 per cent did it wholly as an option. The corresponding figures for 9 year olds are 50 per cent and 4 per cent. Overall, the 9 year olds tended to spend less time on writing than the six year olds.

Table 53

TIME SPENT ON TOPICS (READING AND WRITING MAINLY BASED ON
REFERENCE BOOKS) BY 6 AND 9 YEAR OLDS

	Classes spending these amounts of class time (minutes)							All classes	
	0	*1–30*	*31–60*	*61–90*	*91–120*	*121–150*	*151 or more*	*No.*	*%*
6 year olds Optional time (minutes)									
0	479	192	120	53	23	9	2	878	*62·0*
1–30	95	136	80	23	17	1	3	355	*25·1*
31–60	41	24	32	16	9	2	1	125	*8·8*
61–90	15	2	4	10	5		1	37	*2·6*
91–120	4	2	2	2			3	13	*0·9*
121–150	2		1				2	5	*0·4*
151 or more		1	1				2	4	*0·3*
All classes	636	357	240	104	54	12	14	1,417	
As a percentage of all classes	*44·9*	*25·2*	*16·9*	*7·3*	*3·8*	*0·9*	*1·0*		*100·0*
9 year olds Optional time (minutes)									
0	80	57	99	76	43	22	23	400	*31·9*
1–30	44	65	111	70	42	11	8	351	*28·0*
31–60	53	38	68	61	55	18	6	299	*23·9*
61–90	26	12	14	27	14	12	4	109	*8·7*
91–120	26	2	5	4	8	1	3	49	*3·9*
121–150	13		1	1	2	4		21	*1·7*
151 or more	16	2		1	1		4	24	*1·9*
All classes	258	176	298	240	165	68	48	1,253	
As a percentage of all classes	*20·6*	*14·1*	*23·8*	*19·2*	*13·2*	*5·4*	*3·8*		*100·0*

As many as 66 per cent of the 6 year old classes were doing some topic work, 13 per cent of them spending over an hour of class time a week on it. 45 per cent of the 6 year olds compared with 21 per cent of the 9 year olds had no class time on this work, and the 9 year olds were twice as likely to spend optional time in this way. At age 9 the proportion of children doing no topic work had dropped dramatically to 6 per cent (from 34 per cent at age 6). 42 per cent of 9 year olds had over an hour a week of class time on it, and only 32 per cent no optional time at all. The figure of 42 per cent for over an hour of class time is almost identical with that for time given to personal writing; in the case of the 6 year olds the proportions are 63 per cent for personal writing and 13 per cent for topic work. This seems to indicate a shift towards what is being thought of as more 'serious' work as the children get older. However, the experience of our visits was that much of the writing done in the name of topic work amounts to no more than copying.

394 PART NINE: THE SURVEY

Table 54

TIME SPENT ON INDIVIDUAL READING OF STORIES (EXCLUDING READING PRACTICE) BY 6 AND 9 YEAR OLDS

	Classes spending these amounts of class time (minutes)							All classes	
	0	1–30	31–60	61–90	91–120	121–150	151 or more	No.	%
6 year olds Optional time (minutes)									
0	132	72	34	10	4	1	1	254	17·9
1–30	226	219	121	24	3	1	3	597	42·1
31–60	165	84	90	36	10	2		387	27·3
61–90	55	10	22	15	8		2	112	7·9
91–120	9	10	1	4	1	6	1	32	2·3
121–150	6	2		1	4	2	4	19	1·3
151 or more	9	1		1	2		3	16	1·1
All classes	602	398	268	91	32	12	14	1,417	
As a percentage of all classes	42·5	28·0	18·9	6·4	2·3	0·9	1·0		100·0
9 year olds Optional time (minutes)									
0	58	75	87	34	16	7	2	279	22·3
1–30	118	214	125	42	14	9	2	524	41·8
31–60	85	76	108	47	8	4	1	329	26·3
61–90	27	13	14	13	8	5		80	6·4
91–120	10	1	10	6	5	1		33	2·6
121–150	2	1		1		1		5	0·4
151 or more	2		1					3	0·2
All classes	302	380	345	143	51	27	5	1,253	
As a percentage of all classes	24·1	30·3	27·5	11·4	4·0	2·2	0·4		100·0

9 per cent of the classes with 6 year olds gave no time at all to this experience, 42 per cent no class time and 18 per cent no optional time. The biggest class time allocation was 28 per cent in the 1–30 minutes category for 6 year olds and 30 per cent for 9 year olds. For both age groups the weight of this activity was in optional time, as one would expect. 54 per cent of the 6 year old children devoted more than half an hour of both class and optional time to it, while the corresponding figure for 9 year olds was 63 per cent. Private reading seems to be a well established practice in school for children of both age groups. Among the 9 year olds the percentage spending no time at all upon it has dropped to 5 per cent, and one can only express surprise that there are any children at all in this category. Overall, more of the 9 year olds than 6 year olds were given time for this kind of reading and the amount of time tended on average to be greater for the older children.

Table 55

TIME SPENT ON READING PRACTICE (GRADED AND SUPPLEMENTARY
READERS, PHONIC PRACTICE) BY 6 AND 9 YEAR OLDS

	Classes spending these amounts of class time (minutes)							All classes	
	0	*1–30*	*31–60*	*61–90*	*91–120*	*121–150*	*151 or more*	*No.*	*%*
6 year olds Optional time (minutes)									
0	11	109	212	140	78	55	43	648	*45·7*
1–30	16	104	153	84	44	25	15	441	*31·1*
31–60	25	27	51	44	25	13	11	196	*13·8*
61–90	8	9	14	14	16	10	8	79	*5·6*
91–120		7	5	2	7	6	5	32	*2·3*
121–150	1		1	1	1	5	2	11	*0·8*
151 or more		1		1	1	3	4	10	*0·7*
All classes	61	257	436	286	172	117	88	1,417	
As a percentage of all classes	*4·3*	*18·1*	*30·8*	*20·2*	*12·1*	*8·3*	*6·2*		*100·0*
9 year olds Optional time (minutes)									
0	319	253	164	84	49	30	13	912	*72·8*
1–30	27	68	67	35	14	11	4	226	*18·0*
31–60	17	19	22	14	6	8	1	87	*6·9*
61–90	2	3	8	5	1	1		20	*1·6*
91–120					2	1		3	*0·2*
121–150		1				1		2	*0·2*
151 or more			2				1	3	*0·2*
All classes	365	344	263	138	72	52	19	1,253	
As a percentage of all classes	*29·1*	*27·5*	*21·0*	*11·0*	*5·8*	*4·1*	*1·5*		*100·0*

Fewer than 1 per cent of infant classes had no reading practice, while a further 16 per cent
had less than half an hour a week of class and/or optional time. The remainder did more
than this, although the total of class and optional time seldom exceeded two hours a
week. Most commonly the 6 year olds had between 30 and 60 minutes a week, and for
half of these children the time was supplemented by optional time of up to 30 minutes or
occasionally more. This amounts to no more than about 15 minutes a day on reading
practice. As might be expected, the number of children who had no time on reading
practice has risen to 25 per cent by the age of 9 (compared with less than 1 per cent at
age 6). Most commonly the 9 year olds were given up to half an hour or an hour of
class time on it, and 27 per cent supplemented this with some optional time. The figure of
25 per cent spending *no* time on reading practice is to be compared with the figure of
6 per cent for topic work and 4 per cent for private reading. This reflects the development
of the independent reading ability of the 9 year olds. However, if one considers these
results in another way, it can be said that 75 per cent of the teachers of these children
still think it necessary to spend some time on reading practice.

Table 56

TIME SPENT ON COMPREHENSION AND VOCABULARY EXERCISES (FROM
BOOKS, CARDS, READING LABORATORIES, ETC) BY 6 AND 9 YEAR OLDS

	Classes spending these amounts of class time (minutes)							All classes	
	0	*1–30*	*31–60*	*61–90*	*91–120*	*121–150*	*151 or more*	*No.*	*%*
6 year olds Optional time (minutes)									
0	218	259	228	129	71	28	19	952	*67·2*
1–30	58	74	79	35	18	3	6	273	*19·3*
31–60	28	18	32	20	15	6		119	*8·4*
61–90	5	5	7	6	6	5	2	36	*2·5*
91–120	2	1	3	3	6	4	1	20	*1·4*
121–150	1	2	1	2	1	1	1	9	*0·6*
151 or more		1	1	2		2	2	8	*0·6*
All classes	312	360	351	197	117	49	31	1,417	
As a percentage of *all classes*	*22·0*	*25·4*	*24·8*	*13·9*	*8·3*	*3·5*	*2·2*		*100·0*
9 year olds Optional time (minutes)									
0	92	212	300	137	63	28	18	850	*67·8*
1–30	25	56	92	62	22	9	3	269	*21·5*
31–60	16	10	26	23	7	3	3	88	*7·0*
61–90	9	4	4	6	1	1		25	*2·0*
91–120	9		1	2	2	1		15	*1·2*
121–150	3			1		1		5	*0·4*
151 or more		1						1	*0·1*
All classes	154	283	423	231	95	43	24	1,253	
As a percentage of *all classes*	*12·3*	*22·6*	*33·8*	*18·4*	*7·6*	*3·4*	*1·9*		*100·0*

What is surprising here is the amount of time spent on such work by 6 year olds—most
of it during class time. 67 per cent of all the classes spent no optional time on it, 22 per
cent no class time, and 15 per cent none of either. Over twice as many 6 year olds (15 per
cent) as 9 year olds (7 per cent) did no comprehension and vocabulary exercises. 78 per
cent of the 6 year olds had some of this work in class time, usually up to 30 or 60 minutes,
although over a quarter of them did rather more. The allocation of class time for 9 year
olds was somewhat greater; 88 per cent of them spent time on this work, 23 per cent up
to 30 minutes, 34 per cent 30 minutes to an hour, and 31 per cent more than an hour.
Only about one third of each age group devoted optional time to it. Usually it was up to
30 minutes or, less commonly, 60 minutes or occasionally more. 68 per cent of the 9 year
olds did none of this work in optional time. It is principally a class activity, and 65 per
cent of the sample gave more than 30 minutes a week to it.

Table 57

TIME SPENT ON LANGUAGE USAGE (GRAMMAR, PUNCTUATION, ETC)
BY 6 AND 9 YEAR OLDS .

	Classes spending these amounts of class time (minutes)							All classes	
	0	*1–30*	*31–60*	*61–90*	*91–120*	*121–150*	*151 or more*	*No.*	*%*
6 year olds Optional time (minutes)									
0	673	561	52	11	1			1,298	*91·6*
1–30	45	51	9	4	1			110	*7·8*
31–60		3	2	1	1			7	*0·5*
61–90					1			1	*0·1*
91–120									
121–150						1		1	*0·1*
151 or more									
All classes	718	615	63	16	4	1		1,417	
As a percentage of all classes	*50·7*	*43·4*	*4·5*	*1·1*	*0·3*	*0·1*			*100·0*
9 year olds Optional time (minutes)									
0	183	572	253	64	19	5		1,096	*87·5*
1–30	30	49	29	15	5			128	*10·2*
31–60	5	6	9	4	1			25	*2·0*
61–90		2		2				4	*0·3*
91–120									
121–150									
151 or more									
All classes	218	629	291	85	25	5		1,253	
As a percentage of all classes	*17·4*	*50·2*	*23·2*	*6·8*	*2·0*	*0·4*			*100·0*

As might be expected, as many as 47 per cent of 6 year olds spent no time at all on this work. Of those who did the majority encountered it only in class time, and then seldom for more than half an hour a week. Only 8 per cent of the children spent any optional time on it, and scarcely ever more than 30 minutes a week. At the age of 9 many more children practised this kind of work, largely as a class activity, only 15 per cent spending no time at all on it. 50 per cent of the children were occupied on it in this way for up to half an hour, 23 per cent up to an hour, and 9 per cent over an hour. For a few this class work was supplemented by optional time, though this was seldom ever more than half an hour a week.

Table 58

TIME SPENT ON SPELLING BY 6 AND 9 YEAR OLDS

	Classes spending these amounts of class time (minutes)							All classes	
	0	*1–30*	*31–60*	*61–90*	*91–120*	*121–150*	*151 or more*	*No.*	*%*
6 year olds Optional time (minutes)									
0	499	618	76	14	3		1	1,211	*85·5*
1–30	63	96	20	5	1			185	*13·1*
31–60	3	5	7	1	1			17	*1·2*
61–90			2	1				3	*0·2*
91–120									
121–150			1					1	*0·1*
151 or more									
All classes	565	719	106	21	5		1	1,417	
As a percentage of all classes	*39·9*	*50·7*	*7·5*	*1·5*	*0·4*		*0·1*		*100·0*
9 year olds Optional time (minutes)									
0	129	643	162	19	3			956	*76·3*
1–30	35	184	46	4	2			271	*21·6*
31–60	3	7	8	3	1			22	*1·8*
61–90		2		1				3	*0·2*
91–120									
121–150						1		1	*0·1*
151 or more									
All classes	167	836	216	27	6	1		1,253	
As a percentage of all classes	*13·3*	*66·7*	*17·2*	*2·2*	*0·5*	*0·1*			*100·0*

Of the 6 year olds 35 per cent spent no time at all on spelling, a figure which had dropped to 10 per cent by the age of 9. Most 6 year olds spending time on spelling tended to do so as a class activity of up to half an hour a week, while only 15 per cent did any spelling in optional time. Among the 9 year olds only 13 per cent had no class time on it. Again the biggest representation was in the 1–30 minute band, which accounts for 67 per cent of the children. By the age of 9 the proportion of children spending optional time on spelling had risen from 15 per cent to 24 per cent. As many as 15 per cent of 9 year olds had up to half an hour of both optional and class time on it, and 20 per cent more time than this. Thus the picture is of a marked increase in spelling work from 6 to 9, with spelling still seen as largely a class activity.

Table 59

TIME SPENT ON HANDWRITING BY 6 AND 9 YEAR OLDS

	Classes spending these amounts of class time (minutes)							All classes	
	0	*1–30*	*31–60*	*61–90*	*91–120*	*121–150*	*151 or more*	*No.*	*%*
6 year olds Optional time (minutes)									
0	173	697	189	31	4	4	1	1,099	77·6
1–30	30	137	54	13	6	2	1	243	17·2
31–60	10	13	26	5	3	2		59	4·2
61–90	1	2	1	2	1	2		9	0·6
91–120			1	1				2	0·1
121–150			1		1		1	3	0·2
151 or more	1	1						2	0·1
All classes	215	850	272	52	15	11	2	1,417	
As a percentage of all classes	*15·2*	*60·0*	*19·2*	*3·7*	*1·1*	*0·8*	*0·1*		*100·0*
9 year olds Optional time (minutes)									
0	257	614	137	8	4			1,020	81·4
1–30	45	126	26	6	2	1	1	207	16·5
31–60	3	4	10	2				19	1·5
61–90	1	2	2	2				7	0·6
91–120									
121–150									
151 or more									
All classes	306	746	175	18	6	1	1	1,253	
As a percentage of all classes	*24·4*	*59·5*	*14·0*	*1·4*	*0·5*	*0·1*	*0·1*		*100·0*

12 per cent of 6 year olds had no time allocated to handwriting, and the figure had risen to 21 per cent in the case of 9 year olds. For both age groups the most common pattern was to practise it as a class activity, and for 60 per cent of the children this amounted to no more than half an hour a week. 25 per cent of 6 year olds and 15 per cent of 9 year olds spent more time than this. Only 20 per cent of children practised handwriting in optional time, and then it seldom exceeded half an hour a week. Overall, for both age groups the picture is one of some attention to handwriting, seldom any more than half an hour a week, and certainly less than the 15 minutes every day which was once the pattern in many schools.

25.23   THE SMALL SCHOOL

Among the 936 sample schools were 129 (13.8 per cent) with fewer than 71
children on roll. In England in January 1973 there were 207 one-teacher
schools, 1,809 two-teacher schools and 1,683 three-teacher schools*. Some
of these would be new ones built to serve new housing areas, schools which
had not yet reached their intended total roll, but the majority would be likely
to be established rural schools, very probably with wide agricultural catchment
areas. Some of our questionnaire results have been stratified by size of school
to compare provision in small schools with that in larger ones. In what follows
the word "small" signifies a school with fewer than 71 children on roll.

(i) Teachers

We have already remarked that the smaller schools do not qualify for posts
above Scale 1 for assistant teachers. Consequently these schools are almost
invariably staffed by a full-time teaching head with perhaps one or two
teachers paid on Scale 1, and possibly some part-time assistance. Between
them they cater for all the various needs of the children in their care and it is
unusual to find a small school whose head does not know all the children and
their work in some detail. Our questionnaire data gave no information on
average class size by size of school but an indication of the staffing provision
is given in the fact that the ratio of pupils to teachers in schools of up to
70 pupils in the sample was 17.5:1, compared with 25.5:1 in all schools.
In the smaller schools a wider spread of non-teaching duties is shared between
fewer teachers, but communication between members of staff is a much
simpler matter. 24 per cent of the small schools in our sample had the full-
time equivalent of one teacher over and above the number of registration
classes, while just 2 per cent had 2 "excess" teachers each. The comparative
figures for schools of different sizes appear in Table 60 below.

*These figures refer exclusively to the number of full-time teachers employed in the
schools.

Table 60

PERCENTAGE OF SCHOOLS WITH TEACHERS IN EXCESS OF NUMBER OF
REGISTRATION CLASSES, BY SIZE OF SCHOOL

	Schools with the following number of pupils						*All schools*
	Up to 70	*71–150*	*151–200*	*201–250*	*251–350*	*351 and over*	
Percentage of schools with:							
0 "Excess" teachers	74·4	38·8	6·3	3·6	1·2	1·2	18·2
1 "Excess" teacher	24·0	53·1	50·8	45·0	28·5	17·0	35·3
2 "Excess" teachers	1·6	7·5	36·7	41·4	45·3	31·5	29·2
3 "Excess" teachers	—	0·6	4·7	7·9	21·1	23·3	11·1
4 or more "Excess" teachers	—	—	1·5	2·1	3·9	27·0	6·1
All schools (100%)	129	147	128	140	232	160	936

Note: The "excess" teachers are calculated by counting both full-time and the full-time
equivalent of part-time teachers.

In addition 24 of the 129 small schools had the services of one peripatetic teacher to help with reading. At 19 per cent this was consistent with the average for "all schools", while only 10 of the 936 schools had the services of more than one such peripatetic teacher. The table below shows that the small number of peripatetic teachers of reading was spread fairly evenly across the different sizes of schools, and that the smallest schools fared well in this respect. However, when the figures are taken in conjunction with those in the previous table, it is clear that their small size precludes any real flexibility in deployment of staff.

Table 61
DISTRIBUTION OF PERIPATETIC TEACHERS BY SIZE OF SCHOOL

	Schools with the following number of pupils						*All schools*
	Up to 70	*71–150*	*151–200*	*201–250*	*251–350*	*351 and over*	
Percentage of schools with:							
No peripatetic teachers	*81·4*	*83·0*	*86·7*	*77·9*	*81·5*	*77·4*	*81·2*
1 peripatetic teacher	*18·6*	*16·3*	*12·5*	*21·4*	*16·8*	*20·8*	*17·7*
2 or more peripatetic teachers	—	*0·7*	*0·8*	*0·7*	*1·7*	*1·9*	*1·1*
All schools (100%)	129	147	128	140	232	160	936

Professional contact with other teachers is often a problem for the small school, but one which the teachers themselves seemed to be making efforts to overcome. The survey results showed that 44 per cent of the schools with up to five teachers had had at least one teacher attending a Teachers' Centre for some activity connected with the teaching of English in the five months to January 1973, compared with an average for all schools of 58 per cent.

(ii) Resources

(*a*) *Books*
The questionnaire data were not analysed to give figures of book provision by size of school, because previous studies have shown that the wide variety of provision is attributable to numerous factors which are independent of the size of the school, e.g. local circumstances, parental involvement, and the school's own attitude. Our own views on book provision for small schools appear in paragraph 21.23.

(*b*) *Audio-Visual Aids*
We argue in Chapter 22 that the fact that a school is small does not mean that it thereby needs a narrower range of equipment than a larger school. Table 36 showed the provision of audio-visual equipment by size of school. A digest of that information appears in the table below, and reveals that the smallest schools were in every case worse off than the average of all other schools.

Table 62

PERCENTAGE OF SCHOOLS USING PARTICULAR ITEMS OF AUDIO-VISUAL
EQUIPMENT IN CONNECTION WITH THE TEACHING OF ENGLISH

	Schools with up to 70 pupils	Schools with over 70 pupils
Percentage of schools using:		
Record player	*62·8*	*78·4*
Mains tape recorder	*65·9*	*82·0*
Battery tape recorder	*17·1*	*46·5*
Filmstrip/Slide/Loop projector	*44·2*	*59·4*
Film projector	*11·6*	*25·0*
Radio	*86·1*	*88·2*
Television set	*80·1*	*83·5*
Language Master	*4·7*	*12·4*
Talking Page	*0·8*	*1·7*
Synchrofax	*0·8*	*2·5*
Other teaching machines	*5·4*	*8·9*
All schools (100 per cent)	129	807

III SECONDARY COMMENTARY

25.24 THE SCHOOLS

Table 63

THE SAMPLE SECONDARY SCHOOLS

Type	Number
Modern	165
Grammar	73
Comprehensive	140
Technical	5
Other	9
Total	392

The 'General' sections of the questionnaires provided information about
the schools themselves, their size, staffing and pupil numbers, organisation,
equipment, and the special help they gave to poor readers. The 392 sample
schools had 260,579 full-time pupils on roll, with 14,643 full-time and
1,644 part-time qualified teachers. If one takes part-timers in terms of
equivalents of a full-time teacher, the whole staff complement amounted to
the equivalent of 15,452 full-time teachers, giving an average of 16.9 pupils
per teacher. The pupil/teacher ratio for maintained secondary schools
(excluding middle schools) in England in January 1973 was identical at
16.9:1. (Both figures follow the normal convention of including the head as
a member of the teaching force of the school.)

The 'Individual Pupil' sections of the questionnaires collected information
on the school work and experience of 939 12 year olds and 1,052 14 year olds,

all in different classes. Data on the individual pupils appear throughout this section, and their work in English is examined in paragraph 25.31.

25.25   THE ORGANISATION OF ENGLISH TEACHING

(i) School Organisation of English Teaching

Table 64

SECONDARY SCHOOL ORGANISATION OF ENGLISH TEACHING

Percentage of schools where English teaching is organised:	
A. Under a separate English department	59·7
B. Under a separate department except for remedial	37·0
C. As part of a multi-subject department	1·8
D. As C above except for remedial	0·8
E. In none of these ways	0·8
All schools (100 per cent)	392

It was most common to find English teaching organised by a separate English department, though in over a third of all schools the responsibility for the English of some pupils lay with the remedial department. Other patterns were uncommon.

(ii) English within Integrated Studies

There has been much discussion in recent years of the practice of schools which have abandoned the teaching of English as a separate subject in favour of an integrated approach, where it becomes part of a humanities or a social studies course. We therefore set out to find how widespread was this practice in the schools in our sample. It emerged that 93 per cent of classes containing 12 year olds and 94 per cent of those containing 14 year olds were taught English as a separately time-tabled subject. For only 2 per cent of the classes of 12 year olds and 3 per cent of those of 14 year olds was English assimilated into an integrated scheme of which it was an indistinguishable element. In the remainder English was part of an integrated scheme but still a recognisable element within it.

(iii) School Organisation of Drama

In paragraph 15.9 we mentioned various ways in which drama could be organised. The questionnaire showed that in 84 per cent of schools drama was part of the work of the English department; 10 per cent of schools had separate drama departments; 4 per cent taught it in combination with one or more other subjects excluding English, and the remaining 2 per cent taught no drama at all.

(iv) Type of Classes

Question 4 of the Individual Pupil Section of the questionnaire was designed to make it possible to tabulate much of the data by type of class. For each age-group the separate types of group are exclusive. A pupil in a group with examination objectives is recorded only as in an examination group, even though it is conceivable that he may also be receiving remedial help.

The types of group are as follows:

12 YEAR OLDS

Remedial	Pupils assessed by their teachers as being in need of special help, and receiving it. (11.4 per cent)
Other	Pupils not so assessed. (88.6 per cent)

14 YEAR OLDS

Examination	Pupils in a group some or all of whose members have external examination objectives. (84.7 per cent)
Non-examination	Pupils of varying levels of ability following courses with no examination objectives. (10.2 per cent)
Remedial	Pupils assessed by their teachers as being in need of special help and receiving it. (5.1 per cent)

(The percentages in brackets after each definition show that group as a proportion of the whole age-group.)

(v) Size of English Teaching Groups

Diagram 14

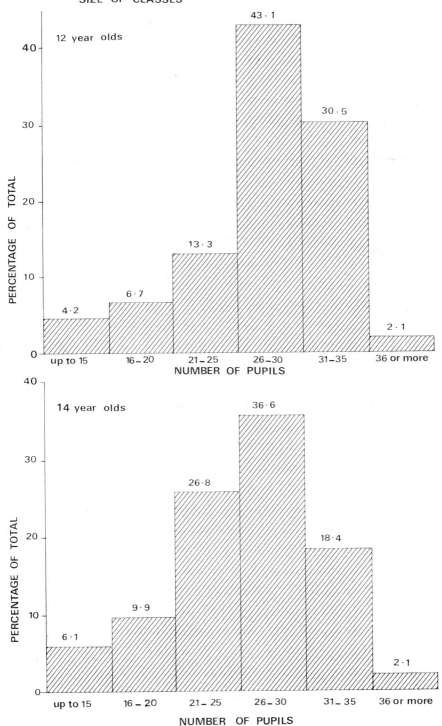

SIZE OF CLASSES

There were 55,978 12 year olds and 55,498 14 year olds in the sample schools. The 12 year olds were organised into 2,010 English teaching groups with an average group size of 28 pupils. The 14 year olds received a more generous staffing allocation, being organised into 2,125 groups with an average size of 26. The full details are given in Table 65 where the differential staffing of classes by age and type is shown.

Table 65

COMPARISON OF CLASS SIZES OF REMEDIAL AND OTHER CLASSES—12 AND 14 YEAR OLDS

	12 year olds			*14 year olds*			
	Reme-dial classes	*Other classes*	*All classes*	*Reme-dial classes*	*Non-exam classes*	*Exam classes*	*All classes*
Average size of class	19	29	28	16	22	27	26
				Percentage of classes			
Size of classes:							
1–5	*1·9*	—	*0·2*	*1·9*	—	—	*0·1*
6–10	*8·4*	*0·1*	*1·1*	*20·8*	—	*0·4*	*1·4*
11–15	*17·8*	*1·0*	*2·9*	*22·6*	*16·8*	*2·1*	*4·6*
16–20	*32·7*	*3·4*	*6·7*	*39·6*	*23·4*	*6·5*	*9·9*
21–25	*28·0*	*11·4*	*13·3*	*9·4*	*32·7*	*27·1*	*26·8*
26–30	*9·4*	*47·5*	*43·1*	*1·9*	*20·6*	*40·6*	*36·6*
31–35	*0·9*	*34·3*	*30·5*	*3·8*	*5·6*	*20·9*	*18·5*
36 and over	*0·9*	*2·3*	*2·1*	—	*0·9*	*2·4*	*2·1*
Total number of classes	107	832	939	53	107	892	1,052

Note: This table includes all classes for whom English was completely assimilated into an integrated scheme.

(vi) Formation of Groups for English Teaching

Heads were asked to say how the 12 and 14 year olds were grouped for the teaching of English. Where more than one method was in operation they were asked to indicate the one which involved the largest number of pupils in the age group. The results of that question appear in Diagram 15 below, where the different forms of grouping have been arranged in descending order of frequency for 12 year olds. This presentation has been adopted in order to show how the relative frequency of different methods of grouping changes from 12 to 14. For the older children the existence of English groups formed according to course or option choice provides an extra dimension. These would include groups formed for English according to their examination options.

Diagram 15

METHODS OF GROUPING FOR THE TEACHING OF ENGLISH IN THE SAMPLE
SECONDARY SCHOOLS—12 AND 14 YEAR OLDS

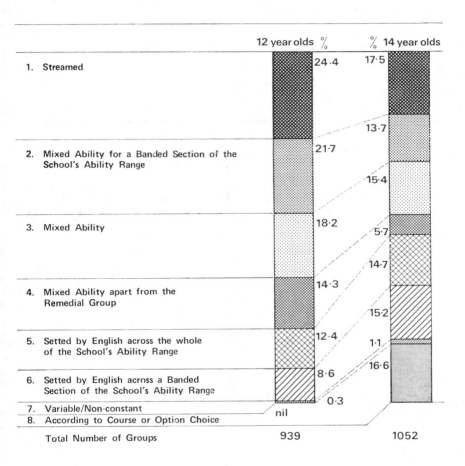

	12 year olds %	% 14 year olds
1. Streamed	24·4	17·5
		13·7
2. Mixed Ability for a Banded Section of the School's Ability Range	21·7	
		15·4
3. Mixed Ability	18·2	5·7
		14·7
4. Mixed Ability apart from the Remedial Group	14·3	
		15·2
5. Setted by English across the whole of the School's Ability Range	12·4	1·1
6. Setted by English across a Banded Section of the School's Ability Range	8·6	16·6
7. Variable/Non-constant	0·3	
8. According to Course or Option Choice	nil	
Total Number of Groups	939	1052

Mixed ability teaching in the sample was evidently very common for 12 year old classes, but less so for 14 year olds, the respective figures being 54.2 per cent and 34.8 per cent. Both totals contain a certain element of selection in that some schools exempt from mixed ability teaching those pupils receiving remedial teaching. The remainder of the schools operated streaming or setting for English in one form or another. Clearly, therefore, some form of selection was still in practice in many secondary schools.

(vii) Time Spent on English

(*a*) *In School*

Information from the Individual Pupil sections of the questionnaire enabled us to construct Table 66, which indicates the amount of time spent on English in school during one week.

Table 66

TIME SPENT ON ENGLISH BY 12 AND 14 YEAR OLDS

	12 year olds		14 year olds			
	Reme-dial classes	*All classes*	*Reme-dial classes*	*Non-exam classes*	*Exam classes*	*All classes*
Average time spent on English	4 hrs. 2 mins.	3 hrs. 22 mins.	3 hrs. 21 mins.	3 hrs. 12 mins.	3 hrs. 16 mins.	3 hrs. 16 mins.
	Percentage of classes					
Minutes						
31–60	—	*0·1*	—	—	*0·1*	*0·1*
61–90	*1·0*	*0·7*	—	*4·4*	—	*0·4*
91–120	*2·0*	*1·2*	*2·2*	*3·3*	*0·9*	*1·2*
121–150	*1·0*	*4·8*	*10·9*	*6·7*	*5·8*	*6·1*
151–180	*10·0*	*25·5*	*19·6*	*21·1*	*26·7*	*25·9*
181–210	*21·0*	*35·7*	*32·6*	*33·3*	*41·5*	*40·4*
211–240	*19·0*	*15·6*	*19·6*	*16·7*	*14·6*	*15·0*
241–300	*28·0*	*12·3*	*10·9*	*14·4*	*8·3*	*9·0*
301–360	*15·0*	*3·6*	*4·3*	—	*1·7*	*1·7*
361 and over	*3·0*	*0·6*	—	—	*0·3*	*0·3*
Total number of classes	100	917	46	90	881	1,017

> *Note:* This table excludes classes for whom English is completely assimilated into an integrated scheme.
>
> See Introduction to this chapter for a reconciliation of this Table and Table 91.

We enquired in some detail into the amount of time spent on English by the sample children, and into the activities which occupied that time. The latter are analysed in paragraph 25.31: The Pupils and Their Work. The evidence of Table 66 is that the majority of the pupils spent between 2½ and 4 hours on English in school. The average weekly time lay between 3 hrs. 12 mins. and 3 hrs. 22 mins. for all except the 12 year old 'Remedial' pupils, who had almost an hour more. Indeed 18 per cent of these pupils were allocated more than 5 hours of English during the week.

Table 67

NUMBER OF PERIODS OF ENGLISH PER WEEK FOR 12 AND 14 YEAR OLDS

	12 year olds			14 year olds			
	Reme-dial classes	Other classes	All classes	Reme-dial classes	Non-exam classes	Exam classes	All classes
Average number of periods per week	6·6	5·4	5·5	5·6	5·1	5·2	5·2
	Percentage of pupils/classes						
Number of English periods per week:							
1	*1·0*	*0·1*	*0·2*	—	*2·2*	*0·1*	*0·3*
2	—	*0·6*	*0·5*	*2·1*	*3·3*	*1·2*	*1·5*
3	*4·0*	*5·3*	*5·1*	*2·1*	*6·6*	*3·1*	*3·3*
4	*4·0*	*14·9*	*13·8*	*10·9*	*10·0*	*16·8*	*15·9*
5	*13·0*	*36·9*	*34·4*	*32·6*	*35·5*	*43·0*	*41·9*
6	*32·0*	*28·3*	*28·7*	*39·1*	*30·0*	*26·8*	*27·6*
7	*12·0*	*8·0*	*8·3*	*2·1*	*8·8*	*5·0*	*5·2*
8	*15·0*	*3·1*	*4·4*	*6·5*	*3·3*	*2·6*	*2·9*
9 or more	*19·0*	*2·8*	*4·6*	*4·2*	—	*1·4*	*1·4*
Total number of classes	100	817	917	46	90	881	1,017

Note: This table omits all classes for whom English was completely assimilated into an integrated scheme.

It would be reasonable to expect from the indications in Table 66 that pupils in remedial groups would have, on average, a greater number of English periods in a week than all other pupils in the two age groups. Table 67 confirms this, but it also shows that the variation within each of the groups is far more marked than any variation between them. If we leave aside these pupils, the table shows that the common experience of over three-quarters of all groups was between 4 and 6 periods of English a week, or on average about one period a day. Of the 12 year old pupils in remedial groups 49 per cent also had 4-6 English periods a week, but 46 per cent of them had more than this, and one in every three had as many as 9 or more periods of English a week. At age 14 there was less difference between the numbers of English periods allocated to 'remedial' and other pupils. The majority of remedial classes were likely to have 6 or more English periods a week, whereas examination classes commonly had no more than 5.

Table 68

ENGLISH LESSONS OVER ONE HOUR IN DURATION FOR 12 AND 14 YEAR OLDS

	12 year olds			14 year olds			
	Reme-dial classes	*Other classes*	*All classes*	*Reme-dial classes*	*Non-exam classes*	*Exam classes*	*All classes*
	Percentage of classes						
Number of English lessons over 1 hour:							
None	*36·0*	*38·9*	*38·6*	*28·3*	*26·7*	*34·4*	*33·4*
1	*20·0*	*25·8*	*25·2*	*19·6*	*18·9*	*22·5*	*22·0*
2	*21·0*	*19·8*	*19·9*	*28·3*	*30·0*	*25·1*	*25·7*
3	*16·0*	*13·0*	*13·4*	*21·7*	*23·3*	*15·7*	*16·6*
4	*6·0*	*1·8*	*2·3*	*2·2*	*1·1*	*2·4*	*2·3*
5 or more	*1·0*	*0·6*	*0·7*	—	—	—	—
Total number of classes	100	817	917	46	90	881	1,017

Note: This table omits all classes for whom English was completely assimilated into an integrated scheme.

As the single school period is normally between 30 and 40 minutes long, it is clear that most lessons of over 1 hour would be timetabled as double periods. In paragraph 15.16 we urged that English should have a due allocation of double periods. Table 68 above shows that on average a third or more of the sample pupils never experienced an English lesson over an hour long. At the other extreme over 20 per cent of the remedial and non-examination groups had 3 or more English lessons of over an hour, which suggests that they may have been allocated almost all their English in double periods. The figures were lower for the examination 14 year olds and the non-remedial 12 year olds, but 18 per cent of the former and 15 per cent of the latter had 3 or more English lessons of over an hour in duration in a week.

(b) Homework

Table 69

TIME ALLOCATED TO HOMEWORK IN A WEEK FOR 12 AND 14 YEAR OLDS

	12 year olds			14 year olds			
	Reme-dial classes	*Other classes*	*All classes*	*Reme-dial classes*	*Non-exam classes*	*Exam classes*	*All classes*
	Percentage of pupils						
Minutes per week:							
None	23·0	11·0	12·3	52·2	51·1	5·3	11·5
Up to 30	27·0	17·4	18·4	13·0	13·3	4·3	5·5
31–60	39·0	52·9	51·4	23·9	28·9	37·1	35·8
61–90	6·0	13·5	12·7	10·9	4·4	37·0	32·9
91–120	3·0	3·9	3·8	—	2·2	13·3	11·7
Over 120	2·0	1·3	1·4	—	—	2·9	2·6
Number of pupils/ classes	100	817	917	46	90	881	1,017

Note: This table excludes classes where English is completely assimilated into an integrated scheme (22 for 12 year olds and 35 for 14 year olds).

A note of caution is necessary here. Whereas the data for the time spent on English in school are derived from the teacher's observation of the sample pupil at work, the homework times are based on less firm foundations, for they can represent no more than the teacher's estimate or the pupil's own report. Given this reservation, an examination of the time spent by different categories of pupils revealed that remedial and non-examination groups were more likely to do little or no homework than examination groups; half the pupils in the 12 year old remedial sample and over 60 per cent of the 14 year old remedial and non-examination groups did up to 30 minutes or less in the week in question. Indeed, for the older pupils homework was the exception rather than the rule unless they had examination objectives, in which case English homework was much more likely.

The examination class 14 year olds had 68 minutes a week, which can be compared with the average of 45 minutes for the total of pupils in the sample who did any homework at all.

25.26 THE TEACHERS OF ENGLISH

(i) Number of Teachers Involved in Teaching English

In paragraph 15.14 we suggested that to a greater extent than any other subject English 'borrows' teachers from other areas of the curriculum. The questionnaire provided the opportunity to discover how many teachers in the sample schools were involved in the teaching of English to any age group (i.e. not simply the 12 and 14 year olds), and how they were deployed. Table 70 shows that 3,397, or 1 in 5, of all the teachers in the secondary schools were involved in the teaching of English. The table should be studied in association with Table 72, which indicates the extent to which these teachers were qualified for this teaching.

Of the 3,397, 9·4 per cent worked only part-time, a proportion slightly lower than that for *all* part-timers in the sample, which was 10·1 per cent. D.E.S. statistics show that the comparable figure for part-time teachers of all subjects in secondary schools in England in January 1973 was 11·3 per cent.

Paragraphs 15.13–15.14 contain our views on the problems for English of employing so many teachers who, whether part-time or not, spend only part of the week working on English.

Table 70

AMOUNT OF TIME SPENT BY TEACHERS IN ENGLISH TEACHING, BY SIZE AND TYPE OF SCHOOL

	Teachers (*both full-time and part-time*) *who teach English:*						All teachers (100%)
	All the time		More than half the time		Up to half the time		
	No.	*%*	*No.*	*%*	*No.*	*%*	
Teachers in:							
Schools of up to 600 pupils							
Modern	195	*23·6*	252	*30·5*	379	*45·9*	826
Grammar	120	*58·3*	44	*21·4*	42	*20·4*	206
Comprehensive	75	*30·5*	64	*26·0*	107	*43·5*	246
All other	26	*49·1*	13	*24·5*	14	*26·4*	53
Total	416	*31·3*	373	*28·0*	542	*40·7*	1,331
Schools of 601–1,000 pupils							
Modern	138	*38·1*	96	*26·5*	128	*35·4*	362
Grammar	118	*63·1*	28	*15·0*	41	*21·9*	187
Comprehensive	188	*35·5*	146	*27·6*	196	*37·0*	530
All other	14	*48·3*	10	*34·5*	5	*17·2*	29
Total	458	*41·3*	280	*25·3*	370	*33·4*	1,108
Schools of 1,001 or more pupils							
Modern	34	*21·8*	36	*23·1*	86	*55·1*	156
Grammar	17	*58·6*	10	*34·5*	2	*6·9*	29
Comprehensive	338	*44·3*	157	*20·6*	268	*35·1*	763
All other	4	*40·0*	1	*10·0*	5	*50·0*	10
Total	393	*41·0*	204	*21·3*	361	*37·7*	958
All schools							
Modern	367	*27·3*	384	*28·6*	593	*44·1*	1,344
Grammar	255	*60·4*	82	*19·4*	85	*20·1*	422
Comprehensive	601	*39·1*	367	*23·9*	571	*37·1*	1,539
All other	44	*47·8*	24	*26·1*	24	*26·1*	92
Total	1,267	*37·3*	857	*25·2*	1,273	*37·5*	3,397

Table 71

NUMBER OF TEACHERS BY WHOM 12 AND 14 YEAR OLDS ARE TAUGHT ENGLISH
IN A WEEK

	12 year olds	14 year olds
	Percentage of pupils/classes	
Number of teachers		
1	70·2	85·7
2	23·4	11·6
3	4·3	1·9
4 or more	2·0	0·8
Number of pupils/classes	917	1,017

Note: This table omits all classes for whom English was completely assimilated
into an integrated scheme.

The table shows that 30 per cent of 12 year olds and 14 per cent of 14 year
olds were taught English by more than one teacher in the course of a week,
but rarely more than two. Had it been common practice within the sample
for the non-specialist English teacher to 'fill in' by taking one or two English
lessons wherever needed, the proportion of pupils meeting two or more
English teachers in the course of a week would undoubtedly have been
higher. Since the great majority of the sample pupils met only one teacher
for English in the week, we must conclude that these non-specialist teachers
were taking them for all their English lessons.

We checked to see whether the pattern for remedial classes differed noticeably
from that of the age-group as a whole. In both age groups rather more of
these classes saw two or more teachers in the course of a week than did the
other groups, but overall only 10 per cent of the remedial classes met *three*
or more.

(ii) Qualifications of Teachers Teaching English

Table 72

QUALIFICATIONS OF TEACHERS TEACHING ENGLISH, AS SUPPLIED BY THE HEADS
OF THE SCHOOLS

	Number	*Percentage*
Teachers of English who have:		
(a) An honours degree in English with a post-graduate certificate in Education	479	*14·1*
(b) A degree in which English is one of the subjects, with a post-graduate certificate in Education	310	*9·1*
(c) Followed a main or advanced course in English (leading to a teaching certificate or B.Ed. degree) at College of Education or Education Department of a Polytechnic, for teaching in:		
(i) secondary schools	745	*21·9*
(ii) junior/secondary schools	331	*9·7*
(iii) junior schools	70	*2·1*
(d) An honours degree in English	105	*3·1*
(e) A degree in which English is one of the subjects	107	*3·1*
(f) A main or advanced qualification in drama	137	*4·0*
(g) None of the above	1,113	*32·8*
All teachers teaching English	3,397	*100·0*

The heads were asked to state how many of all their teachers teaching
English had any of the qualifications listed in Table 72 above, no teacher to be
included in the return more than once. The table shows that almost one-
third of the teachers taking English lessons had none of the qualifications
listed. The implications of this finding are discussed in Chapter 15.14.

> *Note:* It will be seen that the figures do not correspond closely with the
> figures for teacher qualifications in Tables 77 and 78. These were
> derived from a separate return made by the teacher taking English
> with the sample child, and relate only to the 12 and 14 year old age
> groups.

(iii) In-service Education Relating to the Teaching of English

(a) The survey data made it possible to analyse the attendances at in-service
training courses of the 3,397 teachers teaching English. Of this total less than
one third (1,104) had been involved in courses in connection with English
teaching in the three years preceding the survey. Since the total number of
attendances amounted to 2,038, it appears that most of the teachers concerned
had attended more than one course. The great majority of these courses
were very short; nearly half were of only 2-5 sessions and only about 8 per
cent were six weeks or more in length. Table 73 shows that the highest
proportion were on general English, remedial teaching, reading, literature
and practical drama. Spoken English and new areas such as linguistics,
English as a second language, and English within inter-disciplinary studies
had fewer teachers attending. (The questionnaire does not enable us to say
whether this was attributable to lack of supply or lack of demand). Full-
time courses lasting one year or one term accounted for only 6 per cent of all
the course attendances, and the majority of them were on general English or
remedial teaching.

Table 73

TOPICS AND DURATION OF COURSES ATTENDED BY TEACHERS OF ENGLISH DURING THE 3 YEARS TO JANUARY 1973

Subject of course	Full time 1 year*	Full time 1 term*	Full time 6 weeks*	At least 6 sessions	Between 2 and 5 sessions	Total Number of Attendances
Subject of course						
Language and Writing	3	1	4	93	102	203
Literature (including Poetry)	6	—	3	93	100	202
Linguistics	6	1	5	50	47	109
The Teaching of Reading	3	3	—	84	128	218
English as a Second Language	—	2	—	19	15	36
The Place of English in Interdisciplinary Studies	2	3	2	44	86	137
Spoken English	2	1	—	30	56	89
Practical Drama	5	2	2	161	126	296
General English	26	18	16	118	127	305
Remedial Teaching	22	16	8	146	109	301
The School Library	—	3	—	63	76	142
Total number of courses	75	50	40	901	972	2,038

*or equivalents.

(b) *Teachers' Centres*

Another aspect of in-service education is the use of Teachers' Centres, which are not only the venue for a large number of short courses but also the focal point for a variety of activities of other kinds. 280 (71 per cent) of the schools had had at least one teacher attending a Teachers' Centre in connection with the teaching of English in the 12 months to January 1973. This may have been for any one of a number of purposes—from involvement in development work and group study to visiting a book exhibition. It is important to point out that almost a third of the schools made no use of a Teachers' Centre for English work during the 12 months in question.

(iv) Membership of various organisations

The questionnaire enquired about the schools' membership of a selection of professional organisations whose activities are connected with some aspect of English in schools, and the results were as follows:

Table 74

ASSOCIATIONS CONCERNED WITH READING AND THE TEACHING OF ENGLISH, ETC.

Percentage of schools which were affiliated to the following organisations (or which had one or more members of staff who were members)	
The United Kingdom Reading Association	*5·4*
The National Association for the Teaching of English	*49·5*
The School Library Association	*57·1*
The Association for the Education of Pupils from Overseas	*3·1*
The English Speaking Board	*5·6*
The Association of Teachers of Speech and Drama	*5·6*
All schools (100 per cent)	392

The responses for membership of the School Library Association and the National Association for the Teaching of English were encouragingly high. However, information from the two associations themselves suggests that these figures do not reflect *active* membership of local S.L.A. and N.A.T.E. groups. It is probable that for many schools membership means little more than access to the associations' periodical publications.

25.27   THE PUPILS

There were 260,579 pupils in the secondary schools in our survey. Paragraph 25.6 explains how we selected a 'sample pupil' from each class of the relevant age-group. The sampling procedure resulted in the selection of 939 12 year olds and 1,052 14 year olds who became the subjects of the individual pupil questionnaires.

(i) Reading Standards

The teachers were asked to rate each sample pupil in terms of his reading ability and to assume that on average 25 per cent of children were good readers for their age, 50 per cent average, and 25 per cent poor readers. The table of results conforms reasonably closely with this ratio:

Table 75

READING ABILITY OF 12 AND 14 YEAR OLDS AS ASSESSED BY TEACHERS

	12 *year olds*	14 *year olds*
Percentage of pupils whose reading ability was assessed as		
Above average (Top 25 per cent)	24·3	26·4
Average (Middle 50 per cent)	53·1	53·5
Below average (Bottom 25 per cent)	22·6	20·1
Number of pupils (100 per cent)	939	1,052

This information was then used in cross-analysis, to check whether and in which ways the educational provision differed for pupils in each of the three levels of reading ability.

R

(ii) The Pupils' Reading Standards compared with Time Spent on English

Table 76 below shows the results of such an exercise in terms of the time spent on English in a week by children with different reading abilities.

Table 76

TIME SPENT ON ENGLISH BY 12 AND 14 YEAR OLDS, ACCORDING TO READING ABILITY

	12 year olds				14 year olds			
	Above average	*Average*	*Below average*	*All pupils*	*Above average*	*Average*	*Below average*	*All pupils*
Average time	3 hrs. 12 mins.	3 hrs. 17 mins.	3 hrs. 47 mins.	3 hrs. 22 mins.	3 hrs. 12 mins.	3 hrs. 19 mins.	3 hrs. 15 mins.	3 hrs. 16 mins.
	Percentage of pupils/classes							
Minutes								
31–60	*0·5*	—	—	*0·1*	—	0·2	—	0·1
61–90	—	*0·8*	*1·0*	0·7	—	0·4	1·1	0·4
91–120	*1·3*	*1·0*	*1·5*	*1·2*	0·4	1·3	2·2	1·2
121–150	*5·4*	*5·9*	*1·5*	*4·8*	4·7	6·1	8·1	6·1
151–180	*34·4*	*26·5*	*13·3*	*25·5*	33·9	22·7	23·1	25·9
181–210	*36·2*	*34·8*	*28·6*	*35·7*	43·3	39·9	37·6	40·4
211–240	*12·5*	*14·5*	*21·7*	*15·6*	11·6	16·4	16·2	15·0
241–300	*7·6*	*10·8*	*21·2*	*12·3*	3·3	11·4	10·2	9·0
301–360	*2·2*	*1·8*	*9·4*	*3·6*	2·5	1·3	1·6	1·7
Over 360	—	*0·2*	*2·0*	*0·6*	0·4	0·4	—	0·3
Number of pupils/ classes (100 per cent)	224	490	203	917	277	554	186	1,017

Note: This table omits all classes for whom English was completely assimilated into an integrated scheme.

The table shows that pupils in the "below average" category had more time designated for English in their curriculum than those in the "above average" category. One-sixth of the 12 year olds were allocated more than 4 hours of English in a week, and within this group were 33 per cent of the "below average", 13 per cent of the "average" and 10 per cent of the "above average" readers. The difference is more sharply marked for the 12 year olds than for the 14 year olds. From this it might be inferred that, certainly for the pupils in the earlier years of the secondary school, there is a concern to devote extra time and therefore staffing in an attempt to improve the standards of the "below average" readers. Whether this time is being spent in activities likely to effect this improvement is a matter taken up later in paragraph 25.31.

(iii) The Pupils' Reading Ability and the Qualifications of their Teachers

The information in Table 75 was cross-tabulated against the qualifications of the teachers, and the results are given below. As a separate exercise a cross-tabulation was constructed to show the pupil's type of course (whether remedial, examination or non-examination or other) against his teacher's qualifications. These results appear in Table 78.

Table 77

QUALIFICATIONS OF TEACHERS TEACHING ENGLISH TO 12 AND 14 YEAR OLDS, ACCORDING TO PUPILS' READING ABILITY

	12 year old pupils				*14 year old pupils*			
	Reading ability				*Reading ability*			
	Above average	*Average*	*Below average*	*Total*	*Above average*	*Average*	*Below average*	*Total*
Percentage of pupils being taught English by teachers with the following qualifications:								
a Honours Degree in English and post-graduate certificate	*21·9*	*14·7*	*5·9*	*14·5*	*39·0*	*19·0*	*8·6*	*22·5*
b Degree with English and post-graduate certificate	*12·1*	*8·8*	*7·9*	*9·4*	*14·8*	*12·3*	*9·1*	*12·4*
c Teaching certificate or B.Ed. degree with English	*38·0*	*44·5*	*44·3*	*42·9*	*25·6*	*42·2*	*44·1*	*38·1*
d Honours Degree in English	*6·7*	*2·2*	*2·0*	*3·3*	*7·6*	*3·8*	*1·1*	*4·3*
e Degree with English	*3·1*	*3·1*	*2·5*	*2·9*	*1·1*	*1·6*	*3·2*	*1·8*
f Drama qualification	*2·2*	*3·1*	*0·5*	*2·3*	*0·7*	*3·3*	*3·2*	*2·6*
g None of the above	*16·1*	*23·7*	*37·0*	*24·8*	*11·2*	*17·9*	*30·7*	*18·4*
Total number of pupils (equivalent to the number of classes) (100 per cent)	224	490	203	917	227	554	186	1,017

Note: This table omits all classes for whom English was completely assimilated into an integrated scheme.

Table 78

QUALIFICATIONS OF TEACHERS TEACHING ENGLISH TO 12 AND 14 YEAR OLDS, BY TYPE OF CLASS

	12 year old pupils			14 year old pupils			
	Rem-edial clas-ses	*Other clas-ses*	*All clas-ses*	*Rem-edial clas-ses*	*Non-exam clas-ses*	*Exam clas-ses*	*All clas-ses*
Percentage of pupils being taught English by teachers with the following qualifications:							
a Honours Degree in English and post-graduate certificate	*2·0*	*16·0*	*14·5*	—	*4·4*	*25·5*	*22·5*
b Degree with English and post-graduate certificate	*6·0*	*9·8*	*9·4*	*2·2*	*5·6*	*13·6*	*12·4*
c Teaching certificate or B.Ed. degree with English	*43·0*	*42·8*	*42·9*	*52·2*	*45·6*	*36·6*	*38·1*
d Honours Degree in English	*2·0*	*3·4*	*3·3*	—	—	*5·0*	*4·3*
e Degree with English	*2·0*	*3·1*	*2·9*	—	*2·2*	*1·8*	*1·8*
f Drama qualification	*1·0*	*2·5*	*2·3*	*2·2*	*2·2*	*2·6*	*2·6*
g None of the above	*44·0*	*22·4*	*24·8*	*43·5*	*40·0*	*14·9*	*18·4*
Total number of classes (100 per cent)	100	817	917	46	90	881	1,017

Note: This table omits all classes for whom English was completely assimilated into an integrated scheme.

Table 78 shows that the English graduate is more likely to teach English to the above average and average readers of both age-groups. The converse is also true, that teachers with no specific qualifications in English are allocated disproportionately to the "remedial" classes and the "below average" readers. Table 77 shows that 37 per cent of teachers teaching below average readers of 12 years old had "none of the above qualifications". For 14 year olds the comparable figure was 31 per cent. When teachers' qualifications are compared with type of class, in Table 78, it can be seen that 44 per cent of teachers teaching remedial pupils of both 12 and 14 years old had "none of the above qualifications". We cannot say how many of those teachers without any of the listed English qualifications may in fact have had remedial teaching qualifications, but from the number of teachers known to have had additional training it is safe to assume that very few of the sample teachers were so qualified.

Taken together, Tables 77 and 78 indicate that children experiencing reading and language difficulties are much more likely than other pupils to be taught by a teacher without qualifications in English. Discounting for this purpose the teachers in category c who may possess a B.Ed. with English it can be said that the probability of a pupil in a remedial group being taught English by an English graduate is about one in eight at age 12 and negligible at age 14.

25.28 ACCOMMODATION AND RESOURCES

(i) Accommodation and Facilities for the Teaching of English

One important influence on the achievement of an English department is its accommodation, a subject discussed at some length in paragraphs 15.21-15.26. In the questionnaire we asked how many of those teachers who taught any English took most of their English lessons in the same room. We found that 63 per cent of the teachers enjoyed this facility and were therefore in a position to create their own English teaching environment. 27 per cent moved to rooms which were class bases* to take their English lessons, while for the remaining 10 per cent. the location appears to have been determined arbitrarily, with both pupils and teachers lacking a regular base for their English. In Table 79 these categories are compared by size and type of school. The table shows that grammar school teachers were far more likely to teach in class bases than teachers in the other kinds of school, and the larger the school the greater the tendency for this to be true. By comparison the modern, comprehensive and "other" secondary school teachers of English were more likely to teach English mainly in the same room. In the modern school this tendency increased with size of school, so that almost 8 out of 10 teachers in modern schools of up to 1,000 pupils taught in the same room, and more than 9 out of 10 in the schools of over 1,000.

*A class base is a room used regularly by a class, especially for registration purposes. Teachers taking English in class bases therefore have to move from room to room to teach their classes.

Table 79

ALLOCATION OF ROOMS FOR ENGLISH, BY SIZE AND TYPE OF SCHOOL

	Teachers taking English						All teachers teaching English (100%)
	Mostly in the same room		In class bases		In no regular base		
	No.	%	No.	%	No.	%	
Teachers in							
Schools of up to 600 pupils							
Modern	615	74.5	159	19.2	52	6.3	826
Grammar	68	33.0	111	53.9	27	13.1	206
Comprehensive	152	61.8	78	31.7	16	6.5	246
All other	28	52.8	18	34.0	7	13.2	53
Total	863	64.8	366	27.5	102	7.7	1,331
Schools of 601–1,000 pupils							
Modern	264	72.9	70	19.3	28	7.7	362
Grammar	64	34.2	105	56.1	18	9.6	187
Comprehensive	346	65.3	111	20.9	73	13.8	530
All other	19	65.5	10	34.5	—	—	29
Total	693	62.5	296	26.7	119	10.7	1,108
Schools of 1,001 or more pupils							
Modern	131	84.0	10	6.4	15	9.6	156
Grammar	7	24.1	22	75.9	—	—	29
Comprehensive	447	58.6	233	30.5	83	10.9	763
All other	2	20.0	—	—	8	80.0	10
Total	587	61.3	265	27.7	106	11.1	958
All schools							
Modern	1,010	75.1	239	17.8	95	7.1	1,344
Grammar	139	32.9	238	56.4	45	10.7	422
Comprehensive	945	61.4	422	27.4	172	11.2	1,539
All other	49	53.3	28	30.4	15	16.3	92
Total number of teachers teaching English	2,143	63.1	927	27.3	327	9.6	3,397

The general impression given by Table 79 is that on average more teachers of English have their own recognised teaching rooms than might have been expected. However, whether those rooms can seriously be called 'English rooms' remains in question. They may well be general classrooms, used for a variety of purposes and not furnished or equipped in a way that would benefit English teaching. Moreover, we must again point out that over a third (37 per cent) of teachers teaching English had no regular base for their work.

Fewer than 4 out of 5 schools (78.7 per cent) had a store-room for the use of the English department and only 39 of the sample schools had a departmental office. Thus, although 20 per cent of all secondary teachers are involved in teaching some English each week, fewer than 10 per cent of schools have a focal point of this kind for the co-ordination of these efforts. What is more, only 31 (7.9 per cent) of the schools had any clerical time available for the exclusive use of the English department. At a time when English teaching is making increasing use of reproduced material—work-sheets, facsimile documents, and individual copies of poems and prose extracts—there is little evidence of the supply of ancillary help which would take the additional burden off the teacher.

(ii) Books and Library Provision

305 (78 per cent) of the schools in our sample had central libraries, while 83 (21 per cent) had libraries in more than one unit, such as a lower and an upper school library. Four schools reported that they had no library of either type.

Table 80 shows the number of periods in a week for which school libraries were timetabled for purposes other than library use. This table demonstrates that most libraries were free for at least two-thirds of the week. It is nevertheless highly discouraging that for one reason or another over 26 per cent of schools found it necessary to use their libraries as a classroom for a substantial part of the week. A library which is used as a class base for half the week or more simply cannot function as an effective resource centre for the school, a disadvantage which is discussed at greater length in Chapter 21.

Table 80

NUMBER OF PERIODS IN A WEEK WHEN THE LIBRARY WAS TIMETABLED FOR OTHER THAN LIBRARY USE

	Number of periods per week						*All schools*
	None	*1–5*	*6–10*	*11–15*	*16–20*	*21 or more*	
Schools							
Number	183	44	41	21	30	73	392
Percentage	*46·7*	*11·2*	*10·5*	*5·3*	*7·7*	*18·6*	*100·0*

We then sought to discover how well-stocked these libraries were. The results were as follows:

Table 81

PROVISION OF LIBRARY BOOKS

	Number of library books per pupil				*All schools*
	Up to 4	*5–7*	*8–10*	*11 or more*	
Schools					
Number	58	113	105	116	392
Percentage	*14·8*	*28·8*	*26·8*	*29·6*	*100·0*

Note: We explain in Chapter 21 that we do not regard "average number of books per pupil" as a satisfactory measure of book provision. It is given here merely as a rough indication of the book resources available.

Table 81 shows that just 30 per cent of the schools in the sample had 11 books or more per pupil, which means that 70 per cent had fewer than the minima recommended by the Library Association, namely 10 books per pupil and 15 for every sixth form pupil. We regard the 44 per cent of schools with fewer than 8 books per pupil as particularly badly stocked.

64 per cent of schools recorded that they borrowed books from the L.E.A., County, or Borough library, but we are unable to say whether the 36 per cent of schools which did not use these sources chose not to do so or had no external library to call upon.

It is argued in earlier chapters that teachers need to be better informed about children's books. The questionnaire selected two ways in which teachers could improve their knowledge (i.e. through in-service courses and through membership of organisations professionally concerned with books in schools) and aimed to discover how many took advantage of them.

(*a*) In all the in-service training courses attended by teachers in the three years to January 1973, only 142 attendances had been concerned with the school library and only 202 with literature. Details of the length and variety of these courses can be found in Table 73.

(*b*) We found that 224 (57 per cent) of the schools belonged to the School Library Association. This is one of a number of valuable sources of information about books, and well-informed reviews of new material could profitably be used more widely in schools. The local teachers' discussion groups and working parties run by the Association and at Teachers' Centres can also help teachers to keep up-to-date with children's literature, but relatively few groups exist at present.

Finally we enquired whether the schools provided any facilities for the pupils to buy books within the school, such as a paperback book shop. One hundred and twenty seven (32 per cent) of the schools reported that they provided some such facilities. This response was far higher than we would have expected, judging by subjective impressions gained from our visits to schools. It seems to us most likely that in many schools these facilities are available only very occasionally, and that nothing as regular or organised as a paperback book shop was signified by many of the "yes" responses. However, what was encouraging was that by their decision so many schools had recognised the value of such a service.

(iii) Audio-Visual Resources

Table 82

AUDIO-VISUAL EQUIPMENT AVAILABLE FOR THE TEACHING OF ENGLISH

Percentage of schools having the following items available for English:	
Mains tape recorder	*98·0*
Battery portable tape recorder	*57·4*
Record player	*98·2*
Film projector	*92·1*
Strip/Slide/Loop projector	*86·5*
Television set	*91·3*
Video tape recorder	*17·9*
Radio	*82·9*
Reprographic facilities	*75·5*
Teaching machines (including Language Master and Synchrofax)	*13·8*
All schools (100 per cent)	392

The questionnaire asked about the availability of certain items of equipment for the teaching of English, and Table 82 shows the numbers of schools with the items we selected. The list was not intended to be exhaustive but featured the more common items that one might expect to find employed in English teaching. The results show that large numbers of English teachers in the sample have access to most of them. The video recorder was available in almost one in five of the schools, and independent evidence suggests that the rate at which schools are acquiring these is growing rapidly. It is noteworthy that fewer than 3 out of 5 schools had a battery tape recorder available for the teaching of English. The value of this versatile machine is discussed in Chapter 10 and again in Chapter 22, where we suggest that it should be much more widely used than this figure suggests is at present the case. It was interesting to note from the replies to Question 1.C.2 that almost a quarter of the schools had a projection room and 14 per cent a recording room.

25.29   THE TESTING OF READING ATTAINMENT

The questionnaire findings on primary school testing practice were discussed earlier in this Chapter. The secondary survey shows that the incidence of testing decreases progressively as the child gets older. The schools reported the following pattern of testing of reading attainment:

Table 83

TESTING OF READING ATTAINMENT BY STANDARDISED READING TESTS

	Age group			
	11 year olds	*12 year olds*	*13 year olds*	*14 year olds*
Percentage of schools which:				
test all pupils in the age group	*39·1*	*9·2*	*5·8*	*3·4*
test some pupils in the age group	*34·8*	*56·7*	*51·5*	*42·9*
do not test any pupils in the age group	*26·1*	*34·1*	*42·7*	*53·7*
All schools (100 per cent)	368	381	379	378

Note: The total number of schools is not constant because some schools did not have children in each age group.

(a) Only 2 out of 5 secondary schools tested the reading attainment of all their pupils on entry. The remaining 61 per cent comprised 35 per cent who tested selectively and 26 per cent who did not test at all. It should be remembered that the sample contained 73 grammar schools.

(b) After the child's first years in secondary school the percentage of schools testing all their pupils dropped very significantly, though the majority tested at least some of their pupils up to the age of 13.

Table 84 below gives the incidence of each test used.

Table 84

USE OF DIFFERENT READING TESTS

Percentage of schools using each reading test:	
Schonell Silent Reading Test A	*25·5*
Schonell Silent Reading Test B	*26·8*
Schonell Graded Word Reading Test	*48·5*
Burt Rearranged Word Reading Test	*15·3*
Holborn Reading Scale	*25·0*
Neale Analysis of Reading Ability	*17·6*
N.F.E.R. Reading Test A.D.	*4·6*
N.F.E.R. Reading Test E.H.	
1. Vocabulary	*4·8*
2. Comprehension	*5·6*
3. Continuous Prose	*2·8*
N.F.E.R. Reading Comprehension Test D.E.	*4·3*
Manchester Comprehension Test	*0·3*
Young Group Reading Test	*2·3*
Southgate Group Reading Test 2	*3·1*
Other tests	*31·6*
All schools (100 per cent)	392

Of the 14 specific tests we listed, the three Schonell tests were most commonly used. Indeed we found 395 instances of Schonell tests in use in the 392 schools, compared with 336 of all the other 11 tests combined. In addition 124 schools reported using "Other tests", which are likely to have included some lesser-known tests, and possibly a few designed by the schools themselves. The maximum number of schools which carried out any testing of the reading of any age group was 272, and on average schools which *did* test used three different ones.

The fact that several tests are in use suggests a number of possible explanations. Schools may be choosing the tests most appropriate to the pupils' reading ability. The poor readers among the younger children are likely to be given tests with a wide age-span or tests particularly suitable for juniors. On the other hand, teachers within the same school may be using different tests because they are able to choose according to their personal preferences. Where this is the practice it should be remembered that it is important to have continuity and comparability in testing results, an aim which will not be achieved by switching from one to another from year to year.

25.30   PUPILS WITH READING AND LANGUAGE DIFFICULTIES

A brief account of the way the questionnaire identified pupils in need of special help appeared in paragraph 25.25. It is necessary to add only two points here:

(a) Some schools give all their pupils the opportunity to take at least one or two subjects in external examinations, whatever their ability. Where this happens it will have had the effect of including within the "examination" category a number of pupils whose schools normally classed them as "remedial".

(b) Conversely some pupils of average or above average ability choose not to take external examinations; our "non-examination" group may therefore encompass a wide span of ability.

(i) Departmental Organisation of Remedial Groups and Classes

50.7 per cent of the schools had a head of English department or a head of Remedial department part of whose responsibility was to advise specialist teachers in other subjects on the needs of the pupils with low reading ability. This is clearly open to wide interpretation, and the evidence of our visits is that it often meant no more than that the head of department supplied other teachers with the pupil's reading age or a brief note of his progress. 27 per cent of the heads of either English or Remedial department did not undertake this advisory role in any way. The lack of inter-departmental co-operation indicated by these figures must lead us to assume that the very specific reading and language needs of the pupils in remedial classes may well be being overlooked in their other lessons.

Eighty seven (22 per cent) of the schools found this question not applicable to their circumstances, which suggests that they did not consider they had any substantial problem of this kind. Indeed 92 (24.1 per cent) of the schools with 12 year old classes and 115 (30.4 per cent) of the schools with 14 year old classes did not feel the need for any special provision for their children. In this connection it should be remembered that 73 (19 per cent) of the sample schools were grammar schools.

(ii) Incidence of Pupils in Remedial Classes

12 YEAR OLDS

Of the 939 sample pupils, 107 (11.4 per cent) were in remedial classes.

14 YEAR OLDS

Of the 1,052 sample pupils, 53 (5 per cent) were in remedial classes. In addition 107 (10.2 per cent) were in courses which did not lead to any external examination. Thus 15 per cent of the 14 year olds in the sample had no examination objectives.

(iii) Size of Classes

Table 85

SIZE OF CLASSES OF 12 AND 14 YEAR OLDS

	12 year olds		*14 year olds*	
	Remedial classes	*All classes*	*Remedial classes*	*All classes*
Average size of class	19	28	16	26
	Percentage of classes			
Size of class				
1–5	1·9	0·2	1·9	0·1
6–10	8·4	1·1	20·8	1·4
11–15	17·8	2·9	22·6	4·6
16–20	32·7	6·7	39·6	9·9
21–25	28·0	13·3	9·4	26·8
26–30	9·4	43·1	1·9	36·6
31–35	0·9	30·5	3·8	18·5
36 and over	0·9	2·1	—	2·1
Total number of classes (100 per cent)	107	939	53	1,052

In practice the size of all classes is determined by the head, according to what he conceives to be reasonable demands upon his staffing complement and the requirements of different groups of pupils. It is generally recognised that classes of children in need of special help should be smaller than other classes if success is to be achieved in helping individuals to make progress. Among the 12 year olds less than 30 per cent of remedial classes were of 15 or fewer pupils, while a further 33 per cent contained 16-20. The rest were larger and one in 10 contained over 25 pupils. The figures for the 14 year olds showed more favourable ratios; almost half the classes (45 per cent) had 15 or fewer pupils, while scarcely any classes exceeded 20 pupils.

It was pointed out above that pupils without examination objectives are not necessarily always pupils with reading and learning difficulties. Nevertheless there is likely to be a wide range of needs in these classes and it was therefore encouraging to discover that the large majority of their classes (73 per cent) did not exceed 25. However, the smaller numbers in the remedial and non-examination groups appear to be being achieved at the expense of the examination groups. Of these, 3 in 5 contain more than 25 pupils. Full details may be seen in Table 65.

(iv) Time spent on English in a week by remedial and other classes

Table 86

COMPARISON OF TIME SPENT ON ENGLISH IN A WEEK BY REMEDIAL AND OTHER CLASSES—12 AND 14 YEAR OLDS

	12 year olds		14 year olds	
	Remedial classes	*Other classes*	*Remedial classes*	*Other classes*
Average time	4 hrs 2 mins	3 hrs 18 mins	3 hrs 21 mins	3 hrs 16 mins
	Percentage of classes			
Minutes				
31–60	—	0·1	—	0·1
61–90	1·0	0·6	—	0·4
91–120	2·0	1·1	2·2	1·1
121–150	1·0	5·3	10·9	5·9
151–180	10·0	27·4	19·6	26·2
181–210	21·0	37·4	32·6	40·8
211–240	19·0	15·2	19·6	10·7
241–300	28·0	10·4	10·9	8·9
301–360	15·0	2·2	4·3	1·5
361 and over	3·0	0·2	—	0·3
Total number of classes (100 per cent)	100	817	46	971

Note: This table omits all classes for whom English was completely assimilated into an integrated scheme.

In Table 86 the "Other" group refers to all those who are not in remedial classes. It is noticeable that in sharp contrast to the remedial group the total time spent on English by this group follows similar distribution patterns at both age-levels. For the 12 year olds in remedial groups there is a strong concentration on English, to the extent that for almost half of them the time allocated to it exceeds four hours a week. At age 14 there is less contrast between the total time allocated to these groups and that assigned to others. At one extreme a slightly higher proportion of remedial classes exceeded four hours English a week, while at the other 13 per cent of them received less than 2½ hours, the corresponding percentage for the other classes being 7.5. In some schools it is the practice to develop courses of a kind intended to prepare the less able pupil for the time when he leaves school. Such courses sometimes place a considerable emphasis on increased practical work and out of school visiting, so that the amount of time allocated to English lessons is accordingly reduced.

From the evidence of Tables 78, 85 and 86, it can be concluded that the children in need of special help in English tend to lose on the swings what they gain on the roundabouts. Many of them are in smaller than average classes and many may also have the potential advantages of a considerably larger allocation of time for English. On the other hand, their teaching is too often entrusted to teachers who are qualified neither in English nor in remedial teaching. Moreover, as is shown in paragraph 25.31, much of the English work they are asked to perform can be considered unsuitable and may tend to reinforce failure rather than inspire success.

The teachers were asked to state the percentage of the total number of pupils in the two age-groups for whom they were able to make provision for special help. This was then compared with their estimate of the percentage of pupils for whom such provision was desirable. The results were as follows:

Table 87

SPECIAL PROVISION FOR 12 AND 14 YEAR OLDS WITH READING AND LANGUAGE DIFFICULTIES

	12 year olds	*14 year olds*
Percentage of pupils		
(a) for whom special provision was considered desirable	*12·9*	*10·2*
(b) for whom special provision was made	*10·4*	*7·3*

This table gives only the average of the responses, but it indicates that in the case of the 12 year olds the schools were managing to provide for 81 per cent of what they estimated to be the total need for special help, and in the case of the 14 year olds for almost 72 per cent.

Table 88, which follows, gives fuller detail of the returns, and shows that in one-third of the schools special provision fell short of what the heads considered desirable.

Table 88

SPECIAL PROVISION CONSIDERED NECESSARY AND SPECIAL PROVISION ACTUALLY MADE FOR 12 AND 14 YEAR OLDS WITH READING AND LANGUAGE DIFFICULTIES

	Number of schools where special provision is made for								
	No pupils	1–5% pupils	6–10% pupils	11–15% pupils	16–20% pupils	21–25% pupils	26–35% pupils	36% or more pupils	All schools
12 year olds Number of schools where special provision is desirable for									
No pupils	92								92
1–5% pupils	—	22							22
6–10% pupils	4	13	56						73
11–15% pupils	1	2	19	35					57
16–20% pupils	—	—	18	20	30				68
21–25% pupils	—	—	3	4	6	10			23
26–35% pupils	—	1	1	4	6	2	8		22
36% or more pupils	—	1	1	2	6	1	3	10	24
All Schools	97	39	98	65	48	13	11	10	381
14 year olds Number of schools where special provision is desirable for									
No pupils	115								115
1–5% pupils	14	35							49
6–10% pupils	11	22	44						77
11–15% pupils	6	6	10	25					47
16–20% pupils	4	3	10	6	14				37
21–25% pupils	1	1	—	4	5	4			15
26–35% pupils	3	2	2	3	5	2	6		23
36% or more pupils	—	2	2	—	2	1	1	7	15
All schools	154	71	68	38	26	7	7	7	378

Notes: 1. Figures in bold type refer to schools which are able to make available the amount of special provision they consider desirable.

2. "All schools" totals exclude 11 schools which had no 12 year old pupils and 14 schools which had no 14 year old pupils.

(v) Organisation of Special Provision for Pupils with Reading or Language Difficulties

Heads were asked which of the forms of organisation listed in Table 89 were used in their schools to make special provision for pupils with reading or language difficulties. If we subtract from the total of 392 schools the 73 grammar schools and those without pupils of the specified ages there remain 308 schools with 12 year olds and 305 with 14 year olds. It emerged that some schools used more than one form of organisation, particularly for their younger pupils. The percentage (excluding grammar schools) using each was as follows:

Table 89

METHODS OF MAKING SPECIAL PROVISION FOR 12 AND 14 YEAR OLDS WITH READING AND LANGUAGE DIFFICULTIES

	12 year olds	*14 year olds*
Percentage of schools using these methods:		
(a) By withdrawal of individuals or very small groups at certain times of the week for certain purposes	*63·0*	*42·0*
(b) By extraction groups which remain stable for at least a term	*25·6*	*12·1*
(c) Remedial classes formed for part of the curriculum in the course of a week	*17·2*	*13·1*
(d) Remedial classes (or streams) which have the bulk of their work in those classes but are administered by the main school organisation (i.e. not by a Remedial department)	*20·4*	*19·3*
(e) Remedial classes (or streams) which have the bulk of their work in those classes and are administered by a Remedial department	*31·8*	*18·0*
Number of schools	308	305

(vi) Initial Training and In-service Education of Teachers of Pupils in Remedial Groups and Classes

Table 78 compared the qualifications of teachers with the type of class they taught. Comments on the qualifications of staff teaching pupils in remedial classes or groups are to be found earlier in the chapter.

The questionnaires asked how many of the teachers working with these pupils had received specific training (initial or in-service) leading to a qualification in the work in which they were involved. It was found that 167, or precisely 50 per cent, of the 334 teachers taking some work with remedial groups or classes were qualified in these terms. We also asked how many of the teachers who taught any English at all had taken in-service training courses in the 3 years to January 1973. Of the 2,038 course attendances, 301 had been concerned with remedial teaching. A further 218 had been on the teaching of reading and some of these courses may also have involved a remedial reading element.

In the remedial teaching courses the breakdown of teacher participation by length of course was as follows:

Table 90

ATTENDANCE BY TEACHERS AT COURSES ON REMEDIAL EDUCATION

Length of course	Number attending
Full-time 1 year*	22
Full-time 1 term*	16
Full-time 6 weeks*	8
At least 6 sessions	146
Between 2 and 5 sessions	109
Total number of attendances	301

*or equivalent part-time.

(vii) Accommodation for Remedial Groups and Classes

In their written and oral evidence several teachers told the Committee of remedial classes and groups which had their lessons in entirely unsuitable rooms, even at times in corridors and cloakrooms. The questionnaire sought to determine whether the heads of the sample schools felt their accommodation for these pupils to be suitable. In framing the questions we had in mind the recommendation of the Newsom Report that accommodation for remedial pupils should provide them with a stimulus. Commenting in 1971 on the Newsom recommendations, the D.E.S. pamphlet "Slow Learners in Secondary Schools" (Education Survey 15) said:

> "If an imaginative curriculum on Newsom lines is to emerge with good facilities for personal and social development to compensate for the social disadvantages of many of these pupils, a great deal of thought will need to be given to the provision of better designed accommodation than many enjoy at present".

Of the 392 schools, 258 organised withdrawal groups for the teaching of reading and language work, and heads in 61 per cent (158) of these schools felt that all these groups were provided with suitable accommodation. 16 per cent (40) considered that most of their accommodation was satisfactory, while the remaining 23 per cent (60) believed that only certain ones or none at all of their withdrawal groups were suitably housed.

25.31 THE PUPILS AND THEIR WORK

The following table has been derived from the detailed tables of English activities, Tables 96 and 97.

Table 91

TIME SPENT ON DIFFERENT ENGLISH ACTIVITIES BY TYPE OF CLASS—12 AND 14 YEAR OLDS

	All 12 year old classes	*All 14 year old classes*	*12 year old remedial classes*	*14 year old remedial classes*	*14 year old non-exam classes*	*14 year old exam classes*
Oral						
Time in minutes	38·6	43·6	38·3	44·2	47·8	43·1
As a percentage of total time	*18·8*	*22·5*	*14·8*	*22·3*	*23·4*	*22·4*
Writing						
Time in minutes	61·2	57·3	75·5	59·2	68·5	55·7
As a percentage of total time	*29·8*	*29·6*	*29·1*	*29·9*	*33·5*	*29·0*
Language study						
Time in minutes	52·4	42·5	76·7	48·2	39·6	42·5
As a percentage of total time	*25·5*	*22·0*	*29·6*	*24·3*	*19·3*	*22·1*
Reading						
Time in minutes	53·5	50·1	68·8	46·5	48·8	50·7
As a percentage of total time	*26·0*	*25·9*	*26·5*	*23·5*	*23·8*	*26·4*
Total time	3 hrs 26 mins	3 hrs 14 mins	4 hrs 19 mins	3 hrs 18 mins	3 hrs 25 mins	3 hrs 12 mins

Note: See introduction to this chapter for a reconciliation of this and Table 66.

A number of general observations may be made upon this table:

(i) All the 12 year olds were allocated more time in English than the 14 year olds. Most noticeable was the fact that they spent 10 minutes longer on language study than the older pupils.

(ii) 12 year old "remedial" pupils spent almost an hour more on English than "all 12 year old" pupils. The extra time was taken up by 24 minutes more on language study, 15 minutes more on reading and 14 minutes more on writing, while the time spent on oral work remained the same.

(iii) 14 year old "non-exam" pupils spent more time on writing than others of their age. The excess of 11 minutes over the average time on writing for "all 14 year olds" was not reflected in the remedial classes.

(iv) The time given to oral work with 12 year olds was significantly less than that with 14 year olds.

(iii) *Oral English*

The following observations are among those which may be made from an analysis of tables 96 and 97.

(i) Class discussion on the basis of topics chosen by the teacher is the most commonly encountered activity in oral English. With one exception, over half of all the groups were involved in it at some time during the week. In the 12 year old remedial group a lower proportion of the pupils (40 per cent) spent time on this activity, though 24 per cent were allowed to choose their own subjects for class discussion.

(ii) We would have expected that a greater proportion of pupils would be allowed, indeed encouraged, to choose their own topics for discussion, but the teacher-chosen topics remained predominant.

(iii) Group discussion still occupies a relatively minor place, and a higher proportion of classes spent more time on full class discussion than on group discussion. Indeed, no more than 10 per cent of the pupils in any of our categories experienced the latter during the survey week.

(iv) Improvised drama was taken by over one-third of the 12 year olds, but only 17 per cent of the less able 14 year olds. Fewer than 10 per cent of the "examination" 14 year olds spent time on it, which suggests that it was not considered to be truly 'serious' work. Those children who spent time on this activity tended to have about half an hour on it, the "remedial" children of both ages marginally less.

(v) For the older children the emphasis shifted from improvised drama to drama from a printed text, particularly in the classes with examination goals, where nearly three times as many pupils were occupied on the latter as on the former. For remedial and non-exam pupils the shift was less marked.

(vi) Many more of the remedial classes of both age groups listened to broadcasts, records or tapes in schools. In the younger age group this applied to 30 per cent of remedial pupils, compared with 14 per cent of "all 12 year olds". The corresponding figures for 14 year olds were 45 per cent of remedial pupils and 20 per cent of all pupils, with 28 per cent for the non-examination group. The usual amount of time given to this activity was half an hour, though substantially less for the non-remedial 12 year olds.

Writing

(i) From 12 to 14 there was some decline in the amount of the time given to the writing of stories and plays. Nevertheless, it continued to occupy an important place in comparison with the other writing activities.

(ii) A third of 12 year olds and slightly fewer of the older pupils spent time on writing from personal experience. It was most common among the 14 year olds without examination objectives, but this was not equally true of the 14 year old remedial pupils.

(iii) The writing of verse was a relatively uncommon activity, performed more often by the younger and more able pupils. Those few 14 year olds who did produce verse were on average occupied in the activity a little longer than the 12 year olds, and among these older pupils it was most common in the examination classes.

(iv) For each age-group the proportion of pupils engaged in expository writing was similar for all ability groups, the remedial pupils giving only slightly less time to it.

(v) The writing of description was more commonly to be found among the younger pupils and the less able of both age groups. The average times spent on it were 23 minutes for all 12 year olds and 29 minutes for all 14 year olds: for the remedial pupils rather less.

(vi) Letter writing was an activity pursued by a higher proportion of older pupils. The average time for all pupils who did any of this work was 25 minutes, and at both ages it involved a higher proportion of the remedial pupils than the others.

(vii) More than a third of the pupils of both ages and all ability groups were engaged in reproductive writing, which we defined as "writing in pupil's own words of material derived from printed or oral sources". Invariably the work occupied more than half an hour. A higher proportion of the less able pupils was involved, particularly among the 12 year olds, where the comparative figures were 56 per cent of the remedial and 36 per cent of the whole age-group. This pattern was substantially similar to that of pupils occupied with copying printed material and written corrections. A higher proportion of the less able pupils was occupied on these more mechanical and less demanding aspects of English. Taking the three activities together it can be seen from Table 92 below that the less able pupils spent a higher percentage of their writing time in copying and reproductive work and written corrections.

Table 92

PROPORTION OF TIME SPENT BY 12 AND 14 YEAR OLDS ON COPYING AND REPRO-DUCTIVE WORK AND WRITTEN CORRECTIONS, BY TYPE OF CLASS

All 12 year olds	32·8%	12 year old remedial	48·6%
All 14 year olds	33·8%	14 year old remedial	47·1%
14 year old examination	32·0%	14 year old non-examination	40·7%

Language Study

Language work in schools tends to be carried out in one of two ways:

Either: it is taught in the context of the rest of the pupil's English work, as an activity arising naturally from language in use by the pupil or his class, in which case we have termed it "Related Language".

Or: it is the subject of a completely separate study, usually in lessons set aside for that specific purpose. In this case we have called it "Isolated Language".

In order to create Diagram 16 below, the language activities listed in the questionnaire have been divided into two categories.

Table 93

CATEGORIES OF LANGUAGE ACTIVITY

Isolated	*Related*
Grammar exercises	Grammar—Instruction from errors in own work
Punctuation exercises	Punctuation—Instruction from errors in own work
Vocabulary exercises	Vocabulary—Instruction from errors in own work Vocabulary—Arising from literature
Comprehension exercises	Comprehension work from discussion
Spelling from dictation Spelling from lists Spelling tests	Spelling arising from written work
	Linguistics-based language study

From Table 97 we took the proportions of total language time spent on each of the language activities, and divided them into the "isolated" and "related" categories. The totals of the two categories are given in Diagram 16.

Diagram 16

LANGUAGE ACTIVITY BY TYPE OF CLASS—12 AND 14 YEAR OLDS

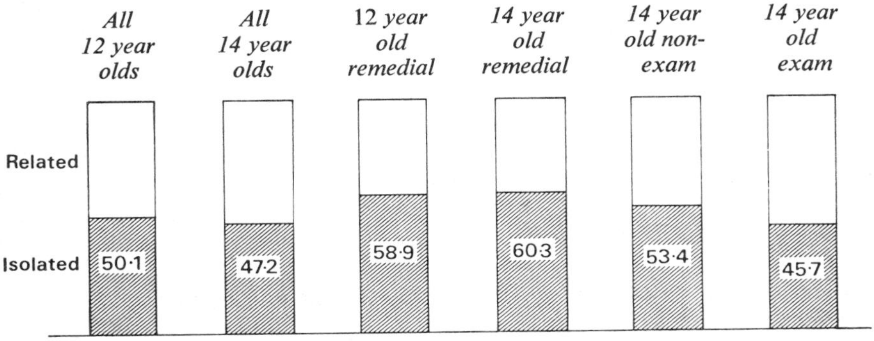

The results in Diagram 16 indicate a preponderance of isolated language work. Only for the 14 year old examination group does the proportion of related language work exceed 50 per cent, while for the remedial and non-examination pupils the scale is weighted, sometimes heavily, in favour of isolated language work.

Expressed in terms of the proportion of total language study time the three most common features are comprehension, vocabulary and grammar. Between them they account for 70 per cent of all the time spent on language study.

Table 94

PROPORTIONS OF TIME SPENT BY 12 AND 14 YEAR OLD PUPILS ON COMPREHENSION, VOCABULARY, AND GRAMMAR, BY TYPE OF CLASS

	All 12 year old classes	*All 14 year old classes*	*12 year old remedial classes*	*14 year old remedial classes*	*14 year old non-exam classes*	*14 year old exam classes*
Comprehension	*29·2*	*40·7*	*26·0*	*34·0*	*37·2*	*41·5*
Vocabulary	*20·8*	*21·9*	*22·5*	*23·0*	*21·0*	*22·0*
Grammar	*23·9*	*16·7*	*22·4*	*12·4*	*14·1*	*17·2*
Percentage of total time spent on language study	*73·9*	*79·3*	*70·9*	*69·4*	*72·3*	*80·7*

The average time devoted to language study declined from age 12 to 14, but comprehension was an exception to the general tendency. In fact the amount of time it received increased slightly between the two age points.

At age 12 a higher proportion of the remedial pupils (56.1 per cent) spent time on comprehension than "All 12 year olds" (34.0 per cent). However, the emphasis was usually strongly in favour of comprehension *exercises*, and it was noticeable how few of the 12 year old remedial classes spent time on comprehension by way of discussion.

Reading

Table 95 below contrasts the reading activities of pupils of different ages and types of class. The table, which is drawn from the data in Tables 96 and 97, divides the reading experience into three parts as follows:

(1) Private Reading—which comprises reading of both fiction and non-fiction, group or class discussion based on *private* reading, and poetry.

(2) Class Reading—which comprises reading of both fiction and non-fiction, group or class discussion based on *class* reading, and poetry.

(3) Reading for Topic Work or Skills.

Table 95

PROPORTIONS OF TIME SPENT BY 12 AND 14 YEAR OLDS ON DIFFERENT KINDS OF READING ACTIVITY BY TYPE OF CLASS

	All 12 year old classes	All 14 year old classes	12 year old remedial classes	14 year old remedial classes	14 year old non-exam classes	14 year old exam classes
Percentage of reading time spent on						
Private reading	*34·2*	*37·8*	*27·2*	*27·9*	*31·4*	*38·7*
Class reading	*44·9*	*46·2*	*25·6*	*23·9*	*34·5*	*48·7*
Reading for Topic Work or Skills	*20·7*	*16·2*	*47·2*	*48·1*	*33·8*	*12·6*

(i)   There is, from the evidence of Table 95, a distinct difference between the opportunities that the different classes have for stimulating reading. The two remedial groups are almost equal in the relatively small proportion they experience, 52.8 per cent for 12 year olds and 51.8 per cent for 14 year olds, compared with 79.1 per cent and 84.0 per cent respectively for all pupils in the age groups.

(ii)   Table 96 shows that two of the most common reading activities for all children are private reading of fiction and class reading of fiction leading to class discussion. Only in the case of the two remedial groups is the frequency of these two activities eclipsed by the proportion of children (68.2 per cent of 12 year olds and 54.7 per cent of 14 year olds) who spend time on reading for skills. Table 97 also shows that the remedial pupils spent almost half their reading time in the kind of reading associated with topics or projects and that which is designed directly to build up reading skills.

(iii) Table 97 makes clear that group discussion based on reading is less common than class discussion for pupils of both ages and all abilities. Thus an opportunity for exploratory talk and the interplay of ideas is relatively little exploited.

(iv) From Table 96 it can be seen that the 14 year olds in remedial groups in our sample had no experience of certain activities in the course of the week. These were the private reading of fiction leading to class or group discussion, class reading of non-fiction leading to group discussion, and the private reading of poetry. This seems to suggest that although these pupils spent about three-quarters of an hour a week on reading they were seldom given an opportunity to develop their understanding of what they had read by talking about it, among themselves or with their teachers.

Table 96

ENGLISH ACTIVITIES OF 12 AND 14 YEAR OLDS BY TYPE OF CLASS (I)

ACTIVITY	Derivation	All 12 year olds		All 14 year olds		Remedial 12 year olds		Remedial 14 year olds		Non Examination 14 year olds		Examination 14 year olds	
		Proportion engaged in activity %	Average time spent by those engaged in activity Minutes	Proportion engaged in activity %	Average time spent by those engaged in activity Minutes	Proportion engaged in activity %	Average time spent by those engaged in activity Minutes	Proportion engaged in activity %	Average time spent by those engaged in activity Minutes	Proportion engaged in activity %	Average time spent by those engaged in activity Minutes	Proportion engaged in activity %	Average time spent by those engaged in activity Minutes
Oral English													
Debates, lecturettes, mock interviews	(I)	12·1	25	12·5	29	5·6	20	9·4	21	10·3	23	12·9	30
Class discussion (teacher chosen topics)	(II)a	53·1	21	56·6	27	40·2	19	58·5	23	63·6	28	55·6	27
Class discussion (pupil chosen topics)	(II)c	11·9	22	10·3	23	24·3	25	24·5	20	15·9	24	8·7	24
Group discussion (teacher chosen topics)	(II)b	11·1	20	13·5	21	10·3	23	15·1	15	18·7	26	12·8	21
Group discussion (pupil chosen topics)	(III)d	5·0	21	5·9	25	7·5	19	7·5	23	5·6	35	5·8	24
Improvised drama	(III)a	35·3	32	10·9	32	39·3	24	17·0	25	16·8	28	9·9	34
Drama from printed text	(III)b	13·9	29	25·0	36	5·6	15	13·2	17	15·0	26	27·0	37
Listening to broadcast/record/tape	(IV)	14·0	23	19·7	29	29·9	31	45·3	30	28·0	30	17·2	29
Writing													
Stories and plays	(I)	40·2	34	25·7	38	44·9	31	32·1	24	29·9	35	24·8	40
Personal experience	(VII)	33·0	28	27·9	31	27·1	36	32·1	17	39·3	31	26·2	32
Verse	(III)	22·2	22	10·4	25	13·1	17	7·5	23	5·6	30	11·1	25
Argument and exposition	(IV)	19·0	26	25·3	29	15·9	29	18·9	24	19·6	32	26·3	25
Description	(IV)	26·3	23	22·2	29	30·8	20	26·4	19	25·2	26	21·6	30
Letters	(VI)	8·5	26	11·8	26	12·1	20	28·3	25	15·0	24	10·4	27
Reproductive	(V)	36·2	32	35·9	36	56·1	36	39·6	39	43·9	35	34·7	36
Copying printed material	(VIII)	14·6	26	9·6	30	29·9	28	28·3	29	20·6	35	7·2	29
Written corrections	(IX)	29·1	17	19·7	17	41·1	20	26·4	15	27·1	18	18·4	17

		C1	C2	C3	C4	C5	C6	C7	C8	C9	C10	C11	C12
Language study													
Grammar exercises	(I)a	24·5	24	10·2	23	28·0	25	13·2	15	7·5	22	10·4	24
Instruction on errors in own work	(I)b	37·7	18	28·4	16	40·2	25	26·4	15	26·2	15	28·8	17
Punctuation exercises	(II)a	16·2	19	10·5	19	15·0	22	13·2	19	12·1	20	10·1	19
Punctuation instructions from written errors	(II)b	20·6	16	15·3	16	12·1	20	13·2	15	14·0	15	15·6	16
Vocabulary exercises	(III)a	21·5	19	18·7	20	43·0	22	35·8	20	24·3	16	17·0	21
Vocabulary study from written work	(III)b	16·3	24	14·3	16	20·6	23	15·1	15	13·1	17	14·3	16
Vocabulary study from literature	(III)c	22·8	16	20·5	16	14·0	21	11·3	15	15·0	15	21·7	16
Comprehension exercises	(IV)a	34·0	26	32·5	30	56·1	29	43·4	25	30·8	27	32·0	31
Comprehension work from discussion	(IV)b	26·6	24	33·0	23	16·8	22	28·3	19	31·8	20	33·4	23
Spelling practice from lists	(V)a	8·5	16	3·1	17	23·4	17	11·3	15	6·5	19	2·2	17
Spelling practice by dictation	(V)b	3·2	16	2·5	19	5·6	19	7·5	30	6·5	19	1·7	17
Spelling practice from written work	(V)c	13·3	17	8·7	16	24·3	20	22·6	15	9·3	15	7·8	17
Spelling tests	(V)d	13·2	16	7·2	16	23·4	16	13·2	19	13·1	17	6·2	15
Linguistics-based language study	(VI)	3·8	24	2·9	26	11·2	25	1·9	15	1·9	15	3·0	28
Reading													
Private reading of fiction	(I)a	47·4	25	39·2	31	57·0	23	47·2	22	39·3	26	38·7	32
Private reading of non-fiction	(I)b	11·2	20	8·7	23	16·8	17	11·3	15	11·2	20	8·3	24
Private reading of fiction—group discussion	(II)a	2·7	17	2·6	27	1·9	15	—	—	1·0	14	2·9	29
Private reading of fiction—class discussion	(II)b	10·1	20	10·1	21	7·5	15	—	—	6·5	15	11·1	22
Private reading of non-fiction—group discussion	(III)a	1·7	23	2·1	18	1·9	15	1·9	15	2·8	15	2·0	19
Private reading of non-fiction—class discussion	(III)b	2·7	22	4·0	18	2·8	15	3·8	15	6·5	15	3·7	20
Class reading of fiction—group discussion	(IV)a	13·5	25	11·7	31	15·0	22	13·2	19	13·1	21	11·4	33
Class reading of fiction—class discussion	(IV)b	47·8	26	38·9	31	39·3	21	26·4	21	32·7	26	40·4	32
Class reading of non-fiction—group discussion	(V)a	2·9	22	1·9	19	7·5	15	—	—	4·7	15	1·7	21
Class reading of non-fiction—class discussion	(V)b	7·2	18	7·2	24	8·4	18	3·8	15	14·0	19	6·6	26
Private reading of poetry	(VI)a	4·7	16	3·4	19	3·7	23	—	—	1·9	29	3·8	19
Class reading of poetry	(VI)b	30·3	21	22·9	23	21·5	15	11·3	20	12·1	17	24·9	23
Reading for topic/project	(VII)	20·3	22	19·7	23	33·6	23	34·0	25	37·4	25	16·7	25
Reading for skills	(VIII)	24·8	27	13·1	25	68·2	37	54·7	28	29·9	23	8·6	25

Table 97

ENGLISH ACTIVITIES OF 12 AND 14 YEAR OLDS BY TYPE OF CLASS (II)

ACTIVITY	Derivation	All 12 year olds		All 14 year olds		Remedial 12 year olds		Remedial 14 year olds		Non-examination 14 year olds		Examination 14 year olds	
		Average time spent	Proportion of total time in activity group	Average time spent	Proportion of total time in activity group	Average time spent	Proportion of total time in activity group	Average time spent	Proportion of total time in activity group	Average time spent	Proportion of total time in activity group	Average time spent	Proportion of total time in activity group
		Minutes	%	Minutes	%	Minutes	%	Minutes	%	Minutes	%	Minutes	%
Oral English													
Debates, lecturettes, mock interviews	(I)	3·0	7·8	3·7	8·5	1·1	2·9	2·0	4·5	2·4	5·0	3·9	9·0
Class discussion (teacher chosen topics)	(II)a	11·1	28·8	15·1	34·6	7·7	20·1	13·3	30·1	17·7	37·0	14·9	34·6
Class discussion (pupil chosen topics)	(II)c	2·6	6·7	2·4	5·5	6·2	16·2	4·8	10·9	3·8	7·9	2·1	4·9
Group discussion (teacher chosen topics)	(II)b	2·2	5·7	2·9	6·7	2·4	6·3	2·3	5·2	4·8	10·0	2·7	6·3
Group discussion (pupil chosen topics)	(II)d	1·1	2·8	1·5	3·4	1·4	3·7	1·7	3·8	2·0	4·2	1·4	3·2
Improvised drama	(III)a	11·2	29·0	3·4	7·8	9·5	24·8	4·2	9·5	4·8	10·0	3·3	7·7
Drama from printed text	(III)b	4·1	10·6	8·9	20·4	0·8	2·1	2·3	5·2	3·9	8·2	9·9	23·0
Listening to broadcast/record/tape	(IV)	3·3	8·5	5·7	13·1	9·2	24·0	13·6	30·8	8·4	17·6	4·9	11·4
Total Oral English		38·6	99·9	43·6	100·0	38·3	100·1	44·2	100·0	47·8	99·9	43·1	100·1
Writing													
Stories and plays	(I)	13·8	22·5	9·8	17·1	14·0	18·5	7·6	12·8	10·4	15·2	9·8	17·6
Personal experience	(II)	9·3	15·2	8·6	15·0	9·6	12·7	5·4	9·1	12·1	17·7	8·3	14·9
Verse	(VII)	4·8	7·8	2·6	4·5	2·2	2·9	1·7	2·9	1·7	2·5	2·8	5·0
Argument and exposition	(III)	5·0	8·2	7·4	12·9	4·6	6·1	4·5	7·6	6·3	9·2	7·7	13·8
Description	(IV)	6·0	9·8	6·5	11·3	6·0	7·9	5·1	8·6	6·6	9·6	6·5	11·7
Letters	(VI)	2·2	3·6	3·1	5·4	2·4	3·2	7·1	12·0	3·6	5·3	2·8	5·0
Reproductive	(V)	11·6	19·0	13·1	22·9	20·2	26·8	15·6	26·4	15·6	22·8	12·6	22·6
Copying printed material	(VIII)	3·7	6·0	2·9	5·1	8·4	11·1	8·2	13·9	7·3	10·7	2·1	3·8
Written corrections	(IX)	4·8	7·8	3·3	5·8	8·1	10·7	4·0	6·8	4·9	7·2	3·1	5·6
Total Writing		61·2	99·9	57·3	100·0	75·5	99·9	59·2	100·1	68·5	100·2	55·7	100·0

		1	2	3	4	5	6	7	8	9	10	11	12
Language Study													
Grammar exercises	(I)a	5·9	11·3	2·4	5·6	7·0	9·1	2·0	4·1	1·7	4·3	2·5	5·9
Instruction on errors in own work	(I)b	6·7	12·6	4·7	11·1	10·2	13·3	4·0	8·3	3·9	9·8	4·8	11·3
Punctuation exercises	(II)a	3·1	5·9	2·0	4·7	3·4	4·4	2·5	5·2	2·4	6·1	1·9	4·5
Punctuation instructions from written errors	(II)b	3·3	6·3	2·4	5·6	2·4	3·1	2·0	4·1	2·1	5·3	2·5	5·6
Vocabulary exercises	(III)a	4·2	8·0	3·7	8·7	9·5	12·4	7·1	14·7	3·9	9·8	3·5	8·2
Vocabulary study from written work	(III)b	3·0	5·7	2·3	5·4	4·8	6·3	2·3	4·8	2·2	5·6	2·4	5·9
Vocabulary study from literature	(III)c	3·7	7·1	3·3	7·8	2·9	3·8	1·7	3·5	2·2	5·6	3·5	8·2
Comprehension exercises	(IV)a	9·0	17·2	9·7	22·8	16·3	21·3	11·0	22·8	8·3	21·0	9·8	23·1
Comprehension work from discussion	(IV)b	6·3	12·0	7·6	17·9	3·6	4·7	5·4	11·2	6·4	16·2	7·8	18·4
Spelling practice from lists	(V)a	1·4	2·7	0·5	1·2	4·1	5·3	1·7	3·5	1·3	3·3	0·4	0·9
Spelling practice by dictation	(V)b	0·5	1·0	0·6	1·4	1·1	1·4	2·3	4·8	1·3	3·3	0·3	0·7
Spelling practice from written work	(V)c	2·3	4·4	1·4	3·3	4·8	6·3	3·4	7·1	1·4	3·5	1·3	3·1
Spelling tests	(V)d	2·1	4·0	1·2	2·8	3·8	5·0	2·5	5·2	2·2	5·6	1·0	2·4
Linguistics-based language study	(VI)	0·9	1·7	0·7	1·6	2·8	3·7	0·3	0·6	0·3	0·8	0·8	1·9
Total Language Study		52·4	99·9	42·5	99·9	76·7	100·1	48·2	99·9	39·6	100·2	42·5	100·1
Reading													
Private reading of fiction	(I)a	12·0	22·4	12·2	24·4	13·0	18·9	10·5	22·5	10·1	20·7	12·6	24·9
Private reading of non-fiction	(I)b	2·2	4·1	2·0	4·0	2·8	4·1	1·7	3·7	2·2	4·5	2·0	3·9
Private reading of fiction—group discussion	(II)a	0·5	0·9	0·7	1·4	0·3	0·4	—	—	0·1	0·2	0·8	1·6
Private reading of fiction—class discussion	(II)b	2·0	3·7	2·2	4·4	1·1	1·6	—	—	1·0	2·0	2·9	4·7
Private reading of non-fiction—group discussion	(III)a	0·4	0·7	0·4	0·8	0·3	0·4	0·3	0·6	0·4	0·8	0·4	0·8
Private reading of non-fiction—class discussion	(III)b	0·6	1·1	0·7	1·4	0·4	0·6	0·5	1·1	1·0	2·0	0·7	1·4
Class reading of fiction—group discussion	(IV)a	3·4	6·4	3·6	7·2	3·4	4·9	2·5	5·4	2·8	5·7	3·7	7·3
Class reading of fiction—class discussion	(IV)b	12·5	23·4	12·2	24·4	8·4	12·2	5·7	12·3	8·6	17·6	13·1	25·8
Class reading of non-fiction—group discussion	(V)a	0·6	1·1	0·4	0·8	1·1	1·6	—	—	0·7	1·4	0·4	0·8
Class reading of non-fiction—class discussion	(V)b	1·3	2·4	1·7	3·4	1·5	2·2	0·6	1·3	2·7	5·5	1·7	3·4
Private reading of poetry	(VI)a	0·7	1·3	0·7	1·4	0·8	1·2	—	—	0·6	1·2	0·7	1·4
Class reading of poetry	(VI)b	6·2	11·6	5·2	10·4	3·2	4·7	2·3	4·9	2·1	4·3	5·3	11·4
Reading for topic/project	(VII)	4·5	8·4	4·8	9·6	7·6	11·0	6·8	14·6	9·5	19·5	4·2	8·3
Reading for skills	(VIII)	6·6	12·3	3·3	6·6	24·9	36·2	15·6	33·5	7·0	14·3	2·2	4·3
Total Reading		53·5	99·8	50·1	100·2	68·8	100·0	46·5	99·9	48·8	99·7	50·7	100·0

IV THE QUESTIONNAIRE FORMS

25.32 We reproduce here the questionnaire forms sent to the schools, together with the replies* we received.

The questionnaire falls into six separate parts:

Primary: Part I School Section
            Part II Class Section—6 year olds
            „   „ Class Section—9 year olds

Secondary: Part I School Section
            Part II Class Section—12 year olds
            „   „ Class Section—14 year olds

When the Primary and Secondary Questionnaires were despatched to the schools the School Section was addressed to the head to complete in relation to the school as a whole. The Class Sections were to be completed by the class teachers of 6 and 9 year olds, or by the English teachers in the case of 12 and 14 year olds. In the following pages each of the four class sections is preceded by the relevant Explanatory Notes which were addressed in the first instance to the head of the school, who was then requested to pass them on to the appropriate teacher.

*It will be noted that some boxes contain an "X" rather than a number. This is because the nature of the question was such that an aggregate number for all the respondents would provide meaningless information.

COMMITTEE OF INQUIRY INTO READING AND THE USE OF ENGLISH

PRIMARY AND MIDDLE SCHOOLS QUESTIONNAIRE

Please ensure that every box or set of boxes is completed, either with a number or with a tick as appropriate.

PART I SCHOOL SECTION

I. General

LEA .... LEA Number

School .... School Number

Head ....

Telephone ....

School Type (please tick one box only)

Infant	207
First	45
Infant with Junior	475
First and Middle	5
Junior	194
Middle	10

Number of full-time pupils on the roll on 25 January 1973 (as Form 7) — 214,494

Number of part-time pupils on the roll on 25 January 1973 (as Form 7) — 1,974

Total number of registration classes — 6,936

II The Teachers

A 1 Number of full-time qualified teachers (including Head) — 7,917

2 Number of part-time qualified teachers — 977

3 Number of part-time qualified teachers as full-time equivalents (please round to the nearest whole number) — 477

B 1 Number of peripatetic qualified teachers (not included at IIA) who visit this school among others at least weekly to assist and advise in the teaching of reading — 188

2 Total number of sessions spent by such teachers in this school in a normal week — 470

C   1 Excluding the Head, how many teachers on the staff, receiving payments above Scale 1, have a special responsibility for the following (do not include teachers with only graduate or E.P.A. allowances)

   a organising the school library | 402 |

   b the teaching of poor readers | 197 |

   c advising other teachers in the teaching of English? | 192 |

   2 How many different teachers are included in C 1? | 704 |

D   How many teachers altogether, excluding the Head, receive payments above Scale 1? | 2,772 |

III   School Affiliations

A   Does the school or any member of staff belong to

	% YES	Yes	No
1 United Kingdom Reading Association	5·6	52	884
2 National Association for the Teaching of English	4·7	44	892
3 School Library Association	12·5	117	819
4 Association for the Education of Pupils from Overseas?	1·9	18	918

B   Have any members of the staff made use of a Teachers' Centre in connection with the teaching of English since September 1972?

	Yes	No
58.1	544	392

IV Audio-Visual Aids

A Are any of these items used in the teaching of English?
Please tick those items of which the school possesses examples that
are used in the teaching of the English language and of reading.

	% YES	Yes	No
1 Record player	76.3	714	222
2 Mains tape recorder	79.8	747	189
3 Battery tape recorder	42.4	397	539
4 Filmstrip/slide/loop projector	57.3	536	400
5 Film projector	23.2	217	719
6 Radio	87.9	823	113
7 Television set	83.1	778	158
8 Language Master	11.3	106	830
9 Talking Page	1.6	15	921
10 Synchrofax	2.2	21	915
11 Other teaching machines?	8.4	79	857

B Which of the following are used by the school in the teaching of
reading

	% YES	Yes	No
1 Initial Teaching Alphabet	9.1	85	851
2 Colour coded schemes	5.9	55	881
3 Diacritical marking	1.9	18	918
4 Key words reading scheme (e.g. Ladybird)	78.9	736	200
5 Other controlled vocabulary (e.g. Janet and John)	89.0	833	103
6 Breakthrough to Literacy	31.3	293	643
7 Reading laboratories (e.g. S.R.A., Ward Lock)	25.3	237	699
8 Stott's Programmed Reading Kit?	29.6	277	659

V   Testing

A Are any of the following tests used in your school	%YES	Yes	No
1 Burt Rearranged Word Reading Test	34.3	321	615
2 Schonell Graded Word Reading Test	72.5	679	257
3 Schonell Silent Reading Test A	24.8	232	704
4 Schonell Silent Reading Test B	23.9	224	712
5 Vernon Graded Word Reading Test	3.6	34	902
6 Holborn Reading Scale	27.2	255	681
7 N.F.E.R. Reading Test AD	15.1	141	795
8 Neale Analysis of Reading Ability	16.6	155	781
9 Standard Test of Reading Skill (Daniels and Diack)	17.7	166	770
10 Word Recognition Test (Carver)	1.5	14	922
11 Group Reading Test (Young)	6.1	57	879
12 Southgate Group Reading Test 1 —Word Selection	6.7	63	873
13 Southgate Group Reading Test 2 —Sentence Completion	4.5	42	894
14 Other	17.3	162	774
15 None?	7.4	69	867

B Is it the school's policy to test ALL children with published tests of reading	%YES	Yes	No
1 During their first term in the school	23.7	222	714
2 During their last year in the school	66.2	620	316
3 At some other point during their time in the school?	75.2	704	232

C Are any children receiving special help in reading this term because they fell below chosen test scores?

Yes	No	Not Applicable
X	X	X

VI **Classes or Groups for Poor Readers** (including classes or groups in centres away from the school).

A Total number of special (or remedial) registration classes for children who are poor readers—

excluding those specially for children whose first language is not English

X

B In some schools children are taught for part of the time in classes, groups or individually outside the registration classes.
(This question does not refer to group work within the class unless an additional teacher is brought in.)

1 Is this being done this term in your school for the teaching of reading Please tick appropriate box

a throughout the full age range

X

b for part of the age range

X

c not at all?

X

2 Is the rearrangement across the whole ability range?

(i.e. are the average and above average readers separated out into groups of similar attainment as well as the poor readers?)

Yes	No	Not Applicable
X	X	X

3 Total number of 'remedial' (or withdrawal) groups this term

3,816

C If you have one or more registration classes or withdrawal groups for poor readers (as described in VI.A and VI.B)

1 What is the total number of children taught in such classes or groups?

22,762

2 How many children attend the largest of these classes or groups? (If children are always withdrawn individually the number should be 1)

X

3 What was the age last birthday of the youngest child in any of these classes or groups?

X

S

4 a How many teachers are engaged in teaching these classes or groups?

| 813 |

b Of these, how many are part-time in this school?

| 557 |

c How many of the teachers engaged in teaching these groups or classes have attended a relevant full-time course (or its part-time equivalent).

i lasting at least 6 months

| 95 |

ii lasting 6 weeks or more, but less than 6 months

| 99 |

iii lasting less than 6 weeks

| 382 |

iv None?

| 237 |

(Please show each teacher once only.)

The Committee of Inquiry would welcome any additional information or opinion which you feel may be of help. A space is provided below.

PRIMARY AND MIDDLE SCHOOL QUESTIONNAIRE: 6 YEAR OLDS

Explanatory Notes

1. The Primary and Middle School Questionnaire is in 2 parts, one to be answered for the school as a whole and headed SCHOOL SECTION, the other relating to certain classes or children within the school and headed CLASS SECTION. Several copies of the latter are enclosed so that one can be completed for each of the relevant classes.

2. The relevant classes are those that contain at least 5 children who were 6 but not 7 on 31 August 1972. If there are fewer than 5 children of the age group in a class, that class should not be included in the survey unless it contains all the children of the relevant age group in the school.

3. It is assumed that the SCHOOL SECTION will be filled in by the Head, or under his/her direct supervision. Each CLASS SECTION is to be filled in by the teacher mainly responsible for the group of children to whom it refers. If 2 or more teachers share the responsibility equally, the teacher whose name is first alphabetically should be the one chosen. It would be helpful to the class teachers if the L.E.A. and school numbers could be filled in at the beginning of the class sections before they are handed over.

4. 25 January has been chosen as the collecting date for certain information because the same figures will need to be returned in Form 7. Unfortunately

it is not possible to use the information directly from Form 7 because the Committee's survey will have to be processed before the Form 7 material, which covers all schools, can be made available.

5.   It is expected that the survey will provide information about the range of teaching practices used in language work (other than a foreign language) with children of the age group. There is no supposition that the survey will say anything about quality, of which the Committee will gain evidence from visits to a smaller number of schools. Nor will the questionnaire returns from a particular school necessarily represent a full range of the work in that school. It is accepted that where a question has to be answered about an individual child the reply may not be typical even of the class. A large number of schools is included in the survey, and the replies should give a fair picture of what is happening over the country as a whole during the week of the survey. Individual returns from schools will not be quoted.

6.   The information given about the school as a whole and about teachers and children will be treated confidentially. The names and telephone numbers have been asked for only in case any query should arise during the processing that requires further information. No names will be transferred to other records.

7.   The questionnaire aims to discover what happens in schools. The fact that a question is asked does not imply that the Committee has already adopted a particular view about what should happen.

8.   It will be found helpful to read the questionnaire throughout before answering. All questions should be answered by completing the boxes on the right-hand side of each page, entering a number or tick as appropriate. Please ignore the small numbers printed beside some of the boxes. No entries should be made in the right-hand margin.

9.   If when completing the questionnaire you should have any difficulty that cannot be resolved in the school, please telephone the Department of Education and Science, Elizabeth House, York Road, London SE1 (telephone 01-928-9222) and ask for the Bullock Committee Survey (ext. 3518).

10.   If the number of class sections you have received is insufficient, please ask your L.E.A. for further copies.

PRIMARY AND MIDDLE SCHOOL QUESTIONNAIRE: 6 YEAR OLDS

Class Section

1.   Separate returns should be made for each registration class that contains at least 5 children who were 6 but not 7 on 31 August 1972. If the school as a whole contains fewer than 5 such children a return should be made for the registration class of which they are members.

2.   This return should be completed by the teacher mainly responsible for the registration class to which it refers. If two or more teachers share the responsibility equally, the one present whose name is first alphabetically

should make the return, with the help of the others where necessary. Information about the teacher (e.g. courses attended) should be answered only in relation to the teacher making the return.

3.   The questionnaire aims to discover what happens in schools. This may of course be less than teachers who work in disadvantageous circumstances would like to do. The fact that a question is asked does not mean that the Committee has formed a view about the practice implied.

Please ensure that every box or set of boxes is completed either with a number or a tick as appropriate.

PART II   CLASS SECTION

I   General

A   LEA .... LEA Number [   ]

B   School   .... School Number [   ]

C   Name of Class.................................
(If the class is known by the name of a
teacher, please give that)

D   Number of children on the class register on
25 January 1973   [X   ]

E   Number of children on the class register that day who
were 6 but not 7 on 31 August 1972   [29,886]

F   How many OTHER registration classes in the school
contain children of this age?   [X   ]

G   The age range within this registration class is

Please tick appropriate box

	%	
6 months or less	10·5	149
between 6 months and 1 year	38.5	546
more than 1 year	50.9	722

	% YES	Yes	No
H Would you describe this class as vertically grouped? (i.e. a class deliberately chosen with an age range of at least 18 months)	22·7	322	1,095

II The Teacher

The questions in this section should be answered with reference to the teacher making the replies.

A   For how long have you taught in this school (if you have had a break of service of 1 year or more, count the time since the break)?

Please tick appropriate box

	%	
less than 1 year	18·3	260
1 to 3 years	32.5	461
more than 3 years	49.1	696

B   Have you, since becoming a qualified teacher, attended a course lasting 6 months full-time or more than 1 year part-time mainly about one or more aspects of teaching English?

%YES	Yes	No
1·6	23	1,394

C   Have you, since becoming a qualified teacher, and within the last 3 years, attended a course mainly about the teaching of one or more aspects of English lasting

	%YES	Yes	No
1 From 30 days to 6 months full-time or 6 months to 1 year part-time	1.6	22	1,395

		Yes	No
2 Shorter than any of the periods above, but of at least 6 half-days or sessions?	28.5	404	1,013

III. Time spent on English work during the week beginning 22 January 1973

This section should be answered in relation to the boy OR girl present for the whole week whose name is first alphabetically (not necessarily first on the register). It is appreciated that the times shown may not be typical of the class as a whole but the intention is to obtain a picture of the range of times for individual children across the country as a whole. Perhaps the child selected (say Albert Aaron) joined in the class poetry lesson on Wednesday afternoon and then, during other times when the children were being given a choice of activities, spent some time reading poetry to himself on Thursday morning, and writing a poem on Friday. The Wednesday time should be entered under "Class Time" i.e. when everyone was engaged on more or less the same kind of activity: the Thursday and Friday times should be entered under "Optional Time (Estimated)" because some children may have been engaged on poetry but others in work associated with other parts of the curriculum. Any time recorded below should be entered once only.

Example

Minutes	Class Time							Optional Time (Estimated)						
	0	1 to 30	31 to 60	61 to 90	91 to 120	121 to 150	151 +	0	1 to 30	31 to 60	61 to 90	91 to 120	121 to 150	151 +
1 Poetry and Verse		√								√				

A Please complete the following

Minutes	Class Time							Optional Time (Estimated)						
	0	1 to 30	31 to 60	61 to 90	91 to 120	121 to 150	151 +	0	1 to 30	31 to 60	61 to 90	91 to 120	121 to 150	151 +
1 Poetry and Verse	53	965	349	45	5	—	—	1,012	370	30	2	—	3	—
2 Stories read or told by the teacher or heard in a school's broadcast (Radio or T.V.)	2	40	141	344	416	318	156	1,180	128	56	27	9	10	7
3 Oral (conversation, language games, planning work, discussion, reporting)	27	213	371	341	200	124	141	580	440	187	91	28	22	69
4 Improvised drama (social/dramatic play, etc.)	408	679	238	53	22	11	6	744	401	166	67	19	9	11
5 Writing (stories, personal accounts, creative, etc.)	146	121	264	308	265	187	126	647	364	200	77	70	27	32

Minutes	Class Time							Optional Times (Estimated)						
	0	1 to 30	31 to 60	61 to 90	91 to 120	121 to 150	151+	0	1 to 30	31 to 60	61 to 90	91 to 120	121 to 150	151+
6 Topics (reading and writing, mainly based on reference books)	636	357	240	104	54	12	14	878	355	125	37	13	5	4
7 Individual reading of stories, excluding reading practice	602	398	268	91	32	12	14	254	597	387	112	32	19	16
8 Reading practice (graded and supplementary readers, phonic practice)	61	257	436	286	172	117	88	648	441	196	79	32	11	10
9 Comprehension and vocabulary exercises (from books, cards, reading laboratories, etc.)	312	360	351	197	117	49	31	952	273	119	36	20	9	8
10 Usage (grammar, punctuation, etc.)	718	615	63	16	4	1	—	1,298	110	7	1	—	1	—
11 Spelling	565	719	106	21	5	—	1	1,211	185	17	3	—	1	—
12 Handwriting	215	850	272	52	15	11	2	1,099	243	59	9	2	3	2

B   Is the child you have referred to above

                                        Please tick appropriate box
                                                    %

a a good reader for his age   30·8 | 437 |

b an average reader for his age   47·0 | 666 |

c a poor reader for his age?   22·2 | 314 |

(a = top 25%, b = middle 50%, c = bottom 25%)

C   How many teachers teach the child (counting all
    subjects) during a normal school week?
                        2·2 average per week | 3,082 |

D   Whether or not you have entered "Class Times"
    above, is it normal for children in the class   % YES   Yes   No
    to do their 'basic work' (or 'skills')
    mainly during the morning sessions?   73·6 | 1,043 | 374 |

IV Ways of Teaching Reading

A   The general approach

Were any of the following approaches used in the class with any of
the children during the week beginning 22 January 1973:

	% YES	Yes	No
1 Alphabetic analysis (letter names)	59·5	843	574
2 Look and Say (word recognition)	96·6	1,369	48
3 Phonic 1 (letter sounds, digraphs, diphthongs)	97·2	1,377	40
4 Phonic 2 (based on syllables)	69·7	987	430
5 Sentence method	51·4	728	689
6 Pre-reading exercises (e.g. to establish left to right eye movement)?	35·4	501	916

B   How many children in the class are still in the early
    stages of learning to read—a reading age of about
    5½ or less?
                                        31% | 9,252* |

*This figure includes a number of 5 year olds in vertically grouped classes.

C How often do the following children in the class normally read to a teacher during a week

	Daily	3 or 4 times	1 or 2 times	Less often
1 the ablest reader in the class	246	510	582	79
2 an average reader in the class	438	761	216	2
3 the poorest reader in the class?	1,009	375	32	1

D Graded reading schemes

Please tick one box only

1 Does reading practice rely on

	%	
a one single, commercially produced, graded reading scheme	19·0	269
b a mixture of books arranged in order by the school and drawing from more than one commercially produced scheme and/or books not in set schemes	52·8	748
c books and materials none of which are arranged in an order of difficulty either by the publishers or the school	0·4	6
d a mixture of b and c?	27·8	394

2 Are the children expected to read from these books

Daily	3 or 4 times weekly	1 or 2 times weekly	Less often	Not applicable
1,049	311	42	12	3
74·0%	21·9%	3·0%	0·8%	0·2%

3 Movement from stage to stage

a Is it usual for children to read supplementary readers between the major steps of the graded series?	% YES	Yes	No	Not applicable
	78·3	1,110	269	38

Whether the books are graded or not

b Are the children usually tested by the
teacher before they move from one   % YES
book to the next?

	Yes	No
87·6	1,241	176

c Do some poor readers ever have to
repeat a book

Please tick one box only

i more than once	41
ii once	458
iii never?	918

d Is phonic practice given when
appropriate to overcome individual
weaknesses detected when the teacher
is listening to reading?

	Yes	No	Not applic-able
% YES 96·8	1,371	29	17

(If you have a systematic class programme for phonic work it will have
appeared under IV A)

V. Books

This section is intended to reveal what books are available to the children
other than graded or supplementary readers, sets of readers, and text books.

A   1 May children borrow, for their individual use in school, books of
fiction and poetry from collections

	% YES	Yes	No
a in the classroom	98.1	1,390	27
b elsewhere in the school (e.g. central library, corridor, etc.)?	76.5	1,084	333

2 May the children borrow books of reference for their use in
school from collections

	% YES	Yes	No
a in the classroom	96.1	1,362	55
b elsewhere in the school?	81.8	1,159	258

3 How many books did the sample child ("Albert
Aaron") have in his/her care at the end of the school

day on 25 January, 1973? (If books are returned to
the shelves each day, show the number of books the
child had immediately before their return.)

3,586

Average 2.5 books per pupil.

4 Are the children allowed to borrow books from elsewhere in
the school

	% YES	Yes	No
a at set times	19.9	282	1,135
b at any time with the class teacher's agreement?	81.8	1,149	268

	%	Yes	No
5 Are books on loan from the L.E.A./ County/County Borough Library?	79.4	1,125	292

	%	Yes	No
6 Are the children allowed to take any books for use at home?	79.7	1,130	287

	%	Yes	No
7 Are any facilities provided in school to enable children or their parents to buy books?	16.3	231	1,186

VI Record Keeping

A Are records kept of	% YES	Yes	No
1 the books read by each child	95.5	1,353	64
2 the occasions when a child has read to a teacher	93.9	1,330	87
3 persistent individual weaknesses that require help from (i) specialist teachers of reading in the school	36.7	520	897
(ii) specialist teachers of reading and/or educational psychologists outside the school	31.6	448	969
4 assessments of written work?	46.5	659	758

	% YES	Yes	No
B　Are examples of a child's written work kept from year to year as a progress record, either by the teacher or more centrally?	39.0	553	864

VII　The Children's Work

A　Which of the following were the subject of poetry, prose or play writing in his/her own words by the sample child ("Albert Aaron") during the week beginning 22 January, 1973?

	% YES	Yes	No
1 Original stories	64.6	915	502
2 Stories or information rewritten in the child's own words	75.4	1,068	349
3 Model making or work in art and craft	41.3	585	832
4 Personal investigations in connection with science or mathematics	36.4	516	901
5 Other aspects of the child's daily life in or out of school	82.6	1,171	246

B　When the children are writing in their own words do they

	% YES	Yes	No
1 ask the teacher for help with spelling	98.7	1,399	18
2 use word lists displayed about the room	87.6	1,242	175
3 use printed dictionaries, including picture dictionaries?	82.8	1,174	243

		% YES	Yes	No
C	1 Is it the practice to give an assessment in writing of at least one piece of written work each week (e.g. 6/10:satisfactory)?	8.4	119	1,298
	2 Are some spelling errors marked each week?	87.5	1,240	177
	(i) Are children expected to learn to spell words from examples of their own errors and/or the errors made by other children in the class and/or lists made by the teacher?	75.0	1,063	354
	(ii) Are the children required to learn to spell words from commercially produced lists?	6.8	96	1,321

(iii) Are the children tested to see that they have learnt these spellings

Please tick one box only

		%	
a	weekly	16.9	239
b	less often	29.1	413
c	not at all?	54.0	765

		% YES	Yes	No
D	1 Are errors of usage (punctuation, grammar, etc.) marked in at least some of the children's writing each week?	87.8	1,244	173

		Yes	No
2 a	Are errors made by the children used as subjects for teaching to the whole class, or to a substantial part of it?	55.1	781	636

		Yes	No
b	Are these errors used as a basis for individual teaching, i.e. teaching the child who made the error?	92.0	1,303	114

3 During the week beginning 22 January, 1973 was any planned attempt made to extend the children's vocabulary by any of the following means

	% YES	Yes	No
a exercises requiring the use of dictionaries	31.6	447	970
b vocabulary exercises	49.6	703	714
c class discussion based on (i) new materials introduced into the classroom	83.3	1,180	237
(ii) a book or topic chosen partly for that purpose?	82.7	1,172	245

PRIMARY AND MIDDLE SCHOOL QUESTIONNAIRE: 9 YEAR OLDS

Explanatory Notes

1. The Primary and Middle School Questionnaire is in 2 parts, one to be answered for the school as a whole and headed SCHOOL SECTION, the other relating to certain classes or children within the school and headed CLASS SECTION. Several copies of the latter are enclosed so that one can be completed for each of the relevant classes.

2. The relevant classes are those that contain at least 5 children who were 9 but not 10 on 31 August, 1972. If there are fewer than 5 children of the age group in a class, that class should not be included in the survey unless it contains all the children of the relevant age group in the school.

3. It is assumed that the SCHOOL SECTION will be filled in by the Head, or under his/her direct supervision. Each CLASS SECTION is to be filled in by the teacher mainly responsible for the group of children to whom it refers. If 2 or more teachers share the responsibility equally the teacher whose name is first alphabetically should be the one chosen. It would be helpful to the class teachers if the L.E.A. and school numbers could be filled in at the beginning of the class sections before they are handed over.

4. 25 January has been chosen as the collecting date for certain information because the same figures will need to be returned in Form 7.   Unfortunately it is not possible to use the information directly from Form 7 because the Committee's survey will have to be processed before the Form 7 material, which covers all schools, can be made available.

5. It is expected that the survey will provide information about the range of teaching practices used in language work (other than a foreign language) with children of the age group. There is no supposition that the survey will say anything about quality, of which the Committee will gain evidence from visits to a smaller number of schools. Nor will the questionnaire returns from a particular school necessarily represent a full range of the work in that school. It is accepted that where a question has to be answered about an individual child the reply may not be typical even of the class. A large

number of schools is included in the survey, and the replies should give a fair picture of what is happening over the country as a whole during the week of the survey. Individual returns from schools will not be quoted.

6. The information given about the school as a whole and about teachers and children will be treated confidentially. The names and telephone numbers have been asked for only in case any query should arise during the processing that requires further information. No names will be transferred to other records.

7. The questionnaire aims to discover what happens in schools. The fact that a question is asked does not imply that the Committee has already adopted a particular view about what should happen.

8. It will be found helpful to read the questionnaire throughout before answering. All questions should be answered by completing the boxes on the right-hand side of each page, entering a number or tick as appropriate. Please ignore the small numbers printed beside some of the boxes. No entries should be made on the right-hand margin.

9. If when completing the questionnaire you should have any difficulty that cannot be resolved in the school, please telephone the Department of Education and Science, Elizabeth House, York Road, London S.E.1. (telephone: 01-928-9222) and ask for the Bullock Committee Survey (ext. 3518).

10. If the number of class sections you have received is insufficient, please ask your L.E.A. for further copies.

PRIMARY AND MIDDLE SCHOOL QUESTIONNAIRE: 9 YEAR OLDS

Class Section

1. Separate returns should be made for each registration class that contains at least 5 children who were 9 but not 10 on 31 August 1972. If the school as a whole contains fewer than 5 such children a return should be made for the registration class of which they are members.

2. This return should be completed by the teacher mainly responsible for the registration class to which it refers. If two or more teachers share the responsibility equally, the one present whose name is first alphabetically should make the return, with the help of the others where necessary. Information about the teacher (e.g. courses attended) should be answered only in relation to the teacher making the return.

3. The questionnaire aims to discover what happens in schools. This may of course be less than teachers who work in disadvantageous circumstances would like to do. The fact that a question is asked does not mean that the Committee has formed a view about the practice implied.

Please ensure that every box or set of boxes is completed either with a number or a tick as appropriate.

PART II   CLASS SECTION

I   General

A   LEA .... LEA Number [   ]

B   School .... School Number [   ]

C   Name of Class..
(If the class is known by the name of a
teacher, please give that)

D   Number of children on the class register
on 25 January 1973 | X |

E   Number of children on the class register that
day who were 9 but not 10 on 31 August, 1972 | 28,466 |

F   How many OTHER registration classes in
the school contain children of this age? | X |

G   The age range within this registration class is   %
(Please tick appropriate box)

	%	
6 months or less	4·2	52
between 6 months and 1 year	46·8	587
more than 1 year	49·0	614

	% YES	Yes	No
H Would you describe this class as vertically grouped? (i.e. a class deliberately chosen with an age range of at least 18 months)	27·8	348	905

II   The Teacher

The questions in this section should be answered with reference to the teacher making the replies.

A   For how long have you taught in this school (if you have had a break of service of 1 year or more, count the time since the break)?
Please tick appropriate box

	%	
less than 1 year	20·8	261
1 to 3 years	32·2	404
more than 3 years	46·9	588

B   Have you, since becoming a qualified   % YES   Yes   No
    teacher, attended a course lasting 6 months   3·1 | 39 | 1,214 |
    full-time or more than 1 year part-time
    mainly about one or more aspects of
    teaching English?

C   Have you, since becoming a qualified teacher, and within the last
    3 years, attended a course mainly about the teaching of one or
    more aspects of English lasting

                                                      % YES   Yes   No

1   from 30 days to 6 months full-time or   2·2 | 27 | 1,226 |
    6 months to 1 year part-time

                                                      % YES   Yes   No

2   shorter than any of the periods above,   25·2 | 316 | 937 |
    but of at least 6 half-days or sessions?

III Time spent on English work during the week beginning 22 January 1973

This section should be answered in relation to the boy OR girl present for
the whole week whose name is first alphabetically (not necessarily first on
the register). It is appreciated that the times shown may not be typical of
the class as a whole but the intention is to obtain a picture of the range of
times for individual children across the country as a whole. Perhaps the
child selected (say Albert Aaron) joined in the class poetry lesson on
Wednesday afternoon and then, during other times when the children were
being given a choice of activities, spent some time reading poetry to himself
on Thursday morning, and writing a poem on Friday. The Wednesday time
should be entered under "Class Time", i.e. when everyone was engaged on
more or less the same kind of activity: the Thursday and Friday times
should be entered under "Optional Time (Estimated)" because some
children may have been engaged on poetry but others in work associated
with other parts of the curriculum. Any time recorded below should be
entered once only.

Example   Class Time   Optional Time
                                                               (Estimated)

Minutes	0	1 to 30	31 to 60	61 to 90	91 to 120	121 to 150	151 +		0	1 to 30	31 to 60	61 to 90	91 to 120	121 to 150	151 +
1 Poetry and Verse		√								√					

A   Please complete the following:

Minutes	Class Time							Optional Time (Estimated)						
	0	1 to 30	31 to 60	61 to 90	91 to 120	121 to 150	151+	0	1 to 30	31 to 60	61 to 90	91 to 120	121 to 150	151+
1 Poetry and Verse	229	793	218	12	1	—	—		848	358	42	3	1	—	1
2 Stories read or told by the teacher or heard in a school's broadcast (Radio or TV)	44	338	502	232	85	34	18	1,092	97	40	13	8	3	—
3 Oral (conversation, language games, planning work, discussion, reporting)	83	379	413	225	93	29	31	706	359	124	35	17	5	7
4 Improvised drama (social/ dramatic play, etc.)	579	449	184	36	1	—	4	1,058	151	39	3	1	1	—
5 Writing (stories, personal accounts, creative, etc.)	73	129	494	312	149	58	38	633	345	185	52	24	8	6
6 Topics (reading and writing mainly based on reference books)	258	176	298	240	165	68	48	400	351	299	109	49	21	24

Minutes	Class Time							Optional Time (Estimated)						
	0	1 to 30	31 to 60	61 to 90	91 to 120	121 to 150	151 +	0	1 to 30	31 to 60	61 to 90	91 to 120	121 to 150	151 +
7 Individual reading of stories, excluding reading practice	302	380	345	143	51	27	5	279	524	329	80	33	5	3
8 Reading practice (graded and supplementary readers, phonic practice)	365	344	263	138	72	52	19	912	226	87	20	3	2	3
9 Comprehension and vocabulary exercises (from books, cards, reading laboratories, etc.)	154	283	423	231	95	43	24	850	269	88	25	15	5	1
10 Usage (grammar, punctuation, etc.)	218	629	291	85	25	5	—	1,096	128	25	4	—	—	—
11 Spelling	167	836	216	27	6	1	—	956	271	22	3	—	1	—
12 Handwriting	306	746	175	18	6	1	1	1,020	207	19	7	—	—	—

B   Is the child you have referred to above

Please tick appropriate box

%

a   a good reader for his age   41.1 | 515 |

b   an average reader for his age   37.4 | 469 |

c   a poor reader for his age?   21.5 | 269 |

(a=top 25%, b=middle 50%, c=bottom 25%)

C   How many teachers teach the child (counting all
subjects) during a normal school week? | 3,961 |

3.2 average per week

| | % YES | Yes | No |

D   Whether or not you have entered "Class
Times" above, is it normal for children in the | 1,009 | 244 |
class to do their 'basic work' (or 'skills')
mainly during the morning sessions?   80.5

IV   Ways of Teaching Reading

A   The general approach

Were any of the following approaches used in the class with any of
the children during the week beginning 22 January 1973:

		% YES	Yes	No
1	Alphabetic analysis (letter names)	31.3	392	861
2	Look and Say (word recognition)	67.0	840	413
3	Phonic 1 (letter sounds, digraphs, diphthongs)	73.7	924	329
4	Phonic 2 (based on syllables)	70.9	889	364
5	Sentence method	30.7	385	868
6	Pre-reading exercises (e.g. to establish left to right eye movement)?	5.3	66	1,187

B   How many children in the class are still in
the early stages of learning to read—a reading
age of about 7 or less?   10.7% | 3,035 |

C   How often do the following children in the class normally read
to a teacher during a week

	Daily	3 or 4 times	1 or 2 times	Less often
1 the ablest reader in the class	15	53	443	742
2 an average reader in the class	34	244	797	178
3 the poorest reader in the class?	599	472	164	18

D Graded reading schemes

Please tick one box only

1 Does reading practice rely on

%YES

		%YES	
a	one single, commercially produced, graded reading scheme	6.0	75
b	a mixture of books arranged in order by the school and drawing from more than one commercially produced scheme and/or books not in set schemes	37.1	465
c	books and materials none of which are arranged in an order of difficulty either by the publishers or the school	2.9	36
d	a mixture of b and c?	54.0	677

2 Are the children expected to read from these books

	Daily	3 or 4 times weekly	1 or 2 times weekly	Less often	Not applicable
	735	352	131	21	14
	58.7%	28.1%	10.5%	1.7%	1.1%

3 Movement from stage to stage

		%YES	Yes	No	Not applicable
a	Is it usual for children to read supplementary readers between the major steps of the graded series?	61.3	768	223	262

Whether the books are graded or not

b   Are the children usually tested by   %YES | Yes | No
    the teacher before they move from
    one book to the next?   77.0 | 965 | 288

c   Do some poor readers ever have to repeat a book

Please tick one box only

i more than once	54
ii once	376
iii never?	823

	%YES	Yes	No	Not applicable
d Is phonic practice given when appropriate to overcome individual weaknesses detected when the teacher is listening to reading?	91.6	1,148	67	38

(If you have a systematic class programme for phonic work it will have appeared under IV A)

V   Books

This section is intended to reveal what books are available to the children other than graded or supplementary readers, sets of readers and text books.

A   1   May children borrow, for their individual use
        in school, books of fiction and poetry from
        collections

	% YES	Yes	No
a in the classroom	94.9	1,189	64
b elsewhere in the school (e.g. central library, corridor, etc.)?	81.6	1,022	231

2   May the children borrow books of reference for
    their use in school from collections

	% YES	Yes	No
a in the classroom	93.9	1,176	77
b elsewhere in the school?	89.5	1,122	131

3   How many books did the sample child ("Albert
    Aaron") have in his/her care at the end of the school day on
    25 January 1973? (If books are returned to the shelves
    each day, show the number of books the child had
    immediately before their return.)

4,584

Average 3.7 books per pupil

4 Are the children allowed to borrow books from elsewhere in the school

	% YES	Yes	No
a at set times	24.6	308	945
b at any time with the class teacher's agreement?	88.7	1,111	142

	% YES	Yes	No
5 Are books on loan from the LEA/County/ County Borough Library?	87.4	1,095	158

	% YES	Yes	No
6 Are the children allowed to take any books for use at home?	92.6	1,160	93

	% YES	Yes	No
7 Are any facilities provided in school to enable children or their parents to buy books?	27.2	341	912

VI Record Keeping

A Are records kept of

	% YES	Yes	No
1 the books read by each child	78.2	980	273
2 the occasions when a child has read to a teacher	69.6	872	381
3 persistent individual weaknesses that require help from i specialist teachers of reading in the school	46.4	582	671
ii specialist teachers of reading and/or educational psychologists outside the school	37.7	472	781
4 assessments of written work?	60.3	756	497

B Are examples of a child's written work kept from year to year as a progress record, either by the teacher or more centrally?

	% YES	Yes	No
	41.7	523	730

VII The Children's Work

A   Which of the following were the subject of poetry, prose or play writing in his/her own words by the sample child ("Albert Aaron") during the week beginning 22 January 1973?

	% YES	Yes	No
1 Original stories	81.7	1,024	229
2 Stories or information rewritten in the child's own words	84.9	1,064	189
3 Model making or work in art and craft	30.6	383	870
4 Personal investigations in connection with science or mathematics	48.2	604	649
5 Other aspects of the child's daily life in or out of school	55.9	700	553

B   When the children are writing in their own words do they

	% YES	Yes	No
1 ask the teacher for help with spelling?	96.3	1,207	46
2 use word lists displayed about the room?	30.9	387	866
3 use printed dictionaries, including picture dictionaries?	97.4	1,220	33

	%YES	Yes	No
C 1 Is it the practice to give an assessment in writing of at least one piece of written work each week (e.g. 6/10: satisfactory)?	43.1	540	713
2 Are some spelling errors marked each week?	97.4	1,221	32
i Are children expected to learn to spell words from examples of their own errors and/or the errors made by other children in the class and/or lists made by the teacher?	95.1	1,192	61
ii Are the children required to learn to spell words from commercially produced lists?	41.4	519	734

iii   Are the children tested to see that they have learnt these spellings

Please tick one box only
% YES

	% YES	
a weekly	59.5	745
b less often	33.1	415
c not at all?	7.4	93

D 1 Are errors of usage (punctuation, grammar etc.) marked in at least some of the children's writing each week?

%YES	Yes	No
99.6	1,248	5

2 a   Are errors made by the children used as subjects for teaching to the whole class, or to a substantial part of it?

%YES	Yes	No
85.3	1,069	184

b   Are these errors used as a basis for individual teaching, i.e. teaching the child who made the error?

%YES	Yes	No
93.7	1,174	79

3 During the week beginning 22 January 1973 was any planned attempt made to extend the children's vocabulary by any of the following means

	%YES	Yes	No
a exercises requiring the use of dictionaries	62.7	786	467
b vocabulary exercises	67.0	839	414
c class discussion based on			
i new materials introduced into the classroom	60.0	752	501
ii a book or topic chosen partly for that purpose?	63.3	793	460

COMMITTEE OF INQUIRY INTO READING AND THE USE OF ENGLISH

SECONDARY QUESTIONNAIRE

Please ensure that every box or set of boxes is completed, either with a number or with a tick as appropriate.

PART I: SCHOOL SECTION

A   GENERAL

L.E.A. .... L.E.A. Number

School .... School Number

Head .... School Type: Modern   165

Telephone ....   Grammar   73

Compre-
hensive   140

Technical   5

Other   9

Age range of school .... Youngest child

Oldest child

Number on roll on 25 January 1973 (i.e. as Form 7)   260,579

Number of full-time qualified teachers (including Head)   14,643

Number of part-time qualified teachers   1,644

Number of part-time qualified teachers as full-time equivalent (please round to the nearest whole number)   809

B   THE TEACHERS OF ENGLISH

(For the purposes of this question please disregard drama which is the subject of Question 2 below.)

1 Is the teaching of English organised

Please tick one box only

	%	
a under a separate English department throughout the school	59.7	234
b under a separate English department except for remedial classes	37.0	145
c as part of a department grouping more than one subject	1.8	7
d as part of a department grouping more than one subject but excluding remedial classes	0.8	3
e in none of these ways?	0.8	3

2 Is drama taught in your school

Please tick one box only

	%	
a as part of the work of the English department	84.4	331
b under a separate department	9.9	39
c in combination with one or more other subjects (excluding English)	4.1	16
d not at all?	1.5	6

For the remainder of Section B please exclude teachers teaching drama as a subject separate from English.

3 a What is the total number of teachers teaching English (including those working with remedial classes)? | | 3,397 |

b How many of these are only part-time in the school? | % 9.4 | 318 |

4 a How many of the teachers teaching English are their first year of teaching? | 11.0 | 375 |

b How many of the teachers teaching English are in their first year of teaching in this school? | 23.6 | 803 |

5   (For the purpose of this question no teacher should be included
     more than once.)
     How many of those teaching English have

                                                                         %

     a an honours degree in English with a post-
        graduate certificate in Education   14.1 | 479 |

     b a degree in which English is one of the subjects,
        with a post-graduate certificate in Education   9.1 | 310 |

     c followed a main or advanced course in English
        (leading to a teaching certificate or B.Ed.)
        at College of Education or Education Department
        of a Polytechnic, for teaching in

        i secondary schools   21.9 | 745 |

        ii junior/secondary schools   9.7 | 331 |

        iii junior schools   2.1 | 70 |

     d an honours degree in English   3.1 | 105 |

     e a degree in which English is one of the subjects   3.1 | 10 |

     f a main or advanced course qualification in drama   4.0 | 137 |

     g none of the above?   32.8 | 1,113 |

6   How many of those teaching English

                                                                         %

     a spend all their teaching time on English   37.3 | 1,267 |

     b spend more than half their teaching time on English 25.2 | 857 |

     c spend up to half their teaching time on English?   37.5 | 1,273 |

7   How many of those teaching English spend
     more than a quarter of their time within school   %
     in administrative or pastoral work outside
     the field of English?   9.4 | 320 |

	Full-time one year	Full-time one term	Full-time 6 weeks	At least 6 sessions	Between 2 and 5 sessions
i Language and Writing	3	1	4	93	102
ii Literature (including Poetry)	6	—	3	93	100
iii Linguistics	6	1	5	50	47
iv The Teaching of Reading	3	3	—	84	128
v English as a Second Language	—	2	—	19	15
vi The place of English in Interdisciplinary Studies	2	3	2	44	86
vii Spoken English	2	1	—	30	56
viii Practical Drama	5	2	2	161	126
ix General English	26	18	16	118	127
x Remedial Teaching	22	16	8	146	109
xi The School Library?	—	3	—	63	76

8 a In the past 3 years, how many of those teaching English have attended an in-service training course of any of the durations shown on any of the following topics

Please give numbers

or equivalents

b How many different teachers are represented in the above? 1,104

% YES Yes No

9 a Have any teachers of English made use of a Teachers' Centre in connection with the teaching of English during the past year? 71·4 280 112

b How many teachers of English are involved in subject panels or committees of examining bodies in connection with English? 8·9 303

c Does the school or any member of staff
belong to

		% YES	Yes	No
i	The United Kingdom Reading Association	5·4	21	371
ii	The National Association for the Teaching of English	49·5	194	198
iii	The School Library Association	57·1	224	168
iv	The Association for the Education of Pupils from Overseas	3·1	12	380
v	The English Speaking Board	5·6	22	370
vi	The Association of Teachers of Speech and Drama?	5·6	22	370

C   ACCOMMODATION AND FACILITIES FOR ENGLISH

1   How many of the teachers of English   % YES

a teach most of their English in the same room   63·1 | 2,143 |

b move to rooms which are class bases to do
their English teaching?   27·3 | 927 |

2   a Are any of the following facilities available for the
teaching of English?

Please tick where appropriate
% YES

i	a drama studio	19·1	75
ii	a projection room	23·7	93
iii	a recording room	13·8	54
iv	a departmental store room	70·7	277
v	a departmental office	10·0	39

	Yes	No	Not Applicable
b Is there any clerical time available for the exclusive use of the English department?	31	349	12

3 Are any of the following available for the teaching of English?
Please tick where appropriate

% YES

	% YES	
a mains tape recorder	98·0	384
b battery portable tape recorder	57·4	225
c record player	98·2	385
d film projector	92·1	361
e strip/slide/loop projector	86·5	339
f television set	91·3	358
g video-tape recorder	17·9	70
h radio	82·9	325
i reprographic facilities	75·5	296
j teaching machines (including Language Master and Synchrofax)	13·8	54

D BOOKS AND LIBRARY FACILITIES

1 Is there a central school library?
Please tick appropriate box

	%	
a Yes, as a single unit	77·8	305
b Yes, in more than one unit (e.g. an upper and a lower school library)	21·2	83
c No	1·0	4

2 In the last week for how many periods was the library time-tabled for purposes other than library use? X

3 How many books are there in stock? Fiction X
Non-fiction X

% YES Yes No

4 Has your school any books on loan from the L.E.A./County/Borough Library? 64·0 251 141

		% YES	Yes	No
5	Do more than half of the rooms where English is taught have class libraries?	26·5	104	288

			Yes	No
6	Are there any facilities for the pupils to buy books within the school (e.g. a paperback "book-shop")?	32·4	127	265

E THE TESTING OF READING ATTAINMENT

1 Are standardised reading tests administered to all or part of the age-group each year:—

Please tick appropriate boxes

Age group	All pupils	Some pupils	No pupils	There are no pupils of this age-range in the school
11–12	144 39·1%	128 34·8%	96 26·1%	24
12–13	35 9·2%	216 56·7%	130 34·1%	11
13–14	22 5·8%	195 51·5%	162 42·7%	13
14–15	13 3·4%	162 42·9%	203 53·1%	14

2   Please indicate which of the following tests are used for any of these age groups:—

Please tick appropriate boxes

	%	
Schonell Silent Reading Test A	25·5	100
Schonell Silent Reading Test B	26·8	105
Schonell Graded Word Reading Test	48·5	190
Burt Rearranged Word Reading Test	15·3	60
Holborn Reading Scale	25·0	98
Neale Analysis of Reading Ability	17·6	69
N.F.E.R. Reading Test AD	4·6	18
N.F.E.R. Reading Test EH 1 Vocabulary	4·8	19
2 Comprehension	5·6	22
3 Continuous Prose	2·8	11
N.F.E.R. Reading Comprehension Test DE	4·3	17
Manchester Reading Comprehension Test	0·3	1
Young Group Reading Test	2·3	9
Southgate Group Reading Test 2	3·1	12
Other?	31·6	124

F   PROVISION FOR PUPILS WITH READING OR LANGUAGE DIFFICULTIES

If you consider that any of your pupils have special difficulties, please answer the following questions. (Please do not include here children whose first language is not English.) If you have no pupils with special difficulties, please continue at Section G.

T

1   By which of the following methods is special provision made for pupils with reading or language difficulties:

	12–13 year age group	14–15 year age group
a by withdrawal of individuals or very small groups at certain times of the week for certain purposes	194	128
b by extraction groups which remain stable for at least a term	79	37
c remedial classes formed for part of the curriculum in the course of a week	53	40
d remedial classes (or streams) which have the bulk of their work in those classes but are administered by the main school organisation (i.e. not by a Remedial Department)	63	59
e remedial classes (or streams) which have bulk of their work in those classes and are administered by a Remedial Department?	98	55

	12–13 year age group	14–15 year age group
2 a For what percentage of the *total* number of pupils in these two age groups are you able to make special provision at the moment?	10·4%	7·3%
b For what percentage of the *total* number of pupils in these two age groups do you consider it desirable to have such special provision?	12·9%	10·2%

	Yes	No	Not applicable
3 Is it a specific part of the responsibility of the head of Remedial Department (or the head of English Department) to advise specialist teachers in other subjects on the needs of pupils with low reading ability?	199	106	87
	50·8%	27·0%	22·2%

	All	Most	Some	None	Not applicable
4 a If there are separate remedial classes (or streams) to which English is taught, do they have regular classroom bases?	158	37	23	18	156
	40·3%	9·4%	5·9%	4·6%	39·8%
b If there are withdrawal groups for the teaching of reading or language work, do they have suitable accommodation?	158	40	38	22	134
	40·3%	10·2%	9·7%	5·6%	34·2%

5 Have any of the teachers working with these pupils received specific training (initial or in-service) leading to a qualification in the work in which they are involved?	% YES	Yes	No
	50·0%	167	167

G   ENGLISH FOR THE 12–13 AND 14–15 AGE GROUPS

	12–13	14–15
1 Number of pupils in these age groups	55,978	55,498
2 How many English teaching groups are there in these age groups?	2,010	2,125

3 By what methods are the groups of pupils formed to which English is taught? If there are two or more grouping methods within the year, tick the one to indicate which covers most of the pupils in the year.

	12–13	14–15
a streamed	230	184
b setted by English across the whole of the school's ability range	116	155
c setted by English across a banded section of the school's ability range	81	160
d mixed ability for the whole of the school's ability range apart from the remedial group	134	60
e mixed ability for the whole of the school's ability range	171	162
f mixed ability for a banded section of the school's ability range	204	144
g according to course or option choice	0	175
h variable/non-constant	3	12

The Committee of Inquiry would welcome any additional information or opinion which you feel may be of help.   A space is provided below.

SECONDARY SCHOOL QUESTIONNAIRE: 12 YEAR OLDS

Explanatory Notes

1.   The questionnaire is in two parts, the first of which is concerned with general organisation, staffing facilities, etc. as they relate to the teaching of English.

2.   The second part relates to a specific child in each group or class to which English is taught in the 12–13 age-group. Several copies of this section have been enclosed, and an explanation as to how the child should be selected is given on each. The relevant classes for this process are those that contain at least 5 children who were 12 but not 13 on 31 August 1972. If there are fewer than 5 such children in a class it should not be regarded as part of the age-group for the purposes of this survey. In this case it should not be included among the classes from which individual children are being selected. This part of the form should be completed for the selected child in each class by the teacher mainly responsible for the teaching of English to that class. If two or more teachers share the responsibility equally for a class, the teacher whose name is first alphabetically should be the one to complete the form. It would be helpful to the teacher if the L.E.A. and school numbers could be filled in at the head of this form before it is handed over.

3.   25 January has been chosen as the collecting date for certain information because the same figures will need to be returned in Form 7. Unfortunately, it is not possible to use the information directly from Form 7 because the Committee's material will have to be processed before that of Form 7 can be made available.

4.   It is expected that this survey will provide information about the range of teaching practices used in English with pupils of the age-group. There is no supposition that the survey will say anything about quality, of which the Committee will gain evidence from visits to a smaller number of schools. Nor will the questionnaire returns from a particular school necessarily represent a full range of the work in that school. It is accepted that where a question has to be answered about an individual child the reply may not be typical even of the class. A large number of schools is included in the survey, and the replies should give a fair picture of what is happening over the country as a whole during the week of the survey. Individual returns from schools will not be quoted.

5.   The information given about the school as a whole and about teachers and children will be treated confidentially. The names and telephone numbers have been asked for only in case any query should arise during the processing that requires further information. No names will be transferred to other records.

6.   The questionnaire aims to discover what happens in schools. The fact that a question is asked does not imply that the Committee has already adopted a particular view about what should happen.

7. It will be found helpful to read the questionnaire throughout before answering.. All questions should be answered by completing the boxes on the right-hand side of each page, entering a number or tick as appropriate. Please ignore the small numbers printed beside some of the boxes. No entries should be made in the right-hand margin.

8. If when completing the questionnaire you should have any difficulty that cannot be resolved in the school, please telephone the Department of Education and Science, Elizabeth House, York Road, London, S.E.1 (telephone 01-928-9222) and ask for the Bullock Committee Survey (ext. 3518).

9. If the number of class sections you have received is insufficient, please ask your L.E.A. for further copies.

PART 2 THE INDIVIDUAL PUPIL: 12–13 AGE GROUP

The purpose of this section is to obtain information about the teaching of English to the 12–13 age-group. Would you please select a single pupil from each of the groups to which English (including English within a remedial context) is taught in this age-group. For each group please answer the questions in relation to the first boy *or* girl who was present for the whole of the week beginning 22 January 1973 and whose name is first alphabetically (not necessarily first on the register). Separate sheets have been sent for each of these pupils. Please read the section throughout before beginning to answer. You will note that the questions relate to the time the pupil spent on various activities during that week. It is recognised that it may have been an untypical week, but such is the nature of the sample that this will not invalidate the results.

1 a Name of class or group...
(If the class is known by the name of the teacher, please give that.)

		Boy?	497

b Is this pupil a

		Girl?	442

2 For this pupil is English

Please tick one box only
%

		%	
a	taught as a separately timetabled subject	93.1	874
b	taught as a separately recognisable element in an integrated scheme	4.6	43
c	completely assimilated into an integrated scheme of which it is an indistinguishable element?	2.3	22

3   How many pupils are there in the group in which this pupil has his/her English?   [X]

	%YES	Yes	No
4 Is this a remedial class or group?	11.4	107	832

5   How would you assess the reading standard of this pupil in comparison with nationally recognised norms?

	Below average (bottom 25%)	Average (middle 50%)	Above average (top 25%)
	212	499	228
	22.6%	53.1%	24.3%

Questions 6–9: If you have ticked c as the answer to question 2 please do not answer questions 6, 7, 8 and 9 below but continue at question 10.

6   a   Total time in minutes allocated to English in respect of this pupil. (Please include drama only if it is taught as an integral part of the work of the English department.)

In school	Home-work
202	43

    b   Number of school periods involved   an average of   [5.5]

7   How many of the English lessons were over an hour's duration?   [X]

8   Does the teacher who takes this pupil for most of his/her English have:

		%	
a	an honours degree in English with a post-graduate certificate in Education	14.4	132
b	a degree in which English is one of the subjects, with a post-graduate certificate in Education	9.4	86
c	a teaching certificate or B.Ed. qualification following a main or advanced course in English at a College of Education or Education Department of a Polytechnic	43.0	393
d	an honours degree in English	3.3	30
e	a degree in which English is one of the subjects	2.9	27
f	a main or advanced course qualification in drama	2.3	21
g	none of the above?	24.6	225

9   How many teachers are involved in teaching
    English to this pupil?   an average of | 1.4 |

10   TIME SPENT ON DIFFERENT ACTIVITIES

Writing

a   What amount of time during the week beginning 22 January 1973 did this pupil devote to any of the following writing activities? (Please do not indicate the same activity under more than one heading.) The amount of time spent in school should be shown at I and the amount of time allocated for homework should be shown at II.

I In School   Minutes

		0	1–30	31–60	61–90	91–120	121–150	Over 150
i	stories and plays	563	181	152	38	5	—	—
ii	from personal experience	630	191	103	14	—	—	1
iii	argument and exposition	761	126	38	14	—	—	—
iv	description	693	191	47	7	1	—	—
v	reproductive, i.e. writing in pupil's own words of material derived from printed or oral sources	600	197	110	23	2	4	3
vi	letters	859	55	23	1	—	1	—
vii	verse	731	166	39	2	1	—	—
viii	copying of existing printed material, e.g. for anthologies or topics	802	100	29	6	1	1	—
ix	written corrections and fair copying of own work	667	256	14	1	1	—	—

II Homework

Minutes

		0	1–30	31–60	61–90	91–120	121–150	Over 150
i	stories and plays	698	176	62	1	2	—	—
ii	from personal experience	747	156	33	3	—	—	—
iii	argument and exposition	860	69	10	—	—	—	—
iv	description	793	126	19	1	—	—	—
v	reproductive, i.e. writing in pupil's own words of material derived from printed or oral sources	777	134	26	1	—	1	—
vi	letters	901	35	3	—	—	—	—
vii	verse	866	66	7	—	—	—	—
viii	copying of existing printed material, e.g. for anthologies or topics	903	31	5	—	—	—	—
ix	written corrections and fair copying of own work	823	112	4	—	—	—	—

b Was the writing to

		%YES	Yes	No
i	titles set by teacher	44.8	421	518
ii	free choice by pupil	10.3	97	842
iii	free choice by pupil within given themes?	57.3	538	401

c   In the correction of the pupil's written work is it the practice to

		%YES	Yes	No
i	correct all errors on the work itself	23.6	222	717
ii	correct some errors on the work itself	71.8	674	265
iii	correct no errors on the work itself	2.4	23	916
iv	discuss the pupil's errors with him/her individually	74.5	700	239
v	require the pupil to write out corrected spellings	59.6	560	379
vi	require the pupil to learn to spell correctly words he/she has misspelt?	47.6	447	492

Oral English

What amount of time during the week beginning 22 January 1973 did the pupil devote to any of the following activities?

Minutes

			0	1–30	31–60	61–90	91–120	121–150	Over 150
i		debates, lecturettes and mock interviews	826	82	26	4	—	1	—
ii	a	class discussion on topics chosen by teacher	442	404	89	3	1	—	—
	b	discussion in small groups on topics chosen by the teacher	835	87	16	1	—	—	—
	c	class discussion on topics of pupil's own choice	828	89	21	—	—	—	1
	d	discussion in small groups on topics of pupil's own choice	892	39	6	2	—	—	—
iii	a	improvised drama	609	171	135	22	2	—	—
	b	drama from a printed text	809	74	50	6	—	—	—
iv		listening to broadcast, record, or tape	808	103	23	3	1	—	1

Language Study

What amount of time during that week did the pupil devote to any of the following activities? The amount of time spent in school should be shown at I and the amount of time allocated for homework should be shown at II.

I   In School

Minutes

		0	1–30	31–60	61–90	91–120	121–150	Over 150
i a	grammar exercises	71C	173	46	6	3	1	—
b	instruction in usage from errors arising from written work	586	333	16	1	1	—	2
ii a	punctuation exercises	787	132	18	2	—	—	—
b	punctuation instruction from errors arising from written work	746	189	3	1	—	—	—
iii a	vocabulary exercises	738	175	22	4	—	—	—
b	vocabulary study arising from written work	786	140	11	1	1	—	—
c	vocabulary study arising from literature	726	203	10	—	—	—	—
iv a	comprehension exercises	621	213	93	9	2	—	1
b	comprehension work arising from discussion of literature or other material	690	194	40	14	1	—	—
v a	spelling practice from lists	859	77	3	—	—	—	—
b	spelling practice by dictation of passages	909	29	1	—	—	—	—
c	spelling practice arising from written work	814	118	6	1	—	—	—
d	spelling tests	815	120	4	—	—	—	—
vi	linguistics-based language study	903	26	10	—	—	—	—

II *Homework*

Minutes

		0	1–30	31–60	61–90	91–120	121–150	Over 150
i a	grammar exercises	869	66	4	—	—	—	—
b	instruction in usage from errors arising from written work	903	36	—	—	—	—	—
ii a	punctuation exercises	896	42	1	—	—	—	—
b	punctuation instruction from errors arising from written work	912	25	2	—	—	—	—
iii a	vocabulary exercises	875	61	2	1	—	—	—
b	vocabulary study arising from written work	883	55	1	—	—	—	—
c	vocabulary study arising from literature	892	46	1	—	—	—	—
iv a	comprehension exercises	826	107	5	1	—	—	—
b	comprehension work arising from discussion of literature or other material	866	70	2	1	—	—	—
v a	spelling practice from lists	881	58	—	—	—	—	—
b	spelling practice by dictation of passages	938	1	—	—	—	—	—
c	spelling practice arising from written work	877	61	1	—	—	—	—
d	spelling tests	925	14	—	—	—	—	—
vi linguistics-based language study		927	10	2	—	—	—	—

PART NINE: THE SURVEY

Reading

What amount of time during the week beginning 22 January 1973 did the pupil devote to any of the following activities? The amount of time spent in school should be shown at I and the amount of time allocated for homework should be shown at II.

I In School

Minutes

	0	1– 30	31– 60	61– 90	91– 120	121– 150	Over 150
i a private reading of fiction	495	306	125	13	—	—	—
b private reading of non-fiction	834	92	10	3	—	—	—
ii private reading of fiction leading to: a group discussion	914	23	2	—	—	—	—
b class discussion	844	81	12	2	—	—	—
iii private reading of non-fiction leading to: a group discussion	923	13	2	1	—	—	—
b class discussion	914	20	4	1	—	—	—
iv class reading (with teacher) of fiction leading to: a group discussion	813	84	40	2	—	—	—
b class discussion	492	296	137	13	1	—	—
v class reading (with teacher) of non-fiction leading to: a group discussion	912	23	2	2	—	—	—
b class discussion	872	55	10	2	—	—	—
vi a private reading of poetry	895	43	1	—	—	—	—
b class reading of poetry (with teacher)	655	234	48	2	—	—	—
vii reading for topic, project, or theme work	749	157	26	2	4	1	—
viii reading to improve reading skills	707	176	38	7	6	2	3

II   Homework

Minutes

	0	1–30	31–60	61–90	91–120	121–150	Over 150
i a private reading of fiction	599	254	67	10	4	1	4
b private reading of non-fiction	896	38	4	—	1	—	—
ii private reading of poetry	906	31	2	—	—	—	—
iii private reading of drama	927	12	—	—	—	—	—
iv reading for topic, project or theme work	809	108	21	1	—	—	—

SECONDARY SCHOOL QUESTIONNAIRE: 14 YEAR OLDS

Explanatory Notes

1   The questionnaire is in two parts, the first of which is concerned with general organisation, staffing facilities, etc. as they relate to the teaching of English.

2   The second part relates to a specific child in each group or class to which English is taught in the 14–15 age-group. Several copies of this section have been enclosed, and an explanation as to how the child should be selected is given on each. The relevant classes for this process are those that contain at least 5 children who were 14 but not 15 on 31 August 1972. If there are fewer than 5 such children in a class it should not be regarded as part of the age-group for the purposes of this survey. In this case it should not be included among the classes from which individual children are being selected. This part of the form should be completed for the selected child in each class by the teacher mainly responsible for the teaching of English to that class. If two or more teachers share the responsibility equally for a class, the teacher whose name is first alphabetically should be the one to complete the form. It would be helpful to the teacher if the L.E.A. and school numbers could be filled in at the head of this form before it is handed over.

3   25 January has been chosen as the collecting date for certain information because the same figures will need to be returned in Form 7. Unfortunately, it is not possible to use the information directly from Form 7 because the Committee's material will have to be processed before that of Form 7 can be made available.

4 It is expected that this survey will provide information about the range of teaching practices used in English with pupils of the age-group. There is no supposition that the survey will say anything about quality, of which the Committee will gain evidence from visits to a smaller number of schools. Nor will the questionnaire returns from a particular school necessarily represent a full range of the work in that school. It is accepted that where a question has to be answered about an individual child the reply may not be typical even of the class. A large number of schools is included in the survey, and the replies should give a fair picture of what is happening over the country as a whole during the week of the survey. Individual returns from schools will not be quoted.

5 The information given about the school as a whole and about teachers and children will be treated confidentially. The names and telephone numbers have been asked for only in case any query should arise during the processing that requires further information. No names will be transferred to other records.

6 The questionnaire aims to discover what happens in schools. The fact that a question is asked does not imply that the Committee has already adopted a particular view about what should happen.

7 It will be found helpful to read the questionnaire throughout before answering. All questions should be answered by completing the boxes on the right-hand side of each page, entering a number or tick as appropriate. Please ignore the small numbers printed beside some of the boxes. No entries should be made in the right-hand margin.

8 If when completing the questionnaire you should have any difficulty that cannot be resolved in the school, please telephone the Department of Education and Science, Elizabeth House, York Road, London, S.E.1 (telephone 01-928-9222) and ask for the Bullock Committee Survey (ext 3518).

9 If the number of class sections you have received is insufficient, please ask your L.E.A. for further copies.

PART 2   THE INDIVIDUAL PUPIL: 14–15 AGE GROUP

The purpose of this section is to obtain information about the teaching of English to the 14–15 age-group. Would you please select a single pupil from each of the groups to which English (including English within a remedial context) is taught in this age-group. For each group please answer the questions in relation to the first boy *or* girl who was present for the whole of the week beginning 22 January 1973 and whose name is first alphabetically (not necessarily first on the register). Separate sheets have been sent for each of these pupils. Please read the section throughout before beginning to answer. You will note that the questions relate to the time the pupil spent on various activities during that week. It is recognised that it may have been an untypical week, but such is the nature of the sample that this will not invalidate the results.

1 a   Name of class or group...
        (If the class is known by the name of the teacher, please give that.)

                                                              Boy? | 578 |
   b   Is this pupil a
                                                              Girl? | 474 |

2   For this pupil is English

                                                    Please tick one box only
                                                         %

   a   taught as a separately timetabied subject   93.8 | 987 |
   b   taught as a separately recognisable element in
        an integrated scheme   2.9 | 30 |
   c   completely assimilated into an integrated scheme
        of which it is an indistinguishable element?   3.3 | 35 |

3   How many pupils are there in the group in which this
    pupil has his/her English? | X |

4   Is this group   Please tick one box only
                                                    %

   a   in the first year of a 2-year "O" level course   21.5 | 226 |

   b   in the first year of a 2-year C.S.E. course   32.2 | 339 |
   c   in the first year of a course which may culminate
        in either "O" level or C.S.E. for some or all of the
        pupils   29.5 | 310 |
   d   on a course which culminates in "O" level in
        Summer Term 1973   1.6 | 17 |

   e   on a course which leads to no examination   10.2 | 107 |

   f   a remedial class or group?   5.0 | 53 |

[If English is one component of a group of subjects which are examined together, e.g. as Humanities, please regard it as a separate subject for the purpose of the above question.]

	Below average (bottom 25%)	Average (middle 50%)	Above average (top 25%)
5 How would you assess the reading standard of this pupil in comparison with nationally recognised norms?	211	563	278
	20.1%	53.5%	26.4%

Questions 6-9: If you have ticked c as the answer to question 2 please do not answer questions 6, 7, 8 and 9 below but continue at question 10.

6   a   Total time in minutes allocated to English
in respect of this pupil. (Please include
drama only if it is taught as an integral
part of the work of the English department.)

In school	Home-work
196	59

     b   Number of school periods involved   An average of   5.25

7   How many of the English lessons were over an hour's
duration?   X

8   Does the teacher who takes this pupil for most of his/her English have

		%	
a	an honours degree in English with a post-graduate certificate in Education	22.5	229
b	a degree in which English is one of the subjects, with a post-graduate certificate in Education	12.3	126
c	a teaching certificate or B.Ed. qualification following a main or advanced course in English at a College of Education or Education Department of a Polytechnic	38.1	387
d	an honours degree in English	4.3	44
e	a degree in which English is one of the subjects	1.8	18
f	a main or advanced course qualification in drama	2.6	26
g	none of the above?	18.4	187

9   How many teachers are involved in teaching English
to this pupil?   an average of   1.2

10   Time spent on different activities

Writing

a   What amount of time during the week beginning 22 January 1973 did
this pupil devote to any of the following writing activities? (Please do
not indicate the same activity under more than one heading.) The
amount of time spent in school should be shown at I and the amount of
time allocated for homework should be shown at II.

I In School

Minutes

	0	1–30	31–60	61–90	91–120	121–150	Over 150
i	stories and plays	782	123	103	33	7	3	1
ii	from personal experience	759	167	104	18	3	—	1
iii	argument and exposition	786	165	82	15	3	1	—
iv	description	818	139	81	13	1	—	—
v	reproductive, i.e. writing in pupil's own words of material derived from printed or oral sources	674	183	141	40	10	1	3
vi	letters	928	84	33	7	—	—	—
vii	verse	943	77	27	4	1	—	—
viii	copying of existing printed material, e.g. for anthologies or topics	951	60	31	10	—	—	—
ix	written corrections and fair copying of own work	845	195	11	1	—	—	—

II Homework

Minutes

	0	1–30	31–60	61–90	91–120	121–150	Over 150
i	stories and plays	859	97	76	10	7	—	3
ii	from personal experience	841	127	78	4	2	—	—
iii	argument and exposition	863	98	82	9	—	—	—
iv	description	908	91	48	5	—	—	—
v	reproductive, i.e. writing in pupil's own words of material derived from printed or oral sources	853	116	68	13	1	1	—
vi	letters	995	45	12	—	—	—	—
vii	verse	995	38	17	2	—	—	—
viii	copying of existing printed material, e.g. for anthologies or topics	1007	34	11	—	—	—	—
ix	written corrections and fair copying of own work	961	84	6	—	1	—	—

b   Was the writing to:

		% YES	Yes	No
i	titles set by teacher	54·1	570	482
ii	free choice by pupil	10·4	109	943
iii	free choice by pupil within given themes?	49·6	522	530

c   In the correction of the pupil's written work is it the practice to

		% YES	Yes	No
i	correct all errors on the work itself	31.0	326	726
ii	correct some errors on the work itself	64.5	679	373
iii	correct no errors on the work itself	1.7	18	1,034
iv	discuss the pupil's errors with him/her individually	78.3	824	228
v	require the pupil to write out corrected spellings	41.1	432	620
vi	require the pupil to learn to spell correctly words he/she has misspelt?	40.5	426	626

Oral English

What amount of time during the week beginning 22 January 1973 did the pupil devote to any of the following activities?

Minutes

			0	1–30	31–60	61–90	91–120	121–150	Over 150
i		debates, lecturettes and mock interviews	921	87	34	6	1	1	2
ii	a	class discussion on topics chosen by teacher	457	395	175	19	5	1	—
	b	discussion in small groups on topics chosen by the teacher	910	119	17	6	—	—	—
	c	class discussion on topics of pupil's own choice	944	81	25	2	—	—	—
	d	discussion in small groups on topics of pupil's own choice	990	46	13	2	—	1	—
iii	a	improvised drama	937	68	31	15	—	—	1
	b	drama from a printed text	789	117	118	23	3	1	1
iv		listening to broadcast, record, or tape	845	129	64	10	3	1	—

Language Study

What amount of time during that week did the pupil devote to any of the following activities? The amount of time spent in school should be shown at I and the amount of time allocated for homework should be shown at II.

Minutes

I *In School*	0	1–30	31–60	61–90	91–120	121–150	Over 150
i a grammar exercises	944	87	14	6	1	—	—
b instruction in usage from errors arising from written work	753	285	14	—	—	—	—
ii a punctuation exercises	942	96	13	1	—	—	—
b punctuation instruction from errors arising from written work	891	156	5	—	—	—	—
iii a vocabulary exercises	855	167	28	2	—	—	—
b vocabulary study arising from written work	902	143	7	—	—	—	—
c vocabulary study arising from literature	839	208	5	—	—	—	—
iv a comprehension exercises	710	197	122	22	1	—	—
b comprehension work arising from discussion of literature or other material	705	267	69	10	1	—	—
v a spelling practice from lists	1019	31	2	—	—	—	—
b spelling practice by dictation of passages	1026	23	2	1	—	—	—
c spelling practice arising from written work	960	88	4	—	—	—	—
d spelling tests	976	73	3	—	—	—	—
vi linguistics-based language study	1022	21	7	2	—	—	—

II Homework

Minutes

	0	1–30	31–60	61–90	91–120	121–150	Over 150
i a grammar exercises	1014	26	12	—	—	—	—
b instruction in usage from errors arising from written work	1025	26	1	—	—	—	—
ii a punctuation exercises	1019	31	2	—	—	—	—
b punctuation instruction from errors arising from written work	1036	16	—	—	—	—	—
iii a vocabulary exercises	979	65	7	1	—	—	—
b vocabulary study arising from written work	1021	27	4	—	—	—	—
c vocabulary study arising from literature	1020	30	1	—	1	—	—
iv a comprehension exercises	916	110	24	1	—	—	—
b comprehension work arising from discussion of literature or other material	946	90	14	1	1	—	—
v a spelling practice from lists	1029	18	5	—	—	—	—
b spelling practice by dictation of passages	1050	2	—	—	—	—	—
c spelling practice arising from written work	1024	28	—	—	—	—	—
d spelling tests	1044	7	1	—	—	—	—
vi linguistics-based language study	1043	8	1	—	—	—	—

Reading

What amount of time during the week beginning 22 January 1973 did the pupil devote to any of the following activities? The amount of time spent in school should be shown at I and the amount of time allocated for homework should be shown at II.

			0	1–30	31–60	61–90	91–120	121–150	Over 150
I	*In School*								
i	a	private reading of fiction	640	238	151	13	2	1	7
	b	private reading of non-fiction	960	70	21	1	—	—	—
ii		private reading of fiction leading to:							
	a	group discussion	1,025	18	8	—	1	—	—
	b	class discussion	946	85	19	2	—	—	—
iii		private reading of non-fiction leading to:							
	a	group discussion	1,030	20	2	—	—	—	—
	b	class discussion	1,010	37	5	—	—	—	—
iv		class reading (with teacher) of fiction leading to:							
	a	group discussion	929	68	48	5	2	—	—
	b	class discussion	643	224	158	20	4	—	3
v		class reading (with teacher) of non-fiction leading to:							
	a	group discussion	1,032	17	3	—	—	—	—
	b	class discussion	976	56	18	1	1	—	—
vi	a	private reading of poetry	1,016	31	5	—	—	—	—
	b	class reading of poetry (with teacher)	811	179	61	1	—	—	—
vii		reading for topic, project, or theme work	845	150	49	7	1	—	—
viii		reading to improve reading skills	914	99	32	6	—	1	—

(Minutes)

II Homework

Minutes

	0	1–30	31–60	61–90	91–120	121–150	Over 150
i a private reading of fiction	632	251	118	22	13	4	12
b private reading of non-fiction	982	38	16	6	4	2	4
ii private reading of poetry	995	53	3	1	—	—	—
iii private reading of drama	1,002	33	12	3	—	—	2
iv reading for topic, project or theme work	853	149	40	5	1	2	2

V   TECHNICAL NOTES

Analysing the Data

25.33   The survey had two main aspects: provision for English teaching in the schools and practice in the classes. Our aim was to make simple statements about the proportions of schools and classes having specified facilities or working on specific activities. In the main, therefore, the analysis of both primary and secondary data has been a simple matter of tabulating frequencies and calculating percentages, with occasional cross-tabulations. In the usual way, mean values derived from the samples have been taken to provide estimates of mean values within the population, and in all instances we have provided information upon the range of responses. This is presented either in full tables within the text and the commentaries or in the reproductions of the questionnaires in paragraph 25.32. In paragraph 25.36 we supply the means to determine the limits of confidence which are appropriate in interpreting any proportion or percentage derived from the data; paragraph 25.37 assists in deciding whether differences in proportion are significant. Certain other statistical tests of significance have been used, and these are described in paragraph 25.40.

25.34   In the secondary section the data on the actual English teaching which takes place could not be analysed in the same manner. The combined effect of having many subdivisions and the possibility of zero or 'nil' returns led us to present the data in two ways. Firstly, we have calculated the average time devoted to each specific activity by all teachers and rendered this as a percentage of the time allocated by all teachers to the main head from which it came (see table 97 in paragraph 25.31). For example, the time devoted to debates, lecturettes and mock interviews by all teachers of 12 year olds was 7·8 per cent of the total time given to Oral English activities. Secondly, however, it was necessary to acknowledge that NOT ALL teachers would have covered every specific activity. Therefore we have also provided the proportion of teachers who did record the specific activity (12.1 per cent in Table 96) during the week in question and have used this to calculate an average teaching time. Thus 25 minutes was the average time spent on "debates, lecturettes and mock interviews" by those teachers who included them in their work during the week of recording.

25.35   Two points had to be considered before we decided to present the data on activities in this fashion. The first was the apparently wide time intervals of 30 minutes provided. The second was the pattern of responses evoked. The data incorporated in the reproduction of the questionnaires in paragraph 25.32 show that the distribution of response was highly skewed, even if the use of the 'nil return' category is ignored. We had to ask whether the width of the time intervals had forced the pattern of responses and rendered suspect our method of calculating average times, i.e. using the mid-point of each interval. However, width of time intervals—30 minutes— does not appear to have operated in this way if we consider that the overall average English time calculated from these returns matches closely the values obtained from an independent question. (See paragraph 25.13.) It thus appears that 30 minutes was a reasonable choice in the context of a week's activities.

The Precision of Estimates

Proportions and Percentages

25.36   Since we wished to be able to state what proportion of schools had certain resources and what proportion of classes were taught in various ways, the results have been quoted in percentage terms, e.g. Table 30 in paragraph 25.18 shows that 59·5 per cent of 6 year olds' classes used Alphabetic Analysis in their approach to reading. If 59·5 per cent is regarded as an estimate of the percentage of all such classes in our sample using this method, it must be understood that a degree of error attends this and all similar stated per-centages. The magnitude of the error is dependent upon the size of the sample and upon how extreme the percentage is, and Table 98 sets out the sizes of error that are possible. The above example can be used here to show how the magnitude of possible error is determined.

The total number of classes upon which the 59·5 per cent is based is 1,417. The nearest sample size quoted in Table 98 is 1,500 and the nearest per-centage quoted is 60 per cent. The table shows the 95 per cent confidence limits for this particular combination of sample size and percentage as being 60 per cent±2·5 per cent. This may be interpreted as meaning that were a census of all schools to be undertaken then there are 19 chances in 20 that the population percentage would lie between 57·5 per cent and 62·5 per cent. In our example, 59·5 per cent of classes of 6 year olds using Alphabetic Analysis was an estimate, based on 1,417 classes, of the propor-tion in the whole population which used this method. This is sufficiently near the 60 per cent of the 1,500 sample shown in the table to enable the statement to be made that there are 19 chances in 20 that the population percentage would lie between 57·0 per cent and 62·0 per cent were a census of all schools to be undertaken and the proportion were measured of 6 year olds' classes using Alphabetic Analysis in their approach to reading.

Differences of Proportions

25.37   The analysis of the data has, in places, been in terms which permit the comparison between differently defined groups. For example, Table 31 shows that 68·9 per cent of deliberately vertically grouped classes with 6 year olds use Alphabetic Analysis compared with 55·6 per cent of classes that are not vertically grouped. The question arises as to whether these two percentages indicate that Alphabetic Analysis is used more in deliberately vertically grouped classes than in classes that are not vertically grouped or whether these two different percentages have resulted merely by chance.

The first step in assessing this is to calculate the weighted average of the two samples, i.e.

$$\frac{n_1 p_1 + n_2 p_2}{n_1 + n_2}$$

which in this example becomes

$$\frac{322 \times 68·9 + 781 \times 55·6}{322 + 781}$$

= 59·5 per cent, i.e. the overall proportion of 6 year olds' classes using Alphabetic Analysis in these two groups.

The next step is to consult Table 99 and locate under the column headed 40/60 per cent the pair of sample sizes nearest to 322 and 781. In this case sample sizes of 1,000 and 400 are shown as having a significant difference (at the 95 per cent probability level) at 5·7 per cent.

The example shown above has a difference of 13·3 per cent (68·9—55·6). Since this greatly exceeds the 5·7 per cent, we may safely conclude that a difference of this magnitude would not have arisen by chance and therefore that deliberately vertically grouped classes are more likely to use Alphabetic Analysis than are classes which are not vertically grouped.

The Basis of the Tables

25.38   Table 98 has been based on the formula for the standard deviation in simple sampling of attributes i.e.

$$\sqrt{\frac{pq}{n}}$$

The ± percentages in Table 98 have been calculated as follows:—

$$\left(1·96 \sqrt{\frac{pq}{n}} \right) \times 100$$

and these percentages have then been added and subtracted from the example percentages at the top of each column.

25.39   Table 99 has been prepared by applying the sample numbers and proportions to the formulae for testing the significance of the differences between proportions.[1]

The percentages shown in the table represent the differences between two sample proportions which could arise from random sampling in 1 in 20 occasions on the assumption that the two samples had been drawn from the same population. It follows that if the differences between two proportions exceed the level shown in the table it may be stated that the difference is significant at the 95 per cent level of significance. This level is commonly taken to mean that larger differences would have been obtained from different populations and therefore that the proportions quoted are different and not merely sampling fluctuations about the same joint proportion. Conversely, smaller differences may well have arisen from sampling fluctuations and thus do not necessarily imply that the two proportions have come from different populations.

An example of the application of the formulae is given below for samples of size 1,000 and 200, where 35 per cent of the 1,000 sample (1) and 25 per cent of the 200 sample (2) exhibited a particular characteristic.

Standard Error of difference
in proportions

$$= \sigma_{(p_1 - p_2)} = \sqrt{p_0 q_0 \left(\frac{1}{n_1} + \frac{1}{n_2} \right)}$$

Where p_0 = weighted average of 2 proportions $\dfrac{n_1 p_1 + n_2 p_2}{n_1 + n_2}$

$$p_0 = \frac{\cdot 35 \times 1,000 + \cdot 25 \times 200}{1,000 + 200}$$

$$= \frac{350 + 50}{1,200}$$

$$= \cdot 30$$

$$\text{Thus } \sigma_{p_1 - p_2} = \sqrt{\cdot 30 \times \cdot 70 \left(\frac{1}{1,000} \times \frac{1}{200} \right)}$$

$$= \cdot 0355 \text{ or } 3 \cdot 55 \text{ per cent.}$$

A difference between two proportions exceeding ($1 \cdot 96 \times 3 \cdot 55$ per cent) $7 \cdot 0$ per cent would be significant at the 95 per cent level of confidence. Any increase in the difference above $7 \cdot 0$ per cent would increase this level of confidence.

Table 98

RANGES OF PERCENTAGES WITHIN WHICH THERE IS A 95 PER CENT CHANCE
THAT THE POPULATION PERCENTAGE WILL LIE

		1	5	10	20	30	40	50	60	70	80	90	95	99
For samples of size														
50	±	3	6	8	11	13	14	14	14	13	11	8	6	3
	From	—	—	2	9	17	26	36	46	57	69	82	89	96
	To	4	11	18	31	43	54	64	74	83	91	98	100	100
100	±	1	4	6	8	9	10	10	10	9	8	6	4	2
	From	—	1	4	12	21	30	40	50	61	72	84	91	97
	To	2	9	16	28	39	50	60	70	79	88	96	99	100
200	±	1·4	3·0	4·2	5·5	6·4	6·8	6·9	6·8	6·4	5·5	4·2	3·0	1·4
	From	—	2·0	5·8	14·5	23·6	33·2	43·1	53·2	63·6	74·5	85·8	92·0	97·6
	To	2·4	8·0	14·2	25·5	36·4	46·8	56·9	66·8	76·4	85·5	94·2	98·0	100·0
500	±	0·9	1·9	2·6	3·5	4·0	4·3	4·4	4·3	4·0	3·5	2·6	1·9	0·9
	From	0·1	3·1	7·4	16·5	26·0	35·7	45·6	55·7	66·0	76·5	87·4	93·1	98·1
	To	1·9	6·9	12·6	23·5	34·0	44·3	54·4	64·3	74·0	83·5	92·6	96·9	99·9
1,000	±	0·6	1·4	1·9	2·5	2·8	3·0	3·1	3·0	2·8	2·5	1·9	1·4	0·6
	From	0·4	3·6	8·1	17·5	27·2	37·0	46·9	57·0	67·2	77·5	88·1	93·6	98·4
	To	1·6	6·4	11·9	22·5	32·8	43·0	53·1	63·0	72·8	82·5	91·9	96·4	99·6
1,500	±	0·5	1·1	1·5	2·0	2·3	2·5	2·5	2·5	2·3	2·0	1·5	1·1	0·5
	From	0·5	3·9	8·5	18·0	27·7	37·5	47·5	57·5	67·7	78·0	88·5	93·9	98·5
	To	1·5	6·1	11·5	22·0	32·3	42·5	52·5	62·5	72·3	82·0	91·5	96·1	99·5

Table 99

PERCENTAGE DIFFERENCES BETWEEN TWO SAMPLES FROM THE SAME
POPULATION THAT COULD BE GIVEN BY 5 PER CENT OF PAIRS OF SAMPLES

Size of Sample 1	Size of Sample 2	5/95	10/90	15/85	20/80	25/75	30/70	35/65	40/60	45/55	50/50
2,000	1,000	5·2	2·3	8·6	3·0	3·3	3·5	3·6	11·8	3·8	3·8
1,500	1,500	1·5	2·1	2·5	2·8	3·1	3·2	3·4	3·4	3·5	3·5
1,000	1,000	1·9	2·6	3·1	3·5	3·8	4·0	4·2	4·3	4·4	4·4
	400	2·5	3·5	4·1	4·6	4·9	5·3	5·5	5·7	5·8	5·8
	200	0·3	4·5	5·4	6·1	6·6	7·0	7·2	7·4	7·5	7·6
	100	4·5	6·2	7·3	8·2	8·9	9·4	9·8	10·1	10·2	10·3
	50	6·2	8·5	10·1	11·3	12·3	13·0	13·5	13·9	14·1	14·2
500	500	2·7	3·7	4·4	4·9	5·4	5·7	5·9	6·1	6·2	6·2
	400	2·9	3·9	4·7	16·6	5·7	6·0	6·3	6·4	6·5	6·6
	300	3·1	4·3	5·1	5·7	6·2	6·5	2·1	7·0	7·1	7·1
	200	3·6	4·9	5·8	6·5	7·1	7·5	7·8	8·0	8·2	8·2
	100	4·7	6·4	7·7	8·6	9·3	9·8	10·2	10·5	10·7	10·7
200	200	4·3	5·9	7·0	7·8	8·5	9·0	9·3	9·6	9·7	9·8
	100	16·5	7·2	8·6	9·6	10·4	11·0	11·4	11·8	11·9	12·0
100	100	6·0	8·3	9·9	11·1	12·0	12·7	13·2	13·6	13·8	13·9
	50	7·4	10·2	12·1	13·6	14·7	15·5	16·2	16·6	16·9	16·9
50	50	8·5	11·8	14·0	15·7	17·0	18·0	18·7	19·2	19·5	16·9

Other Testing

25.40 Elsewhere in the report where figures are provided it has been appropriate to apply one of two other statistical tests of significance to ascertain that apparent differences and relationships are unlikely to be due to chance. Where we have compared mean values—for example, the analysis of different times spent on English (Table 91, paragraph 25.31, Secondary Commentary)—the difference between the means has been tested using the standard t-test. Where 2-way relationships have needed to be tested—for example, the use of teachers' centres by teachers from different sizes of school (Table 27, in paragraph 25.17ii)—the chi-square test has been employed.[2]

The Validity of the Sample

25.41 In order to be assured that the results of this survey may be taken to be representative of all schools in England, we have compared certain characteristics of the schools in the sample with known characteristics of all schools in England. By so doing, and confirming that the characteristics that were checked are unbiased, we may not unreasonably infer that the results of the survey will represent equivalent results for England as a whole, should a census be undertaken.

The comparisons with all schools in England in January 1973 were as follows:

(*a*) Type of school.

(*b*) Regional distribution of schools.

(*c*) Average size of school.

(*d*) Distribution by size of schools.

(*e*) Pupil/teacher ratio.

Table 100

A. A COMPARISON OF THE DISTRIBUTION OF THE TYPES OF SCHOOL IN THE SAMPLE AND IN THE TOTAL IN ENGLAND

January 1973

	England		Sample schools	
	Number	*Percentage*	*Number*	*Percentage*
Primary				
Infant	4,704	*22·2*	207	*22·1*
First	1,131	*5·3*	45	*4·8*
Infant with Junior	10,650	*50·3*	475	*50·8*
First and Middle	143	*0·7*	5	*0·5*
Junior	4,314	*20·4*	194	*20·7*
Middle deemed Primary (8–12)	223	*1·1*	10	*1·1*
Total	21,175	*100·0*	936	*100·0*

$$\chi^2 = 0\cdot8, \text{d.f.} = 5, p = \cdot98$$

January 1973

	England		Sample Schools	
	Number	*Percentage*	*Number*	*Percentage*
Secondary				
Modern	1,841	*40·5*	165	*42·1*
Grammar	783	*17·2*	73	*18·6*
Comprehensive	1,640	*36·1*	140	*35·7*
Technical	43	*0·9*	5	*1·3*
Other	240	*5·3*	9	*2·3*
Total	4,547	*100·0*	392	*100·0*

$$\chi^2 = 4\cdot0, \text{ d.f.} = 4, \text{ p} = \cdot41$$

The questionnaires for the primary schools were to cover the two age groups, 6 years and 9 years. In order to avoid overburdening the sample schools we selected twice as many Infants with Junior and First and Middle Schools: half were required to complete questionnaires for 6 year olds and the other half for 9 year olds, i.e. 964 different schools of this type took part in the survey and are included in the class analysis but only 480 were included in the sample of schools.

Table 101

B.   A COMPARISON OF THE REGIONAL DISTRIBUTION OF SCHOOLS IN THE SAMPLE AND IN THE TOTAL IN ENGLAND

	Primary				Secondary			
	England		Sample schools		England		Sample schools	
	No.	*%*	*No.*	*%*	*No.*	*%*	*No.*	*%*
Region								
North	1,838	*8·7*	78	*8·3*	398	*8·8*	36	*9·2*
Yorkshire and Humberside	2,283	*10·8*	106	*11·3*	437	*9·6*	40	*10·2*
East Midlands	1,818	*8·6*	90	*9·6*	397	*8·7*	34	*8·9*
East Anglia	1,029	*4·9*	43	*4·6*	171	*3·8*	19	*4·8*
Greater London	2,295	*10·8*	89	*9·5*	626	*13·8*	48	*12·2*
Other South East	4,181	*19·7*	191	*20·4*	892	*19·6*	67	*17·3*
South West	2,169	*10·2*	98	*10·4*	385	*8·5*	39	*9·9*
West Midlands	2,398	*11·3*	100	*10·6*	556	*12·2*	47	*12·0*
North West	3,164	*14·9*	143	*15·3*	685	*15·1*	62	*15·8*
England	21,175	*99·9*	936	*100·0*	4,547	*100·1*	392	*100·0*

$$\chi^2 = 4\cdot1 \qquad\qquad \chi^2 = 4\cdot3$$
$$\text{d.f.} = 8 \qquad\qquad \text{d.f.} = 8$$
$$\text{p} = \cdot85 \qquad\qquad \text{p} = \cdot83$$

Table 102

C. A COMPARISON OF THE AVERAGE SIZE OF SCHOOL IN THE SAMPLE AND AVERAGE SIZE OF SCHOOL IN ENGLAND

	Number on roll	
	Primary	*Secondary*
England	230	665
Sample Schools	230	665

Table 103

D. A COMPARISON OF THE SIZES OF SCHOOL IN THE SAMPLE AND IN THE TOTAL IN ENGLAND

	Primary				*Secondary*			
	England		*Sample schools*		*England*		*Sample schools*	
	No.	*%*	*No.*	*%*	*No.*	*%*	*No.*	*%*
Size of School								
Up to 100	4,319	*20·4*	202	*21·5*	7	*0·2*	—	—
101— 200	4,818	*22·8*	212	*22·6*	110	*2·4*	11	*2·8*
201— 300	6,319	*29·8*	274	*29·3*	264	*5·8*	20	*5·1*
301— 400	3,456	*16·3*	141	*15·0*	516	*11·3*	42	*10·7*
401— 500	1,551	*7·3*	81	*8·6*	597	*13·1*	63	*16·0*
501— 600	545	*2·6*	21	*2·2*	759	*16·7*	73	*18·8*
601— 700	120	*0·6*	5	*0·5*	635	*14·0*	51	*13·0*
701— 800	39	*0·2*	1	*0·1*	426	*9·4*	30	*7·6*
801— 900	4	—	—	—	345	*7·6*	23	*5·9*
901— 1,000	2	—	1	*0·1*	241	*5·3*	15	*3·8*
1,001— 1,500	2	—	—	—	545	*12·0*	52	*13·2*
1,501— 2,000	—	—	—	—	96	*2·1*	12	*3·1*
2,001 and over	—	—	—	—	6	*0·1*	—	—
Total	21,175	*100·0*	936	*100·0*	4,547	*100·0*	392	*100·0*

$$\chi^2 = 4\cdot2 \qquad\qquad \chi^2 = 10\cdot4$$
$$\text{d.f.} = 5 \qquad\qquad \text{d.f.} = 9$$
$$\text{p} = \cdot52 \qquad\qquad \text{p} = \cdot32$$

Table 104

E. A COMPARISON OF THE PUPIL-TEACHER RATIO OF SCHOOLS IN THE SAMPLE AND IN THE TOTAL IN ENGLAND

	Primary	*Secondary*
England	25·5	16·9
Sample schools	25·6	16·9

In all the above respects the sample of schools was an unbiased sample.

It was also possible to check on the proportions of boys and girls selected for the secondary schools questionnaire. The survey response gave a higher proportion of boys than would have been expected from a random sample of 1,991 secondary school pupils aged 12 and 14. 54 per cent of the sample pupils were boys, whereas the national proportion at this age is only 51 per cent. The probability of selecting 54 per cent for boys as random sample from the population is less than 1 per cent.

The causes of this bias towards boys are not known, but it may result from (a) the tendency of schools to place boys above girls on registers, (b) the higher rates of absenteeism for girls in the 12–14 year old age group, and (c) the possibility of there being a higher proportion of boys than girls with a forename beginning with an A, B or C.

Despite the tendency for the class data to have favoured boys rather than girls, the effect on the results will be minimal. Reweighting the results to compensate for this small bias by applying 51/54 to the 'boys' data and 49/46 to the 'girls' data would not materially alter any of the findings.

REFERENCES

1. D. G. Lewis: *Statistical Methods in Education:* U.L.P.: 1967, and
   M. J. Moroney: *Facts from Figures:* Penguin: 1951.
2. *Op. cit.*

Part Ten

Summary of
Conclusions and Recommendations

CHAPTER 26

SUMMARY OF
CONCLUSIONS AND RECOMMENDATIONS

We have chosen to present our conclusions and recommendations in a manner which requires some explanation. The form in which they are set out constitutes a summary of the Report, and it was with reluctance that we singled out a smaller number as representing our principal recommendations. Our reason for this reluctance was that we have been opposed from the outset to the idea that reading and the use of English can be improved in any simple way. The solution does not lie in a few neat administrative strokes, nor in the adoption of one set of teaching methods to the exclusion of another. Improvement will come about only from a thorough understanding of the many complexities, and from action on a broad front. We are therefore concerned to emphasise that the selection we have made as representing our principal recommendations should not be regarded as itself a summary of the Report. In the main body of conclusions and recommendations there are many which we consider of equal importance but which do not lend themselves to this kind of direct statement. We are anxious that the complete summary, and the Report it represents, should be read as a whole, for it would be altogether misleading to take these 17 recommendations as a distillation of what we have to say. For this reason they have not been placed in order of priority, but follow the order of the chapters in which they are elaborated. The numbers in brackets draw attention to the more detailed presentation of the recommendation in the ensuing longer list, and these in turn give a reference to the paragraphs in which the proposal is developed. If there is one general summarising conclusion we offer it is that there is nothing to equal in importance the quality and achievement of the individual teacher, to whom most of our suggestions are addressed. All our recommendations are designed to support and strengthen the teachers in the schools, for it is with them that improvements in standards of reading and language most assuredly lie.

Finally, we must again emphasise our awareness that the Report is published at a time of financial difficulty and in a period of serious inflation, and we have deliberately not attempted to cost our proposals. As the Introduction makes clear, we acknowledge that this is not an easy time at which to make recommendations that call for increased expenditure, for national resources are under pressure and local authorities are likely to be faced with stringent restraint. We have felt it essential, however, to indicate plainly what we believe needs to be done, even if some of our recommendations cannot be implemented at once.

PRINCIPAL RECOMMENDATIONS

1 A system of monitoring should be introduced which will employ new instruments to assess a wider range of attainments than has been attempted in the past and allow new criteria to be established for the definition of literacy.

(21-35)

U

2   There should be positive steps to develop the language ability of children in the pre-school and nursery and infant years. These should include arrangements for the involvement of parents, the improvement of staffing ratios in infant schools, and the employment of teachers' aides whose training has included a language element.

(39-55)

3   Every school should devise a systematic policy for the development of reading competence in pupils of all ages and ability levels.

(56-69; 71-90; 93-96; 171)

4   Each school should have an organised policy for language across the curriculum, establishing every teacher's involvement in language and reading development throughout the years of schooling.

(137-139; 190; 89; 171)

5   Every school should have a suitably qualified teacher with responsibility for advising and supporting his colleagues in language and the teaching of reading.

(148-149; 171)

6   There should be close consultation between schools, and the transmission of effective records, to ensure continuity in the teaching of reading and in the language development of every pupil.

(155-167; 198)

7   English in the secondary school should have improved resources in terms of staffing, accommodation, and ancillary help.

(178; 181-188)

8   Every L.E.A. should appoint a specialist English adviser and should establish an advisory team with the specific responsibility of supporting schools in all aspects of language in education.

(191-194; 224)

9   L.E.A.s and schools should introduce early screening procedures to prevent cumulative language and reading failure and to guarantee individual diagnosis and treatment.

(195-203)

10   Additional assistance should be given to children retarded in reading, and where it is the school's policy to withdraw pupils from their classes for special help they should continue to receive support at the appropriate level on their return.

(219-223)

11   There should be a reading clinic or remedial centre in every L.E.A., giving access to a comprehensive diagnostic service and expert medical, psychological, and teaching help. In addition to its provision for children with severe reading difficulties the centre should offer an advisory service to schools in association with the L.E.A.'s specialist adviser.

(213; 224-225)

12 Provision for the tuition of adult illiterates and semi-literates should be greatly increased, and there should be a national reference point for the coordination of information and support.

(228-244)

13 Children of families of overseas origin should have more substantial and sustained tuition in English. Advisers and specialist teachers are required in greater strength in areas of need.

(245-246; 251-252; 254-262)

14 A standing working party should be formed, made up of representatives of the D.E.S. and L.E.A.s, to consider capitation allowances and the resources of schools, and a satisfactory level of book provision should be its first subject of inquiry.

(283-287)

15 A substantial course on language in education (including reading) should be part of every primary and secondary school teacher's initial training, whatever the teacher's subject or the age of the children with whom he or she will be working.

(308-313; 316)

16 There should be an expansion in in-service education opportunities in reading and the various other aspects of the teaching of English, and these should include courses at diploma and higher degree level. Teachers in every L.E.A. should have access to a language/reading centre.

(317-332; 210)

17 There should be a national centre for language in education, concerned with the teaching of English in all its aspects, from language and reading in the early years to advanced studies with sixth forms.

(333)

CONCLUSIONS AND RECOMMENDATIONS

PART 1: ATTITUDES AND STANDARDS

CHAPTER 1: ATTITUDES TO THE TEACHING OF ENGLISH

1 There is no firm evidence upon which to base comparisons between standards of English today and those of before the war, and the comparisons ventured are sometimes based on questionable assumptions. Nevertheless, standards of reading and writing need to be raised to fulfil the increasingly exacting demands made upon them by modern society.

(1.1-1.4; 1.8; 1.10)

2 There appears to be little substance in the generalisation that large numbers of schools are promoting 'creativity' at the expense of the 'basic skills'.

(1.8)

3 Language competence grows incrementally, through an interaction of writing, talk, reading, and experience, and the best teaching deliberately influences the nature and quality of this growth.

(1.10)

4   The pupil should be helped to develop increasing technical control over his language so that he can put it to increasingly complex uses.

(1.10)

5   English in the secondary school is often taught by teachers with inadequate qualifications for the task. English should be recognised as requiring substantial specialist knowledge, and the allocation of teaching assignments should reflect this fact.

(1.11)

CHAPTER 2: STANDARDS OF READING

6   Definitions of the terms 'literate' and 'illiterate' vary to so great an extent as to make them of little value as currently employed.

(2.1-2.2)

7   The level of reading skill required for participation in the affairs of modern society is far above that implied in earlier definitions of literacy.

(2.2)

8   Comparability of levels of 'literacy' between countries is difficult to determine. However, there is no evidence that standards in England are lower than those of other developed countries.

(2.3)

9   There is little empirical evidence to show whether television has had adverse effects upon standards of reading. However, such evidence as exists suggests that in general an increase in television watching has reduced the amount of time spent in private reading.

(2.5-2.7)

10   There is no firm statistical base for comparison of present-day standards of reading with those of before the war; and in terms of today's problems it is questionable whether there is anything to be gained from attempting it.

(2.11)

11   The tests at present in use in national surveys are inadequate measures of reading ability, since they measure only a narrow aspect of silent comprehension.

(2.13)

12   The two most serious limitations of the tests are the effects of ageing (2.14) and their inability to provide adequate discrimination for the more able 15 year olds. (2.14-2.16; 2.19 and 2.31-2.34). The effect of both would be to produce a levelling-off in the rate of increase in scores.

(2.16)

13   The changes in the last decade in the scores of 15 year olds on both tests are not statistically significant, and standards in this age group remained the same over the period 1960/71. In the light of the limitations of the tests this fact is not in itself disturbing.

(2.19)

14   There is no evidence of a decline in attainment over the years in the lowest achievers among 15 year olds. Since national surveys were instituted in 1948 the standards of the poorest readers have risen, and the gap between the most able and least able has narrowed. This reflects upon the capacity of existing tests to measure the achievement of the most able readers.

(2.19; 2.29)

15   There was no significant change in the reading standards of 11 year olds over the decade 1960-1970, but such movement as took place after 1964 was in all probability slightly downwards.

(2.20; 2.29)

16   There is evidence to suggest that this probable slight decline in the scores of 11 year olds may well be linked to a rising proportion of poor readers among the children of unskilled and semi-skilled workers.

(2.22-2.25; 2.29)

17   There is some evidence that children of seven are not as advanced as formerly in those aspects of reading ability which are measured by tests.

(2.26-2.28)

18   It is unrealistic to expect every child to be a competent reader on leaving the infant school. But the foundations of reading should be firmly laid there and not left until the child reaches junior school.

(2.28)

19   It is no longer sufficient to rely upon a 1948 baseline for measuring the movement in reading standards, and the present methods of monitoring them are inadequate.

(2.29)

20   Within schools literacy is a corporate responsibility in which the leadership should be provided by specialist teachers but in which other teachers should share.

(2.30)

CHAPTER 3: MONITORING

21   A system of monitoring should be introduced which will employ new instruments to assess a wider range of attainments than has been attempted in the past and allow new criteria to be established for the definition of literacy.

(3.1-3.3)

22   Responsibility for monitoring should lie with a national research organisation, and 1977 should be the target date for the introduction of the new system.

(3.5)

23   The monitoring procedure should be administered at the ages of eleven and fifteen.

(3.6)

24   The monitoring instruments should be responsive to developments in the curriculum and should avoid setting up 'backwash' effects on the teaching in the schools.

(3.5)

25   The reading test should assess a variety of reading skills in a variety of reading materials, and should contain both multiple choice and open-ended questions.

(3.8)

26   As a temporary expedient the N.S.6. test should remain in operation to ensure a continuing baseline until a new datum can be established.

(3.8)

27   The monitoring of standards of achievement in writing should be introduced, and the test should consist of a variety of tasks requiring different kinds of writing.

(3.9)

28   The scripts should be assessed by:
   i. 'impression marking', a qualitative assessment made by small teams of markers;
  ii. the application of coding schemes to determine accuracy in spelling, punctuation, and grammar.

(3.10-3.12; 3.24)

29   Multiple choice and interlinear tests might be employed as additional items.

(3.12)

30   It is not at present practicable to introduce the monitoring of Spoken English, but research should be conducted into the development of suitable monitoring instruments and economical procedures.

(3.13)

31   In the monitoring of reading and writing the test material should be drawn from a large pool stocked with carefully developed items representing all the skills to be assessed.

(3.15–3.18)

32   The question pool should be constructed by research officers in accordance with the advice of a consultative panel of teachers, L.E.A. advisers and other educationists, and H.M. Inspectorate. The team carrying out the survey will be permanent in the sense that although its members may change it will maintain a continuity of function and experience.

(3.16; 3.23)

33   A system of light sampling should be introduced, with testing carried out at termly intervals to yield a rolling estimate of standards.

(3.19–3.21)

34   When the new monitoring system is firmly established it might, if felt necessary, be selectively applied to give more detailed information about standards in certain areas, e.g. E.P.A.s.

(3.22)

35   Adequate research and development work should precede the introduction of the new system.

(3.24–3.25)

PART 2: LANGUAGE IN THE EARLY YEARS

CHAPTER 4: LANGUAGE AND LEARNING

36   Language has a unique role in developing human learning; the higher processes of thinking are normally achieved by the interaction of a child's language behaviour with his other mental and perceptual powers.

(4.1–4.7)

37   Children learn as certainly by talking and writing as by listening and reading.

(4.8–4.10)

38   The surest means by which a child is enabled to master his mother tongue is by exploiting the process of discovery through language in all its uses.

(4.8–4.10)

CHAPTER 5: LANGUAGE IN THE EARLY YEARS

39   Many young children do not have the opportunity to develop at home the more complex forms of language which school education demands of them. All children should be helped to acquire as wide a range as possible of the uses of language.

(5.4–5.10)

40   Parents should be helped to understand the process of language development in their children and to play their part in it.

(5.10)

41   This understanding should begin in the secondary school, where older pupils should be made aware of the adult's role in young children's linguistic and cognitive development.

(5.11)

42   The study of young children's language by secondary school pupils should wherever possible be firmly based on practical experience in nursery and infant schools.

(5.12–5.13)

43   In ante-natal clinics the question of the child's language development should take its place alongside that of his physical and emotional growth as a matter of vital concern to expectant parents.

(5.14)

44   Health and education authorities should co-operate to devise ways of providing expectant parents with advice and information on the language needs of young children.

(5.14)

45   Authorities should introduce home visiting schemes to help the parents of pre-school children play an active part in the children's language growth.

(5.15–5.18)

46   There should be research into the development of television programmes aimed at making parents aware of their children's language needs and helping them to fulfil them.

(5.19–5.20; and 22.19)

47   In nursery and infant schools there should be planned attention to the children's language development. It should be the school's conscious policy to develop in all children the ability to use increasingly complex forms. A careful record should be kept of their progress.

(5.28–5.29)

48   Language should be learned in the course of using it in, and about, the daily experiences of the classroom and the home, but within this framework teachers might find support in some language programmes and in guidelines or checklists.

(5.24–5.29)

49   There should be more opportunities for children to be in a one to one relationship with adults in school. The additional adults should work in close association with the teacher in helping to carry out the policies she has devised for the children's language development.

(5.32–5.38)

50   The existing language element in the training of nursery nurses and assistants should be extended to take account of the needs outlined in this chapter.

(5.32)

51   In addition to the contribution of nursery nurses and nursery assistants the teacher should have the support of trained aides who have taken a course on language development in the early years. Ideally such a course might be developed as a second-stage course under the administration of the N.N.E.B.

(5.32–5.34)

52   Schools should encourage the involvement of parents to provide additional conversation opportunities for young children. They should build on pre-school contacts where these have been established.

(5.35–5.38)

53   The design of nursery and infant schools should take account of the need for spaces to which adults can withdraw for work with individual children and small groups.

(5.41)

54   In areas of social disadvantage every school should have a pupil-teacher ratio which will make it possible for one or more members of staff to maintain close liaison with the home.

(5.42 and 13.19)

55   As so many of the above recommendations depend on the involvement of an appropriately qualified teacher, the staffing ratio of infant and nursery schools should be improved to allow these additional responsibilities to be undertaken with full advantage.

(5.32–5.43)

PART 3: READING

CHAPTER 6: THE READING PROCESS

56   There is no one method, medium, approach, device, or philosophy that holds the key to the process of learning to read.

(6.1)

57   Too much attention has been given to polarised opinions about approaches to the teaching of reading. What is needed is a comprehensive study of all the factors at work and the influence that can be exerted upon them.

(6.1–6.4)

58   A detailed understanding of the reading process should inform decisions about the organisation of teaching, the initial and in-service education of teachers, and the use of resources.

(6.3)

59   Word recognition is not merely a matter of learning unique whole-word forms, and over-simplified ideas about this aspect of reading are unhelpful as guides to action.

(6.7–6.12)

60   The accurate perception of individual letters and groups of letters is an important factor in learning to read. Young children should be helped to learn the characteristics of letters through a variety of games and activities, not through formal exercises.

(6.7–6.15)

61   The matching of sounds and symbols is of critical importance in learning to read, and the child should steadily acquire an increasing amount of phonic knowledge. However, teaching techniques which fail to recognise the complexity of this process may have an adverse effect on subsequent reading development.

(6.20–6.23)

62   The learning of sound-symbol correspondences should take place in the context of whole word recognition and reading for meaning. It is important, however, that children should first have had a full range of pre-reading experiences.

(6.20; 6.25–6.26; 6.37; 7.24)

63   At the earliest opportunity children should be introduced to morphemic structure, i.e. the relationship between spellings and meaning.

(6.24; 7.23)

64   Fluent reading depends to an important extent on the ability to anticipate that certain sequences of letters, words, or larger units of meaning are likely in a given context.

(6.27–6.36)

65   Failure to develop this competence may partly explain the difficulties experienced by some pupils in making progress beyond a reading age of 8 or 9.

(6.36)

66   The most effective teaching of reading is that which gives the pupil the various skills he needs to make the fullest possible use of context cues in search for meaning.

(6.35)

67   Comprehension skills consist in the interaction between the author's meanings and the reader's purpose, in the course of which the reader confirms or modifies his previous ideas and attitudes.

(6.39; 8.14–8.17)

68   The majority of pupils need a great deal of positive help to develop the various comprehension skills to a high level.

(6.40–6.41; 8.14–8.17)

69   An important aspect of reading behaviour is the ability to use different kinds of reading strategy according to the reader's purpose and the nature of the material. Pupils should acquire the skills which will free them from dependence on single-speed reading.

(6.42; 8.18)

CHAPTER 7: READING IN THE EARLY YEARS

70   Parents have an extremely important part to play in preparing the child for the early stages of reading.

(7.1-7.6)

71   Measures should be taken to introduce children to books in their pre-school years and to help parents recognise the value of reading to their children. Important sources of initiative are Children's Librarians, L.E.A. advisers, nursery and infant schools, voluntary bodies, and radio and television.

(7.2-7.5)

72   Schools should be enabled and encouraged to lend books to the parents of pre-school children and to provide book-buying facilities for them.

(7.4-7.5)

73   It should be established from the beginning in the mind of the child that reading is primarily a thinking process, not simply an exercise in identifying shapes and sounds.

(7.6)

74   The notion of reading readiness needs to be critically examined. It should not be allowed to deny a child access to early experience of reading, provided that the experience carries meaning and satisfaction for him.

(7.7)

75   Learning to read should be seen as a process of gradual evolution in which a variety of pre-reading activities merges imperceptibly with activities that may only at some later stage be unhesitatingly described as reading. A child's readiness for a particular step should be judged by his performance in the one that preceded it, not on a preconceived idea about his mental age or his intelligence.

(7.7-7.11)

76 Children showing signs of visual or auditory impairment should be referred for testing and appropriate treatment.

(7.9-7.10; 17.4)

77 There is great value in using as the children's early reading material their own writing, derived from their school experience and their life outside school.

(7.13-7.15)

78 If reading schemes are used they should be regarded as only an ancillary part of a school's reading programme, which should draw upon a wide range of other resources. Before starting on a reading scheme children should have had a wide range of preparatory reading experiences and acquired certain 'learning sets'.

(7.21; 7.25)

79 Reading schemes which use contrived and unnatural language prevent children from developing the ability to detect sequential probability in linguistic structure.

(6.34; 7.18)

80 In selecting reading schemes schools should take careful account of such features as syntactic structure, the principles followed in selecting the vocabulary, and the attitudes implicit in the content.

(7.17-7.19)

81 A good reading scheme is one which provides a sound basis for the development of all the reading skills in an integrated way. There are disabling limitations in (a) look-and-say schemes which give no direct assistance with phonics, (b) phonic schemes designed on narrowly conceived principles.

(7.22-7.25)

82 We are not unanimous on the value of i.t.a., but believe that schools which choose to adopt it should be given support. Teachers should examine i.t.a. on its merits and not be influenced by the more extreme arguments of its advocates and its opponents.

(7.27-7.29)

83 Most teachers are eclectic in their teaching of reading, making use of both look-and-say and phonic methods. The difference in effectiveness lies not in their allegiance to any one method but in (a) the quality of their relationships with children, (b) their degree of expert knowledge, and (c) their sensitivity in matching their teaching with each child's current learning needs.

(7.20; 7.31)

84 Careful organisation based on clear thinking about sequence and structure is essential in the planning of an appropriate reading curriculum for each individual child as well as for the class as a whole.

(7.30)

85 Every child should spend part of each day in reading or pre-reading activities. The teacher should give each child individual attention several times a week, helping him with his reading and keeping a meticulous check on progress.

(7.31; 17.8; 17.12)

86   Individual attention should not be confined to poor readers, for average and above average children also need it if they are to make optimal progress.

(7.31)

CHAPTER 8: READING: THE LATER STAGES

87   In the middle years there should be an emphasis on (a) reading for pleasure and personal development, and (b) extending the pupils' reading from the general to the more specialised.

(8.1)

88   The extension of reading skills in and through normal learning activities is likely to be more effective than separately timetabled specialist reading periods.

(8.6-8.8; 15.8)

89   There should be certain commonly agreed approaches to the teaching of reading as part of the school's policy for the development of language across the curriculum.

(8.9; 12.7-12.8)

90   The subject teacher in the secondary school should be capable of helping the pupils develop the special reading techniques which will improve the efficiency of their learning within his subject.

(8.2-8.4; 8.9; 8.11-8.19; 12.7-12.8; 15.8)

91   Pupils could be helped to organise their reading by (a) formulating advance questions which lead to disciplined enquiry, (b) surveying and evaluating sources of information, (c) applying organised study methods to the reading material.

(8.11-8.13)

92   Exercises in English text-books or kits of one kind or another are inadequate for developing comprehension.

(8.14)

93   Pupils should acquire a variety of comprehension skills—literal, inferential, and evaluative—in a range of contexts in which they are put to a practical purpose, i.e. in the various subjects of the curriculum.

(8.15-8.17)

94   Flexible reading strategies, i.e. the ability to skim, scan, or read intensively as the occasion demands, should be acquired at school and should be exercised throughout the curriculum.

(8.18)

95   The capacity for self-evaluation is an important instrument for learning. Pupils should be shown how to assess the effectiveness of their own reading.

(8.19)

96   Pupils should acquire while at school the wide variety of skills they will need to cope with the reading demands of adult life.

(8.5; 8.20)

CHAPTER 9: LITERATURE

97   Literature brings the child into an encounter with language in its mu.
complex and varied forms and is a valuable source of imaginative insight. It
should be recognised as a powerful force in English teaching at all levels.

(9.2)

98   There is a strong association between voluntary reading and reading
attainment. Teachers should devise various ways of extending their pupils'
interest in fiction and of increasing the amount and range of their voluntary
private reading.

(9.3-9.4; 9.7-9.8; 9.20-9.21)

99   The teacher should know the pattern of each child's reading and should
keep a record of it to guide him in extending its range. The secondary school
teacher should be informed of the pupils' reading experience in the primary
school and the nature of the work that has grown out of it.

(9.5; 9.20; 14.6; 14.11; 17.21)

100   The supply of narrative books—particularly good modern fiction—
should be increased in primary schools. We believe that narrative is often
neglected in favour of information books.

(9.6)

101   The teacher should have an extensive knowledge of fiction appropriate
for the various needs and levels of reading ability of his pupils.

(9.6)

102   Relevance to the child's own experience is important in young children's
early reading material, but the equal importance of fantasy, fairy tale, and
folk tale should be acknowledged.

(9.10)

103   The experience of literature for many older secondary school pupils is
confined to summaries, model answers, and stereotyped commentaries. The
demands of examinations should not be allowed to distort the experience of
literature.

(9.13-9.14; 9.23-9.24)

104   Thematic work offers valuable opportunities in the teaching of English
and humanities, but it should extend and not restrict the range and quality of
the pupils' experience of literature.

(9.16-9.17)

105   Where English becomes part of a humanities or integrated studies
programme the involvement of an English specialist is essential. There
should be detailed planning and continuous consultation to ensure that
English teaching is maintained at the highest level within the larger context.

(9.18)

106   All pupils should experience poetry in circumstances which emphasise
its enjoyment and its relevance to their lives and their interests.

(9.22-9.24)

107   Teachers should share responsibility for an awareness of recently
published poetry and for building up a collection of poetry in printed form
and on tape, cassette, and disc.

(9.25)

PART 4: LANGUAGE IN THE MIDDLE AND SECONDARY YEARS

CHAPTER 10: ORAL LANGUAGE

Talking and Listening

108   Exploratory talk by the pupils has an important function in the process of learning.

(10.1-10.3)

109   A child's accent should be accepted and attempts should not be made to suppress it. The aim should be to provide him with awareness and flexibility.

(10.5)

110   Children should be helped to as wide as possible a range of language uses so that they can speak appropriately in different situations and use standard forms when they are needed.

(10.6)

111   The teacher's own speech is a crucial factor in developing that of his pupils.

112   A stimulating classroom environment will not necessarily of itself develop the children's ability to use language as an instrument for learning. The teacher has a vital part to play and his role should be one of planned intervention.

(10.10-10.11)

113   Oral work should take place in both large and small group situations, with an emphasis on the latter.

(10.11-10.12)

114   Pupils should learn to regard discussion as an opportunity to investigate and illuminate a subject, not to advance inflexible points of view.

(10.14-10.16)

115   There should be a conscious policy on the part of the teacher to improve the children's listening ability. This is best achieved not through formal exercises but by structuring opportunities within the normal work of the classroom.

(10.20-10.22)

116   Efforts to develop ability in talking and listening should be supported by audio-visual resources on a proper scale.

(10.22-10.23; 22.5; 22.12)

117   External examinations in oral language are of value where they minimise artificiality and help the process of developing ability in a wide variety of uses. There should be further research into the kinds of examination best fitted to achieve this.

(10.25-10.28)

118   As part of their professional knowledge teachers should have:

an explicit understanding of the processes at work
in classroom discourse;

(10.4; 10.29)

the ability to appraise their pupils' spoken language and
to plan the means of extending it.

(10.9-10.10; 10.29)

There should be more opportunities for teachers to study these and other aspects of language in development work and in-service education.

(10.29)

119   There should be further research into the development of children's spoken language and the best means of promoting it.

(10.29)

Drama

120   Drama should be recognised as having a valuable contribution to make to the development of children's language.

(10.31; 10.36-10.37)

121   The written word can provide origin and stimulus for improvisation, and improvisation can illuminate the written word. In dramatic work in school the two should complement one another.

(10.33)

122   Drama in external examinations at 16+ should be substantially based on practical work rather than on the learning of facts.

(10.40)

123   In secondary schools there should be constructive discussion of the place of drama in English teaching and its contribution to other subjects.

(10.41)

Chapter 11: Written Language

124   There is often a lack of a clear rationale for the work to which the term 'creative writing' is applied. The main activity in the area of 'personal' writing should arise from a context created out of the corporate enterprises of the classroom and the experiences of the pupils rather than from prepared stimuli.

(11.3-11.5)

125   The teacher should extend the pupil's ability as a writer primarily by developing his intentions and then by working on the techniques appropriate to them.

(11.5)

126   Progress in writing throughout the school years should be marked by an increasing differentiation in the kinds of writing a pupil can successfully tackle.

(11.8)

127   Pupils should be given the opportunity to write for a variety of readers and audiences. They should be faced with the need to analyse the specific task, to choose the language appropriate to it, and to establish criteria by which to judge what they have achieved.

(11.9)

128   Competence in language comes above all through its purposeful use, not through the working of exercises divorced from context.

(11.19-11.20; 11.25)

129   Extensive reading and writing are the basis of language growth, but pupils should receive specific instruction in such practical matters as punctuation, structure of words, some aspects of usage, and certain technical terms helpful for the discussion of language.

(11.24-11.25)

130   Spelling needs to be taught according to a carefully worked out policy, which should be based upon the needs and purposes of the pupils' own writing, not upon lists of words without context. In individual or small group work the pupil's attention should be directed to the internal structure of the words he needs to learn and to the commonest spelling rules.

(11.12)

131   The ability to spell should be regarded as a part of the common responsibility for language development, which should be shared by teachers of all subjects.

(11.12-11.14; 11.41-11.49)

132   Children should be given instruction and practice in handwriting and encouraged to develop a concern for the appearance of their written work.

(11.50-11.55)

133   Linguistics and other specialist studies of language have a considerable contribution to make to the teaching of English, and they should be used to emphasise the inseparability of language and the human situation. Linguistics should not enter schools in the form of the teaching of descriptive grammar.

(11.26)

134   We endorse the recommendation of earlier Reports that English should be assessed at 16+ and some members believe the opportunity should not be denied to any pupils in ordinary schools, whatever their level of ability.

(11.31-11.38)

135   English requires a wide and flexible range of assessment, a need which is better met by externally moderated school-based assessment than by rigid syllabuses.

(11.39)

136   Post "O" level English syllabuses should contain a language element for all pupils who wish to opt for it, and "A" level or whatever examination may replace it should include a paper on this basis.

(11.40)

CHAPTER 12: LANGUAGE ACROSS THE CURRICULUM
137   In the primary school the individual teacher is in a position to devise a language policy across the various aspects of the curriculum, but there remains the need for a general school policy to give expression to the aim and ensure consistency throughout the years of primary schooling.

(12.3)

138   In the secondary school, all subject teachers need to be aware of:

(i) the linguistic processes by which their pupils acquire information and understanding, and the implications for the teacher's own use of language;

(12.1-12.2; 12.4-12.10)

(ii) the reading demands of their own subjects, and ways in which the pupils can be helped to meet them.

(12.7-12.8; 15.8; 8.9; 8.11-8.19)

139   To bring about this understanding every secondary school should develop a policy for language across the curriculum. The responsibility for this policy should be embodied in the organisational structure of the school.

(12.11-12.12; 6.44; 8.9; 8.11-8.18; 15.33)

PART 5: ORGANISATION

Chapter 13: The Primary and Middle Years

140   There is a very wide variety in the pre-school experience of young children, and this diversity underlines the need for contacts between infant school, nursery, playgroup, and home.

(13.1-13.3)

141   These contacts should include:

(i) exchanges of visits between nursery sohool teachers, infant school teachers, and playgroup leaders;

(13.3)

(ii) opportunities for the parent and young child to spend some time in the infant school in the term preceding admission.

(13.3)

142   Admissions to infant schools should be staggered over a period of some weeks, so that teachers can talk individually to small numbers of parents when they bring their children.

(13.3)

143   At the earliest opportunity parents should be made aware of the value the school places upon books, and should be able to borrow them for reading stories to their children before they start school.

(13.3 and 7.4)

144   There is no one form of organisation of schools, or classes within schools, which will suit all situations. The organisation should be based on the educational needs of the children in question, the strengths and weaknesses of the teachers, and the quality of the other resources, material and human, both inside the school and out.

(13.4-13.12)

145   We believe, however, that the form of classroom organisation best suited to language development is a flexible one in which independent work by individuals and small groups is the principal form of activity.

(13.15)

146   Careful planning should precede any organisational change, and new ways of working should not be introduced until the staff has been able to

prepare for them. Changes in the organisation of a school should be matched by changes in classroom practice, which should be consonant with it in spirit and intent.

(13.12)

147   Throughout the primary and middle years there should be a gradual development from the firmly based class-teacher relationship through co-operative working to a degree of specialism for the older children. Language permeates the curriculum and should not be abstracted from it in the primary school in the form of a specialist subject. Nevertheless, in group work the older children should benefit from the specialist knowledge of a member of staff with responsibility for language.

(13.13)

148   Every school should have a teacher on the staff responsible for supporting his colleagues in language development and the teaching of reading. In the allocation of above-scale posts English should be given a high priority.

(13.14; 13.22-13.23)

149   Authorities should provide these consultant language teachers with in-service training at the level recommended in paragraph 24.14.

150   Schools should be staffed in September according to the largest number of children expected in the ensuing school year.

(13.16)

151   An improvement in the staffing ratio should be related not simply to a reduction in average class size but to the opportunity to create very small groups as the occasion demands.

(13.17)

152   In their staffing policy authorities should take account of the need for additional help in schools which involve parents and/or secondary school pupils in work with young children.

(13.20 and 5.28-36 and 5.11-12)

153   Additional staff should be made available to schools in inner-city areas and other areas where marked social disadvantage affects reading and language development.

(13.20 and 5.38)

154   The design of schools should recognise that educational methods and patterns of organisation are in a continuous process of evolution. A building should provide spaces for large and small group work, including opportunities for reading and writing in the privacy and quiet of the enclosed space.
Design of new buildings and remodelling of existing ones should also take account of the involvement of parents and additional adults in helping with the language development of individuals and small groups.

(13.22)

155 Head-teachers have a vitally important role in the promotion of successful language work and reading in the school. They should fulfil this by:

(i) placing a high priority on language and reading in the curriculum and organisation of the school, and consulting with their staff to produce a planned policy to improve them;

(ii) organising the careful evaluation of new ideas and approaches in language and reading;

(13.29)

(iii) encouraging their colleagues to have positive expectations of every child and to keep careful records;

(iv) encouraging in-service training within the school and ensuring that the benefits from attendance at outside courses are absorbed by the whole staff;

(v) working alongside their colleagues in the classroom.

(13.25)

CHAPTER 14: CONTINUITY BETWEEN SCHOOLS

A. Infant/First School to Junior/Middle School

156 The heads and staffs of infant and junior schools (and first and middle schools) should jointly plan the transition of the children between the two stages. Their planning should include such measures as:

(i) regular inter-staff discussion;

(ii) an exchange of visits and teaching assignments;

(iii) an opportunity for small groups of infants to spend occasional days in the junior school in the term before transfer;

(iv) setting up common working and quiet areas where schools occupy the same building;

(v) joint activities of various kinds.

(14.1)

157 Within this framework of co-operation, there should be special attention to language and reading development.

(14.1)

There should be a common understanding of objectives in the teaching of reading. It should be recognised as a developmental process in which it is unrealistic to expect uniform levels of achievement for every child at a given age.

(14.2)

158 Where possible the schools should jointly plan a programme for the development of reading. At the very least each should have a thorough knowledge of the other's methods and approaches. There should thus be:

(i) an avoidance of sharp breaks in practice, e.g. in the use of the initial teaching alphabet and traditional orthography;

(14.2)

(ii) co-operation to ensure that in addition to the stimulus of new material the child has the security of the familiar when he transfers to his new school.

(14.6)

159   A full set of records should be handed on between schools, giving details of:

  (i) the nursery and infant teachers' appraisal of the child's language development;

(14.3-14.4; 17.8)

  (ii) the specific nature of any reading difficulties which the child is experiencing.

(14.4; 17.15-17.20)

160   The junior or middle school should receive a selection of each child's written work.

(14.5)

161   There should be continuity as far as possible in any policy for:

  (i) involving parents in extending children's language opportunities;
(14.3; 5.35-5.38)

  (ii) arranging book-shop or book-club facilities within the school.

(14.6)

B.   Junior/Middle School to Secondary School

162   There should be close liaison between the secondary school and the junior and middle schools from which it receives its pupils. In addition to joint activities of various kinds, this liaison should include such measures as:

  (i) the appointment of a member of the secondary school staff to maintain contact with the contributory schools;

  (ii) an exchange of visits and teaching assignments between members of the staffs.

(14.7)

Within this framework of co-operation, continuity in respect of language development and reading should receive detailed attention in its own right.
(14.7-14.9)

163   The secondary school should receive from the primary schools detailed information in the form of teachers' assessments and objective data. These should give the secondary school English department a knowledge of:

  (i) the child's language experience over a long period;

  (ii) the extent and range of the pupil's reading;

  (iii) any reading difficulties that may have persisted, and the steps taken to deal with them.   (14.10-14.11)

164   The secondary school English department should receive a selection of each child's writing to provide a cumulative record of his development in the written language over a period of years.

(14.11)

165 Primary and secondary school teachers should meet for discussion and study of children's written and spoken language.

(14.13)

166 There should be an exchange of visits between schools and, where possible, of teaching assignments between primary school staff and members of the secondary school English department.

(14.13)

167 Co-operation between schools should include contacts between children, which might include such activities as:

(i) the writing of stories for young children by older secondary school pupils;

(ii) story-telling, reading, and talking sessions, in which older secondary school pupils work with children in the infant schools under the guidance of the teacher.

(14.14-14.15; 5.10-5.12)

CHAPTER 15: THE SECONDARY SCHOOL

168 Specialised English and integrated studies should not be regarded as mutually exclusive.

(15.6-15.7)

169 Where a school decides to include English in integrated studies it should ensure that:

(i) the English department is fully involved in the planning and operation, and gives guidance, support, and resources to the teachers from other subject areas;

(ii) English retains a valid presence, with the language and literature work recommended in chapters 9, 10, and 11 fully represented.

(15.1-15.4; 15.6)

170 A school deciding that English shall be taught as a separate subject should ensure that it reaches out to other areas of interest, drawing upon them for its material through close co-operation with the teachers concerned.

(15.6)

171 The English department should consider the development of reading skills at all levels as one of its most important responsibilities. As part of the school's policy for language across the curriculum it should offer guidance to colleagues in the extension of reading ability in all the pupil's learning activities. For this purpose it is desirable that there should be at least one member of staff with advanced qualifications in reading.

(15.8; 12.7-12.8; 8.3-8.4)

172 Ideally, secondary school drama should be an essential part of work in English while at the same time having scope as an activity in its own right.

(15.9)

173 Where drama exists only within the English department one of its members should be appropriately qualified and carry the responsibility of

supporting and advising his colleagues. Where it has come to be concentrated within a separate department the teachers should work in very close co-operation with the English department.

(15.9)

174   The majority of the Committee have reservations about arrangements by which pupils are streamed or setted for English according to ability. These members believe that where it is practicable mixed ability grouping offers most hope for English teaching, provided it receives a great deal of thought and planning.

(15.10; 15.12)

175   The complexities inherent in mixed-ability teaching are considerable. If a school decides in favour of mixed ability grouping for the teaching of English it should ensure that:

(i) children with reading difficulties receive the kind of individual help they need;

(ii) there is a flexible pattern of group and individual work, and carefully judged opportunities for learning as a class;

(iii) resources, and particularly the range of books, are adequate to meet the needs of pupils from a wide spectrum of ability and interests;

(iv) the system has the full support of the teachers involved, who should be closely involved in the planning and able to adapt to the new demands the grouping will create.

(15.10-15.12)

176   There is evidence of a substantial turnover among secondary school English teachers and of the employment of a considerable proportion of part-time teachers. These factors work against the continuity so important to English teaching and against collective planning within the English department.

(15.13)

177   The evidence of our survey suggest that:

(i) a third of the teachers involved in the teaching of English have no discernible qualification for the role;

(ii) over a third of the teachers involved in the teaching of English spend less than half their time on it.

It is an unsatisfactory situation in which English is taught by so many teachers without appropriate qualifications.

(15.14)

178   When the timetable is being constructed and the staffing policy devised English should be given a high priority. The indications are that at present it is often sacrificed to the interests of other subjects.

(15.15-15.16)

179   The role of the head of English department has grown in complexity and extends from the management of resources to a concern for the in-service training needs of the department. Recognition of this should be reflected in the support he receives from the head of the school.

(15.17)

180   In some areas, there is a shortage of applicants with the right kind of experience and qualifications for posts of head of English department. There is a particular difficulty in making appointments in very large schools.
(15.18-15.19)

181   Where heads of English department are subject to considerable pressure they should be helped by:

(i) improved staffing ratio within the department to allow more time for consultation and planning;

(ii) generous allocation of above-scale posts to allow the head of department to delegate effectively.
(15.19)

182   English departments should receive ancillary help in:

(i) the preparation of teaching materials, which might be centrally provided through a school resource centre;

(ii) the handling of departmental material, for which 'internal' clerical assistance should be provided on the basis of 20 hours a week for every five forms of entry in an 11-18 school, and pro rata. Where the help mentioned in (i) is not available the department's own ancillary help should be increased.
(15.20; 22.3)

183   A substantial number of teachers of English lack a room of their own in which they can exhibit work, put up illustrations, and mount displays. The needs of English should receive the same consideration as those of any other subject, and as far as possible every teacher with a full programme of English should have his own teaching base.
(15.21)

184   Rooms in which English teaching takes place should have generous space, and where possible they should be grouped to allow teachers to co-operate in various activities and with varying numbers of pupils.
(15.23)

185   The grouping of English rooms should be considered in relation to other subject groupings in order that certain facilities, e.g. projection theatre, sound recording studio, can be shared.
(15.24)

186   Facilities for showing films and videotape should be available at short notice to all teachers of English. Where possible, certain of the grouped English rooms should have equipment built in.
(15.24)

187   English should have a departmental centre to house teaching material and ancillary help, and every English teaching room should have ample storage space.
(15.25)

188   Minimum requirements of the kind suggested cannot be provided at once, but where building improvement or new projects are being planned

they should receive serious consideration. On such occasions there should be full consultation between architects and the authority's English advisory staff and teachers.

(15.26)

189   Every English department should have an 'instrument of policy' making clear its purposes and the means it proposes to fulfil them. This should be a continually evolving document, produced and maintained by the head of department in consultation with his colleagues.

(15.30)

190   The role of the head in the teaching of English is of the greatest importance, and he is uniquely placed to encourage a policy of language across the curriculum.

(15.17; 15.31; 12.11-12.12)

CHAPTER 16: L.E.A. ADVISORY SERVICES

191   Every authority should have an advisory team with the specific responsibility of supporting schools in all aspects of language in education. This would encompass English from language and reading in the early years to advanced reading and English studies at the highest level of the secondary school.

(16.1; 16.6)

192   Each team should have a specialist English adviser, and should draw for its membership from the general primary and secondary advisers, advisory teachers on secondment from schools, and specialists in reading, learning difficulties, drama and 'immigrant' language teaching.

(16.1-16.6)

193   The advisory teachers should be appointed for their special interest in English and should be drawn from among those with responsibility for language in the primary schools (13.23) and from English teachers in secondary schools. They should be seconded for a period of 2-3 years and should spend a substantial part of their time in schools, working with teachers in the classroom.

(16.6)

194   The responsibilities of the advisory team should include:

(i) planning and providing in-service training, and promoting and assisting in development work by teachers;

(16.8)

(ii) giving special encouragement to initiatives in nursery and infant schools to help parents play their part in the development of their children's language;

(16.9; 5.36-5.38)

(iii) co-operation with the Schools Psychological Service in the operation of screening procedures; support to teachers in the diagnosis of reading difficulties and the devising of appropriate measures to deal with them;

(16.9; 17.9; 17.11; 18.14)

(iv) giving support to schools in improving the teaching of reading at all levels and in evaluating new materials;

(16.9)

(v) co-operation with the School Library Service in helping schools to increase voluntary home reading among their pupils;

(16.9; 21.10; 21.11)

(vi) encouraging the development of a language across the curriculum policy in secondary schools;

(Chapter 12; 16.9; 15.30; 15.31)

(vii) providing professional advice on the accommodation needs of English and of language activities in primary schools when new buildings and extensions are being planned;

(13.18; 15.26; 16.9)

(viii) giving support to language and reading work in Teachers' Centres and Language Centres.

(24.15)

PART 6: READING AND LANGUAGE DIFFICULTIES

CHAPTER 17: SCREENING, DIAGNOSIS, AND RECORDING

Screening

195 Early detection of educational failure is of the greatest importance and there should be a far more systematic procedure for the prevention and treatment of learning difficulties.

(17.1-17.4)

196 The infant school should be supplied in confidence with relevant details of the child's medical and developmental history. There should be a well-developed liaison between the school and such sources of information as the school doctor, the health visitor, the social worker, the educational welfare officer and the speech therapist.

(17.10; 7.9-7.10)

197 The first stage of the screening process in school should be systematic observation and recording by the teacher. If the authority introduces a check-list this should be developed by consultation between teachers, advisers and educational psychologists.

(17.8-17.11)

198 The outcome of the observation procedure should be a detailed profile of each child's strengths and weaknesses, and this should be used to plan an appropriate learning programme. This record should accompany the child when he transfers to a different school.

(17.11-17.12)

199 In our view there is no advantage in mass testing and centrally stored data unless the outcome is individualised help directed precisely at the children who need it. As a general principle we prefer that systematised observation should be followed by selective diagnostic testing of those pupils about whom detailed and specific information is required.

(17.13)

200   Such a policy presupposes well developed support services and in-service training of high quality, and until these are available the testing of the whole age group is likely to be seen as the most practical course. Authorities with high teacher mobility and large numbers of children likely to experience learning difficulties may find it an essential feature of their screening procedure.

(17.13)

201   If testing is carried out in this way it should take place not earlier than the middle of the first term of the junior school and not later than the beginning of the second term. The tests should not be restricted to word recognition and should ideally have been developed and evaluated within the last ten years.

(17.7; 17.13)

202   Test results can be used to determine which schools should receive additional resources, but the first priority of any screening policy should be to identify the needs of individual children.

(17.14)

Diagnosis and Recording

203   The screening procedure should be seen as only the first stage in a continuous process of diagnosis, used by the teacher to design appropriate learning experiences.

(17.15)

204   The indications are that only a narrow range of tests is commonly used in schools. Before any test is applied it should be assessed for its appropriateness for the purpose in hand and the practical value of the information it will yield.

(17.16; 17.22)

205   Expert observation cannot be valued too highly; it is a major teaching skill and one upon which all effective diagnosis is founded. One of its important aspects is listening to children read individually, to identify and record the nature of their errors. The development and use of informal reading inventories is one useful way of doing this.

(17.17-17.20)

206   Recording should be in a form which is helpful to other teachers and can be used constructively to advance the child's reading competence.   In a classroom organised on 'informal' lines, with a good deal of individual work in progress, effective recording is of the greatest importance.

(17.21)

207   As pupils grow older there should be increasing opportunities for self-appraisal, and some pupils might be encouraged to record their achievements and difficulties, using the record as an aid to the growth of higher level skills.

(17.21)

208   There is a need for the further development of diagnostic tests which combine the maximum of practical information with ease of administration.

(17.22)

209 A team approach should be developed between teachers, educational psychologist, and doctor. The teacher should be equipped to determine when a difficulty revealed by diagnostic test requires further investigation.

(17.23)

210 Educational psychologists have an important part to play in in-service training, notably in helping teachers to a more detailed knowledge of diagnostic techniques. There is scope for considerable expansion of in-service training activities in which they are jointly involved, and this should entail practical work and follow-up within the schools.

(17.24)

CHAPTER 18: CHILDREN WITH READING DIFFICULTIES

211 It is important to distinguish between different kinds of 'failure' and the needs they generate; namely where (a) success is possible to the child but is eluding him, (b) success at that moment in time is altogether beyond his powers.

(18.3)

212 Delay beyond the age of seven in beginning to read puts a child at educational risk. There is evidence to show that many children who have made little progress in reading on entering the junior school are even further behind at eleven and that this deficiency continues to the end of their statutory school life.

(18.4)

213 A small number of children have severe reading difficulties that cannot be accounted for by limited mental ability or by other readily identifiable factors. All such children should receive a skilled analysis of the nature of their difficulties, followed by intensive and sustained help in a remedial centre or reading clinic.

(18.5; 18.18)

214 Intellectual capacity affects a child's ability to acquire linguistic skills, but as intelligence itself is a developmental concept any child can be expected to make considerable gains with good teaching, sustained support, and positive expectations on the part of the school.

(18.6)

215 There is a close association between retardation in reading and emotional and behavioural disorders, which seems in most cases to be reciprocal. Both reading failure and symptoms of such disturbance should be regarded as cues for action if consequences of a lasting and compounding nature are to be avoided.

(18.7)

216 Low reading achievement and socio-economic circumstances are closely related, and the indications are that the attainment gap between children from favoured and disadvantaged homes widens as they grow older. Early intervention is therefore necessary to compensate as far as possible for the cumulative effect of social handicap.

(18.8)

217 There are marked differences between schools in the success they achieve in the teaching of reading, even where they serve similar populations.

(18.9)

218 A number of research studies have shown the effects of 'remedial' treatment to be disappointing, in that gains have been short-term and progress has not been sustained. However, since the practices and resources described had limitations, it would be unreasonable to conclude from these studies that all efforts are likely to be ineffective. There is evidence in some schools that well-designed measures can be successful.

(18.10-18.11)

219 If the success of remedial measures is to be broad and lasting, a recognition of certain factors is essential:
 (i) the particular nature of each child's difficulties must be seen in relation to his whole linguistic development;
 (ii) the teacher's relationship with the pupils should be such as to give them constant encouragement through the stimulus of success;
 (iii) remedial work is not for the inexperienced or indifferent teacher, but for the teacher who combines a high level of teaching skill with an understanding of the children's emotional and developmental needs;
 (iv) remedial help in learning to read should wherever possible be closely related to the rest of a pupil's learning;
 (v) there should be every effort to involve parents and help them to understand the nature of their children's difficulties.

(18.12)

220 There should be flexibility in the arrangements made in primary schools for teaching children with reading difficulty. These should be designed to ensure that the contribution of peripatetic and part-time teachers is integrated with that of the class teacher.

(18.13-18.14)

221 Every teacher should have a planned reading programme to cater for the various levels of ability of the pupils. If it is the policy to withdraw pupils for special help they should continue to receive support at the appropriate level on their return.

(18.14)

222 In secondary schools the additional assistance given to children retarded in reading should normally be related to the rest of the curriculum and new initiatives should be developed for providing it.

(18.16)

223 In many secondary schools, work with 'slow learners' attracts less than its fair share of resources. General responsibility for these pupils should lie with a senior member of staff able to co-ordinate all the school's resources on their behalf.

(18.17)

224 Every authority should appoint an adviser with special responsibility for children experiencing learning difficulties. This adviser should be involved in the English advisory team activity advocated in Chapter 16.

(18.18)

225   There should be a reading clinic or remedial centre in every authority, giving access to a comprehensive diagnostic service and expert medical, psychological, and teaching help. In addition to its provision for children with severe reading difficulties the centre should offer an advisory service to schools in co-operation with the authority adviser.

(18.18)

226   In areas of social and economic depression the problem of poor attainment is more than one of teaching reading; it requires a combined effort by social services, teachers and administrators throughout the whole period of a child's school life.

(18.19)

227   There will always be children who for various reasons fall behind, but a very great deal can be done to prevent reading disability by raising the quality of teaching generally and by giving skilled individual help before a sense of failure sets in.

(18.19)

CHAPTER 19: ADULT ILLITERACY

228   It is impossible to say with certainty how many adult illiterates and semi-literates there are in the country, but it is clear that only a very small number of them receive instruction. Provision over the country as a whole is inadequate and should be greatly increased.

(19.5; 19.8)

229   Before they leave school pupils with reading difficulties should receive guidance on where to go for continued tuition. It is the responsibility of the school to take the first step to establish continuity of opportunity.

(19.6)

230   There should be an increase in publicity to draw attention to the help available to adults with reading difficulties. References should be made in popular radio and television programmes with large audiences, and specific information at local level should be given through local radio and newspapers.

(19.7; 22.24)

231   L.E.A.s should maintain a continuous service of information on all adult literacy provision to employers and social service agencies.

(19.7)

232   Social service departments, probation officers, youth leaders, and the Careers and Employment services should give advice to young adult illiterates on where to receive help.

(19.7)

233   L.E.A.s should co-ordinate the various sources of advice to adult illiterates and should provide a counselling service to introduce them to the kind of tuition best suited to their needs.

(19.7)

234   Employers, trade unions, and industrial training agencies should investigate the possibility of using the work situation as a place where

literacy improvement could be achieved. There should be an increase in facilities for part-time tuition during working hours.

(19.8)

235   Local authorities should ensure that provision is expanded in antici-pation of the demands created by the increased publicity and the co-ordina-tion of their information services.

(19.12)

236   Authorities should make generous financial grants to voluntary literacy schemes and should help them to maintain and extend their activities.

(19.11)

237   There should be close co-operation between L.E.A.s and voluntary schemes, to develop a range of individual and group provision at different levels to meet individual needs.

(19.12)

238   All adults seeking help with reading should be assured of individual tuition at the beginning of their course and for as long as proves necessary. They should be able to depend upon the continuing personal support of a tutor-counsellor when they have reached the stage of working with a group.

(19.11-19.12)

239   The L.E.A. should provide in-service training for all who are acting as tutors in adult literacy work.

(19.13)

240   There should be a wider range of reading material appropriate to the interests and needs of adult students. Audio-visual aids should be more readily available for tutors who wish to make use of them.

(19.15)

241   Adults of overseas origin add considerably to the numbers requiring help with literacy. They need tutors who have a special understanding of their language difficulties, and these tutors should maintain close contact with those responsible for other types of language instruction at adult education level. There should be more home tutoring facilities for immigrant families.

(19.14)

242   The effectiveness of various forms of provision and of methods and materials should be evaluated, and the results widely disseminated.

(19.15)

243   There should be regional conferences for tutors. The Advisory Councils for Further Education could play a significant part in the development of such opportunities.

(19.15)

244   Provision should be made nationally to develop and evaluate materials and resources, supply information and advice, and organise conferences. We recommend that the Secretary of State should consider ways in which these functions might be carried out most effectively.

(19.15)

CHAPTER 20

CHILDREN FROM FAMILIES OF OVERSEAS ORIGIN

245 Authorities with children from families of overseas origin should carry out regular surveys of their linguistic needs in order to maintain flexibility in the arrangements made to cater for them.

(20.2)

246 In some areas the arrangements do little more than meet the initial language and adjustment needs of new arrivals, whereas these are only the beginning of what for most of the children is a long process.

(20.2)

247 Among families of overseas origin there are considerable differences not only in language and culture but in the stability of their home circumstances and their adaptation to their new country. These differences should be recognised and the stereotype of the 'immigrant child' should be dismissed.

(20.3)

248 Though there has been little sustained research describing the comparative performance of children of minority groups in Britain, there is enough evidence to show a disturbingly low pattern of attainment. In particular, children of West Indian origin are performing well below average.

(20.4)

249 No child should be expected to cast off the language and culture of the home as he crosses the school threshold, and the curriculum should reflect those aspects of his life.

(20.5)

250 All teachers need to be aware of the way books and pictures shape children's attitudes to one another and to society, and of the ethnocentric bias of many books in use in schools. When selecting books for schools teachers and librarians should include books that reflect the experience of children from families of overseas origin and material about their homelands and cultures. There is a general shortage of such books, and publishers could make a valuable contribution by fulfilling this need.

(20.5)

251 Teachers in schools with children of West Indian origin should have an understanding of Creole dialect and a positive and sympathetic attitude towards it. Work relating both to dialect and to improving the ability to use Standard English should be encouraged on a much larger scale.

(20.6)

252 There is an urgent need for research into the specific problems experienced by West Indian children in learning to read, and the results of this study should be disseminated on a wide scale.

(20.7)

253 Schools with pupils of West Indian origin should look for opportunities to draw upon the support that parents and community can give and should acquire a knowledge of the Caribbean and its culture.

(20.8)

254   There is a shortage of teachers able to teach English as a second language and of people to train them.

(20.9)

255   Generally speaking, the teaching of English as a second language begins too late after the child's arrival and ends too soon.

(20.10)

256   Specialist teachers of language should work in close liaison with other teachers in the school and should keep in touch with the child's education as a whole.

(20.10)

257   The teaching of English as a second language should not be discontinued when the pupils have gained a superficial knowledge of it but should be sustained until they have achieved fluency in speaking, reading, and writing.

(20.11)

258   In the secondary school, pupils who are past the initial stage of learning English need help in coping with the linguistic demands made on them by the various specialist areas of the curriculum. To this end there should be close co-operation between subject teachers and language specialist.

(20.12)

259   There should be more initiatives to establish a new role for the language teacher in a multi-racial secondary school, one of consultant and adviser across the curriculum rather than of teacher confined to a single room. Though staffing difficulties and cost are a problem to authorities with large numbers of second-stage language learners, teachers able to carry out this function should be appointed extra to complement where possible.

(20.12)

260   Authorities with areas of immigrant settlement should appoint advisers with special responsibility for the language development of the children, able to provide and sustain in-service education and support the teachers in the schools. These advisers should work closely with the other members of the English advisory team recommended in Chapter 16.

(20.13)

261   The provision of nursery classes in inner city areas has great importance for the early language development of immigrant children. The normal activities of the nursery and infant classroom should be adjusted to suit their individual needs and should be supplemented by specific help with language.

(20.14)

262   Teacher training programmes and in-service education should take account of the need of nursery and infant teachers for an understanding of the specific language difficulties of children from families of overseas origin.

(20.15)

263   There should be a more sustained and systematic linking of home and school, with particular emphasis in the case of young children.

(20.15-20.16)

264   The role of members of the minority communities themselves is vital and it is particularly important that children from families of overseas origin should see people of their own communities in the role of teacher and helper.

(20.16)

265   Every school with pupils whose original language is not English should adopt a positive attitude to their bilingualism and wherever possible help maintain and deepen their knowledge of their mother-tongue.

(20.17)

266   There should be further research into the teaching of their own language to children of immigrant communities and into the various aspects of bilingualism in schools.

(20.17)

PART 7: RESOURCES

CHAPTER 21: BOOKS

267   Every primary school should have a book policy that reflects a set of objectives understood and accepted by the staff.

(21.3)

268   Authorities should devise ways of enabling schools to select books on the basis of first-hand knowledge of the range available. They should consider setting up permanent exhibitions, regularly up-dated, and educational bookrooms which would be sources of guidance to parents as well as to teachers.

(21.4)

269   Responsibility for books in the primary school should be a collective one, but a member of staff with a more specialised knowledge should have an advisory function and the role of giving effect to the book policy which emerges from staff consultation.

(21.5; 13.23)

270   Every primary school classroom should have its own collection of books, constantly refreshed and changing to accommodate new needs. This should be backed by a central collection which contains print and non-print material of various kinds. There should be a recognised system of organisation which makes clear what resources the school possesses and how they are dispersed.

(21.6)

271   The School Library Service is a valuable source of assistance and advice. Its services should not be used passively but as a means of furthering the book policy which the school itself has decided. Books on long-term loan from the Service should become an organic part of the school's resources and not be treated as separate stock.

(21.7-21.8)

272   There should be more initiatives to develop joint courses, study groups, book review panels, and similar activities for teachers and Children's Librarians.

(21.9)

273   School Library Services should be enabled to supply on demand a wider range of resources than books, co-operating where appropriate with such bodies as the museum service and local archives.

(21.9)

274   Activities on the scale we envisage will require an expansion of School Library Services. There should be an appraisal of the kind of support schools can be given, and this will call for close consultation between the education authority's advisers, the schools themselves and the library staff. No authority should be without a Children's Librarian.

(21.10)

275   Pupils should continue to enjoy free access to a wide range of books on transfer from one school to another. Whether they are in primary, middle or secondary school, pupils between 8 and 13 have a common need in terms of book provision and range and this need should receive comparable fulfilment.

(21.11)

276   In a substantial minority of secondary schools the library is used for general teaching purposes for more than half the week, and in others it is open only at certain times of the day. Every secondary school should have library accommodation and ancillary help appropriate to its needs.

(21.12)

277   More extensive use should be made of training facilities for library work in schools, and as a long term aim all school librarians should be doubly qualified in teaching and librarianship.

(21.13-21.14)

278   The school librarian should have a seat at all head of department meetings, and departments should involve him in their own internal planning.

(21.13)

279   Resource centres in schools are an important development, with potentially a considerable contribution to make to the teaching of English. When new buildings are being planned or existing buildings expanded the need for a resource centre should be anticipated.

(21.15-21.16)

280   Retrieval systems should be organised in such a way as to help pupils of all levels of ability to obtain appropriate materials.

(21.15)

281   In some English departments there is an inadequate supply of fiction of the right range and quality. In the department's corporate planning and purchasing policy fiction for the younger pupils should occupy a high priority.

(21.17)

282   Many secondary schools have a disturbingly small number of library books per pupil.

(21.18)

283   There is considerable variation in the expenditure on books between local authorities, and when all qualifications have been made it is clear that

some make inadequate provision. The disparity between individual schools in terms of resources is disturbing.

(21.19-21.22)

284 Schools are finding it increasingly difficult to maintain a good supply of books in the face of rising costs and other factors. Since expenditure on books is part of a larger block of non-teaching costs it is in competition with other demands, and books are in a particularly vulnerable position in times of financial stringency.

(21.20; 21.26)

285 The 'per capita' system of calculating allowances to schools works to the serious disadvantage of small schools, whose needs are not in a linear relationship with the number of pupils.

(21.23-21.24)

286. There should be a detailed examination of the whole question of allowances to schools and how they are distributed. A standing working party, made up of representatives of the D.E.S. and of L.E.A.s, should be formed for this purpose.

(21.25)

287 The suggested working party should as its first task recommend minimal figures for book provision, which should then be kept under annual review to take account of inflation. In the meantime all authorities should make provision according to the figures recommended by the Association of Education Committees, which should be regarded as a minimum.

(21.25-21.27)

CHAPTER 22: TECHNOLOGICAL AIDS AND BROADCASTING

288 Technological aids have a considerable contribution to make to language development and the teaching of reading, but they do not represent a solution in themselves. Their value depends upon the extent to which they can be successfully integrated with the rest of the teacher's work.

(22.1-22.2)

289 Teachers in training should learn how audio-visual aids and broadcasting can be used to good advantage in their work in reading and language.

(22.4)

290 The demand for technological aids should be created by the teacher's curriculum planning; they should not be imposed upon it. There is therefore no simple formula for provision that would apply to all schools.

(22.6-22.12)

291 Where a school has a curricular need for a particular audio-visual aid every effort should be made to provide it. In some instances items of equipment might be shared with other schools, but certain items should be possessed by the individual school and indeed by each class within it where the need is present. Small schools should not be at a disadvantage.

(22.6-22.12)

292 Authorities should provide technical advice, prompt maintenance of equipment, and help with the preparation of materials.

(22.3; 15.20)

293   Reprographic facilities are becoming increasingly important in the teaching of English at all levels. All schools should be able to count on fast high-quality reproduction of the materials they need, and authorities should make provision to ensure this.

(22.11)

294   Television is now part of our culture and therefore a legitimate study for schools. The school has an important part to play in promoting a discriminating approach to it, but it is equally important that children should learn to appreciate the positive values and the variety of experiences the medium can provide.

(22.14)

295   Educational television and radio—both national and local—is a valuable source of stimulus for talking, reading, and writing. It requires careful preparation on the part of the teacher if it is to be effectively integrated with the rest of the children's activity.

(22.13; 22.15)

296   Opportunities for the direct involvement of teachers and pupils in educational radio and television programmes should be taken up more extensively.

(22.16)

297   If radio and television are to be exploited to the best effect every school should have facilities for recording programmes and storing tapes. The needs of nursery and infant schools in particular should be given urgent consideration.

(22.17)

298   There is a need for an extension of copyright agreements to allow schools to record any programmes and use them in ways and at times that suit their purposes.

(22.18)

299   There should be more research and evaluation of programmes, to determine such effects as interest, increase in knowledge or skill, and relative effectiveness with different children and different teachers.

(22.19)

300   There is an urgent need for expansion in educational broadcasting directed at children in the pre-school years and in the early stages of schooling, and at older children with learning difficulties. This can be achieved only by assistance from public funds, possibly with some selective help from charitable foundations.

(22.20-22.22)

301   Programmes should be developed to help the language interaction of parent and child. Schools and social agencies should co-operate to promote interest and participation in homes which would derive particular benefit from such programmes. These and similar programmes should also be shown on video-tape at ante-natal clinics.

(22.21; 5.14)

302   The possibility should be investigated of introducing references to various aspects of literacy into popular television programmes.

(22.23)

PART 8: TEACHER EDUCATION AND TRAINING

CHAPTER 23: PRE-SERVICE TRAINING

303   There is a remarkably wide variation in the importance attached to reading and language development in different teacher training institutions.

(23.2-23.5)

304   Generally speaking, there has been a tendency in the last decade for colleges to develop the 'academic' training at the expense of the professional element. In some colleges this has resulted in little more than nominal attention to language work and the teaching of reading.

(23.4-23.5)

305   Recently, a number of colleges have given much thought to improving the position of language and reading in the professional training, and in some colleges they are now strongly featured.

(23.6-23.7)

306   There should be more highly developed co-operation between colleges and schools, and students should have early access to practical experience. They should have the opportunity to work with individual children and small groups so that theory and practice might be more successfully integrated.

(23.8-23.9)

307   There should be more appointments of the teacher-tutor kind, where lecturers work in both college and school and develop the relationship between theory and practice.

(23.9)

308   All teachers in training, irrespective of the age-range they intend to teach, should complete satisfactorily a substantial course in language and reading.

(23.10-23.12; 23.25-23.26)

309   Some modification to content and scope may be necessary for students taking a one-year post-graduate certificate of education, but their course should include a language and reading component with specified minimum requirements.

(23.13-23.18)

310   This modification should not apply to the one-year course following a Diploma in Higher Education. The language and reading component in this course should be of the substance and extent recommended in 308.

(23.19-23.20)

311   Colleges providing for these students should devise ways of meeting this requirement, either organisationally or by their selection procedures.

(23.20)

312   The staffing of colleges should take account of the need for lecturers qualified by experience and specialist training in language and reading.

(23.21)

313   Language courses in teacher training should have properly equipped accommodation and ancillary help.

(23.22)

314   There are indications that the language competence of some students in training is unsatisfactory. As entry requirements become more stringent this competence should be taken more exactingly into account.

(23.23)

315   In learning about the nature and operation of language, students should be made more explicitly aware of their own practices. Improvement in students' language performance should take place in this context rather than in 'remedial' courses.

(23.23)

316   The understanding of language acquired during pre-service training should be regarded as only the first stage in a continuing process, of which the next phase is the induction year.

(23.24)

CHAPTER 24: IN-SERVICE EDUCATION

317   In his induction year the teacher needs support from his head and colleagues in adjusting to the reading and language policy of the school.

(24.1-24.2)

318   In the light of his practical classroom experience, the newly qualified teacher should receive help in extending his knowledge of the teaching of reading and language. This should take place in the time available for continued study in his induction year.

(24.1-24.2)

319   In their induction year primary school teachers and secondary school teachers of all subjects should meet to discuss continuity and children's language development aspects of the curriculum.

(24.3)

320   More should be done to bring in teachers as full partners in the process of in-service education rather than as the object of a training programme. A necessary implication of this is an increase in activities which involve the teachers in direct participation.

(24.4)

321   The individual school should be seen as an important focal point in in-service education, and there should be an expansion of school-based approaches.

(24.5)

322   School staffs should be encouraged to determine their own in-service education needs, and to share in the evaluation of ideas and information brought back from courses.

(24.5)

323   There should be an increase in the opportunities for heads to attend in-service courses to support them in their vital role in the improvement of reading and language work in their schools. Small schools in particular

should receive help to enable both heads and teachers to take part in in-service education activity.

(24.5)

324   In the secondary school the head of English department has a particular responsibility for helping in the continuing professional education of his colleagues within the department. In this he should receive help and encouragement from the L.E.A. English advisory team.

(24.6)

325   L.E.A.s and other providing agencies should make available more courses on reading and on the various other aspects of English teaching. In particular there is a need for courses on the role of language in the classroom, the use of diagnosis in the teaching of reading, and the teaching of the whole range of reading skills.

(24.7-24.8)

326   In-service courses should take a variety of forms, including half-day release, full-week workshops, and school-based studies. The emphasis should be on a flexible interaction between practice and theory.

(24.9)

327   The regional courses jointly arranged by the Area Training Organisations and the Department of Education and Science have been a valuable development. Under whatever auspices such courses continue in the future there should be an expansion in the number concerned with reading and the various aspects of English teaching.

(24.10)

328   Authorities should do everything possible to second more teachers to one-term or one-year full-time courses on reading, language, and general English, and the number of such courses should be increased.

(24.11)

329   There should be more full-time diploma courses and higher degrees available in language and reading. An expansion at this level is essential for the preparation of people able to give leadership in in-service education at local and regional level.

(24.12)

330   There are not enough teachers equipped to act as language consultants within schools, as advisers and advisory teachers for a local authority, or as specialist lecturers for students in training. If this deficiency is to be made up there must be a systematic and progressive programme of in-service education which opens up possibilities of career development. A suggested pattern would be as follows:

(a) language consultants in schools: local part-time courses continuing over two terms and preferably on the pattern of the A.T.O./D.E.S. courses;

(b) local authority advisory teachers: one-term full-time courses, or their part-time equivalent;

(c) local authority advisers, and lecturers in teacher training: advanced courses at diploma and higher degree level.

(24.14)

331   Teachers in every authority should have access to a language/reading centre.

(24.16)

332   When professional centres are developed their relationship to the language/reading centres must be carefully considered to make them mutually supporting.

(24.17)

333   There should be a national centre for language in education, which includes the teaching of English in all its aspects, from language and reading in the early years to advanced studies with sixth forms. Its siting and funding should be decided by consultation between the Secretary of State and interested parties.

(24.18)

A NOTE ON RESEARCH

A number of developments have taken place in recent years in the area covered by our field of inquiry, and some of these are reviewed in the relevant chapters. Many of them have been the result of teacher activity at teachers' centres, in associations, and in in-service training work, and some have derived their impetus from the findings of research.

Generally speaking, there exists something of an uneasy relationship between research and teaching. The findings of research studies are not always pertinent to the problems of teachers or of much practical value in the classroom. On the other hand, some have had considerable relevance and a great deal to offer to schools and yet have not been taken up. It is sometimes said of teachers that they ignore research findings, and of researchers that they fail to respond to the day-to-day problems of the classroom. There is clearly a pressing need for better communication and a closer understanding, and we would go so far as to say that it is more important to achieve this than to initiate yet more investigation in fields that have already been heavily researched. We do not suggest that there is no room for further research in English in general and in reading and language development in particular; far from it. However, we have allowed our conviction on this vital question of co-operation to temper our general recommendations about research. There is much that remains to be learned; but there is much that has been learned that remains to be used.

Educational research in this country takes three main forms: survey, fundamental analytical research, and action-research. Examples of the first are the N.F.E.R.'s national assessment of reading standards and the National Child Development Study's long-term study of a group of 15,000 + children born in March 1958. Such surveys are characterised by the selection of a large sample of children upon whom a mass of data is collected and analysed and correlated. The researchers may then extrapolate from their findings certain implications for future action. Fundamental analytical researches are generally more limited in scale but deeper in intensity. They vary too widely in type to be easily summed up, but they form the great bulk of research studies in education and are the ones with which teachers are most familiar. Many analytical research studies have produced information of very great value and we have had reason to be grateful to some of these in the course of our inquiry. There is no doubt that the best research of this kind has done and continues to do a great service to reading, language development, and other aspects of English. It is nevertheless true that a substantial number of studies contribute little and lead teachers to say that they confirm the obvious and yield nothing that makes anyone the wiser. The third form is action-research, which is not simply a programme of action with a built-in form of evaluation but consists of a complicated interplay between action and research at all points. The researcher is involved from the outset with the individual or group responsible for action, and dialogue between them is intrinsic to the process. A notable example of action-research in this country is the Educational Priority[1] programme, set up in 1968 and funded jointly by the Department of Education and Science and the Social Science Research Council.

The Plowden Committee examined the relationship between research and educational practice and concluded that:

"Because education is an applied discipline, the relation between research and practice is and should be reciprocal. From studies of what individual teachers are doing, useful pointers can be obtained to fruitful directions for experiment and research: research in education or in such ancillary sciences as child development, social psychology, or learning theory will throw up ideas with which the innovating teacher can experiment. In this very important sense, research and practice are parts of a whole, and neither can flourish without the other."

We believe this statement is a very helpful one, but we would go further. In our view, teachers should be involved not only in experimenting with the outcomes of research but also in identifying the problems, setting up hypotheses, and carrying out the collection and assessment of data. We are glad to see that such enterprises are already taking place in some colleges and university institutes of education in workshop courses as part of in-service training. This kind of participation can help teachers to a better understanding of the discipline, methods, and limitations of research, and can ensure that the outcomes are put to practical use. We should particularly like to see more action-research in which teachers are widely involved, for we believe that this form of activity holds considerable promise for the development of new practices in school.

In paragraph 24.18 we recommended the setting up of a national reference point for language in education. This would be a centre concerned with the teaching of English in all its forms and at all levels, from pre-school language and early reading to advanced reading and sixth form studies. One of the functions we envisage for this centre is to make more widely known the findings of research and to promote co-operation between researchers and teachers. It would have the tasks of assembling information on research in this country and abroad, analysing research needs, supplying information at all levels of demand, and disseminating the results of research and development work. Our own work has led us to the conclusion that none of these services is adequately developed at present. In the early days of the inquiry the Secretary and one of the members produced for the Committee a review of current research and existing research literature relating to projects within our terms of reference. This proved a considerable task, for information on this scale is not co-ordinated nationally. It brought home to us the need for it to be readily available, and we believe that this kind of co-ordination will become increasingly necessary if the most effective use is to be made of steadily accumulating information.

At various points in the Report we have indicated the need for further research into some particular topic. We debated whether we should draw these together and augment them to provide a list of proposed research projects. There seemed to us to be a good case for this, for we are aware that there are certain possible areas for research upon which our discussions did not touch but which clearly merit attention. We nevertheless decided against it, not least because of the likelihood that such a list might have a circumscribing effect. Rather than point the way for further detailed research we prefer to lay emphasis on the need for research and teaching to become more closely interrelated. We see as the first priority the need to give teachers greater insight into educational research, a process which should begin during initial training and find expression in in-service education. Wherever possible this should involve them in the research work itself, from collecting survey data to formulating and testing hypotheses and evaluating results. Secondly, we should like to see a change of emphasis in research within the field with which we are concerned. Many research studies have been, and continue to be, rather remote from the practical experience of teachers in the classroom. While fully acknowledging the value of much analytical research we should like to see more prominence given to research activity likely to have a direct impact in schools and a practical value for teachers.

REFERENCES

1.   *Educational Priority: Vol. 1, E.P.A. Problems and Policies:* HMSO: 1972.

NOTE OF EXTENSION

by Professor J. N. Britton

While the Report clearly acknowledges that the teaching procedures we recommend will not be effective without the co-operation of those who are taught, I believe the implications of this pre-condition need to be further explored. I know a number of English teachers who are succeeding in fostering the initiatives of their students in such a way as to gain the fruitful co-operation of many who have hitherto been hostile to school and everything it stands for. They employ methods which seem to differ from the procedures we have recommended and yet, in my view, what they are doing is in the spirit of the best teaching of the humanities.

Their methods appear to differ from the procedures recommended principally in that they promote the development of language uses which are effective within the narrower context in which they operate and yet are not at this stage directed towards meeting the standards applied in a wider context (whether social or operational). They seem to me to be in the spirit of the best teaching of the humanities in that they are directed towards a student's better understanding of himself and his potential in a multi-cultural and changing society.

Such teachers should in my opinion be encouraged, since the pioneer work they are doing is likely to bear fruit either in modifying the educational system to accommodate the needs of these students or in preparing the way for such provision outside the system as we know it.

I realise that the problem I refer to affects all subjects of the secondary school curriculum and might well be judged to lie outside the Committee's terms of reference. Nevertheless, had there been time I should have welcomed a full discussion of the issue, both in view of its urgency and because work in English lessons may be crucial to any attempt to find a solution. The Report indicates at many points the links between a child's uses of language and the satisfaction of some of his deeply felt, usually unconscious, needs. In paragraph 1.9 the point is made in general terms ("English is rooted in the processing of experience through language"); in paragraphs 5.22 and 5.23 it is made with particular references to the 'consolidation' or 'assimilation' of experience in talk and writing; and it is made quite explicitly in paragraph 11.8 where we outline the satisfactions to be derived from writing. What needs to be further explored are the implications of all this for teachers who face the multi-cultural groups to be found in many of our secondary school classrooms.

I would emphasise that satisfaction of these personal needs is brought about by uses of language built directly upon the speech of the home, and does not depend upon compliance with more widely acceptable standards. In claiming this I take it as axiomatic that any spoken form of English, be it cockney or Creole or anything else, is capable of moving from an expressive into a poetic function—that it can produce spoken or written utterances that have the status of "literature". *Expressive* language (essentially the speech of the home) is the appropriate form, it seems to me, for the development of activities *within a culture group*. In *poetic* language a culture group embodies and refines its essential values, expresses its uniqueness, and in so doing makes that embodiment available for interchange *within a network of culture groups*. *Transactional* language, spoken or written, is the embodiment (at one level) of what is *common across culture groups within a society*—the language of government, of commerce and the professions, of information exchange in all forms from the most practical to the most theoretical. It is here, then, in the use of transactional language, that demands for widely acceptable standards of some kind ('Standard English', for example) are most obviously justified.

Clearly an individual pupil's needs, whatever his culture group, embrace all these uses, and a teacher's concern for him must reach to them. What is at issue is the teacher's priorities, his timing, his tact in the variety of situations that confront him.

NOTE OF DISSENT
by Mr. Stuart Froome

While I agree with the main recommendations of the Report, I find myself bound to dissent from some of the conclusions reached by my colleagues on the Committee. The first concerns the opinion expressed in the chapter on Attitudes to English, where it is claimed there is no firm evidence upon which to make comparisons between standards of English today and those of before the war, and adds that there appears to be little substance in the generalisation that schools are promoting 'creativity' at the expense of the 'basic skills'. These statements, in my view, express a complacency about the teaching of English which is not in accord with some of the evidence which the Committee has received. One indication of declining standards in recent years was contained in evidence received from the Professor of English referred to in paragraph 1.3. He told us that distrust of formal teaching and formal structures of language has had considerable influence on the low standards of English among students today. He talked of "the dilution of English teaching, and the reaction against spelling and grammar". He stated further that students coming into higher education could often be described as semi-literate and he supplied samples of deplorable work to illustrate his contention. He also stated that standards for "O" and "A" level are too low and need to be revised.

From another source the Committee has heard of schools where in the desire to foster creativity, it is held that children will develop the power to use language simply by being encouraged to speak and write, and that any critical intervention will stem the flow. Sometimes work of very poor quality is displayed in such schools, because it is believed that the child's spontaneous effort is sacrosanct and to ask him to improve it is to stifle his creativity.

My own observation in a number of schools leads me to the belief that in the zeal for 'creativity' by teachers today, there is not the rigorous critical marking of spelling, punctuation and grammatical errors which there used to be, while the traditional systematic 'doing of corrections' is fast disappearing. This has led, in my view, to the wretched solecisms exhibited in students' written work, and I believe that the Committee should have made even more of the unfortunate side-effects which the policy of free, uninhibited creativity has engendered. It must be admitted that if teacher-students are as deficient in basic writing skills as our evidence suggests, it can be fairly assumed that the standards of those who do not aspire to be teachers must be correspondingly, dangerously low. The Committee should have been alive to this probability and have stated its concern unequivocally. It could also have been stated with greater force that the more competent children are in the trained accomplishments of spelling, punctuation and the grammatical arrangement of words, the more likely are they to write vividly, gracefully and tellingly, or in short—creatively.

My second point of dissent with the conclusions of the Committee concerns standards of reading. Here I feel more attention has been given to explanation of the limitations of the tests used in national surveys than the subject warrants. The tests may be inadequate but they are the only ones we have. I disagree with the statement that it is questionable whether it is a profitable exercise to compare present-day standards of reading with those of before the war. It is only by such comparisons that we can assess the value of the methods used in the schools, and parents are anxious about such matters. Some will wonder perhaps why the Consultative Committee of 1931 stated that for most children the process of learning to read should be nearly finished by the time the pupil reaches the age of seven, and yet by 1966 the report of the National Child Development Survey showed that 44 per cent of 11,000 seven-year-olds needed the help in reading usually given in the infant school, and 10 per cent had barely begun to read. Others will have read the findings of Dr. Joyce Morris in her reading survey of 1959 that among 3,000 children tested in the first year of the junior school, 45 per cent needed infant school teaching while 19 per cent were virtually non-readers. While these studies are discussed in the Report and the Committee agrees there is some evidence that children of seven are not as advanced as formerly in those aspects of reading ability which are measured by tests, I believe this is an understatement. My own experience, borne out by evidence from Mr. G. E. Bookbinder, alluded to in para. 2.26, is that the average standard reached by today's child of seven was attained by the age of six and a half in 1938, and I believe the Committee should have made an urgent appeal for a return to the methods employed in schools before the war, which seem to have given children at that time a six months' advantage over their counterparts today. It may be true that by the time present-day children have reached the age of eleven, they have caught up the pre-war pupils, but this has only been accomplished by very great effort on the part of the junior schools, many of which make much use of part-time teachers in remedial reading work, a practice quite unknown before the war, when classes were very much larger and super-numerary staff were not available. Moreover, those children who are lagging behind at age seven, even if they do catch up eventually, have in the meantime lost all the accumulated knowledge which has been available to their more fluent peers, and this loss is irretrievable. While the Report advocates a critical reappraisal of the concept of reading readiness, I believe it should have gone further and condemned it as a notion conceived purely as a plausible explanation for pupils' reading retardation.

I am glad the Committee stressed the great advantages to be gained from early reading, but I would like to have seen an even more forthright appeal for a national concerted effort from teachers and their advisers to ensure an acceleration of the reading process in the early stages.

Thirdly, I am in disagreement with the majority of the members of the Committee on their reservations about arrangements by which pupils are streamed or setted for English according to ability, and their belief that mixed ability grouping offers most hope for English teaching. The Committee did not commission a research study of the effects which these two different methods of organisation have on the standard of achievement in schools, and therefore to commend one and by implication reject the other, does not seem to me to be in the spirit of true inquiry. What evidence there is with regard to the effects of streaming is mainly in favour of it, and even the Plowden Report on the Primary School concedes there is some evidence which suggests that in the limited field of measurable attainment, achievement is higher in streamed schools. While we have no information which compares the results of streaming with those of mixed ability grouping in secondary schools, it must be obvious that as children grow older, differences in their inherent ability to cope with the demands of more difficult material, can only accentuate the disparity between the individuals who make up a class. Streaming by ability makes the work of the teacher easier and he and his pupils can therefore advance at a much faster pace. Moreover, it is clearly wasteful of time and manpower for teachers to be spreading their skill and attention thinly across wide spans of ability in separate unstreamed class-rooms, when by judiciously arranging for pupils of similar capacity to be together, more homogeneous groupings can be achieved. Mixed ability grouping makes the teacher's work more difficult because he has the task of reconciling the eagerness of the gifted child with the unavoidable reluctance and occasional hostility of the dull one. As the Report acknowledges (para. 15.11), one of our witnesses pointed out the problems of mixed ability classes. He reminded us that in a first year secondary school form containing the full range of ability, the English teacher may encounter an extraordinarily wide spread of reading age (7-14) and an accompanying wide divergence in maturity of reading interest and taste. Although he did not say this, he was clearly suggesting that it is extremely difficult to fire a group of high ability children with enthusiasm for Shakespeare or Shaw in the same room as another group is struggling with "Janet and John" or "Little Bo-peep".

It is sometimes advanced by those who favour this method of grouping that in the mixed ability class, the children of high ability will be anxious and able to help their less-gifted peers. If this argument contains any truth at infant school level, it most certainly does not apply in the secondary school, where with older children, embarrassment is likely to hamper the would-be helper, and resentment at being patronised may antagonise those who are in need of help. The Report rightly poses (para. 15.11) some penetrating questions that a school ought to be able to answer before introducing mixed ability grouping for English teaching. However, I believe it should have gone further and rejected such grouping as a practice. It seems to me quite illogical to admit that English teaching is rendered difficult in secondary schools by such factors as rapid turnover of staff, excessive use of part-time teachers and the poor qualifications of some personnel, and at the same time to recommend mixed ability grouping where the complexities inherent in the method are considerable.

The move towards mixed ability grouping in British schools is a recent one, and in my view, smacks more of social-engineering than of educational thinking. Like the movement to abolish grades, class positions and pupil competition, it is really a manoeuvre to ensure that no-one is seen to excel. Although the preference for this method was not shared by all members of the Committee, and is not recorded as such, I do not feel it should have been stated at all in the circumstances.

Fourthly, I would question the notion postulated in Chapter 4 that a child can learn by talking and writing as certainly as he can by listening and reading, for it appears to me that in its context it is being used as an attempt to promote the merits of 'discovery methods'. It is doubtful if children's talk in school does much to improve their knowledge, for free discussion as a learning procedure at any age is notoriously unproductive. As for children learning by writing, this seems a very doubtful proposition. The writer can only write from his present knowledge and experience and in the case of children these are very limited. It is true that if a child does some 'research' before writing he is learning by the process, but such an action is strictly 'reading' not 'writing'. Moreover, the Report itself acknowledges that much of children's so-called research in topic or project work is of little practical value. Quite often this work consists in the child seeking encyclopaedias or reference books, and copying out chunks of information without any selective consultation of sources.

It seems to me then that to equate 'talking and writing' with 'listening and reading' as instruments of learning, is to place a value upon the former that has no relation to the experience of practising teachers. I believe that reading is by far the most efficient means of learning, because in addition to its obvious worth in the acquisition of information, it has the additional use of formulating in the reader's mind the principles of the arrangement of words in an orderly sequence to convey their intended meaning. This is why it is so important to ensure that children learn the mechanics of reading at the earliest possible age and are then encouraged to read widely and discriminately, because fluent readers are likely to become fluent writers.

I believe the Committee is in error in putting undue emphasis upon talking as a means of learning language. It has its place, but in my view, one of the causes of the decline in English standards today is the recent drift in schools away from the written to the spoken word. As one author has said: "The cynic may well see the modern trend to use the spoken language in teaching English, rather than reading and writing, as an implied failure of our educational system to teach reading adequately". I fully agree with this conclusion.

In listing the sources of oral and written evidence and the institutions we visited, both here and in the U.S.A., we take a second opportunity to thank all the people who gave us such generous help.

APPENDIX A

LIST OF WITNESSES AND SOURCES OF EVIDENCE

1. WITNESSES WHO GAVE ORAL EVIDENCE

(i) ORGANISATIONS AND ASSOCIATIONS

Association of Teachers in Colleges and Departments of Education.

    Mr. R. W. Sefton-Davies, Chairman of Working Party on evidence to the Committee.
    Mr. D. Farrelly, Member of Working Party on evidence to the Committee.
    Mr. P. Grainge, Member of Working Party on evidence to the Committee.
    Mr. J. Pearce, Member of Working Party on evidence to the Committee.
    Mr. J. Way, Member of Working Party on evidence to the Committee.

Cambridge House Literacy Scheme

    Miss Bridget O'Brien Twohig, Director.
    Mrs. Jenny Stevens, Assistant Director.

Fife L.E.A.

    Miss C. M. Douglas, Organiser of Early Education.
    Mrs. M. Forrest, Assistant Head, Lynburn Primary School, Fife.

Inner London Education Authority

    Mr. Harvey Hinds, Chairman, Schools Sub-Committee.
    Dr. M. Birchenough, Chief Inspector.
    Miss N. Goddard, Staff Inspector for Infant Education.
    Mr. J. Welch, Staff Inspector for English.

Inner London Education Authority: Media Resources Service

    Mr. L. Ryder.
    Miss G. Calloway.

The Joint Four Secondary Association

    Miss M. R. Osborn, Chairman.
    Mr. B. H. Holbeche, Vice-Chairman.
    Mr. A. W. S. Hutchings, Joint Hon. Secretary
    Miss S. D. Wood, Joint Hon. Secretary

National Association of Head Teachers

    Miss G. Belson, Chairman, Professional Advice Committee.
    Mr. P. Bowden, Executive Council Member.
    Mr. J. Holt, Chairman, Education Academic Committee.
    Mrs. M. Richards.

National Association for Remedial Education

Mr. R. Bushell, Chairman, Evidence Sub-Committee and County Advisory Officer, Staffordshire L.E.A.
Mr. J. E. Perry, County Advisory Officer, Devon.
Mr. M. Peterson, Education Guidance Service, Derbyshire.

National Association of Schoolmasters

Mr. F. Smithies, Chairman, Education Committee.
Mr. B. Farrell, Vice-Chairman, Education Committee.
Mr. R. B. Cocking, Ex-President.
Mr. J. D. Marsh, Assistant Secretary.
Mr. C. W. Slater, Executive Member.

National Association for the Teaching of English

Dr. Andrew Wilkinson, Vice-Chairman.
Mr. Anthony Adams, Secretary.

National Council for Educational Standards

Sir Desmond Lee, Hon. Secretary.
Dr. Rhodes Boyson, M.P.
Mr. A. R. Harris.

National Foundation for Educational Research

Mr. A. Yates, Director.
Dr. K. B. Start, Co-author "The Trend of Reading Standards" (N.F.E.R. 1971).
Dr. R. Sumner, Head of Guidance and Assessment Services.

National Union of Teachers

Mr. R. S. Fisher, Chairman, Education Committee.
Mr. F. M. Newrick, Assistant Secretary, Education Committee.
Mr. J. Bowdler, Member, Education Committee.
Miss M. M. Jones, Member, Education Committee.
Mr. P. J. Kennedy, Member, Education Committee.
Mr. M. H. Flannery, Chairman, Advisory Committee for Primary Schools
Mr. P. L. Griffin, Member, Advisory Committee for Primary Schools.
Mr. J. Sloman, Member, Advisory Committee for Special Schools.

Simplified Spelling Society

Mr. S. S. Eustace, Hon. Secretary.
Mr. F. Gibbs, Committee Member.
Mr. G. G. O'Halloran, Committee Member.
Mr. W. J. Reed, Committee Member.
Dr. Zettersten, Cultural Attaché of the Swedish Embassy.

United Kingdom Reading Association

Mr. D. Moyle, President.
Mr. W. Latham, Immediate Past-President.
Dr. Margaret Clark, Past-President.

(ii) INDIVIDUALS

The majority of witnesses also submitted written evidence.

Sir William Alexander, Secretary, Association of Education Committees (now Lord Alexander).

Dr. Miriam Balmuth, Hunter College, City University, New York.

Mrs. D. J. Bantock, Teacher, The Grove School, Melton Mowbray.

Professor G. H. Bantock, Director of the School of Education, University of Leicester.

Mr. Douglas Barnes, Senior Lecturer, Institute of Education, University of Leeds.

Professor Basil Bernstein, Head of the Sociological Research Unit, Institute of Education, University of London.

Mr. R. Bird, Head of English Department, The Thomas Bennet School, Crawley, Sussex.

Mrs. I. Brady, Teacher, Essex Infant School, London Borough of Newham.

Dr. E. W. H. Briault, Education Officer, Inner London Education Authority.

Professor Jerome Bruner, Watts Professor of Psychology, Department of Experimental Psychology, University of Oxford.

Mr. T. Bryans, Educational Psychologist, London Borough of Croydon.

Mr. K. Bunch, Teacher, St. James's C.E. Junior School, London Borough of Newham.

Mr. A. Burgess, Lecturer, Institute of Education, University of London.

Sir Alec Clegg, Chief Education Officer, West Riding of Yorkshire.

Mr. D. Courts, Principal Lecturer and Head of the English Department, St. Peter's College of Education, Saltley, Birmingham.

Professor C. B. Cox, Professor of English Literature, University of Manchester.

Mrs. Joan Dean, Chief Inspector of Schools for Surrey.

Mr. John Dixon, Principal Lecturer in English, Bretton Hall College of Education.

Professor John Downing, Faculty of Education, University of Victoria, British Columbia.

Miss G. E. Evans, Head of English Department, Crown Woods School, Eltham.

Mr. P. Gannon, Senior Lecturer in English, Lady Spencer Churchill College of Education, Oxford.

Dr. Elizabeth Goodacre, Senior Lecturer, Middlesex Polytechnic at Trent Park, and Consultant to the Centre for the Teaching of Reading, School of Education, University of Reading.

Dr. A. H. Halsey, Professorial Fellow and Head of the Department of Social and Administrative Studies, Nuffield College, University of Oxford.

Mrs. E. M. Hawkins, Educational Psychologist, Inner London Education Authority.

Professor Hilde T. Himmelweit, London School of Economics.

Mr. D. Labon, Senior Educational Psychologist, West Sussex County Council.

Miss Nancy Martin, Reader, Institute of Education, University of London.

Mrs. L. McCarthy, Teacher, Carpenters Primary School, London Borough of Newham.

Dr. Joyce Morris, Author and Language Arts Consultant.

Dr. Margaret Peters, Tutor, Cambridge Institute of Education.

Dr. Douglas Pidgeon, Director of the Initial Teaching Alphabet Foundation and former Deputy Director of the National Foundation for Educational Research.

Sir James Pitman, K.B.E., Chairman, Council of Management, The Initial Teaching Alphabet Foundation.

Dr. Mia Kellmer Pringle, Director of the National Children's Bureau.

Mr. M. J. Rankine, H.M.I., Scottish Education Department.

Mr. M. F. Riddle, Senior Lecturer in Linguistics, Department of Arts and Social Studies, Middlesex Polytechnic.

Mr. T. Riley, Teacher, Star Junior School, London Borough of Newham.

Professor H. A. Robinson, Professor of Reading, Hofstra University, New York.

Mrs. Betty Root, Tutor-in-Charge, Centre for the Teaching of Reading, School of Education, University of Reading.

Professor John Sinclair, Professor of Modern English Language, University of Birmingham.

Mr. H. Smith, Institute of Education, University of London.

Dr. R. Sumner, Head of Guidance and Assessment Services, National Foundation for Educational Research.

Mr. B. Thompson, Deputy Head, Lionel Road Junior School, Hounslow. Co-Author of "Breakthrough to Literacy".

Dr. Joan Tough, Lecturer, Institute of Education, University of Leeds.

Mr. J. A. Walker, Head of English Department, Heronswood School, Welwyn Garden City, Hertfordshire.

Mr. Frank Whitehead, Senior Lecturer, Department of Education, University of Sheffield.

Professor Andrew Wilkinson, Institute of Education, University of Exeter.

Mr. S. Wolfendale, Educational Psychologist, London Borough of Croydon.

Mr. J. Worsley, Research Associate, Department of English Language and Literature, University of Birmingham.

Mr. A. Yates, Director, National Foundation for Educational Research.

(iii) DEPARTMENT OF EDUCATION AND SCIENCE

The members of H.M. Inspectorate listed below gave oral evidence. Some of them also submitted papers.

Mr. L. J. Burrows, C.B.E., H.M.I.
Miss K. M. P. Burton, H.M.I.
Mr. C. W. E. Cave, H.M.I.
Mr. R. C. Dove, H.M.I.
Mr. M. Edmundson, H.M.I.
Mr. Eric Lord, H.M.I.
Mr. A. J. Luffman, O.B.E., H.M.I.
Miss E. McDougall, H.M.I.
Mr. P. Phillips, H.M.I.
Mr. N. Thomas, H.M.I.
Mr. E. Whiteley, H.M.I.
Mr. E. Wilkinson, H.M.I.

Other members of the Department of Education and Science helped with information of various kinds, and we are grateful for the co-operation of the staff of the Department's Library.

2. WITNESSES WHO GAVE WRITTEN EVIDENCE

(i) ORGANISATIONS, ASSOCIATIONS AND OTHER BODIES

Advisory Centre for Education.

Assistant Masters' Association.

Association of Educational Psychologists.

Association of Institute and School of Education In-Service Tutors.

Association of Teachers in Colleges and Departments of Education.

Association for the Education of Pupils from Overseas (now National Association for Multi-Racial Education).

Berkshire College of Education, Students' Union.

Bishop Otter College of Education.

Brighton College of Education.

Bristol Association for the Teaching of English.

Bristol Reading Centre.

British Association for Applied Linguistics.

Centre for the Teaching of Reading, Reading University.

Centre for Information on Language Teaching.

City of Cardiff College of Education.

College of Preceptors—Metropolitan Executive.

College of Speech Therapists.

Community Relations Commission.

Community Service Volunteers.

Confederation for the Advancement of State Education.

Confederation of British Industry.

Eastbourne College of Education.

Educational Publishers' Council.

English Speaking Board.

Federation of Children's Book Groups.

FKS Publishers (Film).

Home Office—Prisons Department.

Incorporated Association of Preparatory Schools.

Independent Broadcasting Authority.

Inner London Education Authority.

The Joint Four Secondary Associations.

Kempston Teachers' Centre, Bedford.

Keswick Hall College of Education.

Library Advisory Council for England.

Library Association.

Liverpool University Settlement.

National Association for the Teaching of English.

National Council for Educational Standards.

National Child Development Study.

National Association of Schoolmasters.

National Association of Head Teachers.

National Council for Educational Technology (now The Council for Educational Technology).

National Association for Remedial Education.

National Association of Divisional Executives for Education.

National Association of Inspectors of Schools and Educational Organisers.

National Foundation for Educational Research.

National Union of Students.

National Union of Teachers.

National Book League.

North London Dyslexia Association.

Oxfordshire L.E.A. Primary Schools.

Priory Lane Junior School, Scunthorpe.

Professional Association of Teachers.

St. Albans Teachers' Centre.

School Broadcasting Council for the United Kingdom.

Schools Council Project—The Curriculum Needs of Slow Learning Pupils.

School Library Association.

Simplified Spelling Society.

Sittingbourne College of Education.

Society for Italic Handwriting.

Society of County Librarians.

United Kingdom Reading Association.

Union of Women Teachers.

West Midlands College of Education.

(ii) INDIVIDUALS

This list contains the names of individual witnesses who submitted written evidence. We are also grateful for the 226 letters we received which were an additional source of very helpful opinion and information.

Miss A. M. Adams, Research Worker.

Mr. R. Y. Anderson, Teacher-in-charge, Marsh Remedial Centre, Lancaster.

Mr. H. Armstrong James, Principal, Sunderland College of Education.

Miss S. Augstein, School of Social Sciences, Brunel University.

Mr. P. G. Baker, Curriculum Development Leader, North Oxfordshire Teachers' Centre.

Mr. H. W. Bardens, Teacher, Gordon High School for Boys, Gravesend, Kent.

Mr. J. A. Barnes, Chief Education Officer, Salford, Lancashire.

Mr. C. W. Baty, formerly Her Majesty's Inspector of Schools.

Mr. W. A. Bennett, Lecturer, Department of Applied Linguistics, University of Cambridge.

Mr. G. S. Bessey, Chief Education Officer, Cumberland.

Mr. J. S. Bishop, Chief Education Officer, Royal Borough of Kingston-upon-Thames.

Mr. J. Blackie, formerly Her Majesty's Inspector of Schools.

Mr. F. Blackwell, Director, Primary Extension Programme, Council for Educational Technology.

Mr. E. Bleasdale, Headmaster, St. Osmund's R.C. School, Bolton; and Author.

Mr. J. M. O. Bodmin, Director and General Manager, E.S.A. Creative Learning Limited.

Mr. I. Bolger, Deputy Head, St. Gregory's School, Ealing.

Mr. G. E. Bookbinder, Head of Reading Advisory Service, Salford, Lancashire.

Mr. T. Booth, Research Psychologist, Department of Child Psychology, Guy's Hospital, London.

Dr. R. Boyson, M.P., formerly Headmaster, Highbury Grove Comprehensive School, London.

Mr. S. Bradford, European Manager, Scott Foresman Publishing Company.

Mrs. P. E. Bradley, Part-time Tutor-in-charge, Reading Centre, School of Education, University of Leicester.

Miss M. Brearley, formerly Principal, Froebel Institute.

Mr. W. K. Brennan, Director, Schools Council Project—The Curricular Needs of Slow Learning Pupils.

Mr. B. Bryan, City of Leicester College of Education.

Miss E. M. Brown, Headmistress of an Infant School, Middleton, Manchester.

Mr. D. P. J. Browning, Chief Education Officer, Southampton.

Mr. D. Butts, Head of Department of English Studies, Berkshire College of Education.

Mr. T. Buzan, Principal, College of Advanced Reading.

Mrs. E. Calcutt, Parent.

Mr. B. Cane, Deputy Principal, Sheffield College of Education.

Mr. J. L. Carr, Publisher.

Mr. H. M. C. Carroll, Lecturer in Education, University College of Swansea.

Mrs. K. M. Chacksfield, Headmistress, Chandler's Ford County Infant School, Hampshire.

Mr. P. Chambers, Head of Education Department, West Midlands College of Education.

Mr. M. Chazan, Co-Director, Schools Council Compensatory Education Research and Development Project, University of Swansea.

Sister Christine, Headmistress, St. Anne's R.C. Infant School, Kennington.

Mr. J. A. Clark, Head of Science Department, St. Crispin's School, Wokingham.

Dr. M. Clark, Senior Lecturer, Department of Psychology, University of Strathclyde.

Mrs. E. E. Clarkson, Teacher, Longlevens Secondary School, Gloucester.

Mr. G. H. Clare, Headmaster, St. Mary's Lower School, Caddington, Nr. Luton.

Miss F. M. Coar, Headmistress, Kingsley First School, Bournemouth.

Mr. D. Cookson, Educational Psychologist, Staffordshire County Council.

Miss P. V. Corr, Headmistress, Barrow Island County Infant School, Barrow-in-Furness.

Mr. C. T. Crellin, Head of Education Department, Trent Park College of Education, Barnet, Herts.

Mr. P. W. Daffon, Director, Reading Consultancy Service.

Miss Q. R. A. Daniels, Retired Teacher.

Mrs. J. Dean, Chief Inspector of Schools, Surrey.

Mr. R. Deans, Wurld Langwij Asqsiyon.

Mr. T. Derrick, Lecturer in Education, Post Graduate School of Studies in Research in Education, University of Bradford.

Mr. H. Diack, Senior Lecturer, School of Education, University of Nottingham.

Dr. A. Dickson, Hon. Director, Community Service Volunteers.

Mr. A. Done, Head of English Department, Wilsthorpe Comprehensive School, Long Eaton, Derbyshire.

Miss M. T. Doyle, Teacher, St. Charles' Hospital School, Carstairs, Lanarkshire.

Mrs. R. Driscoll, Member of National Council, Professional Association of Teachers.

Professor E. Edmonds, Professor of Education, University of Prince Edward Island.

Mrs. J. H. Elfer, Remedial Teacher to three schools in Surrey.

Mr. B. Evan-Owen, Oxfordshire Remedial Service.

Mr. J. Fazackerley, Remedial Teacher, Nuffield Clinic, Plymouth.

Mr. D. Nor Ferris, Lecturer in Philosophy, University of Exeter.

Mr. G. Fischer, Managing Director of "Talking Page".

Mr. D. Fiske, Chief Education Officer, Manchester.

Mr. I. S. Flett, Director of Education, Fife.

Mrs. E. D. Foster, Headmistress, Cholsey County Infant School, Wallingford, Berkshire.

Mrs. E. Fraser, Supervising Tutor of the "Speakwell" English classes for foreigners.

Mr. H. Fryer, Educational Sales Manager, Transworld Publishers Limited.

Mrs. D. Gardiner, Principal, Park Lodge School, Helensburgh.

Mrs. B. Gethings, Headmistress, Rendham County Primary School, near Saxmundham, Suffolk.

Mr. T. Gourdie, Teacher and Author.

Mrs. Grabowska, Headmistress, Parklands County Infant School, Long Eaton, Derbyshire.

Mrs. A. C. Greenman, Tutor in College of Education in South America.

Mrs. R. Greensmith, Headmistress, Wheatfields Infant School, Marshalwick, St. Albans.

Mrs. E. C. Greenwood, Principal, Sittingbourne College of Education.

Mr. B. Groombridge, Head of Educational Programme Services, Independent Broadcasting Authority.

Mr. Terry Hall, Ventriloquist.

Dr. A. H. Halsey, Professorial Fellow and Head of Department, Department of Social and Administrative Studies, University of Oxford.

Mr. W. S. Harpin, School of Education, University of Nottingham.

Mr. G. M. A. Harrison, Chief Education Officer, Sheffield.

Mr. M. Harrison, formerly Director of Education, Oldham.

Mr. R. K. Harwood, The British Association for the Teaching of English.

Mr. J. L. Haselden, Chief Education Officer, London Borough of Barking.

Miss E. A. E. Hawes, Deputy Head, Cholsey County Infant School, Berkshire.

Professor E. W. Hawkins, Director, Language Teaching Centre, University of York.

Mr. J. Haynes, Chief Education Officer, Kent.

Mrs. E. Hazlehurst, Teacher, Ashton Park School, Bristol.

Mrs. M. L. Heath, Representative of North London Dyslexia Association.

Mr. B. Heckle, Hon. Registrar, College of Teachers of the Blind.

Miss Janet A. Hill, Children's Librarian, London Borough of Lambeth.

Mr. R. J. Hoare, Tutor/Librarian, St. Mary's College of Education, Twickenham.

Mr. M. E. Holding, Headmaster, Eleanor Palmer Primary School, Tufnell Park, London.

Mr. D. M. Hopkinson, H.M.I.

Mr. D. N. Hubbard, Lecturer in Primary Education, Institute of Education, University of Sheffield.

Mr. A. A. Hughes, Academic Registrar, Bishop Otter College of Education, Chichester.

Mr. J. M. Hughes, Lecturer in Special Education, Caerleon College of Education.

Mrs. M. Hynds, Senior Lecturer, Philippa Fawcett College, London.

Mr. J. Izbicki, Education Correspondent, "The Daily Telegraph".

Mr. Digby Jacks, President of the National Union of Students.

Mr. Brian Jackson, Director, Advisory Centre for Education.

Mr. D. Jackson, Headmaster, New Ash County Primary School, Dartford.

Mr. D. H. Johnson, Manager, Vosper Thorneycroft (Training) Limited.

Mr. R. E. Johnson, Headmaster, Sonning Common Primary School, Reading.

Mr. S. F. Johnson, Head of Teaching Services Division, Social Services Department, Birmingham.

Mr. Kenneth Jones, Author.

Mr. P. Kincaid, Member of Old Palace Group, Oxford (Adult Literacy Tuition).

Mr. J. Kirkham, formerly Principal Lecturer in English, Head of English Department, Kesteven College of Education.

Miss D. Kuya, Senior Community Relations Officer, Liverpool Community Relations Council.

Mrs. J. M. Lander, County Secretary, Cornwall Federation of Women's Institutes.

Mr. J. A. Lane, Headmaster, Micklands County Primary School, Reading, Berkshire.

Mr. H. Y. Larder, Headmaster, Spendlove School, Charlbury, Oxford.

Mr. L. Law, Students' Union, Berkshire College of Education, Earley, Reading.

Mr. D. Lawrence, Educational Psychologist, Somerset.

Mr. A. Lawson, Warden, St. Albans Teachers' Centre.

Mrs. D. J. Leakey, Headmistress, Blagdon Road Nursery School, Reading.

Mrs. F. Leistikow, St. Bernard's School, New York City, U.S.A.

Miss J. Lennox-Barnes, Deputy Headmistress, Flinton Primary School, Hull.

Mr. J. H. K. Lockhart, Head of English Department, Greenford Grammar School, Greenford, Middlesex.

Miss B. Lukasinska, Headmistress, Grimsbury County Infant School, Banbury, Oxon.

Dr. P. Mann, Reader in Sociology, University of Sheffield.

Mr. N. Marten, M.P.

Miss D. Mason, Headmistress, St. Luke's Terrace Infant School, Brighton.

Mr. M. Z. Mavro-Michaelis, Warden, Teachers' Centre, Kempston, Bedford.

Mr. E. W. Maynard Potts, The National Education Association.

Colonel J. K. McConnel, Retired.

Miss S. McCullagh, Author of Children's Stories.

Mr. D. J. McPherson, Head of Education Department, St. Mary's College of Education, Newcastle-upon-Tyne.

Mr. T. W. Messenger, Senior Lecturer in English, Brighton College of Education.

Dr. E. Midwinter, Director of "Priority" and Co-Director, Advisory Centre for Education.

Dr. P. Mittler, Hester Adrian Research Centre.

Professor B. Morris, Professor of Education, University of Bristol.

Mr. H. Morris, Morris Advisory Services, Retford.

Mr. C. Moon, Deputy Head, Yatton Junior School, Bristol.

Mr. D. V. Moseley, Principal Psychologist, Child Guidance Training Centre, London.

Mr. J. Mountford, Lecturer, Department of Education, La Sainte Union College of Education, Southampton.

Mr. D. Moyle, Principal Lecturer in Education, Edge Hill College of Education, Ormskirk.

Miss D. Nash, Headmistress, Sea Mills Infant School, Bristol.

Mr. B. L. Needle, Autoflex Publications.

Mrs. M. Newton, Applied Psychology Department, Aston University.

Mr. J. Nicholls, Head of English Department, Keswick Hall College of Education, Norfolk.

Mrs. R. Nichols, Educational Psychologist, Berkshire.

Professor J. Nisbet, Head of Department of Education, University of Aberdeen.

Mrs. E. W. Norton, Teacher, Claybourne School, Addlestone, Weybridge, Surrey.

Miss M. M. O'Brien, Principal, St. Thomas More's School, Totnes, South Devon.

Miss B. O'Brien-Twohig, Director, Cambridge House Literacy Scheme.

Mrs. C. Obrist, Teacher and Lecturer.

Miss J. O'Neill, Director of "121" Literacy Scheme, Liverpool University Settlement.

Dr. G. M. Owen, Principal, St. Mary's College, The Park, Cheltenham.

Mrs. S. M. Owen, Teacher, Netherhall Girls' School, Cambridge.

Mr. L. H. M. Parsons, Publisher, The Ant and Bee Partnership.

Dr. H. J. Peake, Principal, Sheffield City College of Education.

Mr. G. Peaker, formerly Her Majesty's Inspector of Schools.

Mr. R. C. Phillips, Director, R. C. Phillips Limited.

Mr. G. R. Potter, Chief Education Officer, West Sussex.

Mr. J. Potts, Senior Lecturer, St. Katherine's College, Liverpool.

Mr. E. E. Powell, Headmaster, Llanedeyrn Junior School, Cyncoed, Cardiff.

Mr. J. L. Presland, Educational Psychologist, Warwickshire.

Mr. J. Priest, Retired Headmaster.

Mr. P. D. Pumfrey, Lecturer in Education, University of Manchester.

Sir Lincoln Ralphs, Chairman, Schools Council and formerly Chief Education Officer, Norfolk.

Mrs. M. J. Randle, Teacher, Woodcote County Primary School, Reading, Berkshire.

Mrs. J. M. Ray, Adult Literacy Tutor, East Herts College of Further Education.

Mr. W. Reed, Simplified Spelling Society.

Miss J. Reid, Lecturer in Educational Sciences, University of Edinburgh.

Mr. K. J. Revell, Chief Education Officer, London Borough of Croydon.

Miss M. Richardson, Teacher, Adult Spastic Centre.

Mr. M. F. Riddle, Senior Lecturer in Linguistics, Hendon College of Technology.

Mr. L. V. Rigley, Lecturer in Child Development, University of London.

Mr. J. E. Roberts, Headmaster, Caergeilog County Primary School, Anglesey.

Mr. R. Roberts, Manchester Council of Social Services.

Mr. J. Robertson, Educational Psychologist, Bedfordshire.

Mr. S. J. Rowan, Apprentice Recruiting Officer, Jarrow.

Mr. C. W. Rowley, Senior Lecturer in Remedial Education, St. Peter's College, Saltley, Birmingham.

Dr. M. L. Rutter, Institute of Psychiatry, The Bethlem Royal Hospital and the Maudsley Hospital.

Mr. J. V. Savage, Director, Educational Equipment Association.

Professor D. B. Scott, Professor of Mathematics, University of Sussex.

Mrs. E. Seaman, Norwich Feasibility Study, National Association for the Teaching of English.

Mr. A. M. Shapiro, General Manager, Sight and Sound Education Limited.

Mr. C. Shepheard-Walwyn, Managing Director, Shepheard-Walwyn (Publishers) Limited,

Mrs. M. Shields, Lecturer in Education, Department of Child Development, Institute of Education, University of London.

Mr. N. W. R. Sims, Senior Educational Psychologist, Bristol Reading Centre.

Mr. V. J. Sloman, Headmaster, Riverbank School, Cardiff.

Mrs. E. D. Smelt, Australian Teacher and Author.

Mr. L. S. Smith, Convenor, Language of Failure Sub-Committee, National Association for the Teaching of English.

Mr. R. L. Snowdon, Vice-Principal, Northern Counties College of Education, Newcastle-upon-Tyne.

Mr. J. R. Standeven, Headmaster, Ravensthorpe Secondary Modern School, Dewsbury.

Dr. K. B. Start, Co-Author of "The Trend of Reading Standards" (N.F.E.R.)

Mr. L. Stenhouse, Director, Centre for Applied Research in Education, University of East Anglia.

Mr. H. Stephenson, Assistant Education Officer, Staffordshire.

Dr. W. E. D. Stephens, Chief Education Officer, London Borough of Waltham Forest.

Major C. Stevenson, Royal Army Education Corps.

Mrs. L. M. Tarbox, Speech Therapist.

Mr. D. T. Taverner, General Inspector for Primary Schools, London Borough of Newham.

Mr. M. Temple-Smith, Publisher.

Dr. L. F. Thomas, Director, Centre for the Study of Human Learning, Brunel University.

Mr. N. R. Thomas, Headmaster, Woodhouse Close Junior School, Bishop Auckland.

Mrs. B. Thompson, Headmistress, Northwold Infant School, Clapton, London.

Mr. K. G. Thompson, Librarian, Willowgraph High School, Barnsley, West Riding of Yorkshire.

Mr. G. Thornton, Senior Inspector for English, Cheshire.

Mr. F. A. Thorpe, Publisher, "Trigger Books".

Mr. R. C. Todd, Lecturer in Sociology, Trinity and All Saints Colleges, Leeds.

Mr. J. R. G. Tomlinson, Chief Education Officer, Cheshire.

Mr. N. E. Trowbridge, Head of the Audio-Visual Communication Department, Bishop Otter College, Chichester.

Mr. G. Trump, Headmaster, Chalice School, Glastonbury, Somerset.

Miss B. Tudor-Hart, Teacher.

Mrs. A. L. Tunnadine-Cooper, Chairman of the National Education Association (Surrey Branch).

Mr. E. W. Turner, Headmaster, Rokeby Middle School, Rugby.

Mrs. A. L. Vacher, Headmistress, St. John's Voluntary Controlled Infant School, Glastonbury, Somerset.

Mrs. H. Vegoda, Teacher.

Mr. J. M. Wallbridge, Diagnostic Reading Adviser to the Inner London Education Authority, North Islington Project for Children with Special Difficulties.

Mr. C. D. Waller, Teacher, Gravesend Upper School for Boys.

Mr. A. D. Walters, Principal, Ethel Wormald College of Education, Liverpool

Mrs. B. Wax, formerly Educational Psychologist, London and Surrey.

Mr. J. Webster, formerly Director, The Reading Clinic, St. Helier, Jersey.

Dr. K. Wedell, Senior Lecturer, School of Education, University of Birmingham.

Mr. G. Wells, Research Fellow, School of Education, University of Bristol.

Mr. P. Widlake, Senior Research Assistant, Institute of Education, University of Birmingham.

Professor A. Wijk, Retired Docent in English, University of Stockholm, Sweden.

Mr. J. L. Williams, Dean of the Faculty of Education, University College of Wales, Aberystwyth.

Mrs. M. Wilson, Headmistress, New Denham County Primary School, Uxbridge.

Mr. S. S. Wilson, Lecturer, Department of Engineering Science, University of Oxford.

Mrs. M. Wood, Department of Education, University of Newcastle.

Mr. D. E. Wright, Director, Educational Development Centre.

Mr. P. W. Young, Tutor, Cambridge Institute of Education.

VISITS MADE

1. IN ENGLAND

(i) SCHOOLS

The schools are listed by local authority areas as these existed before Local Government Reorganisation on April 1, 1974.

A. *Counties*

	School	*Head*
Berkshire	Sandy Lane Junior Mixed School, Bracknell	Mr. N. S. Pugsley
	The Grange Nursery School, South Ascot	Miss E. A. Wellbeloved
Buckinghamshire	Gerrards Cross Church of England Primary School	Mr. T. A. Bryan
	John Hampden Infant School, Aylesbury	Mrs. Small
Cornwall	Looe Secondary School	Mr. J. Simmonds
	Sir James Smith's School, Camelford	Mr. D. G. E. Haynes
Cumberland	Hesingham Junior School	Mr. Hind
	Montreal Street School (Junior and Infant), Cleator	Mrs. Jones
	St. Gregory and St. Michael Infant School, Whitehaven	Sister Rose
	St. Michael's Church of England School, Dalston	Mr. Barrow
	Inglewood Junior School, Harraby, Carlisle	Mr. Nichol
Derbyshire	Tibshelf Secondary School	Mr. G. G. Critchlow
	Tupton Hall School, Old Tupton, Chesterfield	Mr. B. F. Rice
Devon	Bickleigh Primary School, Tiverton	Mrs. Scott
	Heathcoat School, Tiverton	Mr. R. C. D. Kingsford
Dorset	Gillingham Comprehensive School	Mr. J. Webster
Durham	Dinsdale Park Residential E.S.N. Special School	Mr. J. H. Morgan
	Greenland Infant School, Stanley	Mrs. M. Robinson
	Greenland Junior School, Stanley	Mr. O. Barras
	Highfield Comprehensive School, Felling	Mr. W. Cooke

APPENDIX B

School	*Head*
Gloucestershire	All Saints' Secondary Modern, Cheltenham	Mr. L. E. J. Taylor
	Fiveways Infant School, New Cheltenham, Kingswood, Bristol	Mrs. D. A. Unwin
Hertfordshire	Gill's Hill Infant School, Radlett	Mrs. A. Blakeley
	Heron's Wood Secondary School, Welwyn Garden City	Mr. R. Bainbridge
Kent	Elvington County Primary School, Kythorne, Dover	Mr. O. P. Baker
Lancashire	Alfred Turner School, Irlam	Mr. M. S. Sealy
	Brookfield Primary School, Skelmersdale	Mr. F. Holmes
Leicestershire	Countesthorpe College	Mr. J. F. Watts
	Fernvale County Junior School, Thurnby	Mr. P. J. Greeve
	Oadby Launde County Infant School	Mrs. J. M. Cooksey
	Oadby Manor High School	Mr. W. Higgins, O.B.E., J.P.
Norfolk	The Belfrey Voluntary Aided Primary School, Overstrand	Mr. Wallace
	St. Andrew's Church of England Primary School, North Pickenham	Mr. R. Linton
	Sheringham Secondary Modern School	Mr. Rowland
	Trowse County Primary School	Mrs. Shaw
Northumberland	Cramlington High School	Mr. T. M. Dines
	Cramlington Parkside Middle School	Mr. W. E. Gowrie
	Linton First School	Miss M. Neil
	Wallsend Central First School	Mr. H. Brown
	Wallsend Central Middle School	Mr. E. A. Snowdon
Shropshire	Madeley Court Education Recreation Centre Madeley Court School (Comprehensive)	} Mr. H. F. Cunningham

	School	*Head*
Somerset	The Chalice School, Glastonbury	Mr. G. Trump
	Nailsea School (Comprehensive)	Mr. D. W. John.
	Swan Mead Middle School	Miss D. Russell
Suffolk East	Stowmarket High School	Dr. R. J. Montgomery
Suffolk West	Tudor Primary (First) School, Sunbury	Mr. D. Evans
Sussex West	Christ's Hospital	Mr. D. H. Newsome
	Midhurst Intermediate School	Mr. M. J. Caton
Westmorland	Kirkby Lonsdale Church of England Primary School	Mr. N. E. Cartwright
	Longlands Boys' School, Kendal	Mr. R. S. Foss
	Queen Elizabeth Grammar School, Kirkby Lonsdale	Mr. P. R. Castle
Wiltshire	Chilton Foliat Church of England Infant and Junior School	Mr. Porter
	Clarendon Junior School, Tidworth	Mr. Rainer
	Tidworth Down County Secondary School	Mr. Fisher Haynes
	Wootton Bassett Comprehensive School	Mr. Shepherd
Yorkshire/North Riding	Huntington Secondary Modern School	Mr. C. E. Browning
	Joseph Rowntree Modern School	Mr. G. Mills

B. *County Boroughs*

Birmingham	Castle Vale Comprehensive School	Mr. W. Barnett
	Chivenor Junior Mixed and Infant School	Miss M. J. Wise
	Pegasus Junior School	Mr. J. L. Harrison
Bolton	The Deane High School	Mr. F. Barwise
Bradford	Hanson Upper School	Mr. Dawson
Bristol	Sea Mills Infant School	Miss M. D. Nash

	School	Head
Burnley	Ightenhill Infant School	Miss I. Stanworth
	Ivy Bank Comprehensive School	Mr. C. Brunton
	Lowerhouse County Primary School	Miss M. Colburn
Carlisle	Inglewood Junior School, Harraby	Mr. J. S. Nichol
Darlington	Hummersknott County Comprehensive School	Mr. L. S. Gordon
Dewsbury	Ravensthorpe Secondary School	Mr. J. R. Standeven
	Thornhill County Primary School	Mr. J. Morris
Halifax	Holy Trinity Infant School	Mrs. N. Clegg
Kingston-upon-Hull	Oldfleet Primary School	Mr. E. E. Senior
	Thorpe Park Primary School	Mr. J. R. Hodgson
Leeds	Brudenell Infant School	Mrs. H. M. Beedel
	Foxwood High School, Seacroft	Mr. R. T. Spooner
Leicester	Crescent Junior School	Mr. S. F. A. Jax
	The Gateway Grammar School	Mr. M. H. Bailey
	Uplands Infant School	Miss P. M. Iliffe
Manchester	Parrs Wood High School	Mr. E. P. Iball
	St. Chrysostom's Infant and Junior School	Mr. G. N. Dodds
Newcastle-upon-Tyne	Snow Street Primary School	Mrs. D. J. Heathcote
Norwich	Trowse County Primary School	Mrs. O. L. Shaw
Nottingham	Douglas Infant and Junior Schools	Mrs. P. Cooper
	Greenwood Junior School	Mr. H. Bradley
	Huntingdon Infant School	Mrs. B. E. Dexter
	Huntingdon Junior School	Mr. G. A. Richardson
	John Player Bi-lateral Secondary School	Mr. D. T. Dowell
	West Player Junior School	Miss L. M. Hollins-head
Plymouth	Camel's Head Secondary School	Mr. V. Machin
	North Prospect Infant School	Mrs. J. Sparey

School	Head
Sheffield	Rowlinson School (Comprehensive)	Mr. P. Dixon
Teesside	Bertram Ramsey Comprehensive School	Mr. D. J. Chalkley

C. *Outer London Boroughs*

Kingston-upon-Thames	The Mount Infant School, New Malden	Miss L. P. Marshall
Newham	Elmhurst Infant School	Miss J. L. Hicks
	Star County Infant School	Miss B. M. Bull

D. *Inner London Education Authority*

Clissold Park School (Comprehensive)   Mr. T. C. Willcocks
Clissold Park Immigrant Language Unit

Grenfell E.S.N. School   Miss K. H. E. Rawlings, O.B.E.

Harrington Hill Junior Mixed and Infants   Mrs. B. A. MacGilchrist
School, London, E.5.

Highbury Grove Comprehensive School   Dr. Rhodes Boyson

Hugh Myddelton Infant School   Miss M. M. Robson, M.B.E.

Lee Church of England Primary School,   Mr. B. C. Secrett
Blackheath

Randal Cremer Junior School   Mrs. G. Shaw

St. Anne's R.C. Infants School, London,   Sister Christine
S.E.11.

Tidemill Junior Mixed School, Deptford   Miss F. M. Lane

(ii) COLLEGES OF EDUCATION

College	Principal
All Saints' and Trinity Colleges, Horsforth, Leeds	Mr. A. M. Kean
Alnwick College of Education, Northumberland	Miss L. K. Hollamby
Avery Hill College of Education, London	Mrs. K. E. Jones
Bedford College of Education	Miss P. B. Dempster
Bretton Hall College of Education, Wakefield, Yorkshire	Dr. A. S. Davies
College of the Venerable Bede, Durham	Mr. K. G. Collier
Culham College of Education, Oxfordshire	Mr. J. F. Wyatt
Darlington College of Education, Co. Durham	Mr. J. Huitson
Digby Stuart College of Education, London	Sister Dorothy Bell

Edge Hill College of Education, Ormskirk, Lancashire	Mr. P. K. C. Millins
Homerton College of Education, Cambridge	Miss A. C. Shrubsole
Kingston-upon-Hull College of Education	Dr. C. Bibby
Maria Grey College of Education, London	Mrs. K. M. Saunders
Newton Park College, Newton St. Loe, Bath, Somerset	Mr. N. P. Payne
Northumberland College of Education, Ponteland	Miss E. M. Churchill
Rachel McMillan College of Education, London	Miss E. M. Puddephat
St. John's College of Education, York	Mr. J. V. Barnett
St. Mary's College of the Sacred Heart, Fenham, Newcastle-upon-Tyne	Sister Prudence Wilson
St. Matthias College of Education, Bristol	Mr. R. A. Adcock
Wall Hall College of Education, Watford, Hertfordshire	Miss A. K. Davies
West Midlands College of Education, Walsall, Staffordshire	Dr. J. Cornwell

(iii) READING AND LANGUAGE CENTRES

Leicester County Borough	Leicester Reading Centre.
Manchester	Reading Centre at George Leigh Street School, Ancoats.
	Reading Centre at Manchester Teachers' Centre, Barlow Moor Road.
Reading	University of Reading, Centre for the Teaching of Reading
London Borough of Croydon	Croydon Language Centre.
Inner London Education Authority	Centre for Language in Primary Education, London, S.W.1.
	Centre for Urban Educational Studies, Aberdeen Park, London, N.5.

2. IN THE U.S.A.

(i) SCHOOLS

Principal

New York

George Washington High School	Mr. S. Kostman
Public School 129	
Public School 234	
Public School 198	Mrs. Charlotte Schiff

Principal

Springfield, Massachusetts
Longmeadow High School   Mr. Edgar G. Craver

Los Angeles Area
McKinley Elementary School, Burbank   Mr. James C. Derrick
Miller Elementary School, Burbank   Mr. Hal Bucklin
Macy School, Lowell Joint School District,   Mr. Marston Ellis
   Whittier
NCL/USC Reading Center School, Los Angeles

San Francisco Area
Oakland High School
Crocker Highlands Elementary School,
   Oakland
Martin Luther King School, Oakland   Dr. Herbert Wong
Washington Elementary School, Berkeley
Everett Junior High School, San Francisco   Mr. Carlos V. Cornejo

(ii) UNIVERSITIES AND OTHER INSTITUTIONS
California State University of San Francisco
University of Southern California
New York Learning Co-operative

(iii) DISCUSSIONS WITH THE FOLLOWING:

Dr. Ruth Love Holloway   Director, The Right to Read Effort, U.S.
                              Office of Education, Washington

Dr. Ralph C. Staiger   Executive Secretary-Treasurer, International
                              Reading Association

Dr. Constance McCullough   President-Elect, International Reading
                              Association

Dr. Edythe Gaines   Director, Learning Co-operative, Board of
                              Education, New York

Dr. Margaret Early   Reading and Language Arts Center,
                              Syracuse University, New York

Dr. Roselmina Indrisano   School of Education, Boston University

Dr. Donald L. Landry   Professor of Education, Westfield State
                              College, Massachusetts

Mr. O. A. Lopes   Chairman of English, Longmeadow High
                              School, Springfield, Massachusetts

Dr. Nila Banton Smith   Distinguished Professor of Education,
                              University of Southern California,
                              Los Angeles

Miss Sue Schrager   University of Southern California, Los
                              Angeles

Dr. Grayce A. Ransom   Associate Professor of Education and
                              Director of the Reading Centers,
                              University of Southern California,
                              Los Angeles

Mrs. Elsie Black   Director of Instruction, Lowell Joint School
                              District, Whittier, California

Dr. Margaret Weymouth   Chairman, Department of Elementary
                              Education, California State University,
                              San Francisco

Dr. James Duggins   Director, External Evaluation Team, School
                              of Education, California State University,
                              San Francisco

Mr. R. Connolly   Assistant Principal, Chairman of English,
                              Oakland High School

Miss Eleanor Robison   Berkeley, California

Discussions with Miss Charlotte Sharp (President) and members of the New England Reading Association at the Association's annual conference, Springfield, Massachusetts.

GLOSSARY

Accent: The way in which language or dialect is pronounced, commonly regarded as indicating the nationality, region, or social class of the speaker.

Accidence: Changes that occur in the forms or inflections of words to indicate tenses, singular and plural, etc.: e.g. climb/climbed, ox/oxen, table/tables.

A.E.C.: Association of Education Committees.

Aides, Teachers': Trained ancillaries whose purpose is to give substantial help to teachers within the school.

Allophone: One of the variant forms of a phoneme or individual speech sound, e.g. the way "n" is sounded in "thin" is different from that in "nose". The two are therefore different allophones of the phoneme "n".

Alphabetic Analysis: A reading method in which the child says the names of the letters, e.g. see-aye-tee "cat".

A.T.C.D.E.: Association of Teachers in Colleges and Departments of Education.

A.T.O.: Area Training Organisation. A regional organisation which is usually part of a university and is made up of colleges of education and departments of education. Its role is to supervise the training of teachers in the region and also to provide courses and conferences for serving teachers.

Auditory Acuity: Sensitivity of hearing.

Auditory Discrimination: The ability to discriminate between the sounds of words or syllables, detecting similarities or differences.

B.B.C.: British Broadcasting Corporation.

B.Ed.: Bachelor of Education. A combined degree and professional teaching qualification which is awarded at the end of a four-year course at colleges of education and various polytechnics. Current proposals are for a three-year course which will entitle the student to a pass degree whilst a four-year course would give an honours degree. Both courses will be recognised for teaching purposes.

Blending: Ability to link together the constituent sounds in a word while pronouncing them separately, as in *gr, pl* and a consonant-vowel blend as in *da, sto.*

Breakthrough to Literacy: A set of materials designed to enable the child to build up words and sentences and to learn to read through using the language he produces himself. This integrated approach derived from a programme set up to study linguistics and the teaching of English.

Burnham Committee: (Properly the Burnham Primary and Secondary Committee). A committee consisting of representatives of teachers, local education authorities and the Secretary of State for Education and Science, constituted to negotiate teachers' salaries.

Capitation Allowance: An annual allowance allocated to schools by the local education authority for the purchase of books, consumable materials, and equipment. The allowance is made on the basis of so much money per pupil, and the sum varies according to age.

Ceiling Effect: A limitation of the value of a test which results from the fact that the most difficult items are too easy for many of the more able pupils (see annex to Chapter 2).

Cloze Procedure: A procedure which involves deleting or omitting words in a text on a systematic basis. The reader is required to insert appropriate words with the help of the context. Cloze procedure can be used to measure reading attainment and the level of difficulty of any given book.

C.N.A.A.: Council for National Academic Awards. This was established by Royal Charter in 1964 to provide more opportunities for students to take degree courses in the colleges of technology. C.N.A.A. degree courses are available mainly in the Polytechnics.

Coding Scheme: A device for assessing accuracy in certain features of a piece of writing, e.g. spelling, punctuation.

Colour Coding: The use of colour to provide additional clues to the value or function of letters in the early stages of learning to read. It may consist of a complex system where every phoneme is represented, or a simpler system in which the more general functions rather than the sound values are signalled.

Comprehensive School: A non-selective school intended to cater for the secondary education of all the children in a given area. The majority of such schools take the children from 11 to 18, but there are alternative forms. In some cases there is a two-tier system with a break at 13 or 14; or a three-tier system involving 'first', 'middle', and 'upper' schools. Another variant is 11-16 followed by sixth form college from 16+.

Context Cues: Words, phrases, or sentences that occur directly before or after a given word and help the reader recognise the word and its meaning.

Controlled Vocabulary: Vocabulary of an early reading book in which the rate of introduction of new words and the number of repetitions of those words are carefully controlled, the principle being that the child can thus 'over-learn' rather than have to cope with an unrestricted number of unfamiliar words.

Creole: A form of language resulting from a mixture of English and the native languages spoken by West Africans who were taken to the West Indies in the 17th and 18th centuries.

C.S.E.: Certificate of Secondary Education. A subject-based examination usually taken at 16+ and administered regionally by fourteen boards in England and Wales, with the option for schools of external or internal syllabuses and assessment. The highest grade awarded is equated with a pass at "O" level of the G.C.E. (q.v.).

C.S.O.: Central Statistical Office.

C.S.V.: Community Service Volunteers.

Day Nursery: Establishments where children under 5 can be left while parents are at work. Most are maintained and staffed by the social services departments of local authorities, but some, attached to hospitals, are run by area health authorities.

Decoding: A term applied to the reading process to signify the translation from unfamiliar written symbols into familiar language.

D.E.S.: Department of Education and Science. (Originally the Board of Education, until 1945, and Ministry of Education, 1945 to 1964).

Diacritical Marking: A system of adding graphic signs to letters to indicate their correct sound value. It preserves traditional spelling, but the marks are added to help the reader cope with situations where the phonemes and graphemes do not correspond.

Dialect: A form of language in which the grammar, pronunciation, and vocabulary associate it with a particular region or social class.

Digraph: Two letters which come together to represent a single sound and lose their individual identity in the process, e.g. *ch* as in *ch*eap.

Diphthong: The continuing of two vowel sounds to make a single sound, e.g. the o and i in 'moisture'.

Dip.H.E.: Diploma in Higher Education: A qualification to be awarded after two years' study in higher education; the standards of entry and of assessment will be comparable with those of the first two years of a degree course. While available as a terminal qualification, it will normally be followed by further study leading to a professional qualification or a degree.

Dyslexic: A term used to describe children who experience a difficulty in learning to read that cannot be accounted for by limited ability or by emotional or extraneous factors. The term is not susceptible to precise operational definition. (See *Children with Specific Reading Difficulties: The Tizard Report:* H.M.S.O.: 1972.)

Elaborated Code: A term devised by Professor Bernstein to describe a form of language which can produce considerable degrees of verbal differentiation.

English Speaking Board: An association devoted to the improvement of speaking ability; as one of its activities it conducts examinations and awards certificates.

E.P.A.s: Educational Priority Areas. A concept introduced in the Plowden Report to denote areas with a high incidence of social and educational deprivation. It recommended that such areas should benefit from positive discrimination—i.e. an allocation of educational resources higher than would ordinarily be provided.

E.S.N.: Educationally subnormal children are "pupils who, by reason of limited ability or other conditions resulting in educational retardation, require some specialised form of education wholly or partly in substitution for education normally given in ordinary school" (Ministry of Education, *The Handicapped Pupils and Special School Regulations*, pamphlet No. 365: H.M.S.O.: 1959).

Education Welfare Officer: An officer employed by the local education authority for school attendance and welfare work.

First School: A school that caters for children from the age of 5 to the age of 8, 9, or 10, and is normally the first stage of a three-tier system.

Functional Literacy: See paragraph 2.2.

G.C.E.: General Certificate of Education. A subject-based examination administered regionally by different boards in England and Wales. Ordinary ("O") level is normally taken at 16 and Advanced ("A") level at 18.

Grammar: The rules and usages of a language which determine the way its words are ordered (syntax), and the changes occurring in those words to make them serve a particular function (accidence).

Grapheme: A printed or written symbol which stands for a particular sound in a language.

Hadow Reports: Reports of the Consultative Committee under the Chairmanship of Sir Henry Hadow: *The Education of the Adolescent* (1926), *The Primary School* (1931) and *Infant and Nursery Schools* (1933).

Health Visitor: Health visitors maintain a link between medical and non-medical social services, visiting children's clinics and the homes of all children under two years of age.

H.M.I.: Her Majesty's Inspector of Schools.

I.B.A.: Independent Broadcasting Authority, formerly Independent Television Authority.

Idiolect: The form of a language spoken by an individual as distinct from a group, class, or nation.

Informal Reading Inventory: A means of determining and recording a child's reading skills by observing his behaviour in a reading situation the teacher has devised for the purpose.

I.L.E.A.: Inner London Education Authority.

Illiterate: See paragraphs 2.1-2.4.

Impression Marking: A process of giving a grade or mark to a piece of a work on general impression and without the use of sub-totals for different aspects or qualities of the performance. It is usually used in multiple-marking, the mark assigned to a piece of work being the sum total of two or more impression marks by different examiners.

I.M.T.A.: Institute of Municipal Treasurers and Accountants, now the Chartered Institute of Public Finance and Accountancy.

Induction Year: The induction year is an improved probation which gives the new teacher a lightened work load, and further training occupying one-fifth of his working time. It is proposed that during this year he should receive guidance and support from a specially appointed 'professional tutor'.

Infant School: A school for pupils aged 5 to 7 years; it is sometimes part of a primary school and sometimes a separate school.

In-Service Education: Continued education and training of serving teachers.

Integrated Day: A form of class or teaching group organisation which provides for a variety of activities (reading, mathematics, art) to be undertaken by different children at the same time. It is usual for the class to be taught together for other parts of the day.

Integrated Studies or Integrated Humanities: An arrangement in a secondary school by which a number of subjects are grouped together and taught in close relationship to one another, e.g. history, geography, religious education and English.

Interlinear Tests: The interlinear test is one of several objective-type methods used to test capacity in English usage. Typically it consists of an ill-written piece of prose which is presented to the candidate with instructions to correct or improve the English.

Intonation: The sequence of pitches that produces the 'tone' of an utterance and plays an important part in conveying the meaning. The intonational tone of a question, for example, usually features a rising pitch at the end.

Item Pooling: Used in monitoring assessment, an item pool is a collection of carefully developed items which are drawn from a variety of sources and which will ensure an extensive coverage of the area to be assessed.

i.t.a.: initial teaching alphabet. Designed to help beginners to learn to read on the basis of 44 visual symbols. The system seeks to avoid the difficulties normally associated with early stages in reading when the child has to cope with the irregularities of English orthography.

James Report: "Teacher Education and Training": Report of a Committee of Inquiry under the chairmanship of Lord James: HMSO: 1972.

Joint Four: The Joint Four Secondary Associations (The Incorporated Association of Head Masters, the Association of Head Mistresses, Assistant Masters Association, Association of Assistant Mistresses).

Kinaesthetic: Perception through the sense of touch and movement.

L.E.A.: Local Education Authority.

Learning Set: An acquired tendency to respond in a way that will produce a successful solution to a particular problem, e.g. learning to look along a line of print from left to right; learning to attend to the shape of a letter while ignoring such irrelevancies as its size.

Lexis: The words of which a language consists; more commonly called "vocabulary".

Linguistics: The scientific study of language, concerned with producing a complete description of a language and obtaining information about the nature of language in general.

Linguistic Method: A term used to describe a method of teaching reading by which words are graded according to the complexity of the spelling.

Logograph: A symbol that stands for a whole word.

Look and Say: A method of teaching reading in which the child is taught to respond to whole words rather than to attend to the separate parts of words.

Medium: In reading terminology the form in which written language is set out on the page. This can be either the conventional form, when it is known as traditional orthography, or one in which a modified alphabet is used, as in i.t.a., or a simplified spelling system. A further variant is the traditional alphabet used with special marks or colours. (See diacritical marking and colour coding.)

Methods: The word used to represent different ways of beginning reading instruction. For examples, see 'Look and Say', Sentence Method, Alphabetic Analysis, and Phonics.

Middle School: A school that caters for pupils in the age ranges 8 to 12, 9 to 13, 10 to 13, or 10 to 14, and is the second stage of a three-tier system.

Miscue: A context cue (q.v.) which in a given situation misleads a reader so that his anticipation of a subsequent word is incorrect.

Monitoring: A term used in the text to denote the measurement of attainment in schools throughout England by means of random sampling.

Morpheme: The smallest unit of language which has a grammatical function; e.g. 'van' and 's' in 'vans', and 'eat' and 'ing' in 'eating' are all morphemes, and each carries meaning.

Morphology: The branch of grammar which is concerned with inflection and word-formation.

Multiple Choice Tests: In a multiple choice test the questions are followed by three or four alternative answers, one of which is the correct or 'preferred response'. The candidate records his answer by indicating one of the answers given.

N.A.H.T.: National Association of Head Teachers.

N.A.R.E.: National Association for Remedial Education.

N.A.S.: National Association of Schoolmasters.

N.A.T.E.: National Association for the Teaching of English.

National Book League: A body whose object is to promote reading and an appreciation of the value of books.

N.C.D.S.: The National Child Development Study is a longitudinal study of the development of a cohort of 15,468 children born in England, Wales and Scotland in March, 1958.

N.C.T.E.: National Council of Teachers of English (U.S.A.).

Newbolt Report: "The Teaching of English in England": Report of the Committee of Inquiry under the chairmanship of Sir Henry Newbolt: H.M.S.O.: 1921.

Newsom Report: "Half our Future": Report of the Central Advisory Council for Education under the chairmanship of Sir John Newsom: H.M.S.O.: 1963.

N.F.E.R.: National Foundation for Educational Research in England and Wales. The functions of the N.F.E.R. are to encourage, organise, co-ordinate and carry out educational research, its primary concern being the study and resolution of such practical problems as arise within the public system of education and are amenable to scientific investigation.

N.N.E.B.: National Nursery Examination Board; a central examining body which grants certificates for qualification as nursery nurse.

Norm: A mean or median score for an age group of a representative population in an intelligence or attainment test.

N.S.6 Test: National Survey Form 6—One of two tests used in the national surveys of reading standards. Devised in 1956 as a multiple-choice test of the incomplete sentence type; it has 60 items and a 20-minute time limit.

Nursery Nurse: A trained person who assists qualified teachers in nursery school, class or group and who holds a certificate of the National Nursery Examination Board.

Nursery Class: A class which is attached to a primary school and contains children aged 3 to 5; there may be more than one such class attached to a school but none must exceed 30 places.

Nursery School: A school providing education for children from 3 to 5.

Nursery Unit: A unit, not exceeding 20 places, which provides nursery education for children from 3 to 5.

N.U.T.: National Union of Teachers.

Orientation: The direction in which letters and words are read along a line of print.

Overlearn: To learn beyond the point at which the skill or process is first shown to have been mastered.

Paralinguistic features: Aspects of spoken communication which do not reside in the words themselves but nevertheless contribute to the meaning, e.g. intonation, loudness and speed of utterance, facial expression.

Percentile: An individual's position on a given dimension, as expressed by the percentage of other people who are at or below that position.

P.G.C.E.: Post Graduate Certificate of Education; a certificate which confers qualified teacher status and is awarded on the results of a one-year course of professional training taken by graduates or those with similar qualification.

Phoneme: The basic sound unit of a language. Phonemes are identified from ʳ ₑe another by contrast.

Phonetics: The study of individual sounds in speech.

Phonic Method: A method of teaching reading where emphasis is placed on the sound values of individual letters, or groups of letters, with the object of helping the child to blend sounds to form words.

Phonic 1 *and Phonic* 2: Terms used in the survey questionnaire to distinguish between phonic approaches which emphasise respectively (*a*) the sound values of individual letters, digraphs and diphthongs, and (*b*) the sounds of syllables.

Plowden Report: "Children and their Primary Schools": Report of the Central Advisory Council for Education (England) under the chairmanship of Lady Plowden: H.M.S.O.: 1967.

Pre-Reading Exercises: Exercises and activities designed to help children acquire the generalised learning sets which provide the essential bases for reading.

Pre-school Play Groups: Voluntary part-time play groups for children under 5.

Primary School: A school at present catering for children from 5 to 11 or 12.

Probationary Year: The first year's full-time service of a qualified teacher, during which he must satisfy the Department of Education and Science of his practical proficiency as a teacher.

Rate Support Grant: The R.S.G. system is the principal means by which the Government gives financial assistance towards the costs of services provided by local authorities. The estimated total expenditure of *all* local authorities on *all* services (education being only one) is determined by annual forecasts made jointly by Government departments and local authority associations. The "relevant expenditure" so determined is then used as a basis for deciding what proportion shall be paid by the Government as R.S.G., and a formula is decided for the apportionment of the total R.S.G. to each local authority.

Readability: The difficulty level of reading materials, usually measured by the familiarity of the words and the length and complexity of the sentences used.

Reading Age: See note 3 to Chapter 2.

Reading Laboratories and Workshops: Collections of assignment cards and other devices designed to give practice in reading comprehension. The material is devised in accordance with some of the principles derived from the field of programmed learning.

Reading Scheme: A graded series of reading books and related materials for the teaching of reading in the early stages.

Received Pronunciation: The least localised pronunciation of English as spoken in Britain.

Redundancy: The presence of more items in a message than the reader or listener needs for the purpose of receiving it.

Register of Language: The kind of language appropriate to use for a particular purpose in a particular situation.

Reliability of Tests: The extent to which a test will give the same scores on different occasions.

Restricted Code: A term devised by Professor Bernstein to describe the language of a group with shared assumptions such that its members do not feel the need to make verbal differentiations.

Reversal: Reversing a letter or word when reading or writing, e.g. *d* for *b*, or *pat* for *tap*.

Sampling: The selection of a proportion of the total population in such a way that the results of a test applied to this proportion will indicate the characteristics of the whole.

Scanning: Reading in such a way as to locate specific information within a piece of writing without reading it in its entirety.

Schools Council: Schools Council for Curriculum and Examinations; a body set up in 1964 to keep under review curricula, teaching methods, and examinations in schools, including aspects of school organisation so far as they affect the curriculum. Its membership includes representatives from local authority and teacher associations and the Department of Education and Science.

School Health Service: Under the terms of the National Health Service Reorganisation Act, 1973, the school health services, previously the responsibility of local education authorities, became part of the child health services provided by Area Health Authorities within the reorganised National Health Service.

S.L.A.: School Library Association; an association devoted to the interests of library work in all its aspects in schools.

School Library Service: A local authority service which maintains a link between schools and the public library, providing schools with long-term book-loans, and providing various other facilities to support teachers in stimulating interest in books.

Screening: The application of certain procedures to a defined population of pupils, usually a whole age group, to identify pupils likely to experience learning difficulties.

Semantic: Relating to the meaning of words.

Semi-literate: See paragraph 2.4.

Sentence Method: A form of the 'Look and Say' method of teaching reading, by which the child is taught to respond to whole sentences in the earliest stages.

Setting: The practice of grouping according to ability for certain subjects, the age group being divided into differently constituted 'sets' for each individual subject concerned.

Sight Words: Words recognised immediately by the reader without his having to go through the process of breaking them into constituent parts.

Skimming: Reading in such a way as to gain a general impression of what a particular piece of writing is about, by going through it rapidly and giving attention to key words, phrases, and sentences.

Specific Reading Retardation: A term which has been used to describe children whose reading ability is characterised by severe difficulties which are not accountable for in terms of low intelligence and which are not explicable merely in terms of the lower end of a normal distribution of reading skills.

Standard Error: A measure of the uncertainty inherent in a sample mean as an estimate of the population mean. It is computed by dividing the standard deviation of the sample by the square root of the number of items. (See note 14 to Chapter 2.)

Standardisation of Tests: The process of establishing norms or standards for a test; this might include norms of administration, size of print, spacing of words/sentences, duration of the test, marking or scoring instructions, and interpretation of scores.

Stochastic Process: Any process governed by the laws of probability. In the case of the language process, the expected probability of occurrence of any single element or sequence, from the point of view of the reader or listener, is governed by the immediate context and his previous personal experience of similar kinds of context.

Streaming: Grouping of children in an age group according to ability.

Structural Grammar: A grammar intended to explain the working of language in terms of the functions of its components and their relationships to each other without reference to meaning.

Syntax: A branch of grammar concerned with sentence structure and the rules governing the relationships between words in a sentence.

Syntactic structure: The arrangement of words in relationship to one another within a sentence.

t.o.: The abbreviation for traditional orthography, which refers to the normal use of the 26 letter alphabet when it is employed according to the accepted rules of the English spelling system.

Teachers' Centre: A centre where teachers meet to exchange ideas and share experiences, prepare materials for use in their work, and receive support in the form of local in-service courses. There are some 500 such centres provided by local authorities in England and Wales, and they differ widely in their activities, accommodation, and facilities.

Transformational Grammar: A grammar that assigns structural description to sentences and relates deep structures to surface structures, i.e. relates the abstract structures postulated as underlying sentences to the actual utterances.

U.D.E.: University Department of Education; university department providing a post-graduate course of professional teacher training.

U.N.E.S.C.O.: United Nations Educational, Scientific and Cultural Organisation.

Validity of Tests: The extent to which a test does in fact test the ability it purports to measure.

Vertical Grouping: An arrangement by which children are not grouped strictly according to age; new pupils, instead of being placed all together in a reception class, are attached to groups containing children ranging in age from, say, 5 to 7.

Visual Discrimination: Ability to detect differences between visual patterns. Involves differentiation of letter forms, word patterns as well as discrimination of gross forms such as pictures and geometrical patterns.

Vocabulary: The words of which a language consists. Applied to an individual child the term stands for the total number of words he is able to use or can recognise when reading or listening.

Watts-Vernon Test: One of the two tests used in the national surveys of reading standards. Devised in 1947 as a silent reading test of the incomplete sentence type; it has 35 items and a ten-minute time limit.

Word Recognition Test: Usually a standardised test of the ability to read aloud single words. The words are graded in difficulty and the tests yield scores which can be converted into Reading Ages.

Index

The references are to paragraphs except where otherwise indicated

Printed in England for Her Majesty's Stationery Office by
Burrup, Mathieson & Co., Ltd.
Dd 496638 K200 4/76